MANAGEMENT
An Introduction

Visit the *Management, Fourth Edition* Companion Website at **www.pearsoned.co.uk/boddy** to find valuable **student** learning material including:

- Multiple choice questions to help test your learning
- Weblinks to key companies mentioned in the text
- An online glossary to explain key terms
- Flashcards to test your understanding of key topics
- Study skills activities and exercises to help you get the most out of the book.

MANAGEMENT
An Introduction

Fourth Edition

David Boddy

University of Glasgow

FT Prentice Hall

FINANCIAL TIMES

An imprint of **Pearson Education**

Harlow, England • London • New York • Boston • San Francisco • Toronto
Sydney • Tokyo • Singapore • Hong Kong • Seoul • Taipei • New Delhi
Cape Town • Madrid • Mexico City • Amsterdam • Munich • Paris • Milan

Pearson Education Limited

Edinburgh Gate
Harlow
Essex CM20 2JE
England

and Associated Companies around the world

Visit us on the World Wide Web at:
www.pearsoned.co.uk

———————————————

First published 1998 under the Prentice Hall Europe imprint
Second edition published 2002
Third edition published 2005
Fourth edition published 2008

© Prentice Hall Europe 1998
© Pearson Education Limited 2002, 2008

ISBN 978-0-273-71106-3

British Library Cataloguing-in-Publication Data
A catalogue record for this book is available from the British Library.

Library of Congress Cataloging-in-Publication Data
Boddy, David.
   Management : an introduction / David Boddy.-- 4th ed.
       p. cm.
   Includes bibliographical references and index.
   ISBN-13: 978-0-273-71106-3 (pbk.)
  1. Management. I. Title.
  HD31.B583 2008
  658--dc22

                                   2007032613

10 9 8 7 6 5 4 3 2 1
12 11 10 09 08

Typeset in 10.5/12.5 pt Minion by 30.
Printed and bound by Mateu Cromo, Artes Graficas, Spain

The publisher's policy is to use paper manufactured from sustainable forests.

Brief contents

Supporting resources

Visit **www.pearsoned.co.uk/boddy** to find valuable online resources

For students
- Multiple choice questions to help test your learning
- Weblinks to key companies mentioned in the text
- An online glossary to explain key terms
- Flashcards to test your understanding of key topics
- Study skills activities and exercises to help you get the most out of the book

For instructors
- Complete, downloadable Instructor's Manual
- PowerPoint slides that can be downloaded and used as OHTs
- Testbank of question material

Also: The Companion Website provides the following features:
- Search tool to help locate specific items of content
- E-mail results and profile tools to send results of quizzes to instructors
- Online help and support to assist with website usage and troubleshooting

For more information please contact your local Pearson Education sales representative or visit **www.pearsoned.co.uk/boddy**

Contents

Part 1
AN INTRODUCTION TO MANAGEMENT

Chapter 1
Managing in organisations

Chapter 2
Models of management

Part 2
THE ENVIRONMENT OF MANAGEMENT

Chapter 3
Organisation cultures and contexts

Chapter 4
Managing internationally

Part 4
ORGANISING

Part 5
LEADING

Chapter 14
Influence and power   454

Chapter 15
Motivation   484

Chapter 16
Communication   522

Chapter 17
Teams   556

Part 6
CONTROLLING

Chapter 18
Performance measurement and control

Chapter 19
Finance and budgetary control

Chapter 20
Managing operations and quality

Guide to the case studies

Chapter/part	Case study	Precis	Country/region	Page no.
1	Ryanair	Examines the roles of managers in building the business and as they interact with the external environment.	Eire and Europe	5
2	Robert Owen	An insight into early management practices which have modern parallels, including some with Innocent Drinks.	UK	37
Part 1	Innocent Drinks	Outlines the decisions the founders faced as they built the business, and relates these to the theories in Chapters 1 and 2.	UK	73
3	Nokia	How the company tries to protect its leading position in a rapidly changing business environment.	Finland	83
4	Starbucks	Alerts students to the range of management issues that face a company operating internationally.	US and global	113
5	Ford Pinto	How managers at Ford misjudged the significance of safety and social responsibility – and how the context at the time influenced decisions.	US	145
Part 2	BP	Contains material on the Part themes of external environment, managing internationally and corporate responsibility.	UK and global	173
6	DSM	A successful Dutch chemicals company that has developed a sophisticated planning process across its many business units.	The Netherlands	181
7	Wipro	Shows the decisions which faced this Indian company as it became a major player in the global IT outsourcing business.	India and global	207
8	Marks & Spencer	Shows the importance of developing and implementing a distinctive strategy if managers are to meet customer expectations.	UK	241
9	Manchester United FC	This global success story shows how effective marketing depends on the right internal structure and on suitable branding.	UK and global	271
Part 3	Virgin Group	The marketing, strategic and organisational issues which have faced Richard Branson as he has built this global business.	UK and global	307
10	Oticon	How the company responded to severe external threat by creating a radical new structure – parallels with W.L. Gore (Part 5 case).	Denmark	317
11	BMW	A distinct and coherent strategy of human resource management supports the success of this European motor company.	Germany	353
12	Google	The company's rise to worldwide prominence since 1997 illustrates the changes made possible by information technology.	US and global	377
13	Vodafone/Ericsson	Insights into managing change from the emerging relationship between two major players in mobile communications.	UK/Sweden	411
Part 4	Royal Bank of Scotland	How one of Europe's largest banks has developed its organisation to meet changing conditions.	UK	445
14	Semco	The charismatic Ricardo Semler provides an unconventional perspective on how a manager can influence others.	Brazil	455
15	IKEA	The company's success is partly due to the way it secures and maintains the enthusiasm and commitment of staff.	Sweden and global	485
16	Carlos Ghosn, CEO of Renault/Nissan	Based on Carlos Ghosn's dramatic time at Nissan, this illustrates the challenge of communicating across different cultures.	France/Japan	523
17	Cisco Systems	The company depends heavily on teams, many of which are made up of members in different continents, who may never meet.	US and global	557
Part 5	W.L. Gore and Associates in Europe	An unusual approach to leading professional staff to ensure their commitment.	US and UK	587
18	AXA	How this global financial services company seeks to control its widely dispersed activities.	France and global	599
19	BASF Group	Illustrates aspects of, as well as the limitations of, financial reporting.	Germany	627
20	Benetton	Examines how the operations systems of this familiar company support its success in the rapidly changing fashion industry.	Italy	653
Part 6	Tesco	How tight systems enable the company to balance the possibly conflicting demands of control and responsiveness.	UK	683

Preface to the first edition

This book is intended for readers who are undertaking their first systematic exposure to the study of management. Most will be first-year undergraduates following courses leading to a qualification in management or business. Some will also be taking an introductory course in management as part of other qualifications (these may be in engineering, accountancy, law, information technology, science, nursing or social work) and others will be following a course in management as an element in their respective examination schemes. The book should also be useful to readers with a first degree or equivalent qualification in a non-management subject who are taking further studies leading to Certificate, Diploma or MBA qualifications.

The book has the following three main objectives:

- to provide newcomers to the formal study of management with an introduction to the topic;
- to show that ideas on management apply to most areas of human activity, not just to commercial enterprises; and
- to make the topic attractive to students from many backgrounds and with diverse career intentions.

Most research and reflection on management has focused on commercial organisations. However, there are now many people working in the public sector and in not-for-profit organisations (charities, pressure groups, voluntary organisations and so on) who have begun to adapt management ideas to their own areas of work. The text reflects this wider interest in the topic. It should be as useful to those who plan to enter public or not-for-profit work as to those entering the commercial sector.

European perspective

The book presents the ideas from a European perspective. While many management concepts have developed in the United States, the text encourages readers to consider how their particular context shapes management practice. There are significant cultural differences that influence this practice, and the text alerts the reader to these – not only as part of an increasingly integrated Europe but as part of a wider international management community. So the text recognises European experience and research in management. The case studies and other material build an awareness of cultural diversity and the implications of this for working in organisations with different managerial styles and backgrounds.

Integrated perspective

To help the reader see management as a coherent whole, the material is presented within an integrative model of management and demonstrates the relationships between the many academic perspectives. The intention is to help the reader to see management as an integrating activity relating to the organisation as a whole, rather than as something confined to any one disciplinary or functional perspective.

While the text aims to introduce readers to the traditional mainstream perspectives on management which form the basis of each chapter, it also recognises that there is a newer body of ideas which looks at developments such as the weakening of national boundaries and the spread of information technology. Since they will affect the organisations in which readers will spend their working lives, these newer perspectives are introduced where appropriate. The text also recognises the more critical perspectives that some writers now take towards management and organisational activities. These are part of the intellectual world in which management takes place and have important practical implications for the way people interpret their role within organisations. The text introduces these perspectives at several points.

Relating to personal experience

The text assumes that many readers will have little if any experience of managing in conventional organisations, and equally little prior knowledge of relevant evidence and theory. However, all will have experience of being managed and all will have managed activities in their domestic and social lives. Wherever possible the book encourages readers to use and share such experiences from everyday life in order to explore the ideas presented. In this way the book tries to show that management is not a remote activity performed by others, but a process in which all are engaged in some way.

Most readers' careers are likely to be more fragmented and uncertain than was once the case and many will be working for medium-sized and smaller enterprises. They will probably be working close to customers and in organisations that incorporate diverse cultures, values and interests. The text therefore provides many opportunities for readers to develop skills of gathering data, comparing evidence, reflecting and generally enhancing self-awareness. It not only transmits knowledge but also aims to support the development of transferable skills through individual activities in the text and through linked tutorial work. The many cases and data collection activities are designed to develop generic skills such as communication, teamwork, problem solving and organising – while at the same time acquiring relevant knowledge.

Preface to the fourth edition

This fourth edition takes account of helpful comments from staff and students who used the third edition, and the suggestions of reviewers (please see below). The book retains the structure of six parts which found favour with the reviewers. The main changes are:

- **Chapters:** In response to reviewer comments I have combined Chapters 10 and 12 into a more accessible Chapter 10. That enabled me to introduce a new chapter on Performance Measurement and Control, which appears as Chapter 18 at the start of Part 6 (Controlling). The chapter on information systems has been substantially rewritten and now appears as Chapter 12, Information Technology and E-business, where it precedes the substantially rewritten and renamed Chapter 13, Managing Change and Innovation. Chapter 3 now contains the material on culture as an important element of the internal context, which leads to the existing (revised) material on external contexts.
- **Academic content:** This remains substantially as before, but has been extended and updated where appropriate. Examples include Yip's model of the growth of international business in Chapter 4, a new section on biases in decision making in Chapter 6, and a model of information system complementarities in Chapter 12.
- **Cases:** These have been revised and updated – and several (such as Robert Owen and Wipro) have been significantly extended throughout their respective chapters. There are three completely new chapter cases – Google (Chapter 12), IKEA (Chapter 15) and AXA Insurance (Chapter 18). There are two new Part Cases – Innocent Drinks in Part 1 and Tesco in Part 6.
- **Features:** Many of the Management in Practice features have been updated and renewed, as have some Key Ideas. There are over 180 new references and additional suggestions for 'further reading'. Several of the Case Questions and Activities have been revised to connect more closely with the theories being presented. The Learning Objectives provide the structure for the Summary section at the end of each chapter.

- **Current themes and issues:** Several reviewers suggested more recurrent treatment through the book of corporate responsibility and international themes. I have taken account of this, and each chapter now ends with a section 'Current themes and issues', with three standard components – performance, responsibility and internationalisation. Each contains new material connecting the topic of the chapter with the theme.
- **Critical thinking:** At the end of the first chapter I present some ideas on the components of critical thinking – assumptions, context, alternatives and limitations. These themes are used systematically to frame many of the learning objectives, and structure the Critical Reflection feature at the end of each chapter.
- **Web-based activities:** Each chapter concludes with a list of the websites of companies that have appeared in the chapter, and a suggestion that students visit these sites (or others in which they have an interest) to find some information and seek new or additional information on some of the themes in the chapter. This should add interest and help retain the topicality of the cases.

Each Part continues to conclude with several skills development activities, drawing on and in some cases integrating ideas from several of the chapters in that Part.

List of reviewers

We would like to express thanks to the original reviewers and review panel members who have been involved in the development of this book. We are extremely grateful for their insight and helpful recommendations.

Reviewers of the second edition

John Clark (London Metropolitan University)
James Edgar (Queens University, Belfast)
Olaf Sigurjonsson (Reykjavik University, Iceland)
Eddie Pargeter (Birmingham College of Food, Tourism and Creative Study)

Bart Bossink (Vrije University, Amsterdam)
Ian Parkinson (Hull College)
Nicky Metcalf (St Martin's College, Lancaster)
Jackie Shaw (Macclesfield College)
Jos Weel (Hogeschool van Amsterdam)
Peter Williams (Leeds Metropolitan University)
Iraj Tavakolo (Brighton University)
Ray Rogers (Coventry)
John Chamberlain (Derby)
Siobhan Tiernan (University of Limerick)
Andrew Godley (University of Reading)

Reviewers of the third edition

Peter Falconer (Glasgow Caledonian University)
Ad van Iterson (Maastricht University)
Gail Shepherd (Coventry University)

Abby Cathcart (University of Sunderland)
Paschal McNeill (University College, Dublin)

Reviewers of the fourth edition

Paul Dudley
Dearbhla Finn
Bobby Mackie
Howard Weston
Colin Combe
Joyce Liddle
Matyna Siiwa
Paul Griseri
Nerys Fuller Love
Frank van Luix
Boon Tan

Custom publishing

Custom publishing allows academics to pick and choose content from one or more texts for their course and combine it into a definitive course text.

Here are some common examples of Custom solutions which have helped over 500 courses across Europe:

- Different chapters from across our publishing imprints combined into one book
- Lecturer's own material combined together with textbook chapters or published in a separate booklet
- Third party cases and articles that you are keen for your students to read as part of the course
- Or any combination of the above

The Pearson Education Custom text published for your course is professionally produced and bound – just as you would expect from a normal Pearson Education text. You can even choose your own cover design and add your university logo. Since many of our titles have online resources accompanying them we can even build a Custom website that matches your course text.

Whatever your choice, our dedicated Editorial and Production teams will work with you throughout the process, right until you receive a copy of your Custom text.

Some Principles of Management lecturers found that the flexibility of Custom publishing has allowed them to include additional material on certain aspects of their course.

To give you an idea of combinations which have proved popular, here is a list of subject areas in which Pearson Education publish one or more key texts that could provide extra chapters to match the emphasis of your course:

- Business Environment / Business in Context
- Organisational Behaviour / Organisational Theory
- Human Resource Management
- Marketing
- Accounting & Finance
- Operations Management
- Information Systems
- Economics / Business Economics
- Business Law and Ethics
- Study Skills

For more details on any of these books or to browse other material from our entire portfolio, please visit: www.pearsoned.co.uk

If, once you have thought about your course, you feel Custom publishing might benefit you, please do get in contact. However minor, or major the change – we can help you out.

You can contact us at: www.pearsoncustom.co.uk
or via your local representative at: www.pearsoned.co.uk/replocator

Guided tour

Navigation and setting the scene

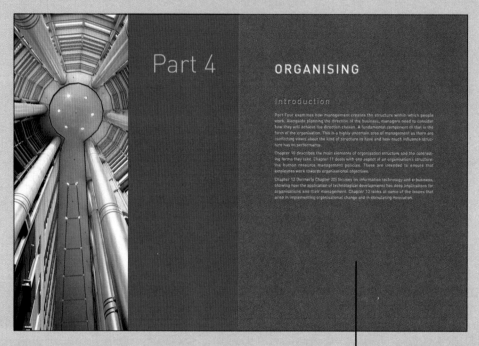

The book is divided into six parts each of which opens with an **introduction** helping you to orientate yourself within the book.

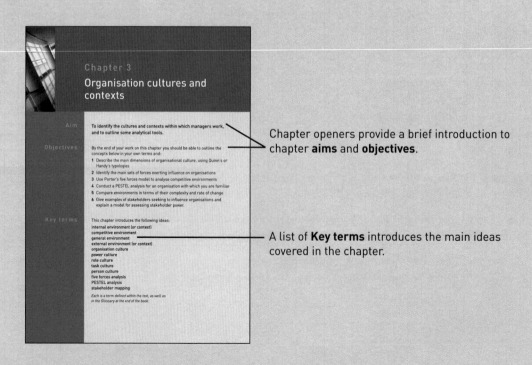

Chapter openers provide a brief introduction to chapter **aims** and **objectives**.

A list of **Key terms** introduces the main ideas covered in the chapter.

Management in context

Case studies engage student interest and encourage critical analysis.

End of Part Case studies enable extended analysis of real business situations, and can form the basis for class discussions.

Activities enable students to personally engage and investigate managerial theory and practice.

Management in practice boxes provide real world examples and encourage students to identify and engage with managerial issues and challenges.

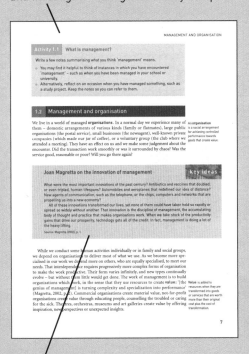

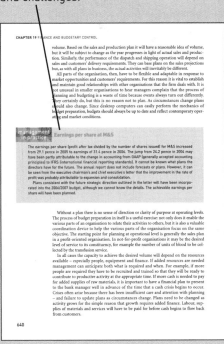

Key ideas are short vignettes which illustrate how developments in management thought influence practice today.

Aiding your understanding

Key terms are defined alongside the text for easy reference and to aid understanding.

Test your knowledge of Key terms using **Flashcards** on the Companion Website. Key terms are also found in the **Glossary** at the back of the book, and on the companion website.

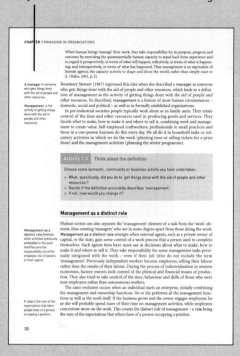

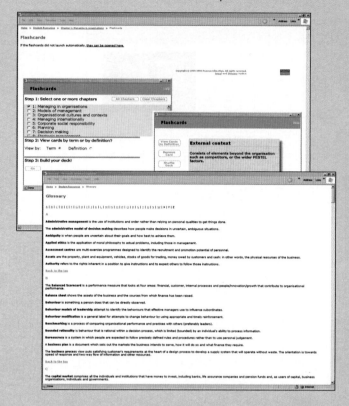

Developing your skills

Skills development sections include tasks which allow students to relate key managerial themes to personal experience.

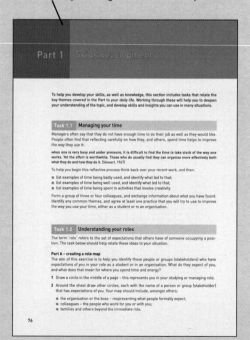

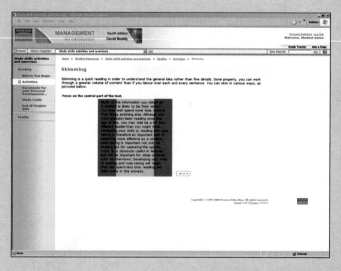

Study skills activities, exercises and guidance are available on the website to help students get the most out of the book. From helping to improve reading to tips for completing assignments, these are essential tools for success on your course.

Companion Website: **wwwpearsoned.co.uk/boddy**

Reinforcing your knowledge and thinking critically

Review questions enable students to check their understanding of the main themes and concepts.

Chapter summaries aid revision by supplying a concise synopsis of the main chapter topics.

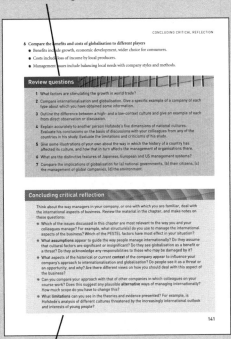

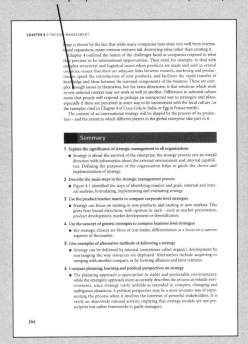

Concluding critical reflections are a series of questions intended to develop critical thinking skills and analysis of key debates.

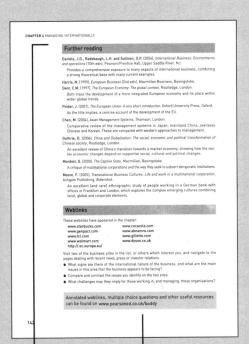

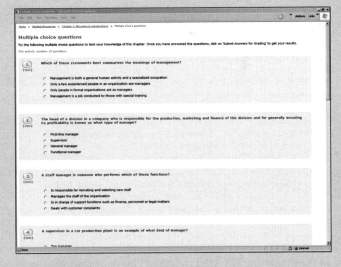

Multiple choice questions on the companion website enable you to check your understanding of the topics covered in each chapter.

Further reading and **Weblinks** provide a starting point for further research and project work. Weblinks can also be found on the Companion Website.

Companion Website: **wwwpearsoned.co.uk/boddy**

Acknowledgements

This book has benefited from the comments, criticisms and suggestions of many colleagues and reviewers of the third edition. It also reflects the reactions and comments of students who have used the material and earlier versions of some of the cases. Their advice and feedback have been of immense help.

Most of the chapters were written by the author, who has also edited the text throughout. These colleagues contributed chapters, for which I thank them: A. C. Muir, Chapter 9; Professor Phil Beaumont, Dr Judy Pate and Sandra Stewart, Chapter 11; Douglas Briggs, Chapter 19; and

Dr Geoff Southern, Chapter 20. I am also grateful to Sheen Bell for pedagogical suggestions and for contributions to the innovation and entrepreneurship themes. Errors and omissions are my responsibility alone. Thank you also to Sylvia Kerrigan for help in producing the manuscript.

Finally, I gratefully acknowledge the support and help that my wife, Cynthia, has provided throughout this project.

David Boddy
University of Glasgow, March 2007

Publisher's acknowledgements

We are grateful to the following for permission to reproduce the following copyright material:

DSM for an extract from the DSM Annual Report 2005, published on www.dsm.com; Marks and Spencer for an extract from a press release, published on their website www.marksandspencer.com, 15th January 2007 and IKEA for an extract published on their company website www.ikea.com.

Figure 2.2 from *Becoming a Master Manager* (Quinn, R.E., Faerman, S.R., Thompson, M.P. and McGrath, M.R. 2003); Figure 2.7 from *Chaos, Management and Economics*, Hobart Paper 125 (Parker, D. and Stacey, R. 1994) reprinted by permission of the Institute of Economic Affairs; Table 4.1 from *The Management of a Multicultural Workforce* (Tayeb, M.H. 1996) © 1996 John Wiley & Sons Limited. Reproduced with permission; Figure 5.1 from *Management*, 6th edition, p.135 (Daft 2000) © 2000. Reprinted with permission of South-Western, a division of Thomson Learning: www.thomsonrights.com. Fax 800 730-2215; Figure 7.4 from *Management*, 7th Edition, fig. 6.8, p.161 (Robbins, Stephen P. and Coulter, Mary 2003) © Pearson Education 2003. Reprinted by permission of Pearson Education, Inc., Upper Saddle River, NJ; Figure 7.5 from *Making Management Decisions*, 2nd edition (Cooke and Slack 1991), with permission from Pearson Education Limited; Figure 7.7 and Table 13.4 from *Organizational Behaviour: An Introductory Text*, 5th edition (Huczynski and Buchanan 2003) © A.A. Huczynski and D.A. Buchanan, 2001, with permission from Pearson Education Limited; Figure 7.8 from *Leadership and Decision-Making*, University of Pittsburgh Press, (Vroom, V.H. and Yetton, P.W. 1973); Table 8.3 from *Marks and Spencer Interim Report to Shareholders 2006*; Figure 8.8 from *The Rise and Fall of Strategic Management*, p.24 (Mintzberg 1994), with permission from Pearson Education Limited; Figures 9.2 and 9.3 from *Marketing Management*, 11th Edition (Kotler, Philip 2003) © Pearson Education 2003. Reprinted by permission of Pearson Education, Inc., Upper Saddle River, NJ; Figure 10.2 from **www.baesystems.com**, *http://www.baesystems.com/ContactUs/index.aspx*; Figure 10.11 from *The Learning Company: A Strategy for Sustainable Development*, 2nd edition, McGraw-Hill Publishing Company, (Pedler, M., Burgoyne, J. and

Boydell, T. 1997) reproduced with the kind permission of The McGraw-Hill Publishing Company; Table 11.1 from *The Occupational Psychologist*, February 1998 (Guest, D. 1987), reprinted by permission of the British Psychological Society; Figure 14.4 from an exhibit in 'How to Choose a Leadership Pattern' in *Harvard Business Review*, 37 (Tannenbaum and Schmidt 1973). Original article translated and reprinted by permission of *Harvard Business Review*. This article was originally published under the English title, 'How to Choose a Leadership Pattern', 37, March-April 1958, reprinted in May-June 1973. Copyright © 1973 by the Harvard Business School Publishing Corporation. All rights reserved. This translation, Copyright © 1973 by the Harvard Business School Publishing Corporation; Figure 15.3 from *Psychological Contracts*, p.2 (Rousseau and Schalk 2000), © 2000 Sage Publications; Figure 15.5 from 'One More Time: How do you Motivate Employees?' in *Harvard Business Review*, 65 (Herzberg, F. 1987). Original article was translated and reprinted by permission of *Harvard Business Review*. This article was originally published under the English title 'One More Time' by Hertzberg (vol. 65) Sept-Oct 1987. Copyright © 1987; Figure 16.5 This article was published in *Group Processes* by Berkowitz, L., 'Communication Networks fourteen years later' Shaw, M.E., copyright Elsevier, 1978; Figure 16.8 from 'The Strategic Communication Imperative' in *MIT Sloan Management Review*, (Argenti, P.A., Howell, R.A. and Beck, K.A. 2005), copyright 2005 by Massachusetts Institute of Technology. All rights reserved. Distributed by Tribune Media Services; Figure 17.2 from *New Patterns of Management*, The McGraw-Hill Companies, Inc, (Likert, R. 1961); Table 17.1 and Figure 17.3 from *The Wisdom of Teams* (Katzenbach and Smith 1993). Original material translated and reprinted by permission of *Harvard Business Review*. The article was originally published under the English title 'The Wisdom of Teams' by Katzenbach and Smith. Copyright ©1993 by the Harvard Business School Publishing Corporation. All rights reserved. This translation, Copyright © 1993 by the Harvard Business School Publishing Corporation; Table 17.2 from *Groups that work (and those that don't)*, Jossey-Bass, San Francisco, CA (Hackman, J.R. 1990), Reprinted with

permission of John Wiley & Sons, Inc; Table 17.3 from *Groups that work (and those that don't)*, Jossey-Bass, San Francisco, CA (Hackman, J.R. 1990), Reprinted with permission of John Wiley & Sons, Inc; Figure 20.3 from 'Operations management: productivity and quality performance', in E.G.C. Collins and M.A. Devanna in *The Portable MBA*, (Sprague, L. 1990);
Chapter 16 W R Grace: Building on the team structure from *The Financial Times Limited*, 21 January 2004, © Rod Newing;

We are grateful to the Financial Times Limited for permission to reprint the following material:
Chapter 3 The drinks are in the house, © *Financial Times*, 23 March 2004; Chapter 4 Inside Track: Italy's firm family ties, © *Financial Times*, 24 March 2003; Chapter 4 Eastern Europe postal sector 'ripe for growth', © *Financial Times*, 19 April 2006; Chapter 5 How BT achieved good migrations, © *Financial Times*, 8 March 2004; Chapter 6 Companies and Finance International: Brewer's head promises to pull no punches, © *Financial Times*, 22 November 2002; Chapter 6 BUSINESS LIFE: The man who has to shake up Merck, © *Financial Times*, 27 March 2006; Chapter 12 Bringing Business Technology out into the open, © *Financial Times*, 17 September 2003;

In some instances we have been unable to trace the owners of copyright material, and we would appreciate any information that would enable us to do so.

Part 1

AN INTRODUCTION TO MANAGEMENT

Introduction

This part considers why management exists and what it contributes to human wealth and well-being. Management is both a universal human activity and a distinct occupation. We all manage in the first sense, as we organise our lives and deal with family and other relationships. As employees and customers we experience the activities of those who manage in the second sense, as members of an organisation with which we deal. This Part offers some ways of making sense of the complex and contradictory activity of managing.

Chapter 1 clarifies the nature and emergence of management and the different ways in which people describe the role. It explains how management is both a universal human activity and a specialist occupation. The purpose of management is to create wealth by adding value to resources, which managers do by influencing others – the chapter shows how they do this. It concludes with some ideas about managing your study of the topic. You are likely to benefit most by actively linking your work on this book to events in real organisations, and the chapter includes some suggestions.

Chapter 2 sets out the main theoretical perspectives on management and shows how these can complement each other despite the apparently competing values about the nature of the management task. Be active in relating these theoretical perspectives to real events as this will help you to understand and test the theory.

The Part Case is Innocent Drinks, an innovative company that was established by three graduates in 1998 and has established a leading position in the smoothies market. The founders have some original and stimulating ideas on managing, which link many themes in this Part.

Chapter 1
Managing in organisations

Aim

To introduce the tasks, processes and context of managerial work in organisations.

Objectives

By the end of your work on this chapter you should be able to outline the concepts below in your own terms and:

1 Summarise the functions of organisations and how management affects their performance

2 Give examples to show how management is both a universal human activity and a distinct role

3 Compare the roles of general, functional, line, staff and project managers

4 Explain how managers influence others to add value to resources through:

 a. the process of managing (Stewart, Mintzberg and Luthans)

 b. the tasks (or content) of managing and

 c. shaping the contexts within which they and others work

5 Evaluate a manager's approach to the role by analysing how they influence others

6 Explain the elements of critical thinking and use some techniques to develop this skill.

Key terms

This chapter introduces the following ideas:

entrepreneur
innovation
organisation
value
management as a universal human
 activity
manager
management
management as a distinct role

role
general manager
functional manager
line manager
staff manager
project manager
stakeholders
management task
critical thinking

Each is a term defined within the text, as well as in the Glossary at the end of the book.

In 2007 Ryanair, based in Dublin, was Europe's leading low-cost airline. It was created in 1985 to offer services between Dublin and London, in competition with the established national carrier, Aer Lingus. In the early years the airline changed its business several times – initially a conventional, though slightly cheaper, competitor for Aer Lingus, then a charter company, at times offering a cargo service. The Gulf War in 1990 discouraged people from travelling by air, and caused financial problems for the company. In 1991 senior managers decided to focus the airline as a 'no-frills' operator, in which many traditional features of air travel (free food, drink, newspapers and allocated seats) were no longer available. It aimed to serve a group of flyers who wanted a functional and efficient service rather than luxury.

In 1997 changes in European Union regulations enabled new airlines to enter markets previously dominated by established national carriers such as Air France and British Airways. Ryanair quickly took advantage of this, opening new routes between Dublin and continental Europe. Managers were quick to spot the potential of the Internet, and in 2000 opened Ryanair.com, a booking site: within a year it was selling 75 per cent of seats online, and now sells almost all seats this way. It also made a long-term deal with Boeing to purchase 150 new aircraft over the next eight years.

Several factors enable Ryanair to offer fares to its customers that are significantly below those of traditional carriers:

- Simple fleet – using a single aircraft type (Boeing 737 – most of which are also quite new) simplifies maintenance, training and crew scheduling.
- Secondary airports – using airports away from major cities keeps landing charges low, sometimes as little as £1 per passenger against £10 at a major airport.
- Fast turnrounds – staff typically turn an aircraft around between flights in 25 minutes, compared to

Thierry Tronnel/Corbis

an hour for older airlines. This enables aircraft to spend more time in the air, earning revenue (11 hours compared to 7 at British Airways).
- Simplified operations – not assigning seats at check-in simplifies ticketing and administrative processes, and also ensures that passengers arrive early to get their preferred seat. Flying directly between cities avoids the problems of transferring passengers and baggage between flights, which is where costly mistakes and delays frequently occur.
- Cabin staff collect rubbish before and after landing, saving the cost of expensive cleaning crews which the established carriers choose to use.

Source: *Economist*, 10 July 2004; O'Connell and Williams (2005); and other published information.

Case questions 1.1

- What functions is Ryanair performing?
- What did 'management' contribute to the growth of the airline?
- Give examples of three points at which managers changed what the organisation does and how it works.

1.1 Introduction

An **entrepreneur** is someone with a new venture, project or activity, and is usually associated with creative thinking, driving innovation and championing change.

The Ryanair case illustrates several aspects of management. A group of **entrepreneurs** created an organisation to offer a new service they believed customers would want to buy. The company does this by bringing resources together and transforming them into something with greater value – which they sell to the customers. They differ from their competitors in that they use a different set of resources (e.g. secondary airports) and have different ways of transforming these into outputs (e.g. short turnrounds). They have been innovative in the way they run the business, such as in identifying what some customers value in a flight – cost rather than luxury – and carried a record 40 million passengers in 2006.

Entrepreneurs such as Michael O'Leary of Ryanair are always looking for ways to **innovate** and make the most of new opportunities. Other managers face a different challenge – more demand with less resources. James Morris, who in 2006 was head of the United Nations World Food Programme, was struggling to raise funds to alleviate the famine in southern Africa. Food aid from global donors has fallen while the number of hungry people has increased. In almost every public healthcare organisation managers face a growing demand for treatment but find it difficult to secure the resources to meet it.

Innovation is the process of taking a creative idea and turning it into a useful product, service or method of operation.

Organisations of all kinds – from rapidly growing operations such as Ryanair to established businesses like Royal Dutch Shell or H&M (the Swedish fashion retailer) – depend on people at all levels who can run the current business efficiently, and also innovate. This book is about the knowledge and skills that enable people to meet these expectations, and so build a satisfying and rewarding management career.

Figure 1.1 illustrates the themes of this chapter. It represents the fact that people draw resources from the external environment and manage their transformation into outputs that they hope are of greater value. They pass these back to the environment and the value they obtain in return (money, reputation, goodwill, etc.) enables them to attract new resources to continue in business (shown by the feedback arrow from output to input). If the outputs fail to attract sufficient resources then the enterprise will fail.

The chapter begins by examining the significance of managed organisations in our world. It then outlines what management means and introduces theories about the nature of managerial work. Finally, it introduces ideas on studying management.

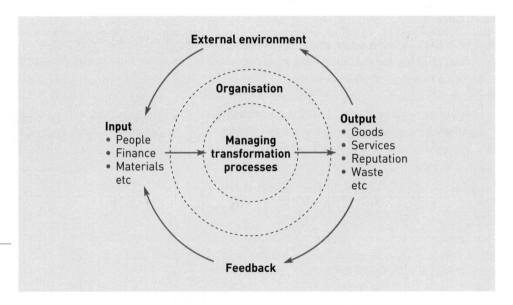

Figure 1.1

Managing organisation and environment

Activity 1.1 What is management?

Write a few notes summarising what you think 'management' means.

- You may find it helpful to think of instances in which you have encountered 'management' – such as when you have been managed in your school or university.
- Alternatively, reflect on an occasion when you have managed something, such as a study project. Keep the notes so you can refer to them.

1.2 Management and organisation

We live in a world of managed **organisations**. In a normal day we experience many of them – domestic arrangements of various kinds (family or flatmates), large public organisations (the postal service), small businesses (the newsagent), well-known private companies (which made our jar of coffee), or a voluntary group (the club where we attended a meeting). They have an effect on us and we make some judgement about the encounter. Did the transaction work smoothly or was it surrounded by chaos? Was the service good, reasonable or poor? Will you go there again?

> An **organisation** is a social arrangement for achieving controlled performance towards goals that create value.

Joan Magretta on the innovation of management

key ideas

What were the most important innovations of the past century? Antibiotics and vaccines that doubled, or even tripled, human lifespans? Automobiles and aeroplanes that redefined our idea of distance? New agents of communication, such as the telephone, or the chips, computers and networks that are propelling us into a new economy?

All of these innovations transformed our lives, yet none of them could have taken hold so rapidly or spread so widely without another. That innovation is the discipline of management, the accumulating body of thought and practice that makes organisations work. When we take stock of the productivity gains that drive our prosperity, technology gets all of the credit. In fact, management is doing a lot of the heavy lifting.

Source: Magretta (2002), p. 1.

While we conduct some human activities individually or in family and social groups, we depend on organisations to deliver most of what we use. As we become more specialised in our work we depend more on others, who are equally specialised, to meet our needs. That interdependence requires progressively more complex forms of organisation to make the work productive. Their form varies infinitely, and new types continually evolve – but without them little would get done. The work of management is to build organisations which work, in the sense that they use resources to create **value**: '[the genius of management] is turning complexity and specialization into performance' (Magretta, 2002, p. 2). Commercial organisations create material value, not-for-profit organisations create value through educating people, counselling the troubled or caring for the sick. Theatres, orchestras, museums and art galleries create value by offering inspiration, new perspectives or unexpected insights.

> **Value** is added to resources when they are transformed into goods or services that are worth more than their original cost plus the cost of transformation.

Well-managed organisations create value in many ways. If you buy a ticket from Ryanair you can easily measure the tangible value of a cheap flight. In other purchases the value is *in*tangible, as people judge a product by its appearance, what it feels or smells like, how trendy it is, or whether it fits the image they want to present to the world. Others value good service, or a clear set of instructions on how to assemble their purchase. Good managers understand what customers value, and build an organisation to deliver it – whether in commercial or non-profit enterprises.

---

management in practice **Creating value in a pub and brewery company**

Ralph Findlay (a former geology student) has been Chief Executive of Wolverhampton and Dudley Breweries since 2001. In 2004 the company owned about 1600 pubs and brewed Banks's and Pedigree ales. Findlay knows that he works in an industry where success often comes down to paying attention to detail – such as a lick of paint or some flower-boxes. He says:

> We are in a business that is not actually that complicated. You can overcomplicate it ... A lot of the time it is about somebody in a place like this who has got a smile on his face and wants to welcome his customers. Provided he makes them feel good about coming in, they will keep coming back and that is what it is really about.

FT

Source: From an article by Adam Jones, *Financial Times*, 25 July 2003.

Although the purpose of managing is to add value and create wealth this does not always happen. People may produce goods and services inefficiently, using more resources than customers are willing to pay for. Their work may create pollution and waste, so destroying wealth: the growth of air travel increases carbon dioxide emissions and so contributes to climate change. Work can create value for some and destroy it for others. Motorway builders create value for road users, residents of by-passed villages, and their shareholders – but destroy value (from their opponents' perspective) if the route damages an ancient woodland rich in history and wildlife. From the latter perspective the company has used resources to destroy natural wealth and has reduced, not created, value. The idea of creating value is subjective and relative.

It is not only commercial organisations that create value by providing goods and services. To a degree that is not commonly recognised, voluntary and non-profit organisations (VNPOs) provide many services in health care, culture, environment, social services and education – Barnado's, The Salvation Army, Age Concern – and thousands more. Osborne (1996) points out that managing such organisations combines issues unique to the sector (maintaining good relationships with donors or funding bodies) with others which are common in commercial organisations (business planning, marketing or quality). Charities such as Oxfam or Greenpeace were created by a few like-minded individuals, and have become worldwide organisations with significant operations to raise funds and manage their activities. Donors and recipients expect them to manage resources well so that they add value (Lewis, 2001).

Other organisations add value by serving particular interests such as Unison, a trade union that represents workers in the UK public sector, or the Law Society, which defends the interests of lawyers. Firms in most industries create trade organisations to protect their interests by lobbying or public relations work. Organisations of all kinds can create value by providing psychological support for members and non-members. Corporate scandals at prominent companies such as Enron and Parmalat have indicated the greed and self-interest of some directors and senior managers, who saw them as vehicles for personal enrichment. Table 1.1 summarises these organisational functions.

Table 1.1

Some functions of organisations

Function	Description	Examples
Create value, wealth or human well-being	By providing goods and services that people value	Commercial, public sector, voluntary and non-profit, and non-governmental organisations (NGOs)
Articulate and implement ideals	Individuals with an interest in a topic, or a passion to change something, usually need the support of others	Charities, protest groups, political parties
Gain power to protect sectional interests	Large organisations have access to political and economic resources beyond those of individuals	Trade unions, professional associations, industry groups
Give people work, status and social contact	A source of jobs, training, careers, contact with others, a wider outlook, a source of structure in life	Any long-lasting and respected organisation
Enrich directors or senior managers	When those in charge work for personal gain by providing misleading information to shareholders or regulators	Scandals at Enron (US), Ahold (The Netherlands) or Parmalat (Italy)

Activity 1.2 Managing in a voluntary organisation

The Charities Commission (which regulates charities in England and Wales) estimates that the 190,000 charities in England and Wales have an annual income of £38 billion – equal to about 3.4 per cent of gross domestic product. Ninety per cent of this income is received by the 10,000 largest charities such as Age Concern and the Royal Society for the Protection of Birds (Charities Commission Annual Report for 2005–06, available at **www.charitycommission.gov.uk**). Running a large charity is at least as demanding a management job as running a commercial business.

- If you are connected with a charity or voluntary group, reflect on how it is managed.
- What management issues have you been aware of in that work?

Whatever its function, how well an organisation performs its value-creating role depends on those who work within it. Luck plays a part, but most of the time it is the quality of management that determines whether an organisation fails or succeeds.

1.3 Meanings of management

Management as a universal human activity

People called managers are not alone in requiring the skills of management. As individuals we run our lives and careers: in this respect we are managing. Family members manage children, elderly dependants and households. Management is both a **universal human activity** and a distinct occupation. In the first sense, people manage an infinite range of activities:

Management as a universal human activity occurs whenever people take responsibility for an activity and consciously try to shape its progress and outcome.

When human beings 'manage' their work, they take responsibility for its purpose, progress and outcome by exercising the quintessentially human capacity to stand back from experience and to regard it prospectively, in terms of what will happen; reflectively, in terms of what is happening; and retrospectively, in terms of what has happened. Thus management is an expression of human agency, the capacity actively to shape and direct the world, rather than simply react to it. (Hales, 2001, p. 2)

A manager is someone who gets things done with the aid of people and other resources.

Rosemary Stewart (1967) expressed this idea when she described a **manager** as someone who gets things done with the aid of people and other resources, which leads to a definition of management as the activity of getting things done with the aid of people and other resources. So described, **management** is a feature of most human circumstances – domestic, social and political – as well as in formally established organisations.

Management is the activity of getting things done with the aid of people and other resources.

In pre-industrial societies people typically work alone or in family units. They retain control of the time and other resources used in producing goods and services. They decide what to make, how to make it and where to sell it, combining work and management to create value. Self-employed craftworkers, professionals in small practices and those in a one-person business do this every day. We all do it in household tasks or voluntary activities in which we do the work (planting trees or selling tickets for a prize draw) and the management activities (planning the winter programme).

> ### Activity 1.3 Think about the definition
>
> Choose some domestic, community or business activity you have undertaken.
>
> - What, specifically, did you do to 'get things done with the aid of people and other resources'?
> - Decide if the definition accurately describes 'management'.
> - If not, how would you change it?

Management as a distinct role

Management as a distinct role develops when activities previously embedded in the work itself become the responsibility not of the employee, but of owners or their agents.

Human action can also separate the 'management' element of a task from the 'work' element, thus creating 'managers' who are in some degree apart from those doing the work. **Management as a distinct role** emerges when external agents, such as a private owner of capital, or the state, gain some control of a work process that a person used to complete themselves. Such agents then have more say in decisions about what to make, how to make it and where to sell it. They take responsibility for some management tasks previously integrated with the work – even if their job titles do not include the term 'management'. Previously independent workers become employees, selling their labour rather than the results of their labour. During the process of industrialisation in western economies, factory owners took control of the physical and financial means of production. They also tried to take control of the time, behaviour and skills of those who were now employees rather than autonomous workers.

A role is the sum of the expectations that other people have of a person occupying a position.

The same evolution occurs when an individual starts an enterprise, initially combining the management and ownership functions. He or she performs all the management functions as well as the work itself. If the business grows and the owner engages employees, he or she will probably spend more of their time on management activities, while employees concentrate more on the work. This creates the distinct role of management – a **role** being the sum of the expectations that others have of a person occupying a position.

This separation of management and non-management work is not inevitable or permanent. People deliberately separate the roles, and can also bring them together. As Henri Fayol (1949) (a French writer, of whom you will read more in Chapter 2) observed:

> Management ... is neither an exclusive privilege nor a particular responsibility of the head or senior members of a business; it is an activity spread, like all other activities, between head and members of the body corporate. (p. 6)

Tony Watson on separating roles

key ideas

All humans are managers in some way. But some of them also take on the formal occupational work of being managers. They take on a role of shaping ... work organisations. Managers' work involves a double ... task: managing others and managing themselves. But the very notion of 'managers' being separate people from the 'managed', at the heart of traditional management thinking, undermines a capacity to handle this. Managers are pressured to be technical experts, devising rational and emotionally neutral systems and corporate structures to 'solve problems', 'make decisions', 'run the business'. These 'scientific' and rational–analytic practices give reassurance but can leave managers so distanced from the 'managed' that their capacity to control events is undermined. This can mean that their own emotional and security needs are not handled, with the effect that they retreat into all kinds of defensive, backbiting and ritualistic behaviour which further undermines their effectiveness.

Source: Watson (1994), pp. 12–13.

Someone in charge of part of an organisation, say a production department, will usually be treated as a manager, and referred to as one. The people who operate the machines will be called something else. In a rapidly growing business such as Ryanair the boundary between 'managers' and 'non-managers' is likely to be very fluid, with all being ready to perform a range of tasks, irrespective of their title.

1.4 Specialisation between areas of management

As an organisation grows, senior managers create separate functions and a hierarchy, so that management itself becomes divided.

Functional specialisation

General managers typically head a complete unit of the organisation, such as a division or subsidiary, within which there will be several functions. The general manager is responsible for the unit's performance, and relies on the managers in charge of each function. A small organisation will have just one or two general managers, who will also manage the functions. At Shell UK the most senior general manager in 2007 was James Smith, the chairman.

Functional managers are responsible for an area of work – either as line managers or staff managers. **Line managers** are in charge of a function that creates value directly by supplying products or services to customers: they could be in charge of a retail store, a group of nurses, a social work department or a manufacturing area. Their performance significantly affects business performance and image, as they and their staff are in direct contact with customers or clients. At Shell, Andrew Kerr was (in 2007) the distribution manager responsible for the storage, scheduling and delivery of Shell's bulk fuel sales in the UK, while Ken Rivers was manager of the Stanlow Refinery.

General managers are responsible for the performance of a distinct unit of the organisation.

Functional managers are responsible for the performance of an area of technical or professional work.

Line managers are responsible for the performance of activities that directly meet customers' needs.

11

A manager with extensive experience of retailing commented:

> The store manager's job is far more complex than it may at first appear. Staff management is an important element and financial skills are required to manage a budget and the costs involved in running a store. Managers must understand what is going on behind the scenes – in terms of logistics and the supply chain – as well as what is happening on the shop floor. They must also be good with customers and increasingly they need outward-looking skills as they are encouraged to take high-profile roles in the community.

Source: Private communication from the manager.

Staff managers are responsible for the performance of activities that support line managers.

Staff managers are in charge of activities such as finance, personnel, purchasing or legal affairs that support the line managers, who are their customers. Staff in support departments are not usually in direct contact with external customers, and so do not earn income directly for the organisation. Managers of staff departments operate as line managers within their unit. At Shell, Rachel Fox was Head of Legal, and Paul Milliken led the unit responsible for UK employment policies including remuneration and benefits.

Project managers are responsible for managing a project, usually intended to change some element of an organisation or its context.

Project managers are responsible for a temporary team created to plan and implement a change, such as a new product or system. Mike Buckingham, an engineer, managed a project to implement a new manufacturing system in a van plant. He still had line responsibilities for aspects of manufacturing, but worked for most of the time on the project, helped by a team of technical specialists. When the change was complete he returned to full-time work on his line job.

Management hierarchies

As organisations grow, senior managers usually create a hierarchy of positions. The amount of 'management' and 'non-management' work within these positions varies.

Performing direct operations

People who perform direct operations do the manual and mental work to make and deliver products or services. These range from low-paid cleaners or shop workers to highly paid pilots or lawyers. The activity is likely to contain some aspects of management work, though in lower-level jobs this will be limited. People running a small business combine management work with direct work to meet customer requirements.

Managing staff on direct operations

Sometimes called supervisors or first-line managers, they typically direct and control the daily work of a group or process, 'framed by the requirement to monitor, report and improve work performance' (Hales 2005, p. 484).

They allocate and coordinate tasks, monitor the pace of work and help to overcome difficulties. Sometimes they become involved with middle managers in making operational decisions on staffing levels or work methods. Examples would include the supervisor of a production team, the head chef in a hotel, a nurse in charge of a hospital ward or the manager of a bank branch. They may continue to perform some direct operations, but will spend less time on these than their subordinates.

Managing managers

Usually referred to as middle managers, they – such as an engineering manager at Ryanair – are expected to ensure that first-line managers work in line with company policies. They translate long-term strategies into short-term operational tasks, mediating between senior management vision and operational reality. They may help to develop strategy by presenting information about customer expectations or suggesting alternative strategies to senior managers (Floyd and Wooldridge, 2000; Currie and Proctor, 2005). They provide a communication link – telling first-line managers what they expect, and briefing senior managers about current issues. Some have close links with managers in other organisations (suppliers or customers) on whom they depend.

In voluntary organisations an important task is to manage relationships with the governing body (similar to the board of directors in a commercial business). Harris and Rochester (1996) describe this as 'one of the most difficult challenges of voluntary and non-profit ... management' (p. 30), since their existence depends on sufficient volunteers being willing to serve as governors, formulating policy and ensuring it raises the necessary resources.

Managing the business

Managing the business is the work of a small group, usually called the board of directors. They establish policy and have a particular responsibility for managing relations with people and institutions in the world outside, such as shareholders, media or elected representatives. They need to know broadly about internal matters, but spend most of their time looking to the future or dealing with external affairs. Depending on local company law, the board usually includes several non-executive directors – senior managers from other companies who are intended to bring a wider, independent view to discussions, supplementing the internal view of the executive directors. Such non-executive directors can enhance the effectiveness of the board, and give investors confidence that the board is acting in their interests. They can 'both support the executives in their leadership of the business and monitor and control executive conduct' (Roberts *et al.*, 2005, p. S6) by challenging, questioning, discussing and debating issues with the executive members. The board will not usually spend time on current operational issues.

The Board of Alliance Boots www.allianceboots.co.uk **management in practice**

The board of directors, which in 2007 consisted of six executive and seven non-executive directors, determines the strategic direction of the company, and meets regularly to review the operating and financial position of the group. The non-executive directors include Guy Dawson, an investment banker who chairs the Audit Committee; Tim Parker, chief executive of the Automobile Association; and Helene Ploix, chairman of a private investment company. The executive directors are led by Richard Baker, the chief executive, and are responsible respectively for Community Pharmacy, Finance, Health and Beauty Retail, and Wholesale and Commercial affairs.

Source: Company website.

1.5 Influencing through the process of managing

Stakeholders
are individuals, groups or organisations with an interest in, or who are affected by, what the organisation does.

Whatever their role, people add value to resources by influencing others, including internal and external **stakeholders** – those parties who affect, or who are affected by, an organisation's actions and policies. The challenge is that stakeholders will have different priorities, so managers need to influence them to act in ways they believe will add value.

They do this directly and indirectly. Direct methods are the interpersonal skills (see Chapter 14) that managers use – persuading a boss to support a proposal, a subordinate to do more work, or a customer to change a delivery date. Managers also influence others indirectly through:

- the process of managing (Rosemary Stewart, Henry Mintzberg and Fred Luthans);
- the tasks of managing (Section 1.6); and
- shaping the wider context (Section 1.7).

key ideas Rosemary Stewart – how managers spend their time

What are managers' jobs like? Do they resemble an orderly, methodical process – or a constant rush from one problem to the next? One of the best-known studies was that conducted by Rosemary Stewart (1967), an academic at Oxford University, who persuaded 160 senior and middle managers to keep a diary for four weeks, which allowed the researchers to establish how the managers spent their time. This showed that managers typically worked in a fragmented, interrupted fashion. Over the four weeks, the managers had, on average, only nine periods of 30 minutes or more alone, with 12 brief contacts each day. They spent 36 per cent of their time on paperwork (writing, dictating, reading, calculating) and 43 per cent in informal discussion. They spent the remainder on formal meetings, telephoning and social activities.

The research team also found great variety between managers when they analysed the data to show different profiles of management work, based not on level or function but on how they spent their time. They identified five profiles:

1 **Emissaries** spent much of their time out of the organisation, meeting customers, suppliers or contractors.
2 **Writers** spent most of their time alone reading and writing, and had the fewest contacts with other managers.
3 **Discussers** spent most of their time with other people and with their colleagues.
4 **Troubleshooters** had the most fragmented work pattern of all, with many diary entries and many fleeting contacts, especially with their subordinates.
5 **Committee members** had a wide range of internal contacts, and spent much time in formal meetings.

They spent half their time in discussions with more than one other person.

Source: Stewart (1967).

Henry Mintzberg – ten management roles

Mintzberg (1973) used structured observations to gather data on how managers spent their time – though from only five chief executives. Despite this limitation others (e.g. Martinko and Gardner, 1990) have supported Mintzberg's main conclusion that managers' work was varied and fragmented (see also Key Ideas). He identified ten management roles in the three categories shown – informational, interpersonal and decisional – all of which are means of influencing other people. Table 1.2 lists these roles, with the right-hand column giving contemporary examples from an account by the manager of a project to distribute funds to schools to improve nutrition.

Table 1.2

Mintzberg's ten management roles

Category	Role	Activity	Examples from a school nutrition project
Informational	**Monitor**	Seek and receive information, scan reports, maintain interpersonal contacts	Collect and review funding applications; set up database to monitor application process
	Disseminator	Forward information to others, send memos, make phone calls	Share content of applications with team members by e-mail
	Spokesperson	Represent the unit to outsiders in speeches and reports	Present application process at internal and external events
Interpersonal	**Figurehead**	Perform ceremonial and symbolic duties, receive visitors	Sign letters of award to successful applicants
	Leader	Direct and motivate subordinates, train, advise and influence	Design and coordinate process with team and other managers
	Liaison	Maintain information links in and beyond the organisation	Become link person for government bodies to contact for progress reports
Decisional	**Entrepreneur**	Initiate new projects, spot opportunities, identify areas of business development	Use initiative to revise application process and to introduce electronic communication
	Disturbance handler	Take corrective action during crises, resolve conflicts amongst staff, adapt to changes	Holding face-to-face meetings with applicants when the outcome was negative; handling staff grievances
	Resource allocator	Decide who gets resources, schedule, budget, set priorities	Ensure fair distribution of grants nationally
	Negotiator	Represent unit during negotiations with unions, suppliers, and generally defend interests	Working with sponsors and government to ensure consensus during decision making

Source: Based on Mintzberg (1973), and private communication from the project manager.

Informational roles

Managing depends on obtaining information about external and internal events, and passing it to others. The *monitor role* involves seeking out, receiving and screening information to understand the organisation and its environment. It comes from papers and reports, and from chance conversations with customers or new contacts at conferences and exhibitions. Much of this information is oral (gossip as well as formal meetings), building on personal contacts. In the *disseminator role* the manager shares information by forwarding reports, passing on rumours or briefing staff. As a *spokesperson* the manager transmits information to people outside the organisation – speaking at a conference, briefing the media or giving the department's view at a company meeting. Michael O'Leary at Ryanair is renowned for flamboyant statements to the media about competitors or officials in the European Commission with whose policies he disagrees.

Interpersonal roles

Interpersonal roles arise directly from a manager's formal authority and status, and shape relationships with people within and beyond the organisation. In the *figurehead role* the manager is a symbol, representing the unit in legal and ceremonial duties such as greeting a visitor, signing legal documents, presenting retirement gifts or receiving a quality award. The *leader role* defines the manager's relationship with other people (not just subordinates), including motivating, communicating and developing their skills and confidence. As one manager commented:

> I am conscious that due to conflicting priorities I am unable to spend as much time interacting with staff members as I would like. I try to overcome this by leaving my door open whenever I am alone as an invitation to staff to come in and interrupt me, and to encourage the staff to come to me to discuss any problems that may arise.

The *liaison role* focuses on contacts with people outside the immediate unit. Managers maintain a network in which they trade information and favours for mutual benefit with clients, government officials, customers and suppliers. For some managers, particularly chief executives and sales managers, the liaison role takes a high proportion of their time and energy.

 **management in practice**   **Strengthening interpersonal roles**

A company restructured its regional operations, closed a sales office in Bordeaux and transferred the work to Paris. The sales manager responsible for south-west France was now geographically distant from her immediate boss and the rest of the team. This caused severe problems of communication and loss of teamwork. She concluded that the interpersonal aspects of the role were vital as a basis for the informational and decisional roles. The decision to close the office had broken these links.

She and her boss agreed to try the following solutions:

- a 'one-to-one' session of quality time to discuss key issues during monthly visits to head office;
- daily telephone contact to ensure speed of response and that respective communication needs were met;
- use of fax and e-mail at home to speed up communications.

These overcame the break in interpersonal roles caused by the location change.

Source: Private communication.

Decisional roles

Creativity is the ability to combine ideas in a unique way or to make unusual associations between ideas.

In the *entrepreneurial role* managers demonstrate **creativity** and initiate change. They see opportunities and create projects to deal with them. Managers play this role when they introduce a new product or create a major change programme – as when Lars Kolind became chief executive of Oticon (Chapter 10 case), determined to change an established and inflexible business, unsuited to deal with new competition. Managers play the *disturbance-handler role* when they deal with problems and changes that are unexpected.

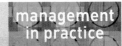

Two examples of handling disturbance

In early 2004 Doreen Tobin, chief financial officer of Vivendi Universal, the French media and communications group that has owned Universal Music Group since 2000, announced that it planned to cut €400 million from its cost base by 2005. The company had just reported a loss of €1.1 billion, which she blamed on the recent contraction in the music industry. The saving will come from cuts in back-office staff, lower royalties to artists, and a reduction in the number of artists whose work it promotes.

In the same year the chief executive of Lego, the Danish toy maker, unveiled a wide-ranging restructuring programme, under which it would cut jobs, reduce costs and sell non-core businesses. He said that it had recently misjudged part of the market and lost substantial sales, but that it now wanted to deal with its serious earnings crisis by improving its competitive edge and returning the focus to basic play materials.

Source: Various published information.

The *resource-allocator role* involves choosing amongst competing demands for money, equipment, personnel and other resources. How much of her budget should the housing manager quoted on p. 23 spend on different types of project? What proportion of the budget should a company spend on advertising or to improve a product? The manager of an ambulance service regularly decides between paying overtime to staff to replace an absent team member or letting service quality decline until a new shift starts. This is close to the *negotiator role*, in which managers seek agreement with other parties on whom they depend. When managers at Ryanair want to change the fees they pay to an airport they try to negotiate a new deal with the owners.

Activity 1.4   Gather evidence about Mintzberg's model

Recall a time when you have been responsible for managing an activity.

- Do the ten roles cover all of the roles you performed, or did you do things that are not included in his list? What were they?
- Give examples of what you did under (say) five of the roles.
- Were there any of these roles to which you should have given more time? Or less?
- If possible compare your results with other members of your course.
- Decide if the evidence you have collected supports or contradicts Mintzberg's theory.

Mintzberg proposed that every manager's job combines these roles, with their relative importance varying between the manager's level and their type of business. Managers usually recognise that they use many of the roles as they influence others to add value.

Managers often highlight two roles missing from Mintzberg's list – manager as subordinate and manager as worker. Most managers have subordinates but, except for those at the very top, they are subordinates themselves. Part of their role is to advise, assist and influence their boss – the role of 'managing up', to influence people over whom they have no formal authority. Managers often cannot wait for a decision to be resolved through formal channels, and need to persuade people higher up the organisation of a proposal's value or urgency. A project manager recalled:

Ryanair – the case continues   www.ryanair.com   C A S E   S T U D Y

The company has continued to grow rapidly, announcing in December 2006 that it had carried a record 40 million passengers that year. Passenger volumes rose by 20 per cent in the year to March 2007 to 42.5 million, following a 26 per cent rise the previous year. However it expected growth in the year to March 2008 to be only about 5 per cent. It was now one of the world's most profitable airlines, and continued to seek new bases from which to operate its growing European network. Despite the growing passenger numbers managers continued to seek ways to cut costs and raise revenues. They decided that their new aircraft would not have window blinds, headrests, seat-pockets or reclining seats: this would save money, and managers believed passengers would not miss these 'frills' as most journeys are less than an hour.

In 2005 the company earned £55 million from selling refreshments to passengers, and in 2006 began to charge customers for checking in their baggage. Each time a passenger rents a car or books a hotel room on the Ryanair website, it earns a commission. It now sells scratch cards on board, plans to offer in-flight gambling and online gaming over its website: the chief executive thinks that gambling could double Ryanair's profits over the next decade. A report by Paul Vallely for *The Independent* in late 2006 noted that:

Currently he's offering advertisers the opportunity to repaint the exteriors of Ryanair's planes. Effectively turning them into giant billboards: Hertz, Jaguar and Vodafone have purchased space on the fuselages of Ryanair's 737s.

Applicants for jobs as first officers are charged £50 to apply online, which is refunded if they are successful. They must also pay a non-refundable £200 for a simulator check. The company expects that in 2007 it will introduce a scheme enabling passengers to use in-flight mobile phones, and believes that revenue from such ancillary activities will continue to grow more rapidly than passenger revenue.

Sources: *Economist*, 10 July 2004; *Independent*, 7 October 2006; *Financial Times*, 7 June 2006; Kumar (2006); and company website.

Case questions 1.2

- Which of Mintzberg's management roles can you identify being exercised in the latest stage of the Ryanair case?
- Decide which two of these roles are likely to be most critical in the next stage of the company's development, and explain why.

This is the second time we have been back to the management team, to propose how we wish to move forward, and to try and get the resources that are required. It is worth taking the time up front to get all members fully supportive of what we are trying to do. Although it takes a bit longer we should, by pressure and by other individuals demonstrating the benefits of what we are proposing, eventually move the [top team] forward.

Many managers spend some time doing the work of the organisation. A director of a small property company helps with sales visits, or an engineering director helps with difficult technical problems. A lawyer running a small practice performs both professional and managerial roles.

Fred Luthans – managers as networkers and politicians

Does the focus of a manager's influencing activities affect performance? Mintzberg's study gave no evidence on this point, but work by Luthans (1988) showed that the relative amount of time spent on specific roles did affect outcomes. The team observed 292 managers in four organisations for two weeks, recording their behaviours in agreed categories.

Managerial work in small businesses

key ideas

O'Gorman *et al.* (2005) studied the work of ten owner-managers of small growth-oriented businesses to establish empirically if the nature of their work differs from those in the large businesses studied by Mintzberg. They concluded that managerial work in these businesses is in some ways similar to that in large organisations, finding brevity, fragmentation and variety; mainly verbal communication; and an unrelenting pace.

Another observation was that managers moved frequently between roles, switching from, say, reviewing financial results to negotiating prices with a customer. They were constantly receiving, reviewing and giving information, usually by telephone or in unscheduled meetings. They reacted immediately to live information by redirecting their attention to the most pressing issues, so that their days were largely unplanned, with frequent interruptions. They spent only a quarter of their time in scheduled meetings compared to Mintzberg's finding that managers in large organisations spent almost 60 per cent of their time in this way. Finally, the owners of these small businesses spent 8 per cent of their time in non-managerial activities – twice that of those in Mintzberg's study.

The research shows that the nature of managerial work in small growth-oriented businesses is in some ways similar to, and in others different from, that in large organisations. There is the same brevity and fragmentation, but more informal communication.

Source: O'Gorman *et al.* (2005).

The research also distinguished between levels of 'success' (relatively rapid promotion) and 'effectiveness' (work-unit performance and subordinates' satisfaction). The behavioural categories were:

Communicating	Exchanging information and paperwork
Traditional management	Planning, decision making, controlling
Networking	Interacting with outsiders, socialising/politicking
Human resource management	Motivating, managing conflict, staffing, training

The conclusion was that *successful* managers spent considerably more time networking (socialising, politicking, interacting with outsiders) than the less successful managers. Human resource management took least time. In contrast, *effective* managers spent most time on communication and human resource management activities. They spent little time networking. These results implied that managers who want to rise to more senior positions should spend relatively large amounts of time and effort on networking and on the political skills of management – confirmed by Aslani and Luthans (2003). Noordegraaf and Stewart (2000) provide an extensive review of research into the managerial role, especially into differences and similarities between contexts, sectors and nations.

1.6   Influencing through the tasks of managing

A second way in which managers influence others is when they manage the transformation of resources into more valuable outputs. Building on Figure 1.1, this involves the **management tasks** of planning, organising, leading and controlling the use of resources to 'get things done'. The amount of each varies with the job and the person, and they do not perform them in sequence: they do them simultaneously, switching as the situation requires.

Management tasks are those of planning, organising, leading and controlling the use of resources to add value to them.

Figure 1.2 illustrates the elements of this definition. It expands the central 'transforming' circle of Figure 1.1 to show the tasks that together make up the transformation process. People draw inputs (resources) from the environment and transform them through the tasks of planning, organising, leading and controlling. This results in goods and services that they pass as output into the environment. The feedback loop indicates that this output is the source of future resources.

Environment

Organisations depend on the external environment for the resources to sustain them. These are most clearly those of finance, people, ideas, materials and information. They also include intangible resources such as goodwill, licences, permissions and authorisations to undertake certain activities. An organisation also depends on people in the external environment being willing to buy or recognise what it produces, and so provide the cash, recognition or reputational resources it needs to survive. Commercial firms sell goods and services and use the revenue to buy resources. Public organisations depend on the authorities being sufficiently satisfied with their performance to provide future budgets. Charities depend on convincing donors that they have used their contributions well. Part 2 of the book deals with the external environment.

Planning

Planning deals with the overall direction of the work to be done. It includes forecasting future trends, assessing resources and developing objectives for performance. It inevitably means making decisions about the areas of work in which to engage, and how to use resources. Managers therefore invest time and effort in developing a sense of direction for the organisation, or their part of it, and express this in a set of objectives. Part 3 of the book deals with planning.

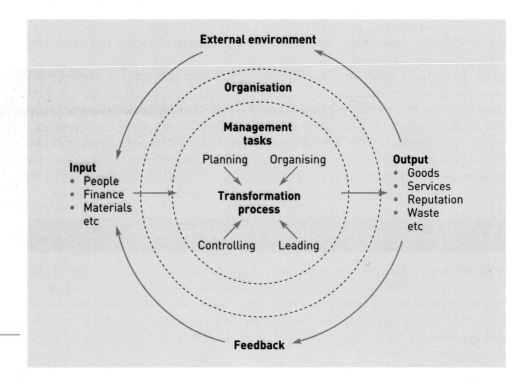

Figure 1.2

The tasks of management

David Simon – planning targets at BP www.bp.com

David Simon was chairman and chief executive of BP from 1992 to 1995. He believes that setting simple goals is an important part of developing a culture of continual performance improvement. He made it clear to BP employees that they should be cost and profit conscious. He has a golden rule for attaining goals: 'Targeting is fundamental to achieving. If you do not target, you do not measure and you do not achieve.' He believes that:

> Picking the right targets is a skill in itself. The difficulty of leadership is picking the targets and having a dialogue as you progress towards that goal so that, when it is achieved, it seems the easiest thing in the world. Then you can pick another target.

One top executive described Simon's accomplishment: 'What he has done so well is pull the company together in a very calming way, setting clear targets and telling people how they can achieve them.'

Source: See BP Case Study at the end of Part 2.

Organising

Organising is the activity of moving abstract plans closer to realisation, by deciding how to allocate time and effort. It includes creating a structure for the organisation, developing policies for HRM and deciding what equipment people need. Part 4 deals with organising.

Reorganising Diageo's distribution in the US www.diageo.com

Diageo, based in the UK, is the world's leading premium drinks business, whose brands include Smirnoff, Guinness, J&B and Baileys. To make the most of its already strong position in the United States it announced in 2004 that it had completed a major reorganisation of its distribution in that country. It had reduced the number of distributors in each state, and in return required those remaining to do more – such as employ some staff who only sell Diageo brands. The benefits included better retail displays – a key influence on a customer's choice of drink. The company believed that this change in organisation had contributed to a 10 per cent growth in sales and a small increase in market share.

Source: Company announcement of half-yearly results, February 2004, available at www.diageo.com.

Leading

Leading is the activity of generating effort and commitment, including motivating individuals and teams. As organisations become more complex, so does the task of securing commitment and action. People exercise choice, and managers cannot assume that they will act as managers would like them to. For David Simon at BP, setting targets was itself a vital part of his leadership. Part 5 deals with this topic.

Controlling

Control is the task of monitoring progress, comparing it with plan, and taking corrective action. Managers set a budget for a housing department, an outpatients' clinic, or for business travel. They then ensure that there is a system to collect information regularly on expenditure or performance – to check they are keeping to budget. If not, they need to decide how to bring actual costs back into line with budgeted costs. Are the outcomes consistent with the objectives? If so, they can leave things alone. But if by Wednesday it is clear that staff will not meet the week's production target then managers need to act. They may deal with the deviation by a short-term response – such as authorising overtime. Other deviations are so severe that the board decides to leave a business altogether – the Prudential decided to sell Egg, their online bank, to Citibank in 2006, as it was losing so much money.

 **The dangers of less control at Shell** www.shell.com

In early 2004 Shell received some damaging publicity when the (then) chairman admitted the company had overstated its oil reserves – a key part of an oil company's value. Many observers believed that the source of the trouble lay in the company's history – including the dismantling of well-established systems of internal controls during a period of growth in the 1990s. As senior managers encouraged growth and a more entrepreneurial spirit ('people were wearing T-shirts saying "grow at 15 per cent a year"') controls were gradually removed as a hindrance. Where previously systems were in place to track projects, it became almost impossible to find out how much money had been committed. Executive committees for main business units were given more responsibility, and were expected to make speedier decisions, with fewer restrictions and checks. This decreased internal control, and opened the way for top management to manipulate data – but it was not seen as dangerous at the time.

Source: Based on an article by Ian Bickerton, *Financial Times*, 18 June 2004.

Control also provides an opportunity to learn from past events. The ability of managers to learn from their experience is crucial to their performance. This does not mean sending people on external courses, but creating and using opportunities to learn from what they are doing. The box gives an example of this; Part 6 deals with control.

 **Encouraging learning**

The organisation is a national charity that runs residential homes for people with severe learning disabilities. It has a high reputation for the quality of the care it gives and for the way it treats the carers. Managers take whatever opportunities they can to help staff gain confidence in the difficult and often stressful work. An example:

> Staff in one area described how their manager supported their studies by creating a file for them containing information on relevant policies and legislation. The same manager recognised that a night-shift worker doing a qualification was not getting the range of experience necessary to complete college assessments: 'So she took me to a review last week and also took me to a referral for a service user. I'd never seen that side before – but now I can relate to the stuff that will come up at college. It's about giving you the fuller picture, because sometimes the night shift can be quite isolating.'

Source: Unpublished research.

The tasks in practice

Managers typically switch between tasks many times a day. They deal with them intermittently and in parallel, touching on many different parts of the job, as this manager in a housing association explains:

> My role involves each of these functions. Planning is an important element as I am part of a team with a budget of £8 million to spend on promoting particular forms of housing. So planning where we will spend the money is very important. Organising and leading are important too, as staff have to be clear on which projects to take forward, clear on objectives and deadlines. Controlling is also there – I have to compare the actual money spent with the planned budget and take corrective action as necessary.

And a manager in a legal firm:

> As a manager in a professional firm, each assignment involves all the elements to ensure we carry it out properly. For example, I have to set clear objectives for the assignment, organise the necessary staff and information to perform the work, supervise staff and counsel them if necessary, and evaluate the results. All the roles interrelate and there are no clear stages for each one.

Activity 1.5   **Gather evidence about the tasks of managing**

Recall your work on Activity 1.4.

- Do the four tasks of managing cover all of your work, or did you do things that are not included? What were they?
- Give an example of something you did in each of the tasks.
- Were there any of these to which you should have given more time? Or less?
- If possible compare your results with other members of your course.

1.7   Influencing through shaping the context

A third way in which managers influence others is through changing aspects of the context in which they work. Changing an office layout, a person's reporting relationships, or the rewards they obtain, alter their context and perhaps their actions. The context is both an influence on the manager and a tool with which to influence others (Johns, 2006):

> It is impossible to understand human intentions by ignoring the settings in which they make sense. Such settings may be institutions, sets of practices, or some other contexts created by humans – contexts which have a history, within which both particular deeds and whole histories of individual actors can and have to be situated in order to be intelligible. (Czarniawska, 2004, p.4)

Managers continually aim to create contexts that they hope will influence others to act in ways that meet their objectives.

Dimensions of context

Internal context

Figures 1.1 and 1.2 showed the links between managers, their organisation and the external environment. Figure 1.3 enlarges the 'organisation' circle to show more fully the elements that make up the internal environment within which managers work. Any organisation contains these elements – they represent the immediate context of the manager's work. For example, as Jorma Ollilia built Nokia into a major business, he and his team made many changes to technology, business processes – and indeed to all the elements shown in the figure (Steinbock, 2001), which later chapters examine:

- **objectives** (Chapters 6 and 8) – a desired future state of an organisation or unit;
- **culture** (Chapter 3) – norms, beliefs and underlying values that characterise the unit;
- **structure** (Chapter 10) – how tasks are divided and coordinated to meet objectives;
- **technology** (Chapter 12) – the facilities and equipment that people use to transform inputs into useful outputs;
- **power** (Chapter 14) – the amount and distribution of power with which to influence others;
- **people** (Chapter 15) – their knowledge, skills, attitudes and goals;
- **finance** (Chapter 19 – the financial resources available;
- **business processes** (Chapter 20) – activities that people and technologies perform on materials and information.

Models such as this show that managers work within constraints – they are to some degree helped or hindered by the elements in Figure 1.3. Effective managers do not accept their context passively – they initiate change to create the combination of elements to meet their objectives (Chapter 13).

Historical context

Managing takes place within the flow of history as what people do now reflects the influence of past events and future uncertainties. Managers typically focus on current issues, ensuring that things run properly, and that the organisation works. At the same time, history exerts an influence through the structure and culture. People remember successes and failures, which affects how they respond to current proposals.

However good the present situation, effective managers look to the future. They question present systems and seek improvements, observe changes in the environment and what they imply. Are resources being wasted, requiring some changes in method? What

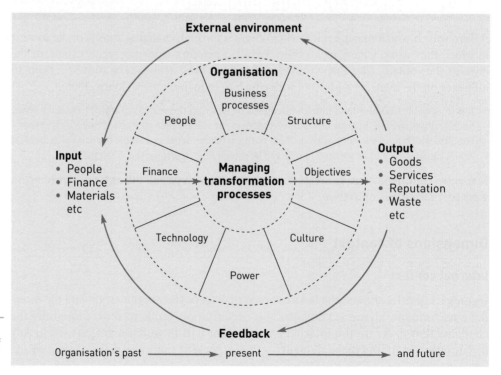

Figure 1.3

The internal and external context of management

are others doing? Questions such as these are resolved through the tasks and processes of management. The arrow at the foot of the figure represents the historical context.

External context

Finally there is the world outside. Chapter 3 shows that the external context includes an immediate competitive (micro) environment and a wider (or macro) environment. All of these affect performance, and part of the manager's work is to identify emerging changes and adapt the organisation. Managers at major food retailers have noted growing consumer interest in healthy food, and are working with suppliers to meet this.

Table 1.3 summarises the last two sections and illustrates how managers can influence others as they perform tasks affecting internal, micro and macro contexts.

	Internal (organisational)	Micro (competitive)	Macro (general)
Planning	Clarifying the objectives of a business unit, and communicating them clearly to all staff	Reducing prices in the hope of discouraging a potential competitor from entering the market	Lobbying for a change in a trade agreement to make it easier to enter an overseas market
Organising	Changing the role of a business unit	Reducing the number of suppliers in exchange for improved terms	Lobbying government to change planning laws to enable longer trading hours
Leading	Redesigning tasks and training staff to higher levels to improve motivation	Arranging for staff to visit customers so that they understand more fully what they need	Sending staff on overseas study tours to raise awareness of changes in the macro context
Controlling	Ensuring the information system keeps an accurate output record	Implementing an information system directly linked to customers and suppliers	Lobbying for tighter procedures to ensure all countries abide by trade agreements

Table 1.3

Examples of managing tasks in each context

Theories of managers and their context

Anyone managing a business uses a theory (even if subconsciously) of the link between context and action. This section sets out three alternative models – determinism, choice and interaction – which Chapter 13 develops more fully.

Determinism

The determinist view is that people have no influence on events, which are the result of forces beyond their control. Performance, on this view, depends on micro and macro factors such as the industry one is in or the rate of economic growth. Managers must adapt to external changes and have little influence over the direction of the business. People expect banks to have cash machines and to offer Internet banking, so banks have little choice but to use these technologies. On this view, the context is an independent variable: Figure 1.4(a) represents this.

Choice

An alternative view is that people have free will and can influence events. People in powerful positions shape their environment, have minds of their own and choose which businesses to enter or leave, and the countries in which they operate. Many observers believe that managers in major companies lobby to influence taxation, regulations and policy generally to serve their interests. On this view, the context is a dependent variable, reflecting human activities – Figure 1.4(b).

Interaction

The interaction approach expresses the idea that people are influenced by, and can themselves influence, the context. People interpret the existing context and act to change it to promote personal, local or organisational objectives. A manager may see a change in the company's external environment, and respond by advocating the purchase of a computer system (technology) or a change in reporting relationships (structure). Others interpret this proposal in the light of *their* perspective. All the players try to influence decisions in a way that suits their interests. The outcomes from these interactions affect the context – which now provides the historical background to future action. The essential idea is that the relationship between the manager and the context works both ways – Figure 1.4(c). People shape the context, and the context shapes people. Throughout the book there are examples of managers interacting with their context.

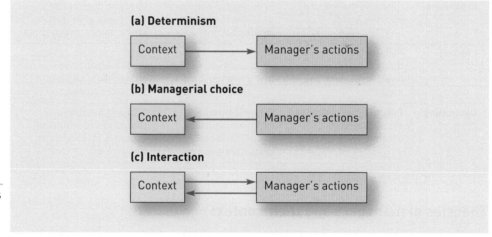

Figure 1.4

Alternative models of managers and their context

Ryanair – the case continues www.ryanair.com   C A S E   S T U D Y

The company depends on securing agreements with airport operators, and also approvals from aviation authorities in the countries to which it flies. This often leads it into public disputes, such as one with the European Commission over subsidies. The regional government and the company operating Charleroi Airport in Belgium offered the company a subsidy to persuade it to fly there. The European Commission ruled that such subsidies were illegal, and the company feared that it would lose subsidies it receives at other airports: 'Bureaucrats in Brussels wish to prevent privately owned airlines from developing low-cost arrangements for the benefit of consumers', said Michael O'Leary, the chief executive. Ryanair's rivals lobbied in support of the Commission, urging them to stand firm against state aid.

In May 2006 Ryanair suspended planned flights between two Italian cities because the Italian National Civil Aviation Authority had refused to allow it to operate the route: the company claimed this was a deliberate attempt to protect the high-cost Italian national airline from competition.

Michael O'Leary takes a deliberately aggressive stance to these controversies, believing that 'as long as its not safety-related, there's no such thing as bad publicity'. He is dismissive of traditional high-cost airlines, the European Commission, airport operators, travel agents, and governments that try to protect established airlines from competition.

The rise in low-cost travel has affected where some people live and work. Some now choose to work in expensive cities such as London for perhaps four days a week, returning at weekends to their families in other countries. Entrepreneurs also offer new services. One

Briton who bought a second home in Slovenia now helps local estate agents to sell properties to English-speaking buyers. Others arrange for Britons to have dental treatment in less expensive eastern European countries.

Source: *Economist*, 10 July 2004; *Business Week*, 8 May 2006; *Independent*, 7 October 2006; and other sources.

Case questions 1.3

- Which aspects of the external general environment have affected the company?
- How has the company affected these environments?

1.8 Critical thinking

As managers aim to add value to resources by influencing others, they continually receive data, information and knowledge about their business and its context – but cannot take what they receive at face value. They must test it by questioning the underlying assumptions, relating them to the context, considering alternatives available and recognising limitations. In doing so they develop the skills of critical thinking.

Critical thinking

Brookfield (1987) stresses the benefits of thinking critically, in that it

> involves our recognizing the assumptions underlying our beliefs and behaviors. It means we can give justifications for our ideas and actions. Most important, perhaps, it means we try to judge the rationality of these justifications ... by comparing them to a range of varying interpretations and perspectives. (p. 13)

Critical thinking is a productive and positive activity that enables people to see a future with many possibilities, rather than as a single, fixed path. Critical thinkers 'are self-confident about their potential for changing aspects of their worlds, both as individuals and through collective action' (Brookfield, 1987, p. 5). He offers four components of critical thinking.

Critical thinking identifies the assumptions behind ideas, relates them to their context, imagines alternatives and recognises limitations.

Identifying and challenging assumptions

Critical thinkers look for the assumptions that underlie taken-for-granted ideas, beliefs and values, and question their accuracy and validity. They are ready to discard those that no longer seem valid guides to action, in favour of more suitable ones. A manager who presents a well-supported challenge to a theory of marketing that seems unsuitable to their business, or who questions the need for a new business division, is engaging in this aspect of critical thinking.

Recognising the importance of context

Critical thinkers are aware that context influences thought and action. Thinking uncritically means assuming that ideas and methods which work in one context will work equally well in others. What we regard as an appropriate way to deal with staff reflects a specific culture: people in another culture – working in another place or at a different time – will have other expectations. Critical thinkers look for approaches suitable for the relevant context.

Imagining and exploring alternatives

Critical thinkers develop the skill of imagining and exploring alternative ways of managing. They ask how others have dealt with a situation, and seek evidence about the effectiveness of different approaches. This makes them aware of realistic alternatives, and so increases the range of ideas that they can adapt and use.

Seeing limitations

Critical thinking alerts people to the limitations of knowledge and proposals. They recognise that because a practice works well in one situation does not ensure it will work in another. They are sceptical about research whose claims seem over-sold, asking about the sample or the analysis. They are open to new ideas, but only when these are supported by convincing evidence and reasoning.

Thinking critically will deepen your understanding of management. It does not imply a 'do-nothing' cynicism, 'treating everything and everyone with suspicion and

 **Techniques to help develop your ability to think critically**

1 **Identifying and challenging assumptions**
   ● Reflect on recent events that worked well or not so well; describing what happened and your reactions to it may help to identify assumptions that were confirmed or challenged by events.
   ● Do the same for an achievement of which you are most proud.
   ● Imagine that you have decided to leave your job, and are advising the committee who will appoint your replacement: list the qualities they should look for in that person. That may indicate the assumptions you hold about the nature of your job, and what it takes to do it well.

2 **Recognising the importance of context**
   ● Select a practice that people in your organisation take for granted; ask people in other organisations how they deal with the matter, and see if the differences relate to context.
   ● Repeat that with people who have worked in other countries.

3 **Imagining and exploring alternatives**
   ● Brainstorming – trying to think of as many solutions to a problem as you can in a short period, by temporarily suspending habitual judgements.
   ● Gather evidence about how other businesses deal with an aspect of management that interests you: the more alternatives you find, the easier it may become to think of alternatives that could work for you.

4 **Seeing limitations**
   ● Acknowledging the limited evidence behind a theory or prescription.
   ● Asking if it has been tested in different settings or circumstances.

Source: Based on Brookfield (1987) and Thomas (2003), p. 7.

doubt' (Thomas, 2003, p. 7). Critical thinking lays the foundation for a successful management career, as it helps to ensure that proposals are supported by convincing evidence and reasoning.

Managing your studies

Studying management is itself a task to be managed. Each chapter sets out some learning objectives – to which you can add. The text, including the activities and case questions, help you work towards these objectives, and you can check your progress by using the review questions at the end of each chapter. The questions reflect objectives of varying levels of difficulty (Anderson and Krathwohl, 2001), which Table 1.4 illustrates. Working on these will help develop your confidence to think critically in your studies and as a manager.

Studying is an opportunity to practise managing. You can plan what you want to achieve, organise the resources you need, generate personal commitment and check your progress. The book provides opportunities to improve your skills of literacy, reflection (analysing and evaluating evidence before acting), critical thinking, communicating, problem solving and teamwork.

The most accessible sources of ideas and theory are this book (including the 'further reading' and websites mentioned), your lectures and tutorials. Draw on the experience of friends and relatives to help with some of the activities and questions. These help you to gather information about current practices, which you can compare with members of your tutorial group and with the theories. As you go about your educational and social lives you are experiencing organisations, and in some cases helping to manage them. Actively reflecting on these experiences will support your study of management.

Table 1.4

Types of learning objective in the text

Type of objective	Typical words associated with each	Examples
Remember – retrieve relevant knowledge from memory	Recognise, recall	State or write the main elements and relationships in a theory
Understand – construct meaning from information	Interpret, give examples, summarise, compare, explain, contrast	Compare two theories of motivation; contrast two strategies, and explain which theory each reflects
Apply – use a procedure in a specified situation	Demonstrate, calculate, show, experiment, illustrate, modify	Use (named theory) to show the issues that managers in the case should consider
Analyse – break material into parts, showing relationship to each other and to wider purpose	Classify, separate, order, organise, differentiate, infer, connect, compare, divide	Collect evidence to support or contradict (named theory); which theory is reflected in (example of practice)?
Evaluate – make judgements based on criteria and standards	Decide, compare, check, judge	Decide if the evidence presented supports the conclusion; should the company do A or B?
Create – put parts together into a coherent whole; reorganise elements	Plan, make, present, generate, produce, design, compose	Present a marketing plan for the company; design a project proposal

Source: Adapted from Anderson and Krathwohl (2001), p. 31.

1.9 Current themes and issues

Each chapter of this book concludes with a section relating the topic to three related themes:

- the challenging performance expectations that many managers face;
- while also acting responsibly in general and over climate change in particular; and
- doing so in an increasingly international economy.

Performance

Many companies are in markets where customers are becoming more demanding, expecting more individual products or services, and who have more opportunities to take their custom elsewhere if they are not satisfied. Managers in the public sector face similar pressures, being expected to provide better services with the same or fewer resources. Taxpayers routinely demand better services but resist higher taxes, while employees may resist attempts to increase efficiency.

To meet these demands managers try to identify trends in the external context, and build an organisation that can meet them, by changing some or all of the elements in Figure 1.3. The next Management in Practice feature illustrates how one company is successfully meeting external demands by developing internal capabilities.

management in practice **Balancing external and internal at H&M** www.hm.com

H&M, the trading name of Swedish fashion retailer Hennes & Mauritz, is one of Europe's top performing companies. In 2005 sales rose by 14 per cent compared to 2004, and profit by 23 per cent. In 2007 it had over 1000 stores in 24 countries, selling fashionable clothes to young, style-conscious customers. The company's secret weapon is its quick turnaround time: H&M's in-house design team of 95 designers can move a garment from the design board to shop floor in as little as three weeks. Quick reflexes enable H&M to stay on the cutting edge of trends and minimise the impact of fashion disasters. Costs are kept low by outsourcing manufacturing to a network of more than 900 apparel contractors in low-wage countries such as Bangladesh, China and Turkey.

Source: *Business Week*, 28 July 2003, 24 June 2004; company website.

The H&M story shows how rapidly improving information and transport systems have enabled them to draw supplies from low-wage countries, while internally they have created processes and structures that allow them to manage a very rapid design-to-delivery system.

Managers meet the challenge of rising performance expectations in conjunction with two other factors – responsibility and internationalisation.

Responsibility

The pressure on H&M managers (as in all commercial companies) originates primarily with those who own the business – the shareholders. They expect managers to focus on adding value to resources in a way that most benefits their (the shareholders') financial interests, and that can be a daunting challenge in itself. As Chapter 5 will show, many other interest groups now expect managers to act in a way that benefits their (the stakeholders') interests. Many now interpret responsible action as that which takes account of a wide range of stakeholders. These wider interest groups press a range of issues: better treatment of employees, dealing fairly with suppliers, selling healthy food, protecting the environment, limiting effects on climate change, or improving the conditions of workers in developing countries. These demands often conflict, in that meeting the performance expectations of one group of stakeholders may make it more difficult to meet the expectations of others.

Internationalisation

The international economy can both help and hinder managers as they balance multiple performance expectations. They can often meet the expectations of their customers and shareholders by moving activities to suppliers in developing countries who are able to supply goods and services much more cheaply than those in the developed world. H&M is typical of this, able to draw suppliers around the world to meet customer demands – which is also profitable for shareholders. However, is that meeting other expectations of responsible behaviour? Workers in the domestic economy have lost employment, the transport of products over vast distances contributes to climate change, and suppliers in developing countries typically work to lower environmental and labour standards than those in developed countries. Meeting social expectations in a European country may mean becoming uncompetitive with companies operating under different regulations. Yet moving production abroad leads trade unions to accuse managers of not acting responsibly towards employees in their home country.

Summary

1 **Summarise the functions of organisations and how management affects their performance**
   - Organisations enable people to create value by transforming inputs into outputs of greater value – though the concept of creating value is subjective and open to different interpretations. Management is the process of building organisations in which inputs are transformed into more valuable outputs.

2 **Give examples to show how management is both a universal human activity and a distinct role**
   - Management is an activity that everyone undertakes to some extent as they manage their daily lives. In another sense management is an activity within organisations, conducted in varying degrees by a wide variety of people. It is not exclusive to people called 'managers'. People create the distinct role when they separate the management of work from the work itself and allocate the tasks to different people. The distinction between management and non-management work is fluid and the result of human action.

3 **Compare the roles of general, functional, line, staff and project managers**
   - General managers are responsible for a complete business or a unit within it. They depend on functional managers who can be either in charge of line departments meeting customer needs, such as manufacturing and sales, or in staff departments such as finance that provide advice or services to line managers. Project managers are in charge of temporary activities usually directed at implementing change.

4 Explain how managers influence others to add value to resources

- The processes of managerial work (Stewart, Mintzberg and Luthans). Rosemary Stewart drew attention to the fragmented and interrupted nature of management work, while Mintzberg identified ten management roles in three groups that he labelled informational, interpersonal and decisional. Luthans observed that successful managers were likely to be those who spent most time networking and politicking.

- Arranging the tasks (or content) of managerial work. Planning is the activity of developing the broad direction of an organisation's work, to meet customer expectations, taking into account internal capabilities. Organising is the activity of deciding how to deploy resources to meet plans, while leading seeks to ensure that people work with commitment to achieve plans. Control monitors activity against plans, so that people can adjust either if required.

- Shaping the contexts within which they and others work. The organisational context consists of eight elements that help or hinder the manager's work – objectives, technology, business processes, finance, structure, culture, power and people. The historical context also influences events, as does the external context made up of the competitive and general environments.

5 Evaluate a manager's approach to the role by analysing how they influence others

- You can achieve this objective by arranging with a manager to discus their role, and organise your questions or discussion around the theories of the processes, contents and contexts of managerial work outlined in the chapter. If possible compare your results with others on your course, and try to explain any differences you find.

6 Explain the elements of critical thinking and use some techniques to develop this skill

- Critical thinking is a positive approach to studying, as it encourages people to develop the skills of identifying and challenging assumptions; recognising the importance of context; imagining and exploring alternatives; and seeing the limitations of any idea or proposal.

7 Current themes and issues

Managers are expected to meet:

- challenging expectations of financial performance or service standards;

- while also acting responsibly in general and over climate change in particular; and

- to do so in an increasingly global economy, where competitors may work to less demanding expectations.

Review questions

1 Apart from delivering goods and services, what other functions do organisations perform?

2 What is the difference between management as a general human activity and management as a specialised occupation? How has this division happened, and what are some of its effects?

3 What examples are there in the chapter of this boundary being changed, and what were the effects?

4 Describe, with examples, the differences between general, functional, line, staff and project managers.

5 Give examples from your experience or observation of each of the four tasks of management.

6 How does Mintzberg's theory of management roles complement that which identifies the tasks of management?

7 What is the significance to someone starting a career in management of Luthans' theory about roles and performance?

8 How can thinking critically help managers do their job more effectively?

9 Review and revise the definition of management that you gave in Activity 1.1.

Concluding critical reflection

Think about the way managers in your company, or one with which you are familiar, go about their work. If you are a full-time student, draw on any jobs you have held or on the management of your studies at school or university. Review the material in the chapter, and make notes on these questions:

- Which of the issues discussed in this chapter are most relevant to the way you and your colleagues manage?

- What **assumptions** about the role of management appear to guide the way you, or others, manage? If these assumptions are supported by the evidence of recent events – have they worked, or not? Which aspects of the content and process of managing are you expected to focus on – or are you unsure? Does your observation support, or contradict, Luthans' theory?

- What aspects of the historical or current **context** of the company appear to influence how you, and others, interpret your management role? Do people have different interpretations?

- Can you compare and contrast your role with that of colleagues on your course? Does this suggest any plausible **alternative** ways of constructing your management role, in terms of where you devote your time and energy? How much scope do you have to change it?

- What **limitations** can you see in the theories and evidence presented in the chapter? For example, how valid might Mintzberg's theory (developed in large commercial firms) be for those managing in small business, or in the public sector? Can you think of ways of improving the model – e.g. by adding elements to it, or being more precise about the circumstance to which it applies?

Further reading

Magretta, J. (2002), *What Management Is (and why it is everyone's business),* Profile Books, London.

This small book by a former editor at the *Harvard Business Review* offers a brief, readable and jargon-free account of the work of general management. Highly recommended.

Thompson, P. and McHugh, D. (2002), *Work Organisations: A critical introduction* (3rd edn) Palgrave, Basingstoke.

Alvesson, M. and Wilmott, H. (1996), *Making Sense of Management,* Sage, London.

Both provide very detailed discussion of management from a critical perspective, with numerous further references.

Handy, C. (1988), *Understanding Voluntary Organizations,* Penguin, Harmondsworth.

This chapter has stressed that management is not confined to commercial organisations, and Handy's book offers a valuable perspective for anyone wanting to consider management in the voluntary sector more fully.

Drucker, P. (1999b), *Management Challenges for the 21st Century,* Butterworth/Heinemann, London.

Worth reading as a collection of insightful observations from the enquiring mind of this great management theorist.

Finkelstein, S. (2003), *Why Smart Executives Fail: And what you can learn from their mistakes,* Penguin, New York.

A thoroughly researched and elegantly written analysis of the causes of failure – from which he draws many valuable insights into the complexities of managing.

Noordegraaf, M. and Stewart, R. (2000), 'Managerial behaviour research in private and public sectors: distinctiveness, disputes and directions', *Journal of Management Studies,* vol. 37, no. 3, pp. 427–444.

A scholarly review of research into the role of managers, which summarises and relates the main contributions, including those who have studied management in the public sector.

Mezias, J.M. and Starbuck, W.H. (2003), 'Studying the accuracy of managers' perceptions: a research odyssey', *British Journal of Management,* vol. 14, no. 1, pp. 3–17.

Since this chapter has stressed the significance of managers interpreting and interacting with their context, this paper is a timely reminder of how fallible those perceptions can be. The other articles in this symposium provide valuable insights into how managers see their world.

Currie, G. and Proctor, S.J. (2005), 'The antecedents of middle managers' strategic contribution: the case of a professional bureaucracy', *Journal of Management Studies,* vol. 42, no. 7, pp. 1325–1356.

An empirical study comparing how middle managers contributed to strategy in three hospitals, showing the ambiguities in their changing roles, and how contextual factors affected performance.

Hales, C. (2005), 'Rooted in supervision, branching into management: continuity and change in the role of first-line managers', *Journal of Management Studies,* vol. 42, no. 3, pp. 471–506.

Reviews the literature on supervisors and first-line managers, as an introduction to an empirical study (135 organisations) of their changing, and continuing, role.

Weblinks

These websites have appeared in the chapter:

www.ryanair.com
www.charitycommission.gov.uk
www.allianceboots.com
www.bp.com

www.shell.com
www.diageo.com
www.hm.com

Visit two of the business sites in the list, or those of other organisations in which you are interested, and navigate to the pages dealing with recent news, press or investor relations.

- What are the main issues which the organisation appears to be facing?
- Compare and contrast the issues you identify on the two sites.
- What challenges may they imply for those working in, and managing, these organisations?

Annotated weblinks, multiple choice questions and other useful resources can be found on www.pearsoned.co.uk/boddy

Chapter 2

Models of management

Aim

To present the main theoretical perspectives on management and to show how they relate to each other.

Objectives

By the end of your work on this chapter you should be able to outline the concepts below in your own terms and:

1 Explain the value of models of management, and compare unitary, pluralist and critical perspectives

2 State the structure of the competing values framework and evaluate its contribution to our understanding of management

3 Summarise the rational goal, internal process, human relations and open systems models and evaluate what each can contribute to a manager's understanding of their role

4 Use the model to classify the dominant form in two or more business units, and to gather evidence about the way this affects the roles of managing in those units

5 Explain the influence on management of uncertain conditions and the assumptions of non-linear models of management.

Key terms

This chapter introduces the following ideas:

model (or theory)	open system
metapho	system boundary
scientific management	feedback
operational research	subsystem
bureaucracy	sociotechnical system
administrative management	contingency approach
human relations approach	non-linear system
system	

Each is a term defined within the text, as well as in the Glossary at the end of the book.

Robert Owen (1771–1856) was a successful manufacturer of textiles, who ran mills in England and at New Lanark, about 24 miles from Glasgow, in Scotland. David Dale built the cotton-spinning mills at New Lanark in 1785 – which were then the largest in Scotland. Since they depended on water power Dale had built them below the Falls of Clyde – a well-known tourist attraction throughout the eighteenth century. Many people continued to visit both the Falls and New Lanark, which combined both manufacturing and social innovations.

Creating such a large industrial enterprise in the countryside meant that Dale (and Owen after him) had to attract and retain labour – which involved building not just the mill but also houses, shops, schools and churches for the workers. By 1793 the mill employed about 1200 people, of whom almost 800 were children, aged from 6 to 17: 200 were under 10 (McLaren, 1990). Dale provided the children with food, education and clothing in return for their working 12 hours each day: visitors were impressed by these facilities.

One visitor was Robert Owen, who shared Dale's views on the benefits to both labour and owner of good working conditions. By 1801 Dale wanted to sell New Lanark to someone who shared his principles and concluded that Owen (who had married Dale's daughter) was such a man. Owen had built a reputation for management skills while running mills in England, and did not approve of employing children in them.

Having bought the very large business of New Lanark, Owen quickly introduced new management and production control techniques. These included daily and weekly measurements of stock, output and productivity; a system of labour costing and measures of work in progress. He used a novel control technique: a small, four-sided piece of wood, with a different colour on each side, hung beside every worker. The colour set to the front indicated the previous day's standard of work – black indicating bad. Everyone could see this measure of the worker's performance, which overseers recorded to identify any trends in a person's work: 'Every process in the factory was closely watched, checked and recorded to increase labour productivity and to keep costs down' (Royle, 1998, p. 13).

Reproduced with kind permission of New Lanark Conservation Trust.www.newlanark.org

Most adult employees, at this stage of the Industrial Revolution, had no experience of factory work, or of living in a large community such as New Lanark. Owen found that many 'were idle, intemperate, dishonest [and] devoid of truth' (quoted in Butt, 1971). Evening patrols were introduced to stop drunkenness, and there were rules about keeping the residential areas clean and free of rubbish. He also had 'to deal with slack managers who had tolerated widespread theft and embezzlement, immorality and drunkenness' (Butt, 1971).

During Owen's time at the mill it usually employed about 1500 people, and soon after taking over he stopped employing children under 10. He introduced other social innovations: a store at which employees could buy goods more cheaply than elsewhere (a model for the Co-operative Movement), and a school that looked after children from the age of 1 – enabling their mothers to work in the mills.

Sources: Butt (1971); McLaren (1990); Donachie (2000).

Case questions 2.1

- What management issues was Owen dealing with at New Lanark?
- What assumptions guided his management practices?

2.1 Introduction

The brief historical sketch of Robert Owen illustrates three themes that run through this book. First, he was active in devising management systems to improve mill performance, and paid particular attention to controlling the workforce to ensure productive activity. Second, Owen engaged with the wider social system: he criticised the effects of industrialisation on that social system and tried to influence local and national policy by advocating the end of child labour. (Providing nurseries for employees' children from the age of 1 would be rare even today.) Third, he was managing at a time of transition from an agricultural to an industrial economy, and many of the practices he invented were attempts to resolve the conflicts between these systems.

Indeed, Owen was an entrepreneur in many ways. His attempts to change worker behaviour was innovative, and he was equally creative in devising management systems and new ways of working. Managers today cope with similar issues. They need to recruit willing and capable staff, and ensure that their work creates value. Many share Owen's commitment to responsible business practice: they see that working conditions affect family circumstances – which in turn affect staff performance – and try to balance the two. Some subsidise child care and offer flexible hours to make it easier for people with family responsibilities to continue working. A new and widespread concern is that climate change will affect all businesses in ways that are not yet clear.

They also operate in a world experiencing changes equal to those facing Owen. In the newer industrial countries of eastern Europe and Asia the transition is again from agriculture to industry. Everywhere the Internet is enabling great changes in how people organise economic activity, equivalent to the Industrial Revolution of which Owen was part. All are coping with the transition to a world in which ever more business is done on a global scale.

In coping with such changes managers, like Owen before them, have searched for ways to manage their enterprises in a way that adds value. They all make assumptions about the best way to do things – and through trial and error develop management methods for their circumstances. Managers today can use their knowledge of these methods in deciding how to manage their business. No single approach will suit all conditions – managers need to draw critically and selectively on several perspectives.

The next section introduces the idea of management models, and how they can support a manager's work. Section 2.3 presents the competing values framework – a way of seeing the contrasts and complementarities between four theoretical perspectives – and the following sections outline the major ideas within each approach. The final section indicates some of the issues facing managers today – and new models that may represent these conditions.

2.2 Why study models of management?

A **model (or theory)** represents a complex phenomenon by identifying the major elements and relationships.

A **model (or theory)** represents a more complex reality. Focusing on the essential elements and their relationship helps to understand that complexity, and how change may affect it. Most management problems can be understood only by examining them from several perspectives, so no model offers a complete solution. Those managing a globally competitive business require flexibility, quality and low-cost production. Managers at Ford or DaimlerChrysler want models of the production process that help them to organise it efficiently from a technical perspective. They also want models of human behaviour which will help them to organise production in a way that encourages enthusiasm and commitment. The management task is to combine both approaches into an acceptable solution.

Managers act in accordance with their model (or theory) of the task. To understand management action we need to know the models available and how people use them, though Pfeffer and Sutton (2006) suggest why people frequently ignore such evidence: see Key Ideas.

Pfeffer and Sutton on why managers ignore evidence  key ideas

In making the case for evidence-based management, Pfeffer and Sutton (2006a) observe that experienced managers frequently ignore new evidence relevant to a decision because they:

● trust personal experience more than they trust research;
● prefer to use a method or solution that has worked before;
● are susceptible to consultants who vigorously promote their solutions;
● rely on dogma and myth – even when there is no evidence to support their value;
● uncritically imitate practices that appear to have worked well for famous companies.

Their paper outlines the benefits of basing practice on sound evidence – similar to the ideas of critical thinking presented in Chapter 1.

Source: Pfeffer and Sutton (2006a).

Models identify the variables

Models (theories) aim to identify the main variables in a situation, and the relationships between them: the more accurately they do so, the more useful they are. Since every situation is unique, many experienced managers doubt the value of theory. Joan Magretta's answer is that:

> without a theory of some sort it's hard to make sense of what's happening in the world around you. If you want to know whether you work for a well-managed organization – as opposed to whether you like your boss – you need a working theory of management. (Magretta, 2002, p. 10)

We all use theory, acting on (perhaps implicit) assumptions about the relationships between cause and effect. Good theories help this universal process by identifying variables and relationships. They provide a mental toolkit to deal consciously with a situation. The perspective we take reflects the assumptions we use to interpret, organise and makes sense of events – see Alan Fox in Key Ideas.

As managers seek to influence others to add value to resources, they use their mental model of the situation to decide where to focus effort. Figure 2.1 develops Figure 1.3 (the internal context within which managers work) to show some variables within each element: 'structure' could include more specific variables such as roles, teams or control systems. In 2006 Willie Walsh took over as chief executive of British Airways, and one of his objectives (set by his predecessor) was to raise operating profits to 10 per cent of sales. Figure 2.1 suggests ways of meeting this:

objectives – retaining a reputation for premium travel (a different market than Ryanair);

people – continuing the policy of reducing the number of employees;

technology – opening Terminal 5 at Heathrow;

business processes – new procedures for dealing with passengers and baggage.

key ideas · Alan Fox and a manager's frame of reference

Alan Fox (1974) distinguished between unitary, pluralist or radical perspectives on the relationship between managers and employees. Which assumption a person holds affects how they interpret the tasks of managing. Fox argued that those who take a:

- **unitary perspective** believe that organisations aim to develop rational ways of achieving common interests. Managerial work arises from a technical division of labour, and managers work to achieve objectives shared by all members.
- **pluralist perspective** believe that the complex division of labour in modern organisations creates groups with distinctive interests. Some conflict over ends and/or means is inevitable, and managerial work involves gaining sufficient consent to meet all interests in some mutually acceptable way.
- **radical perspective** challenge both unitary and pluralist models, arguing that they ignore the fact that the horizontal and vertical division of labour sustains unequal social relations within capitalist society. As long as these exist managers and employees will be in conflict.

Source: Alan Fox (1974).

In each area there are theories about the variables and their relationships – and about which changes will best add value. A change in one element may affect others – the aim of reducing staff will need to be handled sensitively to avoid hindering the aim of providing a premium service. Any change would depend on available *finance* – and on the chief executive's *power* to get things done. External events (Chapter 3) such as rising fuel prices or changes in general economic conditions shape all of these.

Managers need to influence people to achieve their value-adding objectives: people who are aware, thinking beings, with unique experiences, interests and objectives. This affects what information they attend to, the significance they attach to it and how they act. There is an example in Chapter 3 of a retail business in which senior managers, store

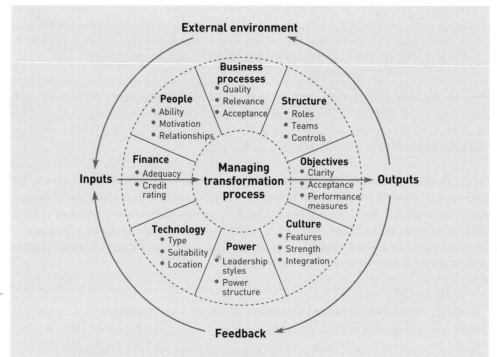

Figure 2.1

Some variables within the internal context of management

managers and shop-floor staff attached different meanings to the culture in which they worked. People interpret information subjectively, which makes it hard to predict how they will react: the Management in Practice feature illustrates two managers' contrasting assumptions about how to deal with subordinates.

Practice reflects managers' theories

These examples illustrate contrasting theories about motivation.

Motivating managers: Tim O'Toole, who became chief executive of London Underground in 2003, put in a new management structure, appointing a general manager for each line to improve accountability.

> Now there's a human being who is judged on how that line is performing and I want them to feel that kind of intense anxiety in the stomach that comes when there's a stalled train and they realise that it's their stalled train.

(From an article by Simon London, *Financial Times*, 20 February 2004)

Motivating staff to be innovative: Joe Roelandts is CEO of Xilinx (a company that makes advanced products in the electronics industry) and which (exceptionally) did not make staff redundant during a period of low industry demand.

> The decision to avoid lay-offs was a better business decision. It protected the minds of the people who work on the future; it keeps their minds free to continue to innovate. No one can innovate when they are worried about their jobs.

(From an article by Simon London, *Financial Times*, 22 January 2003)

Find out more at **www.xilinx.com.**

FT

Case questions 2.2

- Give examples of the variables in Figure 2.1 that Robert Owen was attempting to influence.
- Which of the variables were influencing the performance of his mill?
- Is there a conflict between the need to control workers and Owen's creative approach to management?

Models reflect their context

People develop models in response to circumstances: in this case this means the most pressing issues facing managers at the time. In the late nineteenth century skilled labour was scarce and unskilled labour plentiful: the most pressing problem for managers such as Robert Owen was to recruit and control workers. Entrepreneurs trying to meet growing demand wanted theories about making production more efficient. They looked for ways to simplify tasks so that they could use less skilled employees, and early management theories gave priority to these issues. People often refer to this focus on efficiency as a manufacturing mindset.

Peter Drucker (1954) observed that customers do not buy products, but the satisfaction of needs: what they value may be different from what producers think they are selling. Manufacturing efficiency is necessary, but not sufficient. Managers, Drucker argued, should develop a marketing mindset, focused on what customers want, and how

A **metaphor** is an image
used to signify the
essential characteristics
of a phenomenon.

much they will pay. As managers try to meet changing customer needs quickly and cheaply they seek models of flexible working. As business becomes more global, they seek theories about managing across the world.

key ideas Gareth Morgan's images of organisation

Since organisations are complex creations, no single theory can explain them adequately. We need to see them from several viewpoints, each of which will illuminate one aspect or feature – while also obscuring others. Gareth Morgan (1997) shows how alternative mental images and **metaphors** can represent organisations. Metaphors are a way of thinking about a phenomenon, attaching labels that vividly indicate the image being used. Images help understanding – but also obscure or distort understanding if we use the wrong one. Morgan explores eight ways of seeing organisations as:

- **machines** – mechanical thinking and the rise of the bureaucracies;
- **organisms** – recognising how the environment affects their health;
- **brains** – an information-processing, learning perspective;
- **cultures** – a focus on beliefs and values;
- **political systems** – a view on conflicts and power;
- **psychic prisons** – how people can become trapped by habitual ways of thinking;
- **flux and transformation** – a focus on change and renewal;
- **instruments of domination** – over members, nations and environments.

Critical thinking helps improve our mental models

The ideas on critical thinking in Chapter 1 help managers to improve the accuracy and usefulness of the theories they use to guide their action. Working effectively depends on being able and willing to test the validity of any theory, and to revise it in the light of experience by:

- identifying and challenging assumptions
- recognising the importance of context
- imagining and exploring alternatives
- seeing limitations.

As you work through this chapter, there will be opportunities to practise these components of critical thinking.

2.3 The competing values framework

People have developed a succession of models of management to understand and deal with current management issues. While academics or practitioners put forward new models, many managers continue to use earlier approaches – perhaps because they still suit their situation, or because they are familiar. Quinn *et al.* (2003) believe that successive models (which they term 'rational goal', 'internal process', 'human relations' and 'open systems') complement, rather than contradict, each other as they are all:

symptoms of a larger problem – the need to achieve organizational effectiveness in a highly dynamic environment. In such a complex and fast-changing world, simple solutions become suspect … Sometimes we needed stability, sometimes we needed change. Often we needed both at the same time. (p. 11)

While each model adds to our knowledge of management, none is sufficient in itself – the four are complementary elements in a larger whole. The 'competing values' framework integrates them by highlighting their underlying values – see Figure 2.2.

The vertical axis represents the tension between flexibility and control. Managers seek flexibility as they try to cope with rapid change. Others try to increase control – apparently the opposite of flexibility. The horizontal axis distinguishes an internal focus from an external one. Some managers focus on internal issues, while others focus on the world outside. Successive models of management relate to the four segments.

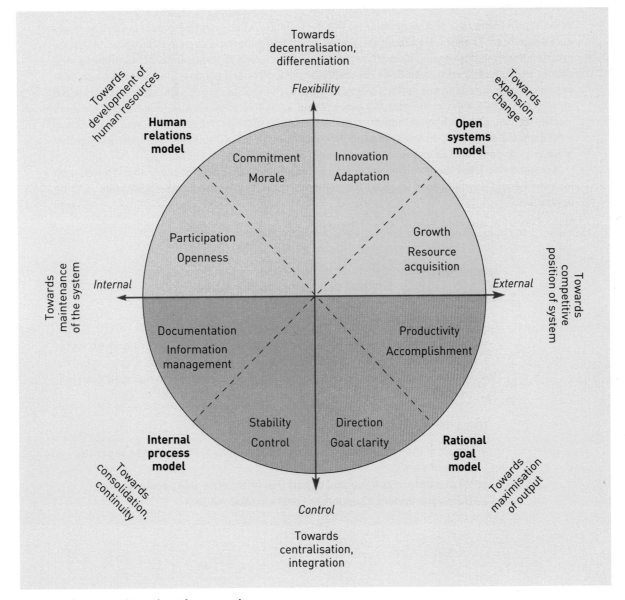

Figure 2.2 Competing values framework

Source: Quinn *et al.* (2003), p. 13.

The labels within the circle indicate the primary criteria of effectiveness that are the focus of models in that segment, shown around the outside. The human relations model, upper left in the figure, stresses the human criteria of commitment, participation and openness. The open systems model (upper right) stresses criteria of innovation, adaptation and growth. The rational goal model in the lower right focuses on productivity, direction and goal clarity. The internal process model stresses stability, documentation and control. Finally, the outer ring indicates the values associated with each model – the dominant value in the rational goal model is that of maximising output, while in human relations it is developing people. Successive sections of the chapter outline theories associated with each segment.

management in practice
Competing values at IMI? www.imiplc.com

When Martin Lamb took control of IMI (the UK's seventh largest engineering group) in 2001 he introduced significant changes. He rebuilt the group, which had suffered a decline in business like many other engineering businesses, by switching more manufacturing to low-cost countries and began to change the culture to encourage close links with key customers and to boost innovation. He also concentrated the business on five sectors of engineering, each associated with high-value products and a strong chance of growth in the next few years. About 40 skilled engineers at 'vision centres' had to identify technologies from other industries that IMI could adapt to its own use. Mr Lamb said: 'This is a fundamental transition, aimed at moving IMI away from an old-established manufacturing enterprise to a company focused on product development and applications of knowledge.'

Someone who knew the company well commented: 'I always had the feeling ... that IMI was a bit introverted and anything that [makes] the company more aggressive on the sales side is to be applauded.'

FT

Source: Extracts from an article in *Financial Times*, 4 February 2004.

Activity 2.1 Critical reflection on the model

Using the model to reflect on IMI

- Which of the competing values were most dominant in 2000, and which were most dominant at the time of this report?
- What examples can you find in the case that correspond to the open systems model?

Using the model to reflect on your organisation

- Which of the competing values are most dominant in, say, three separate departments?
- What evidence can you find of how that affects the way people manage?
- Does your evidence support or contradict the model?

2.4 Rational goal models

A rarely quoted example of early entrepreneurs developing ways to manage large numbers of people is found in the slave plantations in the United States, where several 'modern management practices were to be found in the operation of the ante-bellum plantations' (Cooke, 2003). Cooke quotes a contemporary account of work on a cotton plantation that records how owners divided slaves into gangs according to their abilities, and then allocated predetermined tasks to each:

> 1st the best hands, embracing those of good judgement and quick motion. 2nd those of the weakest and most inefficient class. 3rd the second class of hoe hands. Thus classified, the first class run ahead and open a small hole about seven to ten inches apart, into which the second class drop from four to five cotton seed, and the third class follow and cover with a rake. (Fogel, 1989: quoted in Cooke, 2003, p. 1908)

More widely, the availability of powered machinery during the Industrial Revolution enabled the transformation of manufacturing and mining processes. These technological innovations encouraged, but were not the only reason for, the growth of the factory system. The earlier 'putting-out' system of manufacture, in which people worked at home on materials supplied and collected by entrepreneurs, allowed great freedom over hours, pace and methods of work. However, it was difficult to control the quantity and quality of output. Emerging capitalist entrepreneurs found that they could secure more control if they brought workers together in a factory. Having all workers on a single site meant that:

> coercive authority could be more easily applied, including systems of fines, supervision ... the paraphernalia of bells and clocks, and incentive payments. The employer could dictate the general conditions of work, time and space; including the division of labour, overall organisational layout and design, rules governing movement, shouting, singing and other forms of disobedience. (Thompson and McHugh 2002, p. 22)

This still left entrepreneurs across Europe and later the United States (and now China – see Management in Practice) with the problem of how to manage these new factories profitably. Although domestic and export demand for manufactured goods was high, so was the risk of business failure.

Incentives at TCL, China www.tcl.com

management in practice

TCL Corporation is one of the top producers of electronics products in China, and management is proud of the long hours employees work. Signs posted next to production lines encourage workers to push themselves to do even more. 'If you don't diligently work today', one warns ominously, 'you'll diligently look for work tomorrow'. The company is growing rapidly and has won many awards for design and quality.

Source: Based on 'Bursting out of China', *Business Week*, 17 November 2003, pp. 24–25; company website.

key ideas   Adam Smith and Charles Babbage

Adam Smith, the Scottish economist, had written enthusiastically in 1776 of the way in which pin manufacturers in Glasgow had broken a job previously done by one man into several small steps. A single worker now performed each of these steps repetitively. This greatly reduced the discretion that workers had over their work but, because each was able to specialise, output increased dramatically. Smith believed that this was one of the key ways in which the new industrial system was increasing the wealth of the country.

Charles Babbage supported and developed Smith's observations. He was an English mathematician better known as the inventor of the first calculating engine. During his work on that project he visited many workshops and factories in England and on the Continent. He then published his reflections on 'the many curious processes and interesting facts' that had come to his attention (Babbage, 1835). He believed that 'perhaps the most important principle on which the economy of a manufacture depends is the division of labour amongst the persons who perform the work' (p. 169).

Babbage also observed that employers in the mining industry had applied the idea to what he called 'mental labour'. 'Great improvements have resulted ... from the judicious distribution of duties ... amongst those responsible for the whole system of the mine and its government' (p. 202). He also recommended that managers should know the precise expense of every stage in production. Factories should also be large enough to secure the economies made possible by the division of labour and the new machinery.

Source: Babbage (1835).

Frederick Taylor

Scientific management
The school of management called 'scientific' attempted to create a science of factory production.

The fullest answer to the problems of factory organisation came in the work of Frederick W. Taylor (1856–1915), always associated with the ideas of **scientific management**. An American mechanical engineer, Taylor focused on the relationship between the worker and the machine-based production systems that were in widespread use:

> the principal object of management should be to secure the maximum prosperity for the employer, coupled with the maximum prosperity for each employee. The words 'maximum prosperity' ... mean the development of every branch of the business to its highest state of excellence, so that the prosperity may be permanent'. (Taylor, 1917, p. 9)

He believed the way to achieve this was to ensure that each worker reached their state of maximum efficiency, so that each was doing 'the highest grade of work for which his natural abilities fit him' (p. 9). This would follow from detailed control of the process, which would become the managers' primary responsibility: they should concentrate on understanding the production systems, and use this to specify every aspect of the operation. In terms of Morgan's images, the appropriate image would be the machine. Taylor advocated five principles:

1 use scientific methods to determine the one best way of doing a task, rather than rely on the older 'rule of thumb' methods;
2 select the best person to do the job so defined, ensuring that their physical and mental qualities were appropriate for the task;
3 train, teach and develop the worker to follow the defined procedures precisely;
4 provide financial incentives to ensure people work to the prescribed method; and
5 move responsibility for planning and organising from the worker to the manager.

Taylor's underlying philosophy was that scientific analysis and fact, not guesswork, should inform management. Like Smith and Babbage before him, he believed that efficiency rose if tasks were routine and predictable. He advocated techniques such as time and motion studies, standardised tools and individual incentives. Breaking work into small, specific tasks would increase control. Specialist managerial staff would design these tasks and organise the workers:

> The work of every workman is fully planned out by the management at least one day in advance, and each man receives in most cases complete written instructions, describing in detail the task which he is to accomplish, as well as the means to be used in doing the work ... This task specifies not only what is to be done but how it is to be done and the exact time allowed for doing it. (Taylor, 1917, p. 39)

Taylor also influenced the development of administrative systems such as record keeping and stock control to support manufacturing.

Using work study in the 1990s

Oswald Jones recalls his experience as a work study engineer in the 1990s, where he and his colleagues were deeply committed to the principles of scientific management:

> Jobs were designed to be done in a mechanical fashion by removing opportunities for worker discretion. This had dual benefits: very simple jobs could be measured accurately (so causing [fewer] disputes) and meant that operators were much more interchangeable which was an important feature in improving overall efficiency levels. (p. 647)

Source: Jones (2000).

Managers in industrialised economies adopted Taylor's ideas widely: Henry Ford was an enthusiastic advocate. When he introduced the assembly line in 1914 the time taken to assemble a car fell from over 700 hours to 93 minutes. Ford also developed systems of materials flow and plant layout, a significant contribution to scientific management (Williams *et al.*, 1992; Biggs, 1996).

Increased productivity often came at human cost (Thomson and McHugh, 2002). Trade unions believed Taylor's methods increased unemployment, and vigorously opposed them. Many people find work on an assembly line boring and alienating, devoid of much human meaning. In extreme cases the time taken to complete an operation is less than a minute, and uses few human abilities.

Ford's Highland Park plant

Ford's plant at Highland Park, completed in 1914, introduced predictability and order

> that eliminates all questions of how work is to be done, who will do it, and when it will be done. The rational factory, then, is a factory that runs like a machine. (Biggs, 1996, p. 6)

Biggs provides abundant evidence of the effects of applying rational production methods:

> The advances made in Ford's New Shop allowed the engineers to control work better. The most obvious and startling change in the entire factory was, of course, the constant movement, and the speed of that movement, not only the speed of the assembly line, but the speed of every moving person or object in the plant. When workers moved from one place to another, they were instructed to move fast. Laborers who moved parts were ordered to go faster. And everyone on a moving line worked as fast as the line dictated. Not only were workers expected to produce at a certain rate in order to earn a day's wages but

they also had no choice but to work at the pace dictated by the machine. By 1914 the company employed supervisors called pushers (not the materials handlers) to 'push' the men to work faster.

The 1914 jobs of most Ford workers bore little resemblance to what they had been just four years earlier, and few liked the transformation ... As early as 1912, job restructuring sought an 'exceptionally specialized division of labor [to bring] the human element into [the] condition of performing automatically with machine-like regularity and speed'. (Biggs, 1996, p. 132)

Frank and Lillian Gilbreth

Frank and Lillian Gilbreth (1868–1924 and 1878–1972) worked as a husband and wife team, and enthusiastically promoted the development of scientific management. Frank Gilbreth had been a bricklayer, observing practices that made the work slow and output unpredictable. He filmed men laying bricks and used this to set out the most economical movements for each task. He specified exactly what the employer should provide, such as trestles at the right height and materials at the right time. Supplies of mortar and bricks (arranged the right way up) should arrive at a time that did not interrupt work. An influential book (Gilbreth, 1911) gave precise guidance on how to reduce unnecessary actions (from 18 to 5) and hence fatigue, while laying bricks. The rules and charts would help apprentices:

> [They] will enable the apprentice to earn large wages immediately, because he has ... a series of instructions that show each and every motion in the proper sequence. They eliminate the 'wrong' way [and] all experimenting. (quoted in Spriegel and Myers, 1953, p. 57)

Lillian Gilbreth focused on the psychological aspects of management, and on the welfare of the individual worker. She also advocated the ideas of scientific management believing that, properly applied, they would enable individuals to reach their full potential. Through careful development of systems, careful selection, clearly planned training and proper equipment, workers would build their self-respect and pride. In *The Psychology of Management* (1914) she argued that if workers did something well, and that was made public, they would develop pride in their work and in themselves. She recognised that workers had enquiring minds, and that management should take time to explain the reasons for work processes:

> Unless the man knows why he is doing the thing, his judgment will never reinforce his work ... His work will not enlist his zeal unless he knows exactly why he is made to work in the particular manner prescribed. (quoted in Spriegel and Myers, 1953, p. 431)

Activity 2.2   What assumptions did they make?

What assumptions did Frederick Taylor and Lillian Gilbreth make about the interests and abilities of industrial workers?

Operational research
is a scientific method of providing (managers) with a quantitative basis for decisions regarding the operations under their control.

Operational research

Another practice within the rational goal model is **operational research** (OR). This originated in the early 1940s, when the UK War Department faced severe management problems – such as the most effective distribution of radar-linked anti-aircraft gun emplacements, or the safest speed at which convoys of merchant ships should cross the Atlantic (see Kirby (2003) for a non-technical introduction to the topic). To solve these it formed operational research teams, which pooled the expertise of scientific disciplines such as mathematics and physics. These produced significant results: Kirby points out that while at the start of the London Blitz 20,000 rounds of ammunition were fired for each enemy aircraft destroyed: 'by the summer of 1941 the number had fallen ... to 4,000 as a result of the operational research [teams] improving the accuracy of radar-based gun-laying' (Kirby 2003, p. 94).

After the war, managers in industry and government saw that operational research techniques could also help to run complex civil organisations. The scale and complexity of business was increasing, and required new techniques to analyse the many interrelated variables. Mathematical models could help, and computing developments supported increasingly sophisticated models. In the 1950s the steel industry needed to cut the cost of transporting iron ore: staff used OR techniques to analyse the most efficient procedures for shipping, unloading and transferring it to steelworks.

The method is widely used in both business and public sectors, where it helps planning in areas as diverse as maintenance, cash flow, inventory and crew scheduling (e.g. Lezaun *et al.*, 2006). Willoughby and Zappe (2006) illustrate how a university has used the technique to help allocate students to seminar groups. One difficulty is that some managers find the mathematical basis forbidding. A second is that OR cannot take into account human and social uncertainties, and the assumptions built into the models may be invalid, especially if they involve political interests. The technique clearly contributes to the analysis of management problems, but is only one part of the solution.

Current status

Table 2.1 summarises principles common to rational goal models and their modern application.

Principles of the rational goal model	Current applications
Systematic work methods	Work study and process engineering departments develop precise specifications for processes
Detailed division of labour	Where staff focus on one type of work or customer in manufacturing or service operations
Centralised planning and control	Modern information systems increase the scope for central control of worldwide operations
Low-involvement employment relationship	Using temporary staff as required, rather than permanent employees

Table 2.1

Modern applications of the rational goal model

Examples of rational goal approaches are common in manufacturing and service organisations. Cooper and Taylor (2000) show how the work of accounting staff has been transformed by the steady application of scientific management techniques, while Aquiar (2001) presents a similar story from the building cleaning industry. You may have experienced the frustration of speaking to a customer service adviser on the telephone who is compelled to provide only a scripted response, without deviation, to try to make a further sale.

The methods are widely used in the mass production industries of emergent economies such as China and Malaysia. Gamble *et al.* (2004) found that in such plants 'Work organization tended to be fragmented (on Taylorist lines) and routinized, with considerable surveillance and control over production volumes and quality' (p. 403).

Human resource management policies were consistent with this approach – the recruitment of operators in Chinese electronics plants was

> often of young workers, generally female and from rural areas. One firm said its operators had to be 'young farmers within cycling distance of the factory, with good eyesight. Education is not important'. (p. 404)

2.5   Internal process models

Max Weber

A major contribution to the search for ways of managing organisations efficiently came from Max Weber (1978). Weber (1864–1920) was a German social historian who drew attention to the significance of large organisations. As societies became more complex, responsibility for core activities became concentrated in specialised units. They could only operate with systems that institutionalised the management process by creating rules and regulations, hierarchy, precise division of labour and detailed procedures. Weber was one of the first to observe that the process of **bureaucracy** was bringing routine to office operations just as machines had to production.

Bureaucracy is a system in which people are expected to follow precisely defined rules and procedures rather than to use personal judgement.

Bureaucratic management is usually associated with the characteristics in the next Key Ideas box.

Impersonality Rules leads to impersonality, which protects employees from the whims of managers. Although the term has negative connotations, Weber believed it ensured fairness, by evaluating subordinates objectively on performance rather than subjectively on personal considerations. It limits favouritism.

Division of labour Managers and employees work on specialised tasks, with the benefits originally noted by Adam Smith – such as that jobs are relatively easy to learn and control.

Hierarchical structure Weber advocated a clear hierarchy in which jobs were ranked vertically by the amount of authority to make decisions. Each lower position is under the control of a higher position.

Authority structure A system of rules, impersonality, division of labour and hierarchy forms an authority structure – the right to make decisions of varying importance at different levels within the organisation.

Rationality This refers to using the most efficient means to achieve objectives. Managers should run their organisations logically and 'scientifically' so that all decisions help to achieve the objectives.

Activity 2.4 Bureaucratic management in education?

Reflect on your role as a student and how rules have affected the experience. Try to identify one example of your own to add to those below or that illustrates the point specifically within your institution:

- rules and regulations – the number of courses you need to pass for a degree;
- impersonality – admission criteria, emphasising previous exam performance, not friendship;
- division of labour – chemists not teaching management, and vice versa;
- hierarchical structure – to whom your lecturer reports, and to whom they report;
- authority structure – who decides whether to recruit an additional lecturer;
- rationality – appointing new staff to departments that have the highest ratio of students to staff.

Compare your examples with those of other students and consider the effects of these features of bureaucracy on the institution and its students.

Weber was aware that, as well as creating bureaucratic structures, managers were using scientific management techniques to control production and impose discipline on factory work. The two systems complemented each other. Formal structures of management centralise power, and hierarchical organisation aids functional specialisation. Fragmenting tasks, imposing close discipline on employees and minimising their discretion ensures controlled, predictable performance (Thompson and McHugh, 2002).

Weber stressed the importance of a career structure clearly linked to the position a person held. This would allow them to move up the hierarchy in a predictable, defined and open way, which would increase their commitment to the organisation. Rules about selection and promotion brought fairness to these at a time when nepotism and favouritism were common. He also believed that officials should work within a framework of rules. The right to give instructions was based on a person's position in the hierarchy, and a rational analysis of how staff should work. This worked well in large public and private organisations, such as government departments and banks.

While recognising the material benefits of modern methods, Weber also saw their costs:

> Bureaucratic rationalization instigates a system of control that traps the individual within an 'iron cage' of subjugation and constraint ... For Weber, it is instrumental rationality, accompanied by the rise of measurement and quantification, regulations and procedures, accounting, efficiency that entraps us all in a world of ever-increasing material standards, but vanishing magic, fantasy, meaning and emotion. (Gabriel, 2005, p. 11)

Activity 2.5   **Gathering evidence on bureaucracy**

Rules often receive bad publicity, and we are all sometimes frustrated by rules that seem obstructive. To evaluate bureaucracy, collect some evidence. Think of a job that you or a friend has held, or of the place in which you work.

- Do the supervisors appear to operate within a framework of rules, or do they do as they wish? What are the effects?
- Do clear rules guide selection and promotion procedures? What are the effects?
- As a customer of an organisation, how have rules and regulations affected your experience?
- Check what you have found, preferably combining it with that prepared by other people on your course. Does the evidence support the advantages, or the disadvantages, of bureaucracy?

Henri Fayol

Administrative management is the use of institutions and order rather than relying on personal qualities to get things done.

Managers were also able to draw on the ideas of **administrative management** developed by Henri Fayol (1841–1925), whose work echoes that of Taylor and Weber. While Taylor's scientific management focused on production systems, Fayol devised management principles that would apply to the whole organisation. Like Taylor, Fayol trained as an engineer, graduating at the age of 19 as the most distinguished student in his year. In 1860 he joined Commentry–Fourchambault–Decazeville, a coal mining and iron foundry company, rising rapidly through the company to become managing director in 1888 (Parker and Ritson, 2005). By the time he retired in 1918 it had become one of the success stories of French industry. Throughout his career he kept detailed diaries and notes about his management experiences, and his reflections on these formed the basis of his work after retirement, when he sought to stimulate debate and thinking about management in both private and public sectors. His book *Administration, industrielle et générale* only became widely available in English in 1949 (Fayol, 1949).

Fayol credited his success as a manager to the methods he used, not to his personal qualities. He believed that managers should use certain principles in performing their functions, and these are listed in the next Key Ideas box. The term 'principles' did not imply they were rigid or absolute:

> It is all a question of proportion ... allowance must be made for different changing circumstances ... the principles are flexible and capable of adaptation to every need; it is a matter of knowing how to make use of them, which is a difficult art requiring intelligence, experience, decision and proportion. (Fayol, 1949, p. 14)

In using terms such as 'changing circumstances' and 'adaptation to every need' in setting out the principles, Fayol anticipated the contingency theories that were developed in the 1960s (see Chapter 10). He was also an early advocate of management education: 'Elementary in the primary schools, somewhat wider in the post-primary schools, and quite advanced in higher education establishments' (p. 16).

Fayol's principles of management

key ideas

1 **Division of work** If people specialise, the more can they concentrate on the same matters and so acquire an ability and accuracy, which increases their output. However, 'it has its limits which experience teaches us may not be exceeded'.

2 **Authority and responsibility** The right to give orders and to exact obedience, derived from either a manager's official authority or his or her personal authority. 'Wherever authority is exercised, responsibility arises.'

3 **Discipline** 'Essential for the smooth running of business … without discipline no enterprise could prosper.'

4 **Unity of command** 'For any action whatsoever, an employee should receive orders from one superior only' – to avoid conflicting instructions and resulting confusion.

5 **Unity of direction** 'One head and one plan for a group of activities having the same objective … essential to unity of action, co-ordination of strength and focusing of effort.'

6 **Subordination of individual interest to general interest** 'The interests of one employee or group of employees should not prevail over that of the concern.'

7 **Remuneration of personnel** 'Should be fair and, as far as possible, afford satisfaction both to personnel and firm.'

8 **Centralisation** 'The question of centralisation or decentralisation is a simple question of proportion … [the] share of initiative to be left to [subordinates] depends on the character of the manager, the reliability of the subordinates and the condition of the business. The degree of centralisation must vary according to different cases.'

9 **Scalar chain** 'The chain of superiors from the ultimate authority to the lowest ranks … is at times disastrously lengthy in large concerns, especially governmental ones.' Fayol pointed out that if a speedy decision was needed it was appropriate for people at the same level of the chain to communicate directly, as long as their immediate superiors approved. 'It provides for the usual exercise of some measure of initiative at all levels of authority.'

10 **Order** Materials should be in the right place to avoid loss, and the posts essential for the smooth running of the business filled by capable people.

11 **Equity** Managers should be both friendly and fair to their subordinates – 'equity requires much good sense, experience and good nature'.

12 **Stability of tenure of personnel** A high employee turnover is not efficient – 'Instability of tenure is at one and the same time cause and effect of bad running.'

13 **Initiative** 'The initiative of all represents a great source of strength for businesses … and … it is essential to encourage and develop this capacity to the full. The manager must be able to sacrifice some personal vanity in order to grant this satisfaction to subordinates … a manager able to do so is infinitely superior to one who cannot.'

14 **Esprit de corps** 'Harmony, union among the personnel of a concern is a great strength in that concern. Effort, then, should be made to establish it.' Fayol suggested doing so by avoiding sowing dissension amongst subordinates, and using verbal rather than written communication when appropriate.

Source: Fayol (1949).

Current status

Table 2.2 summarises some principles common to the internal process models of management and indicates their modern application.

Table 2.2

Modern applications of the internal process model

Some principles of the internal process model	Current applications
Rules and regulations	All organisations have these, covering areas such as expenditure, safety, recruitment and confidentiality
Impersonality	Appraisal processes based on objective criteria or team assessments, not personal preference
Division of labour	Setting narrow limits to employees' areas of responsibility – found in many organisations
Hierarchical structure	Most company organisation charts show managers in a hierarchy – with subordinates below them
Authority structure	Holders of a particular post in the hierarchy have authority over matters relating to that post, and not to matters which are the responsibility of others
Centralisation	Organisations balance central control of (say) finance or online services with local control of (say) pricing or recruitment
Initiative	Current practice in some firms is to increase the power and responsibility of operating staff
Rationality	Managers are expected to focus on achieving the organisation's objectives, and assess issues on the basis of evidence, not personal preference

Some organisations use these methods, especially in the public sector and in commercial businesses with geographically dispersed outlets – such as hotels, retailers and banks. Customers expect them to deliver a predictable service in each location, so they centralise design and development activities. Manuals set out how to deliver the service, and the procedures managers should follow – how to recruit and train staff, what the premises must look like and how to treat customers. Walton (2005) found that the model of bureaucratic control outlined by Weber is still widely used (see also Greenwood and Lawrence, 2005), in organisations where predictability and order are important. If managers work in situations that require change, innovation and willing commitment, they need other models.

2.6 Human relations models

In the early twentieth century writers such as Follett and Mayo recognised the limitations of the scientific management perspective.

Mary Parker Follett

Mary Parker Follett (1868–1933) graduated with distinction from Radcliffe College (now part of Harvard University) in 1898, having studied economics, law and philosophy. She took up social work and quickly acquired a reputation as an imaginative and effective professional. She realised the creativity of the group process, and the potential it offered for truly democratic government – which people themselves would have to create.

She advocated replacing bureaucratic institutions by networks in which people themselves analysed their problems and implemented their solutions. True democracy depended on tapping the potential of all members of society by enabling individuals to take part in groups organised to solve particular problems and accepting personal responsibility for the result. Such ideas are finding renewed relevance today in the work of institutions such as community action and tenants' groups.

Mary Parker Follett on groups   key ideas

Follett saw the group as an intermediate institution between the solitary individual and the abstract society, and argued that it was through the institution of the group that people organised cooperative action. In 1926 she wrote:

> Early psychology was based on the study of the individual; early sociology was based on the study of society. But there is no such thing as the 'individual', there is no such thing as 'society'; there is only the group and the group-unit – the social individual. Social psychology must begin with an intensive study of the group, of the selective processes which go on within it, the differentiated reactions, the likenesses and the unlikenesses, and the spiritual energy which unites them.

Source: Graham (1995), p. 230.

In the 1920s Follett became involved in the business world, when managers invited her to investigate business problems. She again advocated the application of the self-governing principle that would facilitate the growth of individuals and the groups to which they belonged. Conflict was inevitable if people brought valuable differences of view to a problem: the group must then resolve the conflict to create what she called an integrative unity amongst the members.

She acknowledged that organisations had to optimise production, but did not accept that the strict division of labour was the right way to achieve this (Follett, 1920), as it devalued human creativity. The human side should not be separated from the mechanical side, as the two are bound up together. She believed that people, whether managers or workers, behave as they do because of the reciprocal response that occurs in any relationship. If managers tell people to behave as if they are extensions of the assembly line they will do so. This implied that effective managers would not manipulate their subordinates, but train them in the use of responsible power: 'managers should give workers a chance to grow capacity or power for themselves'. Graham (1995) provides an excellent review of Follett's work.

Elton Mayo

Elton Mayo (1880–1949) was an Australian who, from 1911 to 1922 taught logic, psychology and ethics at the University of Queensland. In 1922 he moved to the United States, and in 1926 became Professor of Industrial Research at Harvard Business School, applying psychological methods to industrial conflict. He was an accomplished speaker, and his ideas aroused wide interest in the academic and business communities (Smith, 1998).

In 1924 managers of the Western Electric Company initiated a series of experiments at their Hawthorne plant in Chicago to discover the effect on output of changing defined factors in the physical environment. The first experiments studied the effect of lighting. The researchers established a control and an experimental group, varied the level of illumination and measured the output. As light rose, so did output. More surprisingly, as light fell output continued to rise. Even stranger was the fact that output in the control group also rose, even though there had been no change in their lighting. Clearly the physical conditions had only a small effect and the team set up a more comprehensive experiment to identify other factors.

They assembled a small group of workers in a separate room and altered variables in turn. These included the working hours, the length of breaks and the provision of refreshments. The experienced workers were assembling small components into telephone equipment. A supervisor was in charge and there was also an observer to record the experiments and how the workers reacted. Great care was taken to prevent external factors disrupting the effects of the variables under investigation. The researchers were careful to explain what was happening and to ensure that the workers understood what they were expected to do. They also listened to employees' views of working conditions.

The researchers varied conditions every two or three weeks, while the supervisor measured output regularly. This showed a gradual, if erratic, increase – even when the researchers returned conditions to those prevailing at an earlier stage, as Figure 2.3 shows.

Activity 2.6   Explaining the trend

Describe the pattern shown in Figure 2.3. Compare in particular the output in periods 7, 10 and 13. Before reading on, how would you explain this?

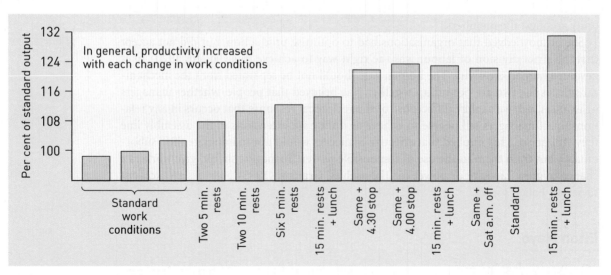

Figure 2.3 The relay assembly test room – average hourly output per week (as percentage of standard) in successive experimental periods

Source: Based on data from Roethlisberger and Dickson (1939). From *Behavior in Organizations*, 6th edition, Greenberg and Baron, © 1997. Reprinted by permission of Pearson Education, Inc. Upper Saddle River, NJ.

In 1928 senior managers invited Mayo to interpret the experiments and present his conclusions to a wider audience (Smith, 1998). Mayo undertook this work enthusiastically, reconciling the different interests in the research teams and bringing additional staff from Harvard into the team now conducting and publicising the research (Roethlisberger and Dickson, 1939; Mayo, 1949).

Their conclusions from the relay-assembly test room experiments were that the increase in productivity was not related to the physical changes, but to a change in the social situation in which the group was working:

> the major experimental change was introduced when those in charge sought to hold the situation humanly steady (in the interests of critical changes to be introduced) by getting the co-operation of the workers. What actually happened was that 6 individuals became a team and the team gave itself wholeheartedly and spontaneously to co-operation in the environment. (Mayo, 1949, p. 64)

The group felt special: managers asked for their views, were involved with them, paid attention to them and they had the chance to influence some aspects of the work.

The research team also observed another part of the factory, the bank wiring room, which revealed a different aspect of group working. Workers here were paid according to a piece-rate system, in which management pays workers a set amount for each item, or piece, that they produce. Such schemes reflect the assumption that financial incentives will encourage staff to work. The researchers observed that employees regularly produced less than they could have done. They had developed a sense of a normal rate of output, and ensured that all adhered to this rate, believing that if they produced, and earned, too much, management would reduce the piece-rate. Group members exercised informal sanctions against colleagues who worked too hard (or too slowly), until they came into line. Members who did too much were known as 'rate-busters' while those who did too little were 'chisellers'. Anyone who told the supervisor about this was a 'squealer'. Sanctions included being 'binged' – tapped on the shoulder to let them know that what they were doing was wrong. Managers had little or no control over these groups, who appointed their leader.

Finally, the research team conducted an extensive interview programme. They began by asking employees about the working environment and how they felt about their job, and then some questions about their life in general. The responses showed that there were often close links between work and domestic life. Work affected people's wider life much more than had been expected, and domestic circumstances affected their feelings about work. This implied that supervisors needed to think of a subordinate as a complete person, not just as a worker.

Activity 2.7   A comparison with Taylor

Compare this evidence with Frederick Taylor's belief that piece-rates would be an incentive to individuals to raise their performance. What may explain the difference?

Mayo's reflections on the Hawthorne studies drew attention to aspects of human behaviour that practitioners of scientific management had neglected. He introduced the idea of 'social man', in contrast to the 'economic man' who was at the centre of earlier theories. While financial rewards would influence the latter, group relationships and loyalties would influence the former, and may outweigh management pressure.

On financial incentives, Mayo wrote:

Man's desire to be continuously associated in work with his fellows is a strong, if not the strongest, human characteristic. Any disregard of it by management or any ill-advised attempt to defeat this human impulse leads instantly to some form of defeat for management itself. In [a study] the efficiency experts had assumed the primacy of financial incentive; in this they were wrong; not until the conditions of working group formation were satisfied did the financial incentives come into operation. (Mayo, 1949, p. 99)

People had social needs that they sought to satisfy – and how they did so may support management interests or oppose them.

Later analysis of the experimental data by Greenwood *et al.* (1983) suggested that the team had underestimated the influence of financial incentives. Becoming a member of the experimental group in itself increased the worker's income. Despite the possibly inaccurate interpretation of the data, the findings stimulated interest in social factors in the workplace, adding another dimension to knowledge of management. Scientific management stressed the technical aspects of work. The Hawthorne studies implied that management should give at least as much attention to human factors, leading to the **human relations approach**. This advocates that employees will work more effectively if management shows some interest in their well-being, such as through humane supervisory practices.

The **human relations approach** is a school of management that emphasises the importance of social processes at work.

> ## Case questions 2.4
> - Which of the practices that Robert Owen used took account of workers' social needs?
> - Evaluate the extent to which he anticipated the conclusions of the Hawthorne experiments.

Current status

The Hawthorne studies have been controversial, and the interpretations questioned (Gillespie, 1991). Also, the idea of social man is itself now seen as an incomplete picture of people at work. Providing good supervision and decent working environments may increase satisfaction, but not necessarily productivity. The influences on performance are certainly more complex than Taylor assumed – but are also more complex than the additional factors Mayo identified in the Hawthorne studies.

Other writers have followed and developed Mayo's emphasis on human factors. McGregor (1960), Maslow (1970) and Alderfer (1972) have suggested ways of integrating human needs with those of the organisation as expressed by management. Some of this reflected a human relations concern for employees' well-being. A much stronger influence was the changing external environments of organisations, which have become less predictable since the time of Taylor and Mayo. These changes encouraged scholars to develop open systems models.

Ricardo Semler and Semco www.semco.locaweb.com.br

Semco is a successful Brazilian company which in 2007 employed 2500 people in three countries. It was founded by Ricardo Semler's father in the early 1950s and is now a federation of about ten companies engaged in highly engineered, high-quality products that they offer in carefully chosen market niches. These include industrial machinery, cooling systems for commercial properties, managing buildings and properties, and environmental consulting.

The most distinctive feature of the company is the philosophy that underlies the way people work. Semler believes that: 'the repetition, boredom and aggravation that too many accept as an inherent part of working can be replaced with joy, inspiration and freedom' (p. x). Semler does not plan the future of the company: he believes that the employees shape it with their effort, interests and initiatives. See the Chapter 14 Case for more on Semco.

Source: Semler (2003).

2.7 Open systems models

The open systems approach builds on earlier work in general systems theory, and has been widely used to help understand management and organisational issues. The basic idea is to think of the organisation not as a **system**, but as an **open system**.

The open systems approach draws attention to the links between the internal parts of a system, and to the links between the whole system and the outside world. The system is separated from its environment by the **system boundary**. An open system imports resources such as energy and materials, which enter it from the environment across this boundary, undergo some transformation process within the system, and leave the system as goods and services. The central theme of the open systems view of management is that organisations depend on the wider environment for inputs if they are to survive and prosper. Figure 2.4 (based on Figure 1.1) is a simple model of the organisation as an open system.

A **system** is a set of interrelated parts designed to achieve a purpose.

An **open system** is one that interacts with its environment.

A **system boundary** separates the system from its environment.

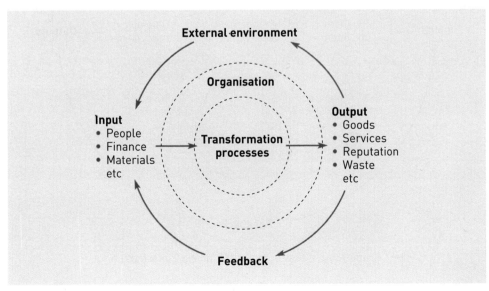

Figure 2.4

The systems model

The figure shows input and output processes, conversion processes and feedback loops. The organisation must satisfy those in the wider environment well enough to ensure that they continue to provide resources. The management task is to sustain those links if the organisation is to thrive. **Feedback** refers to information about the performance of the system. It may be deliberate, through customer surveys, or unplanned, such as the loss of business to a competitor. Feedback enables those managing the system to take remedial action.

Another idea is that of **subsystems**. A course is a subsystem within a department or faculty, the faculty is a subsystem of a university, the university is a subsystem of the higher education system. This in turn is part of the whole education system. A course itself will consist of several systems – one for quality assurance, one for enrolling students, one for teaching, another for assessment, and so on. In terms of Figure 2.1, each of the organisational elements is itself a subsystem – there is a technical subsystem, a people subsystem, a finance subsystem and so on, as Figure 2.5 shows.

These subsystems interact with each other, and how well people manage these links affects the functioning of the whole system: when a university significantly increases the number of students admitted to a popular course, this affects many parts of the system – such as accommodation (*technology*), teaching resources (*people*), and examinations (*business processes*).

A systems approach emphasises the links between systems, and reminds managers that a change in one will have consequences for others. What counts as the environment

Feedback (in systems theory) refers to the provision of information about the effects of an activity.

Subsystems are the separate but related parts that make up the total system.

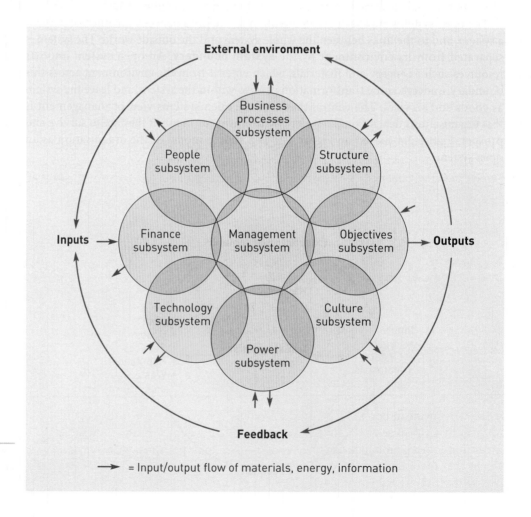

Figure 2.5

Interacting subsystems in organisations

depends on the level at which the analysis is being conducted. If a team at British Airways is discussing a new strategy to concentrate on business passengers, the relevant environmental factors will be mainly external – competing airlines, the expected level of demand, whether they can negotiate suitable facilities at airports. If the discussion is about reservations procedures, then the relevant environment will be mainly internal – such as their information systems, reservations staff and available capacity. In either case the principle is the same: take account of the systems that surround the immediate one. That implies being ready and able to scan those environments, to sense changes in them, and to act accordingly.

Robert Owen – the case continues
www.newlanark.org.uk

CASE STUDY

Owen actively managed the links between his business and the wider world. On buying the mills he quickly became part of the Glasgow business establishment, and was closely involved in the activities of the Chamber of Commerce. He took a prominent role in the social and political life of the city. He used these links in particular to argue the case for reforms in the educational and economic systems, and was critical of the effect that industrialisation was having upon working-class life.

Owen believed that education in useful skills would help to release working-class children from poverty. He provided a nursery for workers' children over 1 year old, allowing both parents to continue working, and promoted the case for wider educational provision. He also developed several experiments in cooperation and community building, believing that the basis of his successful capitalist enterprise at New Lanark (education, good working conditions and a harmonious community) could be applied to society as a whole.

These attempts to establish new communities (at New Harmony in the United States, and at Harmony in Hampshire, England) cost him a great deal of money,

but soon failed (Royle, 1998), because of difficulties over admission, finance and management processes.

More broadly, he sought new ways of organising the economy to raise wages and protect jobs, at a time of severe business fluctuations. In 1815 he persuaded allies in Parliament to propose a bill making it illegal for children under 10 to work in mills. It would also have limited their working hours to ten a day. The measure met strong opposition from mill owners and a much weaker measure became law in 1819.

Sources: Butt (1971), Royle (1998).

Case questions 2.5

- Draw a systems diagram detailing the main inputs, transformation and outputs of Robert Owen's mill.
- What assumptions did Owen make about the difference between running a business and running a community?

Sociotechnical systems

An important variant of systems theory is the idea of the **sociotechnical system**. The approach developed from the work of Eric Trist and Ken Bamforth (1951) at the Tavistock Institute in London. Their most prominent study was of an attempt in the coal industry to mechanise the mining system. Introducing what were in essence assembly line technologies and methods at the coalface had severe consequences for the social system that the older pattern of working had encouraged. The technological system destroyed the social system, and the solution lay in reconciling the needs of both.

A **sociotechnical system** is one in which outcomes depend on the interaction of both the technical and social subsystems.

This and similar studies showed the benefits of seeing a work system as a combination of a material technology (tools, machinery, techniques) and a social organisation (people, relationships, constitutional arrangements). Figure 2.6 shows that an organisation has technical and social systems: it is a socio-technical system. Each affects the other, so people need to manage both.

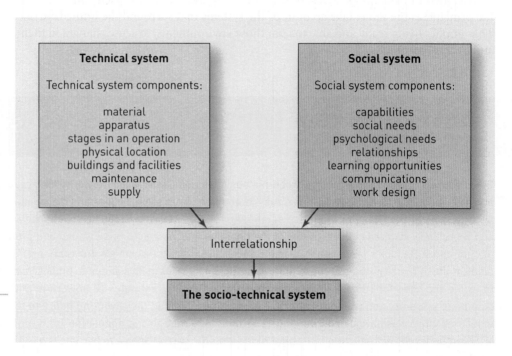

Figure 2.6

The organisation as a socio-technical system

A sociotechnical analysis aims to integrate the social and technical components: optimising one while ignoring the other is likely to be unproductive. Cherns (1987) developed a set of principles for redesigning organisations on socio-technical principles.

Contingency management

A further development of the open systems view is the contingency approach (Chapter 10). This arose from the work of Woodward (1958) and Burns and Stalker (1961) in the United Kingdom, and of Lawrence and Lorsch (1967) in the United States. The main theme is that to perform well managers must adapt the structure of the organisation to match external conditions: 'performance is determined not so much by the environment or the firm's actions, but by the congruence of the two' (Child *et al.*, 2003, p. 4).

Contingency approaches to organisational structure are those based on the idea that the performance of an organisation depends on having a structure that is appropriate to its environment.

The **contingency approach** looks for those aspects of the environment that managers should take into account in deciding how to shape the organisation – see the Management in Practice feature.

As the environment becomes more complex managers can use contingency perspectives to examine what structure best meets the needs of the business. Contingency theorists emphasise creating organisations that can cope with uncertainty and change, using the values of the open systems model: they also recognise that some functions need to work in a stable and predictable way, using the values of the internal process model.

Successful Hong Kong firms adapt to the environment in China

Child *et al.* (2003) studied the experience of Hong Kong companies managing affiliated companies in China, predicting that successful firms would be those that adapted their management practices to suit those conditions. Because the business environment at the time was uncertain and difficult for foreign companies, they proposed that a key aspect of management practice in these circumstances would be the extent to which affiliated companies are controlled by, and integrated with, the parent company. Their results supported this – in the environment of this transitional economy, successful firms kept their mainland affiliates under close supervision, by maintaining frequent contact and allowing them to make few decisions.

Source: Child *et al.* (2003).

Current status

An open systems perspective emphasises that people need to adjust objectives and plans more rapidly to external change, and also find new ways of motivating people to act appropriately in these new conditions. Organisations in themselves achieve nothing: any change depends on the initiative and action of individuals. Open systems models draw attention to the wide range of issues that potentially affect an organisation. Yet these only affect internal affairs when a person notes an issue and in some way ensures that it is on the management agenda – that people begin to take notice of it. It is the goals, interests and power of individuals that determine whether an issue is noticed, interpreted, and acted upon. Factors such as these facilitate employee capability to act creatively and drive innovation.

2.8 Management theories for uncertain conditions

Although theories of management develop at particular times in response to current problems, this does not mean that newer is better. While new concerns bring out new theories, old concerns usually remain. Hence, while current theories are heavily weighted towards ways of encouraging flexibility and change, management still seeks control. Rather than thinking of theoretical development as a linear process, see it as a circular or iterative process in which certain themes recur as new concerns arise. The competing values approach captures the main theoretical developments in one framework and shows the relationships between them – as Table 2.3 shows.

The emerging management challenges come from many sources. One is the increasingly global nature of the economic system. Another is the deregulation of many areas of activity, allowing new competitors to enter previously protected markets (airlines, financial services). Still another is the closer integration between many previously separate areas of business (telecommunications, consumer electronics and entertainment). Consumer expectations are increasing and computer-based information systems are developing rapidly. Managers look for radical solutions – just as at the start of the Industrial Revolution.

Table 2.3

Summary of the models within the competing values framework

Features/model	Rational goal	Internal process	Human relations	Open systems
Main exponents	Taylor Gilbreths	Fayol Weber	Mayo Follett Barnard	Trist and Bamforth Woodward Burns and Stalker Lawrence and Lorsch Peters and Waterman
Criteria of effectiveness	Productivity, profit	Stability, continuity	Commitment, morale, cohesion	Adaptability, external support
Means/ends theory	Clear direction leads to productive outcomes	Routinisation leads to stability	Involvement leads to commitment	Continual innovation secures external support
Emphasis	Rational analysis, measurement	Defining responsibility, documentation	Participation, consensus building	Creative problem solving, innovation
Role of manager	Director and planner	Monitor and coordinator	Mentor and facilitator	Innovator and broker

Peters and Waterman – In Search of Excellence

In 1982 Peters and Waterman published their best-selling book *In Search of Excellence*. As management consultants with McKinsey & Co., they set out to discover the reasons for the success of what they regarded as 43 excellently managed US companies. One of their conclusions was that they had a distinctive set of philosophies about human nature and the way that people interact in organisations. They did not see people as rational beings, motivated by fear and willing to accept a low-involvement employment relationship. Instead, the excellent companies regarded people as emotional, intuitive and creative social beings who like to celebrate victories, however small, who value self-control, but who also need and want the security and meaning of achieving goals through organisations. From this, Peters and Waterman deduced some general rules for treating workers with dignity and respect. This was not out of a sense of philanthropy, but to ensure that people did quality work in an increasingly uncertain environment.

In Search of Excellence had a significant influence on management thinking and practice. It reflected a move away from rational goal approaches that emphasised complex and usually quantitative analytical techniques as the route to effective management. Peters and Waterman believed that management had relied too much on analytical techniques at the expense of the more intuitive and human aspects of business. In this they developed the ideas associated with the human relations school and introduced the idea of company culture – discussed in the next chapter.

Non-linear systems

Another new theme in management thinking in such volatile conditions is to consider the implications of feedback. People in organisations, both as individuals and as members of a web of working relationships, can choose how they react to an event or to an attempt to influence their behaviour. That reaction in turn leads to a further response – setting off a complex feedback process. Figure 2.7 illustrates this for three individuals, X, Y and Z.

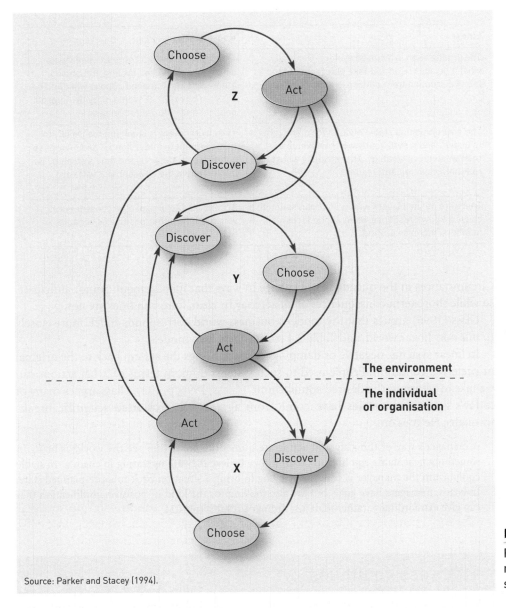

Source: Parker and Stacey (1994).

Figure 2.7

Feedback in non-linear systems

If we look at the situation in Figure 2.7 from the perspective of X, then X is in an environment made up of Y and Z. X discovers what Y and Z are doing, chooses how to respond and then acts. That action has consequences for Y and Z, which they discover. This leads them to choose a response, which has consequences that X then discovers, and acts on. This continues indefinitely. Every act X takes feeds back to have an impact on Y and Z's next action – and the same is true of Y and Z. Hence, as they interact, they make up a feedback system – and what is true of individuals as depicted in the diagram can also be used to indicate the interactions of three groups or three organisations. It can then extend to large numbers of organisations operating in their economic and social environment.

This way of thinking about organisations distinguishes between what are called 'linear' and '**non-linear**' systems. 'Linear' describes a system in which an action leads to a predictable reaction. If you light a fire in a room, the thermostat will turn the central heating down. Non-linear systems are those in which outcomes are less predictable. If managers reduce prices they will be surprised if sales exactly match the forecast – they cannot predict the reactions of competitors, changes in taste, or new products.

Non-linear systems are those in which small changes are amplified through many interactions with other variables so that the eventual effect is unpredictable.

Table 2.4

Contrasting assumptions in linear and non-linear systems

Linear	Non-linear
The organisation is a closed system. Generally, what it decides to do will take place without too much disruption from outside events.	The organisation is a complex open system, constantly influenced by, and influencing, other systems. Intended actions will often be diverted by external events or by the internal political and cultural processes.
The environment is stable enough for management to understand it sufficiently well to develop a relevant detailed strategy. That strategy will still be relevant when implemented.	The environment is changing too rapidly for management to understand it and to develop a detailed strategy. By the time a strategy is implemented the environment will have changed.
There are defined levers within an organisation that cause a known response when applied (cut staff numbers, increase profits).	Actions lead to unexpected consequences, which can be either positive or negative.

Circumstances in the outside world change in ways that management cannot anticipate, so while short-term consequences of an act may be clear, long-run ones are not.

Glass (1996) argues that the modern business world corresponds much more closely to this non-linear world, and Table 2.4 contrasts the two models.

In linear systems, negative or damping feedback brings the system back to the original or preferred condition. People used to such systems think in terms of 'what actions can we take to return to the desired equilibrium?' (Glass, 1996, p. 102). Glass argues many of today's growth industries have come from aggressively exploited scientific break-throughs. He goes on:

> A manager's way of thinking and acting are quite different if they see the world as being in something near stable equilibrium, than if they believe they are operating in chaos ... In stable equilibrium the manager is constantly trying to bring a situation back to a pre-planned state. In chaos, managers have goals but are also looking for the kind of positive amplification that can give extraordinary, rather than just ordinary, results. (p. 102)

Robert Owen – the case continues

www.newlanark.org.uk

CASE STUDY

The mills at New Lanark continued to operate after Owen's departure in 1825. Competition from new sources of supply meant that the mills eventually became unprofitable, and they closed in 1968, threatening the survival of the village community. There had been little new building since Owen left, so the site (with its high mills and rows of workers' cottages) represented a time capsule of industrial and social history. The New Lanark Conservation Trust was created to restore it as a living community, and as a lasting monument to Owen and his philosophies.

Visitors can see the mills and examples of the machinery they contained, visit many of the communal buildings Owen created (such as the store that was the inspiration for the worldwide Co-operative Movement), and some of the workers' housing. New Lanark is not just a tourist destination – it is a living community with most of the houses occupied by people who work elsewhere in the area.

Sources: Published sources and company website.

2.9 Current themes and issues

Performance

The theories outlined in this chapter have usually been developed as a means to improving performance. Many practitioners dismiss the value of theory and systematic evidence, preferring to follow what they call the lessons of experience.

Pfeffer and Sutton (2006a) present the case for basing management actions on substantiated theories and relevant evidence. They acknowledge the difficulties of putting that into practice, given that the demands for decisions are relentless and that information is incomplete. They also acknowledge that evidence-based management depends on being willing to put aside conventional wisdom. They identify practices that help managers to foster an evidence-based approach:

> If you ask for evidence of efficacy every time a change is proposed, people will sit up and take notice. If you take the time to parse the logic behind that evidence, people will become more disciplined in their own thinking. If you treat the organization like an unfinished prototype and encourage trial programs, pilot studies, and experimentation – and reward learning from these activities, even when something new fails – your organization will begin to develop its own evidence base. And if you keep learning while acting on the best knowledge you have and expect your people to do the same – if you have what has been called 'the attitude of wisdom' – then your company can profit from evidence-based management. (p. 70)

Pfeffer and Sutton's advice to demand evidence, examine logic, be willing to experiment and to embrace the attitude of wisdom can guide your approach to using the theories in this chapter. They are all potentially useful as part of an evidence-based approach, but only if you treat them critically, by asking about their underlying assumptions, how well they relate to the context you are considering, examining what alternatives may be available, and recognising the limitations of any theory. Used in that way, they can help you develop the skills of thinking critically about management theory, and using that to enhance performance.

Responsibility

Chapter 5 shows that many observers now believe that performance should be judged against the interests of a wide range of stakeholders, not just those with a financial stake in the enterprise. Although developed long before current concerns over the environment and climate change, the competing values model makes it possible to relate these theories to that topic. Those who believe that managers should act responsibly towards a wider range of stakeholders are taking an open systems view, in that they recognise the wide and interconnected nature of organisational and environmental factors.

There is still considerable scope for understanding the forces that shape managers' responses to these issues – in other words whether they act solely out of philanthropic motives or because they see responsible behaviour and image as helpful to their wider strategy. Applying the techniques of evidence-based management and critical thinking to the topics in Chapter 5 will help clarify how managers can act responsibly while still meeting performance expectations.

Internationalisation

The theories outlined here were developed when most business was conducted within national boundaries, although of course with substantial foreign trade in certain products and services. They take little direct account of the explosion in global trade, and the way in which many organisations are reorganising themselves as international or global businesses. However, the competing values framework provides a useful starting point, by highlighting the importance of underlying assumptions behind a theory, and how this relates to particular contexts. The fact that a theory based on, say, open systems values works well in some economies does not necessarily mean that it will be suitable in others. As Chapters 3 and 4 point out, cultural factors affect performance, yet it is still unclear how multiple national cultures interact with the corporate culture of an international business.

There is no shortage of prescriptions on offer to managers operating in global businesses, offering advice on all aspects of the process, from creating strategies to redesigning the organisation and implementing global changes. Many popular books are based on the practices of successful companies, without explaining the circumstances that enabled them to use the practices advocated. Learning to distinguish good theory and bad is the first step towards a style of management that balances proper regard for theory with respect for the lessons of practice.

Summary

1 **Explain the value of models of management, and compare unitary, pluralist and critical perspectives**

- Models represent more complex realities, help to understand complexity and offer a range of perspectives on the topic. Their predictive effect is limited by the fact that people interpret information subjectively in deciding how to act.

- A unitary perspective emphasises the common purpose of organisational members, while the pluralist draws attention to competing interest groups. Those who take a critical perspective believe that organisations reflect deep divisions in society, and that attempts to integrate different interests through negotiation ignore persistent differences in the distribution of power.

2 **State the structure of the competing values framework and evaluate its contribution to our understanding of management**

- A way of integrating the otherwise confusing range of theories of management. Organisations experience tensions between control and flexibility and between an external and an internal focus. Placing these on two axes allows theories to be allocated to one of four types – rational goal, internal process, human relations and open systems.

3 **Summarise the rational goal, internal process, human relations and open systems models and evaluate what each can contribute to a manager's understanding of their role**

- Rational goal (Taylor, the Gilbreths and operational research):
  - clear direction leads to productive outcomes, with an emphasis on rational analysis and measurement.

- Internal process (Weber, Fayol):
  - routinisation leads to stability, so an emphasis on defining responsibility and on comprehensive documentation and administrative processes.

- Human relations (Follett, Mayo):
  - people are motivated by social needs, and managers who recognise these will secure commitment. Practices include considerate supervision, participation and seeking consensus.

- Open systems (socio-technical, contingency and chaos):
  - Continual innovation secures external support, achieved by creative problem solving.

These theories have contributed to the management agendas in these ways:

- Rational goal – through techniques such as time and motion study, work measurement and a variety of techniques for planning operations; also the narrow specification of duties, and the separation of management and non-management work.

- Internal process – clear targets and measurement systems, and the creation of clear management and reporting structures. Making decisions objectively on the basis of rules and procedures, rather than on favouritism or family connections.

- Human relations – considerate supervision, consultation and participation in decisions affecting people.

- Open systems – understanding external factors and being willing and able to respond to them through individual and organisational flexibility.

4 Use the model to classify the dominant form in two or more business units, and to gather evidence about the way this affects the roles of managing in those units

- You can achieve this objective by asking people (perhaps others on your course) to identify which of the four cultural types in the competing values framework most closely correspond to the unit in which they work. Ask them to note ways in which that cultural type affects their way of working. Compare the answers in some systematic way, and review the results.

5 Explain the influence of uncertain conditions on management and the assumptions of non-linear models of management

- Uncertain conditions mean that it is hard to predict the outcome of an action. Complex feedback loops between the many elements in a situation mean that outcomes are affected by small differences in conditions. The eventual effect is out of all proportion to the initial action or event.

- Linear – closed system, relatively stable environment in which planning is feasible, and identifiable actions with predictable effects are available.

- Non-linear – open system, influenced by other systems; rapidly changing environment, and actions lead to unexpected consequences.

Review questions

1 Name three ways in which theoretical models help the study of management.

2 What are the different assumptions of the unitary, pluralist and critical perspectives on organisations?

3 Name at least four of Morgan's organisational images and give an original example of each.

4 Draw the two axes of the competing values framework, and then place the theories outlined in this chapter in the most appropriate sector.

5 List Taylor's five principles of scientific management and evaluate their use in examples of your choice.

6 What was the particular contribution that Lillian Gilbreth made concerning how workers' mental capacities should be treated?

7 What did Follett consider to be the value of groups in a community as well as business?

8 Compare Taylor's assumptions about people with those of Mayo. Evaluate the accuracy of these views by reference to an organisation of your choice.

9 Compare the conclusions reached by the Hawthorne experimenters in the relay assembly test room with those in the bank wiring room.

10 Is an open system harder to manage than a closed system, and if so, why?

11 How does uncertainty affect organisations and how do non-linear perspectives help to understand this?

Concluding critical reflection

Think about the way your company, or one with which you are familiar, approaches the task of management, and the theories that seem to lie behind the way people manage themselves and others. Review the material in the chapter, and perhaps visit some of the websites identified. Then make notes on these questions:

● What examples of the issues discussed in this chapter are currently relevant to your company?

● In responding to these issues, what **assumptions** about the nature of management appear to guide what people do? Do they reflect rational goal, internal process, human relations or open systems perspectives? Or a combination of several? Do these assumptions reflect a unitary or pluralist perspective, and if so, why?

● What factors such as the history or current **context** of the company appear to have influenced the prevailing view? Does the approach appear to be right for the company, its employees, and other stakeholders? Do people question those assumptions, in the way that Semler does within Semco?

● Have people put forward **alternative** ways of managing the business, or even a small part of it, based on evidence about other companies? Does the competing values model suggest other approaches to managing, in addition to the current pattern? How might others react to such alternatives?

● What **limitations** can you see in the theories and evidence presented in the chapter? For example, how valid might the human relations models be in a manufacturing firm in a country with abundant supplies of cheap labour, competing to attract overseas investment? Will open systems models be useful to those managing a public bureaucracy?

Further reading

Drucker, P. (1954), *The Practice of Management*, Harper, New York.

Still the classic introduction to general management.

Taylor, F.W. (1917), *The Principles of Scientific Management*, Harper, New York.

Fayol, H. (1949), *General and Industrial Management*, Pitman, London.

The original works of these writers are short and lucid. Taylor (1917) contains illuminating detail that brings the ideas to life, and Fayol's (1949) surviving ideas came from only two short chapters, which again are worth reading in the original.

Biggs, L. (1996), *The Rational Factory*, The Johns Hopkins University Press, Baltimore, MD.

A short and clear overview of the development of production systems from the eighteenth to the early twentieth centuries in a range of industries, including much detail on Ford's Highland Park plant.

Graham, P. (1995), *Mary Parker Follett: Prophet of management*, Harvard Business School Press, Boston, MA.

The contribution of Mary Parker Follett has been rather ignored, perhaps overshadowed by Mayo's Hawthorne studies – or perhaps it was because she was a woman. This book gives a full appreciation of her work.

Gillespie, R. (1991), *Manufacturing Knowledge: A history of the Hawthorne experiments*, Cambridge University Press, Cambridge.

Alvesson, M. and **Wilmott, H.** (1996), *Making Sense of Management*, Sage, London.

Thompson, P. and **McHugh, D.** (2002), *Work Organisations: A critical introduction*, Palgrave, Basingstoke.

Morgan, G. (1997), *Images of Organisation*, Sage, London.

These last four books discuss the ideas in this chapter from a critical perspective.

Semler, R. (2003), *The Seven Day Weekend: Finding the work/life balance*, Century, London.

Worth reading for an absorbing insight into a radically different approach to managing.

Gamble, J., Morris, J. and **Wilkinson, B.** (2004), 'Mass production is alive and well: the future of work and organisation in east Asia', *International Journal of Human Resource Management*, vol. 15, no. 2, pp. 397–409.

Smith, J.H. (1998), 'The enduring legacy of Elton Mayo', *Human Relations*, vol. 51, no. 3, pp. 221–249.

Walton, E.J. (2005), 'The persistence of bureaucracy: a meta-analysis of Weber's model of bureaucratic control', *Organisation Studies*, vol. 26, no. 4, pp. 569–600.

Three papers that show the continued application in successful business of early theories of management.

Mumford, E. (2006), 'The story of socio-technical design: reflections on its successes, failures and potential', *Information Systems Journal*, vol. 16, no. 4, pp. 317–342.

A review of socio-technical design from one of its leading practitioners.

Weblinks

These websites have appeared in the chapter:

www.newlanark.org.uk
www.xilinx.com
www.imiplc.com
www.tcl.com
www.semco.locaweb.com.br

Visit two of the business sites in the list, or those of other organisations in which you are interested, and navigate to the pages dealing with recent news, press or investor relations.

● What are the main issues the organisations appear to be facing?

● Compare and contrast the issues you identify on the two sites.

● What challenges may they imply for those working in, and managing, these organisations?

Annotated weblinks, multiple choice questions and other useful resources can be found on **www.pearsoned.co.uk/boddy**

Innocent Drinks

www.innocentdrinks.co.uk

Richard Reed, Jon Wright and Adam Balon founded Innocent Drinks in 1998. The three had known each other since they met during their first week at Cambridge University in 1991. They became instant friends, and continued to keep in touch after they graduated in 1994. Reed worked for an advertising agency, while Balon and Wright worked for (different) firms of management consultants. They also organised events in London (which they had already done while in Cambridge) – such as a music festival called Jazz on the Green in 1997 and 1998. Although they were following different careers, they often joked about starting a company together – and during a winter sports trip to France in March 1998 the topic came up again.

Jon Wright said:

We'd had this conversation so many times. Finally, on the way to France, we said to ourselves: 'We're going in circles here. Let's figure out something to do or forget about it and be happy with our jobs.' Everyone said, 'Great.' Then we realised the problem: we weren't sure what we were qualified to do.

They considered several ideas, rejecting the first two as impractical. The third paid off. They talked about their lifestyles in London – working hard and playing hard. They had a desire to be healthy but didn't have much time to act on it. What about healthier food or drinks? They talked about their habit of buying juice on the way to work in the morning – a little thing that made them feel a bit healthier. They were shocked that none of them could remember the names of the brands they were buying.

Wright recalls:

We thought that if we could come up with a more memorable brand, and with juice that tasted a bit better, that it could be a good business opportunity. No one could think of a reason that it couldn't work.

They had hit on the idea that would lead to the creation of what became in a very few years one of the UK's most successful entrepreneurial companies.

The juice and smoothie market

Smoothies are blends of fruit that include the fruit's pulp and sometimes contain dairy products such as yogurt. They tend to be thicker and fresher than ordinary juice. While some smoothies are made on demand at a juice bar, this was not the market for which Innocent aimed. It focused on the market for pre-packaged smoothies, which has a premium and a standard segment. Premium smoothies contain no water or added sugar and command a higher price than the standard product.

Innocent Ltd.

Most smoothies were sold through three channels – supermarkets, cafés and sandwich shops, and impulse retail (convenience stores and petrol stations).

Early decisions at Innocent

Soon after agreeing on the venture, the three divided the roles: Reed, with advertising agency experience, took care of marketing. Balon, who had recent experience of selling Virgin Cola, took on sales, while Wright (who had studied manufacturing engineering at Cambridge) was in charge of operations. They agreed that rather than have one of them as chief executive all three would jointly lead the company.

They used their 1998 Jazz on the Green festival to do some market research. They prepared a quantity of smoothies using borrowed equipment and set up a stall. In a move that has become part of the company's distinctive image they put a label above two bins for empty bottles (marked Yes and No) asking the question: 'Should we quit our day jobs and start a smoothie company?' The 'Yes' bin overflowed.

One decision concerned pricing. The main competitor at the time was PJ, which sold smoothies made with concentrate. Innocent planned to make a higher-quality product in that it would be fresher and more natural. This made the product more expensive, and the founders doubted if customers would pay the premium required when compared with the cost of a 330ml PJ bottle. The solution came when a designer suggested a 250ml bottle – risky, but marking Innocent as being different from the established brand.

Another issue was finding someone to manufacture the smoothie. There were no smoothie manufacturers in Britain with the facilities to make the fresh smoothies the team wanted, but they came across a small supplier who was keen to diversify away from his current major customers. He also got on well with the Innocent team, and agreed to work for them.

Finally they had to raise capital to finance their growth. Conventional sources were reluctant to invest, but eventually Maurice Pinto, a private investor, put in £235,000 in return for a 20 per cent stake in the company.

The Innocent brand

An old friend of the founders, Dan Germain, joined the business in the summer of 1999. They discussed packaging and came up with the idea of printing off-beat messages on the smoothie labels. These became one of the hallmarks of the Innocent brand, as the tone was offbeat, honest, irreverent and distinctly non-corporate. Germain began to take over as the unofficial voice of the brand – writing most of the labels, a newsletter, and customer communications.

As the company grew it incorporated more traditional marketing approaches, such as bus and London Underground advertisements. One manager noted:

We have to balance Big Brand with Little Brand – the former being a row of cartons on a supermarket shelf, the

latter being an Innocent Fridge covered with grass in a café next door.

An experienced marketing consultant commented: 'They have a really astute understanding of what makes a young metropolitan audience tick. It's almost anti-marketing.'

Company growth

The formula the company had adopted was highly successful, and sales grew rapidly. The original outside investor advised the founders that, despite this success, they should start thinking about opportunities for further growth. Two options were whether to expand in Europe, or to extend the brand to other products (such as ice cream) in the UK. They decided not to diversify, but to concentrate on geographic expansion of the core range. By 2006 they had bases in France and Denmark and planned to launch the smoothies in Germany and Austria in 2007. The table summarises their growth:

	1999	2006
Number of employees	3	105
Number of different recipes on sale	3	24
Market share	0%	62%
Turnover	£0	£75 million
Number of retailers	1 (on first day)	Over 7000
Number of smoothies sold	20 (on first day)	1 million a week

Since 1999 11 competing brands have been launched, and all have withdrawn. Their original main competitor (PJ) was bought by Pepsico, and Coca-Cola is pushing the Minute Maid brand of smoothies in Britain. Several major companies have offered to buy Innocent, but all offers have been refused. The trio are committed to staying with the company for at least the next few years.

Despite the fun image, they run the business very firmly, and are not afraid to fire employees who do not pull their weight. Growth means that they have brought in professional managers from established companies to complement their skills.

Innocent ethics

They want to prove that business can be a force for good. They say:

We want to leave things a little better than we found them. Our strategy for doing so is simple – first, only ever make

100 per cent natural products that are 100 per cent good for people. Second, procure our ingredients ethically. Third, use ecologically sound packaging materials. Fourth, reduce and offset our carbon emissions across our entire business system. Fifth, lead by example at Fruit Towers by doing good things. And finally, give 10 per cent of our profits each year to charities (such as Rainforest Alliance) in countries where our fruit comes from.

Where next?

Founded in 1999, the founders run one of the best-loved and fastest growing businesses in Britain. They have no chief executive, give 10 per cent of profits to charity, and have a constant dialogue with customers – 40,000 of whom have signed up to receive a weekly e-mail. The company is growing so fast that finding the right staff is one factor slowing them down. As one experienced management observer noted:

Consumers are looking for businesses to trust, and they want to reward that trustworthiness. Innocent is a model of the values all businesses should aspire to.

Sources: Based on material from 'Innocent Drinks', a case prepared by William Sahlman (2004), Harvard Business School, Case No. 9-805-031; *Sunday Times*, 24 September 2006; company website.

Part case questions

- How does the management approach of the Innocent founders differ from that of Ryanair and Robert Owen respectively?
- Can you see any similarities?
- Visit the website and check on the latest news about developments in the company.
- What organisational functions does Innocent perform?
- In what ways are managers at Innocent adding value to the resources they use?
- What seems to you unusual about their approach to managing a business?
- In what ways will further growth pose new problems for the company, especially in Europe?
- In what ways, if at all, are the models in the competing values framework supported by the Innocent case?

To help you develop your skills, as well as knowledge, this section includes tasks that relate the key themes covered in the Part to your daily life. Working through these will help you to deepen your understanding of the topic, and develop skills and insights you can use in many situations.

Task 1.1   Managing your time

Managers often say that they do not have enough time to do their job as well as they would like. People often find that reflecting carefully on how they, and others, spend time helps to improve the way they use it:

when one is very busy and under pressure, it is difficult to find the time to take stock of the way one works. Yet the effort is worthwhile. Those who do usually find they can organise more effectively both what they do and how they do it. (Stewart, 1967)

To help you begin this reflective process think back over your recent work, and then:

- list examples of time being badly used, and identify what led to that;
- list examples of time being well used, and identify what led to that;
- list examples of time being spent in activities that involve creativity.

Form a group of three or four colleagues, and exchange information about what you have found. Identify any common themes, and agree at least one practice that you will try to use to improve the way you use your time, either as a student or in an organisation.

Task 1.2   Understanding your roles

The term 'role' refers to the set of expectations that others have of someone occupying a position. The task below should help relate these ideas to your situation.

Part A – creating a role map

The aim of this exercise is to help you identify those people or groups (stakeholders) who have expectations of you in your role as a student or in an organisation. What do they expect of you, and what does that mean for where you spend time and energy?

1 Draw a circle in the middle of a page – this represents you in your studying or managing role.

2 Around the sheet draw other circles, each with the name of a person or group (stakeholder) that has expectations of you. Your map should include, amongst others:

- the organisation or the boss – respresenting what people formally expect;
- colleagues – the people who work for you or with you;
- families and others beyond the immediate role.

Place those where the links are particularly strong nearer the centre, and those that are less critical nearer the edge.

Part B – analysing expectations
Lay out a sheet of paper with the headings below across the top, and a deep row for each main stakeholder. Select three of the stakeholders you identified in Part A, list them in the left-hand column, and make notes on each of the questions in the other columns.

Other person or institution (stakeholder)	[1] What are they expecting of you, and you of them?	[2] In view of (1), what are the three or four study or management tasks you must do well?	[3] Are there situations where the expectations in (1) cause difficulty?	[4] How did you resolve this, or how might you do so?

Part C – comparing with others
Using the role analysis you have carried out, work in pairs or trios with other colleagues on your course. In turn, outline your maps and your analysis in Part B. Your objective is to clarify your awareness of your role, by explaining to your partner(s) what you have written, and then revising it if necessary. Also seek their ideas on the column headed (4).

Part D – connecting theory and practice
Refer to Mintzberg's theory of management roles in Chapter 1. Which (several) of the roles he identified may be most important in helping you to meet the main expectations that others have of you?

Task 1.3   Managing your career

If you have not yet begun your management career, this activity may help you to think about the options and opportunities. Visit major online career websites, such as:

● www.monster.co.uk
● www.fish4jobs.co.uk
● www.prospects.ac.uk

You will be asked to enter a search word for jobs that interest you such as 'marketing' or 'information technology', or to choose a term from a list. This will probably return many possible opportunities – select three, and print the job description. Compile a list of the educational and experience requirements, and of aspects of the job that appeal to you, or which you find unattractive.

Another exercise is to select three of the companies featured on the site, or that are mentioned in this Part, or which interest you. Go to their website and then to the section on 'careers' or 'jobs with us' – again identify some possible jobs, and do as in the previous exercise.

What clues can you find in the information about how the job requirements relate to the tasks of managing (planning, organising, leading and controlling)?

Task 1.4   Identifying what makes a manager effective

You will all have worked with or for people who were managing an activity, either in an organisation or in some other human activity. What makes some people better managers than others? Form a group with three or four others on your course and share your experience of managers – good and bad. List what those who were good managers did, which led you to regard them favourably.

Then answer these questions:

- To which of the management tasks or roles identified in Chapter 1 do these seem to relate?
- Are there any which do not fit the theories?

How would you judge your skills in dealing with the tasks and roles you identified? Be ready to share your conclusions in class.

Part 2

THE ENVIRONMENT OF MANAGEMENT

Introduction

Management takes place within a context, and this Part examines several aspects of the external context of organisations. Managers need to be familiar with that external environment, though they do not need to accept it passively. They can try to influence it by lobbying powerful players, by reaching agreement with competitors or by trying to shape public opinion. Nevertheless, since the organisation draws its resources from the external world, it needs to deliver goods or services well enough to persuade decision makers in that environment to continue their support. This is most obvious in commercial organisations. It is equally relevant in the public service: if a department set up to deliver care is managed badly it will not deliver. Taxpayers or clients will press their elected representatives to improve performance, and they in turn will demand improved performance from management and staff. All those involved with the organisation have some expectations of it. How satisfied they are will affect whether or not they are willing to continue their support. If they do not, the enterprise will fail.

Chapter 3 examines the most immediate aspect of the manager's context – the culture of their organisation – and then offers tools for analysing systematically the competitive and general environments. It also examines what stakeholders expect. Chapter 4 reflects the growing internationalisation of business, by examining some international features of the general environment – political developments such as the European Union, international economic factors and differences in national cultures.

Organisations can no longer act as if their shareholders were the only legitimate external interests. Pressure from interest groups and many consumers has encouraged many companies to take a positive approach to issues of corporate responsibility. There are conflicting interests here and Chapter 5 presents some concepts and tools that help to consider these issues in a coherent and well-informed way.

The Part Case is BP – a leading player in the world oil business. The business itself is inherently international, being affected by political and economic developments around the world. The case also raises issues of responsibility in safety and environmental matters.

Chapter 3

Organisation cultures and contexts

Aim

To identify the cultures and contexts within which managers work, and to outline some analytical tools.

Objectives

By the end of your work on this chapter you should be able to outline the concepts below in your own terms and:

1 Describe the main dimensions of organisational culture, using Quinn's or Handy's typologies

2 Identify the main sets of forces exerting influence on organisations

3 Use Porter's five forces model to analyse competitive environments

4 Conduct a PESTEL analysis for an organisation with which you are familiar

5 Compare environments in terms of their complexity and rate of change

6 Give examples of stakeholders seeking to influence organisations and explain a model for assessing stakeholder power.

Key terms

This chapter introduces the following ideas:

internal environment (or context)
competitive environment
general environment
external environment (or context)
organisation culture
power culture
role culture
task culture
person culture
five forces analysis
PESTEL analysis
stakeholder mapping

Each is a term defined within the text, as well as in the Glossary at the end of the book.

Nokia is the world's leading manufacturer of mobile phones. With an estimated market share of 35 per cent, it sold twice as many handsets in 2006 as second-placed Motorola and many times the number of other rivals such as Samsung and Ericsson. A Finnish company, founded in 1895 as a paper manufacturer, Nokia grew into a conglomerate with interests including electronics, cable manufacture, rubber, chemicals, electricity generation and, by the 1960s, telephone equipment. In the early 1990s senior managers decided to focus on the mobile phone industry, then in its infancy.

Two factors favoured this move. First, the Finnish government had taken a lead in telecoms deregulation and Nokia was already competing vigorously with other manufacturers supplying equipment to the national phone company. Second, the European Union (EU) adopted a single standard – the Global System for Mobile Telephony (GSM) – for Europe's second generation (digital) phones. This became the standard used by two-thirds of the world's mobile phone subscribers. Finland's links with its Nordic neighbours also helped, as people in these sparsely populated countries adopted mobile phones enthusiastically.

Nokia has strong design skills, but above all managers were quick to recognise that mobile phones are not a commodity but a fashion accessory. By offering smart designs, different ring tones and coloured covers Nokia became the 'cool' mobile brand for fashion-conscious people. Nokia has also mastered the logistics of getting millions of phones to customers around the world.

While many competitors subcontract the manufacture of their handsets, Nokia assembles most of its own, with factories in Brazil, Finland and China. Managers believe this gives them a better understanding of the market and the manufacturing process. Nokia buys about 80 billion components a year, and has close relationships with its most important suppliers.

While all of these factors helped Nokia, Matti Alahuhta, Director of Strategy, believes there was a further reason. Although competitors such as Motorola and Ericsson already had advantages of scale, experience and distribution networks, the arrival of the new digital technology changed the rules of the game, forcing all players

© Nokia

to start from scratch. Mr Alahuhta acknowledges that some external factors helped Nokia, but comments that 'good luck favours the prepared mind'.

The company's leading position in the industry owes much to Jorma Ollila, who became chief executive in 1992. He helped to shape the mobile phone industry by pursuing his vision of a mass market for voice communication while on the move. As he prepared to hand over to a new chief executive (Olli-Pekka Kallasvuo) in 2006, he observed that the next challenge would be to enable users to access the Internet, videos, music, games and e-mails through a new generation of 'smart' phones and hand-held devices. In late 2007 the company announced plans to offer new services through its mobiles, including an online music store.

Source: Based on *The Economist*, 16 June 2001; *Financial Times*, 29 June 2001 and 10 October 2005; *Business Week*, 10 September 2007.

Case questions 3.1

- How has the environment favoured the development of Nokia?
- How could the same factors turn to the disadvantage of the company?
- Visit Nokia's website, and read their most recent trading statement (under investor relations). What have been the main developments in the last year?

3.1 Introduction

Nokia's success depends on the ability of its managers to spot and interpret signals from consumers in the mobile phone market, and to ensure that the organisation responds more effectively than its competitors. It also depends on them identifying ideas emerging within the organisation (such as from the research laboratories) that have commercial potential – and working to ensure that consumers are aware of and receptive to the idea when it is incorporated into the next generation of products. The early success of the company was helped by recognising that to many users a mobile was (and still is) a fashion item, and using its design skills to meet that need. It was also helped by a wider change when the European Union established common standards for mobile telephony, which were enthusiastically promoted by the Finnish government.

All managers work within a context that both constrains and supports them. How well they understand, interpret and interact with that context affects their performance. Each business is unique, so the forces with which they interact differ: those who are able to identify and shape them are likely to perform better than those who are not. Figure 3.1 shows four environmental forces. The inner circle represents the organisation's **internal environment (or context)** – which Chapter 1 introduced. That includes its culture, which many now regard as a major contextual feature. Beyond that is the immediate **competitive environment (or context),** sometimes known as the micro-

The **internal environment (or context)** consists of elements within the organisation such as its technology, structure or business processes.

A **competitive environment (or context)** is the industry-specific environment comprising the organisation's customers, suppliers and competitors.

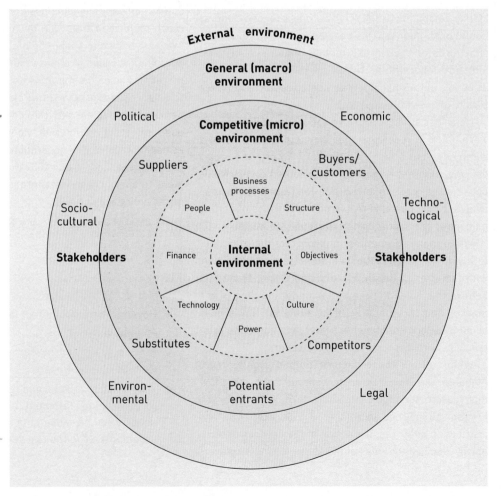

Figure 3.1

Environmental influences on the organisation

environment. This is the industry-specific environment of customers, suppliers, competitors and potential substitute products. The outer circle shows the **general environment (or context)**, sometimes known as the macro-environment – political, economic, social, technological, (natural) environmental and legal factors that affect all organisations. Forces in the internal and competitive environments usually have more impact on, and are more open to influence by, the organisation than those in the general environment.

Together these make up an organisation's **external environment (or context)** – a constantly changing source of threats and opportunities: how well people cope with these affects performance.

Forces in the external environment do not affect practice of their own accord. They become part of the agenda only when internal or external stakeholders pay attention to them and act to place them on the management agenda. In terms of Figure 3.1, they are a fourth set of forces. Managers (who are themselves stakeholders) balance conflicting interpretations of their context. They work within an internal context, and look outside for actual and potential changes that may affect the factors in the centre of Figure 3.1. The figure implies a constant interaction between an organisation's culture and its external environment.

The chapter begins with ideas about organisational culture which, together with many informal arrangements, shapes its distinctive nature. It then shows how to analyse a business's competitive environment, and presents a model for analysing the general environment. It contrasts stable and dynamic environments and concludes with the idea of stakeholder analysis.

> The **general environment (or context)** (sometimes known as the macro-environment) includes political, economic, social technological, (natural) environmental and legal factors that affect all organisations.

> The **external environment (or context)** consists of elements beyond the organisation – it combines the competitive and general environments.

3.2 Cultures and their components

Developing cultures

Interest in **organisation culture** has grown as academics and managers have come to believe that it influences behaviour. Several claim that a strong and distinct culture helps to integrate individuals into the team or organisation (Ouchi, 1981; Deal and Kennedy, 1982; Peters and Waterman, 1982). Deal and Kennedy (1982) refer to culture as 'the way we do things around here' and Hofstede (1991) sees it as the 'collective programming of the mind', which distinguishes one group from another. They claim that having the right culture explains the success of many high-performing organisations.

Someone entering a department or organisation for the first time can usually sense and observe the surface elements of the culture. Some buzz with life and activity, others seem asleep; some welcome and look after visitors, others seem inward looking; some work by the rules, while others are entrepreneurial and risk taking; some have regular social occasions while in others staff rarely meet except at work.

> **Organisation culture** is a pattern of shared basic assumptions that was learned by a group as it solved its problems of external adaptation and internal integration, which has worked well enough to be considered valid and transmitted to new members (Schein 2004, p. 17).

Examples of cultures

management in practice

Michelin www.michelin.com

Our culture is based on a strong belief in our skills. We are industrialists. We have a job, a mission that we have defined more precisely as improving the mobility of goods and people. Everything that rolls affects us. We are like a tyre; supple and strong. We have always stuck to our core business. We never wanted to turn ourselves, like some others, into a conglomerate with media, telephone, energy or yoghurt interests.

Source: The late Edouard Michelin, quoted in *Financial Times*, 25 April 2003.

▶

Heineken www.heineken.com
When Jean-Francois van Boxmeer became chief executive of the Dutch brewing group in 2005 he wanted to accelerate the speed at which managers made decisions.

There is more pressure for results, for achievement. I have changed the way Heineken is managed ... towards more personal accountability; from a northern European way to a more Anglo-Saxon approach. People make the difference, so leave their autonomy, but cultivate their sense of responsibility. Allow for mistakes, but encourage them to say: 'I messed up.' You learn from that and shouldn't hide it.

Source: Mr. van Boxmeer, quoted in *Financial Times*, 9 May 2006.

Cambridge and **MIT**
A partnership between Cambridge University and Massachusetts Institute of Technology uncovered a transatlantic culture clash in teaching and learning, and is encouraging experimentation on both sides.

Engineering courses at MIT seem to be geared towards giving one skills that are ready to be applied in a job without much further training. The preference in Cambridge is to stay conceptual, making problems arithmetically straightforward so that insight can be given a higher profile ... The difference is between the British ideal of asking students to develop their own 'internal compass' for learning, and the US preference for an 'external compass'.

Source: Extracts from an article in *Financial Times*, 20 April 2004.

FT

Figure 3.2 illustrates how a distinctive culture develops; as people develop and share common values they use these to establish beliefs and norms that guide their behaviour towards each other and to outsiders. Positive outcomes reinforce their belief in the values underlying their behaviour, which then become a stronger influence on how people should work and relate to each other: should people have job titles? how should they dress? should meetings be confrontational or supportive?

A shared culture provides members with guidelines about how they can best contribute. The more they work on these issues to develop a common understanding, the better they will perform.

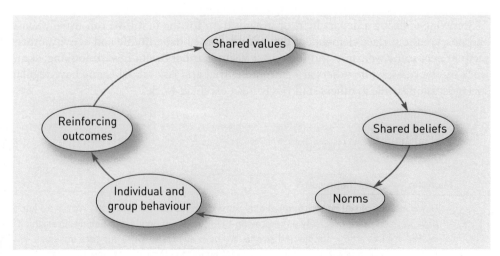

Figure 3.2
The stages of cultural formation

Components of cultures

Schein (2004) identifies three levels of a culture, 'level' referring to the degree to which the observer can see its components.

1 **Artefacts** represent the visible level – elements such as the language or etiquette that someone coming into contact with a culture can observe:
   - visible products;
   - architecture (open-plan offices without doors or private space);
   - technology and equipment;
   - style (clothing, manner of address, emotional displays);
   - myths and stories about the organisation;
   - rituals and ceremonies (leaving events, awards ceremonies and away-days);
   - courses (to induct employees in the culture as well as the content).

   While it is easy to observe and list such artefacts, it is difficult for outsiders to decipher what they mean to the group that created and sustained them, or what underlying assumptions they reflect. That requires an analysis of beliefs and values.

2 **Espoused beliefs and values** are the accumulated beliefs that members hold about the work they are doing, and the situations with which they deal. As a group develops, members refine their ideas about what works in this business: how people make decisions, how teams work together, how they solve problems. Practices that work become the accepted way to behave:
   - 'Quality pays.'
   - 'The customer always comes first.'
   - 'We should stick to our core business.'
   - 'Cultivate a sense of personal responsibility.'
   - 'We depend on close team work.'
   - 'People work best if they have a clear sense of direction.'
   - 'Everyone is expected to challenge a proposal – whoever made it.'

   Some companies go so far as to codify and publish their beliefs and values, to help induct new members and to reinforce them amongst existing staff. Such beliefs and values shape the visible artefacts, though companies vary in the degree to which employees internalise them. The extent to which they do so depends on how clearly they derive from shared basic underlying assumptions.

3 **Basic underlying assumptions** are deeply held by members of the group as being the way to work together. As they act in accordance with their values and beliefs, those that work become embedded as basic underlying assumptions. When the group holds these strongly, members will act in accordance with them, and reject actions based on others:
   - 'We need to satisfy customers to survive as a business.'
   - 'Our business is to help people with X problem live better with X problem.'
   - 'Products we offer to the market must be safe and fit for purpose.'
   - 'Success depends on facing and solving problems, not ignoring them.'
   - 'People can make mistakes, as long as they learn from them.'
   - 'We employ highly motivated and competent adults.'
   - 'Financial markets worry about the short term: we are here for the long term.'

   Difficulties arise when people with assumptions developed in one group work with people from another. Mergers sometimes experience difficulty when staff who have to work together realise they are from different cultures.

management in practice   Cap Gemini and Ernst & Young

When the French company Cap Gemini merged with the information technology consultancy of Ernst & Young (E&Y) they found significant cultural differences. Cap Gemini's chief operating officer commented that accurate statistics from E&Y were scarce: 'They changed their figures repeatedly. We said we needed audited accounts. They said: 'Do you really need audited accounts from a third party?' For them that was somehow traumatic.'

Source: Based on an article by Caroline Daniel, *Financial Times*, 5 February 2001, p.15.

Activity 3.1   Culture spotting

- Identify as many components of culture (artefacts, beliefs and values, underlying assumptions) in an organisation or unit as you can.
- What may the artefacts suggest about the deeper beliefs and values, or underlying assumptions?
- Gather evidence (preferably by asking people) about how the culture affects behaviour, and whether they think it helps or hinders performance.
- Analyse your results and decide which of the four types in the competing values framework most closely reflects that organisation's culture.

3.3   Types of culture

This section outlines three ways of describing and comparing cultures.

Competing values framework

The competing values model developed by Quinn *et al.* (2003) – introduced in Chapter 2 – is based on the inherent tensions between flexibility or control and between an internal or an external focus. Figure 3.3 (based on Figure 2.2) shows four cultural types.

Open systems

This represents an open systems view, in which people recognise that the external environment plays a significant role, and is a vital source of ideas, energy and resources. It also sees the environment as complex and turbulent, requiring entrepreneurial, visionary leadership and flexible, responsive behaviour. Key motivating factors are growth, stimulation, creativity and variety. Examples are start-up firms and new business units – organic, flexible operations.

Rational goal

Members see the organisation as a rational, efficiency-seeking unit. They define effectiveness in terms of production or economic goals that satisfy external requirements. Managers create structures to deal with the outside world. Leadership tends to be directive, goal

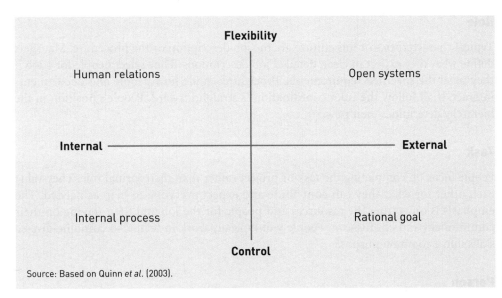

Flexibility

Human relations

Open systems

Internal —————————————————— External

Internal process

Rational goal

Control

Source: Based on Quinn *et al.* (2003).

Figure 3.3

Types of organisational culture

oriented and functional. Key motivating factors include competition and the achievement of predetermined ends. Examples are large, established businesses – mechanistic.

Internal process

Here members pay little attention to the external world, being more focused on internal matters. Their goal is to make the unit efficient, stable and controlled. Goals are known, tasks are repetitive, and methods stress specialisation, rules and procedures. Leaders tend to be conservative and cautious, emphasising technical issues. Key motivating factors include security, stability and order. Examples include utilities and public authorities – suspicious of change.

Human relations

People emphasise the value of informal interpersonal relations rather than formal structures. They try to maintain the organisation and nurture its members, defining effectiveness in terms of their well-being and commitment. Leaders tend to be participative, considerate and supportive. Motivating factors include attachment, cohesiveness and membership. Examples are found in voluntary groups, professional service firms and some internal support functions.

Charles Handy's cultural types

Charles Handy (1993), developing an idea of Roger Harrison, distinguished four cultures, which he designated **power**, **role**, **task** and **person culture**.

Power

A dominant central figure holds power: others follow the centre's policy and interpret new situations in the way the leader would. Many entrepreneurial firms operate in this way, with few rules but with well-understood, implicit codes on how to behave and work. The firm relies on the individual rather than on seeking consensus through discussion.

A **power culture** is one in which people's activities are strongly influenced by a dominant central figure.

A **role culture** is one in which people's activities are strongly influenced by clear and detailed job descriptions and other formal signals as to what is expected of them.

A **task culture** is one in which the focus of activity is towards completing a task or project using whatever means are appropriate.

A **person culture** is one in which activity is strongly influenced by the wishes of the individuals who are part of the organisation.

Role

Typical characteristics of this culture are the job description or the procedure. Managers define what they expect in clear, detailed job descriptions. They select people for a job if they meet the specified requirements. Procedures guide how people and departments interact. If all follow the rules coordination is straightforward. People's position in the hierarchy determines their power.

Task

People focus on completing the task or project rather than their formal role. They value each other for what they can contribute and expect everyone to help as needed. The emphasis is on getting the resources and people for the job and then relying on their commitment and enthusiasm. People will typically work in teams, to combine diverse skills into a common purpose.

Person

The individual is at the centre and any structure or system is there to serve them. The form is unusual – small professional and artistic organisations are probably closest to it, and perhaps experiments in communal living. They exist to meet the needs of the professionals or the members, rather than some larger organisational goal.

Activity 3.2   **Cultural examples**

For each of Handy's four cultural types, identify an example from within this text that seems to correspond most closely to that form.

- What clues about the company have you used to decide that allocation?
- Why do you think that culture is suitable for that organisation?
- What evidence would you seek to decide if that culture was suitable?
- Compare the similarities and differences in the competing values and Handy models.

Multiple cultures

The third perspective introduces the idea that organisations have not one, but several cultures. Early discussions of culture (Peters and Waterman, 1982) explored the benefits to an organisation of a single, unified culture. In contrast, Martin (2002) suggested that observers could take one of three perspectives towards a culture:

1 **Integration** – a focus on identifying consistencies in the data, and using those common patterns to explain events.
2 **Differentiation** – a focus on conflict, identifying different and possibly conflicting views of members towards events.
3 **Fragmentation** – a focus on the fluid nature of organisations, and on the interplay and change of views about events.

Ogbonna and Harris (1998; 2002) provided empirical support for this view, based on interviews with staff at all levels of three retailing companies. They found that the position of a person in the hierarchy determined their perspective on the culture (see Table

3.1), and concluded that attempts to introduce cultural change based on head office values were unlikely to work. As consensus on culture was unlikely, they advised managers to recognise the range of sub-cultures within their oganisation, and only seek to reconcile those differences that were essential to policy. They also observed that culture remains a highly subjective idea, largely in the eye of the beholder 'and is radically different according to an individual's position in the hierarchy' (p. 45).

Table 3.1

Hierarchical position and cultural perspectives

Position in hierarchy	Cultural perspective	Description	Example
Head office managers	Integration	Cultural values should be shared across the organisation. Unified culture both desirable and attainable	'If we can get every ... part of the company doing what they should be doing, we'll beat everybody.'
Store managers	Differentiation	Reconciling conflicting views of head office and shop floor. See cultural pluralism as inevitable	'People up at head office are all pushing us in different directions. Jill in Marketing wants customer focus, June in Finance wants lower costs.'
Store employees	Fragmented	Confused by contradictory nature of the espoused values. See organisation as complex and unpredictable	'One minute it's this, the next it's that. You can't keep up with the flavour of the month.'

Source: Based on Ogbonna and Harris (1998); Ogbonna and Harris (2002).

Culture and performance

Schein, and most other writers on culture, see it as something that can be managed as a tool to improve organisational performance, though others question this link. Kotter and Heskett (1992) studied 207 companies and attempted to relate the strength of their culture to economic performance. Although the variables were positively correlated, the relationship was much weaker than advocates of culture as a factor in performance have predicted. Some doubt the ability of managers to change a culture. The next Key Ideas feature illustrates one of these critical views.

Martin Parker – a critical perspective on culture

Parker (2000) takes a sceptical view of the idea that a strong culture improves performance, while acknowledging that it 'begins to put forward a valuable language which can be used to represent organization and organizing' (p. 10). His book is an attempt to rescue culture from 'managerialism', and includes a valuable historical chapter, and some extended case studies.

    He reviews three popular managerialist works (Ouchi, 1981; Deal and Kennedy, 1982; Peters and Waterman, 1982) and comments critically on their methods (lack of counter-examples, and companies with strong cultures that failed); the limited range of economic sectors; and the sales promotion. ▶

He suggests that one of the attractions of their work may have been that readers saw it as a counter to earlier views that stressed bureaucratic, quantitative and rational methods for controlling staff. Yet promoting culture as an organisational tool, while apparently more humane, may have the same intention: 'to intervene in the identity of the employee just as all organisational control strategies ... have done' (p. 25).

He concluded that rather than the single strong culture advocated by the managerialist writers, organisations have multiple cultures reflecting three divisions by which people distinguish themselves – space/function, generation, and occupation/profession. Even if these overlap, they illuminate the perspectives from which members view events, and that are likely to hinder attempts to develop unified, consensual cultures to control employees.

Source: Parker (2000).

Others suggest that while the link to performance may be unclear the underlying ideas may be more beneficial than harmful – including in not-for-profit settings. Watson (1994) suggested:

> people do not wander away from serving the key purposes of the organisation's founders or leaders. The tightness of control comes from people choosing to do what is required of them because they wish to serve the values which they share with those in charge. These values, typically focusing on quality of service to customers, are transmitted and manifested in the organisation's culture. This culture uses stories, myths and legends to keep these values alive and people tend to be happy to share these values and subscribe to the corporate legends because to do so is to find meaning in their lives. (p. 16)

Thompson and McHugh (2002), while also critical of much writing on the topic, observe that:

> Creating a culture resonant with the overall goals is relevant to any organisation, whether it be a trade union, voluntary group or producer co-operative. Indeed, it is more important in such consensual groupings. Co-operatives, for example, can degenerate organisationally because they fail to develop adequate mechanisms for transmitting the original ideals from founders to new members and sustaining them through shared experiences. (pp. 208–209)

Nokia – the case continues www.nokia.com CASE STUDY

In May 2004 the company had surprised the market by announcing that its share of the handset market had slipped to 29 per cent, against 35 per cent the previous year. However, it also pointed out that demand was growing rapidly in China, India and Russia, and many consumers in established markets were upgrading to colour screens and camera phones. Sales of 3G infrastructure equipment were growing as operators became more confident in the success of that technology.

Since 2004 the company has had four divisions – the main handsets business; mobile infrastructure (which builds networks for operators such as Vodafone); multimedia services: and enterprise solutions. Analysts saw this as an attempt to diversify into new growth areas, and to reduce dependence on handsets. In 2006 Nokia reached a deal with Siemens to merge their network businesses, creating the world's third largest network equipment supplier. By 2007 it appeared to have regained its customary market share of 35 per cent of handset sales.

One factor in the company's sustained success appears to have been a culture that encourages cooperation within teams and across internal and external boundaries. Jorma Ollila, CEO until 2006, believed that Nokia's innovative capacity springs from multi-functional teams working together to bring new insights to products and services. Staff in the four divisions work in teams that may remain constant for many years – but which are from time to time combined with other teams to work on a common task.

The company also encourages a culture of communication by creating small groups from around the company to work on a strategic issue for four months. This helps them to build ties with many parts of the company – some of which continue during later work. The induction process for new employees also encour-

ages team building and cooperation: the newcomer's manager must introduce them to at least 15 people within and outside the team.

Source: *Economist*, 19 June 2004; *Financial Times*, 20 June 2006.

Case questions 3.2

- Which of the cultural types identified by Quinn *et al.* (2003) would you expect to find within Nokia's handset business?
- How will the practices to encourage communication help a culture to develop (refer to Figure 3.2)?

As managers work within a culture, they will also be working in an external context – and perhaps asking whether the internal culture can meet the expectations from outside. To consider that carefully, they need some tools for analysing that external world.

3.4 The competitive environment – Porter's five forces

Managers are most directly affected by forces in their immediate competitive environment. According to Porter (1980a, 1985) the ability of a firm to earn an acceptable return depends on five forces – the ability of new competitors to enter the industry, the threat of substitute products, the bargaining power of buyers, the bargaining power of suppliers and the rivalry amongst existing competitors. Figure 3.4 shows Porter's **five forces analysis**.

Five forces analysis is a technique for identifying and listing those aspects of the five forces most relevant to the profitability of an organisation at that time.

Porter believes that it is the *collective* strength of the five forces that determines industry profitability. The stronger the forces, collectively, the less profitable the industry will be: the weaker they are, the greater the profits. These forces influence profitability through their effects on prices, costs and investment requirements. Buyer power influences the prices a firm can charge, as does the threat of substitutes. The bargaining power of suppliers determines the cost of raw materials and other inputs. Knowing how these forces are likely to affect their industry enables managers to shape their strategy.

Potential new entrants

The extent of this threat depends on how easily they can overcome barriers to entry, including:

- the need for economies of scale (to compete on cost), which are difficult to achieve quickly;
- high entry costs if significant capital investment is required;
- lack of distribution channels;
- subsidies that benefit existing firms at the expense of potential new entrants;

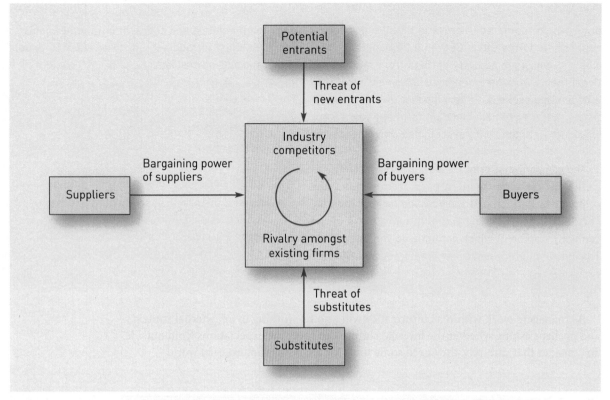

Figure 3.4 The five forces of industry competition

Source: Porter (1980a), p. 5.

- cost advantages of existing firms, such as access to raw materials or know-how;
- strong product or service differentiation – customers are loyal to the brand.

GlaxoSmithKline (an Anglo-American drugs group) is, like all similar companies, facing a growing threat from generic (unbranded) versions of its top-selling drugs, while low-cost airlines in Asia threaten Cathay Pacific.

Intensity of rivalry amongst competitors

Strong competitive rivalry lowers profitability, and occurs when:

- there are many firms in an industry, but none is dominant;
- there is slow market growth, which means companies fight for market share;
- fixed costs are high, encouraging firms to use capacity and overproduce;
- exit costs are high; specialised assets (hard to sell) or management loyalty (in old family firms) can create exit barriers that prolong excess capacity and low profitability;
- products are similar, so customers can easily switch to other suppliers.

A highly competitive market will also be one in which the threat of new entrants is high. While Nokia still dominated the mobile phone industry in 2007, it continued to face pressure from established competitors Motorola, Siemens and Ericsson, and from new entrants in Asia.

Competition amongst Chinese brewers

management in practice

SABMiller and Anheuser-Busch both sought to enter the Chinese market by buying an existing major player, Harbin (with Anheuser-Busch quickly winning the contest). They were attracted by the fact that China is the world's largest market for beer, growing at 6–8 per cent a year. However, it is also fiercely competitive as there are over 400 brewers competing for sales: this keeps prices down, and profits are on average less than 0.5 per cent of sales.

Source: *The Economist*, 15 May 2004.

Buyers (customers)

Buyers (customers) seek lower prices or higher quality at constant prices, thus forcing down prices and profitability. Buyer power is high when:

- the buyer purchases a large part of a supplier's output;
- there are many substitute products, allowing easy switching;
- the product is a large part of the buyer's costs, encouraging the buyer to seek lower prices;
- buyers can plausibly threaten to supply their needs internally.

Wal-Mart's power as a buyer www.walmart.com

management in practice

Wal-Mart (which owns Asda in the UK) is the world's largest company, being three times the size of the second largest retailer, the French company Carrefour. Growth has enabled it to become the largest purchaser in the United States, controlling much of the business done by almost every major consumer products company. It accounts for 30 per cent of hair care products sold, 26 per cent of toothpaste, 20 per cent of pet food and 20 per cent of all sales of CDs, videos and DVDs. This gives it great power over companies in these industries, since their dependence on Wal-Mart reduces their bargaining power.

Source: *Business Week*, 6 October 2003, pp. 48–53, and other sources.

Suppliers

Conditions that increase the bargaining power of suppliers are the opposite of those applying to buyers. The power of suppliers relative to customers is high when:

- there are few suppliers;
- the product is distinctive, so that customers are reluctant to switch;
- the cost of switching is high (e.g. if a company has invested in a supplier's software);
- the supplier can plausibly threaten to extend their business to compete with the customer;
- the customer is a small or irregular purchaser.

Substitutes

In Porter's model, substitute products refer to products in other industries that can perform the same function – using cans instead of bottles. Close substitutes constrain the ability of firms to raise prices, and the threat is high when buyers are able and willing to change their buying habits. Technological change and the risk of obsolescence pose a further threat. YouTube threatens established media companies, while online recruitment threatens the revenues that newspapers receive from job advertisements.

Analysing the forces in the competitive environment enables managers to seize opportunities, counter threats and generally improve their position relative to competitors. They can consider how to alter the strength of the forces to improve their position by, for example, building barriers to entry or increasing their power over suppliers or buyers. Chapter 8 (Strategic Management) examines how managers can position their organisation within the competitive environment.

Activity 3.3   **Critical reflection on the five forces**

Conduct a five forces analysis for an organisation with which you are familiar. Discuss with a manager of the organisation how useful he or she finds the technique.

- Evaluate whether it captures the main competitive variables in his or her industry.
- Compare your analysis with that which you did for Nokia, and present a summary of similarities and differences in the forces affecting the companies.

3.5   Analysing the general environment – PESTEL

PESTEL analysis is a technique for identifying and listing the political, economic, social, technological, environmental and legal factors in the general environment most relevant to an organisation.

Forces in the wider world also shape management policies, and a **PESTEL analysis** (short for political, economic, socio-cultural, technological, environmental and legal) helps to identify these – which Figure 3.5 summarises.

Political factors

Political systems vary between countries and often shape what managers can and cannot do. Governments often regulate industries such as power supply, telecommunications, postal services and transport by specifying, amongst other things, who can offer services, the conditions they must meet, and what they can charge. Regulations differ between countries and are a major factor in managers' decisions.

When the United Kingdom and most European governments altered the law on financial services, non-financial companies such as Virgin and Sainsbury's quickly began to offer banking services. Deregulating air transport stimulated the growth of low-cost airlines, especially in the United States (e.g. Southwest Airlines), Europe (easyJet), Australia (Virgin Blue) and parts of Asia (Air Asia), though as the Ryanair case in Chapter 1 showed, these companies still work in a political environment. The European Union is developing regulations to try to manage the environmentally friendly disposal of the millions of personal computers and mobile phones that consumers scrap each year.

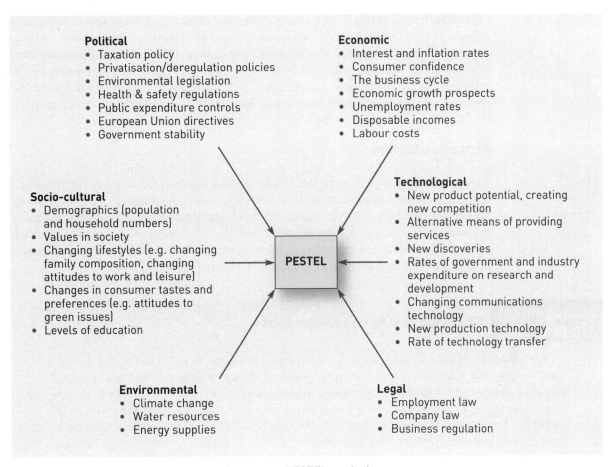

Political
- Taxation policy
- Privatisation/deregulation policies
- Environmental legislation
- Health & safety regulations
- Public expenditure controls
- European Union directives
- Government stability

Economic
- Interest and inflation rates
- Consumer confidence
- The business cycle
- Economic growth prospects
- Unemployment rates
- Disposable incomes
- Labour costs

Socio-cultural
- Demographics (population and household numbers)
- Values in society
- Changing lifestyles (e.g. changing family composition, changing attitudes to work and leisure)
- Changes in consumer tastes and preferences (e.g. attitudes to green issues)
- Levels of education

PESTEL

Technological
- New product potential, creating new competition
- Alternative means of providing services
- New discoveries
- Rates of government and industry expenditure on research and development
- Changing communications technology
- New production technology
- Rate of technology transfer

Environmental
- Climate change
- Water resources
- Energy supplies

Legal
- Employment law
- Company law
- Business regulation

Figure 3.5 Identifying environmental influences – PESTEL analysis

Government and business: compare China with India

management in practice

To [show how] government affects ... the conduct of private enterprise, consider modern China and India ... These have been the world's fastest growing countries for the last twenty years [and] have followed curiously dissimilar approaches in reaching this status. At the root of this dissimilarity is the relative importance of government (vis-à-vis the private sector) and the manner in which government is engaged. The Chinese government has embraced foreign direct investment while discouraging private enterprise. In contrast, India has [avoided] the former but created room for indigenous entrepreneurs ...

A specific look at the two countries' software industries sharpens the point. Most of China's leading software firms are spin-offs of government-owned entities (universities, state-owned enterprises), and government continues to be heavily involved in them. Founder Holdings Limited, for example, is a spin-off from Peking University and remains heavily under the tutelage of the state. India's situation could not be more starkly different. Government has played no role in the formation of India's leading software enterprises. The largest listed software companies, Infosys and Wipro, were launched by entrepreneurs and a family-controlled business enterprise, respectively.

Source: Extracts from Ring *et al.* (2005).

Legislation governing employment rights and environmental practices influences company policy. When General Motors announced in 2006 that it would close a manufacturing plant in the United Kingdom rather than in mainland Europe, many observers believed the choice was influenced by UK legislation that made it relatively easy to dismiss staff. Intergovernmental agreements to control toxic emissions are forcing oil companies to produce cleaner fuels and car manufacturers to improve fuel efficiency.

Economic factors

Economic factors such as wage levels, inflation and interest rates affect an organisation's costs. Increasing competition and the search for cost advantages drive globalisation. Electronics companies such as National Semiconductor or Seagate have switched many production facilities to low-wage economies in Asia to cut costs. Similarly, Marks & Spencer chose to sever long-standing relationships with British clothing manufacturers in favour of suppliers in lower-cost countries such as Turkey and India.

 **Changing tastes challenge pubs**

Across several European markets, people are drinking more alcohol at home and less in bars and pubs – a quiet shift in behaviour that is presenting a big challenge to brewers. The trend is particularly marked amongst the British, a nationality previously noted for 'herd drinking' at public watering holes. Pubs and other licensed venues will soon be usurped as the biggest sellers of beer in the UK, according to the chief executive of a major pub company. By 2008 he reckons the UK will be buying most of its ale and lager from supermarkets and other stores.

FT

Source: *Financial Times*, 23 March 2004, p. 16.

The state of the economy is a major influence on consumer spending, which affects firms meeting those needs. Managers planning capital investments follow economic forecasts: if these suggest slower growth, they may postpone the project.

Socio-cultural factors

Demography is important for organisations where changes in the size and age of the population affect demand. An ageing population increases the demand for health care, pharmaceuticals and financial services. Fidelity Investments changed its strategy to take advantage of demographic change, by offering a broader range of financial advice: this is meant to capitalise on the prediction that by 2010, 75 per cent of the financial assets in the United States would be held by people over 55. More single people affects the design of housing, holidays and life assurance. Demographics also shape an organisation's publicity – to ensure, for example, that advertising acknowledges the racial diversity of a community. Lawyers at leading banks are developing investment and savings schemes that comply with *sharia* law, so that they will be acceptable to devout Muslim investors.

Consumer tastes and preferences change. Commenting on a decision to increase the number of healthier products, the chief executive of Nestlé said: 'I think this shows you where the future direction of the company is. This emphasis on [healthier products] is a strategic decision, reflecting changing economic and demographic conditions.'

The vanishing mass market

Many consumer businesses such as Unilever have prospered by selling standard products to large numbers of consumers – the so-called mass marketing approach. They relied on TV commercials and print advertisements to reach millions of consumers who were all willing to buy the same products. They are now changing direction, and developing many smaller brands directed at small, distinctive groups of consumers. This reflects the growing diversity of the population, with many personal and individual preferences. This in turn has severe implications for media that relied on income from mass market advertising.

Source: *Business Week*, 12 July 2004, where there is more information.

Pepsi promotes healthier snacks www.pepsico.com

In 2006 PepsiCo announced that it was joining a collaborative venture with five leading food manufacturers in the United States to help combat childhood obesity. The alliance would establish first-ever voluntary guidelines for snacks to be sold in schools, and will provide healthier choices for children.

PepsiCo itself will promote the consumption of fruit, vegetables and other healthy products, and will reformulate several of its products to reduce their salt and fat content. The move is part of a broader shift in focus by the US group away from its sugary soft drinks and fatty snacks towards a healthier range of products – a radical change for a business whose brands include Cheetos corn snacks and Lay's potato crisps.

Source: Company website; other published sources.

Technological factors

Companies pay close attention to the physical infrastructure – such as the adequacy of power supplies and transport systems. Even more, they monitor advances in information technology, which are dramatically changing the business environment of many companies. Advances in technology do not only affect data systems. Computers traditionally handled data, while other systems handled voice (telephones) and pictures (film and video). These three devices at the front of the information revolution – the telephone, the computer and the television – have been around for more than half a century. They are familiar to us as separate devices, but the ability to process and transmit information in a common digital format is eroding the boundaries between them. Computers have always handled information this way, while telephones and television used an analogue method. Now that all use digital methods there is a common platform between the three communication devices that greatly increases their ability to exchange information. Digitisation – the packaging of images and sounds into digital form – has profound implications for many industries. Table 3.2 lists just a few of these (see Chapter 12 for a fuller examination).

The growing use of the Internet makes it possible to use new distribution channels for many services, enabling new competitors to enter an industry (such as Virgin Financial Services and Kwik-Fit Insurance Services), often with lower costs than the established players. Technology is changing the nature of work, enabling employees to work at remote locations.

Table 3.2

Examples of digital technologies affecting established businesses

Technology	Application	Businesses affected
Digital Versatile Discs (DVDs)	Store sound and visual images	Sales of stereophonic sound systems decline sharply
IPOD, MP3 and smartphones	Digital downloads of talking books	New markets created for talking books, with titles to suit new audience
Broadband services delivering online content	Advertising expenditure on online media growing much more rapidly than print media	Media companies seek to gain share of that revenue (NewsCorp acquire MySpace, the social networking site)
Voice over Internet Protocol (VoIP)	Enables customers to make telephone calls over the Internet at very low cost	Threat to large part of the revenues of traditional phone companies
Digital photography	Enables people to store pictures electronically and order prints online	Photographic retailers need to add online services to branch networks

Nokia – the case continues www.nokia.com CASE STUDY

While Nokia, like all mobile phone companies, regularly introduces more technically sophisticated devices, these account for a small proportion of the units the industry sells each year. The most rapidly growing demand is for basic models, which often handle just voice and text messaging. In 2005 there were about 2 billion mobile phone users in the world, and market penetration was above 50 per cent in developed countries. Observers expected that as prices for phones and services continue to drop, another billion customers could sign up by 2010 in places such as China, India, Brazil and Russia.

Nokia has been particularly successful in meeting this demand, making great efforts to secure first-time buyers and then build lifelong loyalty to the brand. The scale of its global production allows it to offer basic units very cheaply: even low-cost suppliers in China do not produce enough units to match the efficiency of Nokia, and so cannot match their prices. Moreover, status-conscious buyers in the third world disdain unknown brands: 'Brazilians want brand names and are willing to pay a bit more for Nokia or Motorola' (quoted in *Business Week*, 7 November 2005, p. 21).

More than any other handset maker the Finnish company has connected with consumers in China and India.

Greater China (the mainland, Honk Kong and Taiwan) is the company's biggest market: in 2005 it supplied 31 per cent of all sets sold there, well ahead of the 10 per cent from second-placed Motorola. It has about 60 per cent of the market in India, which it expects will be the company's biggest market by 2010. It owes its strong position in both countries in part to a decentralised organisation that can spot local sales trend very quickly, and an ability to produce sets tailored to local tastes and languages.

Sources: *Business Week*, 7 November 2005 and 27 March 2006.

Case questions 3.3

Gather some information about current developments in the mobile phone industry. Also collect information on Nokia.

- Use Porter's five forces model to outline the competitive environment of the industry.
- Which of these factors may have contributed to Nokia's success?
- Which PESTEL factors are most affecting the development of the industry?

Environmental factors

The natural resources available in an economy – including minerals, agricultural land and the prevailing climate – affect the kind of businesses that managers create: the mills at New Lanark (Chapter 2 Case) were built beside a source of water power. Currently attention focuses on climate change, and what that means for countries and businesses – insurance companies, house builders and water companies are only the most visible examples of companies which are being affected.

Good times for waste management companies

High commodity prices and a tightening ratchet of environmental policy are spurring innovation in waste management and recycling. Governments are setting tough performance targets and are inviting the private sector to commit a large amount of capital. As a result, water and waste markets are growing rapidly, and there is scope for some very attractive investment returns. One of the main drivers is the European Union's landfill directive, which stipulates that from 2007 all waste must be treated before being sent to landfill, while many types of hazardous waste must be dealt with separately.

Source: From a report by Fiona Harvey, *Financial Times*, 11 April 2006.

Legal factors

Governments create the legal framework within which companies operate, most obviously in areas such as health and safety, employment, consumer protection and pollution control. They also create the legal basis for business – such as when the UK Parliament passed the Joint Stock Companies Act in 1862. Previously people were discouraged from putting their money into a business as they were personally liable for the whole of a company's debts if it failed. The Act of 1862 limited their liability to the value of the shares they held in the company – they could lose their investment, but not the rest of their wealth. This stimulated company formation and other countries soon passed similar legislation, paving the way for the countless 'limited liability' companies that exist today (Micklethwait and Wooldridge, 2003).

The PESTEL analysis is just as relevant to public and voluntary sector organisations. Many public service organisations are in business to do things that the market does not, so a PESTEL analysis can identify emerging issues that need attention. An example is the age structure of the population: a country with growing numbers of elderly people has to finance changes in community care services, social services and hospitals. Public sector organisations are often unable to expand their operations where new problems or needs are identified, but the results can be used to lobby for increased funding or to target their existing budgets.

By providing a checklist of possible environmental influences, the PESTEL framework is a useful starting point for analysis. The aim is not to produce a list of forces that might affect performance, but to help managers identify those that seem most relevant, together with possible changes in them.

Conduct a PESTEL analysis for your organisation, or one with which you are familiar.

● Which of the external forces you have identified has most implications for the business?
● Evaluate the extent to which the organisation's policy has taken account of these forces.
● Compare your analysis with that which you did for Nokia, and present a summary of similarities and differences in the forces affecting the companies.

3.6   The nature of the external environment

The axes in Figure 3.6 show two variables (Duncan, 1972) that affect how people see their environment – the degree of complexity and the degree of dynamism. Complexity refers to the number and similarity of factors that people take into consideration when making a decision – the more of these, and the more different they are, the more complex the situation. Dynamism refers to the degree to which these factors remain the same or change.

To consider just the most contrasting cells in Figure 3.6, those who perceive themselves to be in a *simple-stable* environment will experience the least uncertainty. They need only to consider a small number of factors, which do not change much. Competitors offer similar products, newcomers rarely enter the market and there are few technological breakthroughs. Examples include routine legal work such as house sales and wills, and traditional trades such as joinery. The information required for a decision is likely to be available, which will enable them to assess the outcome of a decision quite accurately. They can use past trends to predict the future with a reasonable degree of confidence. Some aspects of health and education, where demand is driven largely by demographic change, may also fit this pattern: the capacity needed in primary and secondary schools is easy to predict several years ahead.

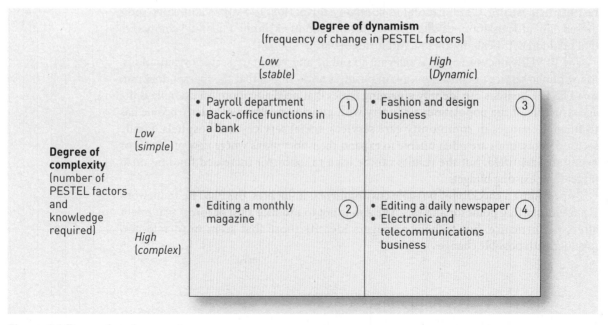

Figure 3.6 Types of environment

Don Sull – active waiting in unpredictable markets

key ideas

Donald Sull (2005) has studied more than 20 pairs of comparable companies in unpredictable industries such as airlines, telecommunications and software development. By comparing similar companies he was able to show how they responded differently to unforeseen threats and opportunities. Successful companies regularly responded more effectively to unexpected shifts in regulation, technology, competitive or macro-environments. They did this by what he termed 'actively waiting', using techniques that included:

● keeping priorities clear to avoid dissipating energy and resources;
● conducting reconnaissance to identify gaps in the market;
● keeping a reserve of cash to fund major opportunities when they emerge;
● using lulls to push through operational improvements;
● declaring that an opportunity is the company's main effort to seize it faster than its rivals.

Source: Based on Sull (2005).

At the other extreme, those working in *complex-dynamic* environments face the greatest perceived environmental uncertainty. They have to monitor a large number of changing factors, which also differ considerably from one another. Competitors offer many different products and services, and it is not clear how customers will react to them. Companies in the mobile phone or entertainment industries fall into this category. Multinationals such as Shell and BP experience great complexity, operating across diverse political, legal and cultural systems. Eric Schmidt (chief executive of Google) has said that in many high-tech and other industries:

> the environment is changing so fast that it requires improvisation in terms of strategy, products and even day-to-day operations. Just when you think you understand the technology landscape, you see a major disruption.

Activity 3.5   Critical reflection on type of environment

Use Figure 3.6 to analyse the environment in which your unit of the organisation works. Then try to do the same analysis for one or two other units of the organisation.

● Compare the nature of these environments.
● What are the implications of that for managing these departments, and the organisation?

Most managers claim to work in dynamic and complex situations. This implies that they face great uncertainty over how the future will unfold. In these circumstances historical analysis is likely to be a less useful guide to the future and managers need to develop different ways of anticipating what may lie ahead.

Case question 3.4

● How would you classify the environment in which Nokia operates? Which factors contributed to your answer?

3.7 Stakeholder mapping

All managers need to deal with stakeholders – individuals, groups or other organisations with an interest in, or who are affected by, what the enterprise does (Freeman, 1984). Organisations depend on being able to acquire resources from their environment, which is made up of a network of stakeholders – the forces in the competitive (micro) environment and in the general (macro) environment shown in Figure 3.1 are represented by stakeholders. Managers (whether in the private or public sector) need to ensure that they understand what stakeholders expect and that they meet those expectations to an acceptable degree. Failing to do so may lead stakeholders to withdraw their support and so deny managers the resources they need to stay in business.

Stakeholders may be internal (employees, managers, different departments or professional groups, owners, shareholders) or external (customers, competitors, bankers, local communities, members of the public, pressure groups and government). The challenge is that:

> Different stakeholders do not generally share the same definition of an organization's 'problems', and hence, they do not in general share the same 'solutions.' As a result, the typical approaches to organizational problem solving, which generally pre-suppose prior consensus or agreement among parties, cannot be used; they break down. Instead a method is needed that builds off a starting point of disagreement ...' (Mitroff, 1983, p. 5)

Stakeholders have expectations of organisations and seek to influence them in various ways. Nutt (2002) studied 400 strategic decisions, and found that half of the decisions 'failed' – that is they were not implemented, only partially implemented or otherwise produced poor results – in large part because decision makers failed to attend to stakeholders:

> Failure to attend to the information and concerns of stakeholders clearly is a kind of flaw in thinking or action that too often and too predictably leads to poor performance, outright failure or even disaster. (Bryson, 2004, p. 23)

As problems in business and the public sector become increasingly interconnected, identifying stakeholders and deciding how to manage relationships with them is a key task of managing.

 **The interests of managers and shareholders**

While senior managers often claim to be trying to align their interests with those of shareholders, the two often conflict. Mergers often appear to benefit senior managers and their professional advisers rather than shareholders. Acquiring companies often pay too much for the target, but executives inside the enlarged company receive higher pay. Professional advisers (investment bankers) make money on both the merger and the breakup.

Using company money to buy the company's shares in the market uses money that cannot be spent on dividends. From the vantage point of many CEOs, paying dividends is about the last thing they would want to do with corporate earnings. In theory, a CEO is carrying out shareholder wishes. In practice, as the spate of recent scandals has shown, the interests of chief executives and their shareholders can diverge widely.

Source: Based on extracts from an article by Robert Kuttner, *Business Week,* 9 September 2002.

Shareholders
- Growth in dividend payments
- Growth in share price
- Growth in asset value

Customers
- Competitive price
- Quality product or service
- Guarantee provisions

Suppliers
- Timely payment of debt
- Adequate liquidity
- Integrity of directors
- Trustworthy purchasing manager

Employees
- Good pay and benefits
- Job security
- Sense of purpose in the job
- Opportunities for personal development

Government
- Adhering to the country's laws
- Paying taxes
- Providing employment
- Value for money in using public funds

Lenders
- Financial strength of the company
- Quality of management
- Quality of assets available for security
- Ability to repay interest and capital

Figure 3.7

Examples of possible stakeholder expectations

Figure 3.7 indicates what stakeholders may expect. Bryson (2004) outlines an extensive range of techniques that managers can use to influence stakeholders. He refers to this as **stakeholder mapping**, which is intended to:

- identify stakeholders and their influence;
- clarify stakeholder views of the organisation;
- identify some key strategic issues; and
- begin to identify coalitions of support and opposition.

Stakeholder mapping is a means of identifying the views and influence of stakeholders, and the major issues that need to be managed.

An important step in influencing stakeholders is to assess their relative power and interest. Figure 3.8 shows a power–interest grid (Eden and Ackerman, 1998), which can be prepared to analyse the relative position of the stakeholders in an issue or project on two dimensions:

- their interest in the issue or activity being proposed; and
- their power to influence the outcomes of the issue or activity.

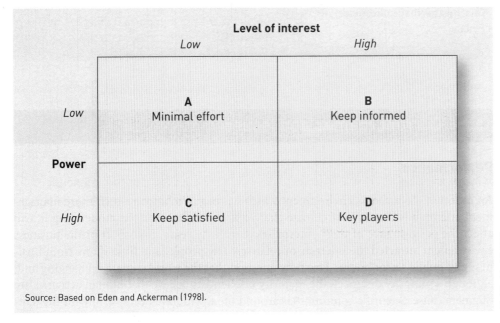

Source: Based on Eden and Ackerman (1998).

Figure 3.8

Stakeholder mapping – the power–interest matrix

Those with both a high level of interest in the issue and high power to influence the outcome are the key players whom the organisation must seek to satisfy. Conversely those with low interest and power may require only minimal attention to ensure their acquiescence in a proposal. Completing this grid helps to determine which stakeholders are the most important to keep on board when taking major decisions. It also implies that communication strategies, ranging from simple provision of information to direct involvement, are likely to differ for each group.

Nokia – the case continues www.nokia.com   CASE STUDY

The manufacture of components for mobile phones is being moved rapidly out of the Nordic country to low-cost locations. Early in 2006 three of Nokia's subcontractors announced that they were cutting more than 1100 jobs in Finland, underlining the dramatic shift in the global telecoms business, in which a rapidly growing share of revenue comes from cost-conscious emerging markets.

This is leading the Finns to reassess their high dependence on the industry. An economist at the Bank of Finland:

Nokia's profits, and the tax revenues they have generated for Finland, have exceeded our wildest dreams in the past 10 years. But it is disappointing that the production has not provided the highly paid, large-scale source of employment we hoped for.

A trade union official:

Nokia puts pressure on the subcontractors to lower prices and requires an increasingly swift response to fluctuations in market conditions. This means that subcontracting becomes unprofitable in Finland.

Nokia is building a new plant in Chennai, India, and many component suppliers are following it there. Arja Suominen, Nokia spokeswoman, speaking from Chennai:

Production has to go where the markets are, otherwise we could not remain competitive.

Source: From an article by Paivi Munter, *Financial Times*, 13 March 2006.

Case questions 3.5

- Who are the main stakeholders in Nokia?
- What are their interests in the success of the company?
- How can management ensure it maintains the support of the most important stakeholders?

3.8   Current themes and issues

Performance

An aspect of the business environment which has begun to attract much more management attention is that of how climate change, and policies aimed at moderating it, will affect the performance of their enterprises. For many years this aspect of the business environment attracted the interests of relatively few people, and little if any from business and public sector bodies. Few now question that the world climate is changing and, although a minority disagrees, the majority of scientists believe that human activities are the main cause. Scientific communities around the world have been warning of the dangers for some time – exemplified in the United Kingdom by the 2007 publication of The Stern Report (HM Treasury, 2007). A consensus is forming that human activity is raising the emission of carbon dioxide at such a rapid rate that it is causing the temperature of the earth's surface to rise, and that unless action is taken, that will become irreversible. Managers need to work out how to respond strategically.

Kolk and Pinske (2005) point out that companies have two strategic options in this area, though their response will depend on the type of the business they are in, and the regulatory regime within which they operate – there are still wide variations between nations within Europe in the policies adopted by government. They distinguish between what they term innovative and compensatory strategies. Innovative approaches attempt to improve the company's performance by developing new technologies or methods of working that reduce emissions – as Marks and Spencer's (see Chapter 8) and many other retailers are planning to do. A compensatory approach involves transferring emissions between companies, so that those whose business inherently produces high emissions can buy permits from other companies who produce lower emissions than they are permitted. How managers respond to this new aspect of the business environment will undoubtedly affect their performance, and work such as that by Kolk and Pinske (2005) helps them to consider the options systematically.

Responsibility

A common prescription is that responsible companies can enhance (or at least protect) performance by taking due account of a wider constituency of stakeholders than was traditionally the case. While the aim may be to *balance* the interests of stakeholders, there are different opinions as to what this means. Campbell (1997) argues that a company's survival ultimately depends on managers' ability to win the loyalty of all the active stakeholders, because they compete for capital, labour and customers.

Others, such as Argenti (1997), argue that some stakeholders are more equal than others. He points out that a retailer contemplating longer opening hours will '*not* attempt to balance the convenience of employees with that of customers', but will instead 'ask what effect each decision might have on profits. That is how all legitimate decisions are made in companies – they are, by definition, profit-making organisations' (p. 443).

Since profit is the objective criterion by which the capitalist company will act, shareholders are, in Argenti's view, the stakeholders whose interests should come first. While he recognises that performance would suffer if companies fail to engage everyone affected by their operations, he maintains that 'an organisation designed to serve more than one set of people will fail to satisfy any' (p. 445).

A variation on this discussion is whether companies should engage all stakeholders in dialogue to ensure that the company's values and actions are in accord with the expectations of society. Hall and Vredenburg (2005) quote a study which identified

> the business opportunities that lie in recognising and integrating the views of 'fringe' stakeholders, defined as those that are disconnected or invisible to the firm because they are remote, weak, poor or disinterested.

Survival depends on meeting stakeholder expectations, but the degree of priority given to each is unequal and changing.

Internationalisation

Models of national culture are highly generalised summaries of diverse populations. Their value is to give some clues about broad differences between the places in which those managing internationally will be working. They encourage people to be ready to adapt the way they work to local circumstances (see also Chen, 2004).

Others take a more robust view of cultural differences and try to eliminate their influence within the organisation. Steve Chang is the Taiwanese founder and chairman of Trend Micro (see page 118), an anti-virus software company operating in many countries: 'The curse is that national cultures are very different. We have to figure out how to convert everybody to one business culture – no matter where they're from' (*Business Week*, 22 September 2003).

However, the study by Laurent – see the next Key Ideas – testifies to the strength of national cultures over organisational ones.

key ideas　National culture or corporate culture?

Laurent (1983) surveyed successive groups of managers on executive development programmes at INSEAD (a leading European centre for management education and development) to assess the relative strength of national or corporate cultures.

The managers came from many nations and organisations. Their responses to a 56 item questionnaire showed that the most powerful determinant of their assumptions about the role of management was their nationality. It had three times more influence on their managerial assumptions than any other characteristics such as age, education, function or type of company.

Laurent concluded that deep-seated managerial assumptions are strongly shaped by national cultures and appear quite insensitive to the more transient culture of organisations.

Source: Laurent (1983).

Moore (2005) provides a valuable new perspective on this dilemma through her study of people working in a German bank with offices in Frankfurt and London. She finds that this leads to the emergence of complex transnational cultures which combine both local, global and corporate elements.

Summary

1　**Describe the main dimensions of organisational culture, using Quinn's or Handy's typologies**

● Quinn *et al.* (2003) – open systems, rational goal, internal process and human relations.

● Handy (1993) – power, role, task and person.

2　**Identify the main sets of forces exerting influence on organisations**

● They include the immediate competitive environment, the wider general (or macro) environment and the organisation's stakeholders.

3　**Use Porter's five forces model to analyse competitive environments**

● This identifies the degree of competitive rivalry, customers, competitors, suppliers and potential substitute goods and services.

4 Conduct a PESTEL analysis for an organisation with which you are familiar

- The PESTEL model of the wider external environment identifies political, economic, social, technological, environmental and legal forces.

5 Compare environments in terms of their complexity and rate of change

- Environments can be evaluated in terms of their rate of change (stable/dynamic) and complexity (low/high).

6 Give examples of stakeholders seeking to influence organisations and explain a model for assessing stakeholder power

- Managers can assess the relative power of stakeholders in terms of their interest in, and power to affect, an issue.

Review questions

1 Describe an educational or commercial organisation that you know in terms of the competing values model of cultures.

2 What is the significance of the idea of 'fragmented cultures' for those who wish to change a culture to support performance?

3 Identify the relative influence of Porter's five forces on an organisation of your choice and compare your results with a colleague's. What can you learn from that comparison?

4 How should managers decide which of the many factors easily identified in a PESTEL analysis they should attend to? If they have to be selective, what is the value of the PESTEL method?

5 Since people interpret the nature of environmental forces from unique perspectives, what meaning can people attach to statements about external pressures?

6 Illustrate the stakeholder idea with an example of your own, focusing on what affects the relative power of the stakeholders to influence an organisation's policy.

Concluding critical reflection

Think about the culture that seems to be dominant in your company, and how managers deal with the business environment and with their stakeholders. Alternatively take another company with which you are familiar, and find out what you can about their culture, and how they monitor and assess the external environment. Review the material in the chapter, and make notes on these questions:

- Which of the issues discussed in this chapter are most relevant to the way you and your colleagues manage? What **assumptions** appear to guide the culture, and the factors in the external environment that managers believe have most effect on the business? Do you all attach the same significance to them, or do views vary? Why is that? How do these views affect your tasks as managers, and indeed the nature of your organisation?

- What factors in the **context** appear to have shaped the prevailing view about which changes in the environment will most affect the business? Why do they think that? Do people have different interpretations?

▶

- Can you compare your business environment with that of colleagues on your course, especially those in similar industries? Does this show up any **alternative** ways of seeing the context, and of dealing with stakeholders?
- What are the **limitations** of the ideas on culture and stakeholders which the chapter has presented? For example, are the cultural types transferable across nations, or how may they need to be adapted to represent different ways of managing?

Further reading

Steinbock, D. (2001), *The Nokia Revolution*, American Management Association, New York.

> This is an authoritative account of the development of the company, and its interaction with the external environment.

Frooman, J. (1999), 'Stakeholder influence strategies', *Academy of Management Review*, vol. 24, no. 2, pp. 191–205.

Pajunen, K. (2006), 'Stakeholder influences on organizational survival', *Journal of Management Studies*, vol. 43, no. 6, pp. 1261–1288.

> These two articles provide a comprehensive theoretical background to case studies of stakeholder management.

Johns, G. (2006), 'The essential impact of context on organizational behavior', *Academy of Management Review*, vol. 31, no. 2, pp. 386–408.

> An overview of the many ways in which writers have expressed the idea of 'context', and how it affects organisational behavior and research. It proposes two ways of thinking about context, one grounded in journalistic practice and the other in classic social psychology.

Weblinks

These websites have appeared in the chapter:

> www.nokia.com
> www.michelin.com
> www.heineken.com
> www.walmart.com
> www.pepsico.com

Visit some of these, or any other companies that interest you, and navigate to the pages dealing with recent news, press or investor relations.

- What can you find out about their culture?
- What are the main forces in the external environment that the organisation appears to be facing?
- What assessment would you make of the nature of that environment?
- Compare and contrast the issues you identify on the two sites.
- What challenges may they imply for those working in, and managing, these organisations?

Annotated weblinks, multiple choice questions and other useful resources can be found on **www.pearsoned.co.uk/boddy**

Chapter 4
Managing internationally

To outline the factors shaping the work of managing internationally.

By the end of your work on this chapter you should be able to outline the concepts below in your own terms and:

1 Summarise the forces stimulating the growth of international business
2 Contrast the ways in which organisations conduct international business
3 Conduct a PESTEL analysis to show countries' contrasting business environments
4 Explain the significance of national cultures, and evaluate the significance of Hofstede's research for managers working internationally
5 Compare and contrast the features of national management systems
6 Compare the benefits and costs of globalisation to different players.

This chapter introduces the following ideas:

international management	arbitrariness (of corruption)
franchising	low-context culture
joint venture	high-context culture
multinational company	power distance
transnational company	uncertainty avoidance
global company	individualism
ideology	collectivism
democracy	masculinity
totalitarianism	femininity
pervasiveness (of corruption)	globalisation

Each is a term defined within the text, as well as
in the Glossary at the end of the book.

Starbucks sells coffee, pastries, confectionery and coffee-related accessories through over 14,000 retail stores. Three entrepreneurs created the company in 1971 to sell coffee in Seattle, and by 1981 they had five stores. The owners decided to sell the business in 1987 and Howard Schultz (a former employee) bought the company which he then expanded rapidly, so that by 1991 there were 114 Starbucks stores. The company was also innovative with new products to attract customers – such as introducing low-fat iced coffee for the diet conscious. It grew by about 20 per cent a year during the 1990s, but some believed that the market in the United States would become saturated.

To maintain rapid growth the company began to expand overseas, through Starbucks Coffee International, a wholly owned subsidary. In 1996 Starbucks entered Japan through a joint venture with Sazaby's Inc. (a leading Japanese teashop company) and it then expanded into south-east Asia, Europe and the Middle East. By 2007 it had 4000 stores (29 per cent of the total) outside the United States.

It entered the Asia Pacific rim first, as the growing eagerness of young people in those countries to imitate western lifestyles made them attractive markets for Starbucks. The company used joint ventures, licensing or wholly owned subsidiaries to enter new markets. Initially it opened a few stores in trendy parts of the area, with the company's managers from Seattle handling the operation. Local *baristas* (brew masters) were trained in Seattle for 13 weeks, to ensure consistent standards across the world. Similar products were stocked, and all stores were 'No Smoking'.

However, the company's managers also took the advice of their partners and adapted the business to local tastes – such as offering curry puffs and meat buns in Asia, where people prefer to eat something while having coffee. In the Middle East the coffee shops had segregated sections for ladies. In 1998 the company opened in Europe, with stores in the United Kingdom, Switzerland, Germany and Greece. By 2007 it had stores in 36 countries, and was planning to enter Egypt and Brazil. The company believed that it was successful not because it was selling coffee, but because it was selling an experience. In many markets it faces local competi-

tion and is subject to the same economic conditions as other businesses of its type.

It has attracted criticism in some overseas markets – in common with many US businesses. In Starbucks' case this also focused on the sources of its coffee. Growers in poor countries complained that they received very low prices for their crops, and that many workers in the coffee plantations were exploited. Advocates of fair trade argued that big coffee buyers such as Starbucks should do more to ensure that they buy coffee at fair prices from growers who do not exploit workers.

Source: Based on published sources.

Case questions 4.1

- What encouraged managers at Starbucks to expand overseas, and what influenced their choice of countries in which to operate?
- What are the main risks that Starbucks faces in expanding rapidly in overseas markets?
- What does the case so far suggest about the management issues it will face in operating internationally?

4.1 Introduction

Managers at Starbucks decided to expand their business overseas, and in doing so are likely to face common problems in moving to a global operation. Having expanded rapidly in their home market, they believe that the best way to maintain that rate of growth is by building the business in other countries. The challenge is that having been successful in their home market, moving to a global operation will bring new and unfamiliar problems. They face choices about their strategy for building a global business, and the organisation they will create to implement that strategy.

Others face the same issues. Major retailers such as Tesco and Carrefour are extending their international operations, despite the problems of understanding different customer tastes and shopping habits. Managers in companies such as Marlboro and H&M with large overseas sales balance the consistency of the global brand with what local customers expect.

Manufacturers such as Ford and service providers like Lloyds TSB Bank have transferred many types of work to low-wage countries such as China and India. That raises new management problems – such as, for Ford, how best to manage a joint venture with the Chong Qing Group in China to manufacture a compact family car. When Tata, the Indian-based multinational group bought the European steel company Corus in 2007 it created the world's largest steel company: it will restructure its operations to ensure that the acquisition adds value. Managers investing overseas consider not only the economic or market aspects, but also whether the legal system will protect their investments and whether the country is politically stable: despite such careful preparation many overseas ventures fail, and so destroy value.

Rapid economic development in China, India and other Asian countries is transforming them into major players in world trade, competing with established companies. For products that are high in value and low in weight the world is one potential market – increasing the possibility of both growth and competition. Even managers in a company that does not trade overseas add an international dimension to their work if they acquire an overseas business, or are themselves acquired.

International management is the practice of managing business operations in more than one country.

From a career point of view, **international management** (managing business operations in more than one country) can mean:

- Working as an *expatriate manager* in another country.
- Joining or managing an *international team* with members from several countries.
- Managing in a *global organisation* whose employees, systems and structures are truly international in that they no longer reflect its original, national base. ABB is an example of this: formed by the merger of a Swiss and a Swedish business, it retains only a small head office in Zurich, and the board deliberately contains people of different nationalities.

This chapter introduces some models that illuminate the task of managing internationally. It begins by outlining the forces driving the growth of international business, and the different ways in which companies take part in it. Later sections outline the context of international business and differences in national cultures. It then distinguishes between national (or regional) management systems, and compares those of the United States, Europe and Asia. It outlines the arguments surrounding globalisation, and considers the winners and losers from that process and concludes by noting some current and emerging themes. Figure 4.1 indicates the main issues of the chapter.

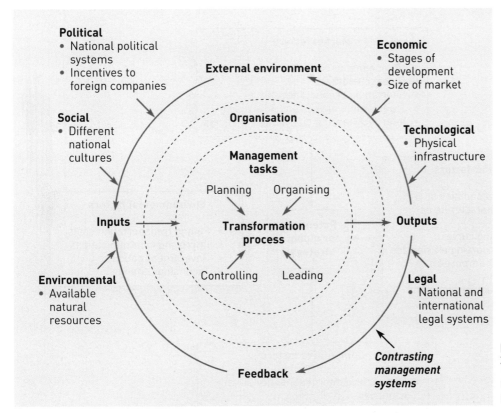

Figure 4.1

Themes in managing internationally

The growth of international business

Driving forces

There has been international trade since the earliest times. The merchants who created the East India Company in London in 1599 to develop trade with the spice islands in south-east Asia (in close and violent competition with the Dutch East India Company, founded in 1602), were putting an established practice on a more formal basis. By the nineteenth century many trading businesses were operating across the world. What is new is the much greater proportion of production that crosses national boundaries, much of it organised by businesses operating not on a national but on a regional or global scale. One estimate is that one-third of all trade takes place within transnational companies, quite apart from external sales of foreign subsidiaries.

In some areas of business global operations are inherent in the task. Transport companies such as Federal Express and Frans Maas work across the globe and develop practices and structures accordingly. Oil companies such as BP and mining companies such as Antofagasta necessarily secure resources in some parts of the world and sell them in others. A newer development is the way businesses trading in a country or region have ambitions to operate on a global scale.

Yip *et al.* (1988) developed a model (Figure 4.2) of the factors that drive globalisation in particular industries – managers (like those at Starbucks) can use such a model to analyse the global potential of a business. Market factors were probably the most significant in Starbucks' case – such as the transferability of brands and advertising, and the ability to develop international distribution channels. While customers around the globe drink coffee, they are not homogeneous, so Starbucks adapts the product to meet local

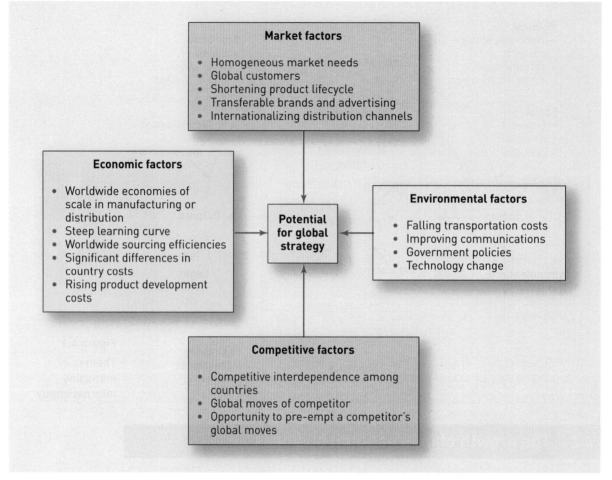

Figure 4.2 Factors driving globalisation in an industry
Source: Yip *et al.* (1988).

tastes. In other industries economic or environmental factors may be more prominent drivers: in motor manufacture the economic factors for globalisation are strong – especially the economies of scale in manufacturing, and the ability to buy components around the world. Environmental factors also encourage this, such as government incentives that persuade companies to relocate manufacturing facilities. Many well-educated people in India speak fluent English and are willing to work for lower pay than people in the United Kingdom or United States: this encourages overseas companies to move there. Developments in information and communication technologies drive globalisation in many industries, by enabling the efficient flow of data on which international operations depend.

Another way to use the Yip model is to distinguish between push and pull factors (Tayeb, 2000). Push factors include saturation and excessive competition in the home market. Starbucks and IKEA are examples of companies whose managers want to grow the business, but believe they can do so only by expanding beyond their traditional markets. Pull factors include lower wages and less rigorous environmental regulations (which attract western companies to move production to China or eastern Europe). Other firms gain competitive advantage by extending their brand to a global scale – consultants such as KPMG or PwC believe they can meet the needs of global clients better if they themselves work as global businesses.

Genpact targets media jobs in the United States and Europe
www.genpact.com

In 2006 Genpact, the largest provider of offshore outsourcing services in India, announced it would offer US and European media companies the opportunity to transfer costly technical, editing and production functions to India. The company has a 50–50 joint venture with New Delhi Television, a leading broadcaster, to market their services to studios and TV networks – at first directed at lowering the costs of digitising their libraries of old programmes – creating graphics and subtitles, editing raw footage and archiving programmes. Hollywood's animated film industry has also shifted significant business to India, benefiting from their animators and visual effects specialists.

Source: Information provided by the company.

4.3 Ways of conducting business internationally

Managers who decide to extend the international operations of their company have several ways of doing so.

Exporting and importing

The longest established way of dealing with overseas customers and suppliers is by transporting physical products (raw materials or finished goods) or delivering services (a retail shop, consultancy or legal advice) across national boundaries. If the final distribution of exports is arranged through a dealer or agent in the receiving country, then the implications for people in the exporting company are limited, apart from those directly involved in managing the transactions.

Foreign direct investment

This is when a firm builds manufacturing or other facilities in a foreign country, and manages them directly. Many motor companies expand in this way – Nissan manufactures at several sites in the United Kingdom, while General Motors is building a plant in India that will start production in 2008 to manufacture the Chevrolet Spark. The Indian car market is growing at about 25 per cent a year and all the major producers wish to share in that growth. If the venture is a wholly owned subsidiary then profits stay within the company. It retains control over expertise, technology and marketing, and can secure local knowledge by employing local staff. In these examples the companies have built and managed the facilities themselves – in others, such as Tata's purchase of Corus, managers achieve the same results by buying the assets of an existing business.

Licensing

Here a business grants the right to (licenses) a firm in another country (the licensee) to produce and sell its products for a specified period – such as the deal between Imperial Tobacco and a Chinese group to produce and distribute Imperial brands in the world's largest cigarette market. The licensing firm receives a royalty payment for each unit sold, while the licensee takes the risk of investing in manufacturing and distribution facilities. **Franchising** is similar, commonly used by firms providing services that wish to expand rapidly beyond their country of origin. With tight conditions the firm wishing to expand allows a company in the target market to use its brand name or designs to build a business in that market: many fast-food outlets are franchises.

Franchising is the practice of extending a business by giving other organisations, in return for a fee, the right to use your brand name, technology or product specifications.

117

Joint ventures and strategic alliances

A **joint venture** is an alliance in which the partners agree to form a separate, independent organisation for a specific business purpose.

These enable firms in two or more countries to share the risks and resources required to do business internationally. Most **joint ventures** involve a foreign firm linking with one in the host country to take advantage of its distribution arrangements and knowledge of local customs, politics and ways of working. Both firms agree their respective investment in the venture and how they will share the profits. Starbucks typically uses joint ventures in overseas markets: in Germany this is with KarstadtQuelle, a department store group. In 2007 Royal Dutch Shell announced a joint venture with a unit of the Shenhua Group, China's largest coal company, to study the possibility of creating a coal-to-liquids facility in western China. The hazards of joint ventures include cultural differences between the partners and misunderstanding what each expects.

---

management in practice   A Chinese company aims to become a global player   www.tcl.com

TCL Corporation is one of the top producers of electronics products in China, and having become one of the most prominent brands at home, the company's entrepreneurial management wants to make the company a global player. In November 2003 they formed a joint venture with French electronics maker Thomson to create the world's largest producer of televisions. For TCL Thomson's brand names – which include RCA and Thomson – were key to the deal. TCL also wants to use Thomson's distribution system to extend its reach.

Source: Based on 'Bursting out of China', *Business Week*, 17 November 2003.

Managers develop different forms of organisation through which to conduct their international business – multinational, transnational and global.

Multinational companies are managed from one country, but have significant production and marketing operations in many others.

Multinational companies are from one country, but have significant production and marketing operations in many others – perhaps accounting for more than one-third of sales. Despite their overseas interests, managers in the home country make the major decisions.

Transnational companies operate in many countries and delegate many decisions to local managers.

Transnational companies also operate in many countries, but decentralise many decisions to local managers. They use local knowledge to build the business while still projecting a consistent company image.

Global companies work in many countries, securing resources and finding markets in whichever country is most suitable.

Global companies work in many countries, securing resources and finding markets in whichever are most suitable. Production or service processes are performed, and integrated, across many global locations. Most significant, ownership, control and top managers are spread amongst many countries and nationalities. Trend Micro, an anti-virus software company, needed to organise in a way that allows its staff to respond rapidly to new viruses that appear anywhere and spread very quickly. Trend's financial headquarters is in Tokyo; product development is in Taiwan (many staff have a PhD); and sales is in California – inside the huge US market. Nestlé is another example since, although its headquarters is in Switzerland, 98 per cent of sales and 96 per cent of employees are not. Manpower, the employment services group, is based in the United States, but generates 85 per cent of its revenues overseas. Such global businesses are often organised on product lines, with those in charge of each line being free to resource their operations from whichever country is most profitable. They typify the globalisation of business – see Section 4.12.

An Indian supplier to Wal-Mart www.walmart.com

Deep in the Punjab heartland, in the town of Barnala, Rajinder Gupta is a star supplier to the world's biggest company – Wal-Mart. Gupta's Abhishek Industries exports Rs 200 crore (2 billion rupees') worth of towels annually and he has twice been judged the Wal-Mart International Supplier of the year. Now he's expanding his product range to rugs and bed-sheets and says: 'We've grown with Wal-Mart since we first began supplying to them five years ago. Now we've created a dedicated capacity for them, with systems geared to their needs.'

From tanneries in Kanpur and rug weavers in Mumbai to shirt manufacturers in Tirupur, Wal-Mart has zeroed in on 142 low-cost quality manufacturing units across India, which will supply to its stores in the United States and 12 other countries. It recently set up Wal-Mart Global Procurement Company in Bangalore where a staff of 54 are working towards further expanding business with India. A company official said: 'Indian suppliers are capable, qualified and quality focused and we intend to grow India as a source of supply, especially in categories like textiles, shoes, jewellery and gift items.'

Source: Based on 'Wal-Mart Effect', *Times of India Corporate Dossier*, 28 May 2004.

Activity 4.1 Choosing between approaches

Consider the different ways of expanding a business internationally.

- For each of the methods outlined above note the advantages and disadvantages.
- Identify a company with international operations, and gather evidence to help you decide which method it has used, and why.
- Compare your research with colleagues on your course, and prepare a short presentation summarising your conclusions.

Case questions 4.2

- Which of Yip's global drivers do you think will have shaped Starbucks' global moves?
- Would you classify Starbucks as a multinational, transnational or global firm?

By whatever method, there has been a steady growth in the volume of business transactions across national borders. These become less significant barriers to the movement of goods and services – especially the growing trade in electronically transmitted information products. These trends mean a steady growth in the proportion of people who work with colleagues from countries, organisations, institutions and cultures widely different from their own. To handle this well means more than learning foreign languages, though that clearly helps. It means being aware of the international aspects of the general business environment outlined in Chapter 3: the PESTEL framework takes on an international flavour, as shown in Figure 4.3.

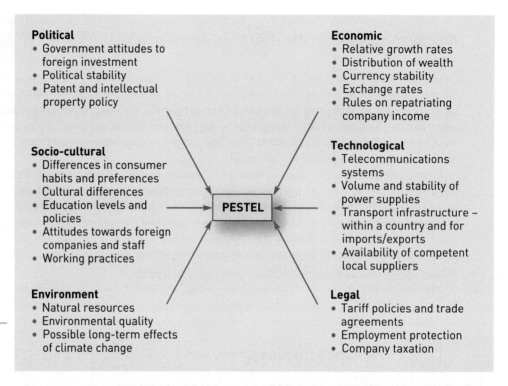

Political
- Government attitudes to foreign investment
- Political stability
- Patent and intellectual property policy

Economic
- Relative growth rates
- Distribution of wealth
- Currency stability
- Exchange rates
- Rules on repatriating company income

Socio-cultural
- Differences in consumer habits and preferences
- Cultural differences
- Education levels and policies
- Attitudes towards foreign companies and staff
- Working practices

Technological
- Telecommunications systems
- Volume and stability of power supplies
- Transport infrastructure – within a country and for imports/exports
- Availability of competent local suppliers

Environment
- Natural resources
- Environmental quality
- Possible long-term effects of climate change

Legal
- Tariff policies and trade agreements
- Employment protection
- Company taxation

Figure 4.3

An international view of a PESTEL analysis

4.4 Political context

The political system in a country has a major influence on business, and managers adapt their policies in the light of the prevailing **ideology**.

An **ideology** is a set of integrated beliefs, theories and doctrines that helps to direct the actions of a society.

Political ideologies are closely linked to economic philosophies and attitudes towards business. In the United States the political ideology is grounded in a constitution that guarantees the rights of people to own property and to have wide freedom of choice. This helped to lay the foundations of a capitalist economy favourable to business. While some countries in western Europe are equally capitalist in outlook others – such as France and Germany – have political ideologies that give more emphasis to social, rather than business, considerations in framing policy.

Democracy is a system of government in which the people, either directly or through elected officials, decide what is to be done.

Totalitarianism is a system of government in which one individual or political party maintains complete control and either refuses to recognise other parties or suppresses them.

Democracy and **totalitarianism** represent contrasting political systems. Democracy is a system of government in which the people, either directly or through elected representatives, decide what is to be done: examples include the United Kingdom, India or The Netherlands. Typical features include: the right to express opinions freely; the election of representatives for a limited period; an independent court system that protects individual and corporate property and rights; and a relatively non-political bureaucracy that ensures the continued operation of the system. Totalitarianism is a system in which one individual or political party retains control and either refuses to recognise other parties or suppresses them. Variants include: communism (Cuba or North Korea) in which the government owns most property, and makes most decisions about the production and distribution of goods and services: and theocracy (Iran or Saudi Arabia) in which a very powerful religious group represses or persecutes those of other faiths.

There are close links between political and economic systems – especially in how they allocate resources and deal with property ownership. In a market-driven economy goods and services are provided in response to demand and supply: as consumers begin to express a preference for Starbucks coffee, Starbucks (or local competitors) will try to meet that demand profitably. In a centrally controlled economy resources are allocated by politicians or public officials: people can only buy what the state decides should be produced or imported. In market economies the productive assets tend to be in private ownership, while in centrally controlled economies the state usually owns them.

These differences in political systems affect business life through:

- the balance between state-owned and privately owned enterprises;
- the amount of state intervention to encourage some kinds of business by subsidies and favourable regulation, or to discourage it by taxes and regulation;
- policies towards foreign companies trading in the country, with or without local partners;
- policies towards foreign companies acquiring local firms;
- policies on employment practices, working conditions and job protection.

The Italian private/public model

Managerial capitalism is taking root in Italy – but the country's tradition of public companies controlled by powerful founding families is not yet ready to bow out. It is almost impossible to exaggerate the importance for the Italian economy of a model widely known as the 'Italian private/public company' – a group of large, publicly quoted companies managed and controlled by founding families.

Italian corporate dynasties have traditionally controlled their industrial and financial groups via a complex structure involving a cascade of holding companies, often quoted, with minimum capital outlay. They further strengthened their hold on their groups through friendly shareholder syndicates and cross-shareholdings based on the principle of 'don't hurt me and I won't hurt you' ...

The tenacity of the family business culture in Italy is such that even Silvio Berlusconi, the prime minister, was unable to resolve a conflict of interest between his extensive business empire ... and his political office.

FT

Source: Extracts from an article by Paul Betts, *Financial Times*, 24 March 2003.

Governments of all forms set the rules that establish what commercial activity takes place within their jurisdiction, and how it can be conducted – whether in a fundamentally capitalist way, in a centrally controlled way, or a mix of the two. All states are affected to some degree by the presence of corruption – when politicians or officials abuse public power for private benefit. Coping with this is part of the job of managers operating internationally, but as Rodriguez *et al.* (2005) point out, 'while corruption is everywhere ... it is not the same everywhere (p. 383).

They introduce a two dimensional framework to help understand the different forms of corruption, and its implications for business – based on its **pervasiveness** and **arbitrariness**. Pervasiveness is the extent to which a firm is likely to encounter corruption in the course of normal transactions with state officials. It indicates the extent to which it is a regular aspect of business behaviour in a given country and the extent to which a firm will need to deal with corrupt behaviour. Arbitrariness is the degree of ambiguity associated with corrupt transactions in a given nation or state. When corruption is arbitrary, laws and rules are applied capriciously and haphazardly – perhaps being strictly enforced in some areas of the country or by some officials, and ignored by others. Figure 4.4 illustrates this.

Pervasiveness (of corruption) represents the extent to which a firm is likely to encounter corruption in the course of normal transactions with state officials.

Arbitrariness (of corruption) is the degree of ambiguity associated with corrupt transactions.

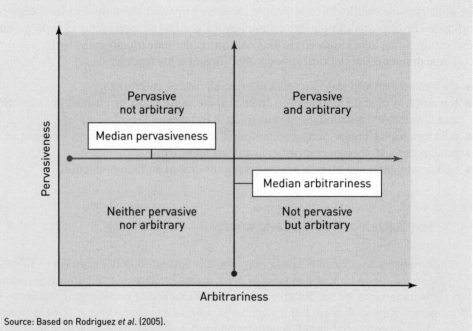

Figure 4.4

Two dimensions of corruption: pervasiveness and arbitrariness

Source: Based on Rodriguez *et al*. (2005).

4.5 Economic context

The economic context of a country includes its stage of economic development, its system of markets, and the current economic situation such as inflation, exchange rates or levels of debt.

Stage of economic development

The measure of economic development usually used is income per head of population – a measure of a country's total production, adjusted for size of population. Lower-income countries are concentrated in the southern hemisphere and include many in Asia, Africa and South America. The richer, developed countries tend to be in the northern hemisphere, where most international firms are located.

---

key ideas The complex forces behind China's transition to capitalism

Doug Guthrie (2006) presents a valuable insight into one of the major business developments in recent years – the transition of China from a state-run towards a market-based system. A distinctive feature of his analysis is the emphasis he places on the links between political, social, cultural and economic forces:

Economic institutions and practices are deeply embedded in political, cultural and social systems, and it is impossible to analyze the economy without analyzing the way it is shaped by politics, culture and the social world. The perspective is essential for understanding the complex processes of economic and social reform in any transforming society, but it is especially critical for understanding China's reform path and trajectory. This position may seem obvious to some, but ... for years, economists from the World Bank, the IMF, and various reaches of academia have operated from a different set of assumptions: they have assumed that a transition to markets is a simple and, basically, apolitical process ... In other words, 'don't worry about the complexities of culture or pre-existing social or political systems; if you put the right capitalist institutions in place (i.e. private property), transition to a market economy will be a simple process'. *The perspective I present here is that the standard economic view of market transitions that defined a good deal of policy for the IMF and the World Bank in the late twentieth century could not be more simplistic or more wrong.* (emphasis added)

Source: Guthrie (2006), pp. 10–11.

Companies from wealthier countries see opportunities in less developed areas – especially their large potential markets. Consumer products companies (especially those in the tobacco business such as British American Tobacco or Phillip Morris) are reaching the limits of their markets in developed countries, but see good prospects in the developing world, whose high birth rates ensure a growing number of young consumers. Companies with strong brands are attracted to large and growing markets in the more prosperous of these countries, such as Malaysia and South Africa. Others see them as sources of cheap labour from which to obtain supplies.

Starbucks – the case continues www.starbucks.com   CASE STUDY

In 2007 the company's presence within Beijing's Forbidden City was threatened, amid complaints that the presence of the chain in the former imperial palace constituted an 'affront to Chinese culture'. China's official media said that the low-key Starbucks outlet near the rear of the sprawling Palace Museum site might be removed following online protests sparked by patriotic views published by a TV anchorman on his personal blog. The controversy surrounding Starbucks' presence in the Forbidden City highlights the risks to foreign companies of offending Chinese nationalist sentiment.

It was unclear why the company was drawing so much attention, as it had lowered its profile and the outlet has no external signage at all. Starbucks said it appreciated the deep history and culture of the Forbidden City and has operated in a respectful manner

that fits within the environment. A Museum spokesperson was quoted as saying that it was working with Starbucks to find a solution in response to the protests.

Starbucks was also experiencing problems elsewhere, with rivals often charging less for similar products. Some also queried the method it used for its overseas expansion, mainly joint ventures. While the company gets a revenue from sales and profits, and also gets a licence income from the sale of its coffee, it is harder to control costs in a joint venture. Moreover, the costs for premises and labour are higher overseas than in the United States. Others questioned the rate of expansion – 'By opening more stores, name recognition will increase but scarcity value, which is crucial in maintaining brand image, will decline'.

Source: *Financial Times*, 19 January 2007; and other sources.

Markets

Managers contemplating international expansion are likely to focus on countries and regions where the market for their service appears strong. Thus Hong Kong Disneyland reflected the company's belief that Asia is a market with high growth potential in media and entertainment. The Chinese government took a 57 per cent stake in the project, which Disney hoped would help it win favourable terms for other business ventures in China – such as TV, motion pictures, advertising and consumer products (from an article by Tim Burt, *Financial Times*, 30 October 2003).

Egg (a UK online bank now owned by Citigroup) discovered the risks of entering an unfamiliar market when it opened an operation in France. The bank hoped to repeat its initial UK success when it bought a French online business in 2002. However, as one analyst observed:

> the market is not yet ready to embrace the concept of a pure online bank. There is a clear attachment to the branch network in France, which is not such a factor in the UK, and means people are not ready to commit their entire banking relationship to a company without a network of branches they can go and visit.

Egg's credit cards were not a success either, as that market was not as fully developed in France as in the United Kingdom. Egg withdrew from the French market in 2004.

4.6   Technological context

Infrastructure includes all of the physical facilities that support economic activities – ports, airports, surface transport and, increasingly, telecommunications facilities. Companies operating abroad, especially in less developed countries, are closely interested in the quality of this aspect of a country as it has a huge effect on the cost and convenience of conducting business in the area.

management in practice   Power shortages in China

During 2004 many parts of China experienced severe shortages of power, and many factories had to close for two days a week as electricity was interrupted. Retailers in the rest of the world who now depend on imports from China found that their supplies were being delayed: one said that 'the cost advantage in China is still so great that we'll continue doing business here, but ultimately if they can't deliver in a timely fashion we'll start looking'.

Demand for power had increased by almost 70 per cent in four years, and other infrastructure problems had contributed to the power shortages – such as an overloaded railway system that could not deliver enough coal to power stations. While plans were in place to increase supplies by 2007, in the meantime the power crisis was damaging company performance.

Source: *Business Week*, 5 July 2004.

A poor infrastructure is an opportunity for those supplying such facilities. European water companies have contracts to apply their expertise to providing water and sanitation services to many developing countries.

4.7   Environmental context

The natural environment is a further aspect of the business context. One aspect of this is the natural resources available in an economy – including oil, coal and other minerals, agricultural land and the prevailing climate. A key distinction in considering natural resources is between those that are renewable and those that are not: land can be used for several purposes in succession, timber is renewable – but oil is not.

These considerations have fundamental impacts on the kind of businesses that people create in different countries, and on the pattern of world trade. Technological developments enable the discovery of previously unknown resources (new oil reserves are being discovered in central Asia) and the fuller use of some that were previously uneconomic. This benefits the countries concerned, and the companies that agree to exploit the resources.

The process is also controversial, as when foreign mining or oil companies come into conflict with local populations whose land they occupy, or over the commercial terms of the concessions. Many also express concern at the environmental degradation that timber or mineral exploitation causes, whose negative effects are felt over much wider areas (such as when rivers are polluted in one country before they flow into another). Economic development itself causes pollution, which is both a problem for people in the area and a business opportunity for foreign businesses that specialise in environmental control and remediation.

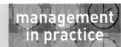

Insurgency that may threaten business growth

management in practice

Just as India is emerging as an economic powerhouse on the world stage, landless revolutionaries committed to the class struggle and the destruction of the state are gaining control of large areas of the country. Maoist groups are estimated by the government to be running parallel administrations, including legal systems, in one-quarter of India's 600 districts, and are imposing high costs on the country's ability to attract investment in mineral-rich states such as Orissa and Jharkand. Motivated by resentment at generations of social injustice and the inequitable distribution of the country's new wealth, the Maoists are identified by Manmohan Singh, India's prime minister, as the single greatest threat to India's security.

Source: From an article by Jo Johnson, *Financial Times*, 26 April 2006, p. 13.

4.8 Legal context – trade agreements and trading blocs

Each jurisdiction has its own regulations affecting business practice, which they expect companies operating in the country to meet. Ensuring that the company complies with this often implies working with a local partner, able to negotiate in the local context.

Companies also query the legal system of a country in which they plan to work, and whether it will give sufficient protection in the event of legal disputes arising. The most significant developments in the political–legal environment are those associated with international trade agreements and regional economic alliances.

GATT and the World Trade Organisation

The General Agreement on Tariffs and Trade (GATT) reduces the propensity of national governments to put tariffs on physical goods to protect domestic companies. Its main tool is tariff concessions, whereby member countries agree to limit the level of tariffs they impose on imports from other GATT members (now more than 100 countries). GATT has also sponsored a series of international trade negotiations aimed at reducing restrictions on trade. The most recent of these was the Uruguay Round, which involved 125 countries and led to the establishment of the World Trade Organisation (WTO).

The World Trade Organisation is a permanent global institution that monitors international trade and arbitrates in disputes between countries over the interpretation of tariffs and other barriers to trade. It is also seeking a world agreement on rules governing foreign investment – both to encourage it and, where thought necessary, to control it.

European Union

The EU is credited with being the model for many other regional trade groupings (Dent, 1997; Mercado *et al.*, 2001). Since the Treaty of Rome was signed in 1959 the aim has been to eliminate tariffs and other restrictions that national governments use to protect domestic industries. This was broadly achieved by 1968, and led to further efforts to bring about closer economic integration between the member states. This culminated in the Single European Act of 1986, which aimed to create a single internal market amongst the member states. Introducing the euro as a common currency for many of the member states encouraged further changes in the European economy by unifying capital markets and making price comparisons more transparent.

The European Commission (responsible for proposing and implementing policy) is encouraging this liberalisation by proposing changes in national laws to make cross-border trade easier. One project will make it easier for investment businesses to sell their products across Europe – most at present operate only in their home country. This and similar deals have encouraged a rapid growth in trade within the region. Car companies such as Ford and DaimlerChrysler have plants in several countries, specialising in particular components or models. They simultaneously import and export these between the countries as part of a region-wide production system.

Enlargement has long been a feature of the EU agenda – Nugent (2004) points out that since the community was founded in the 1950s there has nearly always been an application from at least one potential new member under consideration. The greatest single enlargement occurred in 2004 when ten new members (many from eastern Europe) joined the existing 15. Bulgaria and Romania joined in 2007 and discussions continue about the accession of Croatia and Turkey (Pinder, 2001).

Earlier enlargements were relatively uncontroversial. When Austria, Finland and Sweden joined in 1995 they did not threaten the economic success of the EU: they were liberal democratic states with functioning market economies and above-average incomes. They would be net contributors to the EU budget, and would strengthen the organisation in other ways.

Many observers saw the 2004 enlargement as more problematical. One reason lay in doubts about how quickly the central and east European countries would become effective and efficient EU members. Having emerged fairly recently from the totalitarian Soviet empire with a state-run economy, they lacked an efficient market economy. There was also a fear that enlargement on such a scale would undermine the effectiveness of the EU itself – disproportionately raising costs and slowing down decisions. Compared to the EU-15, the EU-25 has more people (450 million instead of 375 million); wider social and economic disparities; new borders with even poorer countries to the east; and is more diverse politically and ethnically.

At the same time as enlarging the membership the EU is also deepening integration through the development of the internal market, to enable the freer movement of goods and services amongst the member states. The intention is to gradually extend the range of issues affecting business and competitiveness that are covered by common European policies, with the intention of improving the efficiency of business within the EU. Areas covered by this include:

Business opportunities in eastern Europe

Austria's banks are among the market leaders in eastern Europe, having spotted the market potential early. In 2006 the chief executive of the recently privatised post office foresaw huge potential for growing his business as the state-owned post offices in the accession states are sold to private investors and the postal markets are opened to new services:

> The privatisation process hasn't started, [but] I think it will. It will probably be different in each case. It's a highly political issue, but it will open the door for us.

Source: *Financial Times*, 19 April 2006.

FT

- harmonising technical regulations between member states;
- common industrial policy (such as subsidies for local businesses and/or foreign investment);
- liberalising services (such as postal services) across the Union;
- harmonising employment rights and rules on environmental protection;
- facilitating cross-border mergers; and
- recognising professional qualifications (e.g. in medicine and dentistry) between member states to enable freer movement of labour.

Activity 4.2   Access the European Union website   http://ec.europa.eu/

Having accessed the website, go to the page for the internal market and then to the section in which the Commission outlines the benefits it claims have come from the single internal market.

- Which of the benefits it claims for business may have been relevant to Starbucks'?
- Which of the benefits it claims for citizens/consumers have you experienced?
- Which areas of policy remain to be dealt with on the road towards a single market?

4.9   Socio-cultural context

Culture is distinct from human nature (features that all human beings have in common) and from an individual's personality (their unique way of thinking, feeling and acting). It is a collective phenomenon, shared with people in the common social environment in which it was learned. Hofstede and Hofstede (2005) describe it as the unwritten rules of the social game:

> the collective programming of the mind which distinguishes one group or category of people from others (in which 'group' means a number of people in contact with each other, and a 'category' means people who have something in common, such as people born before 1940). (p. 4 and p. 377)

While humans share common biological features those in a particular society, nation or region develop a distinct culture. As a business becomes more international, its managers balance a similar approach to business across the world with the unique cultures of the places in which they operate.

Cultural diversity and evolution

Hofstede and Hofstede (2005) note the wide diversity of cultures between human societies, even though people have evolved from common ancestors. There are recognisable differences between people in geographically separate areas in how they communicate with each other, how they respond to authority, when they go to work – and in countless other aspects of social life. Societies develop these practices as they adapt to their natural environment, experience military or religious conquest, or exploit scientific discoveries in agriculture and industry. These societal developments are usually overlaid by the relatively recent creation of nations:

> strictly speaking, the concept of a common culture applies to societies, not to nations ... yet rightly or wrongly, properties are ascribed to the citizens of certain countries: people refer to 'typically American,' 'typically German,' 'typically Japanese' behaviour. Using nationality is a matter of expediency. (pp. 18–19)

Nations develop distinct institutions – governments, laws, business systems and so on. Some argue that these in themselves account for differences in behaviour between countries, implying that institutions (such as a legal or banking system) that work in one country will do so elsewhere. A counter view is that institutions reflect the culture in which they developed: something that works well in one country may fail in another: 'Institutions cannot be understood without considering culture, and understanding culture presumes insight into institutions' (p. 20).

Managers and those who work for them are part of a nation, and to understand and work with them we need to understand their respective cultures – what types of personality are common, how they see work in relation to family life, their dominant values, what they regard as important.

 **Cultural variety in the European Commission**

Marcello Burattini was head of protocol for the European Commission. On the 40th anniversary of the Treaty of Rome he recalled the early days of the Commission:

> At the beginning of the 1960s the rules, based on the principles of Franco-Prussian administration, were strict, formal modes of address, and ties were *de rigueur* ... Then certain political leaders decided to enlarge [the Community]. Thus the British and the Irish arrived, bringing with them the English language, humour, simplicity in human relations, many original ideas – for example, pragmatism – somewhat softening the rigorous orthodoxy. The Danes taught us to be less formal, and were astonished by our way of doing things – and by the fact that secretaries made coffee for their bosses.

Source: *The European*, 27 March 1997.

Activity 4.3   Comparing cultures

Form a group amongst your student colleagues made up of people from different countries.

- Identify the main characteristics of the respective cultures in your group.
- Gather any evidence about how members think they affect the work of managing.
- Compare your evidence on cultural differences with that from Hofstede's research (see below).

Tayeb (1996) distinguishes between high- and low-context cultures.

High-context and low-context cultures

A **high-context culture** is one in which information is implicit, and can only be fully understood in conjunction with shared experience, assumptions and various forms of verbal codes. High-context cultures occur when people live closely with each other, where deep mutual understandings develop, that then provide a rich context within which communication takes place. In a **low-context culture** information is explicit and clear. These cultures occur where people are typically psychologically distant from each other, and so depend more on explicit information to communicate:

> Japanese, Arabs and Mediterranean people, who have extensive information networks among family, friends, colleagues and clients and who are involved in close personal relationships, are examples of high context cultures. Low context peoples include Americans, Germans, Swiss, Scandinavians and other northern Europeans; they compartmentalise their personal relationships, their work and many aspects of day-to-day life. (Tayeb, 1996, pp. 55–56)

High-context cultures are those in which information is implicit and can only be fully understood by those with shared experiences in the culture.

Low-context cultures are those where people are more psychologically distant so that information needs to be explicit if members are to understand it.

Attitude to conflict and harmony

Disagreements and conflict arise in all societies. The management interest is in how different societies have developed different ways of handling conflict. Individualistic cultures such as those of the United States or The Netherlands see conflict as healthy, on the basis that everyone has a right to express their views. People are encouraged to bring contentious issues into the open and to discuss conflicts rather than suppress them. Other cultures place greater value on social harmony and on not disturbing the way things are:

> The notion of harmony is central in almost all East Asian cultures, such as Korea, Taiwan, Singapore and Hong Kong, through their common Confucian heritage. In ... Korea the traditional implicit rules of proper behaviour provide appropriate role behaviour for individuals in the junior and subordinate roles of an interpersonal relationship. (Tayeb, 1996, p. 60)

The significance of cultural issues for managers depends on the nature of the firm's involvement in international business – Table 4.1 sums up the options.

Character of the firm	Relevance of national culture to foreign culture
Domestic, single-nation firm with no foreign interests	nil
Single-nation firm with import/export activities	low to moderate
Multinational firm with franchising and licensing activities	moderate to high
Multinational firm with manufacturing and/or service units abroad	high
Global firm with business activities in most parts of the world	high

Source: Tayeb (2000), p. 87.

Table 4.1

Company strategies and relevance of national culture

Several scholars have developed formal instruments to classify and compare national cultures, notably Trompenaars (1993), Hofstede (2001) and House *et al.* (2004). Hofstede's work has been the most widely used and replicated in management research (Kirkman *et al.*, 2006), and is outlined in the following section.

key ideas   Overemphasising diversity?

The chapter has illustrated the diversity of national cultures. There is another view: that the underlying fundamentals of management outweigh cultural variations in detailed processes. One powerful constraint on diversity is the economic context of an essentially capitalist economic system. This places similar requirements on managers wherever they are. They have to provide acceptable returns, create a coherent organisational structure, maintain relations with stakeholders and try to keep control.

Further, if managers work in a multinational organisation that has developed a distinctive corporate culture (Chapter 3), will that influence their behaviour more than the local national culture?

Another constraint is the use of integrated information systems across companies (and their suppliers) operating internationally, which can place common reporting requirements on managers irrespective of their location. This ties units more closely together, and may bring more convergence in the work of management.

These are unresolved questions: look for evidence as you work on this chapter that supports or contradicts either point of view.

Activity 4.4   Reflecting on PESTEL factors

If you have worked in a company operating internationally, which of the PESTEL factors had most effect on the management of the venture?

- Within each PESTEL heading, which items had most impact, and why?
- Which items that are *not* listed had a significant impact, and why?
- Evaluate the usefulness of the model as a guide to those managing internationally.

4.10   Hofstede's comparison of national cultures

Geert Hofstede is a Dutch academic who has conducted widely quoted studies of national cultural differences. The second edition of his research (Hofstede, 2001) extends and refines the conclusions of his original work, which was based on a survey of the attitudes of 116,000 IBM employees, one of the earliest global companies. The research inspired many empirical studies with non-IBM employees in both the original countries in which IBM operated and in places where they did not. Kirkman *et al.* (2006) reviewed many of these and concluded that 'most of the country differences predicted by Hofstede were supported' (p. 308), and Hofstede and Hofstede (2005, pp. 25–28) make a similar point: that book also provides an accessible account of the research method.

Hofstede (2001), as already noted, defined culture as a collective programming of people's minds, which influences how they react to events in the workplace. He identified five dimensions of culture and sought to measure how people in different countries vary in their attitudes to them.

Power distance

Power distance (PD) is 'the extent to which the less powerful members of ... organisations within a country expect and accept that power is distributed unevenly' (Hofstede and Hofstede, 2005, p. 46). One of the ways in which countries differ is in how power and authority are distributed. Related to this is how people view the resultant inequality. In some the existence of inequality in boss/subordinate relationships is seen as undesirable while in others people see it as part of the natural order of things. The questionnaire allowed the researchers to calculate scores for PD, countries with a high PD being those where people accepted inequality. Those with high scores included Malaysia, Mexico, Venezuela, Arab countries, China, France and Brazil. Those with low PD scores included Australia, Germany, Great Britain, Sweden and Norway.

> **Power distance** is the extent to which the less powerful members of organisations within a country expect and accept that power is distributed unevenly.

Uncertainty avoidance

Uncertainty avoidance is 'the extent to which the members of a culture feel threatened by ambiguous or unknown situations' (Hofstede and Hofstede, 2005, p. 167). People in some cultures tolerate ambiguity and uncertainty quite readily – if things are not clear they will improvise or use their initiative. Others are reluctant to move without clear rules or instructions. High scores, indicating low tolerance of uncertainty, were obtained in the Latin American, Latin European and Mediterranean countries, and for Japan and Korea. Low scores were recorded in the Asian countries other than Japan and Korea, and in most of the Anglo and Nordic countries – such as the United States, Great Britain, Sweden and Denmark.

> **Uncertainty avoidance** is the extent to which members of a culture feel threatened by uncertain or unknown situations.

Individualism/collectivism

Hofstede and Hofstede (2005) distinguish between **individualism** and **collectivism**:

> Individualism pertains to societies in which the ties between individuals are loose: everyone is expected to look after himself or herself and his or her immediate family. Collectivism as its opposite pertains to societies in which people, from birth onwards, are integrated into strong, cohesive in-groups which throughout people's lifetime continue to protect them in exchange for unquestioning loyalty. (p. 76)

Some people live in societies in which the power of the group prevails: there is an emphasis on collective action and mutual responsibility, and on helping each other through difficulties. Other societies emphasise the individual, and his or her responsibility for their position in life. High scores on the individualism dimension occurred in wealthy countries such as the United States, Australia, Great Britain and Canada. Low scores occurred in poor countries such as the less developed South American and Asian countries.

> **Individualism** pertains to societies in which the ties between individuals are loose.

> **Collectivism** 'describes societies in which people, from birth onwards, are integrated into strong, cohesive in-groups which ... protect them in exchange for unquestioning loyalty' (Hofstede, 2005, p. 76).

Activity 4.5   Implications of cultural differences

- Consider the implications of differences on Hofstede's first two dimensions of culture for management in the countries concerned. For example, what would Hofstede's conclusions lead you to predict about the method that a French or Venezuelan manager would use if he or she wanted a subordinate to perform a task, and what method would the subordinate expect his or her manager to use?
- How would your answers differ if the manager and subordinates were Swedish?

Masculinity
pertains to societies in which social gender roles are clearly distinct.

Femininity
pertains to societies in which social gender roles overlap.

Masculinity/femininity

A society is called masculine when emotional gender roles are clearly distinct: men are supposed to be assertive, tough and focused on material success, whereas women are supposed to be more modest, tender and concerned with the quality of life. A society is called feminine when emotional gender roles overlap (i.e. both men and women are supposed to be modest, tender and concerned with the quality of life). (Hofstede and Hofstede, 2005, p. 120)

The research showed that societies differ in the desirability of assertive behaviour (which they label masculinity) and of modest behaviour (femininity). Many societies expect men to seek achievements outside the home while women care for things within the home. Masculinity scores were not related to economic wealth: 'we find both rich and poor masculine countries, and rich and poor feminine countries' (p. 120). The most feminine countries were Sweden, Norway, The Netherlands and Denmark. Masculine countries included Japan, Austria, Germany, China and the United States.

Long-term and short-term orientation

Long-term orientation (LTO) stands for the fostering of virtues oriented towards future rewards – in particular perseverance and thrift. Its opposite pole, short-term orientation, stands for the fostering of virtues related to the past and present – in particular respect for tradition, preservation of 'face', and fulfilling social obligations. (Hofstede and Hofstede, 2005, p. 210)

Countries with high LTO scores include China, Hong Kong, Taiwan and Japan. Great Britain, Australia, New Zealand, the United States and Canada have a short-term orientation, in which many people see spending, not thrift, as a virtue.

Limitations of Hofstede's work

Other scholars have drawn attention to some limitations of Hofstede's work, including:

- the small (and so possibly unrepresentative) number of respondents in some countries;
- reducing a phenomenon as complex as a nation's culture to five dimensions;
- basing the original sample on the employees of a single multinational;
- the possibility that cultures change over time;
- the variety of cultures within a country (e.g. between religious or ethnic groups); and
- the likelihood of differences of culture within IBM (McSweeney, 2002).

Case question 4.3

Below are some of the countries in which Starbucks operates. If Hofstede's analysis is accurate, what may be the implications for managing the business in each of those countries, and for a manager who needs to work with colleagues in each? Check the text for the cultural features that Hofstede identified for each country, and then compare them.

- United States
- Japan
- France
- United Kingdom.

Even if the precision of the results is questionable, they are a useful starting point for those working internationally to think about the culture in which they operate, and to reflect on their own cultural biases. People operating internationally need to develop an ability to deal with the different cultural contexts.

Activity 4.6 Critical reflection on cultural differences

If you have worked in an organisation with international operations, reflect on whether your experience leads you to agree or disagree with the ideas in this section. For example:

- Can you recognise the differences in national cultures identified by Hofstede?
- If so, in what ways did they affect the way people worked?
- How did company culture and national culture interact?

4.11 Contrasting management systems

Despite the growth of international trade and the growing interdependence of business across the world, countries vary substantially in the way they organise economic activities. There are major differences in the way business is organised in Japan, Korea and Taiwan, as compared with the United States or the United Kingdom. Within western Europe business in the United Kingdom operates in different ways from that in Germany, France or Italy – even though all are capitalist economies. As Whitley (1999) explains:

> Different patterns of industrialization developed in contrasting institutional contexts and led to contrasting institutional arrangements governing economic processes becoming established in different market economies ... Partly as a result, the structure and practices of state agencies, financial organizations and labour-market actors [in different] countries continue to diverge and to reproduce distinctive forms of economic organization. (p. 5)

At one extreme are the Japanese networks of interdependent relations, with a tradition of mutual ownership between different, but friendly, business units. Companies have close financial and obligational links with each other and the Ministry of Industry actively supports and guides the strategic direction of major areas of business. Firms create a network of mutually dependent organisations and decide strategy by negotiation with their stakeholders – other companies and financial institutions.

At the other extreme, firms in the United Kingdom and the United States work in a more isolated way. They receive less direct support from banks, which have traditionally avoided long-term investments and whose boards rarely contain representatives of companies with common interests.

The level of dependence affects companies' attitudes towards growth and profitability. Whitley suggests that a high dependence on the state encourages growth but discourages concern over profit, and cites France as an example. In Japan firms seek market share and growth within their sector, but not beyond it. The network of relations between Japanese firms and their customers and suppliers restricts unrelated diversification, but there is a strong collective interest in expansion. The more isolated UK and US firms, where owners operate as portfolio holders, find growth limited by the need to meet profit targets and the expectations of the capital market.

key ideas Whitley's elements of national institutional features

State structure and policies
- Dominance of the state and its willingness to share risk with private owners
- State antagonism to institutions enabling cooperation between firms
- Extent of formal regulation of entry to and exit from markets.

Financial system
- Capital market or credit based.

Skill development and control system
- Strength of public training system and of state–employer–union collaboration
- Strength of independent trade unions
- Strength of labour organisations based on certified expertise
- Centralisation of bargaining.

Trust and authority relations
- Strength of institutions governing trust relations and collective loyalties
- Predominance of paternalist authority relations
- Importance of communal norms governing authority relations.

Source: Whitley (1999), p. 48.

Mayer and Whittington (2004) examined the effects of national styles in their study of the spread of the multi-divisional form of organisation. First developed in the United States this form, in which firms divide their separate activities (perhaps directed at different markets or customer groups) into relatively autonomous divisions, had been adopted by most large European firms by the early 1990s. However, its distribution varies across advanced European economies: it is widely used in the United Kingdom, but is less common in Germany. Mayer and Whittington conclude that while the multi-divisional form is spreading, it has done so more slowly than originally expected, at least in part because of differences in national management systems. This is consistent with a study of the variation in human resource management practices amongst European firms (Gooderham *et al.*, 1999).

4.12 Views on globalisation

The globalisation of markets?

If you travel to another country, you immediately see many familiar consumer products or services – things that epitomise the idea that global brands are steadily displacing local products. In several industries identical products (Canon cameras, Famous Grouse whisky) are sold across the globe without modification. This trend towards **globalisation** was observed by Theodore Levitt – see the next Key Ideas.

Globalisation refers to the increasing integration of internationally dispersed economic activities.

Levitt's argument soon influenced practice in many global businesses. In the mid-1980s British Airways developed an advertisement ('The world's favourite airline') and (after dubbing it into 20 languages) showed it in identical form in all 35 countries with a developed TV network. Consumer companies such as Coca-Cola and McDonald's began promoting themselves as identical global brands, with standard practices and a centralised management structure.

By the end of the 1990s managers began to change their approach. Customers were finding that new local brands offered better value and, as producers adopted western methods, good quality. Global brands, offering standard products regardless of local tastes, lost market share. So rather than 'going global' they began to 'go local' – Coca-Cola, for instance, owns not one brand but 200, many of them in only one or two markets; McDonald's varies its menu to suit local tastes; Nestlé has about 200 varieties of its instant coffee; and MTV varies programming to suit different countries and regions.

The globalisation of markets

Theodore Levitt, a Professor at Harvard Business School, argued that advances in communications technology were increasingly inspiring consumers around the world to want the same things. 'The world's needs and desires have been irrevocably homogenised. This makes the multinational corporation obsolete and the global corporation absolute' (p. 93). He believed therefore that international companies should cease to act as 'multinationals' that customised their products to fit local markets and tastes. Instead they should become 'global' by standardising the production, distribution and marketing of their products across all countries. Sameness meant efficiency and would be more profitable than difference. From economies of scale would flow competitive advantage.

Source: Based on Levitt (1983).

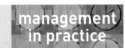

Coca-Cola finds formula for India   www.cocacola.com

Coca-Cola India totally misjudged rural India, home to two-thirds of the country's 1 billion population, when it re-entered the country in 1993. It paid a high price for the then market leader, Thumbs Up, and then tried to kill it off in the mistaken belief that this would pave the way for Coca-Cola's rise. The approach failed – best illustrated by the fact that India is one of the few markets where Pepsi-Cola leads Coca-Cola. 'We were just not addressing the masses', admitted Sanjeev Gupta, Coca-Cola's operations chief. In 2000 management decided to change their approach – by focusing on the distinctive needs of the Indian rural consumer. This meant using smaller bottles, lower prices, more outlets and an advertising campaign (featuring Bollywood stars) that makes sense to villagers as well as city dwellers.

Source: Extracts from an article by Khozem Merchant, Financial Times, 18 June 2003.

Rugman (2000) offers another view on globalisation, arguing that the world has become divided into three regions – North America, the European Union and Japan/East Asia. He notes that almost three-quarters of exports from EU members went to other EU countries – and exports to North America accounted for less than 10 per cent of the total. He concluded that we are seeing not so much globalisation as regionalisation – with the three groupings having very different traditions and ways of doing business. 'Only in a few sectors is globalization a successful firm strategy ... For most manufacturers and all services, regionalisation is much more relevant than globalization' (p. 18).

The globalisation of production

Since the 1960s a growing number of firms in the developed world have noted that labour-intensive manufacturing and service operations in their home country are costly ways of working. This was especially the case in electrical and electronic goods, clothing, footwear and toys, which faced growing competition from cheaper imports. Managers looked for new sources of supply, and received a very positive response from a small group of Asian countries – Taiwan, Hong Kong, South Korea and especially Singapore. These countries took the opportunity over the next 30 years to become major 'outsourcing' centres, supplying finished goods and components to companies around the world. They have also developed their education systems so that they can do work of higher value, so that the range of products has also widened greatly – including a growing trade in services such as software development and the back-office functions of airlines and banks. Table 4.2 gives some examples.

Table 4.2

Examples of the globalisation of production

Company	Years	Work transferred	Reasons given
ABN Amro www.abnamro.com	2006–08	Relocate 2400 jobs in back office operations to India	'To meet cost-saving targets and remain competitive'
Gillette www.gillette.com	2005–07	Close three factories (two UK and one German) and transfer work to new factory in eastern Europe	'Significantly reduce costs and improve operating efficiency'
Dyson www.dyson.co.uk	2003–04	Moved production of vacuum cleaners and washing machines from UK to Malaysia	'Reduce manufacturing costs and help protect UK jobs in design and development'

Concerns about globalisation

Supporters of more liberal world trade argue that it brings benefits of wider access to markets and cheaper goods and services. The growth in trade that follows benefits both consumers and workers by encouraging innovation and investment. It has given many consumers a much wider choice of goods, by being able to attract supplies from around the world, often much more cheaply than those produced locally. Others take a much more critical view, pointing out that moves towards liberalisation through bodies such as the WTO are driven by the rich countries. They believe the agreements reached serve the interests of multinational businesses and richer economies rather than indigenous producers in local economies.

Starbucks – the case continues www.starbucks.com CASE STUDY

In late 2006 Chairman Howard Schultz announced that the world's largest coffee-shop chain would be bigger yet: he plans to more than triple the number of stores, to 40,000, with half in the United States and half overseas. Starbucks' executives had earlier announced that the company had reached an agreement with Apple to give consumers the ability to preview, buy and download a variety of Starbucks' Hear Music titles from the iTunes store. The company's success was being reflected in the share price, which in late 2006 was at an all-time high.

It was however facing opposition from activists in several countries. Some criticise it for an apparently relentless expansion, offering a similar global brand that tends to push out local companies, reducing the variety of local shopping areas.

Others cast doubt on its claims to treat coffee growers fairly. In 2000 it was pressed by groups campaigning on behalf of coffee growers to introduce Fair Trade coffee into its stores. Partly to avoid bad publicity it agreed to do so – despite having concerns about quality, and its relationship with its coffee suppliers as a whole. In 2004 the company purchased 4.8 million pounds of Fair Trade Certified™ coffee, a figure that increased to 11.5 million pounds in 2005. Nevertheless, it attracted criticism again in late 2006 when it opposed an attempt by Ethiopian coffee growers to trademark three brands of high quality coffee in the United States. This would have enabled producers to sell it for a higher price than if it was sold as an unbranded commodity product.

Sources: Argenti (2004); *BBC News* website, 26 October 2006; *Fortune*, 13 November 2006; company website.

Activity 4.7 Debating globalisation

Arrange a debate or discussion on these questions:

- Has globalisation increased people's power as consumers, or diminished their power as employees?
- Has it lifted millions out of poverty, or has it widened the gap between rich and poor?
- Has it widened consumer choice, or has it encouraged levels of industrialisation and consumption that make unsustainable demands on the earth's natural resources?
- Does globalisation heighten aesthetic awareness of different cultures, or does it expose people to a stream of superficial images?
- Does it enable more people to experience diversity, or does it lead to a bland homogenisation of local cultures into a global view?

Globalisation: what it means to small nations

In July 1996 the then prime minister of Malaysia, Dr Mahathir, gave a lecture in which he questioned whether globalisation would bring benefits to poorer countries. Some extracts from his speech follow.

A globalised world is not going to be democratic, but will belong to powerful, dominant countries. Those countries would impose their will on the rest who will be no better off than when they were colonies. Fifty years ago, the process of decolonisation began and in about 20 years it was virtually completed. But before any have become truly and fully independent, recolonisation has begun. This is what globalisation may be about. It does not contain much hope for the weak and poor. But unfortunately it is entirely possible.

As interpreted by developed countries, globalisation meant breaking down boundaries so that every country had access to others. The poor countries will have access to the markets of the rich, unrestricted. In return the rich will have access to the markets of the poor. This sounds absolutely fair. The playing field will be level, it will be a borderless world, and everyone would be equal citizens. But will they be truly equal?

Dr Mahathir said that, after 30 years or more of 'independence', the former colonies of the west have found the emptiness of their independence. They have found that their politics, their economy, their social and behavioural systems are all under the control, directly or indirectly, of the old colonial masters and the great powers. It was clear that the developed countries wished to use the World Trade Organisation to impose conditions on the developing countries. This will not improve their ▶

human rights, labour practices or care for the environment: instead it will stunt their growth and mean more suffering for their people. If the developing countries were competing with the west in any way then their records were scrutinised and threats issued. The net effect is to prevent the development of these newly industrialising economies.

Dr Mahathir said globalisation would leave these countries totally exposed and unable to protect themselves against increasing foreign investment. The effect would be the demise of the small companies based in the developing countries: 'Large international corporations, originating in the developed countries, will take over everything.'

Source: *New Straits Times*, July 1996.

Activity 4.8   Understanding a critic of globalisation

Malaysia has attracted much foreign direct investment, especially from IT companies. It is a leading player in south-east Asia with little unemployment. Yet the architect of its economic success clearly has serious doubts about the emergence of the global economy.

- What are his main concerns?
- Can you find examples of global companies using their economic bargaining power to take advantage of the weaker countries in which they operate?

All of these developments imply much greater patterns of contact between managers in different countries. Legislative changes and treaties remove some barriers to trade, but they do not solve the management problems of making those economic activities work efficiently. Above all, they bring many managers face to face with the need to manage cultural differences.

4.13   Current themes and issues

Performance

As companies choose to respond to apparent international opportunities they need to deal with structural issues such as:

- managing matrix structures where products are made and sold in several countries;
- improving the links between research, marketing and production to speed the introduction of new products;
- facilitating knowledge transfer between the national components of the business;
- encouraging tactical and local flexibility while maintaining strategic coherence.

These issues are complex enough in themselves, but since they are working internationally managers aim to balance theories and methods that they believe support performance in one national context with approaches which suit other contexts. People in countries with high power distance scores will expect managers to make plans and subordinates to implement them without complaint or disagreement. Attempts to involve subordinates in discussing the alternatives would be greeted with puzzlement. Similar challenges arise in developing appropriate structures for international business.

People in high power distance countries may expect structures to be centralised, formal and with strict job descriptions. People in low power distance countries will prefer more fluid structures that allow them to use their initiative.

Responsibility

The internationalisation of business confronts managers with several issues of corporate responsibility (see Chapter 5), such as outsourcing, dealing with corruption, and corporate governance arrangements. While some managers and companies are genuinely motivated by a commitment to social or environmental goals, responsible corporate action is only sustainable in the long run if it can be made consistent with the organisation's overall strategy. If the costs outweigh the benefits (which may be intangible) this will make the firm less profitable than those who are less scrupulous.

Outsourcing is one example. The motivation for outsourcing is usually to reduce labour costs, but also to avoid the environmental regulations that add significantly to costs in the developed world. Those who receive the outsourced work, and their families, clearly benefit, even though working in conditions that would be illegal in most western countries. Because of their poverty they will be less concerned about the pollution and waste that their work generates, and which is a cost to the surrounding community. However the danger for the outsourcing firm is that controversies about the practices of its subcontractors may lead to negative publicity amongst its customers.

Many of those involved in international business experience face the dilemmas of bribery – from the trivial 'speed money' to allegations of serious corruption in securing construction or military contracts. Most companies establish procedures to deal with this through their systems of corporate governance. In doing so they face the dilemma of which standards they should apply. Activities that are illegal in some countries are regarded as normal business practice in others. One way of resolving this is the doctrine of ethical relativism: while from the point of view of the company ethical relativism may secure the business, it may cause difficulties for individual managers if their personal ethical views are more universal than relative.

Internationalisation

As business becomes increasingly international, do managers respond passively to aspects of the environment in the countries where they do business, or do they try to shape it? The first view stresses how features of the political or other environments can constrain choice, especially in economies with a tradition of significant government involvement in business. It sees managers as having a rather passive role, reacting to pressures from their environment. An alternative view regards managers as proactive, in the sense that they can influence the policies that form part of their context: the Management in Practice feature reports a study which gives some empirical support for the proactive view.

The idea that companies can proactively try to influence their environment applies equally to other elements. Companies can try to influence suppliers, customers, local communities or national governments in ways that support their strategy, through a variety of active influencing methods. The essential idea is that the relation between the manager and the context works both ways. People shape the context, and the context shapes people.

 **MNCs and environmental policy in China and Taiwan**

In a study of the interaction between companies and government institutions over environmental policy, Child and Tsai compared the experience of companies in China and Taiwan. They examined three multinational corporations (MNCs) in the chemicals sector, each with plants in China and Taiwan – which have different environmental policies. In examining how these policies affected companies, and how companies affected the policies, they found that:

- MNCs took a broad view of the stakeholders to whom they paid attention, including suppliers, customers, local communities and especially non-governmental agencies (NGOs) who could affect public opinion.
- Non-governmental organisations (NGOs) played a major role in mobilising public concerns.
- MNCs engaged in proactive political action, often in conjunction with NGOs, to influence environmental policy.

Source: Based on Child and Tsai (2005).

Summary

1 **Summarise the forces stimulating the growth of international business**
   - Yip proposes that these factors are market, economic, environmental and competitive.

2 **Contrast the ways in which organisations conduct international business**
   - Exporting, licensing, joint ventures, wholly owned subsidiaries.
   - Multinational (independent operations in many countries, run from centre); transnational (independent operations in many countries, decentralised); global (linked and interdependent operations in many countries, closely coordinated).

3 **Conduct a PESTEL analysis to show countries' contrasting business environments**
   - This would involve gathering data and information about political, economic, socio-cultural, technological, environmental and legal.

4 **Explain the significance of national cultures, and evaluate the significance of Hofstede's research for managers working internationally**
   - This would involve gathering evidence (as in the Activities) on differences in national culture (using Hofstede or a similar model), and on whether the cultural differences had a noticeable effect on the task of managing.
   - Low context – information explicit and clear; high context – information is implicit and can only be understood through shared experience, values and assumptions.
   - Hofstede distinguished between cultures in terms of power distance (acceptance of variations in power); uncertainty avoidance (willingness to tolerate ambiguity); individualism/collectivism (emphasis on individual or collective action); and masculinity/femininity (preferences for assertive or modest behaviour); and long-/short-term orientation.

5 **Compare and contrast the features of national management systems**
   - These shape the way people interpret generic activities of management:
     - United States – individualistic, rational approach, contingent design of organisations;
     - Europe – collective, rational approach, pragmatic;
     - Japan – collective responsibility, trust of subordinates, consensus building.

6 Compare the benefits and costs of globalisation to different players

- Benefits include growth, economic development, wider choice for consumers.

- Costs include loss of income by local producers.

- Management issues include balancing local needs with company styles and methods.

Review questions

1. What factors are stimulating the growth in world trade?

2. Compare internationalisation and globalisation. Give a specific example of a company of each type about which you have obtained some information.

3. Outline the difference between a high- and a low-context culture and give an example of each from direct observation or discussion.

4. Explain accurately to another person Hofstede's five dimensions of national cultures. Evaluate his conclusions on the basis of discussions with your colleagues from any of the countries in his study. Evaluate the limitations and criticisms of his study.

5. Give some illustrations of your own about the way in which the history of a country has affected its culture, and how that in turn affects the management of organisations there.

6. What are the distinctive features of Japanese, European and US management systems?

7. Compare the implications of globalisation for (a) national governments, (b) their citizens, (c) the management of global companies, (d) the environment.

Concluding critical reflection

Think about the way managers in your company, or one with which you are familiar, deal with the international aspects of business. Review the material in the chapter, and make notes on these questions:

- Which of the issues discussed in this chapter are most relevant to the way you and your colleagues manage? For example, what structure(s) do you use to manage the international aspects of the business? Which of the PESTEL factors have most effect in your situation?

- What **assumptions** appear to guide the way people manage internationally? Do they assume that cultural factors are significant or insignificant? Do they see globalisation as a benefit or a threat? Do they acknowledge any responsibilities to those who may be damaged by it?

- What aspects of the historical or current **context** of the company appear to influence your company's approach to internationalisation and globalisation? Do people see it as a threat or an opportunity, and why? Are there different views on how you should deal with this aspect of the business?

- Can you compare your approach with that of other companies in which colleagues on your course work? Does this suggest any plausible **alternative** ways of managing internationally? How much scope do you have to change this?

- What **limitations** can you see in the theories and evidence presented? For example, is Hofstede's analysis of different cultures threatened by the increasingly international outlook and interests of young people?

Further reading

Daniels, J.D., Radebaugh, L.H. and Sullivan, D.P. (2004), *International Business: Environments and operations* (10th edn), Pearson/Prentice Hall, Upper Saddle River, NJ.

> Provides a comprehensive exposure to many aspects of international business, combining a strong theoretical base with many current examples.

Harris, N. (1999), *European Business* (2nd edn), Macmillan Business, Basingstoke.

Dent, C.M. (1997), *The European Economy: The global context*, Routledge, London.

> Both trace the development of a more integrated European economy and its place within wider global trends.

Pinder, J. (2001), *The European Union: A very short introduction*, Oxford University Press, Oxford.

> As the title implies, a concise account of the development of the EU.

Chen, M. (2004), *Asian Management Systems*, Thomson, London.

> Comparative review of the management systems in Japan, mainland China, overseas Chinese and Korean. These are compared with western approaches to management.

Guthrie, D. (2006), *China and Globalization: The social, economic and political transformation of Chinese society*, Routledge, London.

> An excellent review of China's transition towards a market economy, showing how the visible economic changes depend on supportive social, cultural and political changes.

Monbiot, G. (2000), *The Captive State*, Macmillan, Basingstoke.

> A critique of multinational corporations and the way they seek to subvert democratic institutions.

Moore, F. (2005), *Transnational Business Cultures: Life and work in a multinational corporation*, Ashgate Publishing, Aldershot.

> An excellent (and rare) ethnographic study of people working in a German bank with offices in Frankfurt and London, which explores the complex emerging cultures combining local, global and corporate elements.

Weblinks

These websites have appeared in the chapter:

www.starbucks.com	www.cocacola.com
www.genpact.com	www.abnamro.com
www.tcl.com	www.gillette.com
www.walmart.com	www.dyson.co.uk
http://.ec.europa.eu/	

Visit two of the business sites in the list, or others which interest you, and navigate to the pages dealing with recent news, press or investor relations.

- What signs are there of the international nature of the business, and what are the main issues in this area that the business appears to be facing?
- Compare and contrast the issues you identify on the two sites.
- What challenges may they imply for those working in, and managing, these organisations?

Annotated weblinks, multiple choice questions and other useful resources can be found on www.pearsoned.co.uk/boddy

Chapter 5
Corporate responsibility

Aim

To introduce the dilemmas of ethical and responsible behaviour that managers face, and offer some analytical tools to help manage them.

Objectives

By the end of your work on this chapter you should be able to outline the concepts below in your own terms and:

1 Give examples of contrasts in business practice, including those that damage firms' reputation
2 Decide which ethical theory someone is using to justify an action
3 Use a model of ethical decision making to identify organisational influences on ethical choice
4 Compare an organisation's policies with alternative views of the role of business in society
5 Explain an organisation's policy on responsible behaviour in terms of its stakeholders
6 Outline the structures and frameworks for corporate governance that managers can use to encourage responsible behaviour.

Key terms

This chapter introduces the following ideas:

philanthropy
enlightened self-interest
applied ethics
ethical relativism
ethical decision-making models
social contract
corporate responsibility
ethical investors
ethical consumers
ethical audit

Each is a term defined within the text, as well as in the Glossary at the end of the book.

In the late 1960s Lee Iacocca, then president of Ford, sought to improve the company's market position by having a new car, the Ford Pinto, on the market by the 1971 model year. This would be a basic vehicle selling for $2000, which meant that it had to be produced very cheaply, with a small margin between production costs and selling price.

The designers placed the petrol tank at the back of the car, six inches from a flimsy rear bumper. Bolts were placed just three inches from the tank. Other sharp metal edges surrounded the tank, and the filler pipe tended to break loose from the tank in low-speed crashes. These features could have been redesigned, but the extra expense would go against Iacocca's aim of 'a 2000 pound car for $2000'.

In testing its new design Ford found that when it was struck from behind at 20 mph the bumper would push the bolts into the tank, causing it to rupture. This posed a significant risk to those inside and contravened proposed legislation that required cars to withstand an impact at 30 mph without fuel loss. No one informed Iacocca of these findings, for fear of being fired. He was fond of saying 'safety doesn't sell'.

The car went on sale and in 1976 a magazine exposed the dangers of the Pinto petrol tank. This prompted the National Highway Traffic Safety Administration (NHTSA) to launch an investigation, which in 1977 identified 28 rear-end crashes in which petrol had leaked and caused a fire; 27 occupants had died and 24 suffered burns.

Feeling some pressure to fix the tank, Ford officials devised a polythene shield to prevent it from being punctured by the bolts, and a jacket to cushion it against impact. The engineers calculated that these improvements would cost $11 per car, and had to decide whether to recall the cars to make these repairs. They conducted a cost–benefit analysis. Using NHTSA figures for the cost to society of death or serious injury, and an estimate of the likely number of future deaths and serious injuries, Ford's calculations were:

Bettmann/Corbis

Benefits of altering design

Savings:	180 deaths; 180 serious injuries; 2100 vehicles
Unit cost:	$200,000 per death; $67,000 per serious injury; $700 per vehicle
Total benefit:	$49.5 million

Costs of altering the design

Sales:	11 million cars; 1.5 million light trucks
Unit cost:	$11 per car; $11 per truck
Total cost:	$137.5 million

Since the costs of recalling and altering the cars outweighed the benefits they decided not to do so, continuing to produce the Pinto in its original form. They reasoned that the current design met federal safety standards at the time. While it did not meet proposed legislation, it was as safe as current competing models.

In 1977 the proposed fuel tank legislation was adopted and Ford decided to recall all 1971–76 Pintos to modify their fuel tanks. A month before the recall began three people in a Pinto were struck from behind in a low-speed crash and burned to death. A $120 million lawsuit followed, but Ford escaped on a technicality. Ford won the lawsuit, but its reputation suffered badly.

Source: Based on Shaw (1991) and Nutt (2002).

Case questions 5.1

- As a marketing or production manager at Ford at the time, what dilemmas would you face?
- How would you express these dilemmas within the company?

5.1   Introduction

Ford managers dealing with the Pinto chose to put profit before safety. Yet they did not act illegally, and customers were not as interested in safety features then as they are today. A manager who tried to delay the model launch would have damaged their career, their family economy – and the livelihood of other Ford workers. But the managers' decisions led to death and injury.

Most people only become conscious of business ethics when there is a problem. Events such as the collapse of Enron (Swartz and Watkins, 2002), Arthur Andersen (Toffler and Reingold, 2003) and Parmalat (an Italian dairy company with wide international operations), or the high pay and pensions paid to senior managers who lose their jobs, increase distrust of corporate bodies (Clarke, 2003). Controversies about food safety or the use of child labour in the Far East to produce clothing sold in western stores raise questions about the companies' sense of corporate responsibility.

While such situations seem clear-cut, there are many ambiguities:

> there is no consensus on what constitutes virtuous corporate behavior. Is sourcing overseas to take advantage of lower labor costs responsible? Are companies morally obligated to insist that their contractors pay a 'living wage' rather than market wages? Are investments in natural resources in poor countries with corrupt governments always, sometimes or never irresponsible? More broadly, is it ever responsible for companies to use their shareholders' resources to provide public goods if doing so makes them less profitable? Or are corporations acting most responsibly when they seek to maximize shareholder wealth? (Vogel, 2005, pp. 4–5)

Should BP be praised for acknowledging climate change before many of its competitors, or criticised for its poor recent safety record? Is it at fault for producing the oil that consumers demand? Is Shell acting responsibly by extracting oil in Nigeria and so contributing to the national economy, when this activity sometimes brings it into conflict with local communities?

Discussions of corporate responsibility often focus on working conditions in developing countries, on the environment, and on human rights – but ethical issues arise at each stage of the value-adding chain. Dilemmas can arise over inputs (e.g. whether to use existing staff or to outsource work), transformation (e.g. treatment of employees, use of energy, transport and other resources) and outputs (e.g. waste and pollution, honest treatment of customers).

The chapter begins with examples of contrasting business behaviour, introduces ideas on personal ethics and sets out an ethical decision-making model that places individual behaviour within its context. It then presents contrasting views about the role of busi-

 **Scandal at Farepak**

In October 2006 customers of Farepak received unwelcome news. They had paid regular amounts to the company since January, in return for which they would receive a hamper of food and drink before Christmas. This is a common method by which people, often on low incomes, can save towards the cost of the holiday. The company announced that due to financial difficulties it was no longer trading, and would not be distributing the hampers. Senior management blamed their bank for the difficulty, claiming that it had been unwilling to extend sufficient credit to the company to enable it to meet its obligations. Administrators of the collapsed firm estimated that those who had lost money would probably receive 5p for every £ they had invested.

Source: Published sources.

ness in society, and relates this to identifying and managing stakeholders. Later sections examine practices that can encourage more responsible behaviour, including a framework of corporate governance.

5.2 Contrasts in business practice

The Pinto case is a prominent example of irresponsible corporate action, and Table 5.1 notes some other recent notable examples of financial irregularities.

Table 5.1

Recent financial scandals at major companies

Company	Incident	Outcome
Enron, 2001, a US trading company	Company collapsed in 2001, amid allegations of accounting practices that artificially inflated earnings and share prices, to benefit top managers.	Employees lost jobs and pensions, directors received large financial benefits. Founder Ken Lay and CEO Jeff Skilling convicted of fraud in May 2006.
Arthur Andersen, 2002, accounting and consulting firm, worked for Enron	Shredded thousands of documents to hide malpractice at Enron.	Found guilt of obstructing justice, CEO resigns, firm collapses, and 85,000 staff lose their job.
Parmalat, 2003, an Italian dairy company	Managers claimed assets in bank accounts that did not exist, to cover growing liabilities. CEO accused of diverting £600m to his own use.	Senior managers convicted of fraud, and others pleaded guilty to charges of misleading investors. Company continues to trade under new management.
Shell, 2003, oil company	Admits overstating its oil reserves, which investors use in valuing such businesses.	Chairman resigns, accused of creating a culture that encouraged misreporting, and for delay in admitting the error.
Ahold, 2006, Dutch retailer	Conceals documents about joint ventures from auditors, so that revenues appeared higher than they should have been.	Chief executive and chief financial officer convicted of fraud. Shareholder groups criticised lenient sentences.
Volkswagen, 2007, car maker	Former head of personnel admits illegal payments to trade union leaders, managers and prostitutes.	Initially denies involvement, then resigns and pleads guilty; receives short jail sentence. Trade union leaders charged.

Sources: *Business Week*, 12 January 2004; *Financial Times*, 20 February 2004, 23 May 2006, 26 May 2006, 18 January 2007.

There is an equally long tradition of ethical behaviour in business, when people have challenged the actions of others on ethical grounds – Robert Owen (Chapter 2) campaigned against the employment of children under the age of 10 in the mines and mills of nineteenth-century Britain. From the start of the Industrial Revolution some entrepreneurs acted with philanthropy:

1803–76	Titus Salt	Textiles	Employee welfare; Saltaire Village
1830–98	Jeremiah Coleman	Mustard	Charities; Salvation Army; YMCA
1839–1922	George Cadbury	Chocolate	Employee welfare; Bournville Village
1836–1925	Joseph Rowntree	Chocolate	Employee welfare; New Earswick Village
1851–1925	William Lever	Soap	Employee welfare; Port Sunlight Village

Philanthropy is the practice of contributing personal wealth to charitable or similar causes.

Enlightened self-interest is the practice of acting in a way that is costly or inconvenient at present, but which is believed to be in one's best interest in the long term.

Applied ethics is the application of moral philosophy to actual problems, including those in management.

They recognised the social impact of industry and its potential to improve social conditions. By fostering an ethos of care, these industrialists offered a different business model and showed society what was possible. Their **philanthropy** helped define **enlightened self-interest** as a viable approach to business.

Some of today's business leaders give substantial donations to charities. Bill Gates (founder of Microsoft) gives very large sums to health and educational causes, and Jeff Skoll (ex-president of eBay, the online auction business) gave £5 million to the Said Business School at Oxford University. Lord Sainsbury, former head of the UK supermarket chain, is the country's most generous charitable donor – having already put £400 million into his Gatsby Charitable Foundation and planning to give another £600 million before he dies.

Growing public interest in corporate behaviour has encouraged more companies to manage issues of corporate responsibility, and to report publicly on how they do so. Some, such as The Body Shop and the Co-operative Bank, make a point of testing decisions against criteria of responsible corporate behaviour. Problems of **applied ethics** are complex, and some choose to ignore the problem by invoking economic imperatives rather than grapple with ethical concerns.

Activity 5.1   **Looking for responsible business activity**

Collect two examples of organisations that seem to be taking the matter seriously by introducing explicit policies on environmental, social or ethical matters. You could check some of the websites listed at the end of the chapter to see what they say about the companies' policies on corporate responsibility.

- What aspects of the business (e.g. inputs, transformation, outputs) does the policy cover?
- How did management develop the policy (e.g. which people or groups took part in forming it)?
- How do they ensure that people follow the policy, and that it has the expected effects?

Compare what you find with colleagues on your course and present a short summary, with questions for further research.

5.3   Perspectives on ethical behaviour

Before looking at some tools for exploring the ethical dilemmas facing management, use Activity 5.2 to locate your ethical position.

Three domains of human action

'Ethics' refers to a code of moral principles and values that guide human action by setting standards of what is acceptable. We can understand this more clearly if we compare ethics with actions that are governed by law and by free choice, which Figure 5.1 illustrates. Some actions fall within the domain of codified law – they are the subject of legislation that can be enforced in the courts. It is illegal in most European countries for managers to allow factory waste to pollute rivers. At the other extreme are actions in the domain of free choice – anyone can apply for another job.

Activity 5.2   Reflecting on your ethics

You are walking down the street. There is no one nearby and you see: (a) a 50 pence piece, (b) a £5 note, (c) a £50 note, (d) £100, (e) £1000.

- Do you keep it? Yes or no?
- The money you find was actually in a wallet with the owner's name and address in it. Does this make a difference?
- That name indicates to you that it belongs to: (a) a wealthy person, (b) a pensioner of modest means, (c) a single parent. Does this make a difference?
- Suppose there were some people nearby. Does this make a difference?

Explore your reasons for each of your decisions.

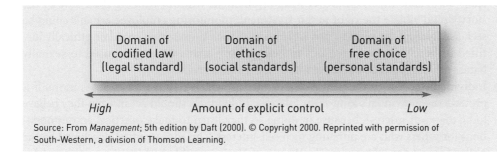

Source: From *Management*; 5th edition by Daft (2000). © Copyright 2000. Reprinted with permission of South-Western, a division of Thomson Learning.

Figure 5.1

Three domains of human action

In between are acts that have an ethical dimension. Laws do not prescribe action, but nor are people free to act as they wish: they are to some degree constrained by shared principles and values about acceptable behaviour in those circumstances. An ethically acceptable action is one that is legal *and* meets the shared ethical standards of the society – which raises the question of how people in that society form and express those standards: a standard that you think should be respected may be ignored by others.

Most ethical dilemmas involve a conflict between the needs of the part and the whole – the individual and the organisation, or the organisation and society:

- Should a company monitor websites to check that staff are not downloading paedophilia?
- Should airlines routinely test pilots for alcohol before they go on duty?
- Should food companies design and advertise products that make children obese?
- Should a company extend a quarry (and provide employment) in a national park?

The fact that people will give different answers to those questions shows that they are evaluating them against different criteria: what might they be?

Four criteria for justifying an action as ethical

Philosophers have identified four principles that people use to justify an action – moral principles, utilitarianism, human rights and individualism.

- **Moral principles** This approach evaluates whether a decision is consistent with an accepted moral principle. Societies develop rules that members generally accept (e.g. that people do not rob or deliberately injure each other) and which are valid in many situations, including organisations. If a decision fits such an accepted principle, it is ethically justified. This implies that a senior manager who accepts a high salary and bonus even if the company has performed badly would be acting unethically, as most people would feel it violated accepted ideas of fairness and equity.

- **Utilitarianism** This looks at an action from the point of view of its effect on overall human well-being: an act is morally right if it produces as great a balance of pleasure over pain as any alternative action. On this view, a manager who makes 20 per cent of a company's workforce redundant during a business downturn could justify their action as ethical if it enabled the company to survive, and so save the jobs of the others. The manager would be acting unethically (on this principle) if the savings were used to increase his or her salary.

- **Human rights** This is the idea that people have fundamental rights and liberties, and an ethically correct decision is one that best maintains the human rights of those affected. These rights could include those of consent, privacy, conscience, free speech, fair treatment, and to life and safety. Decisions that violate these rights may be unethical – so penalising an employee after an incident without hearing their side of the story would violate the right to fair treatment; monitoring employee e-mails could be seen as violating the right to privacy. However such monitoring could be ethically justified if there were good reasons to believe the e-mails were being used to sexually harass other people, so violating one of *their* human rights.

- **Individualism** This is the 'ethics of self-interest', which claims that an act is moral if it protects the individual's long-term interests. Individuals should act in what they believe to be their self-interest, because in doing so they learn to make practical accommodations for others who are pursuing *their* self-interest. This idea was first developed by the philosopher Adam Smith in *The Wealth of Nations*, published in 1776, reflecting his belief that following this principle will, paradoxically, result in the general good. The assumption is that people will only maximise their personal self-interest if they do things that others value and are willing to pay for. A counter-argument is that this assumption may be incorrect in some instances – such as if someone uses a position of privilege to enrich themselves, with no benefit to others.

Activity 5.3 Justifying actions

Think of actions which you have justified on the grounds that:

(a) it was fair to those affected
(b) it was the right thing to do
(c) it was the best option for yourself
(d) more people gained than lost.

Explain which of the ethical philosophies outlined above matches each reason.

These tools from moral philosophy enable a more analytical insight into management dilemmas, even if they lead to more questions than answers, which Table 5.2 illustrates. As in much of management, there are no right or wrong answers. These philosophical tools only enable people to recognise the arguments that others use to support an action. They can then evaluate them critically, and suggest an alternative philosophy that would lead to a different action. This makes the debate about management decisions with a moral dimension more transparent.

Table 5.2

Questions within
each philosophy

Philosophy	Dilemma
Moral principles	Who determines that a moral principle is 'generally accepted'? What if others claim that a principle leading to a different decision is equally 'accepted'?
Utilitarianism	Who determines the majority, and the population of which it is the greatest number? Is the benefit to them assessed over the short term or the long term?
Human rights	Actions usually involve several people – what if the decision would protect the rights of some, but breach the rights of others? How do you compare them?
Individualism	Whose self-interest is central to the debate? What if the action of one damages the self-interest of another?

Activity 5.4 Visualising a management dilemma

Capacity in the European motor industry exceeds demand by 7 million units, so many manufacturers are considering closing at least one plant. Imagine you are the chair of a global motor company. Your shareholders expect profits, and as a global company you are profitable: but you are losing money in Europe and need to reduce costs. While you and other companies are considering plant closures, trade unions and governments oppose them.

- Your company has several plants in Europe. What criteria should you use to select the one to close? Do you ask for further information on the social impact that any closure might have?
- Might it be better to reduce the size of several plants rather than close one? Should you take social concerns into account in your decision?
- What solution would each ethical philosophy justify?

Imagine the problem is not one of reducing capacity but of relocating it. Demand in the developing world is growing rapidly, and major companies are tempted to move capacity to these areas.

- Should a (profitable) plant be moved from an economically poor European region to a country in south-east Asia whose government offers incentives? It could operate with a cheaper workforce, fewer rules about health, safety and environmental protection, and weak trade unions. It would be more profitable and would improve living standards of people in the area.

Carroll (1989) notes that whenever people make decisions about what is ethical, they are likely to come to different conclusions, for the reasons shown in Figure 5.2. This shows three elements – the action being evaluated; prevailing norms of acceptability; and the person's value judgements about both of these. It would be surprising if two people considering the rightness of an action did *not* reach different conclusions.

There is an additional philosophy called **ethical relativism** that managers, especially of companies operating in many countries, use to justify what they do.

Ethical relativism is the principle that ethical judgements cannot be made independently of the culture in which the issue arises.

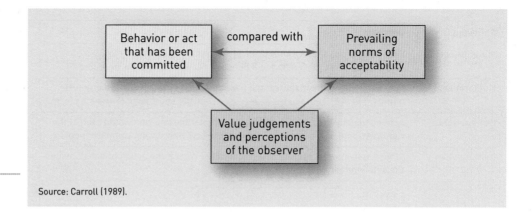

Figure 5.2

Making ethical judgements

Source: Carroll (1989).

Universal or relative ethics?

People face a difficulty when an action that is acceptable in the country where they are working would not be accepted in their home country. On the universal perspective, people should act in an ethically consistent way irrespective of where they are. The opposite view – relativism – stresses the role of national context, arguing that people should incorporate local conditions and norms in making ethical decisions because they have a duty to follow local moral standards. If local and home country norms conflict, people should follow the local norms. For companies that operate internationally ethical relativism is a convenient philosophy, especially when their competitors are from countries where bribes are an expected part of business. The issue arises in dramatic ways when major deals for armaments or construction projects are offered to competitive tender from international companies. While from the point of view of the company ethical relativism may secure the business, it may cause difficulties for individual managers if their personal ethical views are more universal than relative.

Strict ethics at Wipro www.wipro.com

Wipro (Chapter 7 case) is one of India's leading hi-tech businesses, and in the early days its founder, Azim Premji, took a firm stand on ethics. Steve Hamm (2007) writes:

> In the late 1960s and early 1970s corruption was rampant in the Indian economy. Government officials asked for kickbacks. Farmers bribed clerks to tamper with weighing machines ... Premji set a zero-tolerance policy for bribes and any form of corruption or corner-cutting – from top managers to laborers ... 'We said anybody committing a breach of integrity would lose their job. It's open and shut and black and white,' Premji says. It took several firings before people believed it. But finally they did. The company stood out, and not just from the local Indian outfits. Some of the multinationals had fallen into the trap of paying bribes as well. (p. 35)

Source: Hamm (2007).

Think again about some of the ethical decisions you have considered in this chapter. Does ethical relativism help a decision on corporate gifts? Some consider that if it is standard industry practice to exchange gifts this creates a level playing field, so that giving cannot be an incentive. Others have a policy that no gift to employees from any other company is acceptable as it may affect employees' judgement.

Activity 5.5 Accepting a gift

In your job as a buyer for a multinational company you receive a gift from one of your suppliers at Christmas. It is: (a) a calendar with their brand name on it, (b) a pen set with their brand name on it, (c) a bottle of whisky, (d) a case of whisky, (e) an invitation to a major sporting event, (f) an invitation to a luxury holiday at the supplier's expense.

- Which offer can you accept, if any? What should you do with it? What would stop you accepting these gifts?
- Should your employer have a policy that outlines solutions to such ethical problems?
- Research a chosen company to find out whether they have an ethics policy. What areas of concern are highlighted?

Ethical decision-making models

Setting out ethical criteria such as these focuses attention on the beliefs of the individual, but ignores the social context in which people face ethical decisions. Conversely, arguing that ethics reflect the culture of the organisation, which can put pressure on people to accept established practices, however unethical, ignores the scope for individual choice and action. A way of reconciling these perspectives is to adopt an **ethical decision-making** framework. This examines the influence of both individual characteristics (such as personal value systems) and organisational contexts (such as its structure and distribution of power) on ethical choices. For example Trevino (1986) sees ethical (or unethical) action as the result of individual and situational components – shown in Figure 5.3. Faced with an ethical dilemma (such as those in Activity 5.4), an individual's action is shaped by individual and situational moderators. Bartlett (2003) contains an extensive review of this and similar models.

> **Ethical decision-making models** examine the influence of individual characteristics and organisational policies on ethical decisions.

The Ford Pinto – the case continues www.ford.com   CASE STUDY

Court records showed that Ford's top managers knew that the Pinto was unsafe, but concluded that it was cheaper to incur the losses from lawsuits than to fix the cars. Production staff also knew of the risks, but were never given the opportunity to tell top management about it. Ford's 'profit drives principle' philosophy of the time discouraged staff from drawing attention to risks. Actions were guided by the original aim for the Pinto – '2000 pounds for $2000' – and a 'safety doesn't sell' mindset. Insiders believed they were acting in line with company values. Richard Pascale (1990) noted that during the 1970s:

The company was financially focused. Cost accounting drove suboptimal design decisions at the front edge of the product development process. In the factories, a system tied a large percentage of plant managers' compensation to volume, driving plants to build cars as rapidly as possible and worry about the defects later. (Pascale, 1990, pp. 116–117)

These practices were rooted in the distant past, and did not address the issues the company was facing in the late 1970s, when consumers were more concerned about safety and less concerned about price.

When a new chief executive took over, he went to great lengths to consult with top managers about major ▶

decisions. He wanted to break away from the previously autocratic 'do as I say' style of management, and to encourage debate and discussion: which may enable people to raise ethical issues early in the decision-making process.

Sources: Pascale (1990); Nutt (2002).

Case questions 5.2

● Does the ethical decision-making model help explain the decisions made by Ford at that time?

● How did the style of the new chief executive alter the likelihood of a similar scandal arising?

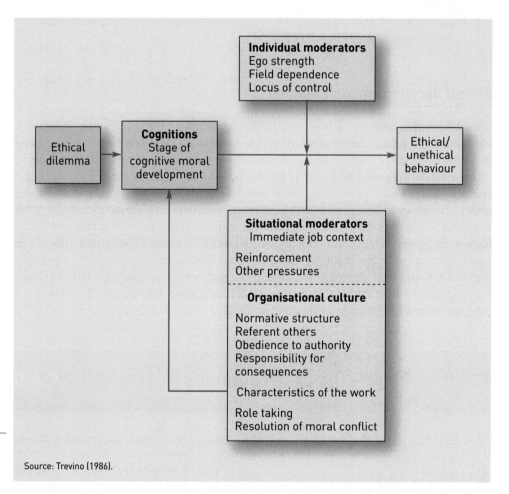

Figure 5.3

Trevino's model of ethical decision making

Source: Trevino (1986).

5.4   The role of business in society

The chapter now moves from individual ethical choices to the wider issue of corporate responsibility. The discussion begins by outlining the contrasting criteria people can use to judge performance, and hence what they expect of business behaviour, and then presents the 'Friedman' and 'wider responsibility' positions.

Positioning corporate responsibility

Figure 5.4 presents a way of analysing how managers can respond to ideas and opportunities of socially responsible behaviour. Four possibilities (Carroll, 1999) are in a continuum, from economic responsibilities on the left-hand side through to discretionary responsibilities on the other. This builds on the ideas in Figure 5.1, and locates ethical issues between the areas of legal and discretionary actions.

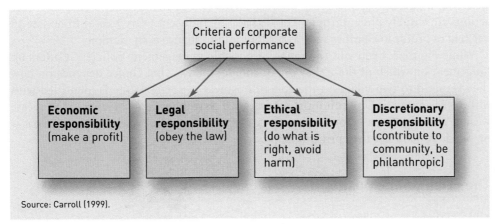

Source: Carroll (1999).

Figure 5.4
Criteria of corporate social performance

Economic responsibilities

Here managers focus on serving the economic interests of the company and its shareholders. They act to support that aim, regardless of the effects on communities or other considerations. An example was when Burberry, the luxury goods retailer, decided to close one of its few remaining UK factories. The finance director was questioned by the media about the decision, and she commented:

> Ultimately if a factory isn't commercially viable you have to take the decision to close ... that's what your obligations to your shareholders dictate. When you know you've made the right decision commercially, you have to stay true to that. These are the facts – commercial realities reign. (*Financial Times*, 15 February 2007, p. 3)

Legal responsibilities

Society expects managers to obey the law – by not polluting rivers, selling faulty goods or providing misleading information to investors. These issues reflect areas that society has decided were sufficiently important to pass laws regulating company behaviour in the wider interest. Some companies will take these responsibilities seriously – but will go no further. If what they do is legal, then that is their only criterion – even if the decision has damaging consequences for others. Managers involved with the Ford Pinto scandal took this view.

Ethical responsibilities

This area includes actions that are not specified by law, and may not serve a company's narrow economic interests. Managers take these actions because they believe they meet some wider social interest, such as discouraging tobacco consumption, protecting the natural environment or supporting a socially disadvantaged group. They may do so in the belief that these will complement their economic responsibilities by, for example, enhancing their reputation with customers or local communities. Announcements by companies such as Marks & Spencer (Chapter 8 case) or Tesco that they will trade in a carbon-neutral way are examples.

Discretionary responsibilities

This covers actions that are entirely voluntary, not being shaped by economic, legal or ethical considerations. They include anonymous donations with no expectation or possibility of a payback, sponsorship of local events and contributions to charities – the actions are entirely philanthropic. The decision by Innocent (Part 1 case) to donate 10 per cent of profits to charities such as the Rainforest Alliance is an example.

While Figure 5.4 sets out the range of possible management policies, it offers no judgement on which of these they do, or should, follow. That choice depends on how they respond to two views on the role of business in society. One is identified with Milton Friedman, a US economist who argued that the role of business is to create wealth. The other is based on the idea of corporate responsibility, where the emphasis is on public good rather than private gain.

The Friedmanite position

Milton Friedman was clear:

> [In a free economy] there is one and only one social responsibility of business – to use its resources and engage in activities designed to increase its profits so long as it stays within the rules of the game, which is to say, engages in open and free competition, without deception or fraud. (1962, p. 133)

As an economist, Friedman believed that operating business 'without deception or fraud' provided sufficient social benefit through the creation of wealth or employment. In terms of Figure 5.4, managers should concern themselves only with the two left hand boxes – economic and legal responsibilities. For a business to give money away to charitable purposes was equivalent to self-imposed taxation. He argued that the board of directors in charge of a business should concentrate on generating wealth for shareholders, and distributing it to them. Shareholders could then decide if they wished to use that income to support social causes (Margolis and Walsh, 2003).

Henderson (2001) develops this view, arguing that for business to take on responsibilities which are the domain of government harms, rather than enhances, human welfare. Others point out that meeting stringent environmental or other regulations inevitably increases costs, and makes a business less competitive than those operating in countries with less interest in the topic (Stavins, 1994). Investing in socially responsible but unprofitable ventures will ultimately damage the firm and so be unsustainable.

Corporate responsibility as a moral obligation

Others disagree, taking the view that corporations have both the resources and the moral obligations to act in ways that benefit others – such as by ensuring suppliers treat staff fairly, minimising environmental damage, treating customers honestly and giving generously to charity. They maintain that while society depends on business for goods and services, business in turn depends on society. It requires inputs – employees, capital and physical resources – and the socially created institutions that enable business to operate – such as a legal and education system.

The moral case for corporate responsibility reflects this interdependency: society and business have mutual obligations within a **social contract**. What people expect of companies changes. The Ford Pinto case shows that producers had little interest in safety in the late 1960s – and nor did motorists. Pressure groups can persuade governments to legislate to protect consumers from undesirable selling practices or faulty goods and services. Public demand for recycled or more environmentally friendly goods has prompted changes in corporate behaviour and products.

> The **social contract** consists of the mutual obligations that society and business recognise they have to each other.

Activity 5.6   Critical reflection on the role of business

Try to gather information from acquaintances or relatives in business about which of these views (Friedman and corporate responsibility):

- they personally favour
- they believe has most influence on practice in their company.

- If you work in an organisation, which view guides policy?
- Do you agree with that balance?
- How would practice change if the other view was dominant?

Case questions 5.3

- Did Ford act unethically at that time? Should the law be the only influence on a corporation's actions? What responsibilities do you think a major company has?
- Ford used cost–benefit analysis to decide what to do – could this have been improved? Was it a useful decision tool in this case?
- Imagine you were a Ford manager at this time. What would you have done, and why? List the social costs and benefits to the company and society of the alternatives to help you determine your answer.
- Imagine you worked for Ford as an engineer and were aware of this potential design fault. What would you do? What, if any, are your responsibilities to the customer and/or your employer?

Taking a Friedmanite position implies a relatively simple prescription for managers – do what is best for the business and the shareholders. The alternative perspective regards responsible corporate behaviour as a form of enlightened self-interest, in the sense that it can satisfy both economic *and* moral expectations. Managers may add more value (and serve their shareholders better) if they interpret their responsibilities more widely than implied by the Friedmanite position, but do so in ways that bring economic benefits to the business. Which of these approaches managers adopt will reflect how they interpret the relative power and interests of their stakeholders.

key ideas   **David Vogel on responsibility and strategy**

Vogel (2005) examines the claims for and against the idea that corporations should act responsibly, by analysing the forces driving the corporate responsibility (CR) movement. He concludes that while the managers of businesses that are prominent advocates of CR (The Body Shop or Co-operative Financial Services amongst many others) are genuinely motivated by a commitment to social goals, CR is only sustainable if 'virtue pays off'. He acknowledges that not every business expenditure or policy needs to directly increase shareholder value, and that many of the benefits of responsible action are difficult to quantify. But ultimately responsible action is both made possible, and constrained, by market forces.

Market forces encourage and also limit responsible corporate action. Encouraging forces include demand for responsibly made products, consumer boycotts, challenges to a firm's reputation by non-governmental organisations (NGOs) such as Greenpeace, pressure from ethical investors and the values of managers and employees. This has led many firms to accept that they need to be accountable to a broad community of stakeholders. Virtuous behaviour can make business sense for some firms in some areas in some circumstances:

> Many of the proponents of [CR] mistakenly assume that because some companies are behaving more responsibly in some areas, [more] firms can be expected to behave responsibly in more areas. This assumption is misinformed. There *is* a place in the market economy for responsible firms. But there is also a large place for their less responsible competitors. (p. 3)

While some companies can benefit from acting responsibly, market forces alone cannot prevent others from acting in less responsible ways, and profiting from doing so.

Source: Vogel (2005).

5.5   Stakeholders and corporate responsibility

A stakeholder perspective on CR

Corporate responsibility is the awareness, acceptance and management of the wider implications of corporate decisions.

Ethical investors are people who only invest in businesses that meet specified criteria of ethical behaviour.

How managers respond to ideas of **corporate responsibility** may be understood by recalling stakeholder theory, introduced in Chapter 3. This expresses the idea that organisations have internal and external stakeholders with an interest in, or who are affected by, what the organisation does. As well as shareholders these will typically include customers, employees, suppliers and the communities in which the organisation works. Many now add **ethical investors** and pressure groups advocating care for the natural environment to the list. Table 5.3 lists and illustrates the stakeholders with an interest in the extent to which managers aim to act responsibly.

These stakeholders can make things uncomfortable if they disapprove of managers' policies by, amongst other things:

- negative publicity in local and national media
- direct action and protests – blockading premises
- threats or actual legal action
- withholding planning or other permissions necessary for operations.

If managers can satisfy stakeholders' (often conflicting) expectations to an acceptable degree, they will retain their support. As Egan and Wilson (2002) point out, some companies are able to balance:

responsibility and corporate success, and that the enlightened shareholder understands that it is in his or her best long-term interests that the company performs [in a way that satisfies all stakeholders]. (p. 174)

Table 5.3

Stakeholders and interests in relation to corporate responsibility (CR)

Stakeholders	Expectations
Employees	Employment, security, safe working conditions, rewarding work, fairness in promotion, security and pay
Shareholders	Financially centred investors: high return on investment Ethical investors: strong CR policies and reputation
Suppliers	Fair terms, prompt payment, long-term relationships
Customers	Majority – price, quality, durability and safety Minority (ethical consumers) – Fairtrade sources, fair treatment of staff, care for environment
Communities	Employment, income, limits on pollution and noise
Competitors	Fair competition, follow the norms of behaviour in the industry
Governments	Pay taxes, obey laws, provide economic opportunities
Environmental campaigners	Minimise pollution, emissions, waste, and assist recycling
NGOs	Actions that support policies
Charities and causes	Donations and gifts in kind

Case questions 5.4

- What did customers of Ford expect of the Pinto at that time?
- Would customers today have different expectations?
- Does that affect your view of the company's actions?
- What other stakeholders would have been affected by Ford's decisions?

Stakeholder power and corporate policy

Stakeholders vary in their ability to influence managers. If the most powerful expect a company to follow a Friedmanite position managers will deliver that, perhaps with some public commitment to socially acceptable practice. Many businesses fall into this group. At the other extreme, some people (stakeholders) create organisations to promote an interest – working conditions, inequality, Third World debt or care for the natural environment. Their managers will focus on policies and practices that support those aims. In between are managers who are aware that shareholders expect an acceptable financial return, but believe that they can best deliver that return by meeting, to some degree, the expectations of other stakeholders. This may have a cost, but can also avoid negative publicity, enhance reputation, or attract customers – it is enlightened self-interest: 'Firms with this perspective will invest in social initiatives because they believe that such investments will result in increased profitability' (Peloza, 2006). Companies follow a range of policies as part of the enlightened self-interest approach – mission; target specified customers; as part of wider strategy; and to avoid negative publicity.

Responsible action as the corporate mission

Some companies have positioned corporate responsibility at the heart of their business, reflecting the beliefs and values of founders and senior managers. They gain media attention and increase customer loyalty with little advertising. Familiar examples are The Body Shop and the Co-operative Bank. This approach worked for The Body Shop, and helped it become a major retailing group. However, its unique position was eroded – partly by its own success. Animal testing of cosmetics (one of the firm's early campaigns) was stopped, and more people are aware of environmental issues. So a strategically valuable position, benefiting those it aimed to help, came under competitive threat – the company is now owned by the French cosmetics group, L'Oréal.

management in practice   **The Body Shop**   www.the-body-shop.com

Anita Roddick (1943–2007) founded The Body Shop to show that ethical behaviour could co-exist with a profitable business. The company mission was: 'To dedicate our business to the pursuit of social and environmental change'. She wrote:

Social and environmental issues are woven into the fabric of the company itself. Not a single decision is taken in Body Shop without considering them. We have an Environmental Projects Department which monitors the company's practices and products to ensure they are environmentally sound. We have a simple credo. You can run a business differently from the way most businesses are run: you can share your prosperity with your employees; you can rewrite the book of how a company interacts with the community; you can rewrite the book on third world trade ... You can do all this and still raise money, and give shareholders a wondrous return on their money. (p. 24)

Source: Roddick, 1991.

Another example of a company that was founded on social rather than purely commercial principles is the Co-operative Bank (now known as Co-operative Financial Services) which was founded as a cooperative enterprise in the 1870s. It launched its present ethical policy in May 1992 and is now one of the leading examples of this approach.

Activity 5.7   **Critical reflection on ethical policies**

Visit the CFS website (**www.cfs.co.uk**).

- Which partners does it identify?
- Take any one of those partners, and find out from the site what the company believes to be their main concerns, and how it tries to meet them.
- How does CFS monitor its ethical performance?

If you work in an organisation:

- Which, if any, of these sources of pressure have influenced management practice?

Activity 5.8   Revising Activity 5.4

- Using the stakeholders listed above, try again to solve the dilemma of closing the factory in Activity 5.4. Whose 'stake' within the company should be given priority above the others? What did you decide?
- Do you think that, as a global company, you have specific local responsibilities or a major responsibility to maintain a profitable company for the good of shareholders, customers and workers worldwide?

Responsible action to meet customer needs

Other companies, while not focused on responsibility as a mission, focus on meeting the needs of **ethical consumers** – those who take ethical issues into account when making a purchase, and try to avoid buying products from companies that damage the environment, deal with oppressive regimes, have a poor record on animal rights or pay low wages. Such consumer action is not solely a negative response to corporate activities. Many shoppers use their 'ethical purchase votes' (Smith, 1990) to support the actions of companies that conduct business responsibly. Café Direct and Green & Black Chocolate have been the biggest successes of 'fairly traded' products. Co-operative Financial Services produces an annual survey on the shopping habits of a sample of consumers who join their ethical panel: the latest 'ethical consumerism research report' is available on the ethical policy pages of the website.

Ethical consumers are those who take ethical issues into account in deciding what to purchase.

Red – Bono and the fight against Aids in Africa

management in practice

In 2006 Bono, lead singer with U2, announced the creation of his new brand – Red – which will dedicate some of its revenue to fight Aids in Africa. The effort will include a series of joint ventures with companies such as American Express, Georgio Armani and Gap to sell products under the brand (go to www.gap.com and you will see the red brands featured). They will be marketed first in the United Kingdom to an estimated 1.5 million 'conscience consumers' who are seen as more likely to buy products associated with a social benefit. Other products available will include Converse sports shoes made with African mud-cloth, a new line of Gap vintage T-shirts and wraparound Armani sunglasses.

'I think doing the Red thing, doing good, will turn out to be good business for them', said Bono, who has long been associated with campaigns on African debt relief, Aids, and unfair trading rules that hurt the continent's poor. This and similar efforts are being supported by big companies worried that television advertising is losing its punch. The idea is that using good works or services will gain consumer attention – what some call 'corporate social opportunity'.

Sources: *Financial Times*, 26 January 2006, *Independent*, 13 May 2006.

Responsible action as part of strategy

Others follow sustainable policies not out of philanthropy but because it fits their business strategy. Using energy efficiently, avoiding waste and treating staff with respect are established daily practices in many companies – some of whom now present such practices as part of a responsible image. Reebok and Nike introduced codes of practice to eliminate child labour in manufacturing their products, reflecting wide concerns about the exploitation of children in the developing world. Major supermarkets now stock Fair-trade products. In 2006 Wal-Mart, long criticised (though not by its customers) for focusing on low prices at the expense of everything else, announced targets for reducing greenhouse gas emissions and cutting waste. The chief executive also committed the company to working with its suppliers to promote good environmental practices. Tesco announced a long-term plan to label all its products to show the amount of carbon dioxide emitted during their production, transport and consumption.

 **management in practice** Sustainable coffee www.kraft.com

Kraft Foods, which buys about 10 per cent of the world's coffee, has agreed to blend sustainably produced beans into its main European brands, which include Kenco, Jacobs and Carte Noire. The deal with the non-profit Rainforest Alliance is the most serious attempt by a big coffee purchaser to tackle the crisis that has pushed down the commodity price, which is often below the cost of production. This threatens the livelihood of 25 million coffee farmers, and the long-term supply of beans. Said a senior Kraft commodity manager:

> We need to make sure we can get the coffees we need 20 years from now. This is not philanthropy. This is about incorporating sustainable coffee into our mainstream brands as a way to have a more efficient and competitive way of doing business.

Kraft will buy £5 million worth of Rainforest Alliance-certified coffee in the first year, paying farmers a premium of 20 per cent. The company also plans to introduce a brand of coffee aimed at the away-from-home market, which includes universities and other institutions seen as sensitive to issues of global equity.

Brokers said the deal would send a signal to the entire supply chain, particularly producers, that roasters are concerned about more than just the purity of the coffee and may pay more knowing that the beans have been produced using good environmental practices by workers who are adequately paid.

Source: *Financial Times*, 7 October 2003; company website.

Some firms invest in educational projects to improve the social climate in which the firm operates, or to ensure long-term supply of staff. In coordinating such a programme, Cisco (a big supplier of switching equipment for computer networks) aligns its economic and social goals by ensuring a supply of well-trained employees.

Responsible action to avoid negative publicity

Another way in which responsible behaviour may enhance performance is through its effect on company reputation. Many companies differentiate themselves less by their products than by the ideas, emotions and images that their brand conveys. Managers who allow their brand to become associated with being hostile to people, communities or the natural environment are taking a grave risk. Adopting responsible practices enables a firm to imbue the brand with positive themes that coincide with the beliefs of many customers. The value of a positive reputation is 'precisely because [developing one] takes considerable time and depends on a firm making stable and consistent investments' (Roberts and Dowling, 2002).

This valuable asset can be damaged if activists target the company. Companies such as Nike, Shell, McDonald's and Starbucks have all faced well-organised campaigns. In 2007 students at many UK universities banned the sale of Coca-Cola in their student union bars and shops in protest at the company's activities in India, including taking water from rivers, water that would otherwise have been used by farmers (*Independent*, 10 March 2007, p. 13).

5.6 Managing company ethics

Managers who wish to improve the level of socially responsible behaviour in their company use several methods to do so, including: leading by example; codes of ethics; ethical structures and reporting; and inclusion in the FTSE4Good Index Series.

Leading by example

Leaders set the tone for an organisation by their actions. If others see they are acting in line with stated ethical principles their credibility will rise and others are likely to follow. Leaders who are known to be engaging in malpractice are likely to encourage its spread throughout the business.

Code of ethics

A code of ethics is a formal statement of the company's values, setting out general principles on matters such as quality, employees or the environment. Others set out procedures for situations – such as conflicts of interest or the acceptance of gifts. Their effectiveness depends on the extent to which top management supports them with sanctions and rewards.

Ethical structures and reporting

These are the formal systems and roles that a company may create to support ethical behaviour. An ethics committee is a group of executives appointed to oversee and communicate a company's ethics policy. It may provide rulings on difficult issues, and discipline transgressors. Most companies now include a corporate responsibility statement in their annual report, and may include in this an **ethical audit** profiling current practice.

Ethical audits are the practice of systematically reviewing the extent to which an organisation's actions are consistent with its stated ethical intentions.

Director of corporate responsibility at Vodafone
www.vodafone.com

Charlotte Grezo was appointed as director of corporate responsibility at Vodafone in 2001. Her brief was to create a group-wide strategy for corporate responsibility. Her team works closely with staff in the operating companies to decide the issues to put to the group operational review committee that sits just below board level. She refers to corporate responsibility simply as being 'responsible in the way we run our business and interact with society and the environment'. In the Corporate Responsibility Report for the year to 31 March 2006 she wrote:

> We have come a long way since we started in 2001, our business is highly dynamic and as we enter new markets and embrace new technologies we encounter new CR issues.

Amongst the concerns raised by investors was 'adult content'. The company is working to address these concerns, but as a multinational must be careful not to impose moral standards or limit customer choice. Current areas of activity for the corporate responsibility group include: supply chain standards (such as ensuring that raw materials for handsets are mined in a sustainable way); responsible marketing (preventing children accessing pornography via a handset); electro-magnetic fields and health; energy efficiency; handset recycling; waste management; and wireless applications with social benefits.

Source: Company website.

Inclusion in the FTSE4Good Index Series www.FTSE4Good.com

The FTSE4Good Index Series provides investors with guidance on companies that meet defined criteria of social responsibility. These are developed in consultation with NGOs, governments and others, and to be included in the Index companies need to show they are:

- developing positive relations with stakeholders
- working towards environmental sustainability
- upholding and supporting universal human rights
- ensuring good supply-chain labour standards, and
- countering bribery.

Simon Sproule, corporate vice-president at Nissan, comments:

> Trust is fast becoming one of the most valued assets in any organisation. Without the trust of our stakeholders, the sustainability of our business is at risk. Being included in the FTSE4Good Index is a key element for Nissan to demonstrate its commitment to a sustainable business that inspires trust from all our stakeholders.

5.7 Corporate governance

How managers deal with corporate responsibility will be influenced by the framework of corporate governance within which they work. This establishes who the organisation is there to serve, how this should be decided, and by whom. The issue arises because in capitalist economies ownership is separated from control. The founder provides the initial capital but growth requires further capital that is supplied (depending on the local economic system) by external parties.

In Anglo-American economies this usually means issuing shares so that ownership becomes diffuse – with shares held by many individuals and institutions who cannot supervise management decisions closely. It then becomes possible for managers to run a corporation to serve their own ends. Scandals such as those at Enron and Parmalat give new urgency to the task of creating mechanisms to ensure that managers act in the interests of shareholders.

While some see corporate governance as being essentially a matter between managers and shareholders (Sternberg, 2004), others broaden the debate to include a range of stakeholders and considerations (Egan and Wilson, 2002). On this view, the framework of governance should be designed to ensure that managers act in the interests not only of shareholders but of a wider range of stakeholders.

Whichever view people take, the key concept in corporate governance is accountability – 'that individuals and institutions are answerable for what they do: they must account to others for their conduct and for their use of resources' (Sternberg, 2004, p. 41). In Anglo-American systems the main mechanisms for corporate governance are:

- the powers and responsibilities of directors
- the requirement that directors report periodically to shareholders
- the requirement that certain appointments and types of action require explicit shareholder approval.

Directors and senior executives

There is a fundamental difference between the responsibilities of directors and those of senior executives. The main responsibility of the board of directors is to set policy, authorise key decisions, appoint senior executives and auditors, monitor executive performance and decide executive pay. The responsibility of senior executives is to implement decisions of the board. A key issue is the extent to which directors are able and willing to challenge executive actions: several scandals have arisen when directors, for whatever reason, failed to probe sufficiently closely the information that executives provided.

As well as the main board, large companies will usually have several board committees, overseeing different aspects of the business – see Management in Practice.

Corporate governance at BP   www.bp.com

BP's governance policies require a majority of the board to be composed of independant non-executive directors – people with relevant experience from outside the organisation. BP has five board committees, each of which is made up entirely of non-executive directors, and none of BP's executive directors may serve as a member of a board committee.

Chairman's committee	Comprises all the non-executive directors and deals with broad issues of governance, including matters referred to it for an opinion from any other board committee.
Audit committee	Monitors all reporting, accounting, financial and control aspects of the executive management's activities.
Safety, ethics and environment assurance	Monitors all non-financial aspects of the executive management's activities.
Remuneration committee	Determines the terms of engagement and remuneration of the executive directors
Nomination committee	Identifies and evaluates candidates for appointment and reappointment as directors or company secretary of BP.

Source: *BP Annual Report and Accounts 2006.*

Periodic reports

A second mechanism for ensuring accountability is through providing information about performance to stakeholders. The annual report and accounts are intended to give shareholders the information they need to judge the performance of the directors and senior executives. These are scrutinised by specialist firms of external auditors (appointed by the shareholders at the annual meeting) to ensure they give a true and fair view. Many companies now include Corporate Responsibility Reports, setting out how well they have met their targets in these areas.

Annual meeting

The annual general meeting (AGM) is another mechanism for ensuring directors are accountable to shareholders, as they are an opportunity for the shareholders to review company performance. These meetings can be attended by anyone holding shares in the company. Many pressure groups buy a token share in companies of which they disapprove and attend the AGM to challenge certain company actions, notably on environmental issues.

Governance systems and responsibility

The accountability systems sketched above reflect the methods typically used in countries modelled on UK and US practice, and there is a debate about the respective merits of alternative governance systems. In the present context, some argue that the Anglo-American system encourages a short-term view of the business, since shareholders can press managements to pursue short-term gains at the expense of long-term investment, and thus discourage them from giving due weight to environmental or other issues. Continuing concern about corporate performance, whether from a shareholder or broader stakeholder perspective, ensures that governments will continue to look closely at ways of strengthening corporate governance frameworks.

5.8   Current themes and issues

Performance

One part of the debate about corporate responsibility is whether it affects performance – as measured by company profitability. A meta-analysis found a generally positive relationship between responsible corporate behaviour and financial performance (Orlitzky *et al.*, 2003), but Vogel (2005) is more sceptical. He found some studies showing a positive relationship between, for example, the level of emission reduction and financial performance for firms in manufacturing and mining. However, the direction of causality was unclear – it could be that profitable firms were able to invest in expensive equipment to reduce emissions. Another possibility is that other variables not included in the research affected both variables under study. Some other studies showed a positive relationship, some a negative one, and others a mixed one. Overall the relationship between corporate responsibility and profitability is inconclusive.

Vogel drew attention to several limitations in studies of the relationship between CR and performance, including:

- different measures of financial performance (one review of 95 studies found that they had 49 different accounting measures);
- different measures of corporate responsibility (95 studies used 27 different data sources);
- the validity of some of the measures is questionable (some rankings only represent the views of executives in the industry);
- many rankings are subjective.

His overall conclusion is that the relationship between responsible behaviour and performance must be treated with caution:

> just as firms that spend more on marketing are not necessarily more profitable than those that spend less, there is no reason to expect more responsible firms to outperform less responsible ones. (p. 33)

Responsibility

An aspect of corporate responsibility that is currently attracting great interest is climate change – which some see as the greatest challenge facing the world. Governments and international bodies are developing policies to slow the release of carbon dioxide emissions, and one aspect of this has been the launch of emission trading schemes. These enable companies to buy or sell certified emission reductions (CERs) in the market which, Kolk and Pinkse (2005) point out, gives companies some clear strategic choices in how they respond to the problem. They can change their processes to reduce emissions (an 'innovation' approach); they can buy emissions certificates from other companies (a 'compensation' approach); or they can do both. Any of these approaches can be made by the company acting alone or in conjunction with other organisations.

A company that takes the innovative approach would try to improve its operating processes to reduce emissions, or it could develop new products (such as Shell investing in systems to produce solar energy). If it reduced emissions sufficiently, it could earn CERs that it could then sell to other companies. These could be companies that were big energy users, or which found it hard to change their processes quickly. It might then be more profitable for them to retain their existing process much as they are, and compensate for this by buying CERs in the market – which would give them the right to continue operating.

Such schemes are in their early stages, but illustrate a broader point from this chapter that management decisions on corporate responsibility can best be understood by relating them to the wider strategic interests of the company.

Internationalisation

A common response by firms to such competitive pressure on performance has been to outsource parts of their operation to countries overseas, where labour is cheaper and environmental controls lax or non-existent. This reduces costs and helps them meet customer demands. However in doing so they may damage the interests of staff in their home country, and their local communities. Their overseas suppliers may employ child labour, exploit their staff, and cause environmental damage that would be unacceptable in the home country. The Management in Practice feature shows how BT tried to manage this dilemma.

BT – responsible offshoring?

management in practice

When BT implemented its decision to open call centres in India, consolidating its UK centres led to the loss of 2000 jobs. Within a year, however, all but four had found new jobs within BT, taken voluntary redundancy, or left for other reasons, such as changing domestic circumstances. BT had signed an agreement with the union representing professional and managerial staff, ruling out forced redundancies and undertaking to ensure that overseas suppliers treat their workers well. It has two call centres in India, which must follow an agreed code of practice, and work to ensure employee development and satisfaction.

However a review of BT outsourcing did recommend that in future BT should give stakeholders, including trade unions, more say at an earlier stage of the outsourcing process. **FT**

Source: *Financial Times*, 8 March 2004.

Another theme is that internationalisation has enabled some MNCs to become progressively more powerful, such that they can no longer be monitored or controlled by national governments. Many critics also see little effective international regulation. To some extent this gap is filled by NGOs and other activists, who attempt to encourage changes in business practice that governments and international agencies have been unable or unwilling to introduce. Some favour the use of trade agreements to restrict imports of irresponsibly produced goods, either because of the natural resources or the labour practices used in their production.

Conversely, internationalisation can make some companies more vulnerable to activists' campaigns, especially where they have created global brands that are recognised and consumed in many countries. NGOs can use this to put pressure on the companies concerned: they pass information to consumers in many countries about, for example, Coca-Cola's dispute over the damage its production practices have done to nearby farms in India, or about BP's weak safety record in the United States.

Summary

1 **Give examples of contrasts in business practice, including those that damage firms' reputation**

- Negative examples include poor treatment of suppliers or staff, wasteful uses of energy and other resources during transformation, and unfair treatment of customers. Reputations are also damaged by cases of senior management fraud or high compensation to failed managers.

- In contrast there are many examples of philanthropy, in which people give to charities and other causes without expecting any specific benefit in return.

2 **Decide which ethical theory someone is using to justify an action**

- Moral principles – the decision is consistent with generally accepted principles.

- Utilitarianism – the decision that benefits the greatest number of people is the right one to take.

- Human rights – decisions that support one of several human rights (such as privacy) are right.

- Individualism – decisions that serve the individual's self-interest are right – in the long run they will benefit society as well.

3 **Use a model of ethical decision making to identify organisational influences on ethical choice**

- Trevino's model combines individual factors with those in their organisational context to take account of the range of factors that shape individual actions as ethical or otherwise.

4 **Compare an organisation's policies with alternative views on the role of business in society**

- Milton Friedman's view that the only function of business is to act legally in the interests of shareholders.

- The social responsibility view that business has wider responsibilities, since it depends on aspects of the society in which it operates. It recognises the legitimate claims of a range of stakeholders and seeks an acceptable balance between them.

5 Explain an organisation's policy on responsible behaviour in terms of its stakeholders

- To explain an organisation's interpretation of responsible behaviour, use the concept of stakeholders. Those with most power will have most influence on the approach used.

- The chapter then distinguished between those that interpret responsible behaviour as their mission, as an attempt to satisfy particular customer groups, or as part of their wider commercial strategy.

6 Outline the structures and frameworks for corporate governance that managers can use to encourage responsible behaviour

- Structures for encouraging ethical behaviour include leading by example, codes of ethics, ethics committees, ethical audits and ethical reporting.

- Corporate governance frameworks depend on systems for providing adequate information, and this implies clarifying the roles of directors in relation to executives, annual reporting and annual meetings of shareholders.

Review questions

1 Identify two recent examples of corporate philanthropy. What are the benefits to the donor and the recipient?

2 List the reasons why you think 'business ethics' is important to the success of firms.

3 Summarise the Friedman and social contract positions on social responsibility with an example of each being applied.

4 List three major ethical issues facing management at the present time, and give reasons for your choices.

5 Describe in your own terms each of the four schools of ethical thought and illustrate each with an example of how it has been used to justify a decision.

6 Outline the ways in which the consumer can affect business practice, and decide whether this is effective or not.

7 List the stakeholders in the Ford Pinto case and prioritise them in order to justify the decision to manufacture.

8 What could Ford staff have done to promote the communication of these difficult issues to higher management?

9 Who should determine a company's level of acceptance of social responsibilities?

Concluding critical reflection

Think about the way your company, or one with which you are familiar, approaches issues of corporate responsibility. Review the material in the chapter, and perhaps visit some of the websites identified. Then make notes on these questions:

- What examples of the issues discussed in this chapter are currently relevant to your company?

- In responding to these issues, what **assumptions** about the role of business in society appear to have guided what people have done? Are they closer to the Friedmanite or the social responsibility view?

- What factors such as the history or current **context** of the company appear to have influenced the prevailing view? Does the approach appear to be right for the company, its employees, and other stakeholders? Have any stakeholders tried to challenge company policy?

- Have people put forward **alternative** ways of dealing with these issues, based on evidence about other companies? If you could find such evidence, how may it affect company practice?

- What **limitations** do you find in the ideas and theories presented here? For example, while it is easy to advocate that a company should act responsibly, Vogel points out that managers' willingness to do so is constrained by the potential threat of competitors who act less responsibly – perhaps offering cheaper products from less sustainable sources. Can you find evidence for and against Vogel's view?

Further reading

Megone, C. and Robinson, S.J. (2002), *Case Histories in Business Ethics*, Routledge, London.

Clarke, F.L. (2003), *Corporate Collapse: Accounting, regulatory and ethical failure*, Cambridge University Press, Cambridge.

Egan, J. and Wilson, D. (2002), *Private Business – Public Battleground*, Palgrave, Basingstoke.

  Develops the case for companies that are structured in a way that takes account of a range of stakeholder interests.

Jackall, R. (1998), *Moral Mazes: The world of corporate managers*, Oxford University Press, Oxford.

  Focuses on the managerial role in tackling the complexity of ethical issues.

Ackroyd, S. and Thompson, P. (1999), *Organizational Misbehaviour*, Sage, London.

  Looks at the larger corporate view of 'organisational misbehaviour'.

Bartlett, D. (2003), 'Management and business ethics: a critique and integration of ethical decision-making models', *British Journal of Management*, vol. 14, no. 3, pp. 223–235.

  Useful as an overview of recent attempts to resolve the dilemmas between organisational and individual approaches to ethical questions.

Vogel, D. (2005), *The Market for Virtue: The potential and limits of corporate social responsibility*, Brookings Institution Press, Washington, DC.

  Places issues of corporate responsibility within a wider consideration of company strategy. Many current examples support the discussion.

Weblinks

These websites have appeared in the chapter:

www.ford.com

www.wipro.com

www.the-body-shop.co.uk

www.cfs.co.uk

www.gap.com

www.kraft.com

www.vodafone.com

www.FTSE4Good.com

www.bp.com

Visit two of the sites in the list, and navigate to the pages dealing with corporate responsibility, sustainability or corporate governance.

- What are the main concerns that they seem to be addressing?
- What information can you find about their policies?
- Compare and contrast the concerns and policies expressed on the sites.
- Gather information from the media or pressure group websites that relate to these companies. What differences are there between these perspectives? What dilemmas does that imply managers in these companies are dealing with?

Annotated weblinks, multiple choice questions and other useful resources can be found on **www.pearsoned.co.uk/boddy**

In 2007 BP was the world's second largest oil and natural gas producer, having recently grown through mergers and joint ventures – such as its deal with a major Russian producer in 2003 to create a 50–50 joint venture, TNK-BP. By its nature it is engaged in international business, with a strong interest in managing the political, economic and technological aspects of the environment. Some criticise the oil industry for contributing to climate change – though the companies can point out that they are only meeting the growing demand that people in all countries have for energy.

BP is a British registered company, but 40 per cent of its assets are in the United States, and it is that country's largest gas producer. It does 80 per cent of its business outside the United Kingdom, and is inevitably involved with political considerations. For example, in 2001 the company argued that while BP would be perfectly entitled to follow Royal Dutch Shell and make production agreements with Iran, it would be 'inappropriate' for the company to ignore US sanctions on Iran.

John Browne was chief executive of the company from 1995 until 2007, when he admitted that he had lied to a court about aspects of his private life. The strong position of the company (recognised in a *Financial Times* survey as one of the world's best-managed companies) is the culmination of a period of radical change in line with the changing environment.

When David Simon took over in 1992 he believed the organisation needed to revise its strategy to reverse losses and repay large debts. Simon moved fast to implement a three-year plan with a simple name: '1-2-5' – cut debt by $1 billion per year, build profits to $2 billion per year and keep capital spending below $5 billion per year. Over the following two years he sold many marginal businesses and reduced staff by almost 50 per

cent, with a large reduction in middle management. He narrowed BP's core interest to petroleum only – 'finding it, extracting it, shipping it, refining it, converting it and selling it', as he put it – through three main divisions: exploration, oil and chemicals. Simon made it clear to BP employees that they should be cost and profit conscious. He has a golden rule for attaining goals: 'Targeting is fundamental to achieving. If you do not target, you do not measure and you do not achieve.' An outside analyst commented: 'I think you have to put an awful lot of BP's recovery down to him. A complete cultural change has been put into place.'

BP PLC.

John Browne took over from Simon in 1995, and continued to persuade the board and managers that BP must keep changing. He has stated that:

To achieve distinctive performance from a portfolio of first-class assets requires continuous development of our organisation and management processes. We are further decentralising the organisation in order to encourage personal initiative and creativity. Simultaneously, we are strengthening the sharing of experience and best practice so that BP's total competitive strength is greater than the sum of its parts.

The firm prides itself on its collegiate management style, with large amounts of power passed to senior managers below CEO level. Browne is said to lead by power of intellect. Everything pivots around his ability to absorb vast amounts of information, keeping on top of what is happening anywhere in the company. He carries a heavy workload, even by the standards of multinational bosses.

He is extremely bright, extremely well organised and is a very good lateral thinker. Very strong on the numbers side, financially extremely astute, but the same also goes for the technological side. He understands geopolitics and has the nose for a deal.

He greatly increased BP's oil reserves not only by exploration but also by acquisitions and joint ventures. The deal with TNK was strategically important as apart from its intrinsic merits it opened the way for further deals related to Russian oil and gas reserves – which are the largest in the world. It also fitted a wider political strategy of developing Russian fields to reduce the west's dependence on Middle Eastern supplies. Rather than own the new company, the deal is for BP to own 50 per cent, and take management control. This was to help ensure that Russian investors felt equally treated, and to secure their help in lobbying the Russian government, which is trying to secure greater control of the country's natural resources.

Although the company refines some 4 million barrels of oil a day, it sells almost 6 million through its 29,000 service stations and other distribution systems around the world. It therefore has to buy refined products from other companies to fulfil its needs. One observer noted: 'most of the majors trade oil to balance their own systems, BP is far more ambitious. They look on trading as a profit-generating centre'.

A unique trading culture has developed within the company, setting it apart from rivals such as Shell and Exxon – in 2005 it made $2.97 billion pre-tax profit on its trading activities, out of a total profit of $22.3 billion. A culture of aggressive trading is said to have developed, fuelled by above-average incentives for traders, which has its roots in the company's origin as Anglo-Persian Oil in the 1900s. The company then produced oil in what is now Iran, but had few outlets to refine and market it. The company therefore needed to build up its trading operations to sell the oil on. It is now the most active energy trader among its peers. In 2006 BP suspended three Houston-based gas traders at the centre of an alleged price manipulation scheme.

Dealing head on with the industry's impact on the environment became one of the principles of John Brown's leadership.

These are issues of tremendous complexity. Do you want a clean environment or do you want hydrocarbons? False trade-off. You have to ask if you want both, and in the service of gaining both usually comes technology and better ways of doing things. The industry hasn't handled it well. Consumers want to consume more, they recognise the consequences of consumption, they don't want to shoulder the burden of that themselves, so they transfer it on to the shoulders of the oil and gas companies ... The reality is it's a shared responsibility. We can do a lot but so must consumers.

One potentially controversial aspect of the deal with TNK is that some of the facilities they will now be managing in Russia are old, and could raise serious environmental concerns. While no longer a member of the group lobbying to open the Alaskan National Wildlife Refuge for drilling, Browne believed it should be opened. Although he claimed that new technology would allow this to be done with minuscule damage, he recognised it would bring BP into conflict with some environmental lobby groups: 'While this would dent Sir John's ... "green" image, he claims to have always been in the business of pragmatic trade-offs between nature and the world's insatiable thirst for oil.'

The company's reputation suffered in March 2005 when an explosion at the Texas City refinery, its biggest in the United States, killed 15 people and injured about 500, making it the deadliest US refinery accident in more than a decade. An investigation by the Department of Labor uncovered more than 300 violations at the refinery. An internal BP report found that senior managers at the plant had ignored advice to spend money on safety improvements, though boasting internally that the plant had just had its most profitable year.

There was further damage a year later when a pipeline spilled 270,000 gallons of crude oil into Alaska's Prudhoe Bay, North America's largest oilfield. The Alaska Department of Environmental Conservation blamed corrosion for the spill, something which workers had for years complained that management were neglecting. BP denied this, saying that its expenditure on corrosion inspection and maintenance had increased over the years. The authorities then began criminal investigations into aspects of the company's Alaskan operations, after representations on behalf of workers who complained about the company's Corrosion Inspection and Control Division.

In August 2006, after further leaks, BP announced that it would close half the Alaskan oilfield until it had solved the corrosion problem. It had earlier announced its intention to close the whole field, but changed the plan after local protests about the effect of the loss of jobs and revenue for the state: 90 per cent of the state's revenue comes from oil royalties and taxes, which fund most services provided by the state. Almost half of that revenue comes from BP's Prudhoe Bay.

In July 2006 the company appointed Bob Malone to be chairman and president of BP America. In an early message to staff he said that he would be establishing a US health, safety, security and environment adviser to include accountability for crisis management in the United States, reporting directly to him. He also planned to build stronger, direct links with the US press team. The company ensured that Mr Malone could focus on repairing its reputation in the United States by giving some of the responsibilities traditionally associated with the job to another manager.

Towards the end of his term as CEO it became clear that Browne's image had been damaged by the Texas explosion and the leaking pipes in Alaska. Browne's successor, Tony Howard, stressed that his priority was simple and clear: 'BP had to implement strategy by focusing like a laser on safe and reliable operations.'

Sources: European Case Clearing House Case No. 497-013-1, 'British Petroleum: transformational leadership in a transnational organisation', by Elizabeth Florent-Treacy and Manfred Kets de Vries, 1997; *Financial Times*, 30 June 2006, 4 July 2006, 14 August 2006; 7 March 2007: and other sources.

Part case questions

- Analyse the five forces acting on BP. Which of them appear to bring the greatest threat to the company?
- Construct a PESTEL analysis to establish the main aspects of the external environment that affect BP.
- Make a list of stakeholders for BP. Assess their sources of power, and rank them according to the likely degree of influence they hold.
- In what ways will managing in BP, with such international exposure, be different from managing in a national company with no international business? List the three most significant.
- What has BP done to indicate that it is acting in a socially responsible manner?
- A major issue for the company is to balance different stakeholder groups. What argument, from an ethical standpoint, could BP use to support the case for opening new oilfields in the Alaskan Wildlife Reserve?

Part 2 Skills development

Task 2.1 Dimensions of the competitive environment

Select an industry in which you have an interest (perhaps for a potential career), and write a one- to two-page paper describing the main competing players in that industry, and the major issues the industry is facing. Identify the companies in which you are interested by checking articles about the industry in sources such as **www.hoovers.com**, **www.ft.com** or **www.economist.com** (these sites are mainly subscription only once you get beyond the headlines) and then go to the companies' websites for more detailed information.

Task 2.2 Dimensions of the general environment

Changes in a country's demography have significant implications for managers, as they affect the resources available as inputs to organisations, the outputs that are likely to be in demand, and aspects of the transformation process (such as the growing desire for flexible working times). Information about these trends is available from official websites – such as (in the United Kingdom) **www.statistics.gov.uk**.

Go to that site, or the equivalent in your country, and find out: (1) the total number of people in the country now, and the predictions for five and ten years on; (2) the changing age distribution; (3) the number of people with Internet access; (4) other data that interest you as a student of management.

What implications may your results have for business in five years' time?

Task 2.3 Comparing industry environments

While all organisations face opportunities and threats from their competitive and general environments, these differ. Summarise the work you have done in the earlier activities so that you can set out the main threats and opportunities facing one industry. Then compare your conclusions with another student who has studied a different industry. List those factors that are the same, and those which are different.

Task 2.4 Tracking multinationals

Since an increasing amount of business is done through multinational businesses, it pays to become familiar with some of them. Select three businesses that have a major international presence (preferably not limited to the most obvious ones) and go to their websites. Find out about their main products and services, the countries in which they operate, the broad structure of the organisation, and their statements about social responsibility. You could also check their careers page.

Compare what you have found with a colleague, identifying what is similar about the companies, and what is different.

Task 2.5 Country studies for a multinational

Suppose that one of the companies you have worked with in Task 2.4 is considering launching a valuable new product in one of the following countries: Malaysia, Singapore, Brazil or Australia. One issue in their decision will be the status of regional trading alliances affecting these countries. Use the Internet to establish whether these countries are part of any such alliances. If so, compile a one-page report on that alliance for presentation to the company. The managers of the company would also like information on the main PESTEL factors in each country. Prepare a one-page report outlining the main PESTEL factors for one of the countries identified. Managers are also interested in what environmental constraints they may face in that country – try to include a commentary on this aspect, if you can find adequate information, as in some industries it will be a critical part of an investment decision.

Part 3

PLANNING

Introduction

This part examines the generic management activities of planning and decision making, and then looks at two substantive applications of these ideas – to strategy and marketing respectively. Both areas depend on understanding the environment of the business and the stakeholders within it. They also both depend on building an internal capability to deliver the chosen strategy.

Chapter 6 provides an overview of planning in organisations, setting out the purposes of planning, the types of plan and the tasks of planning. While all these tasks are likely to be part of the process, their shape will always depend on the circumstances for which a plan is being made.

Decision making is closely linked to planning, made necessary by finite resources and infinite demands. People in organisations must continually decide on inputs, transformation processes and outputs – and the quality of those decisions affects organisational performance. Chapter 7 therefore introduces the main decision-making processes, and contrasts several theories of decision making in organisations.

Chapter 8 outlines the strategy process, and introduces techniques that managers use to analyse the options facing businesses of all kinds. This analysis can then lead to clearer choices about future direction.

A critical aspect of that is the markets the organisation chooses to serve. Chapter 9 argues that marketing is not just a functional area within the organisation, but is closely allied to the core strategy process. Like strategy, it uses external and internal analysis to establish a way forward, and like strategy it depends on other functions if the organisation is to meet customer expectations profitably.

The Part Case is The Virgin Group, illustrating the interaction of the external environment with the developing corporate and marketing strategies.

Chapter 6

Planning

Aim

To describe the purposes of planning in organisations, and illustrate the iterative tasks in the planning cycle.

Objectives

By the end of your work on this chapter you should be able to outline the concepts below in your own terms and:

1 Explain the purposes of planning and the content of different types of plan
2 Compare alternative planning processes, and evaluate when each may be most suitable
3 Outline the seven iterative steps in planning, and describe techniques used in each
4 Use theory to evaluate the motivational effect of the goals stated in a plan
5 Use a framework to evaluate whether a plan is sufficiently comprehensive
6 Evaluate the context that will affect the ability of managers to implement a plan.

Key terms

This chapter introduces the following ideas:

planning
goal (or objective)
business plan
strategic plan
strategic business unit
operational plans
corporate strategy
planning system
SWOT analysis
critical success factors
sensitivity analysis
scenario planning
mission statement
stated goal
real goal

Each is a term defined within the text, as well as in the Glossary at the end of the book.

© DSM

In 1902 the Dutch government created Dutch State Mines (DSM) as a state-owned coal mining company. Although it stopped mining coal years ago, its headquarters are at Heerlen in the south of The Netherlands, close to the original mines. It has been through many changes since then, and is now a speciality chemicals business. The Dutch government sold the firm in 1989 and it now operates entirely in the private sector.

By 2007 the company had almost 22,000 employees working in over 200 offices and production sites in 40 countries. It has a decentralised structure, with 13 business groups that are empowered to perform all business functions. They form four strategic clusters – Nutrition, Pharma, Performance Materials and Industrial Chemicals. Each of the 13 companies is headed by a business group director, who reports directly to the managing board of directors. This has five members, responsible for strategy, the portfolio (the range of businesses in the company) and resource allocation.

Until the mid-1990s the company operated a traditional strategic planning process, with a corporate planning department setting out three- to five-year plans, supplemented by an annual budget cycle. Senior managers became dissatisfied with this as it was 'owned' by the corporate planning department, and had become a routine 'numbers' exercise.

The company therefore introduced a new arrangement. There is a Corporate Strategic Dialogue (CSD)

every three years, in which about 50 executives take part. It develops a long-term strategy for the business, deciding on the portfolio, investment priorities and geographical spread. The result of the last such exercise – 'Vision 2010: Building on Strengths' – is now being implemented through the business groups.

This strategic plan will build on Vision 2005, through which the company's portfolio shifted towards speciality products in the areas of life sciences and performance materials, in the search for higher and more stable earnings. The plan is to accelerate growth in the most profitable and innovative areas, by investing heavily in research and development and in new production facilities and staff.

Source: Based on Bloemhof *et al.* (2004). Copyright 2004 INSEAD, Fontainebleau, France; *DSM Annual Report, 2005* (on website).

Case questions 6.1

Visit the DSM website.

- What are the main elements of 'Vision 2010: Building on Strengths'?
- What effects may the plan have on what managers in the business do?
- What kind of environment do you think the company is operating in (Chapter 3, Section 3.4)?

6.1 Introduction

The DSM story outlines how managers in that company developed an approach to planning that seeks to balance the need for overall strategic direction with a high degree of autonomy for the main business units. DSM operates around the world in several technologically advanced businesses – like many other prominent companies. They too face the issue of how to identify external trends and plan changes accordingly.

Changes in external forces create uncertainty, and planning offers a systematic way to cope with that, and to adapt to new conditions. It enables people to set objectives, to specify and coordinate actions to achieve them, and to monitor progress. It is concerned with both ends (what to do) and means (how to do it).

Some plans are informal – not written down, nor widely or consistently shared. This can work perfectly well in managing domestic and social life, or in small businesses where the owner-manager and a few staff can see what everyone is doing and adapt to changing circumstances. Some larger organisations also manage with little formal planning – though they run the risk of duplication or of ignoring important information.

The focus here is on more formal plans, which express the goals of a business or unit for some future period, and the actions to achieve them, in written form. Warburton's, a family-owned Lancashire-based bread company, has a goal of reaching every UK household, challenging the two dominant firms. To achieve this it had to plan and build new capacity – it opened a bakery in North London in 2003, and is now searching for a site to the south of London. When two entrepreneurs decided to create the City Inn hotel chain they planned in detail the kind of hotels they would be – contemporary, city centre, newly built, 'active and open' atmosphere, and a consistent room design across the group. Plans like this can then be communicated to relevant players, to ensure they act consistently.

Figure 6.1 provides an overview of the themes. At the centre are seven generic tasks in planning – but people vary the order, and how much attention they give to each. How they manage these issues will affect whether planning helps or hinders performance.

The chapter outlines the benefits of planning and distinguishes the content of plans. Later sections examine the process of planning, and its seven generic steps – stressing throughout that these take place iteratively, and that their form depends on circumstances.

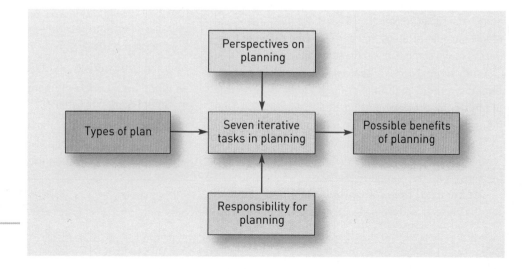

Figure 6.1

An overview of the chapter

6.2 Purposes of planning

While people use different terms, the activity of **planning** essentially involves establishing the **goals** (or **objectives**) for the task being planned, specifying how to achieve them, implementing the plan and evaluating the results. Goals represent the desired future state of an activity or organisational unit, and planning to meet them typically includes allocating the resources and specifying what people need to do.

Planning, if done well, brings four main benefits in that it:

- it clarifies direction;
- motivates people;
- helps to use resources efficiently; and
- provides a way to measure progress.

The act of planning may in itself add value, by ensuring that people base decisions on a wider range of evidence than if there was no planning system (Sinha, 1990). If done badly, planning has the opposite effect, leading to confusion, frustration and waste.

Good plans give direction to the people whose work contributes to their achievement. If everyone knows the purpose of a larger activity and how their task contributes, they can work more effectively. They can adjust their work to the plan (or vice versa), and cooperate and coordinate with others. It also helps them cope with the unexpected, since if they understand the end result they can respond to unexpected changes – without having to ask or waiting to be told. People like to know how their task fits into the larger whole, as it adds interest and enables them to take more responsibility.

> **Planning** is the task of setting objectives, specifying how to achieve them, implementing the plan and evaluating the results.
>
> **A goal** (or **objective**) is a desired future state for an activity or organisational unit.

---

management in practice

More planning at SABMiller   www.sabmiller.com

South African Brewers (SAB) purchased the US brewer Miller in 2002, to form SABMiller. The chief executive of SAB, Graham Mackay, was reported to be very critical of the company he had bought, saying that it was not a finely tuned, focused, effective organisation. In recent years it had lost market share to Anheuser-Busch and Coors. He would be exporting the South African company's direct management style to Miller's Milwaukee home, bringing a tighter focus on planning, objective setting and appraisal of Miller staff. The typical middle manager at Miller will be working to clearer objectives as well as having their pay more closely linked to performance: 'There will be a very much stronger management of consequences than there has been in the past. People will be held accountable for performance.'

FT

Source: *Financial Times*, 22 November 2002.

Planning reduces overlapping activities, and at the same time ensures that someone is responsible for each activity. A plan helps people coordinate their separate tasks, so saving time and resources; without a plan they may work at cross purposes. If people are clear on the end result they can spot inefficiencies or unnecessary delays in the activity, and correct or eliminate them.

Finally, planning establishes goals and standards that help people to monitor progress towards them. Setting final and interim goals lets people know how well they are progressing, and when they have finished. Comparing actual progress against the intended goals enables people to adjust the goal or change the way they are using resources.

key ideas   **Does planning help new ventures?**

Delmar and Shane (2003) studied whether planning helps new ventures, gathering data from over 200 new firms in Sweden. They hypothesised that planning would support new ventures by:

- enabling quicker decisions;
- providing a tool for managing resources to minimise bottlenecks;
- identifying actions to achieve broader goals in a timely manner.

They gathered extensive data from the firms at their start-up in 1998, and then at regular intervals for three years. The results supported each of their hypotheses, leading them to conclude that planning did indeed support the creation of successful new ventures.

Source: Delmar and Shane (2003).

The content of a plan is the subject matter – *what* aspect of the business it deals with: the next section distinguishes strategic, business unit, operational and special purpose plans. The one after that focuses on the process of planning.

Activity 6.1   **Critical reflection on the purpose of plans**

Gather examples of the plans that people prepare in an organisation – try to get one example of each of the types listed here.

- For one of the plans, ask someone who is familiar with it what the purpose of the plan is, and whether it achieves that purpose.
- Ask whether the plan is too detailed, or not detailed enough.
- What do they regard as the strengths and weaknesses of the planning process?

6.3   The content of plans

A **business plan** is a document that sets out the markets the business intends to serve, how it will do so and what finance they require.

People starting a new business or expanding an existing one prepare a **business plan** – a document that sets out the markets the business intends to serve, how it will do so and what finance they require (Blackwell, 2004). They do so to convince potential investors to lend money. Managers in divisions of a business (such as DSM) seeking capital investment or other corporate resources need to convince senior managers to allocate a share of the capital budget to them – which they do by presenting a convincing divisional plan. People in the public sector do the same – a director of roads (for example) needs to present a plan to convince the chief executive or elected members that planned expenditure on roads is a better use of resources than competing proposals from (say) the director of social work or cultural services. Service managers inevitably compete with each other for limited resources, and develop plans to support their case.

A **strategic plan** sets out the overall direction for the business, is broad in scope and covers all the major activities.

Plans vary in the level and breadth of the business they cover and in how far ahead they look. **Strategic plans** apply to the whole organisation or business unit. They set out the overall direction and cover major activities – markets and revenues, together with plans for marketing, human resources and production. Chandler (1962, p. 13) defined strategic plans as determining 'the basic long-term goals and objectives of an enterprise and the adoption of courses of action and the allocation of resources necessary for carrying out these goals'. Strategy is concerned with deciding what business an organisation should be in, where it wants to be and how it is going to get there. These decisions involve major resource commitments and usually require a series of consequential operational decisions. The benefits of central planning, especially at the strategic level, have long been advocated (Ansoff 1965, 1991; Armstrong, 1982) to coordinate actions and to spur adaptive strategic thinking. Glaister and Falshaw (1999) found that most senior managers regularly engage in strategic planning.

DSM – the case continues www.dsm.com   CASE STUDY

In October 2005 DSM presented its new five year strategy – 'Vision 2010' – which was the outcome of the regular corporate strategic dialogue (CSD). This focuses on accelerating the profitable and innovative growth of its specialties portfolio, with the overall objective of strong value creation. This will be accomplished in three ways:

1 **Market-driven growth and innovation** Based on existing product leadership, DSM plans to grow sales in four *emerging business areas* – personalised nutrition, speciality packaging, biomedical materials and industrial biotechnology. This growth will be accelerated by innovation in the target markets. The company plans that by 2010 60 per cent of sales will come from speciality products, compared with 40 per cent in 2005. To boost innovation, 250 people will be recruited to work in business-driven innovation teams. About 15 per cent of capital expenditure will be dedicated to this effort.

2 **Increased presence in emerging economies** DSM plans to continue the trend of improving its globally balanced presence by accelerating the internationalisation of its asset base and workforce. Identified growth in demand in selected emerging economies has led the company to significantly increase its growth efforts in these regions. When evaluating investment proposals DSM will take this aim into account.

3 **Operational excellence** The company plans to continue building on its strong operational skills to enhance the cost competitiveness of the business. Over the previous five years it had implemented several operational excellence programmes, standardising business processes in manufacturing, order fulfilment, finance, and information technology. These will be extended to purchasing, pricing and productivity.

Source: DSM *Annual Report 2005* (on website).

Case questions 6.2

● How are the strategic plans being supported by operational plans?

● Visit the company website and look for information about recent developments in the business that may affect these plans.

In a large business there will be divisional plans for each major unit. If subsidiaries operate as autonomous **strategic business units** (SBUs) they develop their plans with limited inputs from the rest of the company, as it manages distinct products or markets.

Strategic plans are usually long term in form, looking up to three years ahead – though in businesses with long lead times (energy production or aircraft manufacture) they look much further ahead. Ryanair plans to grow capacity rapidly to meet demand, and makes a plan showing the financial and other implications of enlarging the fleet, recruiting staff and opening new routes.

A **strategic business unit** consists of a number of closely related products for which it is meaningful to formulate a separate strategy.

management in practice Fiat's restructuring plan www.fiat.co.uk

In 2003 Fiat Group, owner of the Italian car maker, decided to retain the struggling Fiat Auto, and to invest in returning the company to profit. The plan included:

- cutting manufacturing costs by £700 million
- increasing research and development expenditure by £750 million
- reducing European capacity to 1.6 million vehicles a year
- boosting sales in Europe by 9 per cent with the launch of new models
- investing £100 million a year for three years to expand the dealer network.

Within that broad plan, the sports car division that makes the Alfa-Romeo was making its own plans to restore excitement to the range before re-entering the US market in 2007.

Source: *Business Week*, 21 April 2003.

Operational plans detail how the overall objectives are to be achieved, by specifying what senior management expects from specific departments or functions.

Corporate strategy 'is concerned with the firm's choice of business, markets and activities' (Kay, 1996), and thus it defines the overall scope and direction of the business.

Operational plans detail how the overall objectives are to be achieved. They are narrower in scope, indicating what senior management expects individual departments or functions to do, so that they support the overall plan. So there may be a family of related plans forming a hierarchy – a strategic plan for the organisation and main divisions, and several operational plans for departments or teams. Each will contain linked objectives and plans that become more specific as they move down the organisation, but aiming to be consistent with the overall **corporate strategy**. Table 6.1 shows this hierarchical arrangement, and how the character of plans changes at each level.

Most organisations also prepare annual plans that deal mainly with the financial aspects of the business and set out budgets for the coming year, but necessarily include sales, marketing, production or technology plans as well. These short-term plans are expected to be consistent with the longer-term strategy, but take account of immediate developments and changes since the strategic plan was prepared.

Activity plans are short-term plans that deal with immediate production or service delivery – a sheet scheduling which orders are to be dealt with next week, or planning who is on duty when. Some use a method called enterprise resource planning to integrate the day-to-day work of complex production systems – Chapter 12 describes this technique in section 12.6.

Table 6.1

A planning hierarchy

Type of plan	Strategic	Operational	Activity
Level	Organisation or business unit	Division, department, function or market	Work unit or team
Focus	Direction and strategy for whole organisation	Functional changes or market activities to support strategic plans	Actions needed to deliver current products or services
Nature	Broad, general direction	Detail on required changes	Specific detail on immediate goals and tasks
Timescale	Long term (2–3 years?)	Medium (up to 18 months?)	Very short term (hours to weeks?)

Figure 6.2 contrasts specific and directional plans. Specific plans have unambiguous, mainly quantified objectives and leave little room for discretion in how to achieve them. A manager who seeks to increase his or her unit's work output by 8 per cent over the next 12 months could establish clear procedures, budgets and schedules of activities to reach that goal.

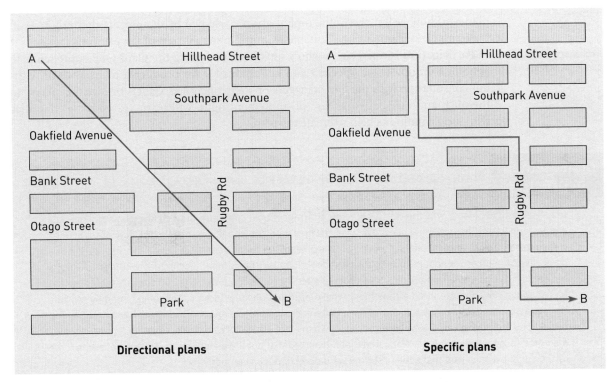

Figure 6.2 Specific and directional plans

In uncertain conditions management will need to respond to unexpected changes, and then directional plans are preferable. They give a looser guidance – providing focus but not directing managers to specific actions. The Chapter 7 case (Wipro) describes how in the early days of the company the founder, Azim Premji, held weekly telephone conversations with his regional managers, in which he set their targets for the following week – but they were free to decide how to meet them. He held them accountable for meeting the target, but not for how they did so (provided they met his high ethical standards).

Managers also prepare special-purpose plans for projects or aspects of the business. They may have plans for disaster recovery (after, say, a major computer failure or terrorist action), and develop project plans to organise and implement specific changes, such as introducing a new computer system or launching a new product. When The Royal Bank of Scotland took over NatWest Bank managers quickly developed a collection of over 160 interlocking plans to incorporate NatWest operations into those of RBS to secure the cost savings they had promised investors (Kennedy *et al.*, 2006). On a smaller scale, a manager who needs to recruit a new member of staff will make a simple plan to organise the task. Standing plans specify how to deal with routine, regularly recurring issues such as recruitment or dealing with customer complaints. People plan throughout an organisation, at all levels and in all degrees of formality.

6.4   The process of planning

The process of planning refers to the way plans are produced – are they developed from the top of the organisation, or from the bottom up? How frequently are they revised? Who takes part in creating them? The organisation's **planning system** organises and coordinates the activities of those involved in the planning process. The content of a plan, and how well it serves the organisation, is shaped by the process that produces it. Designing and maintaining a suitable planning system is part of the planning task.

A **planning system** refers to the processes by which the members of an organisation produce plans, including their frequency and who takes part in the process.

Participation is one issue – who is involved in making the plan? One approach is to appoint a group of staff specialists to be responsible for producing plans, with or without consultation with the line managers or staff concerned. Others believe the quality of the plan, and especially the ease of implementing it, will be increased if staff familiar with local conditions help to create the plan.

management in practice   A new planning process at Merck   www.merck.com

In the early 1990s Merck was the world's leading pharmaceutical company, but by 2006 it was ranked only eighth. Dick Clark, the new chief executive, was charged with reviving the company: one of his first actions was to make radical changes in its planning process. Teams of employees were asked to present the business cases to senior managers to test possible directions for the company – such as whether to build a generic drugs business. This process was vital, said Mr Clark, as it showed the 200 senior executives that Merck would now operate in an atmosphere where assumptions would be openly questioned by anyone. He has also changed the way the company sets its earnings projections. Formerly set by top managers, projections are now set by lower-level teams. 'It wasn't like Dick Clark said "We're going to have double-digit growth, go out and find it!" We tested it and tweaked it ... but it was legitimate and we believe in it, so let's go public with it. And that's the first time we'd done that as a company.'

FT

Source: From an article by Christopher Bowe, *Financial Times*, 27 March 2006, p. 10.

key ideas   The benefits of participation and communication

Ketokivi and Castañer (2004) studied the strategic planning process in 164 manufacturing plants in five countries and three industries (automotive supplies, machinery and electronics). It has long been recognised that organisational members tend to focus on the goals of their unit or function, rather than on those of the enterprise – known as 'position bias'. The study sought to establish empirically whether position bias existed, and, more importantly, whether strategic planning reduced this. The evidence confirmed the tendency to position bias. It also showed that having employees participate in strategic planning, and communicating the outcome to them, significantly diminishes it. If top management wants to reduce position bias, they should incorporate participation and communication into the strategic planning process.

Source: Ketokivi and Castañer (2004).

A related debate (developed more fully in Chapter 8, Section 8.6) is between those who advocate a rational approach to planning and those who favour what are variously called learning or emergent approaches (also called logical incrementalism (Quinn, 1980)). They argue that when a company is in dynamic context plans must be essentially temporary and provisional, so that managers can adapt them to suit changing circumstances, drawing on new information from the frequent interaction of a wide range of participants (Fletcher and Harris, 2002; Papke-Shields *et al.*, 2006).

Jennings (2000) shows how companies change their approach to planning as conditions change. A study of the UK electricity generating company PowerGen (now owned by the German company E.on) that was privatised in 1991 traced the evolution since then of the company's corporate planning process. It had retained a formal process with a five-year planning horizon, but it was more devolved. A small central team focuses on overall strategy while business units develop strategy for their particular situations. Business unit plans have become shorter and are no longer required to follow a prescribed format. The overall planning cycle is completed in a shorter period of time. All of these developments have created a more adaptive style of planning that is consistent with the increased uncertainty of the company's business environment.

Figure 6.3 shows the seven generic tasks that people can perform when they make a plan. They use them iteratively, often going back to an earlier stage when they find new information which implies, say, that they need to reshape the original goals. And of course they may miss a stage, or spend too little or too much time on each: the figure only indicates a way of analysing the stages of planning.

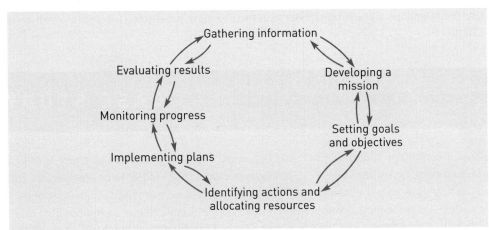

Figure 6.3

Seven iterative tasks in making a plan

6.5 Gathering information

Any plan depends on information that people can use to guide their choices in building the plan. This includes both informal, soft information gained from casual encounters with colleagues, competitors and customers, and from formal analyses of economic and market trends. This will reflect the form of plan, but an indication of the range available can begin with the strategic level – people use a simpler version for plans that are more limited in level or scope.

Chapter 3 outlined the competitive and general environments, and those involved in planning will usually begin by drawing on information about these, collecting, analysing and interpreting information from internal and external sources. Computer-based information systems usually hold a great deal of valuable information about a company's customers. The main benefit of loyalty cards for retailers is that they can track each customer's purchasing patterns and map them against the personal information in the database, obtained when they applied for the card. Tesco has been particularly skilled at analysing customer data, enabling planners to predict likely demand, especially for new products.

management in practice

Electrolux asks its customers www.electrolux.com

When Hans Straberg became chief executive of Electrolux, the world's second largest maker of domestic appliances, he faced major problems with both costs and product design. He tackled the former by closing many western European and US manufacturing plants and transferring the work to countries with lower costs. To ensure the company designed products that customers wanted, the company conducted in-depth interviews with 160,000 customers from around the globe. To analyse the data 53 employees, including designers, engineers and marketers gathered in Stockholm in November 2005 for a week-long brainstorming session to search for insights to stimulate the next generation of new products. This open, cross-functional approach to dealing with information was a radical departure from traditional ways of planning at the company.

Source: *Business Week*, 27 February 2006, pp. 42–43.

External sources include government economic and demographic statistics, industry surveys and general business intelligence services. Managers also commission market research on, for example, individual shopping patterns, attitudes towards particular firms or brand names, and satisfaction with existing products or services. Many firms use focus groups to test consumer reaction to new products (for more on this see Chapter 9).

DSM – the case continues www.dsm.com

CASE STUDY

The new strategy presented in October 2005 was the outcome of the corporate strategy dialogue. This 12-month process thoroughly analysed global economic and social trends and conditions, technological developments, and price scenarios for energy and raw materials. It also studied likely differences in growth in the various geographical regions and end markets, fac-tors that might affect the company's portfolio, and likely developments within each of DSM's business areas. This led to a clear set of conclusions about the future of each business area, and specifically to the need to focus more on those speciality innovative products in which it had a leading position in the industry.

Source: DSM *Annual Report 2005* (on website).

SWOT analysis

A **SWOT analysis** is a way of summarising the organisation's strengths and weaknesses relative to external opportunities and threats.

At a strategic level, planning will usually combine an analysis of external environmental factors with an internal analysis of the organisation's strengths and weaknesses. A **SWOT analysis** does this, bringing together the internal strengths and weaknesses and the external opportunities and threats. Internally, managers would analyse the strengths and weaknesses of the resources within, or available to, the organisation (Grant, 1991) – such as a firm's distinctive research capability, or its skill in integrating acquired companies. The external analysis would probably be based on PESTEL and Porter's (1980a) five forces model (see Chapter 3). These tools help to identify the main opportunities and threats that people believe could affect the business.

A SWOT analysis at Cable & Wireless   www.cw.com

Cable & Wireless is a global telecommunications business. One of its most successful areas has been its Caribbean operation, but in 2002 it experienced growing competition from new rivals, especially a company called Digicel. C&W took the threat sufficiently seriously to commission a report that compared the company with Digicel, using the SWOT technique. This provides a useful public example of the technique.

Strengths
- Established customer base
- Diversified revenue structure that can absorb losses
- Strong knowledge of local culture
- Strong technical support

Weaknesses
- C&W network not as good as Digicel's
- Capital spending restrictions
- Poor image across the Caribbean
- Low motivation of sales team

Opportunities
- Take advantage of regionalisation and economies of scale
- Offer more coverage before Digicel arrives
- Market growth potential
- Ability to remain the market leader

Threats
- Global entrants to market
- Loss of key staff to competitors
- Rapid technological innovation
- Poor market image

Source: Based on *Financial Times*, 10 December 2002.

While the method appears to be a rational way of gathering information, its usefulness depends on recognising that it is a human interpretation of internal and external factors. It is only a representation of reality – and participants are likely to differ about the significance of a factor, or even if it should be included at all. Debate about the factors is itself a potentially valuable part of the planning process.

Activity 6.2   Conducting a SWOT analysis

Choose one of the companies featured in the text (or any that interests you).

- Gather information from the company's website and other published data to prepare a SWOT analysis.
- Compare your analysis with that of a colleague on your course.
- Identify any differences between you in terms of the factors identified, and the significance given to them. What do those differences tell you about the value of the SWOT method?

Given the diversity and complexity of organisational environments it is easy to have too much information. Managers need to focus on the few trends and events that are likely to be of greatest significance. De Wit and Meyer (2004) report that planners at Royal Dutch/Shell focus on critical factors such as oil demand (economic), refining capacity (political and economic), the likelihood of government intervention (political) and alternative sources of fuel (technological).

Critical success factors analysis

Critical success factors are those aspects of a strategy that *must* be achieved to secure competitive advantage.

In considering whether to enter a new market, a widely used planning technique is to assess the **critical success factors** (Hardaker and Ward, 1987) in that market. These are the things which customers in that particular market most value about a product or service – and they therefore play a key role as people plan whether to move into a line of business. Some value price, others quality, others some curious aspect of the product's features – but in all cases they are things that a company must be able to do well to succeed in that market.

Forecasting

Forecasts or predictions of the future are often based on an analysis of past trends in factors such as input prices (wages, components, etc.), sales patterns or demographic characteristics. All forecasts are based on assumptions. In relatively simple environments people can reasonably assume that past trends will continue, but in uncertain conditions they need alternative assumptions. A new market might support rapid sales growth, whereas in a saturated market (e.g. basic foods, paid-for newspapers) it might be more realistic to assume a lower or nil growth rate.

Forecasting is big business, with several organisations selling analyses to business and government, using techniques such as time-series analysis, econometric modelling and simulation. However, because forecasts rely heavily on extrapolating past trends, users learn to question the assumptions inherent in them.

Sensitivity analysis

A **sensitivity analysis** tests the effect on a plan of several alternative values of the key variables.

One way of testing the assumptions is by including a **sensitivity analysis** of key variables in a plan to increase confidence in the choice made. A plan may assume that the company will attain a 10 per cent share of a market within a year: what will be the effect on the calculations if they secure 5 per cent, or 15 per cent? What if interest rates rise, increasing the cost of financing the projects? This enables those making the decision to compare the robustness of the options they are examining and so be better able to assess the relative risks. It gives people greater confidence in the decision, or alternatively may show that it is too risky to be worthwhile. Johnson *et al.* (2006) give a worked example that illustrates the method (pp. 372–373).

Scenario planning

Scenario planning is an attempt to create coherent and credible alternative stories about the future.

Forecasting is still relevant in dynamic and complex situations but cannot be relied on as uncertainty increases and where the rate of environmental change shows signs of discontinuity (marked and often rapid changes from trend). In these situations some companies build scenarios of what the future may look like. Cornelius *et al.* (2005) note that: '**scenarios** are not projections, predictions or preferences; rather they are coherent and credible stories about the future.'

Scenarios typically begin by considering how some major forces in the external environment such as the Internet, an ageing population, global terrorism or climate change might affect a company's business over the next five to ten years. Doing so can bring new ideas about their environment into the heads of managers, thus enabling them to recognise new and previously unthinkable possibilities. No one can predict the future, but advocates (Van der Heijden, 1996; Schwartz, 2005) claim two main benefits of scenario planning. The first is that it discourages reliance on what is sometimes referred to as 'single-point forecasting' – a single view of the future; second it encourages managers to develop contingency plans to cope with outcomes that depart from the most likely scenario. However, few companies use the technique as it is time consuming and costly. Moreover, while systematic thinking about possible futures may yield new information, that only becomes useful if senior managers make noticeable adjustments to strategy as a result.

Scenario planning at Shell   www.shell.com

management in practice

In today's global and fast-changing environment, extrapolating from historical performance using medium- and long-term forecasting techniques has not proved very reliable, and managers in some companies use scenarios to test their plans. Royal Dutch/Shell was one of the earliest to adopt this approach. Traditionally, Shell planners would forecast refining plant requirements for several years ahead by extrapolating from current demand. However, the volatility in the oil market makes accurate prediction difficult. Shell underestimated oil demand in the 1950s and 1960s and overestimated it in the 1970s.

Rather than rely on one projection, Shell develops a range of possible scenarios for, say, future crude oil supply. One scenario could be that it continues as now, another that many new fields become available and a third that Saudi Arabia experiences major political turmoil and ceases to export oil. Major capital investment projects are evaluated against each scenario, with the aim of ensuring that they have a positive return under each. Scenario planning helps generate projects that are more robust under a variety of alternative futures. It also encourages people to ask deeper questions – for example about whether the oil companies, or the political leaders in the oil-rich countries where the wells are drilled, would be deciding the supply of oil.

Scenario thinking now underpins the established way of thinking at Shell. It has become a part of the culture, such that people throughout the company, dealing with significant decisions, normally will think in terms of multiple, but equally plausible, futures to provide a context for decision making. (Van der Heijden, 1996, p. 21)

Source: Van der Heijden (1996).

A combination of PESTEL and five forces analysis should ensure that managers recognise all the major influences in the external environment. Forecasting and scenario planning then enable them to consider the possible implications for the business at the start of the planning process.

DSM – the case continues   www.dsm.com

CASE STUDY

The planning process introduced at DSM requires that each business group conducts a business strategy dialogue (BSD) about every three years. The purpose of a BSD is to provide a consistent method and terminology to structure the development process and improve its quality. Usually the whole management team of the business group conducts the dialogue, supported by specialists from within the organisation. The reviews have five phases:

1 **Characterising the business situation** Collecting information on questions such as what business are you in, who are the competitors, how attractive is the industry in terms of growth and profitability, how do you compare with competitors, what are the main trends?

2 **Analysing the business system (macro)** Analysing the industry in which the business unit competes, using Porter's five forces model. It also analyses the strategies that competitors are using, to identify the ▶

different ways in which a business could compete in an industry.

3 **Analysing the business system (micro)** This looks at the internal processes of the business, including its internal value chain, benchmarking of functions, and the strengths and weaknesses of the unit.

4 **Options and strategic choice** This phase compares the results of earlier phases – the competitive environment and the key success factors required, and its internal capabilities. This allows the unit to choose which strategic option it should pursue and what is required for successful implementation.

5 **Action planning and performance measurement** The chosen strategy is then turned into an action plan and linked to performance measurement. The team sets performance indicators such as market share, new product development, customer satisfaction and cost per unit of output. These enable managers to monitor the implementation of the strategy.

Each unit reviews progress on the implementation of

its BSD quarterly in its management reporting, and annually in the annual strategic review (ASR). With these building blocks from the businesses, the ASR monitors progress on DSM's overall execution of its strategic plan.

Source: Based on Bloemhof *et al.* (2004). Copyright 2004 INSEAD, Fontainebleau, France.

Case questions 6.3

- Comment on the main features of the content and process of planning at DSM.
- What are their main methods of gathering information?
- The process must be very costly to the company. What features of their business explain why they are willing to incur these costs?
- How does it compare with the planning process at your organisation?

6.6 Developing a mission and goals

Mission statements

A clear plan depends on being clear about the ultimate purpose of a task – whether this concerns the whole organisation or a single unit. This seems obvious, but studies of managerial work (Stewart, 1967) show that managers are drawn towards action rather than planning – especially the ambiguities of agreeing on purposes. Yet until a team has spent time thinking, debating and clarifying the wider purpose, they will find it difficult to agree on details.

A fashionable medium for expressing purpose at the level of the whole organisation is the **mission statement** – a way of expressing a vision of what the future could be if the plan were to succeed. The same idea can be expressed at departmental or business unit level – setting out what participants see as distinctive about their activities.

A **mission statement** is a broad definition of an organisation's operations and scope, aiming to distinguish it from similar organisations.

Goals

Goals turn the generalities of mission statements into specific commitments – what is to be done by when. They provide the focus or reference point for other decisions and the criteria against which to measure performance. Most plans include quantified objectives in the areas of financial objectives – such as earnings per share, return on shareholders' funds and cash flow. They are also likely to quantify sales targets, cost reductions, and R&D expenditure. Table 6.2 lists some stated goals of high-profile projects.

Table 6.2

Examples of published goals

Company	Published goals
Merck Pharmaceuticals – Recovery plan to 2010	Annual earnings growth of at least 10% Focus drug research on 9 disease areas, rather than 32 Restructure manufacturing operations
British Airways – Future shape and size (2001–2005)	Deliver operating margins of at least 10% Reduce capacity and destinations served Reduce aircraft fleet by 10%
Volkswagen – Recovery plan to 2008	Pre-tax profit target of €5.1 billion (up from €1.1 billion in 2004) Reduce jobs by at least 30,000 A restructuring 'more drastic than people can imagine' (company executives)
Nestlé – long-term growth target	In 2003 set new targets of 5–6% organic growth over three to five years, to focus managers' efforts on profit margins rather than sales

Source: Company announcements.

Activity 6.3   Developing a mission and goals

- Go to the websites of some companies that interest you and collect examples of mission statements.
- Does the organisation you work for have a mission statement? If so, how was it developed?
- Gather examples of goals at either organisational, operational or activity levels. If you can, ask those affected by them about the process by which they were set. Also ask if this has affected their attitudes towards them.

A hierarchy of goals

A way of relating goals to each other is to build them into a hierarchy, in which the overall goals are transformed into more specific goals for different parts of the organisation – such as marketing, finance, operations and human resources. Managers in those areas develop plans setting out the actions they must undertake to meet the overall goal. Figure 6.4 illustrates this by using IKEA's plan to expand in Japan. To meet its planned sales growth managers intend to open many stores across Asia, of which the first group will be in Japan. That has evolved into a plan for their probable location, and then into a precise plan for two near Tokyo, for which land has been bought. That in turn is leading managers to develop progressively more detailed plans for the thousands of details that will need to be in good order if the venture is to succeed.

Plans of this sort need to be flexible, as there is no knowing what may change between design and completion. Managers often stress their firm commitment to the highest-level goals – but leave staff with much more discretion over the lower-level plans through which they achieve them.

However convincingly set out, statements of goals only have value if they guide action. Effective goal setting involves balancing multiple goals, considering whether they meet the SMART criteria (see below), and evaluating their likely motivational effects.

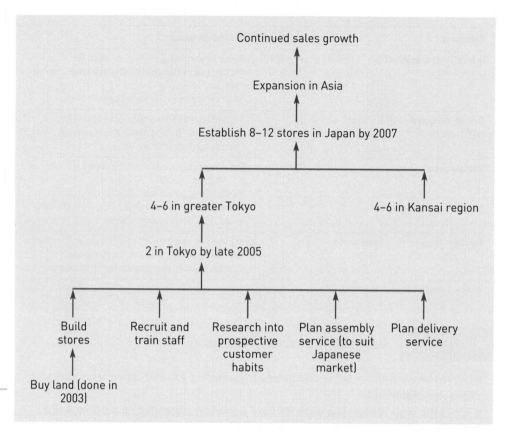

Figure 6.4

Developing a plan for IKEA (Japan)

Single or multiple goals?

Company statements of goals – whether long term or short – are usually expressed in the plural, since a single measure cannot indicate success or failure. Emphasis on one goal, such as growth, ignores others such as dividends for shareholders. Growth takes time and investment – which takes away from profits available for distribution to shareholders now. Managers have to balance multiple, possibly conflicting objectives, of even one group of stakeholders. As Gerry Murphy, who became chief executive of Kingfisher (a UK DIY retailer) in 2004, recalled:

> Alan Sheppard, my boss at Grand Metropolitan and one of my mentors, used to say that senior management shouldn't have the luxury of single point objectives. Delivering growth without returns or returns without growth is not something I find attractive or acceptable. Over time we are going to do both. (*Financial Times*, 28 April 2004, p. 23)

As senior managers try to take account of stakeholders other than those with shares in the company, they anticipate their various expectations. This means balancing profits (or growth) to satisfy shareholders, quality to satisfy customer interests, and sustainability to satisfy environmental interests. All are legitimate, but mean that managers are juggling conflicting goals. This can lead to conflict between stated goals, as reflected in public announcements, and real goals, which are those to which people work. **Stated goals** are those that appear and are given prominence in company publications and websites. Establishing the **real goals** – those to which people give most attention – depends on observing what they do. Actions reflect the priorities that senior managers express through what they say and do within the company, and how they reward and discipline managers.

Stated goals are those that are prominent in company publications and websites.

Real goals are those to which people give most attention.

Criteria for assessing goals

The SMART acronym summarises some criteria for assessing a set of goals. What form of each is effective depends on circumstances (specific goals are not necessarily better than directional ones). The list simply offers some measures against which to evaluate a statement of goals.

- **Specific** Does the goal set specific targets? People who are planning a meeting can set specific goals for what they hope to achieve, such as:

  By the end of the meeting we will have convinced them to withdraw their current proposal, and to have set a date (within the next two weeks) at which we will start to develop an alternative plan.

  Having a clear statement of what the meeting (or any other activity in a plan) is intended to achieve helps people to focus effort.
- **Measurable** Some goals may be quantified ('increase sales of product X by 5 per cent a year over the next three years') but others, equally important, are more qualitative ('to offer a congenial working environment'). Quantitative goals are not more useful than qualitative ones – what can be measured is not necessarily important. The important point is that goals be defined precisely enough to measure progress towards them.
- **Attainable** Goals should be challenging, but not unreasonably difficult. If people perceive a goal as unrealistic, they will not be committed. Equally goals should not be too easy, as that too undermines motivation. Goal-setting theory (see Key Ideas) predicts the motivational consequences of goal setting.
- **Rewarded** People need to see that attaining a goal will bring a reward – this gives meaning and helps ensure commitment.
- **Timed** Does the goal specify the time over which it will be achieved, and is that also a reasonable and acceptable standard?

Practical uses of goal-setting theory | key ideas

Goal-setting theory offers some practical implications for those making plans:

- **Goal difficulty**: set goals for work performance at levels that will stretch employees but are just within their ability.
- **Goal specificity**: express goals in clear, precise and if possible quantifiable terms, and avoid setting ambiguous or confusing goals.
- **Participation**: where practicable, encourage staff to take part in setting goals to increase their commitment to achieving them.
- **Feedback**: provide information on the results of performance to allow people to adjust their behaviour and perhaps improve their achievement of future plans.

Source: Locke and Latham (2002).

Activity 6.4 **Critical reflection on goals**

Choose a significant plan that someone in your organisation has produced within the last year. Assess the goals that it expresses – are they mutually consistent? Do they meet the criteria of being motivational? Are they SMART? Then try to set out how you would amend the goals to meet these criteria more fully. Alternatively, comment on how the criteria set out in the text could be modified, in the light of your experience with these goals.

6.7 Identifying actions and communicating the plan

This part of the planning process involves deciding what needs to be done, who will do it, and communicating that. In a small activity such as planning a project in a club this would just mean listing the tasks and dividing them clearly amongst a few able and willing members. At the other extreme, Ford's plan to build a new car plant in China probably runs to several volumes.

Identifying what needs to be done and by whom

Figure 1.3 (reproduced as Figure 6.5) provides a model to help envisage the implications of a goal, by enabling managers to ask what, if any, changes need to be made to each element.

If the goal is to launch a new product, the plan could identify which parts of the organisation will be affected (structure), what investment is needed (finance), how production will fit with existing lines (business processes) and so on. New technology

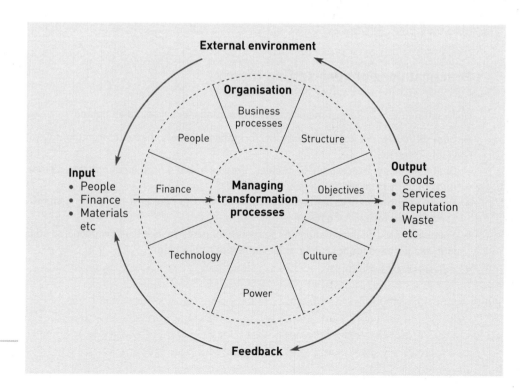

Figure 6.5

Possible action areas in a plan

projects often fail because those planning them pay too much attention to the techno-logical aspects, and too little to the human aspects of structure, culture and people (Boddy *et al.*, 2005). Each main heading will require further actions that people can identify and assign.

Lynch (2003) points out that managers handle this aspect of planning comprehen-sively, incrementally or selectively.

- **Comprehensive (specific) plan** This happens if managers decide to make a clear-cut change in direction, in response to a reassessment of the market, a financial crisis or a technological development. They assume that success depends on driving the changes rapidly and in a coordinated way across the organisation – which implies a compre-hensive plan.
- **Incremental (directional) plan** People use this approach in uncertain conditions – such as volatile markets or when direction depends on the outcome of research and development. Tasks, times and even the objective are likely to change as the outcomes of current and planned activities become known – 'Important strategic areas may be left deliberately unclear until the outcomes of current events have been established' (Lynch, 2003, p. 633).
- **Selective plan** This approach may work when neither of the other methods is the best way forward – such as when managers wish to make a comprehensive change, but are unable to do so because of deep opposition in some area affected by the plan. They may then try to implement the major change in only some areas of the business which, while not their preferred choice, may enable them to make some progress towards the objectives.

Communicating the plan

In a small organisation or where the plan deals with only one area, communication in any formal way is probably unnecessary. Equally, those who have been involved in devel-oping the objectives and plans will be well aware of it. However, in larger enterprises managers will probably invest time and effort in communicating both the objectives and the actions required throughout the areas affected. They do this to:

- ensure that everyone understands the plan;
- allow them to resolve any confusion and ambiguity;
- communicate the judgements and assumptions that underlie the plan;
- ensure that activities around the organisation are coordinated in practice as well as on paper.

6.8 Implementing plans and monitoring results

However good the plan, nothing worthwhile happens until people implement it, acting to make visible, physical changes to the organisation and the way people work within it. Many managers find this the most challenging part of the process – when plans, however well developed, are brought into contact with the processes people expect them to change. Those implementing the plan then come up against a variety of organisational and environmental obstacles – and possibly find that some of the assumptions in the plan are incorrect. When a new chief executive took over at Woolworths he commented that he had joined the group because of the great opportunities it offered to recover after a difficult trading period:

but I did not know how much of the work to be done was executional and how much about strategic positioning. Now I know that it is 80 per cent executional.

Organisations are slower to change than plans are to prepare – so events may overtake the plan. Miller *et al.* (2004) tracked the long-term outcomes of 150 strategic plans to establish how managers put them into action and how that affected performance. They defined implementation as

> all the processes and outcomes which accrue to a strategic decision once authorisation has been given to ... put the decision into practice (p. 203)

Their intention was to identify the conditions in which implementation occurs, the managerial activities involved in putting plans into practice, and the extent to which they achieved the objectives. They concluded that success was heavily influenced by:

- managers' experience of the issue; and
- the readiness of the organisation for the change.

> Having relevant experience of what has to be done ... enables managers to assess the objectives [and to] specify the tasks and resource implications appropriately, leading [those affected to accept the process]. (p. 206)

Readiness means a receptive organisational climate that enables managers to implement the change within a positive environment.

The statistical results were illustrated by cases that showed, for example, how managers in a successful company were able to implement a plan to upgrade their computer systems because they had *experience* of many similar changes. They were 'able to set targets, detail what needed doing and allocate the resources ... That is, they could plan and control the implementation effectively'. In another illustration, a regional brewer extending into the London area had no directly relevant experience, and so was not able to set a specific plan. But people in the organisation were very *receptive* to new challenges, and could implement the move with little formal planning.

The authors concluded that the activities of planning do not in themselves lead to success, but are a means for gaining acceptance of what has to be done when it is implemented. Planning helps by inducing confidence in the process, leading to high levels of acceptability. 'Planning is a necessary part of this approach to success, but it is not sufficient in itself' (Miller *et al.* (2004) p. 210).

The final stage in planning is to set up a system that allows people to monitor progress towards the goals. This happens at all levels of planning – from a project manager monitoring and controlling the progress of a discrete project to a board committee monitoring the progress of a broad strategic change that affects many parts of the business – such as integrating an acquisition, or entering a new line of business. This is sometimes called a programme, and monitoring then focuses on the interdependencies between many smaller specific projects.

Project plans define and display every task and activity, but someone managing a programme of linked projects would soon become swamped with such detail. The programme manager needs to maintain a quick-to-understand snapshot of the programme. This should show progress to date, the main events being planned, interdependencies, issues, and expected completion dates. This also helps the programme manager to communicate with senior executives and project managers. One way to do this is to create a single chart with a simplified view of each project on an indicative timeline. Figure 6.6 illustrates this. Details vary but the main features are usually:

- an indicative timeline, along which the individual projects are plotted;
- a simplified representation of the major milestones in each project or change;
- descriptions of progress made against that expected for each project;
- indications of interdependencies between projects.

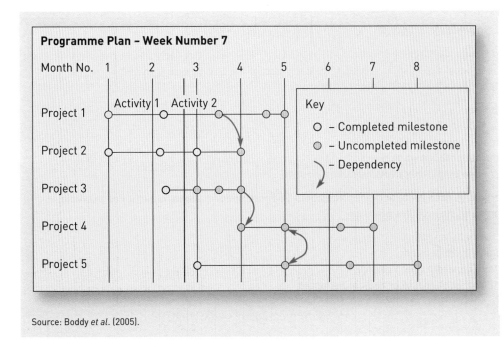

Figure 6.6

A programme overview chart

Source: Boddy *et al.* (2005).

Performance

Section 6.3 introduced the continuing controversy over whether planning affects performance, especially in conditions which are so uncertain that they are likely to change before a plan lasting longer than a year has been implemented. While most managers regularly engage in some form of strategic planning (Glaister and Falshaw, 1999), an influential group of writers (notably Mintzberg, 1994a) question the role of centralised planning, instead focusing on the autonomous actions of managers throughout the organisation. They argue that action by those familiar with local circumstances are the sources of significant strategic change, which planning tends to inhibit.

Andersen (2000) sought to reconcile these views by studying the use of strategic planning and autonomous action in three industries with different external conditions. He concluded that strategic planning was associated with superior organisational performance in all industrial settings. Whether industries were complex and dynamic or stable and simple, companies that planned performed better than those that did not. In addition, he found that in complex dynamic industries a formal planning process was accompanied by autonomous actions by managers, which further enhanced performance.

Responsibility

Many companies are now responding to the challenges posed by climate change, and are developing policies to reduce carbon emissions and other environmentally damaging practices. Such policy statements will depend on the quality of the plans managers develop – unless they make detailed plans they will be no more than good intentions. Some idea of the planning required to make a difference can be gained from Marks & Spencer's 'Plan A', announced in 2007 (see Chapter 8 case), illustrated in the Management in Practice feature.

The M&S 'Plan A'   www.marksandspencer.com

Plan A is a business-wide 'eco-plan' that will affect every part of the business over the next five years. The 100-point plan means that by 2012 the company will:

- become carbon neutral
- send no waste to landfill
- extend sustainable sourcing
- set new standards in ethical trading
- help customers and employees live a healthier lifestyle.

The plan sets targets in each area, and specifies about 20 more specific plans in each. For example, the item on reducing waste includes plans to:

- stop sending waste to landfill
- reduce packaging by 25 per cent
- use food waste to generate green energy
- use packaging from sustainable or recycled sources.

Source: Company press release, 15 January 2007 (on website).

In each of these areas more detailed plans will be required to bring the plan into reality – including ensuring that suppliers also plan changes in the way they operate.

Internationalisation

A theme in all international businesses is the extent to which they should plan the business on a global scale, or leave local managers with autonomy to adapt to local conditions. As Chapter 4 pointed out, the globalisation of markets was observed, and advocated, by Theodore Levitt, who noted the trend in the early 1980s for global brands to displace local products, with identical goods being sold across the globe without modification. This enabled consumer companies such as Coca-Cola and McDonald's to develop as identical global brands, with standard practices and a centralised management structure: it also implied a high degree of centralised planning, with major decisions being made at the centre and local companies implementing them.

This approach began to lose favour as local companies fought back, with customers often finding that new local brands offered better value. Global brands, offering standard products regardless of local tastes, lost market share. So rather than 'going global' they began to 'go local' – adapting products to suit local tastes.

The dilemma this raises is how far to plan globally, and how much to leave to local managers. Managers typically identify some features that are important to the overall health of the brand – such as ingredients or design, advertising or promotional style, and to the health of the business – such as financial performance. They are likely to plan these issues at the global level. They leave other matters, such as choice of suppliers or methods of distribution, to local planners. Establishing that balance in planning is likely to affect the value they add to resources.

Summary

1 Explain the purposes of planning and the content of different types of plan

- Effective plans can clarify direction, motivate people, use resources efficiently and allow people to measure progress towards objectives.

- Plans can be at strategic, tactical and operational levels, and in new businesses people prepare business plans to secure capital. Strategic business units also prepare plans relatively independently of the parent. There are also special-purpose or project plans, and standing plans. All can be either specific or directional in nature.

2 Compare alternative planning processes, and evaluate when each may be most suitable

- Plans can be formal/rational/top down in nature, or they can be adaptable and flexible (logical incrementalism); accumulating evidence that a combination of approaches is most likely to suit firms in volatile conditions.

3 Outline the seven iterative steps in planning and describe techniques used in each

- Recycling through the tasks of gathering information, developing a mission, setting goals, identifying actions and allocating resources, implementing plans, monitoring progress and evaluating results.

- Planners draw information from the general and competitive environments using tools such as Porter's five forces analysis. They can do this within the framework of a SWOT analysis, and also use forecasting, sensitivity analysis, critical success factors and scenario planning techniques.

4 Use theory to evaluate the motivational effect of the goals stated in a plan

- Goal-setting theory predicts that goals can be motivational if people perceive the targets to be difficult but achievable.

- Goals can also be evaluated in terms of whether they are specific, measurable, attainable, rewarded and timed.

5 Use a framework to evaluate whether a plan is sufficiently comprehensive

- The 'wheel' provides a model for recalling the likely areas in an organisation that a plan should cover, indicating the likely ripple effects of change in one area on others.

6 Evaluate the context that will affect the ability of managers to implement a plan

- The value of a plan depends on people implementing it, but Miller's research shows that that depends on the experience of those implementing it, and the receptivity of the organisation to change.

Review questions

1 What types of planning do you do in your personal life? Describe them in terms of whether they are (a) strategic or operational, (b) short or long term, (c) specific or directional.

2 What are four benefits that people in organisations may gain from planning?

3 What are the main sources of information that managers can use in planning? What models can they use to structure this information?

4 In what ways can a goal be motivational? What practical things can people do in forming plans that take account of goal-setting theory?

5 What is meant by the term 'hierarchy of objectives', and how can that idea help people to build a consistent plan? What else would managers need to do once they have agreed a hierarchy of objectives?

6 Explain the term 'organisational receptivity', and how people can use the idea in developing a plan that is more likely to work.

7 What are the main ways of monitoring progress on a plan, and why is this so vital a task in planning?

8 As environments become more uncertain, will planning become more or less useful? How can managers plan effectively in a rapidly changing environment?

Concluding critical reflection

Think about the way your company, or one with which you are familiar, makes plans. Review the material in the chapter, and perhaps visit some of the websites identified. Then make notes on these questions:

● What examples of the themes discussed in this chapter are currently relevant to your company? What types of plans are you most closely involved with? Which of the techniques suggested do you and your colleagues typically use, and why? What techniques do you use that are not mentioned here?

● In responding to these issues, what **assumptions** about the nature of planning in business appear to guide your approach? Are the prevailing assumptions closer to the planning or emergent perspectives, and why do you think that is?

● What factors in the **context** of the company appear to shape your approach to planning – what kind of environment are you working in, for example? To what extent does your planning process involve people from other organisations – and why is that?

● Have you compared your planning processes with those in other companies to check if they use **alternative** methods to yours? How do they plan?

● Have you considered the **limitations** of your approach – such as whether you plan too much, or too little? What limitations can you see in some of the ideas presented here – for example the usefulness of scenario planning or SWOT analyses?

Further reading

Johnson, G., Scholes, K. and Whittington, R. (2006), *Exploring Corporate Strategy* (7th edn.), Financial Times/Prentice Hall, Harlow.

> The best-selling European text on corporate strategy. Although more detailed than required at introductory level, a number of sections usefully build on this chapter.

Dobson, P., Starkey, K. and Richards, J. (2004), *Strategic Management: Issues and cases*, Blackwell, Oxford.

Smith, R.J. (1994), *Strategic Management and Planning in the Public Sector*, Longman/Civil Service College, Harlow.

> Both cover the main elements in the strategic planning process and explain, with the use of examples, some planning tools in addition to those covered in this chapter. Smith's book also contains useful chapters on definitions and terminology and options analysis.

Weblinks

These websites have appeared in the chapter:

www.dsm.com
www.sabmiller.com
www.fiat.co.uk
www.merck.com
www.electrolux.com
www.cw.com
www.shell.com
www.powergen.co.uk
www.marksandspencer.com
www.cocacola.com

Visit two of the sites in the list, and navigate to the pages dealing with corporate news, or investor relations.

● What planning issues can you identify that managers in the company are likely to be dealing with?

● What kind of environment are they likely to be working in, and how will that affect their planning methods and processes?

Annotated weblinks, multiple choice questions and other useful resources can be found on **www.pearsoned.co.uk/boddy**

Chapter 7

Decision making

Aim

To identify major aspects of decision making in organisations and to outline alternative ways of making decisions.

Objectives

By the end of your work on this chapter you should be able to outline the concepts below in your own terms and:

1 Explain the tasks in making a decision and how decision processes affect the outcome
2 Explain, and give examples of, programmed and non-programmed decisions
3 Distinguish between certainty, risk, uncertainty and ambiguity
4 Contrast rational, administrative, political and garbage can decision models
5 Give examples of common sources of bias in decisions
6 Explain the contribution of Vroom and Yetton, and of Irving Janis, to our understanding of decision making in groups.

Key terms

This chapter introduces the following ideas:

decision	ambiguity
decision making	rational model of decision making
problem	administrative model of decision
opportunity	making
decision criteria	bounded rationality
decision tree	satisficing
programmed decision	incremental model
procedure	heuristics
rule	prior hypothesis bias
policy	representativeness bias
non-programmed decision	illusion of control
certainty	escalating commitment
risk	groupthink
uncertainty	

Each is a term defined within the text, as well as in the Glossary at the end of the book.

Wipro provides a growing range of IT services to companies around the world. In the year to March 2006 it reported that sales had reached $US 2.4 billion – 33 per cent above the previous year. It employed over 50,000 staff (23,000 in 2004). Azim Premji is chairman of the company and follows an exhausting work routine even though he is India's richest person:

[His day begins at 7 with] meetings with visiting customers or government officials. That's followed by meetings where he focuses on the minutiae of business. Before the sun is overhead Premji has already worked seven hours, with another seven to go. Frequently he ends his day on a commercial flight – there is no corporate jet – to Bombay, San Francisco or London – anywhere his sales team needs a boost.

The company has grown from being a small producer of cooking oil (Western India Vegetable Products) founded by his father. He took charge in 1966 when he was 21 and immediately began to professionalise the company. He held staff meetings by telephone every Monday morning at which regional managers reported on their performance and were set new goals for the following week.

He empowered his managers. They were free to set prices in their regions as they saw fit. But they were also held accountable for their performance. These were innovations for India, which (had a tradition of bureaucracy and government control). (Hamm, 2007, p. 34)

Sales grew, but Premji wanted to broaden the business. He had no long-term plan, but saw opportunities in new areas – diversifying into toilet soaps and beauty products, and into manufacturing construction equipment. His next diversification laid the foundations for the modern company.

In 1977 the Indian government passed new rules that required foreign companies to operate through local, Indian-owned partners. IBM, then the world's dominant computer company, left the country, creating an opportunity for Indian companies to enter the market for computer hardware. Premji recalls: 'When IBM left, it created a vacuum. So we decided to zero in on info tech.'

By 1981 the company was selling the computers it had designed, which were India's top-selling machines for several years. In 1984 it moved into software with a spreadsheet and word-processing package.

Wipro

In the early 1990s the rules changed again, with serious consequences. The Indian government liberalised its business regulations, which enabled the world's top computer companies to move into the country again. Their R&D resources and sales volumes would soon allow them to overcome Wipro. The head of the IT unit, Sridhar Mitta, had the idea of selling the company's expertise to the world's top tech companies:

We saw that while the door was open for others to come in, it was also open for us to go out. So we decided to become a global company.

As a relatively unknown company growth was slow, but a large contract from a major US company, General Electric in 1990 helped Wipro's credibility. Initially the work was in low-value software coding and maintenance, but has extended into more advanced areas of designing software and complete IT systems. Premji has also expanded his reach into the Middle East where US companies are unwelcome.

Recent decisions have involved moving the technology division's HQ to California to be closer to the customers, and acquiring smaller companies that will add to the range of expertise and services it can offer.

Sources: Based on *The Economist*, 6 February 2003; Hamm (2007); Wipro *Annual Report 2005-06* from the company website.

Case questions 7.1

- Make a note of the decisions that Mr Premji has made in the story so far.
- How have they affected the development of the business?
- Visit Wipro's website, and note examples of recent decisions that have shaped the company.

7.1 Introduction

The case recounts the recent history of one of India's biggest and most successful companies, which is now a global player in the market for IT services. To develop the business from a local cooking oil firm to its present position senior managers at Wipro needed to decide where to allocate time, effort and other resources. Over the years their decisions paid off and they now face new issues, such as how to attract customers and well-qualified staff against competition from established global companies. Wipro also faces political reactions from foreign governments about the loss of local jobs when work is outsourced. How managers decide to deal with matters such as these will shape Wipro's future.

The performance of every organisation reflects (as well as luck and good fortune) the decisions that people make, and there are many studies of the activity – Buchanan and O'Connell (2006) provide a historical review. People continually make choices (including that of ignoring an issue and avoiding a decision), as they see problems that may need attention, and ideas or proposals they may be able to use. Resources are limited, there are many demands on them, and people have different goals. Their choices relate to all aspects of the management task – decisions about inputs (how to raise capital, who to employ), outputs (what products to make, how to distribute them) and transformations (how to organise the delivery of a new service, how to manage the finances). Decisions affect how well the organisation uses resources, and whether it transforms them in a way that creates sufficient value (as seen by customers) to ensure it survives: 'Like management itself, decision-making is a generic process that is applicable to all forms of organised activity' (Harrison, 1999, p. 8). Choice is a source of tension as it makes us worry about 'what if' we had selected the other option (Schwartz, 2005).

J.K. Rowling (estimated, in 2007, to be the wealthiest person in the media business) offered the manuscript of the original Harry Potter story to several leading publishers, whose editors decided to reject it: an editor at Bloomsbury decided to accept it. The managers of the European Airbus 380 project decided in July 2004 to increase production from 20 to 30 a year. By 2007 technical difficulties were delaying deliveries by two years – so airlines that had ordered the aircraft needed to decide whether to cancel their order or accept the delay and seek compensation.

Figure 7.1 illustrates the themes of the chapter, showing that decision making involves:

- identifying the type of decision
- identifying the conditions surrounding the decision
- using one or more models to guide the approach
- selecting a decision-making style
- working through the process and implementing the decision.

The chapter begins with the tasks through which people make decisions and identifies types of decision. It compares four models of the decision-making process, and finally examines a method for deciding how much to involve others in making decisions.

7.2 Tasks in making decisions

A **decision** is a specific commitment to action (usually a commitment of resources).

A **decision** is a specific commitment to action (usually a commitment of resources). People make such choices at several levels – individual, group, organisational and societal (Harrison, 1999) – and will be influenced to some extent by decisions made at the other levels.

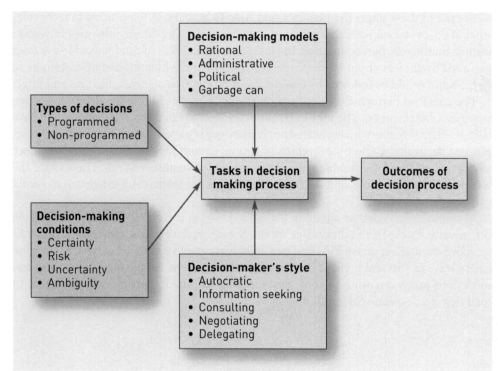

Figure 7.1

An overview of
decision making in
organisations

- **Individual** People make individual choices about all aspects of their lives, and in relation to organisations they make choices about careers, whether to change job or not, how hard to work, whether to apply for promotion or make a complaint.
- **Group** Members of a group continually make decisions about how to work together, accomplish a task or choose a new member. They are still individuals, but their decisions reflect relationships and mutual expectations.
- **Organisational** These decisions are made by people in their organisational roles. They are still individuals and will often be part of a team resolving a problem – but will be aware of what others expect, and of organisational policies and practices.
- **Societal** People outside the organisation make decisions that affect those within it – either directly (awarding a contract) or indirectly (changing a tax). People within organisations also seek to influence, and be part of, these external processes.

Managers at Nokia, seeking to maintain the company's dominant position in the mobile phone market, constantly have to choose between several possible models to launch. In 2003 they made some wrong decisions, favouring models that customers did not like, and lost sales. Later choices must have been better, since by 2007 sales were rising again and the company had recovered its position. Such decisions are part of a wider process of **decision making** – which includes identifying problems, opportunities and possible solutions. It involves effort before and after the actual choice. In deciding whether to select Jean, Bob or Rasul for a job the manager would probably, amongst other things, have to:

Decision making is the process of identifying problems and opportunities and then resolving them.

- identify the need for a new member of staff
- perhaps persuade his or her boss to authorise the budget
- decide where to advertise the post
- interview candidates
- select the preferred candidate
- decide whether or not to agree to their request for a better deal, and
- arrange their induction into the job so that they work effectively.

At each of these stages the manager may have to go back in the process to reconsider what to do, or to deal with another set of decisions – such as the sensitive area of who to include on the selection committee. In Nokia's case the choice of model would have been preceded by choices about the basic design concept and which groups of customers to target – and would be followed by choices about production volumes, features and price.

The effect on performance depends on the actions that follow the decision – when someone implements it. The visible, public actions that tell us about a decision will have been preceded by many invisible choices. A manager is making small but potentially significant decisions all the time – which of several urgent jobs to deal with next, whose advice to seek about them, which report to read, which customer to call. These shape the way people use their time, and the issues they decide are sufficiently important to earn a place on the agenda.

As we make decisions we attend to the tasks shown in Figure 7.2 – the arrows showing the iterative nature of the process, as we move back and forwards between the tasks. As we move through an activity we find new information, reconsider what we are doing, go back a stage or two and perhaps decide on a different route. People may also miss a step, or pay too much attention to some and too little to others. Putting enough time into each step is a decision-making skill.

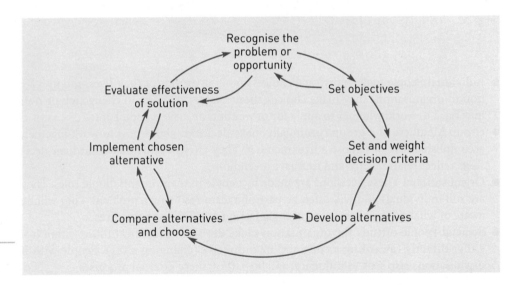

Figure 7.2

Tasks in making decisions

Paul Nutt on why decisions fail

Paul Nutt studied over 400 decisions involving major commitments of resources. He distinguished between a 'discovery process' that usually led to success, and an 'idea imposition process' which usually led to failure. Decision makers select tactics that push their process towards one or other of these types, and Nutt argues that by being aware of these managers have a better chance of success than failure.

Those following a discovery process spend time at the start looking beyond the initial claim that 'a problem has arisen that requires a decision': they spend time *understanding the claims* – by talking to stakeholders to judge the strength of their concerns and their views. This leads to a better-informed expression of the 'arena of action' on which to take a decision. They also identify at the outset the forces that may block them from *implementing the preferred idea*, as this helps to understand the interests of stakeholders whose support may be required.

These early actions enable decision makers *to set a direction* – an agreed outcome of the decision. Dealing thoroughly with these three stages makes the remaining stages – *uncovering and evaluating ideas* – comparatively easy, as they help build agreement on what the decision is expected to achieve. Those following an idea imposition process

skip some stages ... jump to conclusions and then try to implement the solution they have stumbled upon. This bias for action causes them to limit their search, consider very few ideas, and pay too little attention to people who are affected, despite the fact that decisions fail for just these reasons. (Nutt, 2002, p. 49)

Source: Nutt (2002).

Recognising a problem and setting objectives

People make decisions that commit time and other resources towards meeting an objective. They do so when they become aware of a **problem** – a gap between an existing and a desired state of affairs, or an **opportunity** – the chance to do something not previously expected. An example to illustrate the steps would be a manager who needs to decide whether to buy new laptops for members of their sales team. The team have been complaining that their present machines are too slow and do not have enough capacity for the volume of work. The sales manager now has a problem, but in real life few problems are that obvious. Is a 5 per cent drop in sales a problem? Identifying a problem as significant is a subjective, possibly contentious matter. Before a problem (or opportunity) gets on to the agenda, enough people have to be aware of it and feel sufficient pressure to act. Managers at Microsoft were slow to realise that Linux software was a serious threat to their growth, and this delay lost valuable time.

A **problem** is a gap between an existing and a desired state of affairs.

An **opportunity** is the chance to do something not previously expected.

Denial at P&G   www.pg.com

Procter & Gamble (P&G), the world's largest consumer products company (brands include Tide, Pampers and Crest), is undergoing radical change to increase profitability. This drive is being led by A.G. Laffley, a long-term manager at the company, who became CEO in 2000.

For most of its history P&G was one of the United States' leading companies, with brands that have become household names in many parts of the world. Many of its management techniques have also been widely adopted – such as the idea of having competing brands within the same company, to encourage performance. But by the 1990s P&G was in danger of becoming another Eastman Kodak or Xerox, a once-great company that had lost its way. Sales of most of its top 18 brands were slowing; the company was losing ground to more focused rivals such as Kimberly-Clark and Colgate-Palmolive. At the same time, the dynamics of the industry were changing as power shifted from manufacturers to massive retailers.

Through all of this, much of senior management was in denial. Laffley says: 'Nobody wanted to talk about it. Without a doubt [I and a few others] were in the camp of "We need a much bigger change".'

Source: *Business Week*, 7 July 2003.

Managers become aware of a problem as they compare existing conditions with the state they desire. If things are not as they should be – the sales reps are complaining that their slow laptops prevent them doing their jobs properly – then there is a problem.

People are only likely to act if they feel pressure to do so – such as a rep threatening to leave or a customer complaining about the time it takes to download the latest prices. Pressure comes from many sources – and people differ in whether they pay attention to the signals: some will react quickly, others will ignore uncomfortable information and postpone a difficult (to them) decision.

Setting and weighting the decision criteria

Decision criteria define the factors that are relevant in making a decision.

To decide between two or more options people need some **decision criteria** – the factors that are relevant to the decision. Until people set these, they cannot choose between options: in the laptop case criteria could include usefulness of features, price, delivery, warranty, compatibility with other systems, ease of use and many more. Some criteria are more important than others and the decision process needs to represent this in some way – perhaps by assigning 100 points between the factors depending on their relative importance. We can measure some of these criteria (price or delivery) quite objectively, while others (features, ease of use) are subjective.

Like problem recognition, setting criteria is subjective: people vary in the factors they wish to include, and the weights they assign to them. They may also have private and unexpressed criteria – such as 'will cause least trouble', 'will do what the boss expects', 'will help my career'. Changing the criteria or their relative weights will change the decision – so the manager in the laptop case also has to decide whether to set and weight the criteria herself, or to invite the views of the reps.

Developing alternatives

Another task is to identify several alternative solutions to the problem. In the laptop case this is a matter of identifying currently available brands and is not difficult. In more complex problems the alternatives themselves may need to be developed. A practical issue is how many alternatives to develop – and how much time and effort to put into the process. Developing too few limits choice, but developing too many will be costly and may overwhelm decision makers. Barry Schwartz (2005) found this in his study of individual decision making – giving people more choices beyond a certain point can be counter-productive. More choice means more stress, frustration and anxiety that they may make the wrong decision – see Key Ideas.

 **key ideas   Too many jams to choose**

Iyengar and Lepper (2000) demonstrated that consumers protect themselves from the stress of too much choice by refusing to purchase. In an experiment conducted in a food store, they set up a tasting booth offering different types of jam. When 24 types were on display, about 60 per cent of passers-by stopped at the booth, compared with just 40 per cent when only 6 jams were shown. But when it came to choosing a pot of jam to buy, the proportions changed. Just 3 per cent of the visits to the 24 jam booth resulted in a purchase, while 30 per cent of those who visited the smaller display made a purchase. The limited selection was the most effective in converting interest into sales.

Source: Iyengar and Lepper (2000).

Comparing alternatives and making a choice

As in daily life, management decisions depend on a system for comparing alternatives and making a choice. Which bar, where to holiday, whether to bid for a house – people compare alternatives and decide between them. In a simple case, the chosen criteria may quickly show the best choice. Since criteria and their weights are subjective, a choice that is made by several people can end in argument and disagreement – those who do not like the choice may reopen the debate by proposing different criteria.

Figure 7.3 illustrates the tasks in making a decision through a simple personal example. Although superficially simple, people find these choices difficult – mainly in the area of setting criteria. Some are easy to state and compare (price, warranty) but others are inherently subjective (in fashion?) and so are open to wide differences of interpretation. The more people involved, the more difficult it may be to resolve these issues.

Another way to structure a situation in which there are several alternative actions is to draw a **decision tree**. This helps to assess the relative suitability of the options by assessing them against identified criteria – successively eliminating the options as each relevant factor is introduced. Figure 7.8 is an example of a decision tree – it shows how a manager can decide the most suitable method of solving a problem by asking a succession of questions about the situation, leading to the most likely solution for those circumstances. The main challenge in using the technique is to identify the logical sequence of intermediate decisions and how they relate to each other.

A **decision tree** helps someone to make a choice by progressively eliminating options as additional criteria or events are added to the tree.

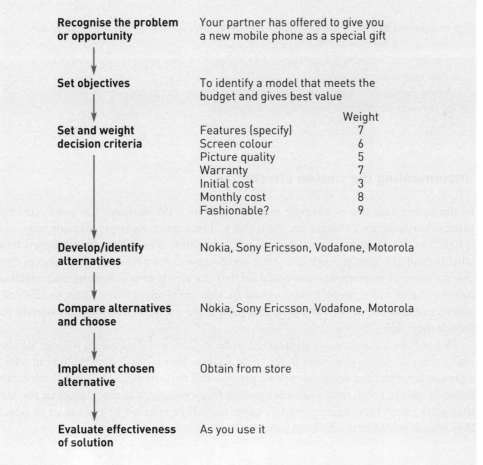

Figure 7.3

Illustrating the decision-making tasks – a new mobile phone

| Activity 7.1 | Critical reflection on making a decision |

Work through the steps in Figure 7.3 for a decision you currently face – such as where to go on holiday, which courses to choose next year, or which job to apply for. Then do the same for a decision that involves several other people, such as which assignment to do in your study group or where to go for a night out together.

If you work in an organisation, select two business decisions as the focus of your work.

- How did working through the steps affect the way you reached a decision?
- Did it help you think more widely about the alternatives?
- How did the second decision, involving more people, affect the usefulness of the method?
- Then reflect on the technique itself – did it give insight into the decision process? What other tasks should it include?

| key ideas | Mintzberg's study of major decisions |

Henry Mintzberg and his colleagues studied 25 major, unstructured decisions in 25 organisations, finding that rational techniques could not cope with the complexity of strategic decisions. They concluded that:

- Whether people recognised the need for a decision depended on the strength of the stimuli, the reputation of the source and the availability of a potential solution.
- Most decisions depended on designing a custom-made solution (a new organisation structure, a new product or a new technology).
- The choice phase (see Figure 7.2), was less significant than the design phase: it was essentially ratifying a solution that was determined implicitly during design.

Source: Mintzberg *et al.* (1976).

Implementing the chosen alternative

In the laptop case this is a simple matter – provided the manager has conducted the process satisfactorily. In bigger decisions this will be a much more problematic stage as it is here that the decision is translated, or not, into visible action. Even then it depends on what is meant by 'implementation'. If the decision concerns a new computer system then one measure of implementation could be that the equipment is bought and installed. Another (and more useful) view would be that implementation refers to the wide acceptance and use of the system so that people are using it effectively to improve the service they offer.

This will be a much more protracted process, and will depend on people making many other decisions elsewhere in the organisation. This is also where the way in which a person conducts the decision-making process will become evident. If implementation depends on the cooperation of other people (for example, a major change in the way they work) then their willingness to cooperate will be affected by the extent to which they were involved in the decision process.

Wipro – the case continues   www.wipro.com   CASE STUDY

Decide quickly, and don't be afraid to switch

A company facing rapidly changing technical and business conditions needs to be able to make decisions quickly. Wipro has evolved a management rhythm that is organised around the type of decisions managers have to make. There are:

- weekly meetings in each business unit about spotting and fixing problems, or exploiting opportunities (continuing the meetings with regional managers in the cooking oil business);
- monthly IT management meetings to introduce and adjust tactics;
- quarterly strategy council meetings to decide longer-term issues.

In each of these meetings, the spirit of experimentation is pervasive. Managers are inclined to try things and get them going fast – essentially pilot projects. They track the projects closely, so if something doesn't work, they spot it quickly and make adjustments, or even pull the plug. (Hamm, 2006, p. 286)

Source: Hamm (2007).

Case questions 7.2

- Compare this account with Nutt's analysis (p. 210) of why decisions fail, and try to identify how closely Wipro's approach matches Nutt's recommendations.
- What are the advantages and disadvantages of quick decision making?

Evaluating the decision

The final stage is evaluation – looking back to see if the decision has resolved the problem, and what can be learned. It is a form of control, which people are often reluctant to do formally, preferring to turn their attention to future tasks rather than reflect on the past. That choice inhibits their ability to learn from experience.

Having given this simplified overview of the process, the following sections outline different types of decisions, and some models that seek to explain how people make them.

7.3   Types of decisions

Strategic and operational decisions

Strategic decisions have greater implications for the organisation than operational ones. As Chapter 8 shows, strategy is the business of developing the future direction of the organisation, by committing major resources to one area rather than another. Strategic decisions relate to the world outside the organisation – to develop a new product, acquire a competitor, enter an overseas market or increase a price. Strategic decisions affect the future of large parts of the organisation – such as when managers at Philips decided to change from being a traditional electronic manufacturer to a healthcare and technology group. This in turn led to the disposal of its interests in semiconductor manufacturing and the purchase of medical equipment companies.

Activity 7.2 **Critical reflection on types of decisions**

Reflect on your experience and identify new examples of these types of decision:

- **Clear choice** – choosing between two candidates
- **Competing choice** – whether to appoint new staff, outsource the work or close the service
- **Choice avoidance** – not acknowledging that current staff cannot provide adequate service
- **Choice suppression** – not introducing feedback forms that would make complaints visible.

Compare your examples with those of other students. Are these categories the only ones? Do some of your examples not fit any of them? How did those involved make each decision?

management in practice **McDonald's decides on a new menu** www.mcdonalds.com

In 2004 McDonald's, the world's largest fast food chain and a popular target for those concerned about obesity, announced that it would introduce a new range of salads in its European restaurants. Dennis Hennequin, executive vice-president for Europe, promised that space for the new products would be created by eliminating two traditional burgers from the menu. The company has also stopped selling several super-size portions of fries and drinks. Mr Hennequin had taken on his present job earlier in the year, in recognition of his success in turning France into McDonald's fastest-growing European market. His decisions there to upgrade restaurants and modernise menus will be the template for what will be done elsewhere in Europe. The menu will include many new ingredients and reflect Hennequin's belief that the company must start catering to a new customer awareness of the need for a well-balanced diet.

Source: Based on *Financial Times*, 9 March 2004.

Operational (or activity-related) decisions are shorter term, often on day-to-day matters, and within established policy: whether to recruit staff, to replace a machine or to offer a discount to a customer.

Programmed and non-programmed decisions

A **programmed decision** is a repetitive decision that can be handled by a routine approach.

A **procedure** is a series of related steps to deal with a structured problem.

A **rule** sets out what someone can or cannot do in a given situation.

A **policy** is a guideline that establishes some general principles for making a decision.

Programmed decisions (Simon, 1960) deal with problems that are familiar, and where the information required is easy to define and obtain – the situation is well structured. If a store manager notices that a product is selling more than expected there will be a simple, routine procedure for deciding how much extra to order from the supplier. Decisions are structured to the extent that they arise frequently and can be dealt with routinely by following an established **procedure** – a series of related steps, often set out in a manual, to deal with a structured problem. They may also reach a decision by using an established **rule**, which sets out what someone can or cannot do in a given situation. They may also refer to a **policy** – a guideline that establishes some general principles for making a decision.

People make programmed decisions to resolve recurring problems – to reorder supplies when stocks drop below a defined level, to set the qualifications required for a job, to decide whether to lend money to a bank customer. Once managers formulate procedures, rules or policies others can usually make the decisions. Computers handle many decisions of this type – the checkout systems in supermarkets calculate the items sold and order new stock.

Simon (1960) also observed that people make **non-programmed decisions** to deal with situations that are unstructured, and so require a unique solution. The issue has not arisen in quite that form, and the information required is unclear, vague or open to many interpretations. Major management decisions are of this type – such as the choice that managers at Virgin faced over whether to delay their order for Airbus 380 planes for 18 months until the weight of the new airliner was reduced to that originally promised. Several solutions were being tested, but it was not clear when they would be ready, nor how passengers would react to them. Most issues of strategy are of this type, because they involve great uncertainty and many interests.

> A **non-programmed decision** is a unique decision that requires a custom-made solution when information is lacking or unclear.

People need to deal with programmed and non-programmed decisions in different ways. The former are amenable to procedures, routines, rules and quantitative analytical techniques such as those associated with operational research. They are also suitable for resolution by modern information systems. Non-programmed decisions depend on judgement and intuition.

Figure 7.4 relates the type of decision to the levels of the organisation. Those lower in the organisation typically deal with routine, structured problems that they can resolve by applying procedures. As people move up the hierarchy they face correspondingly more unstructured decisions. It is easy to see why this happens – lower-level staff hand decisions that do not fit the rules to someone above them to deal with; those higher up pass routine matters to subordinates.

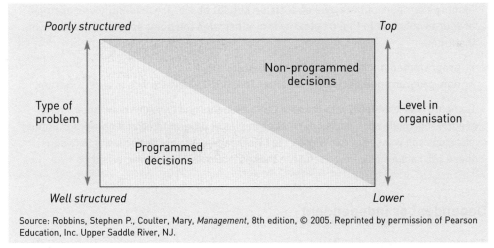

Source: Robbins, Stephen P., Coulter, Mary, *Management*, 8th edition, © 2005. Reprinted by permission of Pearson Education, Inc. Upper Saddle River, NJ.

Figure 7.4

Types of decision, types of problem and level in the organisation

Many decisions have elements of each type – non-programmed decisions probably contain elements that can be handled in a programmed way.

Wipro – the case continues   www.wipro.com   C A S E   S T U D Y

Non-programmed decisions – growth goals and the Wipro way

In 1999 Premji hired Vivek Paul (from GE Medical Systems) as head of Wipro Technologies, with the goal of accelerating growth. Paul had seen the capabilities of Wipro staff, and was eager for the chance to run the global technology business. However, other tech businesses were also growing rapidly, and he feared this would make it difficult to retain and excite staff. He decided that Wipro was not thinking big enough. He and his aides came up with a challenging growth goal – to be a $4 billion company by the end of 2004 (the 4 × 4 plan): 'We decided to dream big, and people had the confidence we could actually achieve it.'

Paul left in 2005, and the company faced challenges from other Indian companies such as Tata and Infosys, and from overseas competitors. To attack these issues, Premji took personal charge of the technology business, deciding that Wipro needed to be more aggressive about growing revenues, both organically and through acquisition. He sought more innovative solutions, and continued the practice of frequent reorganisations.

He and his executive team also decided to formalise the company's core philosophy – the Wipro Way. This gives all managers and employees a clear target at which to aim. It identifies Wipro's four pillars of strength – customer centred, process excellence, people management and career development. Then it sets a high bar for each of them – such as to have the best customer satisfaction ratings of any company in the industry.

Source: Hamm (2007).

Activity 7.3   Programmed and non-programmed decisions

Identify examples of the types of decision set out above. Try to identify one example of your own to add to those below or that illustrates the point specifically within your institution:

- **programmed decision** – whether to reorder stock
- **non-programmed decision** – whether to launch a new service in a new market.

Compare your examples with those of other students and consider how those responsible made each decision. What examples of programmed and non-programmed decisions can you see in the Wipro case? How easy is it to divide decisions between these two categories – how useful are they as distinguishing characteristics?

Dependent or independent

Another way to categorise decisions is in terms of their links to other decisions. People make decisions in a historical and social context and so are influenced by past and possible future decisions and the influence of other parts of the organisation.

Many decisions are influenced by previous decisions – that constrain, or enable, what can be done now. When Hutcheson began to offer third-generation (3G) mobile services in 2004 it was able to offer more competitive prices than established companies. The latter were concerned that if they cut charges on their third-generation services this would affect revenues from existing customers. Hutcheson, as the new entrant, did not depend on revenues from earlier decisions. Legacy computer systems (the result of earlier decisions) frequently constrain how quickly a company can adopt new systems.

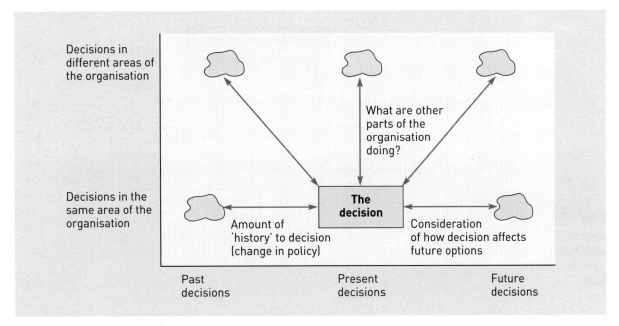

Figure 7.5 Possible relationships between decisions
Source: Cooke and Slack (1991), p. 24.

Some decisions have few implications beyond their immediate area, but others have significant ripples around the organisation. Changes in technology, for example, usually require consistent, supportive changes in structures and processes if they are to be effective – but decisions on these areas are harder to make than those affecting the technology. More generally, local units may be limited in their decisions by wider company policies. Figure 7.5 illustrates this.

7.4 Decision-making conditions

Decisions arise within a wider context, and the conditions in this context, as measured by the degree of **certainty, risk, uncertainty** and **ambiguity,** materially affect the decision process.

A major factor distinguishing structured from unstructured decisions is the degree of certainty managers deal with in making the decision. Some aspects of a decision are unknowable – what Nokia's competitors will be charging next year, whether GSK's pharmaceutical research programme will deliver the new drugs the company needs to keep revenue growing. Decisions based on assumptions about these future conditions may not turn out as people hope. Managers try to obtain information about the options facing them to reduce this uncertainty.

Figure 7.6 relates the nature of the problem to the type of decision. People can deal with conditions of certainty by making programmed decisions, but many situations are both uncertain and ambiguous. Here people need to be able to use a non-programmed approach.

Certainty describes the situation when all the information the decision maker needs is available.

Risk refers to situations in which the decision maker is able to estimate the likelihood of the alternative outcomes.

Uncertainty is when people are clear about their goals but have little information about which course of action is most likely to succeed.

Ambiguity is when people are uncertain about their goals and how best to achieve them.

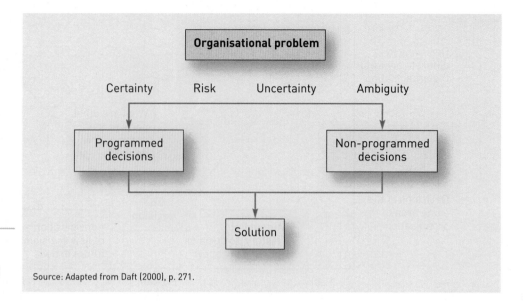

Figure 7.6

Degree of
uncertainty and
decision-making
type

Source: Adapted from Daft (2000), p. 271.

Certainty

Certainty is when the decision maker has all the information they need – are fully
informed about the costs and benefits of each alternative. A company treasurer wanting
to place reserve funds can readily compare rates of interest from several banks, and calculate exactly the return from each. Few decisions are that certain, and most contain risk
and/or uncertainty.

Risk

Risk refers to situations in which the decision maker can estimate the likelihood of the
alternative outcomes, possibly using statistical methods. Banks have developed tools to
assess credit risk, and so reduce the risk of a borrower not repaying a loan. The questions
on an application form for a loan (home ownership, time at this address, employer's
name, etc.) enable the bank to assess the risk of lending money to that person.

Uncertainty

Uncertainty means that people know what they wish to achieve but do not have enough
information about alternatives and future events to estimate the risk confidently. Factors
that may affect the outcomes of deciding to launch a new product (future growth in the
market, changes in customer interests, competitors' actions) are difficult to predict.

Managers at GSK, the pharmaceutical group, experienced great uncertainty in a decision to allocate research funds. Scientists who wished to develop a new range of
vaccines had to persuade the board to divert resources to their project. Uncertainties
included the fact that the science was evolving rapidly, discoveries could be made elsewhere, and it would be many years before the research produced commercial results.
The board approved the investment, and the line of work is now a major product
within GSK Biologicals.

Ambiguity

Ambiguity describes a situation in which the intended goals are unclear, and so the alternative ways of reaching them are equally fluid. Ambiguity is by far the most difficult decision situation. Students would experience ambiguity if their teacher created student groups, told each group to complete a project, but gave them no topic, direction or guidelines. Ambiguous problems are those where people have difficulty in coming to grips with the issues, and they are often associated with conflicts over ends and means, rapidly changing circumstances and unclear links between decision elements – see Management in Practice.

Ambiguity at EADS defers a decision www.eads.com

EADS is the parent company of Airbus, and has experienced long-running conflicts between French and German shareholders. In 2007 the board was under pressure to approve a cost-cutting plan proposed by the chief executive of Airbus, necessary because of the delays to the A380, which has increased losses at the company. It is also trying to launch a project to build a new fleet of aircraft to compete with Boeing's Dreamliner, but has been unable to agree how to divide the work between operations in France, Germany, Spain and the United Kingdom. National political conflicts at the highest level over this long-term issue were preventing the board from deciding the short-term restructuring issue.

Source: *Financial Times*, 20 February 2007.

Case questions 7.3

- Reflect on the decisions at Wipro that you identified earlier. What risks, uncertainties or ambiguities were probably associated with them?
- When the company moved its technology division to California, what dependencies would that have involved (use Figure 7.5 to structure your answer)?
- If the company expands its business in the Middle East, what dependencies might that raise?

7.5 Decision-making models

James Thompson (1967) distinguished decisions on two dimensions – agreement or disagreement over goals, and the beliefs that decision makers hold about the relationship between cause and effect. A decision can be mapped on these two dimensions – whether or not there is agreement on goals, and how certain people are about the consequences of their decisions. Figure 7.7 shows these, and an approach to making decisions that seems best suited to each cell.

Computational strategy – rational model

The **rational model of decision making** is based on economic assumptions. Traditional economic models suggested that the role of a manager was to maximise the economic return to the firm, and that they did this by making decisions on economically rational criteria. The assumptions underlying this model are that the decision maker:

The **rational model of decision making** assumes that people make consistent choices to maximise economic value within specified constraints.

● aims for goals that are known and agreed, and that the problem is structured;
● strives for conditions of certainty, gathering complete information and calculating the likely results of each alternative;
● selects the alternative that will maximise economic returns;
● is rational and logical in assigning values, setting preferences and evaluating alternatives.

	Consensus on goals or problem definition?	
	Agree	*Disagree*
Certainty	I Computational strategy Rational model	III Compromise strategy Political model
Beliefs about cause-and-effect relationships *Uncertainty*	II Judgemental strategy Incremental model	IV Inspirational strategy Garbage can model

Figure 7.7
Conditions favouring different decision processes

Source: Huczynski and Buchanan (2007, p. 754).

The rational model is normative, in that it defines how a decision maker should act – it does not describe how managers actually make decisions. It aims to help decision makers act more rationally, rather than rely solely on intuition and personal preferences, and is most valuable for programmed decisions where there is little conflict. Where the information required is available and people can agree the criteria for choice, the approach can work well.

key ideas   Evidence-based management?

Pfeffer and Sutton (2006a) note that managers frequently make decisions without considering the evidence about what works, and what does not. They often base decisions on:

experience (which may or may not fit current circumstances);
solutions with which they are familiar;
accepting commercially motivated claims about a technique;
dogmas or beliefs for which there is no reliable evidence.

After enumerating the possible reasons for this, they advocate that evidence-based management could change the way every manager thinks and acts:

We believe that facing the hard facts and truth about what works and what doesn't, understanding the dangerous half-truths that constitute so much conventional wisdom about management, and rejecting the total nonsense that too often passes for sound advice will help organizations perform better. (p. 74)

Source: Pfeffer and Sutton (2006a).

Developments in technology have encouraged some observers to anticipate that computers would be able to take over certain types of decisions from managers and professionals. While many early attempts to apply artificial intelligence or decision support systems failed, Davenport and Harris (2005) report new applications in many organisational settings. They are well suited where decisions depend on the rapid analysis of large quantities of data, with complex relationships – such as in power supply, transport management and banking. Automated decision systems: 'sense online data or conditions, apply codified knowledge or logic and make decisions – all with minimal amounts of human intervention' (Davenport and Harris, 2005, p. 84). Table 7.1 gives examples.

Table 7.1

Examples of the application of automated decision systems

Type of decision	Example of automated decision application
Solution configuration	Mobile phone operators who offer a range of features and service options: an automated programme can weigh all the options, including information about the customer, and present the most suitable option to the customer.
Yield optimisation	Widely used in the airline industry to allow companies to vary prices frequently depending on available capacity and present time relative to departure. Spreading to companies in transport generally, retailing and entertainment to increase revenue.
Fraud detection	Credit card companies and tax authorities use some automated screening techniques to help detect and deter possible fraud.
Operational control	Power companies use automated systems to sense changes in the physical environment (power supply, temperature or rainfall), and respond rapidly to changes in demand, by redirecting supplies across the network.

Source: Based on Davenport and Harris (2005).

Such applications will continue to spread, supporting companies where many decisions can be handled by using rational, quantitative methods. When decisions are more complex and controversial, the rational approach itself will not be able to resolve a decision – it can play a part, but only as one input to a wider set of methods.

A behavioural theory of decision making

key ideas

Richard Cyert, James March and Herbert Simon (Simon, 1960; Cyert and March, 1963; March, 1988) developed an influential model of decision making. It is sometimes referred to as the behavioural theory of decision making since it treats decision making as an aspect of human behaviour. Also referred to as the administrative model, it recognises that in the real world people are restricted in their decision processes, and therefore have to accept what is probably a less than perfect solution. It introduced the concepts of bounded rationality and satisficing to the study of decision making.

Judgemental strategies – administrative, incremental and intuitional

Administrative models

Simon's (1960) **administrative model of decision making** aims to describe how managers make decisions in situations that are uncertain and ambiguous. Many management problems are unstructured and not suitable for the precise quantitative

The **administrative model of decision making** describes how people make decisions in uncertain, ambiguous situations.

223

analysis implied by the rational model. People rely heavily on their judgement to resolve such issues.

Simon based the model on two central concepts – bounded rationality and satisficing. **Bounded rationality** expresses the fact that people have mental limits, or boundaries, on how rational they can be. While organisations and their environments are complex and uncertain, people can process only a limited amount of information. This constrains our ability to operate in the way envisaged by the rational model, which we deal with by **satisficing** – we choose the first solution that is 'good enough'. While continuing to search for other options may eventually produce a better return, identifying and evaluating them costs more than the benefits. Suppose we are in a strange city and need coffee before a meeting. We will look for the first acceptable coffee shop that appears to provide what we need. We have neither the time nor the knowledge to explore several alternatives for variety and price – we satisfice by choosing one that looks good enough for the immediate problem. In a similar fashion, managers generate alternatives for complex problems only until they find one they believe will work.

The administrative model focuses on the human and organisational factors that influence decisions. It is more realistic than the rational model for non-programmed, ambiguous decisions. According to the administrative model, managers:

> **Bounded rationality** is behaviour that is rational within a decision process which is limited (bounded) by an individual's ability to process information.

> **Satisficing** is the acceptance by decision makers of the first solution that is 'good enough'.

- have goals that are typically vague and conflicting, and are unable to reach a consensus on what to do – as indicated by the EADS example on p. 221;
- have different levels of interest in the problems or opportunities facing the business, and interpret information subjectively;
- rarely use rational procedures, or use them in a way that does not reflect the full complexity of the issue;
- limit their search for alternatives;
- usually settle for a satisficing rather than a maximising solution – having both limited information and only vague criteria of what would be 'maximising'.

The administrative model is descriptive, aiming to show how managers make decisions in complex situations rather than stating how they should make them.

 **Satisficing in an IT project**

Symon and Clegg (1991) studied a project to introduce a computer-aided design and computer-aided manufacturing (CAD-CAM) system into a manufacturing plant. The system itself was technically complex, but to secure the fullest benefits managers would also need to make significant changes throughout the organisation. The processes for managing orders would need to change, as would the work of staff and the responsibilities of managers. After several years of operation the system was producing some modest benefits, but nothing like the benefits that investment could have produced. The research team concluded that managers had unconsciously decided to satisfice – it was working, and producing some benefits that they could demonstrate: to secure the full potential would require more effort than they were willing to give.

Source: Symon and Clegg (1991).

Incremental models

Charles Lindblom (1959) developed what he termed an **incremental model**, which he observed people used when they were uncertain about the consequences of their choice. In the rational model these are known, but people face many decisions in which they cannot know what the effects will be. Lindblom built on Simon's idea of bounded rationality to show that if people made only a limited search for options their chosen solution would differ only slightly from what already existed. Current choices would be heavily influenced by past choices – and would not move far from them.

People use an **incremental model** of decision making when they are uncertain about the consequences. They search for a limited range of options, and policy unfolds from a series of cumulative small decisions.

On this view, policy unfolds not from a single event but from many cumulative small decisions. Small decisions help people to minimise the risk of mistakes, and to reverse the decision if necessary. Lindblom called this incrementalism, or the 'science of muddling through'. Instead of looking rationally at the whole problem and a range of possible ways forward, the decision maker simplifies the problem by contemplating only marginal changes. The incremental model (like the administrative one) recognises human limitations.

Intuitional models

George Klein (1997) studied how effective decision makers work, including those working under extreme time pressure such as surgeons, fire fighters and nurses. He found they rarely used classical decision theory to weigh the options: instead they used pattern recognition to relate the situation to their experience. They acted on their intuition – a subconscious process of making decisions on the basis of experience and accumulated judgement – sometimes called 'tacit knowledge'. Klein concluded that effective decision makers use their intuition as much as formal processes – perhaps using both formal analysis and intuition as the situation demands. Experienced managers can act quickly on what seems like very little information. Rather than do a formal analysis, they draw quickly on experience and judgement to decide what to do. It may be that intuition is better described as 'recognition'.

When people build a depth of experience and knowledge in an area the right decision often comes quickly and effortlessly, as the subconscious mind recognises information that the conscious mind has forgotten. Jurgen Schrempp, CEO of DaimlerChrysler, is said to be such a person – a risk-taker who always trusts his instincts, and to whom the need for bold moves is so evident that he becomes annoyed when investors question his strategy. In similar vein Sadler-Smith and Shefy (2004) argue that both rationality and intuition have a part to play in making decisions.

Compromise strategy – political model

The political model examines how people make decisions when managers disagree over goals and how to pursue them (Pfeffer, 1992; Buchanan and Badham, 1999). It recognises that an organisation is not only a working system, but also a political system, which establishes the relative power of people and functions. A significant decision will enhance the power of some people or units and limit that of others. People will pursue goals relating to personal and sub-unit interests, as well as those of the organisation as a whole. They will evaluate a decision in terms of its likely effects on those possibly conflicting objectives. Chapter 13 contains an example in Section 13.4 – the Management in Practice feature on 'Pensco'.

They will often try to support their position by building a coalition with those who share their interest. This gives others the opportunity to contribute their ideas and enhances their commitment if the decision is adopted.

The political model assumes that:

- Organisations contain groups with diverse interests, goals and values. Managers disagree about problem priorities and may not understand or share the goals and interests of other managers.
- Information is ambiguous and incomplete. Rationality is limited by the complexity of many problems as well as personal interests.
- Managers engage in the push and pull of debate to decide goals and discuss alternatives – decisions arise from bargaining and discussion.

Inspirational strategy – garbage can model

This approach is likely when those concerned are not only unclear about cause-and-effect relationships, but are also uncertain about the outcome they seek. James March (1988) observed that in this situation the processes of reaching a decision become separated from the decisions reached. In the other models there is an assumption that the processes that the decision makers pass through lead to a decision. In this situation of extreme uncertainty the elements that constitute the decision problem are independent of each other, coming together in random ways.

March argued that decisions arise when four independent streams of activities meet – and when this happens will depend largely on accident or chance. The four streams are:

1	Choice opportunities	Organisations have occasions at which there is an expectation that a decision will be made – budgets must be set, there are regular management meetings, etc.
2	Participants	A stream of people who have the opportunity to shape decisions.
3	Problems	A stream of problems that represent matters of concern to people – a lost sale, a new opportunity, a vacancy.
4	Solutions	A stream of potential solutions seeking problems – ideas, proposals, information – that people continually generate.

In this view, the choice opportunities (scheduled or unscheduled meetings) act as the container (garbage can) for the mixture of participants, problems and solutions. One combination of the three may be such that enough participants are interested in a solution, which they can match to a problem – and take a decision accordingly. Another group of participants may not have made those connections, or made them in a different way, so creating a different outcome.

This may at first sight seem an unlikely way to run a business, yet in highly uncertain, volatile environments this approach may work. Creative businesses depend on a rapid interchange of ideas, not only about specified problems but on information about new discoveries, research at other companies, what someone heard at a conference. They depend on people bringing these solutions and problems together – and deliberately foster structures that maximise opportunities for face-to-face contact and rapid decisions. The practical implication is that encouraging frequent informal contact between creative people will improve decisions, and performance.

Oticon builds a better garbage can www.oticon.com

Oticon, a leading maker of sophisticated hearing aids, underwent a massive transformation in the early 1990s, in which the chief executive, Lars Kolind, broke down all barriers to communication. He realised that the key to success in the face of severe competition was to ensure that the talents of staff in the company were applied to any problems that arose. In March's terms, problems were expressed as a project, for which a member of staff (a participant) took responsibility, depending on other staff to suggest or help develop a solution.

> Any and all measures were taken to encourage contact and informal communication between employees. Elevators were made inoperable so that employees would meet each other on the stairs, where they were more likely to engage in conversation. Bars were installed on all three floors where coffee was served and meetings could be organised – standing up. Rooms with circular sofas were provided, complete with small coffee tables, to encourage discussion. (Rivard *et al.*, 2004, p. 170)

These discussions centred on reaching fast and creative decisions about problems and new product ideas – and the arrangement is credited with helping the continuing success of the company.

Source: Rivard *et al.* (2004); see also Chapter 10 Case.

Table 7.2 summarises these four models.

Table 7.2 Four models of decision making

Rational	Administrative/incremental	Political	Garbage can
Clear problem and goals	Vague problems and goals	Conflict over goals	Goals and solutions independent
Condition of certainty	Condition of uncertainty	Uncertainty/conflict	Ambiguity
Full information about costs and benefits of alternatives	Little information about costs and benefits of alternatives	Inconsistent views about costs and benefits of alternatives	Costs and benefits unconnected
Rational choice to maximise benefit	Satisficing choice – good enough	Choice by bargaining amongst players	Choice by accidental merging of streams

7.6 Biases in making decisions

Since people are subject to bounded rationality (limited capacity to process information) they tend to use **heuristics** – simple rules, or short cuts, that help us to overcome our limited capacity to deal with information and complexity (Khaneman and Tversky, 1974). While these short cuts help us to make decisions, they expose us to the danger of biases – four of which are prior hypothesis, representativeness, illusion of control and escalating commitment (Schwenk, 1984).

Heuristics Simple rules or mental short cuts that simplify making decisions.

Prior hypothesis bias

People who have strong prior beliefs about the relationship between two variables tend to make decisions based on those beliefs, even when presented with evidence that shows the beliefs are wrong. In doing so they fall victim to the **prior hypothesis bias**: their bias

Prior hypothesis bias results from a tendency to base decisions on strong prior beliefs, even if the evidence shows that they are wrong.

227

is strengthened by a tendency to use information consistent with their beliefs, and ignore or discredit that which is inconsistent. People recall vivid events more readily that ones that stir no particular emotions or did not have a memorable outcome. The ones they recall will bias decisions about the likelihood of an event occurring, even if circumstances have changed.

Representativeness bias

Representativeness bias results from a tendency to generalise inappropriately from a small sample or a single vivid event.

A common source of bias is to generalise from a small sample or a single episode. It uses the similarity of one object to another to infer that the first object acts like the second, and this can lead people to ignore other relevant information. Examples include:

- believing that expensive-looking packaging means a high-quality product;
- predicting the success of a new product on the basis of an earlier success;
- appointing someone with a certain type of experience because a previous successful appointment had a similar background.

Illusion of control

The **illusion of control** is a source of bias resulting from the tendency to overestimate one's ability to control activities and events.

Other errors in making decisions result from the **illusion of control**, which is the human tendency to overestimate our ability to control activities and events. Those in senior positions, especially if they have a record of successes, seem particularly prone to this. Having worked their way to the top, they tend to have an exaggerated sense of their ability to shape destiny. This bias causes them to overestimate the odds of a favourable outcome, and so end up making poor decisions – such as the ability to grow a company successfully by acquisition.

Escalating commitment

Escalating commitment is a bias that leads to increased commitment to a previous decision despite evidence that it may have been wrong.

Having already made decisions that have committed significant resources to a project, some managers continue to commit more resources even though there is abundant evidence that the project is failing. Feelings of personal responsibility for a project, and the resources already consumed bias their analysis and lead to an escalating commitment – see Management in Practice. They may also be influenced by the phenomenon known as the **escalation of commitment**, which is an increased commitment to a previous decision despite evidence that it may have been wrong (Drummond, 1996). People are reluctant to admit mistakes, and may persist in committing further resources to a project despite its evident failure. Rather than search for a new solution, they increase their commitment to the original decision.

management in practice   A study of escalation – Taurus at the Stock Exchange

Helga Drummond studied the attempt by management at the London Stock Exchange to implement a computerised system to deal with the settlement of shares traded on the Exchange. The project was announced in May 1986 and was due to be completed by 1989 at a cost of £6 million. After many crises and difficulties, the Stock Exchange finally abandoned the project in March 1993. By that time the Exchange had spent £80 million on developing a non-existent system. Drummond interviewed many key participants to explore the reasons for this disaster – which occurred despite the commitment of the system designers.

She concluded that the project suffered from fundamental structural problems, in that it challenged several powerful vested interests in the financial community, each of whom had their own idea about what should be done. Each new demand, reflecting this continuing power struggle, made the system more complicated. However, while many interests needed to work together, structural barriers throughout the organisation prevented this. There was little upward communication, so that senior managers were largely unaware of staff concerns about the timetable commitments being made.

Senior managers continued to claim the project was on track until a few days before it was finally, and very publicly, terminated. The lack of proper mechanisms to identify pressing issues lulled those making decisions into a false sense of security about the state of the project.

Source: Drummond (1996).

7.7 Group decision making

Many organisational decisions are made by groups, rather than by individuals acting alone, as groups have several potential advantages over individuals. When managers work as a team they are less likely to experience the biases which the previous section identified: other members are more likely to challenge them. They are also able to draw on a wide range of experience and perspectives, and so more likely to deal fully with dimensions of a decision that an individual may overlook. There is also evidence that if the group includes those who will be responsible for implementing the decision, the chances of acceptance are greater.

However, groups can take longer than individuals to reach decisions, and not all decisions are suitable for a participative approach. In addition, groups too can be liable to bias, which reflects the phenomenon of groupthink.

Vroom and Yetton's decision model

The idea behind Vroom and Yetton's (1973) contingency model of decision making is to influence the quality and acceptability of decisions. This depends on the manager choosing how best to involve subordinates in making a decision – and being willing to change their style to match the situation. The model defines five leadership styles and seven characteristics of problems. Managers can use these characteristics to diagnose the situation. They can find the recommended way of reaching a decision on that problem by using the decision tree shown in Figure 7.8. The five leadership styles defined are:

1 *AI (Autocratic)* You solve the problem or make the decision yourself using information available to you at that time.
2 *AII (Information seeking)* You obtain the necessary information from your subordinate(s), then decide on the solution to the problem yourself. You may or may not tell your subordinates what the problem is in getting the information from them. The role played by your subordinates in making the decision is clearly one of providing the necessary information to you rather than generating or evaluating alternative solutions.
3 *CI (Consulting)* You share the problem with relevant subordinates individually, getting their ideas and suggestions without bringing them together as a group. Then *you* make the decision that may or may not reflect your subordinates' influence.
4 *CII (Negotiating)* You share the problem with your subordinates as a group, obtaining their collective ideas and suggestions. Then you make the decision that may or may not reflect your subordinates' influence.

5 *G (Group)* You share the problem with your subordinates as a group. Together you generate and evaluate alternatives and attempt to reach agreement (consensus) on a solution. Your role is much like that of a chairperson. You do not try to influence the group to adopt 'your' solution, and you are willing to accept and implement any solution that has the support of the entire group.

The idea behind the model is that no style is in itself better than another. Some believe that consultative or delegating styles are inherently preferable to autocratic approaches, as being more in keeping with democratic principles. Vroom and Yetton argue otherwise. In some situations (such as when time is short or the manager has all the information needed for a minor decision) going through the process of consultation

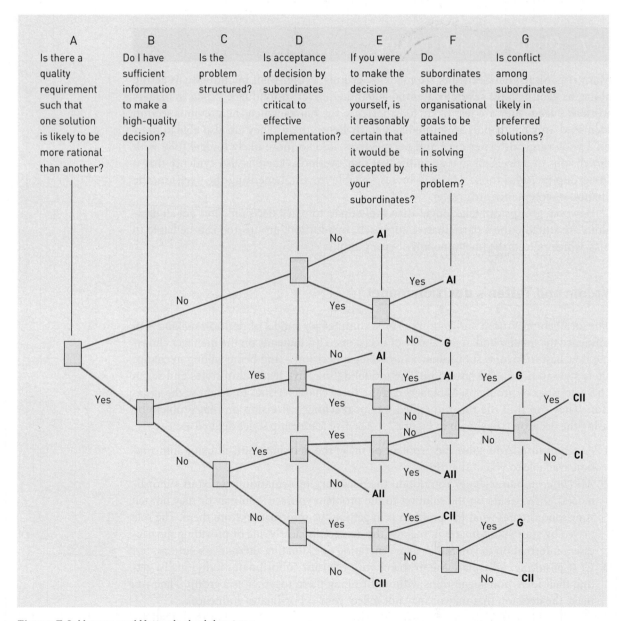

Figure 7.8 Vroom and Yetton's decision tree

Source: Reprinted from Vroom and Yetton (1973), p. 188 by permission of the University of Pittsburgh Press, copyright © 1973 by University of Pittsburgh Press..

will waste time and add little value. In other situations, such as where the subordinates have the relevant information, it is essential to consult them. The point of the model is to make managers more aware of the range of factors to take into account in using a particular decision-making style.

The problem criteria are expressed in seven diagnostic questions:

1 Is one solution likely to be better than another?
2 Does the manager have enough information to make a high-quality decision?
3 Is the problem structured?
4 Is acceptance of the decision by subordinates critical to effective implementation?
5 If the manager makes the decision alone, is it likely to be accepted by subordinates?
6 Do subordinates share organisational goals?
7 Is conflict likely amongst subordinates over preferred solutions?

The Vroom–Yetton decision model implies that managers need to be flexible in the style they adopt. The style should be appropriate to the situation rather than consistent amongst all situations. The problem with this is that managers may find it difficult to switch between styles, perhaps several times a day. Although the approach appears objective, it still depends on the manager answering the questions. Requiring a simple yes or no answer to complex questions is too simple, and managers often want to say 'it all depends' – on other historical or contextual factors.

Decision-making style at Rexam   www.rexam.com

Rexam is a UK-based packaging business (and the world's leading beverage can maker), run by Chief Executive Swede Rolf Borjesson from 1996 until 2004 (when he became chairman). His management style is described by colleagues as collegial, combined with ruthlessness in delivering results. When it comes to key decisions about the business he says:

> I want to test where the organisation is, or where my closest colleagues are, when it comes to important decisions, and then I have to make up my mind what to do. It is very, very critical to the success of the company that the team is very much involved. If you try to run it yourself and you take all the decisions, you turn around to look back and there is no one behind you.

Source: *Financial Times*, 18 November 2002.

Nevertheless the model is used in management training to alert managers to the style they prefer to use and to the range of options available. It also prompts managers to consider systematically whether that preferred style is always appropriate. They may then handle situations more deliberately than if they relied only on their preferred style or intuition.

Delegation

The model also relates to the issue of *delegation* that managers frequently face – whether or not to delegate more of their tasks to others, including how far to enable them to participate in decisions. As managers cope with increasingly demanding and uncertain conditions and as staff become more educated and confident, it will often make sense to widen the range of people taking part in decisions. This enables a wider range of experience and perspectives to be brought into consideration, as well as the motivational and development benefits.

However, the model indicates that this may not always be the best approach – such as if time is too short for wide consultation, or if conflicting views would delay, but not necessarily affect, the implementation of a decision. Equally if the decision is in effect already made for reasons beyond the manager's control, staff would see a show of participation as an empty gesture. The model brings in the notion of management style being contingent on the specific situation, a topic to which later parts of the book will return.

Irving Janis and groupthink

Groupthink is 'a mode of thinking that people engage in when they are deeply involved in a cohesive in-group, when the members' striving for unanimity overrides their motivation to realistically appraise alternative courses of action' (Janis, 1972).

Groupthink is a pattern of biased decision making that occurs in groups which become too cohesive – members strive for agreement amongst themselves at the expense of accurately and dispassionately assessing relevant, and especially disturbing, information. An influential analysis of how it occurs was put forward by the social psychologist Irving Janis. His research (Janis, 1972) began by studying major and highly publicised failures of decision making, looking for some common theme that might explain why apparently able and intelligent people were able to make such bad decisions – such as President Kennedy's decision to have US forces invade Cuba in 1961. One common thread he observed was the inability of the groups involved to consider a range of alternatives rationally, or to see the likely consequences of the choice they made. Members were also keen to be seen as team players, and not to say things that might end their membership of the group. Janis termed this phenomenon 'groupthink', and defined it as:

> a mode of thinking that people engage in when they are deeply involved in a cohesive in-group, when the members' striving for unanimity overrides their motivation to realistically appraise alternative courses of action. (Janis, 1972, p. 9)

He identified eight symptoms of groupthink, shown in Key Ideas.

---

key ideas   Irving Janis on the symptoms of groupthink

Janis (1977) identified eight symptoms that give early warning of groupthink developing – and the more of them that are present the more likely it is that the 'disease' will strike. The symptoms are:

1 **Illusion of invulnerability** The belief that any decision they make will be successful.
2 **Belief in the inherent morality of the group** Justifying a decision by reference to some higher value.
3 **Rationalisation** Playing down the negative consequences or risks of a decision.
4 **Stereotyping out-groups** Characterising opponents or doubters in unfavourable terms, making it easier to dismiss even valid criticism from that source.
5 **Self-censorship** Suppressing legitimate doubts in the interest of group loyalty.
6 **Direct pressure** Strong expressions from other members (or the leader) that dissent to their favoured approach will be unwelcome.
7 **Mindguards** Keeping uncomfortable facts or opinions out of the discussion.
8 **Illusion of unanimity** Playing down any remaining doubts or questions, even if they become stronger or more persistent.

Source: Based on Janis (1977).

Groupthink in medicine

An experienced nurse observed three of the symptoms of groupthink in the work of senior doctors:

- **Illusion of invulnerability** A feeling of power and authority leads a group to see themselves as invulnerable. Traditionally the medical profession has been very powerful and this makes it very difficult for non-clinicians to question their actions or plans.
- **Belief in the inherent morality of the group** This happens when clinical staff use the term 'individual clinical judgement' as a justification for their actions. An example is when a business manager is trying to reduce drug costs and one consultant's practice is very different from those of his colleagues. Consultants often reply that they are entitled to use their clinical judgement. This is never challenged by their colleagues, and it is often impossible to achieve change.
- **Self-censorship** Being a doctor is similar to being in a very exclusive club, and none of the members want to be excluded. Therefore doctors will usually support each other, particularly against management. They are also extremely unlikely to report each other for mistakes or poor performance. A government scheme to encourage 'whistle blowing' was met with much derision in the ranks.

Source: Private communication.

When groupthink occurs, pressures for agreement and harmony within the group have the unintended effects of discouraging individuals from raising issues that run counter to the majority opinion. An often-quoted example is the Challenger disaster in 1986, when the space shuttle exploded shortly after take-off. Investigations showed that NASA and the main contractors, Morton Thiokol, were so anxious to keep the Shuttle programme on schedule that they ignored or discounted evidence that would slow the programme down. When two Thiokol engineers warned that a component was likely to fail in cold weather, endangering safety, they were overruled by the team, which authorised the launch in cold weather. Turner and Pratkanis (1998) review research on groupthink, including studies that have taken a critical view of the phenomenon.

7.8 Current themes and issues

Performance

As performance standards become more demanding and circumstances more volatile, the task of making decisions becomes correspondingly more challenging. Nutt's analysis (Nutt, 2002) identifies the causes of failure in decision making and points towards practices that he claims increase the chances of a successful outcome. His suggestions include:

- Avoid making premature commitments – the hazard of grabbing hold of the first idea that comes up.
- Maintain an exploratory mindset – keep an open mind towards other possibilities.
- Let go of the quick fix – defer choice until understanding has been gained.
- Pause to reflect – even if this means resisting demands for a quick fix.
- Use resources to evaluate options, not just the preferred solution (or current quick fix).
- Pay attention to both the rational and the political aspects of a decision process.

Adopting such practices would undoubtedly add to the quality of anyone's approach to decision making: the challenge is whether they will be able to resist the pressures from others to deal with issues quickly, to deal with rapid external change. Wipro has developed the approach of making decisions quickly – and being willing to change quickly if the decision turns out to be wrong. Defending a wrong decision in the face of evidence is a sure way to destroy value.

Responsibility

Decisions often raise ethical issues – which can arise at any point in the process. A problem that may appear ethically neutral to those promoting a project – to alter recruitment policies, to build a manufacturing or distribution facility or to launch a new consumer product – may not seem like that to others. Ethical issues often arise when there is a mismatch between those who benefit from a decision and those who lose. Failure to take account of ethical concerns in the decision-making process can lead to delay, protest and a diversion of management time.

One way of addressing this is to attend to the structure of the decision-making process, to ensure that those whose interests will be affected are included from the outset. Including relevant stakeholders in the decision-making process may seem like a costly investment, but it could pay off if it brings better and more acceptable decisions. Some companies ensure that ethical issues have a higher place on the management agenda by appointing a director with an explicit remit in the area of ethics or corporate responsibility.

Internationalisation

The structure of decision-making processes also arises as companies become international. Decisions will cross the boundaries between managers at global headquarters, those in local business units and perhaps a regional grouping in between. Neither of the extreme possibilities is likely to work. If decision making tilts too far in favour of global managers at the centre, local preferences are likely to be overlooked, and local managers are likely to lack commitment to decisions in which they have had no say. Leaving too many decisions to local managers can waste opportunities for economies of scale or opportunities to serve global clients consistently.

A solution may be to identify the major ways in which the company adds value to resources, and align the decision-making processes to make the most of them. For example, it may be that procurement can best be done on a global scale, with contracts being negotiated at the centre to supply the whole of the company's needs. Once supply contracts are agreed, however, responsibility for operating them could pass back to the local level. Conversely, they might leave decisions on pricing or advertising expenditure to local managers. The central issue is to spend time on the difficult choices about the location of each set of decisions, to achieve an acceptable balance between global and local expectations.

Summary

1 Explain the tasks in making a decision and how decision processes affect the outcome

- Decisions are choices about how to act in relation to organisational inputs, outputs and transformation processes. The chapter identifies seven *iterative* steps in the process:

  1 Recognise the problem – which depends on seeing and attending to ambiguous signals.

  2 Set and weight criteria – the features of the result most likely to meet problem requirements, and that can guide the choice between alternatives.

  3 Develop alternatives – identify existing or develop custom-built ways of dealing with the problem.

  4 Compare and choose – using the criteria to select the preferred alternative.

  5 Implement – the task that turns a decision into an action.

  6 Evaluate – check whether the decision resolved the problem.

  7 Most decisions affect other interests, whose response will be affected by how the decision process is conducted, in matters such as participation and communication.

2 Explain, and give examples of, programmed and non-programmed decisions

- Programmed decisions deal with familiar issues within existing policy – recruitment, minor capital expenditure, small price changes.

- Non-programmed decisions move the business in a new direction – new markets, mergers, a major investment decision.

3 Distinguish between certainty, risk, uncertainty and ambiguity

- Certainty – decision makers have all the information they need, especially the costs and benefits of each alternative action.

- Risk – where the decision maker can estimate the likelihood of the alternative outcomes. These are still subject to chance, but decision makers have enough information to estimate probabilities.

- Uncertainty – when people know what they wish to achieve, but information about alternatives and future events is incomplete. They cannot be clear about alternatives or estimate their risk.

- Ambiguity – when people are unsure about their objectives and about the relationship between cause and effect.

4 Contrast rational, administrative, political and garbage can decision models

- Rational models are based on economic assumptions which suggest that the role of a manager is to maximise the economic return to the firm, and that they do this by making decisions on economically rational criteria.

- The administrative model aims to describe how managers actually make decisions in situations of uncertainty and ambiguity. Many management problems are unstructured and not suitable for the precise quantitative analysis implied by the rational model.

235

- The political model examines how people make decisions when conditions are uncertain, information is limited, and there is disagreement amongst managers over goals and how to pursue them. It recognises that an organisation is not only a working system, but also a political system, which establishes the relative power of people and functions.

- The garbage can model identifies four independent streams of activities that enable a decision when they meet. When participants, problems and solutions come together in a relevant forum (a 'garbage can'), then a decision will be made.

5 Give examples of common sources of bias in decisions

- Sources of bias stem from the use of heuristics – mental short cuts that allow us to cope with excessive information. Four biases are:

    1 representativeness bias – basing decisions on unrepresentative samples or single incidents;

    2 prior hypothesis bias – basing decisions on prior beliefs, despite evidence they are wrong;

    3 illusion of control – excessive belief in one's ability to control people and events;

    4 escalating commitment – committing more resources to a project despite evidence of failure.

6 Explain the contribution of Vroom and Yetton, and of Irving Janis, to our understanding of decision making in groups

- Vroom and Yetton introduced the idea that decision-making styles in groups should reflect the situation – which of the five ways to use of involving subordinates in a decision (Autocratic, Information seeking, Consulting, Negotiating and Delegating) depended on identifiable circumstances – such as whether the manager has the information required.

- Irving Janis observed the phenomenon of groupthink, and set out the symptoms which indicate that it is affecting a group's decision-making processes.

Review questions

1 Why does the quality of decisions that people make in an organisation affect its performance?

2 Explain the difference between risk and ambiguity. How may people make decisions in different ways for each situation?

3 List three decisions you have recently observed or taken part in. Which were programmed, and which unprogrammed?

4 The Vroom–Yetton model describes five styles. How should the manager decide which style to use?

5 What are the major differences between the rational and administrative models of decision making?

6 What is meant by satisficing in decision making? Can you illustrate the concept with an example from your experience? Why did those involved not try to achieve an economically superior decision?

7 What did Henry Mintzberg's research on decision making contribute to our understanding of the process?

Concluding critical reflection

Think about the ways in which your company, or one with which you are familiar, makes decisions. Review the material in the chapter, and perhaps visit some of the websites identified. Then make notes on these questions:

- What examples of the issues discussed in this chapter struck you as being relevant to practice in your company?

- Are people you work with typically dealing mainly with programmed or non-programmed decisions? What **assumptions** about the nature of decision making appear to guide their approach – rational, administrative, political or garbage can? On balance, do their assumptions accurately reflect the reality you see?

- What factors such as the history or current **context** of the company appear to influence the way people are expected to reach decisions? Does the current approach appear to be right for the company in its context – or would a different view of the context lead to a different approach? (Perhaps refer to some of the Management in Practice features for how different contexts encourage different approaches.)

- Have people put forward **alternative** approaches to decision making, based on evidence about other companies? If you could find such evidence, how may it affect company practice?

- Can you identify **limitations** in the ideas and theories presented here – for example are you convinced of the 'garbage can' model of decision making? Can you find evidence that supports or challenges that view?

Further reading

Bazerman, M.H. (2005), *Judgment in Managerial Decision Making* (6th edn), Wiley, New York.

Comprehensive and interactive account, aimed at developing the skill of judgement amongst students, thus enabling them to improve how they make decisions.

Harrison, E.F. (1999), *The Managerial Decision-Making Process* (5th edn), Houghton Mifflin, Boston, MA.

Comprehensive interdisciplinary approach to the generic process of decision making, with a focus on the strategic level. The author draws on a wide range of scholarly perspectives and presents them in a lucid and well-organised way.

Schwartz, B. (2005), *The Paradox of Choice*, Ecco, New York.

An excellent study of decision making at the individual level. It shows how people in modern society face an ever-widening and increasingly bewildering range of choices, which is a source of increasing tension and stress. Many of the issues the author raises apply equally well to decision making in organisations.

Buchanan, L. and O'Connell, A. (2006), 'A brief history of decision making', *Harvard Business Review*, vol. 84, no. 1, pp. 32–41.

Informative overview, placing many of the ideas mentioned in the chapter within a historical context. Part of a special issue of the *Harvard Business Review* devoted to decision making.

Weblinks

These websites have appeared in the chapter:

www.wipro.com
www.pg.com
www.mcdonalds.com
www.eads.com
www.oticon.com
www.rexam.com

Visit two of the business sites in the list, or any other company that interests you, and navigate to the pages dealing with recent news or investor relations.

● What examples of decisions that the company has recently had to take can you find?

● How would you classify those decisions in terms of the models in this chapter?

● Gather information from the media websites (such as **www.ft.com**) that relate to the companies you have chosen. What stories can you find that indicate something about the decisions the companies have faced, and what the outcomes have been?

Annotated weblinks, multiple choice questions and other useful resources can be found on www.pearsoned.co.uk/boddy

Chapter 8

Strategic management

Aim

To describe and illustrate the main elements of strategy and to show the flexible nature of the process.

Objectives

By the end of your work on this chapter you should be able to outline the concepts below in your own terms and:

1 Explain the significance of strategic management to all organisations
2 Describe the main steps in the strategic management process
3 Use the product/market matrix to compare corporate level strategies
4 Use the concept of generic strategies to compare business level strategies
5 Give examples of alternative methods of delivering a strategy
6 Compare planning, learning and political perspectives on strategy.

Key terms

This chapter introduces the following ideas:

strategic management
strategy
competitive strategy
value for money
institutional advantage
mission statement
strategic capability
tangible resource
intangible resource
unique resources
competences
core competences
value chain
cost leadership strategy
differentiation strategy
focus strategy
emergent strategy

Each is a term defined within the text, as well as in the Glossary at the end of the book.

Originating in 1884 as a market stall, Marks & Spencer (M&S) is today one of the UK's leading retailers of clothes, food, home products and financial services, with a turnover of £7.8 billion in the year to April 2006. There are 455 UK stores, employing 65,000 people. Each week, 15 million people shop at M&S and three-quarters of UK adults have shopped there in the last 12 months. There are 198 M&S-branded franchised stores in Europe, the Middle East, Asia and the Far East. Until April 2006 the company owned the US supermarket group Kings Super Markets. Following an unprecedented programme of expansion at home and abroad in the late 1990s, profits started to slide.

Clothing accounts for 45 per cent of M&S's UK retail sales. There is a wide range of clothing for all ages and, although sales fell in 2003, the company still held an 11 per cent share of the UK market. Food sales account for 50 per cent of UK turnover and grew by 5 per cent in 2003. New 'metro' store concepts were being tested in city centre and high street stores.

At the 2004 AGM the new CEO, Stuart Rose, conceded that the brand was in decline and that customer relationships were weakening due to confusion and disappointment. Although it still had a high share of the market, there was intense rivalry with competitors who can establish strong brands in well-defined segments. Some thought that M&S was targeting too many segments and losing understanding of customer needs.

The traditional bases for competition (quality, trust) for which customers paid a premium appeared to be changing: differentiating competitors (Next, Gap) offered more attractive ranges at similar prices; cost competitors (Matalan, TK Maxx, Tesco) offered basic clothing at lower prices.

The new management team were debating whether to change the traditional strategy and if so, how. Another possibility was that the traditional strategy was still valid, but had been poorly implemented in recent years. By the end of 2006 the new strategy appeared to be paying off, with the company reporting a strong growth in sales and profits, and M&S was about to begin

a large investment programme to make the stores more attractive.

Source: M&S *Annual Reports* 2003–2006; company website; *Financial Times* (various, 2006–2007).

Case questions 8.1

Visit an M&S store, and also visit their website – especially the section on 'the company'.

- Note the sales and profit performance in the most recent period compared to an earlier one.
- What do the chairman and chief executive write about the company's current strategy?
- What challenges do they say the company is facing?

8.1 Introduction

Strategic management is the set of decisions and actions intended to improve the long-run performance of an organisation.

Marks & Spencer illustrates the value of **strategic management**. For many years it occupied a leading position in the UK retailing industry, but in the late 1990s its performance declined. Some reasons were external – new competitors and changing customer tastes – while others were internal – little investment in modern stores and poor clothing design. New senior managers were appointed in 2003, and began to adjust the company's strategy – investing to improve the stores, making the all-important women's clothing line more fashionable and developing a new line of 'Just Food' stores. By 2007 the company was doing well again, as the new strategies began to show through in rising sales and profits. It still faces strong challenges from new brands that focus on a cheaper range or a narrower group of customers. Managers also know that entrepreneurs such as Phillip Green could use any sign of trading weakness as an opportunity to try to take the company over (as he attempted to do in 2005).

All organisations (not just those in trouble) face issues of strategic management. Established businesses such as BT are in a growing and diversifying telecommunications market – but face new competition that threatens their core business. Should the company try to compete in all areas, or concentrate on one sector, as Vodafone has done? Should Virgin continue to extend the brand into ever more diverse areas of activity, or would it gain more by building profits in the existing areas, and achieving more synergies across the group? Some charities face declining income – should their managers continue as they are now, or will they serve their cause better by initiating a radical review of their strategy? Strategic management enables companies to be clear about how they will add value to resources, even though much is changing in their world. Table 8.1 gives examples of the strategic issues managers face, and how they have responded: you can easily collect current examples. Comparing the performance of companies serving similar markets shows the importance of strategy: while all work in the same business and competitive environment, some perform better than others – probably because they adopted a more suitable strategy.

Table 8.1

Examples of organisations making strategic changes

Organisation and strategic issue	Strategic decisions or moves
BAE Systems (UK military equipment) – how to increase sales in the US www.baesystems.com	Acquired United Defense, US armoured vehicles maker in 2005, becoming sixth biggest contractor to Pentagon.
Procter & Gamble (world's largest supplier of consumer goods e.g. soap and toothpaste) – how to ensure long term-growth **www.pg.com**	Changed from focus on people in rich economies to those in poor countries – affects R&D, market research and manufacturing to identify and make suitable products.
Nestlé (global food and beverage company) – how to stimulate sales and profits in a mature business www.nestle.com	Increased emphasis on healthy foods, by adapting current products and taking over companies with established reputations for healthy products.

Strategy links the organisation to the outside world, and Chapter 3 showed how this influences management practice. Porter's model (1985) identifies the forces specific to an industry's competitive environment while the PESTEL framework summarises factors common to all organisations. Changes in these represent opportunities and threats: understanding strategic management enables you to observe more analytically the moves that companies make, and to think about possible alternatives.

Linn Products, suppliers of hi-fi equipment   www.linn.co.uk

Linn Products was founded in 1972 with a clear purpose: 'to reproduce, through superior sound, the thrills and emotion of a live performance'. The commitment is to quality and accurate performance. Linn is an independent precision-engineering company specialising in top-performance sound reproduction. It makes a portfolio of products, including CD players, tuners, amplifiers and speakers, which it exports to more than 50 countries. Linn entertainment systems can be found throughout the world in royal residences, luxury homes, performance motorcars and yachts.

A market leader in specialised sound systems, Linn exhibits a clear, consistent philosophy, being true to the music and being directly coupled to its sources. As the sound technology leader, Linn has earned a unique reputation in the world of specialist hi-fi and multi-channel sound recording and reproduction, providing pitch-accurate sound reproduction. Linn has its own record label with a list of 275 jazz, classical and Celtic titles: artists include Claire Martin, Barb Jungr and Carole Kidd. This helps Linn to control, monitor and compare every stage in the sound reproduction process, from performance to listener.

Market channels are strictly controlled: agents and distributors are intensively trained in the Linn philosophy. The jeans-clad, single-minded founder and CEO, Ivor Tiefenbrun:

> the traditional [dealer] approach is inadequate to sustain growth in our industry. And retailers who want to build a business, or who want to grow with their customers, have to meet their changing requirements.

Today, the Linn mission is 'To thrill customers who want the most out of life from music, information and entertainment systems that benefit from quality sound'. Reflecting changes in technology, it now offers digital downloads of all its music titles, allowing customers to receive high-quality music more quickly than through traditional channels, and making the titles more widely available around the world.

Competition is growing more active. Tiefenbrun says:

> I don't think there's much wrong with the way hi-fi's sold now in the sense that the people who sell it and the people who buy it are quite happy with that programme. But hi-fi is falling down people's lists of priorities. Our customers are changing, and we recognise that the world has changed from the time of the classic enthusiast like myself 20 years ago. There are more products and more issues competing for those individuals' attention.

Source: Interviews with managers, published information and company website.

Activity 8.1   Comparing practice with the model

- What features of Linn's business could be a source of challenge in formulating strategy?
- What are the bases of competition in this market?

The chapter begins by outlining the strategic management process, and then examines each step – mission, external and internal analyses, formulating, implementing and review. It compares structured, emergent and political theories of the strategy process and concludes with a commentary on three current themes.

8.2   Purposes of strategy – and how they vary with context

Benefits of setting strategy

A structured approach to strategy can benefit all organisations, though its nature varies with circumstances. Common benefits are that it:

- **Reduces uncertainty** It obliges managers to look ahead, anticipate change and develop appropriate responses; it also encourages them to consider the risks of each option.
- **Links long term and short term** It helps people to relate current operational activities and decisions to the longer-term strategic objectives they are intended to support.
- **Clarifies and unifies purpose** By setting the overall strategic objectives and what these imply for those at operational level it helps departments to work towards common goals.
- **Enables control** By setting clear objectives, it provides standards against which to measure performance.

Strategy is concerned with deciding what business an organisation should be in, where it wants to be, and how it is going to get there.

While people use different terms, the activity of **strategy** essentially involves dealing with what is to be achieved, for whom and how. In traditional strategic planning, people establish a vision and/or mission, set some more tangible goals, and then design the strategy – how to achieve the goals. As you will see, strategic planning is rarely as neat as this – strategies can emerge, alter and disappear, sometimes very quickly.

For most organisations the purpose of developing strategy is to perform well against competitors over the long term. It helps to identify the factors that give it a sustained advantage, the basis for higher levels of profitability or other measures of performance. Identifying sustainable sources of competitive advantage clarifies the organisation's **competitive strategy**. This sets the direction and scope of the organisation, by establishing how it will use resources to meet the expectations of stakeholders.

Competitive strategy is concerned with the basis on which an organisation (or unit within it) might achieve competitive advantage in its market.

Strategy and type of business

While the common benefits of developing a strategy are clear, the process varies with the type of organisation. One difference is that the concept of competitive advantage does not apply directly to not-for-profit (NFP) organisations (Goold, 1997). While NFPs have some similar characteristics to the profit-seeking firm, there are fundamental differences in (a) their goals, (b) their funding and external influence, and (c) their internal power relationships (Bowman and Asch, 1996). Some NFPs have direct competitors: Oxfam competes for donations and for customers through shop and mail order networks. Others compete for resources, media attention and volunteers.

A **value for money** service is one that is provided economically, efficiently and effectively.

The analogue to profit in the public and NFP sector (Smith, 1995) is frequently **value for money**, that is, providing a project or service as economically, efficiently and effectively as possible. Goold (1997) suggests that in these sectors a better term is **institutional advantage**, which 'is held when a not-for-profit body performs its tasks more effectively than ... comparable organisations'.

Institutional advantage 'is when a not-for-profit body performs its tasks more effectively than comparable organisations' (Goold, 1997).

Porter (1990) has also written about competition between nations. Nation states (and cities within them) compete with each other to secure investment by multinational companies, the right to host events such as the Olympic Games, or to hold titles such as 'European City of Culture'. Such events can bring valuable income and to gain this countries and cities identify sources of their competitive advantage, such as an educated workforce or an attractive physical environment. Table 8.2 summarises the strategic issues that arise in different settings.

Table 8.2

Strategic issues in different settings

Type of organisation	Distinctive strategic issues	Examples in this text
Large multinational corporations (MNCs)	Structure and control of global activities Allocating resources between units	Procter & Gamble (this chapter); BP (Part 2 case)
Small and medium enterprises (SMEs)	Strongly influenced by founders or owners; lack of capital limits choices	Linn Products (this chapter)
Manufacturing	Relative contribution to competitive advantage of the manufacturing (physical product) or service aspect (delivery, customer support) of the offer.	Wipro (Chapter 7 case); BMW (Chapter 11)
Firms in innovative sectors	Competitive advantage depends on ability to change the rules of the game, and so on creating a culture of questioning and challenge	Nokia (Chapter 3); Oticon (Chapter 10)
Public sector	Competition centres on fight for resources, and so on ability to demonstrate best value in outputs; problems increasingly require cooperation between agencies, complicating strategy.	HM Revenue and Customs (Chapter 11)
Voluntary and NFP sector	Balancing the influence of ideology and values with interests of funding sources; balancing central control (consistency) with local commitment (volunteers and local staff).	Charity with residential homes (Chapter 1); Housing Association (Chapter 10); The Big Issue (Chapter 9)
Professional service organisations	Strategy process influenced by partnership nature of their structure, requiring time to reach consensus.	

8.3   Steps in the strategic management process

Figure 8.1 illustrates the six steps in the strategic management process – which will be carried out iteratively and, in many circumstances, continually.

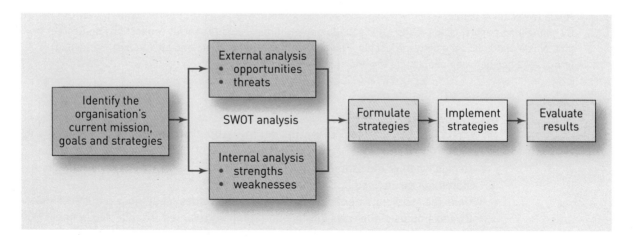

Figure 8.1 The strategic management process

Identifying current mission, goals and strategies

A **mission statement** is a broad statement of an organisation's scope and purpose, aiming to distinguish it from similar organisations.

Defining an organisation's mission is intended to identify the scope of its customers, products or services: it provides a focus for work. A broad statement of mission (or purpose) can guide those setting more specific goals and the strategies to achieve them. A useful **mission statement** also expresses the underlying beliefs and values held within the organisation – the emphasis given to matters such as innovation, customer care or climate change. Dobson *et al.* (2004) suggest that a mission statement should clarify:

- principal business or activities
- key aims or objectives
- key beliefs and values – what it represents
- main stakeholders.

Missions should be short and easy to understand: the Management in Practice feature gives examples.

management in practice   Examples of mission and vision statements

IKEA (www.ikea.com)
A better everyday life. The IKEA business idea is to offer a wide range of home furnishings with good design and function at prices so low that as many people as possible will be able to afford them. And still have money left!

Unilever (www.unilever.com)
Unilever's mission is to add vitality to life. It meets the everyday needs for nutrition, hygiene and personal care with brands that help people feel good, look good and get more out of life.

Royal Society for the Protection of Birds (www.rspb.org.uk)
The RSPB is the UK charity working to secure a healthy environment for birds and wildlife, helping to create a better world for us all.

Higher Education Funding Council for England (www.hefce.ac.uk)
Working in partnership, HEFCE promotes and funds high-quality, cost-effective teaching and research, meeting the diverse needs of students, the economy and society.

Nokia (www.nokia.com)
By connecting people, Nokia helps fulfil a fundamental human need for social connections and contact. Nokia builds bridges between people – both when they are far apart and face to face – and also bridges the gap between people and the information they need.

Activity 8.2   Critical reflection on mission statements

- Decide whether the examples above satisfy the requirements of a good mission statement (as defined by Dobson *et al.*, 2004).
- Does the M&S statement of vision, mission and values meet those requirements?
- Give examples of the ways in which the company's values are reflected in its business activities.
- Does your organisation have a mission statement, and does it meet the criteria of Dobson *et al.* (2004)? If not, edit it so that it would fit, or suggest why it is better as it is.

The dangers of mission statements

Some question the value of mission statements, especially if they are an idealistic aspiration rather than a realistic guide to action. A study of local government in Britain (Leach, 1996) found that while in some authorities mission statements had clarified the dominant values and culture, in others staff saw them only as symbolic public relations documents. Another danger is that management fails to develop a belief in the mission throughout the organisation. People only come to believe in, and act upon, the mission statement if they see others doing the same – especially senior managers. The mission needs to be cascaded through the structure to ensure it guides day-to-day actions.

Marks & Spencer – the case continues
www.marksandspencer.com

CASE STUDY

The M&S brand is strongly associated with the company's values of quality, value, service and trust. These were severely tested during the difficulties between 2001 and 2004, but the new management team built their recovery plan on the company's 'unique fundamental strengths'. One of these is that it works to high ethical trading standards and a strong sense of environmental and social responsibility. In January 2007 it announced 'Plan A', a five-year plan to tackle some of the biggest challenges facing the business and the world. It covered:

climate change – aiming to become carbon neutral by minimising energy use and using renewable energy sources where possible;
waste – aiming to stop sending waste to landfill and reducing the amount of packaging on products;
raw materials – ensuring that raw materials come from the most sustainable resources possible;

fair partner – trading fairly to improve the lives of hundreds of thousands of people in its supply chain and in its local communities;
healthy eating – continuing to set good food standards, helping customers and employees to live a healthier lifestyle.

Sources: M&S *Annual Reports* 2003–2006; company website, *Financial Times* (various, 2006–2007).

Case questions 8.2

● What encouraged the company to extend its ethical policies by launching Plan A (see the website)?

● Do you think these commitments will give M&S a competitive advantage? How?

External analysis

Chapter 3 established that the external environment is made up of competitive and general environments. At the micro-level, Porter's five forces analysis helps management to assess the state of competition within the industry. At the macro-level, the PESTEL framework helps to identify the major drivers of change. Lei and Slocum (2005) distinguish industries in terms of the stage of their life cycle, and their rate of technological development. In the early stages of an industry's growth there are few barriers to entry, so many firms enter the market and seek different ways of attracting consumers. These will change as the industry matures, growth slows, and customers become familiar with the product. Their second point is that industries vary in their rate of technological change. At one extreme, firms experience a slow accumulation of minor changes, while at the other they face a constant stream of radical new technologies that change the basis of competition. The chapter also showed that external stakeholders, such as government and pressure groups, also influence organisations.

Case questions 8.3

Referring to the analytical frameworks in Chapter 3:

● What are the main external factors affecting M&S at present?

● How do these differ between the food and clothing businesses?

Kay (1996) defined strategy as the match between the organisation's external relationships and its internal capabilities, describing 'how it responds to its suppliers, its customers, its competitors, and the social and economic environment within which it operates'. Before establishing a direction, managers need an internal analysis to show how well they can cope with external changes.

Internal analysis: resources and capabilities

Managers analyse the internal environment to identify the organisation's strengths and weaknesses. This means identifying what the organisation does well, where it might do better and whether it has the resources and competences to deliver a preferred strategy. Those that are considered essential to outperforming the competition constitute critical success factors.

Johnson *et al.* (2006) define **strategic capability** as the ability to perform at the level required to survive and prosper. That depends on the resources available to the organisation, and its competence in using them. **Tangible resources** are the physical assets such as buildings, equipment, people or finance, while **intangible resources** include reputation, knowledge or information. **Unique resources** are those which others cannot obtain – such as a powerful brand or access to a unique source of raw material.

While the amount and quality of these resources matter, how people use them has a more sustained effect on performance. If a manager encourages staff to develop higher skills, cooperate with each other, be innovative and creative, the company is likely to perform better than one where staff are unable to use their talents. The first company gains because it has developed **competences** – activities and processes that enable it to deploy resources effectively.

Understanding competitive advantage requires a further distinction between those capabilities (resources and competences) that are at the threshold level and those that give competitive advantage. Threshold capabilities are those an organisation must have to compete in a market – adequate IT systems, for example. **Core competences** are the activities and processes which people use to deploy resources in ways that gain them a competitive advantage, because others cannot imitate them. Ryanair has prospered not just because it has a fleet of modern, standard aircraft – other airlines could have a similar resource, but be unprofitable. The difference is that Ryanair has developed core competences that enable it to use its aircraft more efficiently than competitors.

Management's task in internal analysis is to identify those strengths (capabilities) that distinguish the organisation in the minds of the customer and thereby support its competitive advantage. One of these strengths is the overall balance of activities that the organisation as a whole undertakes – the product or service portfolio. Does it have sufficient interests in growing rather than declining markets? Does it have too many new products (which tend to be a drain on resources) relative to established ones?

At the divisional or strategic business unit level, the ability to compete effectively depends on:

Strategic capability is the ability to perform at the level required to survive and prosper, and includes resources and competences.

Tangible resources are physical assets such as buildings, equipment, people or finance.

Intangible resources are non-physical assets such as reputation, knowledge or information.

Unique resources are resources that are vital to competitive advantage and which others cannot obtain.

Competences are the activities and processes through which an organisation deploys resources effectively.

Core competences are the activities and processes through which resources are deployed to achieve competitive advantage in ways that others cannot imitate or obtain.

- **The resource base**: includes physical resources (buildings and production facilities), human resources (employees' skills, knowledge, attitudes, etc.), financial resources (growth prospects, debt–equity mix, liquidity position, financial control systems, etc.) and intangibles (such as 'goodwill', or good relationships with suppliers). Each can be assessed for their adequacy in supporting a strategy.
- **The competence base**: how the organisation performs the activities of designing, producing, marketing, delivering and supporting its products or services – and manages the linkages between them. These are critical since the key to performance lies in the competences that add extra value to the resources available to the organisation.

Value chain analysis

The concept of the **value chain**, introduced by Porter (1985), is derived from an accounting practice that calculates the value added at each stage of a manufacturing or service process. Porter applied this idea to the activities of the whole organisation, as an analysis of each activity could identify sources of competitive advantage.

Figure 8.2 shows primary and support activities. *Primary* activities transform inputs into outputs and deliver them to the customer:

- **Inbound logistics**: activities such as receiving, storing and distributing the inputs to the product or service. They include material handling, stock control, etc.
- **Operations**: transforming these into the final product or service, such as machining or packing.
- **Outbound logistics**: moving the product to the buyer – collecting, storing and distributing; in some services (a sports event) these activities will include bringing the customers to the venue.
- **Marketing and sales**: activities to make consumers aware of the product.
- **Service**: enhancing or maintaining the product – installation, training, repairs.

> A **value chain** 'divides a firm into the discrete activities it performs in designing, producing, marketing and distributing its product. It is the basic tool for diagnosing competitive advantage and finding ways to enhance it' (Porter, 1985).

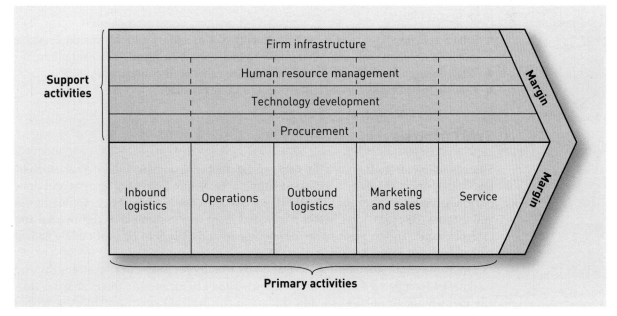

Figure 8.2 The value chain

Source: Porter (1985), copyright © 1985 Michael E. Porter, reprinted with permission of The Free Press, a division of Simon & Schuster.

These depend on four *support* activities:

1 **firm infrastructure:** organisational structure, together with planning, financial and quality systems;
2 **human resource management:** recruitment, training, rewards, etc.;
3 **technology development:** relate to inputs, operational processes or outputs;
4 **procurement:** acquiring materials and other resources.

Case questions 8.4

As part of the recovery plan, M&S improved the design of its products, outsourced the supply of many to cheaper suppliers overseas, improved store design, spent heavily on training, and introduced an online service.

● How do these changes fit into the value chain?
● What new challenges may they have raised for the linkages between stages in the chain?

Value chain analysis enables managers to consider which activities are of particular benefit to customers, and which are more troublesome – perhaps destroying value rather than creating it. It might, say, be good at marketing, outbound logistics and technology development – but poor at operations and human resource management. That awareness may lead managers to consider which activities in the value chain it should concentrate on – perhaps outsourcing the others to specialist firms. Even if they decide to outsource, say, after-sales service they must still ensure that those who deliver that service on its behalf do so in a way that contributes to overall quality.

Each activity in the chain 'can contribute to a firm's relative cost position and create a basis for differentiation' (Porter, 1985) – the two main sources of competitive advantage. While a threshold level of competence is necessary in all value chain activities, management needs to identify the core competences that the organisation has (or needs) to compete effectively. Analysing the separate activities in the value chain helps management to consider:

● Which activities have most effect on reducing cost or adding value? If customers value quality more than costs, then that implies a focus on ensuring quality of suppliers.
● What linkages do most to reduce cost, enhance value or discourage imitation?
● How do these linkages relate to the cost and value drivers?

SWOT analysis

Strategy follows from finding a 'fit' between external environment and internal capabilities. Management therefore needs to identify the key issues from each analysis and draw out the strategic implications. A SWOT analysis (strengths, weaknesses, opportunities and threats – discussed) in Chapter 6 is a convenient way to summarise the internal and external issues, and to identify the developments most likely to be profitable – shown schematically in Figure 8.3.

The value chain and comparative analysis usually identify internal strengths and weaknesses (compared with the competition). The PESTEL and five forces analyses usually identify the opportunities and threats in the external environment. A potential customer locating a plant near a firm might constitute an opportunity, but competition from cheaper imports could pose a threat.

Figure 8.3

Identifying the organisation's opportunities

Formulate strategy

Once the SWOT analysis is complete, managers can develop and evaluate strategic alternatives, aiming to select those that make the most of internal strengths and external opportunities. These may need to be developed for corporate, business and functional levels.

Managers are usually advised to focus on identifying strengths that give the company an edge over its competitors and constitute its core competences, which can be sustained in the long term. If there is a threat from an external factor that could erode them, can they be enhanced (e.g. through technology or training) or protected from imitation (e.g. patenting of innovation)? If erosion is inevitable then a new strategy is required. Management also needs to assess the critical success factors to ensure they have the resources and competences needed to achieve the strategy.

Case questions 8.5

Drawing on your answers to previous questions:

- Make a summary SWOT analysis for Marks & Spencer's clothing business.
- Consult the website to read recent statements from the CEO and other information.

Examples of objectives

The Kingfisher Group's mission is to be the world's best international home improvement retailer. It has three core objectives for its home improvement division: (1) major growth at B&Q, Costorama, Brico and Screwfix; (2) driving best practice and scale benefits throughout the sector; and (3) building an international store network beyond the United Kingdom and France.

With a more specific set of objectives to hand, managers can then plan how to achieve them. Given its stated mission to be the best in the world, Kingfisher, for example, could expand internationally by building new stores, by buying overseas companies, or both.

Implement strategy

Implementation turns strategy into action, moving from corporate to operational levels. Many strategies fail to be implemented, or fail to achieve as much as management expected. A common mistake is to assume that formulating a strategy will lead to painless implementation. Sometimes there is an 'implementation deficit', when strategies are not implemented at all, or are only partially successful. A common reason for this is that while formulating strategy may appear to be a rational process, it is often a political one. Those who were content with the earlier strategy may oppose the new one if it affects their status, power or career prospects. Chapter 13 shows how implementing major change is a complex, often conflicting process.

Evaluate results

Managers, shareholders (current and potential) and financial analysts routinely compare a company's performance with its published plans. Only by tracking results can these and other interested parties decide if performance is in line with expectations or if the company needs to take some corrective action. Many targets focus on financial and other quantitative aspects of performance, such as sales, operating costs and profit. Table 8.3 shows the highlights of the Marks & Spencer results for the half-year to 30 September 2006.

Table 8.3

Summary of Marks & Spencer results for 26 weeks to end September 2006

Indicator	2006 (£m)	2005 (£m)	Growth (%)
Total revenue	3,929	3,542	11
Profit before tax	407	306	33
Earnings per share	16.6p	12.7p	31
Interim dividend per share	6.3p	4.8p	31

Source: M&S *Interim Report to Shareholders* on company website.

Given the wide-ranging interests of stakeholders, companies do not restrict their reporting to this type of information. In the public services, measures of quality and fairness of service outcomes may be more important to consumers and service users, but financial performance may be of greater interest to government and other funders.

Although monitoring is shown as the last stage in the strategy model, it is not the end of the process. This is continuous as organisations adjust to changes in their business environment. Regular monitoring alerts management to the possibility that targets might not be achieved and that operational adjustments are needed. Equally, and in conjunction with continuous scanning of the external environment, performance monitoring can prompt wider changes to the organisation's corporate and competitive strategies.

Case questions 8.6

Review Marks & Spencer's most recent annual reports (on the website), including the summary financial statements (not the detailed version).

- What measures does the company use to assess performance?
- What measures does it use (or is it planning) in respect of its commitment to society?
- Is the emphasis on hard (quantitative) or soft (qualitative) measures?

8.4 Levels of strategy

Managers in large enterprises will typically develop strategies at corporate, business and functional levels, though in smaller organisations there will be less complexity. Figure 8.4 shows this.

Corporate level strategy

At corporate level the strategy reflects the overall direction of the organisation, and the part which the respective business units will play in that. Should it remain focused on a small range of activities or diversify? Should it remain a local or national business, or seek to operate internationally? These decisions establish the direction of the organisation.

Strategies can aim for growth, stability or renewal. A growth strategy seeks to increase the organisation's business by expanding the number of products offered or markets served. A stability strategy is one in which the organisation plans to continue offering the same products and services to much the same group of customers. A commercial business may do this after a period of rapid growth (perhaps through acquisition), and it wishes to conserve managerial resources to manage the current business, rather than seek further growth in the short term. Many public sector organisations operate a stability strategy: since resources are limited, they will usually have little opportunity to engage in growth. Many owners of small businesses wish to retain their business at its present size so that they are able to remain in sole control.

A renewal strategy often follows a period of trouble within a business: if performance has been poor management will be required to make major changes to the strategy to return profits to an acceptable level – perhaps involving significant changes to the business to secure the required turnround.

Managers can decide how to achieve their chosen option by using the product/market matrix, shown in Figure 8.5. They can achieve growth by focusing on one or more of the quadrants; stability by remaining with existing products and services; and renewal by combining withdrawal from some existing products and markets, followed (perhaps) by entry into some new products or markets.

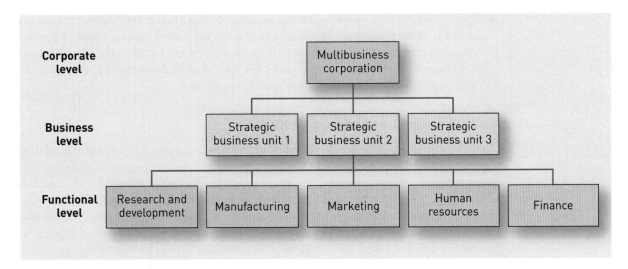

Figure 8.4 Levels of organisational strategy

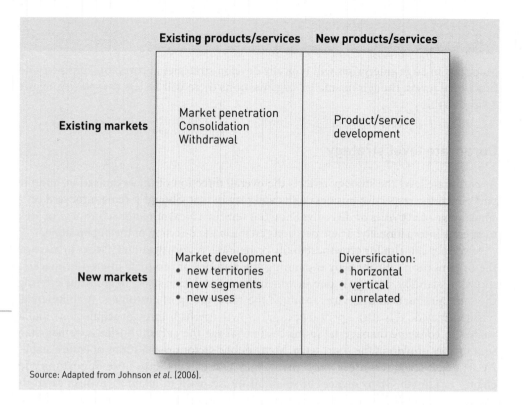

	Existing products/services	**New products/services**
Existing markets	Market penetration Consolidation Withdrawal	Product/service development
New markets	Market development • new territories • new segments • new uses	Diversification: • horizontal • vertical • unrelated

Figure 8.5

Strategy development directions – the product/market matrix

Source: Adapted from Johnson *et al.* (2006).

Existing markets, existing product/service

Choice within this segment depends on whether the market is growing, mature, or in decline. The box shows several possibilities:

● A market penetration strategy aims to increase market share, which will be easier in a growing than in a mature market. It could be achieved by reducing price, increasing advertising or improving distribution.

● Consolidation aims to protect the company's share in existing markets. In growing or mature markets this could mean improving efficiency and/or service to retain custom. In declining markets management might consolidate by acquiring other companies.

● Withdrawal is a wise option when, for instance, competition is intense and the organisation is unable to match its rivals: staying in that line of business would destroy value, not create it. In the public sector, changing priorities lead to the redeployment of resources. Health boards have withdrawn accident and emergency services from some hospitals to make better use of limited resources.

Existing markets, new products/services

A strategy of product or service development allows a company to retain the relative security of its present markets while altering products or developing new ones. In retail sectors such as fashion, consumer electronics and financial services, companies continually change products to meet perceived changes in consumer preferences. Car manufacturers compete by adding features and extending their model range. Some new products, such as 'stakeholder pensions' in the United Kingdom, arise out of changes in government policy. Many new ideas fail commercially, so that product development is risky and costly.

New markets, existing products/services

Market development aims to find new outlets by:

- extending geographically (from local to national or international);
- targeting new market segments (groups of customers, by age, income or lifestyle); or
- finding new uses for a product (a lightweight material developed for use in spacecraft is also used in the manufacture of golf clubs).

P&G targets poorer customers   www.pg.com

Procter & Gamble, the world's largest consumer goods company, built its success on selling detergent, toothpaste and beauty products to the world's wealthiest 1 billion consumers. When Chief Executive AG Lafley arrived in 2002 and said, 'We're going to serve the world's consumers' he surprised the company's staff. One recalled:

> We realised that we didn't have the product strategy or the cost structure to be effective in serving lower-income consumers. What's happened in the last five years has been one of the most dramatic transformations I've seen in my career. We now have all of our functions focused on meeting the needs of poorer consumers.

By 2005 it was devoting 30 per cent of the annual research and development budget to low-income markets, a 50 per cent increase on five years earlier. Developing markets are expected to grow twice as fast as developed markets over the next five years. The transformation has been evident in three areas:

1 how the company finds out what customers want;
2 how this affects R&D; and
3 manufacturing facilities.

Source: Published sources and company website.

New markets, new products/services

Often described as diversification, this can take three forms:

1 **Horizontal integration** Developing related or complementary activities, such as when mortgage lenders extend into the insurance business, using their knowledge of, and contact with, existing customers to offer them an additional service. The advantages include the ability to expand by using existing resources and skills – such as Kwik-Fit's use of its database of depot customers to create a motor insurance business.
2 **Vertical integration** Moving either backwards or forwards into activities related to the organisation's products and services. A manufacturer might decide to make its own components rather than buy them from elsewhere. Equally, it could develop forward, for instance into distribution.
3 **Unrelated diversification** Developing into new markets outside the present industry. Virgin has used its strong brand to create complementary activities in sectors as diverse as airlines, trains, insurance and soft drinks. The extension by some retailers into financial services is another example. It is a way to spread risk where demand patterns fluctuate at different stages of the economic cycle, and to maintain growth when existing markets become saturated.

Alternative development directions are not mutually exclusive: companies can follow several at the same time. Nevertheless, managers need to decide where to focus their effort, as some directions will bring higher sales than others. Terri Dial was appointed as head of retail banking at Lloyds TSB in 2005, charged with introducing a three-year turnround programme. Commenting on her job she said: 'I am a big believer that what you aspire to be is a diversified retail financial services firm ... Diversification is important as the only way to meet customers' needs.'

> Sales through branches were declining in the third quarter of last year, but by the first quarter of 2006 she had reversed the trend and sales were increasing. Ms Dial believes Lloyds has concentrated too much on cross-selling more products to existing customers, and not enough on innovation and attracting new customers. (*Financial Times*, 16 August 2006, p. 17)

Marks & Spencer – the case continues
www.marksandspencer.com

CASE STUDY

Appointed as chief executive in 2003, Stuart Rose and his new management team built their three-year recovery plan on the company's strengths, while also looking for new opportunities. The company's scale facilitates innovation and also gives it buying power, although the close supplier relationships for which M&S is renowned were damaged by its decision to increase overseas sourcing in search of cost advantage.

It has a good record of product development. In food it has a leading share in fast-growing markets, such as ready meals; it has strong food development capabilities, changing a quarter of its food range every year, and has introduced bakeries, butcher's shops and hot food counters. Of the company's lines, 40 per cent are suitable for vegetarians and it was the first retailer in the world to respond to customers' health and nutrition concerns by appointing food technologists and animal welfare specialists.

In clothing, product ranges are constantly upgraded and the company is proud of its innovative 'magic fabrics' such as non-iron cotton, machine-washable wool and non-polish shoes. In 2006 the number of people visiting the stores had risen to the levels last achieved in 2002, as the company improved its core women's wear range with up-to-date fashion at Limited Collection and a buoyant Per Una:

'We had been making tractors for people who wanted wheelbarrows,' joked Mr Rose, saying he was pleased with the current designs. He also said he was thinking about broadening the range by experimenting with branded electrical products.

In April 2006 M&S completed the sale of the Kings Super Markets in the United States, the last part of the programme to refocus the group.

By 2006 financial analysts were becoming enthusiastic about the business again, as it appeared that the plan was six months ahead of target. Results for the year to April 2006 showed that group sales were higher than the previous year, while pre-tax profits had risen from £556 million to £751 million. Observers noted that the new team had increased both total sales and the profit margin on those sales – a significant milestone on the road to recovery. It was growing market share in all clothing categories, including the vital women's wear collection.

The recovery plan centred on reviving the existing business of selling high-quality clothing, food and household items through large, well-designed stores. In 2007 the company was continuing to develop its 'Simply Food' concept – a range of smaller stores aimed at those who wanted easy access to that part of the company's product range. It was also planning an e-commerce initiative in conjunction with Amazon.com.

Sources: M&S *Annual Reports* 2003–2006; company website; *Financial Times* (various, 2006–2007).

Case questions 8.7

- Use the product/market matrix to classify the elements of Marks & Spencer's current strategy.
- How has the company chosen to deliver changes in strategic direction?
- In the light of your reading and answers to previous questions, what kind of competitive strategy do you think M&S is following in respect of clothing and foods? Provide examples to support your answer.

Business level strategy

At the business unit level, firms face a choice about how to compete. Porter (1980b, 1985) identified two basic types of competitive advantage: low cost or differentiation. From this he developed the idea that there are three generic strategies that a firm can use to develop and maintain competitive advantage: cost leadership, differentiation and focus. Figure 8.6 shows these strategies. The horizontal axis shows the two bases of competitive advantage. Competitive scope, on the vertical axis, shows whether company's target market is broad or narrow in scope.

Cost leadership

Cost leadership is a strategy whereby a firm aims to compete on price rather than on, say, advanced features or high levels of customer service. Firms following this strategy typically sell a standard no-frills product and place a lot of emphasis on minimising direct input and overhead costs. This requires economies of scale in production and close attention to efficiency and operating costs, although other sources of cost advantage, such as preferential access to raw materials, also help. However, a low cost base will not in itself bring competitive advantage – consumers must see that the product represents value for money. Retailers that have used this strategy include Wal-Mart (Asda in the United Kingdom), Argos and Superdrug; Dell Computers is another example, as is Ryanair (Chapter 1 case).

A **cost leadership strategy** is one in which a firm uses low price as the main competitive weapon.

Differentiation

A **differentiation strategy** is seen when a company offers a service that is distinct from its competitors, and which customers value. It is 'something unique beyond simply offering a low price' (Porter, 1985) that allows firms to charge a high price or retain customer loyalty. Chatterjee (2005) shows the strategic benefits of identifying very clearly

Differentiation strategy consists of offering a product or service that is perceived as unique or distinctive on a basis other than price.

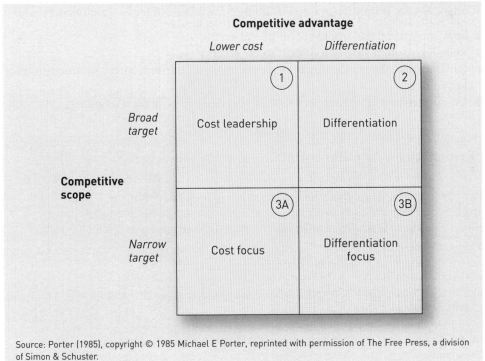

Competitive advantage

	Lower cost	Differentiation
Broad target	① Cost leadership	② Differentiation
Narrow target	③A Cost focus	③B Differentiation focus

Competitive scope

Source: Porter (1985), copyright © 1985 Michael E Porter, reprinted with permission of The Free Press, a division of Simon & Schuster.

Figure 8.6

Generic competitive strategies

key ideas The experience curve

An important feature of cost leadership is the effect of the experience curve, in which the unit cost of manufacturing a product or delivering a service falls as experience increases. In the same way that a person learning to knit or play the piano improves with practice, so 'the unit cost of value added to a standard product declines by a constant percentage (typically 20–30 per cent) each time cumulative output doubles' (Grant, 2002). This allows firms to set initial low selling prices in the knowledge that margins will increase as output grows and costs fall. The rate of travel down the cost experience curve is a crucial aspect of staying ahead of the competition in an undifferentiated market and underlines the importance of market share – if high volumes are not sold, the cost advantage is lost. Examples of products where costs have fallen as volumes have risen are semiconductors, watches, cars and online reservations.

the outcomes that customers value, and Sharp and Dawes (2001) contrast companies' methods of differentiation:

- Nokia achieves differentiation through the individual design of its product.
- Sony achieves it by offering superior reliability, service and technology.
- BMW differentiates by stressing a distinctive product/service image.
- Coca-Cola differentiates by building a widely recognised brand.

The form of differentiation varies. In construction equipment durability, spare parts availability and service will feature in a differentiation strategy, while in cosmetics differentiation is based on images of sophistication, exclusivity and eternal youth. Cities compete by stressing differentiation in areas such as cultural facilities, available land or good transport links.

Focus

A focus strategy is when a company competes by targeting very specific segments of the market.

A **focus strategy** involves targeting a narrow market segment, either by consumer group (teenagers, over-60s, doctors) or geography. The two variants – cost focus and differentiation focus – are simply narrow applications of the broad strategies. Examples include:

- Saga offers travel and insurance for those over 50.
- Rolls-Royce offers luxury transport to the wealthy.
- NFU Mutual offers insurance for farmers, Female Direct offers motor insurance for women.
- Co-operative Financial Services appeals to consumers with social concerns.

management in practice British Airways' differentiation strategy www.ba.com

After several years of poor performance British Airways has been renewing its strategy. It is seeking to differentiate itself from other airlines by focusing on business travellers rather than those travelling in economy class. Business passengers pay the full fare for their ticket, and expect a high-quality service. BA gradually reduced the number of seats available in economy class, and took fewer low-cost passengers travelling on connecting flights with other airlines. It sold GO (its low-cost airline) in early 2001, as this was not consistent with the new strategy. Through this clear differentiated strategy, BA has lost passenger volume to the low-cost airlines but sustains the higher-paying business passenger, who needs flexibility.

At the same time, BA has cut many fares on its website, even though they still provide some frills. In its desire to satisfy multiple segments, the company is essentially hyper-differentiating, a situation in which competitive companies must respond more rapidly to customers' changing demands.

Porter initially suggested that firms had to choose between cost leadership and differentiation. Many disagreed, observing how companies often appeared to follow both strategies simultaneously. By controlling costs better than competitors, companies can reinvest the savings in features that differentiate them. Porter (1994) later clarified his view:

> Every strategy must consider both relative cost and relative differentiation ... a company cannot completely ignore quality and differentiation in the pursuit of cost advantage, and vice versa ... Progress can be made against both types of advantage simultaneously. (p. 271)

However, he notes that there are trade-offs between the two and that companies should 'maintain a clear commitment to superiority in one of them'.

Is the Porter model valid in the Internet age?

Kim *et al.* (2004) asked whether strategy perspectives developed when the competitive landscape contained only offline firms are still relevant in the Internet age. The Internet allows firms to overcome barriers of time and distance, to serve large audiences more efficiently while also targeting groups with specific needs, and to reduce many operating costs. However Kim *et al.* also noted that some things stay the same – especially the need to invest in a clear and viable strategy. Their analysis led them to propose that the generic strategies of differentiation and cost leadership still apply to online businesses. However the strategy of focus will not be as viable as it has been for offline firms: since the Internet enables companies to reach both large and tightly defined audiences very cheaply, focus will be a competitive imperative rather than an option.

They also proposed a third approach – an 'integrated strategy' – that combines features of cost leadership and differentiation, and which will be superior to both. They suggested that online strategies could form a continuum, as shown in Figure 8.7.

Source: Kim *et al.* (2004).

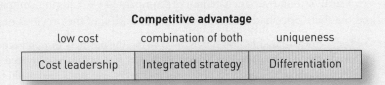

Figure 8.7 E-business competitive strategy as a continuum
Source: Kim *et al.* (2004).

Functional level strategy

Business level strategies need the support of suitable functional level strategies – Chapters 9 (Marketing) and 11 (Human Resources) give examples.

8.5 Alternative ways to deliver strategy

Corporate and business strategies can be delivered by internal development, acquisition or alliance – or a combination.

Internal development

The organisation delivers the strategy by expanding or redeploying relevant resources that it has or can employ. This enables managers to retain control of all aspects of the development of new products or services – especially where (such as at Linn Products) the product has technologically advanced features. Microsoft develops its Windows operating system in-house.

Public sector organisations typically favour internal development, traditionally providing services through staff whom they employ directly. Changes in the wider political agenda have meant that these are often required to compete with external providers, while some – such as France Telecom, Deutsche Post or the UK Stationery Office – have been partially or wholly sold to private investors.

Merger and acquisition

One firm merging with, or acquiring, another allows rapid entry into new product or market areas and is a quick way to build market share. It is also used where the acquiring company can use the other company's products to offer new services or enter new markets. Companies such as Microsoft and Cisco Systems frequently buy small, entrepreneurial companies and incorporate their products within the acquiring company's range. A company might be taken over for its expertise in research or its knowledge of a local market. Financial motives are often strong, particularly where the merger leads to cost-cutting. When The Royal Bank of Scotland acquired NatWest it achieved major economies by merging the two companies' computer systems. Other mergers extend the range of activities. Vodafone made several large acquisitions in its quest to become the world's largest mobile phone company.

Mergers and acquisitions frequently fail, destroying rather than adding value. When Sir Roy Gardner took over as chairman of Compass (a UK catering company) at which profits and the share price had fallen rapidly, he was critical of the previous management:

> [They] concentrated far too much on growing the business through acquisition. They should have stopped and made sure [that] what they had acquired delivered the expected results. Compass was being run by its divisional managers, which resulted in a total lack of consistency. (*Financial Times*, 19 January 2007, p. 19)

Joint developments and alliances

Organisations sometimes turn to partners to cooperate in developing products or services. Arrangements vary from highly formal contractual relationships to looser forms of cooperation but there are usually advantages to be gained by both parties. One attraction of this method is that it limits risk. For example, the large UK constructor John Laing announced an infrastructure joint venture in July 2004 with the Commonwealth Bank of Australia. It is a 50:50 joint venture with the bank to invest in UK hospital and European road projects, which allows both parties to limit the risk and to operate in areas in which they are strong. Rather than simply borrow from the bank, Laing shares the risk (and the reward) with the bank.

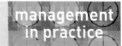

GSK's drug development strategy www.gsk.com

Half of the new drug discovery projects at GlaxoSmithKline may be undertaken by external partners by the turn of the decade as part of a radical overhaul designed to improve the pipeline of new drugs at the group. The research and development will be coordinated by GSK's Centre of Excellence for External Drug Discovery (CEEDD) which the company created in 2005 to boost innovation. The company's research director estimated that between one-quarter to one-third of GSK's existing research pipeline of new drugs already involved work conducted with external partners and a growing role would be played by the CEEDD, managing a 'virtual' portfolio of research run by such companies: 'In the future we are going to have many more external projects.'

Source: *Financial Times*, 31 May 2006, p. 22.

A second reason for joint ventures (JVs) is to learn about new technologies or markets. Alliances also arise where governments want to keep sensitive sectors, such as aerospace, defence and aviation, under national control. Airbus, which competes with Boeing in aircraft manufacture, was originally a JV between French, German, British and Spanish manufacturers. Alliances – such as the Star Alliance led by United Airlines of the United States and Lufthansa of Germany – are also common in the airline industry, where companies share revenues and costs over certain routes. As governments often prevent foreign ownership, such alliances avoid that barrier.

Other forms of joint development include franchising (common in many retailing activities – M&S has 198 franchised stores overseas), licensing and long-term collaboration between manufacturers and their suppliers.

Alliances and partnership working have also become commonplace in the public sector. In many cities alliances or partnerships have been created between major public bodies, business and community interests. Their main purpose is to foster a coherent approach to planning and delivering services. Public bodies often act as service commissioners rather than as direct providers, developing partnerships with organisations to deliver services on their behalf.

8.6 Perspectives on the strategy process

While most managers recognise the steps outlined earlier as the basic content of strategic planning there are differing views on how the *process* actually works in practice. Some views are *prescriptive* in that they seek to explain how management *should* make strategy, while others are *descriptive* in that they try to set out how management *does* make strategy. Table 8.4 shows three perspectives.

Table 8.4 Alternative perspectives on the strategy process

	Planning	Learning	Political
Approach	Prescriptive; assumes pure rationality	Descriptive; based on bounded rationality	Descriptive; based on bounded rationality
Content	Extensive use of analytical tools and techniques; emphasis on forecasting; extensive search for alternative options, each evaluated in detail	More limited use of tools and techniques and more limited search for options: time and resources don't permit	As learning view, but also some objectives and options disregarded as politically unacceptable
Nature of process	Formalised, systematic, analytical; top down – centralised planning teams	Adaptive, learning by doing; bottom up and top down	Characterised by bargaining and negotiation; use of power to impose objectives and strategies; top down and bottom up
Outcomes	Everything planned in advance; plans assumed to be achieved as set out	Plans are made but not all are 'realised'; some strategies are not planned but emerge in course of 'doing'	Plans are made but often couched in ambiguous terms to secure agreement; need interpretation in course of implementation; outcomes reflect compromises
Context/ environment	Stable environment; assumption that future can be predicted; if complex, use of more sophisticated tools	Complex, dynamic, future unpredictable	Stable or dynamic, but complex; stakeholders have diverging values, objectives and solutions

Planning view

The 'planning view' is prescriptive and based on a belief that the complexity of strategic decisions requires an explicit and formalised approach to guide management through the process. In the 1960s and 1970s a wide literature, most notably the work of Ansoff (1965), espoused this structured approach. At this time, strategy was seen as a systematic process, following a prescribed sequence of steps and making extensive use of analytical tools and techniques. This was the 'one best way' to develop strategy that, if followed, was believed almost to guarantee corporate success. Implicit in this view are assumptions that people behave rationally and that events and facts can be expressed or observed objectively. Those who challenge assumptions of rationality and objectivity advocate two possible alternative views – the learning and the political (Brews and Hunt, 1999).

Learning view

The learning view sees strategy as an *emergent* or adaptive process. Mintzberg (1994a, b) regards formal strategic planning as a system developed during a period of stability, and designed mainly for centralised bureaucracies typical of manufacturing industry. This style of planning may be appropriate for them, but not for businesses in more rapidly changing sectors: they require a more flexible approach.

Emergent strategies are those that result from actions taken one by one which converge in time in some sort of consistency or pattern.

Mintzberg (1994a) distinguished between intended and **emergent strategy** (see Figure 8.8). He acknowledges the validity of strategy as a plan, setting out intended courses of action, and recognises that some deliberate intentions may be realised. But he challenges managers to review how closely their realised strategies fit the original intention. As well as realising some intended strategies, it is also likely that some plans were not implemented (unrealised strategies) and that others which he describes as 'emergent strategies' were not expressly intended. They resulted from 'actions taken one by one, which converged in time in some sort of consistency or pattern' (p. 25).

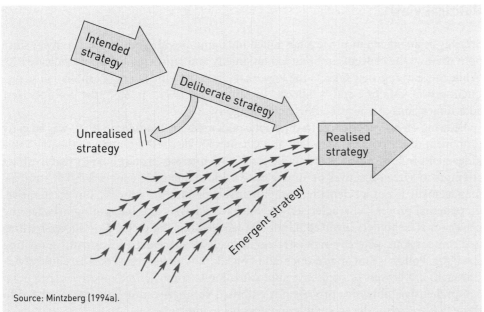

Source: Mintzberg (1994a).

Figure 8.8

Forms of strategy

A flexible approach to strategy is one which recognises that 'the real world inevitably involves some thinking ahead of time as well as some adaptation en route' (Mintzberg, 1994a, p. 26). The essence of the learning view is this process of adaptation, the ability to react to unexpected events, to exploit or experiment with new ideas 'on the ground'. Mintzberg gives the example of a salesperson coming up with the idea of selling an existing product to some new customers. Soon all the other salespeople begin to do the same, and 'one day, months later, management discovers that the company has entered a new market' (p. 26). This was not planned but learned, collectively, during implementation.

 **Emergent strategy at IKEA**

Barthélemy (2006) offers an insight into the strategy process at IKEA (Chapter 15 case). Their strategy has clearly been highly successful, but how did it come about? A close examination of the company's history shows that many of the specifics of the strategy were not brought about through a process of deliberate formulation followed by implementation:

> Instead, the founder, Ingvar Kamprad started with a very general vision. IKEA's specific strategy then emerged as he both proactively developed a viable course of action and reacted to unfolding circumstances. (p. 81)

Examples include:

- The decision to sell furniture was an adaptation to the market, not a deliberate strategy – furniture was initially a small part of the retail business, but was so successful that he soon dropped all other products.
- The flat-pack method which symbolises the group was introduced to reduce insurance claims on the mail order business – its true potential only became clear when the company started opening stores, and realised that customers valued this type of product.
- The company only began to design its own furniture because other retailers put pressure on established furniture companies not to sell to IKEA.

Source: Barthélemy (2006).

Political view

Strategy as an emergent process has much in common with political perspectives, since both draw on the concepts of bounded rationality and satisficing behaviour (Chapter 7). While the learning view reflects the logic that 'prior thought can never specify all subsequent action' (Majone and Wildavsky in Mintzberg, 1994a, p. 289), the political view adds dimensions of power, conflict and ambiguity.

Drawing on his experiences in the public policy sphere, Lindblom (1959) was an early proponent of the political view (see also Chapter 7). He drew attention to the way value judgements influence policy and to the conflicting interests of stakeholders that frustrate attempts to agree objectives or strategies to achieve them. He concluded that strategic management is not a scientific, comprehensive or rational process, but an iterative, incremental process, characterised by restricted analysis and bargaining between the players or stakeholders involved. Lindblom labelled this the method of 'successive limited comparisons' whereby 'new' strategy is made by marginal adjustments to existing strategy: 'Policy is not made once and for all; it is made and remade endlessly ... [through] ... a process of successive approximation to some desired objectives.' It is not a comprehensive, objective process but a limited comparison of options, restricted to those that are politically acceptable and possible to implement.

> ### Activity 8.4 Reviewing mission statements
>
> Refer back to the examples of mission statements earlier in the chapter. Do you consider any of these stated intentions to be unclear or vague? If so, consider why they might have been expressed in this way.

Both the learning and the political views of strategy oppose the rigid planning view of strategy, but ultimately accept that a structured approach to strategy has its place: 'Too much planning may lead us to chaos, but so too would too little, and more directly' (Mintzberg, 1994a, p. 416). The planning style of the 1960s seemed to suit the relative stability that characterised the period. The highly competitive, increasingly global and fast-moving markets that characterise the present time may be better matched by a learning, adaptive or even 'real-time strategy' (Taylor, 1997).

8.7 Current themes and issues

Performance

Several studies have claimed to show that strategic planning improves company performance, though a review of research by Greenley (1986) was more sceptical, concluding that the evidence of a link between planning and performance was at best inconclusive. Pfeffer and Sutton (2006b) suggest that strategic planning can be valuable in providing a focus for a business and its staff, helping them to set priorities and allocate resources – provided it is done intelligently. Strategy is typically seen as an activity of senior managers and their advisers, with details of implementation left to those lower in the hierarchy:

the view that strategy setting is top management's central activity remains dominant. Because of the obvious importance of focus and the need to optimize the allocation of scarce resources, it became almost axiomatic that strategy was the most important single cause of a firm's success. (Pfeffer and Sutton, 2006b, p. 138)

In view of the inconclusive evidence, they advocate supplementing top down approaches with more flexible, responsive methods. While some top down planning is valuable, there are other ways of ensuring that effort is focused and scarce resources are allocated productively. These include:

● ensuring that managers listen to customers and employees, and act on what they say;
● not confusing implementation problems with the need to change strategy;
● expressing strategies in simple, actionable terms;
● balancing attention to strategy with attention to the details of implementation:

too many companies overemphasize strategy which detracts time, resources and focus from the less glamorous and gritty details of implementation and undermines adaptation to shifting conditions. (2006, p. 156)

Responsibility

Issues of corporate responsibility arise in many aspects of management, and managers debate how these relate to strategy. Chapter 5 contrasted the 'Friedmanite' and 'stakeholder' perspectives – the former arguing that the business leaders should focus on the financial interests of shareholders, while the latter believe that managers have responsibilities to a wider constituency. Claims for and against the idea that corporations should act responsibly often reflect deeply held moral and ethical principles, and this makes it a challenge to relate them to a company's strategic decisions. A perspective that can help to clarify the issue was suggested by Vogel (2005), who concludes that while advocates of corporate responsibility are genuinely motivated by a commitment to social goals, CR is only sustainable if 'virtue pays off'. Responsible action is both made possible and constrained by market forces.

Virtuous behaviour can make business sense for some firms in some areas in some circumstances, but does not in itself ensure commercial success. Companies that base their strategy on acting responsibly may be commercially successful, but equally they may fail – responsible behaviour carries the same risks as any other kind of business behaviour. While some consumers or investors will give their business to companies that appear to be acting responsibly, others will not. Some customers place a higher priority on price, appearance or any other feature than they do on whether goods are produced and delivered in a sustainable way. As Vogel (2005) observes: 'There *is* a place in the market economy for responsible firms. But there is also a large place for their less responsible competitors' (p. 3).

While some companies can benefit from a strategy based on acting responsibly, market forces alone cannot prevent others from having a less responsible strategy, and profiting from doing so.

Internationalisation

As the business world becomes ever more international, companies inevitably face difficult strategic choices about the extent to which they develop an international presence, and the way in which they develop their international strategy. The nature of the challenge is shown by the fact that while many companies have done very well from international expansions, many overseas ventures fail, destroying value rather than creating it.

Chapter 4 outlined the nature of the challenges faced as companies respond to what they perceive to be international opportunities. They need, for example, to deal with complex structural and logistical issues when products are made and sold in several countries, ensure that there are adequate links between research, marketing and production to speed the introduction of new products, and facilitate the rapid transfer of knowledge and ideas between the national components of the business. These are complex enough issues in themselves, but the extra dimension is that solutions which work in one national context may not work as well in another. Differences in national culture mean that people will respond in perhaps an unexpected way to strategies and plans, especially if these are perceived in some way to be inconsistent with the local culture (as the examples cited in Chapter 4 of Coca-Cola in India or Egg in France testify).

The content of an international strategy will be shaped by the process of its production – and the extent to which different players in the global enterprise take part in it.

Summary

1 **Explain the significance of strategic management to all organisations**
  - Strategy is about the survival of the enterprise; the strategy process sets an overall direction with information about the external environment and internal capabilities. Defining the purposes of the organisation helps to guide the choice and implementation of strategy.

2 **Describe the main steps in the strategic management process**
  - Figure 8.1 identified the steps of identifying mission and goals, external and internal analysis, formulating, implementing and evaluating strategy.

3 **Use the product/market matrix to compare corporate level strategies**
  - Strategy can focus on existing or new products, and existing or new markets. This gives four broad directions, with options in each – such as market penetration, product development, market development or diversification.

4 **Use the concept of generic strategies to compare business level strategies**
  - Key strategic choices are those of cost leader, differentiation or a focus on a narrow segment of the market.

5 **Give examples of alternative methods of delivering a strategy**
  - Strategy can be delivered by internal (sometimes called organic) development by rearranging the way resources are deployed. Alternatives include acquiring or merging with another company, or by forming alliances and joint ventures.

6 **Compare planning, learning and political perspectives on strategy**
  - The planning approach is appropriate in stable and predictable environments; while the emergent approach more accurately describes the process in volatile environments, since strategy rarely unfolds as intended in complex, changing and ambiguous situations. A political perspective may be a more accurate way of representing the process when it involves the interests of powerful stakeholders. It is rarely an objectively rational activity, implying that strategy models are not prescriptive but rather frameworks to guide managers.

Review questions

1 Distinguish between a corporate and an operating strategy.

2 In what ways does the concept of competitive advantage apply to for-profit organisations, non-profits, cities and countries?

3 Describe the main elements in the strategy process in your own terms.

4 Discuss with a manager from an organisation how his or her organisation developed its present strategy. Compare this practice with that set out in the model. What conclusions do you draw from that comparison?

5 Compare the strategies of Marks & Spencer and The Body Shop, and list any similarities and differences.

6 What are the main steps to take in analysing the organisation's environment? Why is it necessary to do this?

7 Can you describe clearly each of the stages in value chain analysis and illustrate them with an example? Why is the model useful to management?

8 The chapter described three generic strategies that organisations can follow. Give examples of three companies each following one of these strategies.

9 Give examples of company strategies corresponding to each box in the product/market matrix.

Concluding critical reflection

Think about the way your company, or one with which you are familiar, approaches issues of strategy. Review the material in the chapter, and perhaps visit some of the websites identified. Then make notes on these questions:

● What examples of the issues discussed in this chapter are currently relevant to your company – such as whether to follow a differentiation or focus strategy, or the balance between planning and learning?

● In responding to these issues, what **assumptions** about the strategy process appear to have guided what people have done? To what extent do these seem to fit the environmental forces as you see them? Do they appear to stress the planning or the learning perspectives on strategy?

● What factors such as the history or current **context** of the company appear to have influenced the prevailing view? Is the history of the company constraining attempts to move in new directions? How well are stakeholders served by the present strategy – how would they benefit from a significantly different one?

● Have people put forward **alternative** strategies, or alternative ways of developing strategy, based on evidence about other companies? If you could find such evidence, how may it affect company practice?

● What limitations can you see in any of the ideas presented here? For example, does Porter's value chain adequately capture the variable most relevant in your business, or are there other features you would include? What limitations are there in the way strategy is formed in an organisation with which you are familiar?

Further reading

Johnson, G., Scholes, K. and Whittington, R. (2006), *Exploring Corporate Strategy* (7th edn.), Financial Times/Prentice Hall, Harlow.

The best-selling European text on corporate strategy. Although more detailed than required at introductory level, a number of sections usefully build on this chapter.

Smith, R.J. (1995), *Strategic Management and Planning in the Public Sector* (2nd edn), Longman/Civil Service College, Harlow.

Covers the main elements in the strategic planning process and explains, with the use of examples, some tools of strategic analysis in addition to those covered in this chapter. It also contains useful chapters on definitions and terminology, and on options analysis.

Kay, J. (1996), *The Business of Economics*, Oxford University Press, Oxford.

Presents a readable account of competitive strategy written from an economic perspective, illustrated by a wide range of European and other international examples.

Mintzberg, H., Ahlstrand, B. and Lampel J. (1998), *Strategy Safari*, Prentice Hall Europe, Hemel Hempstead.

Excellent discussion of the process of strategy-making from various academic and practical perspectives.

Moore, J.I. (2001), *Writers on Strategy and Strategic Management* (2nd edn), Penguin, London.

Summarises the work of the major contributors to the fields of strategy and strategic management – Part One contains a useful overview of the work of the 'movers and shakers', including Ansoff, Porter and Mintzberg.

Greenley, G.E. (1986), 'Does strategic planning improve company performance?', *Long Range Planning*, vol. 19, no. 2, pp. 101–109.

Valuable study that shows the benefits of a sceptical view towards claims about the planning–performance link, and also a good example of a systematic literature analysis.

Cummings, S. and Angwin, D. (2004), 'The future shape of strategy: lemmings or chimera?', *Academy of Management Executive*, vol. 18, no. 2, pp. 21–36.

Based on research amongst executives in Europe and Australasia, this article develops an approach to strategy formulation that takes account of the current need to manage multiple customer groups in complex environments.

Weblinks

These websites have appeared in the chapter:

www.marksandspencer.com
www.baesystems.com
www.pg.com
www.nestle.com
www.linn.co.uk
www.ikea.com
www.unilever.com
www.rspb.org.uk
www.hefce.ac.uk
www.nokia.com
www.ba.com
www.gsk.com

Visit two of the business sites in the list, or any other company that interests you, and navigate to the pages dealing with news or investor relations.

- What are the main strategic issues the companies seem to be facing?
- What information can you find about their policies?

Annotated weblinks, multiple choice questions and other useful resources can be found on **www.pearsoned.co.uk/boddy**

Chapter 9

Managing marketing

Aim

To explain the benefits that all organisations gain if they give a prominent role to marketing, and how they can organise the activity.

Objectives

By the end of your work on this chapter you should be able to outline the concepts below in your own terms and:

1 Compare and contrast marketing with alternative organisational orientations

2 Describe the benefits to any organisation of adopting a marketing orientation

3 Explain why marketing is an information-intensive activity

4 Identify the responsibilities of the marketing manager

5 Explain market segmentation and the practice of selecting a target market

6 Describe the components of the marketing mix

7 Explain what is meant by product positioning

Key terms

This chapter introduces the following ideas:

marketing
marketing orientation
consumer
consumer centred
marketing environment
marketing information system
market segmentation
target market
marketing mix
product life cycle

Each is a term defined within the text, as well as in the Glossary at the end of the book.

Manchester United FC www.manutd.com

With over 50 million fans across the globe, Manchester United Football Club (MU) is one of the best-known soccer clubs. Founded in 1878, it rose to prominence in the early 1950s. Since then the club has never been out of the sports headlines, hiring a series of almost legendary managers (including Sir Matt Busby and Sir Alex Ferguson) and buying or developing world-recognised players (including David Beckham, Ruud van Nistelrooy and Wayne Rooney).

In May 2005 the club was taken over in a £790 million bid by American sports tycoon Malcolm Glazer in a deal that was heavily financed by debt. The 2006 annual turnover was £173 million, generated from a wide range of football-related businesses (gate and TV revenues, sports clothes, etc.) and brand-related activities (MUTV, mobiles, travel, finance). Manchester United Football Club is only a part of worldwide operations: the holding company (Manchester United) owns MU, Manchester United Catering (Agency Company) and Manchester United Interactive. MUTV, the club's official channel, is a joint venture between Manchester United, Granada and BSkyB.

The club's ambition is to be the most successful team in football. Its business strategy is to do this by having the football and commercial operations work hand in hand, both in existing and new domestic markets and in the potential markets represented by the club's global fan base, especially Asia. The marketing strategy is built on maintaining success on the field and leveraging global brand awareness through new products and partnered services designed to appeal to MU's worldwide fans. A substantial partner is Nike, whose development and marketing channels are used to generate new value from the MU trademarks (for example, replica kits) by supplying the millions of MU fans in the United Kingdom and Asia.

PA Photos: Kin Cheung/AP.

MU attempts to control and develop its own routes to market for media rights (for example, MUTV), thereby exploiting the club's own performance and reputation rather than relying on the collective appeal of competition football. The management believes this enhances the ability to deliver branded services to customers anywhere in the world. They rely strongly on IT-based CRM (customer relationship management) technology to convert fans into customers.

Source: Based on material from Butterworth Heinemann Case 0181, *Manchester United and British Soccer: Beautiful Game, Brutal Industry*; 'Can football be saved?', *Business Week*, 19 July 2004; published Manchester United material.

Case questions 9.1

- Consider the marketing implications of MU's activities. What is it offering to customers?
- What groups would MU see as competitors? Are they simply other successful football clubs?
- How might MU improve its marketing?

Activity 9.1   **Describing marketing**

Before reading this chapter, write some notes on what you understand 'marketing' to be.

Think of some recent purchases, and consider the different ways in which you came across marketing before, during or after your purchase.

Keep your notes safe as you will use them again at the end of the chapter.

9.1   Introduction

Manchester United is very successful in raising awareness and reputation amongst fans and other customer groups. Its strategy revolves around the loyalty and trust that customers have in the club and the MU brand. There is a question as to what product or service customers think they are getting when they purchase an MU product. Different groups of consumers attribute differing benefits to the MU brand. An MU football fan might buy a season ticket to fulfil a psychological need to be part of a group with a common purpose, while a person with no interest in football might use an MU mobile phone because they trust the product, based on the MU reputation.

How should MU management manage the brand in these complex and sometimes unrelated markets? Might it be in the interests of the PLC to position the brand away from direct success on the football field, as that success cannot be guaranteed and the brand could be contaminated by a disaster (such as demotion from the Premier League)? How should MU promote itself? Standard advertising campaigns – based on the product's advantages over the competitor's offerings – are inappropriate.

Marketing is a management process that identifies, anticipates and supplies consumer requirements efficiently and effectively.

Manchester United depends on good **marketing**. Originally conceived as a local football team to keep working men occupied and interested on Saturday afternoons, it is now a worldwide business managed by trained business managers rather than by retired football players. MU marketing managers are aware that they are satisfying psychological needs: when fans buy replica MU football jerseys as T-shirts, they are not keeping themselves warm and dry – they are making indirect statements about their personality. In a highly differentiated market such as this, buyers are not as price sensitive as they are in commodity markets. A football shirt which costs less than £2 to make and deliver can sell for up to £40.

All organisations face the challenge of understanding what customers want, and ensuring that they can meet those expectations. Managers of profitable firms of any size will usually attribute much of their success to marketing; marketing is often closely tied to the business strategy. IKEA, the Swedish furniture retailer, has found and refined a formula that appeals to its target market. In 40 years it has grown from a single store to a business with over 230 outlets in 35 countries. Virgin Direct, the financial services joint venture with Norwich Union, has become a major player. Successful not-for-profit organisations such as Oxfam and the Royal Society for the Protection of Birds also demonstrate the benefits of understanding a market and communicating with it effectively. All organisations need to give value for money, and so need to be aware of their customers, sensitive to changing needs and organised to deliver those needs.

The chapter opens by considering a marketing orientation, identifying the benefits of the concept to all organisations, and how they can make it the focus of their activities. It then discusses the management of marketing information and the roles of marketing management. It concludes with an explanation of the marketing mix and brand management.

9.2   What is marketing?

People often confuse marketing with a range of sales techniques such as:

- glossy brochures;
- the latest promotional offer at a supermarket;
- sponsorship of popular television programmes by branded products, such as Toyota's relationship with Channel 4's weekend youth programming;
- endorsement of products or services by celebrity names, such as Gary Lineker (broadcaster and former England football captain) advertising Walker's crisps, or Gordon Ramsay (three-star Michelin chef and TV presenter) promoting Victoria Wine;
- e-mail messages from companies promoting travel offers or new books.

These techniques illustrate the way in which marketers try to sell products or services – but there is more to marketing than promotion. All definitions of marketing emphasise the need to identify and satisfy customer requirements. Kotler and Keller (2006) define it as 'a social and managerial process by which individuals and groups obtain what they need and want through creating and exchanging products and value with others'. Peter Drucker (1999a) places the activity even more firmly at the centre of business:

> Because the purpose of business is to create and keep customers, it has only two central functions – marketing and innovation. The basic function of marketing is to attract and retain customers at a profit.

These definitions imply that marketing refers both to a marketing function within the organisation and to a more deeply embedded marketing orientation that shapes other activities of the organisation. The former view that the marketing was done by marketing people is not suitable for today's competitive environment. As David Packard, co-founder of Hewlett-Packard, said: 'Marketing is too important to be left to the marketing department', i.e. the entire organisation should be marketing the company, from the company receptionist as 'Director of First Impressions' to the chief executive as 'Director of Shareholder Interests'.

Consumer marketing and industrial marketing

There are two categories of organisational marketing: (a) consumer marketing, which concerns creating and delivering products to satisfy consumers, and (b) industrial or business-to-business (B2B) marketing, which aims to satisfy the needs of businesses. The marketing concept is similar for both but this chapter is mainly concerned with consumer marketing.

A marketing orientation

Most commercial organisations have a marketing function – usually a group of people who focus on activities such as market research, competitor analysis, product strategy or promotion. Those which recognise the full significance of marketing incorporate it deeply in the organisation, adopting not only a marketing function but a **marketing orientation**. They concentrate their activities on the market and the **consumer**, being '**consumer centred**' or 'consumer driven'.

Levi have positioned themselves as a successful manufacturer of fashion clothing by making marketing a central organisational activity. With products like Levi's jeans, they

Marketing orientation is an organisational orientation that believes success is most effectively achieved by satisfying consumer demands.

Consumers are individuals, households, organisations, institutions, resellers and governments that purchase the products offered by other organisations.

Consumer-centred organisation is focused upon, and structured around, identifying and satisfying the demands of its consumers.

respond to the changing needs, wants and demands of consumers by investing in product development and marketing communications. They watch the customers to see how their clothes are worn: studies like this resulted in the popular hipster jeans, when marketers noticed that female jeans wearers were pulling the jeans down on their hips and responded with a line of products cut this way.

Charities such as Oxfam (**www.oxfam.co.uk**), Greenpeace (**www.greenpeace.com**) and Médecins sans Frontières (**www.msf.org**) pay attention to the interests of their supporters. As well as promoting established lines of work, they survey their donors to ensure an acceptable match between the charity's campaigns and the issues that matter to those who donate the funds. Adopting a customer-focused orientation enables them to continue achieving their goals (Kottasz, 2004).

 **Financial services become consumer centred**

Prior to the 1980s, bank and financial service providers were not noted for their customer friendliness. Customers regarded them as organisations that almost had to be persuaded to carry out their core business, such as providing a loan. Today's financial services industry is an aggressive and competitive market. Faced with intense competition, encouraged by deregulation and the demutualisation of many building societies, most high street retail banks adopted a more consumer-centred approach. Rather than having to be persuaded to make loans, they trumpet the advantages of taking out a loan with them and listen to the (often changing) needs of their consumers. By investing in new products and widening access to their services through telephone and Internet banking, organisations such as the Co-operative Bank (**www.co-operativebank.co.uk**) have successfully responded to the new business and marketing environment and the competition that comes with it.

management in practice **Marketing and the voluntary sector**

Many staff and volunteers in charities are still uncomfortable with the idea that they are in marketing – preferring to see themselves as helpers or carers. Yet as Keaveney and Kaufmann (2001) say:

> donors, local authorities, opinion formers, the media, all have the choice of whether or not to support a particular charity. They also, through exercising that choice ... can change parts of what the charity does. They make up the markets within which the charity operates. Without knowledge and understanding of those markets, the charity, quite simply, will fail. This does not mean charities operate in a value-free vacuum; rather that by knowing themselves and their mission, and by knowing the markets they exist to serve or work in, charities can match their activities to external needs and make sure that they achieve as much as possible for their beneficiaries. (p. 2)

Source: Keaveney and Kaufmann (2001).

Alternative orientations

Table 9.1 summarises these alternative orientations.

Table 9.1

Alternative
organisational
orientations

Organisational orientation	Focus	Benefit	Disadvantage
Product	Product features	High-quality products	Research may not have identified demand for the product and it may not sell
Production	Production	Low costs	Costs determine price and production, not consumer demands. Production may not match consumer demand
Sales	Turnover and shifting product	Sales targets met; good for cash flow in the short term	High-pressure sales techniques may meet current targets but lose future ones if users find product unsatisfactory
Marketing	Continually on consumers and consumer demands	Product offering determined by consumer demands; organisational goals achieved	Initial investment in becoming consumer centred

Source: Based on Lancaster *et al.* (2002); Dibb *et al.* (2006); Jobber (2007).

Product orientation

Organisations operating with a product orientation focus on their technological strengths and expertise. They stress the products and product features that these strengths allow them to make. They pay less attention to the demands of the market and can often find themselves in a position similar to that of the De Lorean car:

> This stainless steel car was built in Northern Ireland with government grants and Lotus expertise. Targeted for the American market, it received free publicity from its appearance in the film *Back to the Future*. When the manufacturers introduced the car to the market they found that there was no demand. Nobody wanted to buy the car. (*Car Magazine*, supplement, April 1997)

While a product orientation is focused on products for which there may or may not be demand, a marketing orientation is focused on identifying consumer demands for particular products.

Production orientation

The production orientation holds that consumers will buy products that are highly available and low cost. Therefore, an organisation operating under the production orientation uses production efficiency and cost of materials to determine the quantity and price of goods to be produced. The production orientation focuses on efficiency and costs; it is relevant when the market has high growth prospects and the firm can benefit from economies of scale.

Sales or selling orientation

An organisation operating under the sales orientation aims to shift as much of a product as it can as quickly as possible. Levitt (1960) provides a clear understanding of the differences between selling and marketing philosophies:

Selling focuses on the needs of the seller; marketing on the needs of the buyer. Selling is a pre-occupation with the seller's need to convert his product into cash; marketing with the idea of satisfying the needs of the consumer by means of the product and the whole cluster of things associated with creating, delivering and finally consuming it.

As Kotler and Keller (2006) point out, the selling concept is typically practised with *unsought* goods, those that consumers do not normally think of buying, such as encyclopedias.

Marketing orientation

Putting the consumer at the beginning rather than the end of the production–consumption cycle enables organisations to discover what consumers want. They can then decide how best to use the strengths of the organisation to *return* to the marketplace with a product for which a demand exists. They use market information about demand and the price that consumers are prepared to pay to determine how much to produce and what production costs must be to offer a price acceptable to consumers. While the sales orientation focuses on shifting products, the marketing orientation focuses on satisfying consumers and building mutually satisfying relationships. To paraphrase Kotler and Keller (2006), the marketing concept takes an *outside-in* perspective rather than the *inside-out* perspective of the selling concept.

Satisfying latent need

Taking the marketing approach means meeting the consumers' needs. In some instances, consumers will not be aware of the usefulness or value of a product which they do not know about or that has not been brought to market. Demand that is waiting to happen is called latent demand. Examples of widely used products that satisfy a formerly latent demand include mobile phones, electric toothbrushes and organic foodstuffs.

Activity 9.2   **Identifying consumers**

A marketing orientation suggests that organisational success is best achieved by focusing on the consumer. Identify each of the following organisations' consumers and suggest the benefits that a focus on their consumers will bring to each organisation: Microsoft, easyJet (**www.easyjet.com**), Sainsbury's (**www.sainsburys.co.uk**), and Cancer Research UK (**www.cancerresearchuk.org**).

Benefits of a marketing orientation

Marketers assert that the most effective way of achieving organisational objectives is through consumer satisfaction. Organisations with a marketing philosophy still have to assess product features, efficient levels of production and sales targets (see the study by Shaw *et al.*, 2004 of the relationship between marketers and engineers in German and UK organisations), but decisions about these matters are not the focus of organisational activities. Instead, consumer demands determine product development, levels of production and sales targets.

Adopting a marketing orientation ensures that the whole organisation commits to achieving organisational goals by *continually* satisfying consumer demands. Aware of this objective and their potential contribution, functional areas cooperate and coordinate their activities towards a common goal – for a recent comparative study of two fashion retailers, see Newman and Patel (2004). Organisations such as Manchester United, Linn Products (see Chapter 8) and Sony Ericsson anticipate changing demands and are able to develop new products to meet them.

Apple   www.apple.com/uk

With its share price tripling in 2004, doubling in 2005, and up 16 per cent in 2006, Apple is doing well. There appear to be two main drivers of its current success. First, the success of its iPod, which has sold over 90 million units since 2001: second, the revival of its personal computer business with the success of its laptops and desktops. Apple demonstrates a marketing orientation by continually satisfying customer demands.

The iPod is now in its fifth generation and has been improved every year since release, becoming smaller and more powerful. There are now different iPods to meet personal requirements: Shuffle, for those who seek the smallest and lightest music player; Nano, for those looking for style; and the main iPod, which has huge memory capacity (up to 80G) and can carry photos and video. Combined with this is the Apple Online Music Store that allows consumers to buy music legally online as opposed to illegal file sharing; as well as free iTunes that allow both Mac and PC users to control and play their music from their computer.

Apple has successfully responded to consumer demands for a seamless digital music experience before its rivals, giving it very high market share (up to 80 per cent of the UK market alone).

Sources: Company website; www.macobserver.com.

By identifying and monitoring consumer demands, marketing-oriented organisations are able to respond to these demands and ensure that the products they offer satisfy consumers. Above all else, the adoption of the marketing orientation offers stability in the marketplace (Figure 9.1).

Figure 9.1

Benefits of marketing as an organisational orientation

This concept has been extended to include network marketing, which recognises a web of interdependencies between firms. While relationship marketing depends on managing relationships with customers, network marketing recognises that meeting their needs depends on a wider range of stakeholders – such as raw materials suppliers or delivery companies. Manchester United is an example of multiple stakeholders and relationship marketing combining to create network marketing.

key ideas Transactional marketing and relationship marketing

Gronroos (2000) distinguishes between transactional marketing and relationship marketing. To ensure a stable position many organisations have replaced their focus on transactions (exchange of value, e.g. a purchase) with one that seeks to develop long-term relationships with their consumers. They argue that a focus on one-off transactions encourages organisations to concentrate on short-term profit maximisation and to pay less attention to their long-term position. Organisations that move towards a relational focus have a better understanding of consumer needs. They concentrate on developing a 'long-term, continuous series of transactions' that help them maintain stability in the market and achieve their objectives in the long term.

Others (such as Zolkiewski, 2004) argue that relationship marketing is not suitable for all organisations, and that not all long-term relationships are as beneficial or necessary as advocates of this approach claim.

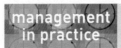

management in practice Ted Baker   www.tedbaker.co.uk

One of the fast-growing 'lifestyle' brands in the United Kingdom, Ted Baker offers stylish men's and women's wear and accessories. To build relations with its customers the company has heavily promoted its store card, offering discounts on purchases and invitations to evening events launching its new collections. Enjoying rapid growth since its formation in 1987 as a specialist shirt shop in Glasgow, the strategy appears to be working: it now has outlets all over the United Kingdom and has expanded into over ten countries. By keeping in touch with customers, their preferences and where they live, the firm is able to tailor its offerings more exactly. It also encourages them to be part of the Ted 'family' through regular events.

Source: Company website; other sources.

9.3 What types of organisation can use marketing?

The benefits offered by the marketing orientation apply to all types of organisations, including charities, churches and sports teams. Writing about the Health Service, Moutinho (1995) states:

> the present day marketing concept views marketing as a social process ... [to identify] consumer needs and satisfy them through integrated marketing activities ... Marketing thinking will lead to a better understanding of the needs of different client segments; to a more careful shaping and launching of new services; to a pruning of weak services; to more flexible pricing approaches; and to higher levels of patient satisfaction.

Some health care organisations now apply marketing to a broader set of problems by asking questions such as:

- Where should we locate a clinic or an ambulatory care unit?
- How can we estimate whether a new service will draw enough patients?
- What should we do with a maternity wing that is only 20 per cent occupied?
- How can we attract more consumers to preventive care services such as annual medical check-ups and cancer-screening programmes?

Church marketing www.churchmarketing.com

Started in 1993, John Manlove's Church Marketing consultancy aims to offer churches a clear mission, vision, values and strategy statement. The company uses its experience in advertising and transfers many of the terms used in marketing to one not associated with business terms. On brand development for example, JMCM offers to 'bring essential information and ideas to the task of translating the church's identity and direction into a visual brand for the church's communication media'.

Source: Company website.

Activity 9.3   Evaluating market research

- What kind of information would a firm involved in church marketing seek to obtain? How would it go about doing this and what are the cost implications?
- Can you identify another social care organisation that could use market research to assist it?

Organisations with social or charitable aims are beginning to take a marketing orientation, including those raising awareness of the dangers of smoking, increasing charitable donations and promoting the benefits of an active lifestyle. Not-for-profit organisations focus on understanding the opinions, perceptions and attitudes of people whose opinions, attitudes or behaviours they want to change, or whose support they seek.

Andreasen and Kotler (2002) have expressed the not-for-profit transaction in terms of *favourable exchange*, where one party (the marketing organisation) can induce behaviour changes in another (equivalent to the consumer) by working on the assumption that people behave in ways that they believe will leave them better off than the alternatives. The authors believe that in attempting to understand consumer behaviour it is critical to differentiate between the exchange as a process and the exchange as an outcome. The latter is simply a transaction. The management of the exchange *process* is marketing.

A marketing orientation helps the homeless

The Big Issue was established to tackle the problem of homelessness in a progressive and entrepreneurial manner. Rather than campaigning to raise funding and donations that could be used to address homelessness, *The Big Issue* sought to challenge conventions. By adopting a marketing orientation *The Big Issue* has successfully approached the challenge of homelessness in a novel and unique manner: by developing a new product, a street magazine that homeless vendors sell to the public, *The Big Issue* has addressed several objectives. Vendors earn money from the magazines they sell, which highlights the extent of homelessness; the public purchase an informative magazine and also support a social cause. Using the Andreasen and Kotler model, managing the exchange process is the main task. The newspaper sale transaction is almost incidental in terms of the consumer benefits. The exchange process in contrast is to be a complex mix of a desire to reduce homelessness, a desire to help the individual vendor, assuaging of guilt at the position of someone worse off, or even the reduction of mild fear at perceived aggressive selling.

9.4 Creating a marketing orientation

Michaels warned back in 1982 that: 'No one person, system, or technique will make a company marketing orientated' and stresses that a marketing orientation cannot be achieved overnight (Michaels, 1982). Advising on the implementation of a marketing orientation, he emphasises the following requirements:

- **Investment by top management** Before marketing can be instilled throughout the whole organisation, senior managers must commit themselves to the marketing orientation or other managers will not implement the necessary changes.
- **Injection of outside talent** Managements that successfully implement a marketing orientation have brought in new personnel. These have helped to educate other staff about the possible benefits of the new orientation.
- **A clear sense of direction** As with any change, it is essential that management takes a planned approach to its implementation. It must set objectives and timescales to guide the introduction.

Kotler and Keller (2006) continue to stress the importance of structuring the organisation to focus on the consumer. Managers need to educate themselves and their staff about the idea and how it may support long-lasting success in the marketplace. This applies to all levels and functions who must share a common commitment if they are to work together in the interests of the consumers. Without the support of top management, the focus on consumer satisfaction advocated by the marketing orientation will not become the guiding orientation for organisational decisions.

Manchester United – the case continues
www.manutd.com

CASE STUDY

One of the challenges facing Manchester United is the best organisational marketing structure to design and the internal culture to induce in managing its huge operation. At corporate level, the Glazer family owns football-related and non-football-related businesses and is involved with various joint ventures in TV, financial services and mobile phones. At business and product levels, management have to deal directly with their target segments. Promotional campaigns for individual products have to be sensitive to the image of

sister MU products. Hoarding adverts of a noisy football crowd having a good time will be exciting to other potential fans but could be off-putting for someone who has to produce their MU credit card at local stores.

Preserving the perceived value of the brand is also important: the replica jersey product manager will not want stores such as Tesco to sell them at a discount. This raises important questions of channel management and relationship with suppliers whose strategy might be more cost focused than differentiated. In 2006

MU signed a record deal for £56 million over four years with the American Investment Group (AIG) to be their shirt sponsor. This represents a substantial increase from their previous £9 million a year tie-in with Vodafone, who were able to withdraw from their contract with MU after the Glazer takeover.

The structure of the organisation may have to change to allow all departments to become focused on and work together for the achievement of consumer satisfaction. Compare Figures 9.2 and 9.3. Figure 9.2 shows marketing as an important function within

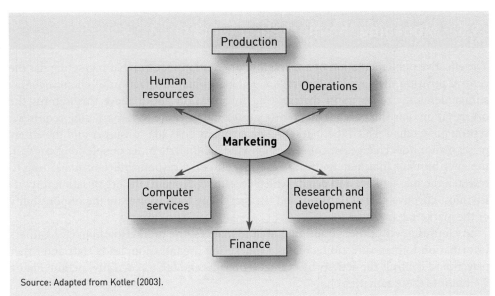

Source: Adapted from Kotler (2003).

Figure 9.2

Marketing as an important function

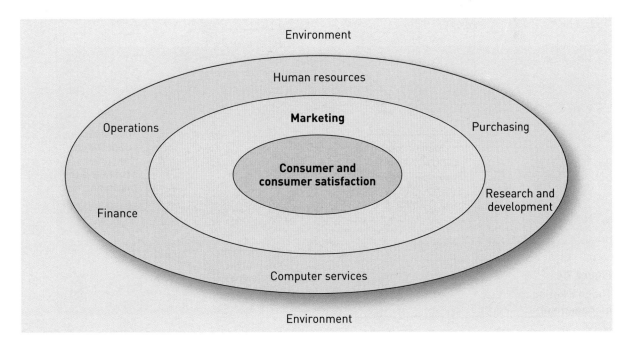

Figure 9.3 Structure of a consumer-centred organisation

Source: Adapted from Kotler (2003).

the organisation and Figure 9.3 is the structure required if an organisation is to become consumer centred. Such restructuring includes developing systems and procedures to collect, analyse and distribute data about the changing demands of consumers. It also requires that achieving organisational objectives through consumer satisfaction becomes the basis of decisions. An important area of organisational study is the management of the boundaries between marketing and the other functional areas, due to differences in culture. Tension can arise, for example, between the R&D team and the marketing team when new products need to be rapidly modified at concept stage to meet changing customer demands. Shortened product life cycles are a feature of today's markets, which exacerbates internal tensions and highlights the need for a flexible structure and a communicative culture.

9.5 Managing the marketing function

The effective implementation of a marketing orientation requires that marketing has the central position displayed in Figure 9.3. The continual satisfaction of changing consumer demands relies upon distributing information about these throughout the organisation. For this reason, marketing professionals claim that marketing requires a central position, in which the marketing department links the consumer and the enterprise. It monitors changes in consumer demands and alerts other people to changes in the environment that may require a response. It is the responsibility of marketing to research the marketplace and decide which consumer demands the organisation can satisfy most effectively. That decision, and the marketing tools to use, are the responsibility of the marketing manager.

In common with other functional area managers, the marketing manager gathers information to plan direction, creates a marketing organisation, leads staff and other players and controls the activity by evaluating results and taking corrective action. Figure 9.4 outlines these activities.

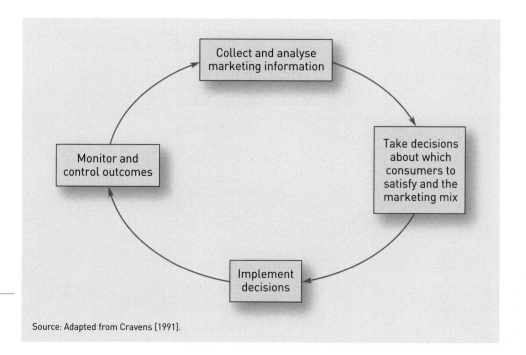

Figure 9.4

The marketing management process

Source: Adapted from Cravens (1991).

The figure shows that the marketing function is responsible for (a) identifying those consumers whose demands the organisation can satisfy most effectively, and (b) selecting the marketing mix that will satisfy consumer demands and succeed in achieving organisational objectives.

Case questions 9.2

- What customer demands were Manchester United seeking to satisfy at the time of the case study?
- What other demands does the business have to satisfy?
- What marketing tools are mentioned in the case?
- What management structure do you think would suit (a) the Glazers and (b) the football club?

In order to take these decisions, managers need information about consumer demands, competitor strategies and changes in the **marketing environment** (Armstrong and Kotler, 2006) that are likely to impact upon consumer demands. The marketing environment contains micro and macro components. The micro-environment is that part of an organisation's marketing environment to which it is close and within which it directly operates. Each organisation will have a micro-environment unique and specific to it; as shown in Figure 9.5, it comprises the stakeholders with which the organisation regularly interacts, including employees, suppliers, distributors, consumers, competitors and publics such as pressure groups and the general public. All organisations, including small and medium-sized enterprises, have some control over changes in their micro-environment and the likely impact these will have upon their marketing activities.

The macro component of an organisation's marketing environment is more remote and will be similar for all those in the same industry. Organisations have little direct influence over their macro-environment, which consists of the PESTEL factors outlined in Chapter 3 – repeated in Figure 9.6.

The **marketing environment** consists of the actors and forces outside marketing that affect the marketing manager's ability to develop and maintain successful relationships with its target consumers.

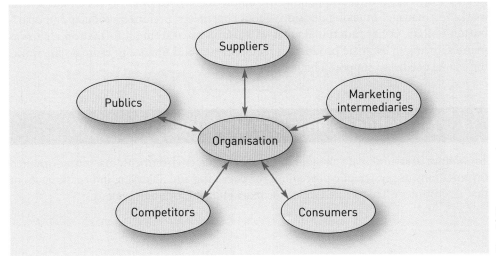

Figure 9.5

The micro-environment

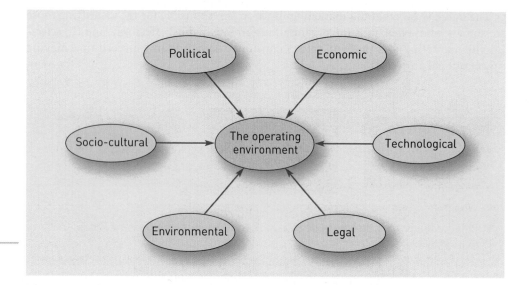

Figure 9.6

The macro-
environment

Such frameworks are useful in identifying whether changes in the environment will
have a positive or negative impact on the marketing activities of an organisation. This is
because they can be useful in identifying both the *opportunities present in the environment*, such as those presented to multimedia organisations by developments in
e-commerce, as well as *threats*, such as the impact of a natural disaster on a country's
tourism industry.

Providing environmental information regularly makes marketing an *information-
intensive activity*. Information about the marketing environment is used to assist the
marketing manager in taking decisions about consumers' preferred products and distribution outlets. Other functional areas will also use marketing information – such as
manufacturing to estimate production requirements, and finance to estimate the working capital needed to support a higher demand.

A **marketing
information system** is
the systematic process
for the collection,
analysis and distribution
of marketing information.

9.6   Marketing as an information-intensive activity

To monitor and anticipate changes in the marketing environment, marketing-oriented
organisations use systematic procedures for collecting and analysing information about
that environment. This is often called the **marketing information system**.

Marketing information systems

To keep in touch, marketing managers need a marketing information system to provide accurate and up-to-date information. They need to have systematic processes to collect, analyse and distribute information about the marketing environment throughout the organisation. Cannon (1996) defines such a system as:

> The organised arrangement of people, machines and procedures set up to ensure that all relevant and usable information required by marketing management reaches them at a time and in a form to help them with effective decision making.

Figure 9.7 details the typical component parts of such a system.

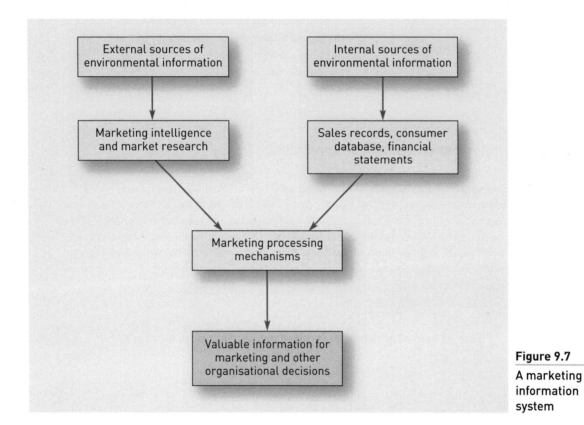

Figure 9.7

A marketing information system

A marketing information system contains internal and external sources of data and mechanisms to analyse and interpret the data. As Chapter 12 explains, data is not the same as information. Data in itself has no meaning. A company may discover that in December 2004, 59 per cent of a sample of people were aware of their product. In itself that has no value – but it does become useful information if it can be compared with similar data from earlier or later periods or with competing products. Management may then see a trend, and be able to decide if it needs to act. Table 9.2 summarises the main sources of marketing information.

Table 9.2

Sources of marketing information

Source	Description and examples
Internal records	Size and regularity of orders, cost of each level of production, customer complaints, quality statistics
Marketing intelligence	Data on micro- and macro-environments. Usually secondary data from newspapers, trade associations and industry reports. Informal sources from staff or customers are also valuable guides to, for example, competitor plans
Market research	Involves five stages: 1 specifying information required (how many people with X income, living in place Y, are aware of product Z?) 2 developing hypotheses (is awareness higher or lower in area B where the product has been advertised than in C?) 3 collecting quantitative or qualitative data to refute or confirm 4 analysing the data and 5 presenting the results

Information on food shopping habits

All major supermarkets have for a long time monitored activity at point of sale so that they can order supplies close to when they will be needed. Loyalty cards keep a record of the frequency, value and type of food shopping bought by individuals, and small incentives reward customers for their store loyalty. Marketing departments use (a) the application form information (address, income bracket, family size, etc.) and (b) the regular information about buying patterns. This helps them to manage their inventory and their marketing communications, such as on sales promotions. There is more information on Tesco in the Part 6 case.

Figure 9.8 shows the processes involved in a market research project.

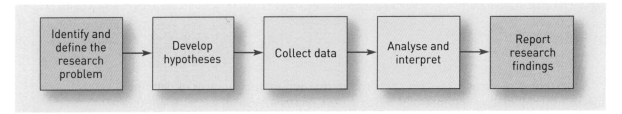

Figure 9.8 The market research process

Case question 9.3

- Suppose that Manchester United is approached by a snack food company wishing to manufacture 'Man U' breakfast bars for children and young people to have as snacks or in school lunch boxes. What type of market research would you recommend using?

9.7 Understanding the consumer – buyer behaviour

The marketing information system provides information on the marketing environment. The results of market research projects indicate solutions to precise marketing questions. Organisations with a marketing orientation also want to understand how customers decide to buy something.

Activity 9.5 Why did you buy that?

Pick a product that you buy regularly – such as a magazine, soft drink or chocolate bar. Think of the last time you bought that product and try to identify the factors which influenced your choice, such as the product features, your mood or other psychological state, your physical state (e.g. hunger), the company you were in (if any), etc.

Buyer behaviour research (Howard and Sheth, 1969; Engel *et al.*, 1978) has identified that consumers work through the series of decisions shown in Figure 9.9.

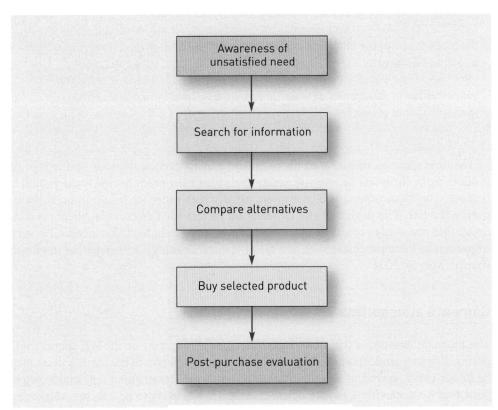

Figure 9.9

A model of consumer buying behaviour

Awareness of unsatisfied need

Consumers become aware of a need that they want to satisfy in two ways. The first is self-discovery. Stomach rumbles or a dry throat are physical signals that you are hungry and thirsty and need to satisfy these feelings. Consumers also become aware of an unsatisfied need by receiving some marketing communication from an organisation. For example, until 3M made you aware of 'Post-It pads' did you identify the need to have a small piece of paper on which you could write messages and stick to a surface? This is an example of latent need referred to earlier.

Theories of human motivation described in Chapter 15 give marketing managers guidance on the needs of potential customers. They use this to ensure that the product or service is helping consumers satisfy a need – for status, recognition, a sense of achievement and so on.

Search for information

Aware of a need, consumers search for information that will help them decide which product to buy. Many sources provide this information – personal experience is one powerful source; that of family and friends is another. A third source of information is from organisations providing products that may satisfy the need – by advertisements and other promotional activities. The information source at this stage in the buying process has great influence on the purchase decision. The poor service to a friend at a restaurant will usually dissuade a potential customer.

Activity 9.6   Reflecting on consumer information

Select from one of the following expensive products: a DVD player, a mountain bike, a round-the-world air ticket. For your selected product describe the type of information you would want before deciding which brand to buy, and why. Which of your information categories do you think would be useful for the marketing manager of that product?

The time spent on this stage of the consumer buying process depends on the type of product that consumers believe will satisfy their identified need. Buying some products is more risky than others, and customers usually seek more information on them to reduce the risk. The degree of risk depends on factors such as expense, effect on self-image and knowledge of the product. Self-image (or 'psychological closeness') is very important in some purchases such as a car or fashion clothing – or in whether to give to charity (Kottasz, 2004).

Compare alternatives

The more information a consumer has collected, the longer he or she will spend comparing different products against set criteria. For a new television, the main criteria may be brand name, surround sound, Internet access, wide screen and a reasonable price. Note that for a television, psychological closeness is less likely to be a factor. Marketing managers will take that into account in designing product ranges and variants.

Buy selected product

Having compared the alternatives and decided which will best satisfy their need, the customer makes the purchase. Even at this stage of the process other factors may intrude –

out of stock, a price cut on an alternative, or the advice of the salesperson may influence decisions. Note that the way a purchase is financed is a product feature, e.g. no-interest loans to purchase the product.

Manchester United – the case continues – what makes people buy? www.manutd.com

CASE STUDY

A football game is not a tangible product. A regular and significant intangible purchase by a Manchester United football fan is the £23–£38 ticket to see a home game at Old Trafford or £10 on a pay-per-view TV basis. There is no guarantee of satisfaction and no exchange or refund. No promotional advertising is needed and the ticket demand is relatively 'inelastic', i.e. prices can increase without sales volumes necessarily falling.

An important question for a marketing manager is 'How does a fan reach the decision to buy this experience and how is value measured?' The buyer behaviour framework described above can help: domestic UK fans are typically lifelong, acquiring perceptions of and loyalty to the club at school or in the home. Influencers would include peers and older pupils. Although football was formerly male dominated, young females are an increasing part of the market. Most fans travel in groups of two or more, so this is a segment attribute that can be managed in raising awareness and favourability. Publicity photos can depict fans celebrating or commiserating together and the whole emphasis of attending a football match can be positioned away from 'did we win?' to 'did we have a good time?' This approach is one of MU's declared marketing strategies.

Post-purchase evaluation

The final stage of the buying process is when the customer compares pre-purchase expectations with post-purchase reality. If expectation matches reality then the consumer is more likely to buy in the future. At this stage, consumer communications can affect future decisions. The quality of after-sales service might convince the car purchaser whether he or she made the right decision or not.

When thinking about the post-experience evaluation, marketing managers should be aware of the potential difference between how consumers think (rationally) about their product and how they feel (emotionally) about it. It is possible, for example, for football fans to think rationally that the home game they just saw was very poor but still to retain great affection and warmth for the experience and the team. This apparent dichotomy can be turned to advantage when planning promotional campaigns.

Internal and external influences shape the decisions consumers make at each stage. Table 9.3 describes these, and Figure 9.10 illustrates them.

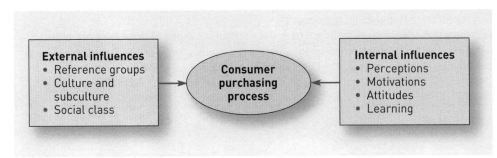

Figure 9.10

Influences on buyer behaviour

Table 9.3 Internal and external influences on buying behaviour

Influence	Description	Example
Internal influences **Perception**	How people collect and interpret information	Affects reaction to advertisements – images, colours, words. See Chapter 16 on communication
Motivation	Internal forces that shape purchasing decisions to satisfy need	Marketers design products to meet needs. Insurers remind people of dangers against which a policy will protect them. See Chapter 15
Attitudes	Opinions and points of view that people have of other people and institutions	Marketers design products to conform. Attitudes against testing cosmetics on animals led firms to stop this practice. Similarly for environmental issues
Learning	How people learn affects what they know about a product, and hence their purchasing decisions	Marketers help people to 'learn' to associate a product with unique colours or images – such as Coke with red and white, and Nike with its 'Swoosh' symbol
External influences **Reference groups**	Other people with whom the consumer identifies	Marketers establish the reference groups of their consumers, and allude to them in promotions – e.g. sponsoring athletes in return for product endorsement
Culture	The culture to which a consumer belongs affects their values and behaviour	Subcultures associated with music or cars influence buying behaviour – which marketers use in positioning products for those markets
Social class	People identify with a class based on income, education, where they live, and so on.	Purchase decisions confirm and reaffirm the class to which people belong, or to which they aspire. Marketers use this information in promotional material

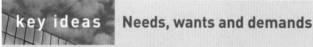 **key ideas**   **Needs, wants and demands**

A marketing orientation implies that to satisfy the consumer it is necessary to identify the products for which there is *demand* and to understand the *needs* and *wants* which the product will satisfy for the consumer. Marketers distinguish between needs, wants and demands as follows:

- **Needs** These are the core feelings that consumers 'need' to satisfy; for example, thirst is a physical requirement that needs to be satisfied.
- **Wants** These are the preferences that individual consumers have about the ways in which they 'want' to satisfy the needs that they share in common with others. Consumers will want different liquids to satisfy the thirst that makes them need a drink.
- **Demands** The money that individual consumers have determines the types of drink they are able to buy. An individual who needs a drink may want to buy a Red Bull energy drink. The money in their wallet determines that their demand (their actual purchasing power) is for an own-label soft drink.

To satisfy consumers, marketers need to understand their needs, wants and demands. If they define demand too narrowly they may be unable to satisfy consumers.

9.8 Taking marketing decisions

The marketing manager now has information about the marketing environment, possible opportunities and threats, and the buying behaviour of consumers. The next stage is to decide which demands to satisfy and how to do this. The first decision is about market segmentation and targeting. The second is about choosing the correct mix of marketing tools to position products and make them attractive to consumers (Figure 9.11).

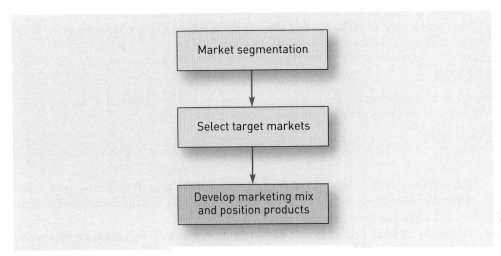

Figure 9.11

Taking marketing decisions

Segmenting markets

Organisations are increasingly using **market segmentation** strategies to satisfy the different needs that exist within the marketplace. Airlines offer consumers the choice of flying first class, business class or economy class. Notice that although the basic product attribute (transport from A to B) is the same for all passengers in the plane, the total offering is not: premium passengers pay for a premium service. Universities offer degrees by full-time, part-time and distance learning study. Athletic shoe companies offer shoes specifically for running, aerobics, tennis and squash as well as 'cross' trainers for the needs of all these sports.

Market segmentation is the process of dividing markets comprising the heterogeneous needs of many consumers into segments comprising the homogeneous needs of smaller groups.

Segmentation is based on the fact that consumers have different needs: it is more efficient for management to treat them as homogeneous groups, for the purposes of communication, advertising and so forth. The personal computer market consists of all the individuals who need a personal computer. Within that market people with similar needs can be grouped into distinct segments: travellers needing a laptop form one distinct segment; parents wanting a low-cost personal computer with Internet connection to help their children learn form another. Segmentation is very efficient when allocating the promotional budget. For example, note the number of beer sponsors involved with sports such as rugby, where both industries are targeting the same demographic profile, namely young men aged 18–35.

Segmenting the personal computer market (and any other market) relies on identifying the variables that distinguish consumers with similar needs, as follows:

● **Demography** The easiest way to segment a consumer market is by using demographic variables such as age, gender and education level. Magazine companies use gender and age variables to ensure that within their portfolio they have magazine titles which

key ideas   Segmenting markets in the public sector

The idea of segmentation is highly relevant to managers providing public services, such as further and higher education, school meals and leisure centres. They need to know who uses the services, who might use them and how provision relates to demand. To understand these questions, public sector providers need to understand the needs and behaviours of current and potential users. A particular feature of the public sector is that services meet two types of demand (Chapman and Cowdell, 1998, pp. 122–126):

● non-discretionary demand – services that satisfy community demands which everyone needs, such as refuse collection, basic health care and street lighting;
● discretionary demand – services that people can choose to use, such as leisure and cultural services or public transport.

Market segmentation techniques apply equally to both – providers need to understand the needs of users and purchasers if they are to create value with the resources they use.

Source: Chapman and Cowdell (1998).

will suit the needs of females as well as males and those of different ages. Local authorities use information on age and family structures to help decide the distribution of facilities in their area.

● **Geography** This segmentation variable is commonly used by organisations competing in a global market. By segmenting markets by country, organisations such as HSBC (hsbc.com) have been able to 'think global but act local'. While maintaining uniform global standards of service and hygiene, the company competes differently in each country by varying the menu available to suit local tastes.
● **Socioeconomic** Segmentation on the basis of socioeconomic variables – such as income, social class and lifestyle. Lifestyle segmentation includes identifying groups of consumers who share similar values about the way in which they wish to live.

When segmenting consumer markets, marketers typically use a mix of these variables to provide an accurate profile of distinct groups. The magazine *Marie Claire*, for example, uses age, gender, education, lifestyle and social class to attract a readership of educated, independently minded women between the ages of 25 and 35, in income brackets ABC1.

Activity 9.7   Identifying market segments

● What market segments have the following identified: Swatch, Amazon.com, Borders Books?
● What marketing management benefits do you think their segmentation strategies offer?

A **target market** is the segment of the market selected by the organisation as the focus of its activities.

Having segmented a market using the variables described above, marketers have to decide which of those segments to select as **target markets** – those to be the focus for their activities. Marketing managers usually select target markets that meet the following three criteria:

● contain demands that the resources of the organisation can satisfy
● are large enough to provide a financial return
● have growth potential.

Ultimately, segments selected as target markets are those that offer the greatest potential for achieving management goals.

Manchester United FC – the case continues
www.manutd.com

In 2005 Manchester United launched a Chinese website and appointed china.com as their official partner. Two hundred million Chinese regularly watch the team on TV. MU saw this as an opportunity for mail order sales to China and the rest of south-east Asia. As well as watching the games on TV, Asian fans frequently place bets on the outcome.

Source: Company website.

Case question 9.4

- What segmentation criteria would you have recommended for MU in this burgeoning sector?

9.9 Using the marketing mix

The final decision facing the marketing manager is the selection of the combination of price, product, promotion and place. This is known as the **marketing mix.**

> The **marketing mix** is the mix of decisions about product features, prices, communications and distribution of products used by the marketing manager to position products competitively within the minds of consumers.

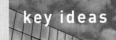

The marketing mix

key ideas

The marketing mix comprises four levers that marketing managers can control. The mix *positions* products in the market in a way that makes them attractive to the target consumers. The **position** that a product has within a market reflects consumer opinions of that product and the comparisons that they make between it and competing products. The aim is to position products *within the minds of consumers* as more attractive, and better able to satisfy their demands, than competing products.

To position products effectively, the marketing manager develops a coordinated marketing mix. Kotler and Keller (2006) define an organisation's marketing mix as 'a set of tools that work together to affect the marketplace'. The marketing mix has traditionally been presented as consisting of the so-called 4 Ps: product, price, promotion and place.

However, Gronroos (2000) points out that

during the last two decades marketing researchers have increasingly found that the list of 4 Ps is too restrictive and more ... variables have been suggested ... such as people, processes and physical evidence. (pp. 240–241)

He suggests that adding further categories (see, for example, Judd 2003) is a symptom of the weakness of the marketing mix approach, although it may still be useful in certain types of market such as consumer packaged goods. The main problem with the approach, in Gronroos's view, is that it restricts marketing to a limited number of decision areas, and leads to the neglect of many aspects of what he calls the 'customer relationship life cycle' (pp. 242–243).

Marketing mix – product

Decisions about which products to develop will establish the range of goods and services an organisation offers. Some are physical products; others intangible personal services. Most are a mixture of the two. Note that the product can include non-core items such as packaging, after-sales service, maintenance and insurance.

 **Swatch** www.swatch.com

The development and introduction of Swatch is a classic example of marketing techniques being used by a traditional industry to launch a new product. Faced with competition from low-cost producers SMH, an established Swiss watchmaker (brands included Longines and Omega) urgently needed a new product line. Its engineers developed a radically new product that was much cheaper to make than traditional models. The company worked closely with advertising agencies in the United States on product positioning and advertising strategy. In addition to the name 'Swatch', a snappy contraction of 'Swiss' and 'watch', this research generated the idea of downplaying the product's practical benefits and positioning it as a 'fashion accessory that happens to tell the time'. Swatch would be a second or third watch used to adapt to different situations without replacing the traditional 'status symbol' watch.

Swatch continues to reposition itself through new products and collections, and sponsorship of the Olympic Games as official timekeeper. Revenue was up 12 per cent in 2006 with sales exceeding $5 billion for the first time.

Source: Based on 'Swatch', Case No. 589-005-1, INSEAD-Cedep, Fontainebleau; and company website.

The extent to which offerings are tangible or intangible affects how marketing staff deal with them. Services present marketing with particular challenges because of their characteristics of perishability, intangibility, heterogeneity and inseparability.

Perishability

Perishable services cannot be held in stock for even the shortest amount of time. If a plane flies with empty seats these cannot be stored for another flight – empty seats are permanently lost sales.

Intangibility

Intangible services present the marketing manager with the greatest challenge. They cannot usually be viewed, touched or tried before their purchase. One way for consumers to 'try before buying' is to be given leaflets with attractive information on the service benefits: the financial services industry relies on information packs about features and benefits of mortgages, insurance policies and bank accounts. Consumers also have little information on which to assess the product benefits relative to their demands. A common source of service information is reference groups: organisations such as health clubs encourage existing members to invite friends and family to their fitness clubs for trial membership.

Heterogeneity and inseparability

Services are labour intensive. They rely on the skills, competences and experiences of the people who provide them, and this creates particular challenges for the marketing manager. *Heterogeneity* refers to variations in what in principle should be an identical service each time it is provided, e.g. a pedicure. *Inseparability* refers to a product or service that is consumed as it is produced, e.g. a haircut. Service providers and consumers will meet for some amount of time. For a doctor's appointment, it is necessary to meet with the doctor to discuss your health.

Organisations operating through branch systems such as banks or fast-food restaurants have to overcome the hazards of inseparability and heterogeneity to ensure consistent delivery standards. Both service providers and consumers have personalities, opinions and values that make them unique. This can create differences in the levels of service and standards that consumers experience when buying services. Organisations such as Pizza Hut and UCI cinemas try to minimise differences by providing staff with company uniforms, decorating premises in a similar way and setting firm guidelines for the way staff deliver the service.

Consumer products (both goods and services) can be classified as convenience, shopping, speciality or unsought products. Each poses a different marketing challenge, which Table 9.4 summarises.

Table 9.4

Market challenges by type of product using the marketing mix

Type of product	Examples	Marketing challenge
Convenience	Regular purchases, low price – bread, milk, magazines	Widely available, and easy to switch brands. Managers counter this by heavy advertising or distinct packaging of the brand
Shopping	Relatively expensive, infrequent purchase – washing machines, televisions, clothes	Brand name, product features, design and price are important and managers will spend time searching for best mix. Managers spend heavily on advertising and on training sales staff
Speciality	Less frequent, often luxury purchases – cars, diamond rings, houses	Consumers need much information. Sales staff vital to a sale – management invest heavily in them, and in protecting image of product by restricting outlets. Also focused advertising and distinctive packaging
Unsought	Consumers need to buy, but don't get much pleasure from – insurance, a car exhaust	Managers need to make customers aware that they supply this need, and distinct product features

The **product life cycle** suggests that products pass through the stages of introduction, growth, maturity and decline.

Product life cycle

key ideas

In managing the organisation's product decisions, marketing managers use a concept called the **product life cycle** (Figure 9.12). The central assumption upon which the product life cycle rests is that all products have a limited life, which could vary from years to decades. Depending on the stage reached by a product in its life cycle, a known set of competitive and consumer conditions exists that helps the marketing manager to specify the marketing activities required at that stage. Mapping the sales and profit generated, the product life cycle suggests that products pass through the stages of introduction, growth, maturity and decline.

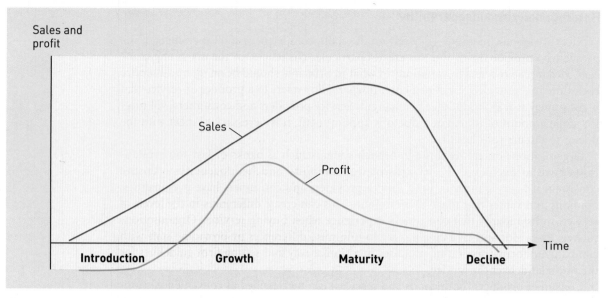

Figure 9.12 The product life cycle

Introduction

This is the stage at which products enter the marketplace. Profits are negative because sales from the early adopters have not reached the level needed to pay back investment in researching and developing the product. Few consumers are aware of – and therefore interested in – buying the product and few organisations are involved in producing and distributing it. The aim of the marketing manager at this stage is to invest in marketing communication and make as many potential consumers as possible aware of the product's entry into the marketplace.

Growth

At this stage consumers have become aware of and started buying the product. Sales rise quickly and profits peak. As people buy the product, more consumers become aware of it and the high profit levels attract new competitors into the industry. The aim of the marketing manager at this stage is to fight off existing competitors and new entrants. This can be done by (a) encouraging consumer loyalty, (b) distributing the product as widely as is demanded by consumers, and (c) cutting selling prices: production costs fall as total units increase, due to the learning curve effect. Competitors arriving later have not had time to cut costs so may baulk at entering the market.

Maturity

With profits peaking during the growth stage, profit and sales start to plateau and then decline towards the end of this stage. By this stage in a product's life cycle many consumers are aware of and have bought the product and there are many organisations competing for a decreasing amount of consumer demand for the product. The aim of the marketing manager is to fight competition by reducing the price of the product or by differentiating it by, for example, altering its packaging and design. Swatch continues to add value to its product in the later stages of its product life cycle with items such as the Infinity Concept watch launched in early 2007.

At this stage product differentiation can successfully reposition products to an earlier stage in their life cycle. It is also important that the marketing manager begins to consider ideas for replacement products and to select ideas for research and development.

Decline

In the decline phase, there is little consumer demand and all competing organisations are considering removing the product from the marketplace. It is important that, by this stage, the marketing manager has a new product ready to enter the marketplace and replace the product that is being removed. Certain rarity products can still generate profits in the decline phase, e.g. spare parts for old cars.

An awareness of the stage which a product is at in its life cycle can assist the marketing manager in deciding upon the course of marketing action to take. For example, aware that a product is at the maturity stage, the marketing manager might decide to reposition the product by changing the packaging or image created by the branding of the product. Consider the repositioning of Lucozade. Traditionally marketed as a health drink for older people, product modifications together with new packaging and celebrity endorsement have successfully repositioned Lucozade as a youth sports drink (www.lucozade.com).

Lynx/Axe

key ideas

Lynx (known as Axe throughout the rest of the world) has been a phenomenon since its launch it 1983. Much of its success is down to its iconic and award-winning advertising which has helped the brand gain 75 per cent market penetration of the 15–24-year-old male segment in the United Kingdom. However, Lynx faces a challenge: how to stay fresh and stylish, and avoid the fate of previous brand leaders in this category such as Brut – which is no longer produced.

The firm must continue to recruit a new customer base of 15–19-year-olds, but also constantly strive to improve its product offering. Lynx's method is clever yet straightforward: the advertising themes have followed UK male culture as it has evolved into the twenty-first century; and the weakest selling of six varieties of deodorant is removed and replaced every year. Thus the brand remains up to date and relevant to consumers, and allows the firm to charge a significant price premium. While Lynx has probably reached the maturity stage of the product life cycle, its focus on brand equity is preventing it moving into the decline stage.

Sources: www.unilever.co.uk/ourbrands/personalcare/lynx.asp; published sources.

Activity 9.8   Using the product life cycle

State the stage that you believe each of the following products to be in and comment on how long, in years, you believe their life cycle to be: drawing pins, iPods, umbrellas, hand soap.

Activity 9.8 shows that some products do not have a limited lifespan and other products can be repositioned to an earlier stage. Despite these criticisms, the product life cycle offers the marketing manager a useful aid to many product decisions.

Marketing mix – price

Price is the value placed upon the goods, services and ideas exchanged between organisations and consumers. For most products, price is measured with money, though consumers do not identify all the purchases they make as having a 'price': for example, accessing BBC television programmes is the cost of a television licence, and the price of street lighting and cleaning is the council tax that individual households are responsible for paying. Not-for-profit marketing can involve a time price (volunteering to work in a charity shop) or a psychological price for behaviour change (government campaigns to discourage drink driving).

In selecting the price that will position a product competitively within consumers' minds, the marketing manager must be aware of the image that consumers have of the product. Consumers have expected price ranges for certain types of product. In particular, for safety products, products for children, those associated with health or connected to their self-image, consumers have a *minimum* price they expect to pay. If the price is below this, consumers will not purchase the product because they perceive such products as being of inferior quality or lower value.

The price charged must also cover the costs of producing, distributing and promoting products. It must provide the organisation with an acceptable profit yet leave an acceptable margin for distributors and retailers.

Marketing mix – promotion

Properly referred to as marketing communications, this element of the marketing mix involves taking decisions about the information that will encourage consumers to buy a product or change attitudes and behaviours in some way. Organisations can communicate with their target markets in many ways. Packaging can provide information, a company logo may transmit a particular message, and sponsoring a football team or a concert indicates an organisation's values and attitudes. The most frequent modes of encouraging consumers to buy products include advertising, sales promotions, personal selling and publicity.

- *Advertising* is the form of communication commonly selected when an organisation wishes to transmit a message to a large audience. It is impersonal, as it does not involve direct communication between an organisation and a potential consumer. Advertising is effective in creating awareness of the offering but is less effective in persuading consumers to buy. It is, however, a cost-effective method of communicating with potential consumers in a mass market.
- Organisations typically use *sales promotions* to encourage consumers who are considering a product to take the next step and buy it. Both McDonald's and Burger King

---

management in practice A Department of Trade and Industry (DTI) advertising campaign

The UK government launched an online campaign to promote its new Consumer Direct telephone, online and e-mail information service for consumers. Consumer Direct provides advice on consumer protection issues, including what rights consumers have or how to get redress for faulty goods. Run in partnership with local authorities and existing services, including Trading Standards, there are 11 contact centres across the United Kingdom.

Source: *Marketing Week*, 9 September 2004; www.consumerdirect.gov.uk.

frequently offer special promotions to encourage consumers to buy their brand. Companies also use promotions to encourage repeat buys and to encourage consumers to try out new products of which advertising has made them aware.

- Marketing departments use *personal selling* when consumers require first-hand information before making a purchase. It is particularly useful for infrequently purchased products such as DVD players and cars – and in industrial marketing. Personal selling is a direct transfer of product information to potential consumers: it is able to respond to questions that consumers might have and to explain complicated or technical product features. Personal selling requires that managers train salespeople properly, especially on specific product features. It is useful for expensive or technically sophisticated products.

- *Publicity* or PR (public relations) is effective in supporting a positive image of the organisation. It involves building good working relationships with the media and using them to promote a positive image of the organisation. The aim is to ensure that positive events of media interest (such as launching a new product) are fully reported, and that negative ones do as little damage as possible.

Marketing mix – place

'Place' refers to decisions about the ways in which products can be most effectively distributed to the final consumer, either directly or through intermediaries. Decisions about marketing channels concentrate on whether the distribution of products should be owned by the producing organisation or whether products should be distributed by external parties. These decisions depend on the products involved and the costs of distribution. If product quality and image are vital to market positioning then the organisation must maintain control over distribution.

Protecting the brand

management in practice

Paul Mitchell hair products maintain the image of quality that consumers attach to the name by detailing on the product packaging that authenticity cannot be guaranteed unless purchased from a Paul Mitchell approved outlet. Similarly, brands such as Calvin Klein, Nike and Clarins have expressed concerns about the distribution of their products through such stores as Tesco and Superdrug, which they believe detract from rather than add to the value of their branded products.

Distributor cost is a consideration in channel management. Having identified the price at which consumers demand to buy particular products, the costs involved in distributing products in-house relative to external providers must be considered.

A third channel decision is whether to make purchase of products available electronically through the Internet. This decision has been embraced by organisations such as easyJet, amazon.com and lastminute.com. Such organisations have decided to use electronic channels of distribution as a differentiation tool, on the grounds that consumers prefer online convenience and see this as a product feature. For many organisations electronic product distribution is a complementary channel used, for example, to widen product access to geographically remote markets. The major supermarkets and retailers all have busy websites, often offering discounts over store prices. This market channel also allows easy gathering of data for relationship marketing.

In developing a marketing mix that will place products competitively within the minds of consumers the marketing manager must be aware that changes in one element will create changes in other areas. For example, if the price of a product is reduced, consumer perceptions of the product might change. Creating an effective marketing mix with which to position products relies upon integration and coordination of each element.

management in practice   Maintaining consistency

In positioning their products as **value for money**, organisations ensure that each part of the marketing mix supports and reinforces this image. This means that products must not be highly differentiated, prices should be low, and promotion messages should stress the low price and value for money. The stores in which products are distributed should be simple in design. This avoids sending a message that the costs of creating a smart place in which to buy products will be reflected in the prices. A good example is the Asda supermarket (www.asda.co.uk).

9.10 Current themes and issues

Performance

The chapter has presented the benefits to organisations of adopting a marketing orientation, in the sense of incorporating marketing deeply into all of its activities. A marketing orientation requires that the whole organisation commits to achieving organisational goals by *continually* satisfying consumer demands. Aware of this objective and of their contribution towards it, different areas within the organisation are able to cooperate and coordinate their activities.

The challenge in moving to this position lies in the nature of the organisational changes that will be required. Chapter 13 examines this, including the view that organisations must change radically and relentlessly. Managers are advised that to survive they must continually review their missions and objectives, their processes, their structures and cultures, their relations with suppliers, and with their employees. 'Change or perish' is the rationale of those who propose unrelenting change. While the arguments may sometimes be valid, the counter-view is that disruptive change is costly, and does not necessarily improve performance, as excessive change may lead to initiative overload, change-related chaos and employee cynicism.

Responsibility

The adoption of a marketing orientation can clearly bring significant benefits to the commercial or other success of organisations. Commentators have also been critical of marketing. They argue that marketing manipulates consumer choices and encourages materialism and over-consumption. Food manufacturers have faced criticism for promoting the sale of foods with a high fat and sugar content, thus contributing to obesity: in response to such criticism, Mars announced in 2007 that it would stop advertising aimed at children under the age of 12. Chapter 5 (Corporate responsibility) also includes ideas relevant to marketing, such as the influence of ethical consumers, the success of the Fairtrade brand, and of individual products such as Café Direct, which promise producers a fair return.

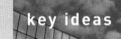

Naomi Klein's *No Logo: Taking Aim at the Brand Bullies*

key ideas

Klein (2000) presents a powerful argument against the growing dominance of some global brands in consumer markets, and how many use advertising to exploit impressionable teenagers. She argues that companies such as Microsoft, Gap and Starbucks now present themselves as purveyors of lifestyles, images and dreams rather than products. In doing so they harm both the cultures in which they operate and the workers they employ. She also reports a growing backlash by ethical shareholders, human rights activists and McUnion organisers demanding a citizen-centred alternative to the rule of the brands.

However, not everyone agrees that Klein is correct. She is accused of overstating her case, and brand advocates point out the many positives brands have for consumers, manufacturers and retailers. What is not in dispute, however, is that companies are now facing up to social and ethical responsibility as never before.

The debate on marketing's role within society will continue to run. Those concerned with environmental and public health issues will criticise organisations they perceive to be damaging the environment or knowingly causing harm to people's health. Others argue that adopting a marketing orientation in itself is not an ethical issue, as long as it is used to inform consumers and widen their choice. Responsible marketers do not advocate that consumers should be tricked into making purchases. Nevertheless it is a fact that some people use marketing concepts to sell pornography, traffic drugs and invade privacy.

Internationalisation

If you travel to another country, you immediately see many familiar consumer products or services – things that epitomise the idea that global brands are steadily displacing local products. In several industries identical products (Canon cameras, Sony Walkman, Famous Grouse whisky) are sold across the globe without modification. This trend was observed by Theodore Levitt (1983), a professor at Harvard Business School, who argued that advances in communications technology were increasingly inspiring consumers around the world to want the same things. Companies should become 'global' by standardising the production, distribution and marketing of their products across all countries. Sameness meant efficiency and would be more profitable than difference. From economies of scale would flow competitive advantage.

Levitt's argument soon influenced practice and many consumer companies, such as Coca-Cola and Marlborough, began promoting themselves as identical global brands, with standard practices and a centralised management structure.

By the end of the 1990s, managers began to change their approach. Customers were finding that new local brands offered better value and, as producers adopted western methods, good quality. Global brands, offering standard products regardless of local tastes, lost market share. So rather than 'going global' they began to 'go local': Starbucks varies its menu to suit local tastes; Nestlé has about 200 varieties of its instant coffee; and MTV varies programming to suit different countries and regions.

Activity 9.9   Revising your definition

- Having completed this chapter, how would you define marketing?
- Compare this definition with the one that you were asked to make in Activity 9.1 and comment on any changes.

Summary

1 Compare and contrast marketing with alternative organisational orientations

- Adopting a marketing orientation makes the customer the centre of attention and is different from product, production and sales philosophies. It becomes a guiding orientation for the whole organisation. If management wishes a marketing orientation to pervade the organisation, all activities are focused on meeting customer needs. Activity is monitored and controlled to ensure that work is done in a way which meets the needs of customers.

- Implementing the approach involves precise targeting of defined market segments. It also implies restructuring to ensure that the whole organisation focuses on the customer, with organisation-wide information systems to handle marketing data.

2 Describe the benefits to any organisation of adopting a marketing orientation

- A marketing orientation implies that in major business decisions management hears a consumer perspective, through mechanisms for involving the relevant players. A firm with a consumer-centred marketing orientation focuses all activities on meeting consumer needs and is organised with that in mind.

3 Explain why marketing is an information-intensive activity

- To meet consumer needs effectively, marketing is an information-intensive activity. A major element in marketing is the management of communications, i.e. ensuring that information about external developments and customer needs is gathered, processed and transferred around the organisation. Consumers also have to be informed of the offerings and their benefits.

4 Identify the responsibilities of the marketing manager

- The primacy of marketing can create organisational tension with other professional groups within the firm, whose status and position may be threatened by the primacy. Other departments are, however, expected to support and be committed to the central position of marketing.

5 Explain market segmentation and the practice of selecting a target market

- Greater consumer understanding enables a company to segment the market in various ways, and to target certain segments in the hope of meeting their distinctive needs.

6 Describe the components of the marketing mix

- The chapter then outlined the components of the marketing mix – product, price, promotion and place – that a company can use to position its offerings to consumers.

7 Explain what is meant by product positioning

- Marketing places particular emphasis on keeping in touch with external (micro and macro) developments that affect customers' needs and the organisation's objectives.

Review questions

1 What advantages does the marketing orientation have over each of the following organisational philosophies: production, product and sales?

2 Outline the benefits that the marketing orientation can offer each of the following organisations: a global brand, a football team, a university, a charity, a small firm and a high street retailer.

3 What are the key responsibilities of the marketing manager?

4 In what way is an organisation's micro-environment different from its macro-environment? Comment on which of these organisations' marketing environments have the greatest impact upon their marketing activities: LivingWell health clubs (www.livingwell.com), McDonald's (www.mcdonalds.com), your local library.

5 Outline various sources of marketing information and compare and contrast alternative ways of collecting and analysing information about an organisation's market environment.

6 Describe the process of buying decisions involved and identify the factors that might influence the purchase of a new car, a soft drink, a present for a friend's 30th birthday, a new clothes outfit for work.

7 What are the advantages of market segmentation and what are the variables upon which consumer markets are commonly segmented?

8 How are target markets identified and what is meant by product positioning?

9 What position does each of the following have in the marketplace and what mix of marketing tools has each used to achieve this position: Asda supermarkets (www.asda.co.uk), Tango soft drinks (www.tango.co.uk), Save the Children Fund (www.savethechildren.org.uk), Surf washing powder (www.surf.co.uk)?

Concluding critical reflection

Think about the ways in which your company, or one with which you are familiar, manages marketing. Review the material in the chapter, and perhaps visit some of the websites identified. Then make notes on these questions:

● What examples of the marketing issues discussed in this chapter struck you as being relevant to practice in your company?

● Considering the people you normally work with, what **assumptions** about the nature of the business and its customers appear to guide their approach – a production, sales or marketing orientation? How does this affect the way the business operates?

● What factors such as the history or current **context** of the company appear to influence this? Does the current approach appear to be right for the company in its context – or would a different view of the context lead to a different approach? What would the implications for people in the company be of a distinctive marketing orientation?

● Has there been any pressure to adopt a more customer-focused approach, perhaps based on evidence about similar organisations? If you could find evidence about such **alternatives**, how ▶

may it affect company practice? What would be the obstacles to a greater emphasis on marketing?

● The chapter has stressed the benefits of a marketing orientation, and of understanding customer needs in ever greater detail. What **limitations** can you identify in this philosophy, or others within the chapter? Are people only to be valued in their roles as consumers? How valid might ideas on marketing be in other cultures? What, if any, limitations can you now identify in the way an organisation with which you are familiar approaches marketing?

Further reading

Armstrong, G. and Kotler, P. (2006), *Marketing: An introduction* (8th edn), Financial Times/Prentice Hall, Harlow.

Provides a detailed introduction to marketing.

Baker, M. (2002), *The Marketing Book* (5th edn), Butterworth/Heinemann, London.

Contains an excellent selection of classic marketing articles.

Gronroos, C. (2000), *Service Management and Marketing: A customer relationship management approach*, 2nd edn, Wiley, Chichester.

Highly recommended to students wishing to read more about services marketing from one of Europe's leading writers on marketing.

Jobber, D. (2007), *Principles and Practices of Marketing* (5th edn), McGraw-Hill, London.

The most popular European-centred marketing textbook.

Judd, V.C. (2003), 'Achieving customer orientation using people power – the 5th P', *European Journal of Marketing*, vol. 37, no. 10, pp. 1301–1313.

Examines how employees can have a powerful influence on the value the organisation delivers to customers – and complements the '4Ps' outlined in the chapter.

Kottasz, R. (2004), 'How should charitable organisations motivate young professionals to give philanthropically?', *International Journal of Non-Profit and Voluntary Sector Marketing*, vol. 9, no. 1, pp. 9–27.

An example of how research can uncover consumers' motives – in this case finding that wealthy young men were more likely to be motivated to give to charities if they received some social benefits in return – such as invitations to black tie dinners, and being associated with a well-known charity.

Kotler, P. and Keller, K. (2006), *Marketing Management* (12th edn), Financial Times/Prentice Hall, Harlow.

The biggest selling marketing textbook worldwide, aimed at MBA or honours undergraduate level.

Mellahi, K., Jackson, P. and Sparks, L. (2002), 'An exploratory study into failure in successful organizations: the case of Marks and Spencer', *British Journal of Management*, vol. 13, no. 1, pp. 15–29.

Detailed empirical research into the deep-rooted internal problems that led to the difficulties which the company experienced in the late 1990s.

Newman, A.J and Patel, D. (2004), 'The marketing directions of two fashion retailers', *European Journal of Marketing*, vol. 38, no. 7, pp. 770–789.

Fascinating comparison of the recent performance of Topshop and Gap, relating the variation to their success (or not) in developing a marketing orientation throughout the business.

Schor, J.B. (2004), *Born to Buy: The commercialized child and the new consumer culture*, Scribner, New York.

A revealing account of the ploys some marketers use to sell products to children – turning them, she argues, into miniature consumption machines.

Weblinks

These websites have appeared in the chapter:

www.manutd.com
www.oxfam.co.uk
www.greenpeace.com
www.msf.org
www.co-operativebank.co.uk
www.easyjet.com
www.sainsburys.co.uk
www.churchmarketing.com
www.cancerresearchuk.org
www.apple.com
www.macobserver.com
www.ryanair.com
www.diesel.com
www.hsbc.com
www.swatch.com
www.lucozade.com
www.consumerdirect.gov.uk
www.livingwell.com
www.lynxeffect.co.uk
www.asda.co.uk
www.mcdonalds.com
www.tango.co.uk
www.savethechildren.org.uk
www.surf.co.uk

Visit two of the sites in the list (or that of another organisation in which you have an interest).

● What markets are they in? How have they segmented the market?

● What information can you find about their position in their respective markets, and what marketing challenges do they face?

● Gather information from media websites (such as www.ft.com) that relate to the organisations you have chosen. What stories can you find that relate to the marketing decisions they have made, and what the outcomes have been?

Annotated weblinks, multiple choice questions and other useful resources can be found on **www.pearsoned.co.uk/boddy**

The Virgin Group

www.virgin.com

Virgin is known all over the world and is seen by the public as fun, daring and successful. The first record shop was opened in 1971 and the record label launched in 1973. Virgin Atlantic Airways began operating in 1984, quickly followed by Virgin Holidays. In 1995 the company entered a joint venture offering financial services. By 1997 it was an established global corporation with airline, retailing and travel operations. The original record business was launched shortly after the UK government had abolished retail price maintenance, a practice that had limited competition and kept prices high. Richard Branson saw the opportunity and began a mail order business offering popular records at prices about 15 per cent below those charged by shops.

The business prospered until there was a postal strike. Branson's response was to open a retail outlet, which was an immediate success, and the start of Virgin Retail. These retail interests were later consolidated around the Megastore concept in a joint venture with a major retailer. In prestige locations in major cities Megastores began to sell home entertainment products – music, videos and books – on a large scale. The success of the Megastore concept was exported to major cities

Visual Media.

throughout the world, frequently through joint ventures.

In the early 1980s Branson was approached by Randolph Fields, who was seeking additional finance for his cut-price airline. The airline business then was tightly regulated, with routes, landing rights, prices and service levels established and maintained by inter-governmental arrangements. These regulations were mainly used to protect inefficient, often state-owned, national 'flag carriers', keeping fares high. After three

months of intense activity Branson and Fields had gained permission to fly, arranged to lease an aircraft and recruited staff. The first flight was in June 1984. To grow, Branson needed more landing rights, and would need to persuade government ministers to secure them at both ends of each route. Those ministers would also be lobbied by the established airlines, to persuade them not to approve the low fares that Branson was proposing. Alternatively, they could undercut his fares and subsidise the losses from profits on other routes.

Virgin Atlantic grew successfully and by 1990, although still a relatively small player, it competed with the major carriers on the main routes from London, winning awards for innovation and service. The airline was now the focus of Branson's interests and was becoming a serious threat to the established airlines. It now serves 29 destinations around the world. The company is also a leading player in the low-cost airline business through Virgin Express based in Brussels and

Virgin Blue in Australia. The latter was founded in 1999 with an investment of $8 million and in 2003 was valued at $2 billion.

The Virgin brand

Research on the Virgin brand name demonstrated the impact over time of quirky advertising and publicity stunts. The brand was recognised by 96 per cent of UK consumers, and Richard Branson was correctly identified by 95 per cent as the company's founder. The Virgin name was associated by respondents with words such as fun, innovation, success and trust, and identified with a range of businesses, confirming what Branson and others had believed: in principle there were no product or service boundaries limiting a brand name, provided it was associated with a quality offering.

Encouraged by the research, Virgin began entering new sectors outside its core activities of travel and retail. Virgin businesses as diverse as radio broadcasting, book publishing and computer games found a home in the same stable as well as hotels, railways, personal computers, cola drinks, cinemas and financial services. Branson continued to work at the centre, supported by a small business development group, a press office, and advisers on strategy and finance. The early Virgin style of informality and openness remains – ties are rarely worn, denim jeans are common, and everybody is on first-name terms.

The Virgin organisation

Having a centre did not mean a centralised operation. Each operating unit was expected to stand alone, having little interaction with either head office or other units. Unit managers networked informally (usually at parties or similar events), but were not obliged to follow prescriptive corporate policies; these were 'understood' rather than codified. For example, there was no common human resource policy. Managers knew that employees must be treated 'fairly' since 'that is what Richard would want', and they complied in their own way. Similarly there was no group information technology strategist or central purchasing function, because Branson believed that those roles would constitute interference and discourage managerial creativity. Nor was there any systematic seeking out of synergy, either at the centre or by unit managers.

In 1999 a remark by one of his senior executives made Branson rethink his approach. The executive mentioned that the head of a rival organisation had commented that if Virgin enterprises ever decided to collaborate they would be unstoppable. To test whether this was true Branson immediately – and for the first time – brought together all his managing directors (some 30 in all) for a retreat at his hotel in Mallorca. The agenda was open, but two themes dominated: a unifying document, the Virgin Charter, and e-commerce.

The Virgin Charter is an agreement between Virgin Management Ltd (in effect the holding company) and the subsidiaries. It defines the role of the centre in relation to the subsidiaries in such matters as taxation, legal affairs, intellectual property and real estate. It also outlines closer links in areas previously left to individual units: IT, people, purchasing. Thus the Charter sets out ways for the many Virgin companies to tackle common activities with a common approach. Nearly all are private and owned entirely by the Virgin Group or Branson's family trusts. Business should be 'shaped around people', Branson believes, citing his experience of subdividing the record company as it grew. Each new record label was given to up-and-coming managers, creating in-house entrepreneurs who were highly motivated to build a business with which they identified.

Branson believes that expanding by creating discrete legal entities gives people a sense of involvement with, and loyalty to, the small unit to which they belong. He gives substantial autonomy to those running the subsidiaries and offers them share options – Virgin has produced many millionaires. Branson does not want his best people to leave the company to start a venture outside; he prefers to make millionaires within. He has created a structure of numerous small companies around the world operated quasi-independently. Both systems embody the maxims 'small is beautiful' and 'people matter'.

Virgin.com

During the Mallorca meeting participants realised that, more by chance than planning, Virgin was in businesses 'that were ideally suited to e-commerce and in which growth is expected to occur – travel, financial services, publishing, music, entertainment'. To exploit this potential the participants decided to streamline their online services with a single Virgin web address: Virgin.com.

Branson believed that the Virgin name, known for its consumer-friendly image and good service, would translate well across a range of businesses – 'Virgin isn't a company, it's a brand', commented one senior manager in the company. This is attractive to partners, who provide the expertise and capital for a joint venture in their area of business (such as insurance or share trading), while

Virgin provides the brand image. By putting all Virgin's business on one easily accessible site Branson hopes to cross-promote a wide range of offerings. The site groups these under headings such as online shopping, finance and money, media and telecommunications, leisure and pleasure, travel and tourism, and health.

Virgin is also using the web to streamline internal operations. The airline and the stores now order inventory electronically as they need it, rather than keeping it in physical form. Airline mechanics can use the Internet to source local suppliers of a required part and have it available in hours – an impossible task with earlier technologies. The Megastores only stock the most popular products. The rest are held at a fulfilment house – ready to send to customers who order them, enabling the stores to offer a wide range of products. Advertising staff in each company use the Internet to coordinate their advertising spending and strategy before booking the business with a central agency.

In October 2006 Richard Branson, at a meeting of the Clinton Global Initiative, announced that he would invest all future profits of the Virgin Group's transportation businesses – mainly airlines and trains – into renewable energy initiatives. These would be within the Virgin transportation companies and in new biofuel research and development projects. He had earlier announced the creation of Virgin Fuels, which will invest up to $400 million in renewable energy initiatives over the next three years.

A new venture announced in 2007 was a plan to build a £1.5 billion casino resort in Macau, the Chinese administrative region. Opening in 2010 the entertainment complex would include three hotels and a casino, the group's first. Other parts of the company were continuing to expand, Virgin Atlantic announcing new routes. Virgin Mobile continued to grow, offering free music downloads in early 2007 to customers with 3G handsets. The range of products in the Virgin Megastores was being extended to include clothes, mobile phones and consumer electronics aimed at teenagers.

Source: Based on material from INSEAD Case 400-002-1, *The House that Branson Built: Virgin's entry into the new millennium*; 'Branson's brash new gambit', *Business Week*, 8 March 2004; and other published material.

Part case questions

- What examples does the case give of links between Branson's strategy for Virgin and the environment in which it operates?
- What environmental influences have particularly affected the Virgin Group?
- Which of these are similar to, and which are different from, those facing Marks & Spencer?
- Are the decisions mentioned in the case programmed or non-programmed? How do you sense, from the information in the case, that the company ensures the quality of those decisions?
- What common themes link the different businesses in the group?
- Which generic strategy has Virgin followed at different periods in its history?
- On balance, does the Virgin story support the planned or the emergent view of strategy?
- Why does Branson use joint ventures with other companies to realise the Virgin strategy? Are there any disadvantages in this method of working?
- To what extent has Virgin implemented a marketing orientation?
- Visit Virgin's website and comment on how it has used this to support its marketing activities.
- Where do Richard Branson's publicity stunts fit into the company's marketing strategy?

To help you develop your skills, as well as knowledge, this section includes tasks that relate the key themes covered in the Part to your daily life. Working through these will help you to deepen your understanding of the topic, and develop skills and insights that you can use in many situations.

Task 3.1   Clarifying objectives for a task

Chapter 6 pointed out that one difficulty in planning is being clear about the longer-term objectives of the project or task. A useful skill to help reconcile apparently conflicting objectives is to try to relate them to a wider set of purposes by developing a 'why/how network'. This can make it easier to relate immediate, tangible and possibly conflicting objectives to a wider, and perhaps less conflicting, set of purposes for the activity.

Select a project from your work, or perhaps concerned with your career plans. Write the name of the project at the bottom of a large sheet of paper, and then ask 'Why?' Answer by one or more sentences beginning with the phrase 'in order to ...', and write these answers above the project task. For each of these answers, repeat the process of asking 'Why?', and answering with 'in order to ...', writing your answers on the sheet. Repeat this several times, until it makes sense to stop – by which time you will probably have some broad, long-term purposes that the project can serve.

Figure 1 illustrates the method, and you will need to work over the chart several times to ensure it is clear.

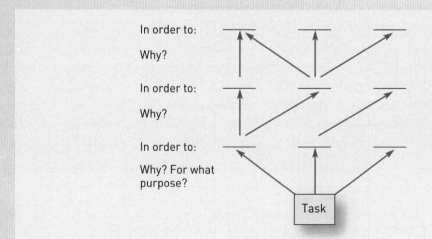

Figure 1   A method for clarifying objectives

Task 3.2 Developing an outline plan for a task

The proposed investment by Virgin in Macao (mentioned in the Part case) has been agreed, and the project is under way. Use Figure 6.5 to outline (one page only) the main issues that the Virgin managers responsible should have on their agenda for managing this project.

Then use Figure 6.6 to sketch a programme overview chart to show how the different projects within the programme might fit together. Check the company website to see if you can find any information about the progress of the investment.

Task 3.3 How to reach a decision

This activity allows you to practise using Vroom and Yetton's model of the different ways in which managers can involve staff in reaching a decision. Review that section of Chapter 7. Then read the following four cases and decide which of Vroom and Yetton's decision-making methods would generate the most effective decision. Note your choice, and your reasons. You could then work through the decision tree and discuss your answers with other students.

Case 1

You are the manager of a small television, radio and electronics business. For some time you have had complaints from your sales staff about the need to redecorate the large shop in which they work. You recently agreed to this and you have received three tenders from reliable and well-known local contractors. They are all able to do the work to the required standard and there is little difference in the quoted costs or times for the job.

You recently asked your employees for their suggestions on suitable colour schemes and there was considerable difference of opinion. You now have to decide which tender to accept, and tell the contractor the colour scheme.

Which decision method would you use, and why?

Case 2

You are an engineer in charge of commissioning a chemical plant. You need to estimate the rate of progress of the stages of the work to schedule the materials and equipment. You are familiar with the work and you possess all the information you need to estimate when materials and equipment will be required at the various commissioning stages. It is very important that your estimates are accurate, since if materials are not available at the right time work will be held up. Equally, if materials and equipment arrive too soon they will be lying around idle. Your team are all committed to the plant being commissioned on time.

Which decision method would you use, and why?

Case 3

You are a training manager employed by a firm of consultants. You have to select three of your eight training advisers to work on an assignment abroad. The assignment involves a training needs analysis, preparation of training programmes and training local instructors.

The assignment is expected to last about six months. It is in a remote part of the Middle East with poor facilities and a ban on the consumption of alcohol. Your advisers are all experienced personnel and each of them is capable of performing the task satisfactorily.

Which decision method would you use, and why?

Case 4

You are a project leader and you need to decide which operators to transfer to a new plant, Line 2. Your objective is to commission this on time without adversely affecting production on the existing plant, Line 1. Most of the operatives working on Line 1 want to transfer to Line 2 because working conditions will be better and the rates of pay higher. Senior operatives working on Line 1 expect to be given preference over less senior ones, and all those on Line 1 expect to be given preference over operatives working in other departments.

You, however, want to transfer only the best operatives from Line 1 to Line 2 and make up the balance with operatives from other departments. Your reason for wanting to do this is that Line 2 will work much faster than Line 1. This means that operatives working on Line 2 will need to be much more skilled at fault rectification than those working on Line 1. The ability to react quickly to control panel and video display unit (VDU) cues is essential.

Which decision method would you use, and why?

Task 3.4   Growth through mergers

Chapter 8 showed that one popular way of implementing strategy is through a merger or acquisition. Use the Internet (such as by accessing the online versions of the *Financial Times* (**www.ft.com**) or *The Economist* (**www.economist.com**)) to identify mergers and acquisitions announced within the past month. For a selection of these, list the companies involved, the industries in which the companies worked, and how the acquiring company relates the acquisition to its broader strategy. Which of the strategic directions shown in Figure 8.5 is best represented by the stated strategy in this case? Follow the story over the coming months.

Part 4

ORGANISING

Introduction

Part Four examines how management creates the structure within which people work. Alongside planning the direction of the business, managers need to consider how they will achieve the direction chosen. A fundamental component of that is the form of the organisation. This is a highly uncertain area of management as there are conflicting views about the kind of structure to have and how much influence structure has on performance.

Chapter 10 describes the main elements of organisation structure and the contrasting forms they take. Chapter 11 deals with one aspect of an organisation's structure: the human resource management policies. These are intended to ensure that employees work towards organisational objectives.

Chapter 12 (formerly Chapter 20) focuses on information technology and e-business, showing how the application of technological developments has deep implications for organisations and their management. Chapter 13 looks at some of the issues that arise in implementing organisational change and in stimulating innovation.

Chapter 10
Organisation structure

To introduce terms and practices that show the choices managers face in shaping organisational structures.

By the end of your work on this chapter you should be able to outline the concepts below in your terms and:

1 Outline why the structure of an organisation affects performance

2 Give examples of management choices about dividing and coordinating work, with their likely advantages and disadvantages

3 Compare the features of mechanistic and organic structures

4 Use the 'contingencies' believed to influence choice of structure to evaluate the suitability of a form for a given unit

5 Summarise the work of Woodward, Burns and Stalker, Lawrence and Lorsch and John Child, showing how they contributed to this area of management theory

6 Explain and illustrate the features of a learning organisation.

This chapter introduces the following ideas:

organisation structure
organisation chart
formal structure
informal structure
vertical specialisation
horizontal specialisation
formal authority
responsibility
delegation
span of control
centralisation
decentralisation
formalisation

functional structure
divisional structure
matrix structure
network structure
mechanistic structure
organic structure
contingencies
technology
differentiation
integration
determinist
structural choice

*Each is a term defined within the text, as well as
in the Glossary at the end of the book.*

This Danish company is the world's second largest producer of hearing aids with about 1,200 staff in Denmark (the parent company, William Demant Holdings, has about 4400 employees worldwide). Oticon has research and production facilities that help ensure the high-quality design and manufacture of its products. Competition intensified during the 1980s and the company began to lose market share to larger rivals such as Siemens. Lars Kolind was appointed chief executive in 1988. In 1990 he concluded that a new approach was needed to counter the threats from larger competitors that were becoming stronger. Oticon's only hope for survival and prosperity was to be radical in all aspects of the business. Kolind intended the changes to turn Oticon from an *industrial* organisation producing hearing aids into a *service* organisation with a physical product.

He organised product development work around projects. The project leader was appointed by the management team and recruited people to do the work. Employees chose whether or not to join – and could only do so if their current project leader agreed. Previously most people had a single skill; they were now required to be active in at least three specialties – one based on professional qualification and two others unrelated to the first. A chip designer could develop skills in customer support and advertising, for example. These arrangements allowed the company to respond quickly to unexpected events and to use skills fully.

Previously Oticon had a conventional hierarchical structure, and a horizontal structure of separate functional departments. The only remnant of the hierarchy is the ten-person management team, each member of which acts as an 'owner' to the many projects through which work is done. Kolind refers to this as 'managed chaos'. The company tries to overcome the dangers of this by developing a strong and clear mission – 'to help people with X problem to live better with X'; and a common set of written values. Examples include: 'an assumption that we only employ adults (who can be expected to act responsibly)', and 'an assumption that staff want to know what and why they are doing it', so all information is available to everyone (with a few legally excepted areas).

There are no titles – people do whatever they think is right at the time. The potential for chaos is averted by building underneath the flexible organisation a set of clearly defined business processes, setting out essential tasks: 'The better your processes are defined, the more flexible you can be.' The absence of departments avoids people protecting local interests and makes it easier to cope with fluctuations in workload.

Oticon was one of the earliest companies to redesign the workplace to maximise disturbance. This was most visible in the 'mobile office', in which each workstation was a desk without drawers (nowhere to file paper). There were no installed telephones, though everyone had a mobile. The workstations were equipped with powerful PCs through which people worked (staff had a small trolley for personal belongings that they wheeled to wherever they were working that day). Although common today, this arrangement was revolutionary at the time.

Source: Based on Bjorn-Andersen and Turner (1994); Rivard *et al.* (2004); and company website.

Case questions 10.1
- What factors persuaded management to change the structure at Oticon?
- How would you expect staff to react to these changes?

10.1 Introduction

Managers at Oticon had to adapt its structure to survive new competition. This required not only lower costs, but also an ability to respond more quickly to the needs of individual customers and to broader changes in technology and in the market.

Senior managers of companies that have not been performing well frequently announce structural changes. When Shell was trying to recover from the 2004 oil reserves crisis the board first dismissed the three senior executives involved in the failure – and then started to change the structure to prevent a recurrence. In 2007 Cadbury Schweppes announced that it would split the drinks and confectionery parts of the business into separate companies, in the belief that this would allow both to perform better. Management at Philips, the Dutch electronics group, has been working to ensure that the fiercely independent units in the company cooperate more closely with each other to improve performance.

When an owner-manager is running a small business he or she decides what tasks to do and coordinates them. If the enterprise grows the entrepreneur usually passes some of the work to newly recruited staff, though the division will probably be flexible and informal. Owner and staff can easily communicate directly with each other, so coordination is easy. If the business continues to grow, new structural questions arise about how best to use available resources. Managers divide the enterprise into distinct units of activity – which brings the possibility of misunderstanding between people in separate units with less direct contact: they need to establish some mechanisms to ensure coordination. How they do this reflects their theory about organisation structure.

This chapter outlines the structural issues that managers in all organisations need to resolve, and which Figure 10.1 illustrates. Managers create a formal structure when they decide how to divide and coordinate the work of the organisation. These decisions in part reflect their interpretation of contingencies affecting the business, and in part the views of stakeholders. Together with many informal arrangements, these decisions create a structure that balances mechanistic and organic forms, which affect organisational performance.

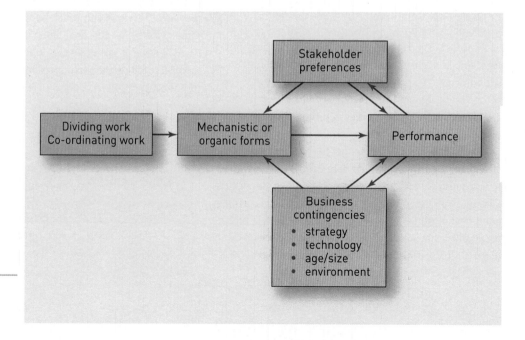

Figure 10.1

Alternative structures and performance

10.2 Designing a structure

Organisation structure describes the way work is divided, supervised and coordinated. When people join a department or take a job within the structure this gives a fairly clear signal about what they should do. The director of marketing is expected to deal with marketing, not finance. Various 'operating policies' reinforce the signal from the basic structure. These cover matters such as recruitment, selection, appraisal and reward (Chapter 11) which managers design to influence employees to act in ways that support wider objectives.

Organisation structure 'The structure of an organisation [is] the sum total of the ways in which it divides its labour into distinct tasks and then achieves co-ordination among them' (Mintzberg, 1979).

The organisation chart

The **organisation chart** shows the structure as a picture. It shows the main departments and positions, with lines linking senior executives to the departments or people for whose work they are responsible. It shows who people report to, and clarifies four features of the **formal structure**:

1 tasks – the major tasks or activities the organisation undertakes;
2 subdivisions – how the major tasks are further divided;
3 levels – the position of each post within the management hierarchy;
4 lines of authority – the lines linking the boxes show who has formal authority over whom, and to whom people report.

Organisation charts give a convenient (though transient) summary of the current allocation of tasks and who is responsible for them. Figure 10.2 shows the chart for an aircraft factory within what is now BAE Systems, a UK defence contractor. The chart shows it has six main departments – design, production engineering, purchasing, inventory, production and human resources. It also shows the chain of command within the plant and the tasks of the respective departments (only some of which are shown). In this case the chart includes direct staff such as operators and engineers, and shows the lines of authority throughout the factory. It does *not* show the **informal structure** – the many patterns of work and communication that are part of organisational life.

An **organisation chart** shows the main departments and senior positions in an organisation and the reporting relations between them.

Formal structure is the official guidelines, documents or procedures setting out how the organisation's activities are divided and coordinated.

Informal structure is the undocumented relationships between members of the organisation that inevitably emerge as people adapt systems to new conditions and satisfy personal and group needs.

Work specialisation

'Job specialisation ... is an inherent part of every organisation, indeed every human activity' (Mintzberg, 1979, p. 69). Management divides work into smaller tasks, with people or departments specialising in one or more of these. They become more expert in one task than they could be in several and are more likely to come up with improved ideas or methods. Taken too far specialisation leads to the negative effects noted in Chapter 15.

Figure 10.2 shows the specialisation of work in the BAE factory. At the top is specialisation between design, production, purchasing and so on. It shows a **vertical specialisation** in that people at different levels deal with distinct sets of activity. It also shows a **horizontal specialisation**. Within production engineering some specialise in electrical problems and others in mechanical, within which groups specialise in structures, systems and fittings. Although Multi-show Events is still a very small company, they too have begun to create a structure showing who is responsible for what.

Vertical specialisation refers to the extent to which responsibilities at different levels are defined.

Horizontal specialisation is the degree to which tasks are divided among separate people or departments.

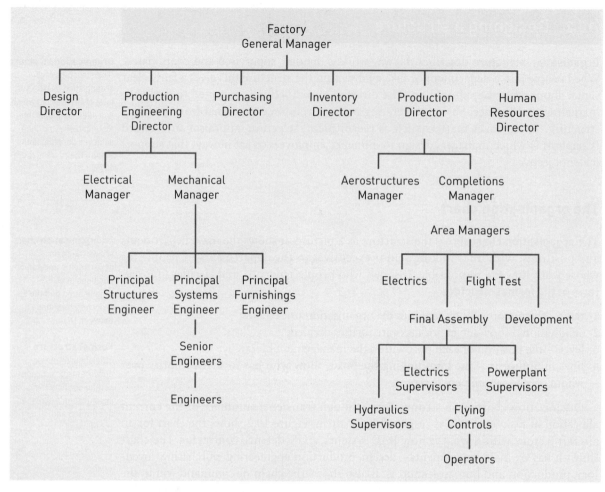

Figure 10.2 The structure within a BAE aircraft factory (www.baesystems.com)

Multi-show Events

Multi-show Events employs 11 people providing a variety of entertainment and promotional services to large businesses. When Brian Simpson created the business in 1990 with a full-time staff of 2 the company obviously had no formal structure. He reflected on the process of growth and structure:

> While the company was small thinking about a structure never occurred to me. It became a consideration as sales grew and the complexity of what we offered increased. There were also more people around and I believed that I should introduce a structure so that clear divisions of responsibility would be visible. It seemed natural to split sales and marketing from the actual delivery and production of events as these were two distinct areas. I felt that by creating 'specialised' departments we could give a better service to clients as each area of the company could focus more on their own roles. [Figure 10.3 shows the structure.]

> We had to redesign the office layout and introduce a more formalised communication process to ensure all relevant information is being passed on – and on the whole I think this structure will see us through the next stage of business growth and development.

Source: Private communication.

Chain of command

The lines of authority show the links between people – who they report to and who reports to them. It shows who they can ask to do a piece of work, who they can ask for help – and who will be expecting results from them. In Figure 10.2 the production director can give instructions to the aerostructures manager, but not to the electrical manager in production engineering. Figure 10.3 shows the lines of authority in Multi-show Events. In both there are many informal contacts in the course of normal human activity, which bring the organisation to life and help people cope with unplanned events.

The lines of authority show the allocation of **formal authority** within the organisation – the right a person has to make decisions, allocate resources or give instructions. It is based on the position, not the person. The production engineering director at BAE has formal authority over a defined range of matters – and anyone else taking over the job would have the same amount of formal authority.

> **Formal authority** is the right that a person in a specified role has to make decisions, allocate resources or give instructions.

Subordinates – those below someone else in the hierarchy – comply with instructions or requests because they accept the person has the formal (sometimes called legitimate) authority to make them. An operator in the hydraulics area of final assembly would accept an instruction from the hydraulics foreman, but probably not from the power-plant foreman (he or she may help them as a personal favour, but that is different from accepting formal authority). If managers attempt to give instructions beyond their area of formal authority they are likely to meet resistance.

Responsibility is a person's duty to meet the expectations associated with a task. The production director and the hydraulics foreman are responsible for the tasks that go with those positions. To fulfil those responsibilities they require formal authority to manage relevant resources.

> **Responsibility** refers to a person's duty to meet the expectations others have of them.

Accountability means that people with formal authority over an area are required to report on their work to those above them in the chain of command. The principal systems engineer is accountable to the mechanical manager for the way he or she has used resources: have they achieved what was expected as measured by the cost, quantity, quality or timeliness of the work?

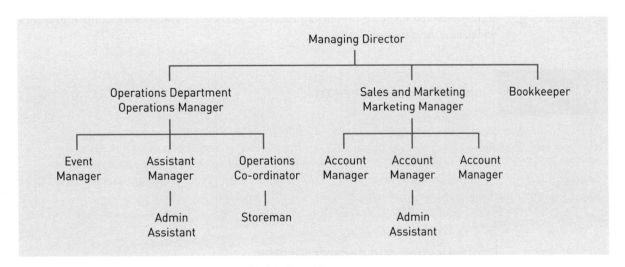

Figure 10.3 The organisation structure at Multi-show Events

Before the change the company had six distinct hierarchical levels, with privileges based on rank:

Not only was there a specific company car assigned to each management level, but other material signs existed ... prestige and reward were very apparent: in the length of the curtains, the type of carpet ... the size of people's desks. It all gave status. And that was what people strove for. (Rivard *et al.*, 2004, p. 181)

Horizontal boundaries were also strong, as the two main divisions – Electronics (product development) and International (sales) communicated poorly. Within these divisions work was organised round specific departments and tasks: 'People were locked into specific roles and responsibilities and were rewarded only for those – nobody took initiatives' (Rivard *et al.*, 2004, p. 180).

Source: Based on Bjorn-Andersen and Turner (1994); and Rivard *et al.* (2004).

Delegation occurs when one person gives another the authority to undertake specific activities or decisions.

Delegation is the process by which people transfer responsibility and authority for certain parts of their work to people below them in the chain of command. While the production director is responsible and accountable for all the work in that area, they are only able to do this by delegating. They are still accountable for the results, but they pass the responsibility, and the necessary authority, to subordinates – and this continues down the hierarchy. If managers delegate more to their subordinates this enables quicker decisions and more rapid responses to new conditions – though some managers are reluctant to delegate in case it reduces their power (Chapter 14).

The span of control

A **span of control** is the number of subordinates reporting directly to the person above them in the hierarchy.

The **span of control** refers to the number of subordinates reporting to a supervisor. Where staff are closely supervised there is a narrow span of control – as shown in the top half of Figure 10.4. If staff have more autonomy and responsibility they need less direct supervision, so more can report to the same manager – the span of control becomes wider, and the structure flatter.

Centralisation and decentralisation

When an organisation grows beyond the smallest operation management divides work vertically, as those at the top delegate more of their work to those below them – and so begin to create a hierarchy such as that shown in Figure 10.4. As the business grows the hierarchy becomes more complex, but it is often possible to see three levels – corporate, divisional and operating – such as at Cadbury Schweppes (**www.cadburyschweppes.com**).

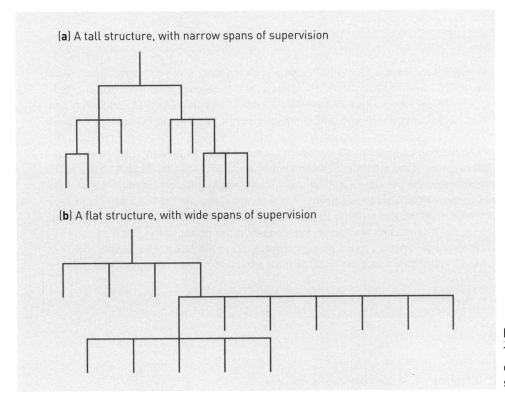

(a) A tall structure, with narrow spans of supervision

(b) A flat structure, with wide spans of supervision

Figure 10.4

Tall and flat organisation structures

- *Corporate* The most senior group, such as the board of Cadbury Schweppes, who are responsible for managing the overall direction of the organisation. This includes not only guiding and monitoring the performance of the organisation but also maintaining links with significant external institutions such as banks and political bodies.
- *Divisional* Responsible for implementing broad areas of policy and for allocating budgets and other resources. Cadbury Schweppes is organised geographically so the managers in, for example, the Europe, Middle East and Africa (EMEA) division are responsible for meeting the targets which the board sets for that division. Divisional managers represent the division's interests to the board and also monitor and control the performance of the operating units.
- *Operating* The level responsible for the technical work of any organisation – making products, catching thieves, caring for patients or delivering services. Within EMEA at Cadbury's there is a team responsible for the Dairy Milk brand in the United Kingdom – ensuring it is produced and sold successfully in that market; other teams look after other products.

The vertical hierarchy establishes what decisions people at each level can make. **Centralisation** is when those at the top make most decisions, with managers at divisional level ensuring those at operating level follow the policy.

    Decentralisation is when a relatively large number of decisions are taken in the divisions or operating units. Branch managers in ATMays, a chain of retail travel agents (now part of Going Places) had considerable freedom over pricing and promotional activities, but were required to follow very tight financial reporting routines.

Centralisation is when a relatively large number of decisions are taken by management at the top of the organisation.

Decentralisation is when a relatively large number of decisions are taken lower down the organisation in the operating units.

Philips www.philips.com

After a period of heavy losses during the 1990s Philips, the Dutch electronics company, appointed a new chief executive in 2001 – Gerard Kleisterlee. He acted quickly to restructure the company, including reducing staff by 25 per cent. The company has a rich 113-year history of innovation and pioneered electric shavers, medical X-rays and compact disks: it symbolised European technical prowess.

But the same engineering culture has also produced failures (such as an early rival to the now-standard VCR) and revenues today are little higher than they were 10 years ago. To pick up the pace, Kleisterlee has reorganised the company – selling unprofitable areas, outsourcing much electronics manufacture (see Section 10.6). Now he is refocusing the company around the most profitable sectors, especially medical systems, and pushing all products to a digital format. This focus is backed up by breaking down the walls separating the fiercely independent divisions and getting them to communicate. 'We're transforming ourselves into a single company', says Mr. Kleisterlee. Under the 'One Philips' slogan, he is centralising functions such as marketing and human resources to eliminate duplication.

Source: *Business Week*, 3 May 2004.

Johnson & Johnson www.jnj.com

This leading health care products company has three divisions – drugs, medical devices and consumer products. Although widely known for products such as Band-Aid and baby powder, its deeper strength lies in scientific research and innovation.

J&J's success has hinged on its unique culture and structure ... Each of the far-flung units operates pretty much as an independent enterprise. Businesses set their own strategies; they have their own finance and human resources departments, for example. [While this is costly] Johnson & Johnson has been [successful] precisely because the businesses it buys, or the ones it starts, are given near-total autonomy. That independence fosters an entrepreneurial attitude that has kept J&J ... competitive as others around it have faltered.

Source: *Business Week*, 5 May 2003.

In practice, organisations display a mix of both. Many have moved towards a more decentralised structure in the belief that those closest to the action will make better decisions. Others limit the power of divisions and operating units by taking more decisions at the centre. Hewlett-Packard had a tradition of local autonomy ('The HP Way'). The company founders believed that 'smart people will make the right choices if given the right tools and authority' and so pushed strategic decisions down to the managers in each business. The company appointed a new CEO, Carleton Fiorina, in 1999. She created a strategy council to advise her on strategy and to allocate resources – a big change from 'The HP Way'.

There is always a tension between centralisation and decentralisation. The profile at any point reflects the shifting power of these forces, as managers weigh the benefits of a move in one direction or the other (including career interests). Table 10.1 summarises these.

Table 10.1

Advantages and disadvantages of centralisation

Factor	Advantages	Disadvantages
Response to change	Thorough debate of issues	Slower response to local conditions
Use of expertise	Concentration of expertise at the centre makes it easier to develop new services and promote best practice methods	Less likely to take account of local knowledge
Cost	Economies of scale in purchasing Efficient administration if use common systems	Local suppliers may be better value than corporate suppliers
Policy implications	Less risk of local managers breaching legal requirements	More risk of local managers breaching legal requirements
Staff commitment	Backing of centre ensures wide support	Staff motivated by greater local responsibility
Consistency	Provides consistent image to the public – less variation in service standards	Local staff discouraged from taking responsibility – can blame centre

Formalisation

Formalisation is the practice of using written or electronic documents to direct and control employees. Documents include rule books, procedures, instruction manuals, job descriptions – anything that sets out what people must do in designated circumstances. They include the scripts that operators in most call centres must use to guide their conversation with a customer. The intention of these formal methods (consistent with the ideas of Max Weber discussed in Chapter 2) is to bring consistency and predictability to organisational work.

There is always tension between formality and informality. If people want to respond to individual needs or local conditions, they favour informal arrangements with few rules, as this seems the best way of meeting those needs. Other requirements, such as those of industry regulators or consumer legislation, pull towards more formality. They may specify detailed procedures and guidelines to protect customers against unsuitable selling methods or to protect staff against unfounded complaints. This leads to formal systems and recording procedures.

Formalisation is the practice of using written or electronic documents to direct and control employees.

Critical reflection on structures

Select an organisation with which you are familiar, or one of those mentioned in this text. Gather information about aspects of the structure, such as:

- Does the organisation chart look tall, or flat?
- What evidence is there of high or low levels of formality?
- Which decisions are centralised, and which are decentralised?

Share your information with colleagues on your course, to increase your awareness of the range of ways in which people have designed structures.

10.3 Grouping jobs into functions and divisions

While work specialisation divides the tasks of the enterprise into smaller jobs for individuals, an opposite process groups jobs together in functional, divisional or matrix forms. Two other forms use teams and networks as the basis of structure. Figure 10.5 shows these alternatives.

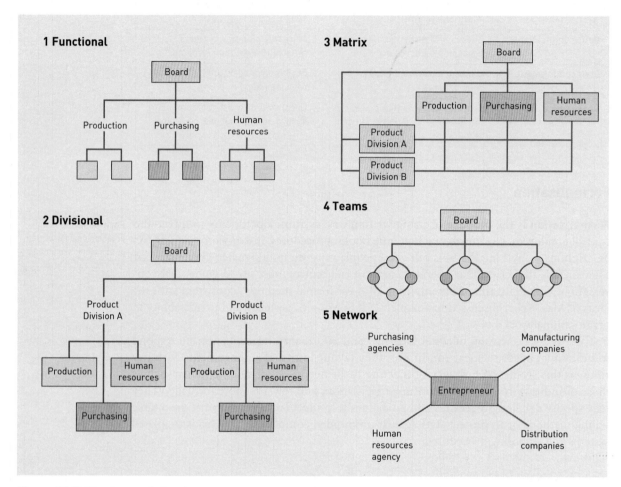

Figure 10.5 Five types of structure

Specialisation by function

A **functional structure** is when tasks are grouped into departments based on similar skills and expertise.

In a **functional structure** managers group activities and staff according to their profession or function – such as production, finance or marketing. The BAE chart shows design, production engineering, purchasing, inventory, production and human resources functions. Figure 10.6 shows a hospital chart, with a functional structure at senior level.

The functional approach can be efficient as people with common expertise work together, sharing and seeing a professional career path. A difficulty is that it may be a source of conflict (Nauta and Saunders, 2001) if the separate functions develop different perceptions of organisational goals. The same may happen as an organisation grows and diversifies into a range of different products, markets or geographical areas. Managers

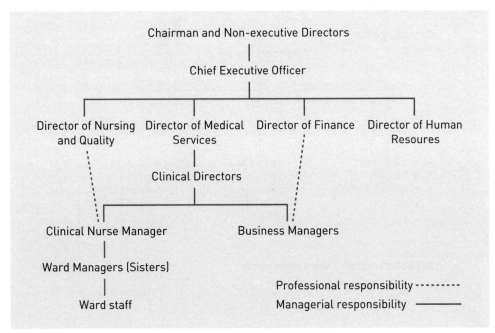

Figure 10.6

Partial organisation structure in a hospital

responsible for these areas expect functional staff to give them priority – leading to competition between business units for functional services.

Specialisation by divisions

Managers create a **divisional structure** when they arrange the organisation around its main products, services or customer groups. In a divisional structure senior managers give each unit the authority to design, produce and deliver the product or service. Functions within the division are likely to cooperate as they depend on satisfying the same set of customers, though duplicating functions make it expensive.

A **divisional structure** is when tasks are grouped in relation to their outputs, such as products or the needs of different types of customer.

Product or customer

Divisional structures enable staff to focus on a distinct group of customers. Banks know that wealthy clients have different needs from other people – and have created divisions to focus on meeting those needs. Hospitals can use what they term the 'named-nurse' system, in which one nurse is responsible for several identified patients. That nurse is the patient's point of contact with the system, managing the delivery of services to the patient from other (functional) departments. Figure 10.7 contrasts the approaches.

Geographic divisions

Here managers group tasks by geography – a common approach in companies with many service outlets – supermarkets, hotels or pub chains. It allows people to focus on identifying and meeting different customer requirements in the region, and it is also easier for divisional managers to monitor and control the many outlets – see Table 10.2.

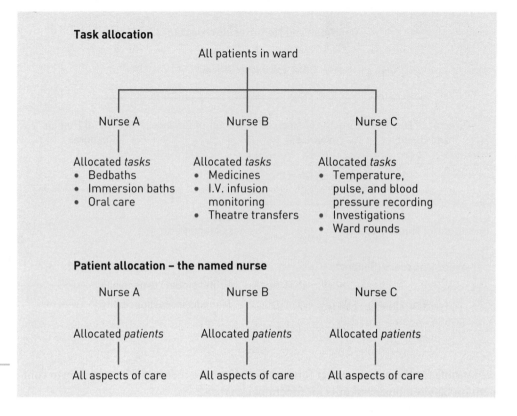

Figure 10.7

Task and named-nurse structures

Table 10.2

Advantages and disadvantages of functional and divisional structures

Structure	Advantages	Disadvantages
Functional	Clear career paths and professional development Specialisation leads to high standards and efficiency Common professional interests support good internal relations	Isolation from wider interests damages promotion prospects Conflict over priorities Lack of wider awareness damages external relations
Divisional	Functional staff focus on product and customer needs Dedicated facilities meet customer needs quickly Common customer focus enables good internal relations	Isolation from wider professional and technical developments Costs of duplicate resources Potential conflict with other divisions over priorities Focus on local, not corporate, needs

Activity 10.2 Choosing between approaches

Go to the website of a company that interests you, and gather information about the structure of the company.

- Gather evidence to decide whether it has a functional or divisional structure – and if the latter, is that based on products or geography?
- If it has international operations, how are they shown in the structure?

Compare your research with colleagues on your course, and prepare a short presentation summarising your conclusions.

10.4 Grouping jobs in matrices, teams and networks

Matrix structure

A **matrix structure** combines functional and divisional structures: function on one axis of the matrix and products or projects on the other. Functional staff work on one or more projects, moving between them as required. They report to two bosses – a functional head and the head of the current project.

> A **matrix structure** is when those doing a task report both to a functional and a project or divisional boss.

Product development at Toyota www.toyota.com

management in practice

Toyota used to organise its product development in a matrix form. The product planning division employed about 7000 people working on 16 current projects. Each represented a new model and employed a chief engineer and several hundred staff. There were also 16 functional engineering divisions.

> A chief engineer had to co-ordinate people in 48 departments in 12 divisions to launch a new product ... In addition, relatively young chief engineers did not always get sufficient co-operation from senior functional managers ... For their part, functional managers found it difficult to spend the time on managing details on so many projects. Most of these managers had to oversee work for about 15 different projects at the same time.

Source: Cusumano and Nobeoka (1998, pp. 22–24).

Teams

In their search for more flexibility, lower costs and faster response some companies organise work into teams – most evident in companies that depend on a steady flow of new products – such as Johnson & Johnson or Philips. Management delegates significant responsibilities and authority not to individual workers but to an identifiable team, which is then accountable for the results (Chapter 17).

Networks

Network structures refer to situations in which organisations remain independent but agree to work together to deliver products or services. Sometimes this happens when managers arrange for other companies to undertake certain non-core activities on their behalf. The remaining organisation concentrates on setting strategy direction and managing the core units. Abbey (a Spanish-owned UK bank) has an agreement with computer services company Unisys to manage the 1.5 million insurance policies it has sold. Large electronics producers such as Dell or Sun Microsystems have their products made under contract by companies that specialise in such work. The arrangement is becoming common in personal services – such as when Care UK runs schools for disturbed children on behalf of local government.

> A **network structure** is when tasks required by one company are performed by other companies with expertise in those areas.

A similar structural form is when managers sell one of their services to another company, but still deliver the service to customers under their own name. Abbey sold its credit card business to MBNA as the cost of updating its systems to compete effectively in the card business was too high. The company continues to offer cards with the Abbey logo, but MBNA operates the service.

An **organic structure** is one where people are expected to work together and to use their initiative to solve problems; job descriptions and rules are few and imprecise.

that those at the centre must depend on those nearest the action to find the best solution. Communication is likely to be horizontal amongst those familiar with the task. There may not be an organisation chart, so fluid is the division of work. Burns and Stalker (1961) called this an **organic structure**. Table 10.3 compares mechanistic and organic forms.

Table 10.3

Characteristics of mechanistic and organic systems

Mechanistic	Organic
Specialised tasks	Contribute experience to common tasks
Hierarchical structure of control	Network structure of contacts
Knowledge located at top of hierarchy	Knowledge widely spread
Vertical communication	Horizontal communication
Loyalty and obedience stressed	Commitment to goals more important

Source: Based on Burrns and Stalker (1961).

management in practice A more organic structure at Philips www.philips.com

The Dutch group Philips is the world's third largest consumer electronics company – renowned for its innovative products. It has faced many crises in recent years, and in 2002 was trading at a heavy loss. Gerard Kleisterlee became chief executive in 2001 and has made radical changes in the company's structure. He reduced the many separate divisions to just five, and is breaking down long-established internal divisions' barriers to communication, so that expertise in one can be used in another. For example the lighting group is working with the consumer electronics division to produce a room lighting system that changes colour according to what is being shown on the TV.

Source: *The Economist*, 12 June 2004.

Within a large organisation some units will correspond to mechanistic forms and others to organic. A company may have a centralised information system and tightly controlled policies on capital expenditure – while also allowing divisions considerable autonomy on research or advertising.

Case questions 10.2

● What was the role of strategy and technology in encouraging the change at Oticon?

● What features of the present form correspond to the organic model?

● How does management hope that the new structure will support their strategy?

Contingencies are factors such as uncertainty, interdependence and size that reflect the situation of the organisation.

Why do managers favour one form of structure rather than another? A widely held (though disputed) view is that it depends on certain **contingencies**:

the essence of the contingency paradigm is that organizational effectiveness results from fitting characteristics of the organization, such as its structure, to contingencies that reflect the situation of the organization. (Donaldson, 2001, p. 1)

10.4 Grouping jobs in matrices, teams and networks

Matrix structure

A **matrix structure** combines functional and divisional structures: function on one axis of the matrix and products or projects on the other. Functional staff work on one or more projects, moving between them as required. They report to two bosses – a functional head and the head of the current project.

A **matrix structure** is when those doing a task report both to a functional and a project or divisional boss.

Product development at Toyota www.toyota.com

Toyota used to organise its product development in a matrix form. The product planning division employed about 7000 people working on 16 current projects. Each represented a new model and employed a chief engineer and several hundred staff. There were also 16 functional engineering divisions.

A chief engineer had to co-ordinate people in 48 departments in 12 divisions to launch a new product ... In addition, relatively young chief engineers did not always get sufficient co-operation from senior functional managers ... For their part, functional managers found it difficult to spend the time on managing details on so many projects. Most of these managers had to oversee work for about 15 different projects at the same time.

Source: Cusumano and Nobeoka (1998, pp. 22–24).

Teams

In their search for more flexibility, lower costs and faster response some companies organise work into teams – most evident in companies that depend on a steady flow of new products – such as Johnson & Johnson or Philips. Management delegates significant responsibilities and authority not to individual workers but to an identifiable team, which is then accountable for the results (Chapter 17).

Networks

Network structures refer to situations in which organisations remain independent but agree to work together to deliver products or services. Sometimes this happens when managers arrange for other companies to undertake certain non-core activities on their behalf. The remaining organisation concentrates on setting strategy direction and managing the core units. Abbey (a Spanish-owned UK bank) has an agreement with computer services company Unisys to manage the 1.5 million insurance policies it has sold. Large electronics producers such as Dell or Sun Microsystems have their products made under contract by companies that specialise in such work. The arrangement is becoming common in personal services – such as when Care UK runs schools for disturbed children on behalf of local government.

A **network structure** is when tasks required by one company are performed by other companies with expertise in those areas.

A similar structural form is when managers sell one of their services to another company, but still deliver the service to customers under their own name. Abbey sold its credit card business to MBNA as the cost of updating its systems to compete effectively in the card business was too high. The company continues to offer cards with the Abbey logo, but MBNA operates the service.

Mixed forms

Large organisations typically combine functional, product and geographical structures within the same company – the structure of Unilever, the Anglo-Dutch conglomerate that produces a vast range of consumer products throughout the world, is an example – see Management in Practice.

---

management in practice Mixed structure at Unilever   www.unilever.com

During the year ended 31 December 2005 Unilever's top management team consisted of regional, category and functional presidents, and was headed by the group chief executive. He was accountable for all aspects of Unilever operations, managing business performance and overall profit responsibility for the group.

The three regional presidents (the Americas, Asia/Africa and Europe) are responsible for profit, implementing proven brand mixes in their region, and single-mindedly focusing on growth through excellent go-to-market execution.

The categories presidents (Food and Home and Personal Care) are responsible for category strategy and brand development (including R&D and innovation): 'The interdependence between the regions and the categories allows us to capitalise on our global scale while building on our deep roots in local markets.'

Finance and HR presidents ensure excellence in their functional areas and provide support to the regions, categories and corporate centre.

Source: Extracts from *Unilever Annual Report, 2005.*

The counterpart to the task of dividing work is that of coordinating it – without which there will be confusion and poor performance.

Activity 10.3   **Comparing structures**

Think of an organisation you have worked in, or about which you can gather information.

● Which of the five structural forms did it correspond to most closely?
● What were the benefits and disadvantages of that approach?

Compare your conclusions with colleagues on your course, and use your experience to prepare a list of the advantages and disadvantages of each type of structure.

10.5   Coordinating work

There are five ways to coordinate the activities of people working on different tasks.

Direct supervision

This is where a manager ensures coordination by directly supervising his or her staff to ensure they work together in line with company policy. The number of people whom a manager can effectively supervise directly reflects the idea of the span of control – that beyond some (variable) point direct supervision is no longer sufficient.

Hierarchy

If disputes or problems arise between staff or departments, they can be reconciled by putting the arguments to their common boss in the hierarchy. It is the boss's responsibility to reach a solution. At BAE (Figure 10.2), if the engineer responsible for structures has a disagreement with the systems engineer, they can ask the mechanical manager to adjudicate. If that fails they can escalate the problem to the production engineering director. The weakness of this is that it takes time to get a response, and meantime the issue is unresolved. In rapidly changing circumstances the hierarchy cannot cope with the volume of issues requiring attention, and becomes slow at making decisions.

Standardising inputs and outputs

This involves making sure that what goes into the system, and what managers expect it to produce, are standardised. If the purchaser of components specifies accurately what is required, and the supplier meets that specification, coordination between users will be easier. If staff work to precise specifications that helps coordination with the next stage. If they receive the same training they will need less direct supervision, as their manager can be more confident that they will be working consistently.

Rules and procedures

Another coordination method is to prepare rules or procedures, such as that shown in the Management in Practice feature. Organisations have procedures for approving capital expenditure. To compare proposals on a common basis they set strict guidelines on the questions a bid should answer, how people should prepare a case, and to whom they should submit it. Companies developing computer software have coordination problems if several designers are working on a project, so use strict change control procedures to ensure that the sub-projects fit together.

Safety procedures in a power station

The following instructions govern the steps that staff must follow when they inspect control equipment in a nuclear power station:

1. Before commencing work you must read and understand the relevant Permit-to-Work and/or other safety documents as appropriate.
2. Obtain keys for relevant cubicles.
3. Visually inspect the interior of each bay for dirt, water and evidence of condensation.
4. Visually inspect the cabling, glands, terminal blocks and components for damage.
5. Visually check for loose connections at all terminals.
6. Lock all cubicles and return the keys.
7. Clear the safety document and return it to the Supervisor/Senior Authorised person.

Information systems

Information systems help to ensure that people who need to work in a consistent way have common information, so that it is easier to coordinate their activities. The Internet offers a radical way of moving information and knowledge between organisations, as the Siemens example shows.

management in practice   Internet coordination at Siemens   www.siemens.com

Mr von Pierer, chief executive of Siemens, is enthusiastic about the way the company is using the Internet to coordinate different parts of the company. One example is online purchasing, which enables the company to save huge amounts of money by pooling the demands of several purchasing departments, using a company-wide system called click2procure.

Another is encouraging customers to buy online. They can click on 'buy from Siemens' on the website home page and place orders for most Siemens products. The automation and drives division, for example, generates some 30 per cent of its sales online. The strategy also helps to improve internal administrative processes – such as by handling 30,000 job applications a year online, or expecting employees to book their business travel arrangements over the Internet.

> There is more to this than paperless administration. The idea is to make sure that the whole supply chain – from customers, through Siemens, and then on to its suppliers – runs smoothly.

Von Pierer also wants customers to have a single, coordinated view of the company:

> I don't think that in the future customers will tolerate four or five different views about Siemens. They want one view of our capabilities. Even if a customer is buying things from several different Siemens divisions, it should deal directly with only one, which should act as a lead manager within the company. Inside Siemens, the customer should be identified by only one code.

However he acknowledged that reorganising all the internal processes would be a major task.

Source: Boddy *et al.* (2005) and company website.

Many companies now conduct their purchasing over the Internet, ensuring that new instructions to hundreds of suppliers flow almost automatically as the manufacturing programme changes to match current orders. This was previously a laborious task in which people easily made mistakes: the Internet makes it tightly coordinated.

Direct personal contact

The most human form of coordination is when people talk to each other. Mintzberg (1979) found that people use this method in both the simplest and the most complex organisation. There is so much uncertainty in the latter that information systems cannot cope – only direct contact can do this, by enabling people to making personal commitments to each other across business units (Sull and Spinosa, 2005).

Coordination in a social service

management in practice

The organisation cares for the elderly in a large city. Someone who had worked there for several years reflected on coordination:

> Within the centre there was a manager, 2 deputies, an assistant manager, 5 senior care officers (SCOs) and 30 officers. Each SCO is responsible for 6 care officers, allowing daily contact between the supervisor and the subordinates. While this defines job roles quite tightly, it allows a good communication structure to exist. Feedback is common as there are frequent meetings of the separate groups, and individual appraisals of the care officers by the SCOs. Staff value this opportunity for praise and comments on how they are doing.
>
> Contact at all levels is common between supervisor and care officers during meetings to assess the needs of clients – for whom the care officers have direct responsibility. Frequent social gatherings and functions within the department also enhance relations and satisfy social needs. Controls placed on the behaviour of the care officers come from senior management, often derived from legislation such as the Social Work Acts or the Health and Safety Executive. Performance is measured – outsiders regularly assess how the Quality of Practice code is working – and there are internal measures of absenteeism and lateness.

Source: Private communication.

Activity 10.4 Comparing coordination

Think of an organisation you have worked in, or about which you can gather information.

- Which forms of coordination did it use?
- What were the benefits and disadvantages of that approach?

Compare your conclusions with colleagues on your course, and use your experience to prepare a list of the advantages and disadvantages of each method of coordination.

The accumulation of decisions on the division and coordination of work lead to organisations that can be analysed in terms of how closely they correspond to mechanistic or organic forms.

10.6 Mechanistic and organic structures

The purpose of structure is to encourage people to act in ways that management hopes will support its objectives. Some organisations have a structure that emphasises the vertical hierarchy, by defining responsibilities clearly, taking most decisions at the centre, delegating tightly defined tasks and having rigorous reporting requirements. This enables those at the centre to know what is happening, and ensuring that staff apply policies consistently. This enables them to present a uniform image, to ensure that customers receive consistent treatment and that best practices are shared. Communication is mainly vertical, as the centre passes down instructions and staff send queries to those above them. Burns and Stalker (1961) called this a **mechanistic structure**.

Others develop a structure with broadly defined, flexible tasks, many cross-functional teams, and base authority on expertise rather than position. Management accepts

A **mechanistic structure** means there is a high degree of task specialisation, people's responsibility and authority are closely defined and decision making is centralised.

333

An **organic structure** is one where people are expected to work together and to use their initiative to solve problems; job descriptions and rules are few and imprecise.

that those at the centre must depend on those nearest the action to find the best solution. Communication is likely to be horizontal amongst those familiar with the task. There may not be an organisation chart, so fluid is the division of work. Burns and Stalker (1961) called this an **organic structure**. Table 10.3 compares mechanistic and organic forms.

Table 10.3

Characteristics of mechanistic and organic systems

Mechanistic	Organic
Specialised tasks	Contribute experience to common tasks
Hierarchical structure of control	Network structure of contacts
Knowledge located at top of hierarchy	Knowledge widely spread
Vertical communication	Horizontal communication
Loyalty and obedience stressed	Commitment to goals more important

Source: Based on Burrns and Stalker (1961).

management in practice

A more organic structure at Philips www.philips.com

The Dutch group Philips is the world's third largest consumer electronics company – renowned for its innovative products. It has faced many crises in recent years, and in 2002 was trading at a heavy loss. Gerard Kleisterlee became chief executive in 2001 and has made radical changes in the company's structure. He reduced the many separate divisions to just five, and is breaking down long-established internal divisions' barriers to communication, so that expertise in one can be used in another. For example the lighting group is working with the consumer electronics division to produce a room lighting system that changes colour according to what is being shown on the TV.

Source: *The Economist*, 12 June 2004.

Within a large organisation some units will correspond to mechanistic forms and others to organic. A company may have a centralised information system and tightly controlled policies on capital expenditure – while also allowing divisions considerable autonomy on research or advertising.

Case questions 10.2

● What was the role of strategy and technology in encouraging the change at Oticon?

● What features of the present form correspond to the organic model?

● How does management hope that the new structure will support their strategy?

Contingencies are factors such as uncertainty, interdependence and size that reflect the situation of the organisation.

Why do managers favour one form of structure rather than another? A widely held (though disputed) view is that it depends on certain **contingencies**:

the essence of the contingency paradigm is that organizational effectiveness results from fitting characteristics of the organization, such as its structure, to contingencies that reflect the situation of the organization. (Donaldson, 2001, p. 1)

Successful organisations appear to be those in which managers maintain a good fit between contingent factors (such as strategy, technology, size/life cycle and environmental uncertainty) and the structure within which people work. Figure 10.1 illustrated these contingent factors – strategy, technology, age/size and environment.

Strategy

Chapter 8 outlined Porter's view that firms adopt one of three generic strategies – cost leadership, differentiation or focus. With a cost leadership strategy managers concentrate on increasing efficiency to keep costs low. A mechanistic structure is likely to be the best support for this strategy, with closely defined tasks in an efficient functional structure. There is likely to be a hierarchical chain of command to ensure that people work to plan and vertical communication to keep the centre well informed. PowerGen, a privatised electricity utility, initially took a cost–leadership approach and adopted a tight functional structure with detailed rules and performance measures.

A differentiation strategy focuses on innovation – developing new products rapidly and imaginatively. An organic structure is most likely to support this, by enabling ideas to flow easily between people with something to contribute, regardless of their function. Oticon moved towards this team-based structure, as has Microsoft in its efforts to maintain high levels of innovation in its research organisation. As PowerGen diversified into different businesses it supported this with a structure of autonomous product divisions, able to respond quickly to new demands. Hill and Pickering (1986) showed that companies in which business units had relatively high decision-making authority were more successful than those that were centralised. The Management in Practice feature shows how GlaxoSmithKline (GSK) followed this approach when the board restructured its R&D activities into six autonomous, but tightly focused, units.

GlaxoSmithKline   www.gsk.com

In February 2001 Tachi Yamada, head of R&D at GlaxoSmithKline (GSK), set out the company's plan to split the company's research organisation ('the engine room of any pharmaceutical company') into six 'internal biotechnology companies'. These units will compete for resources. Divided along therapeutic lines, they will operate autonomously. GSK is the world's second largest drugs company, and employs 15,000 scientists with an annual budget of £2.5 billion. Jean-Paul Garnier, chief executive, said that organising this research group required a radical new structure. Early research, where scarce skills and expensive equipment are applied across a range of diseases, needed to stay big. So did late-stage development where huge dossiers of clinical trial data were prepared for regulators. However, the section in the middle, where bright ideas were honed into drugs, would work best as competing, autonomous units: 'We start big, we move to small and then back to big again. Nobody has attempted this before.'

The job of the six autonomous units is to deliver drugs with 'proof of concept' – after small-scale clinical tests on patients – to GSK's development organisation. That will put drugs through full clinical trials, aimed at winning regulatory approval and maximising sales potential.

The business units, called Centres of Excellence for Drug Discovery (CEDDs), can deliver molecules invented at GSK or brought in from academia or external biotech groups. Dr Yamada said: 'They have complete autonomy. They can have 100 chemists per project, or 5. It doesn't matter to me how they do it, so long as they produce drugs.'

Clinical trials are undertaken on a massive scale, often across continents, and must comply with strict regulatory conditions. Thus corporate control, uniformity and economies of scale are preeminent. The other area where scale will be leveraged is early research, where hundreds of millions of pounds are spent on platform technology. Two divisions, Genetics Research and Discovery Research, will work on understanding basic biology and on producing leads to set drug discovery units on their way. Figure 10.8 illustrates the new structure.

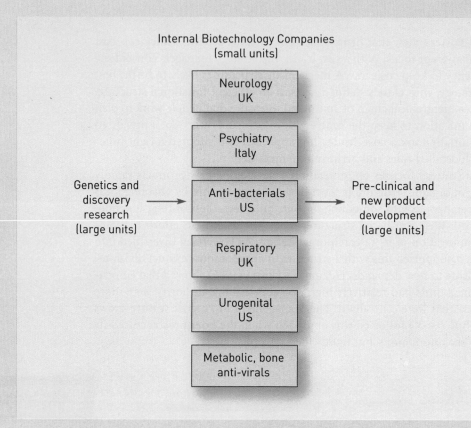

Figure 10.8 The structure introduced at GlaxoSmithKline

In 2007 Jean-Pierre Garnier was able to report that the change in structure was paying off – the company now had a strong pipeline of new drugs, and was planning five major product launches during the year. It was also creating additional CEDDs for inflammatory diseases and infection.

Source: Based on *Financial Times*, 24 October 2002 and 9 February 2007.

Figure 10.9 expresses the idea that different strategies require different structures. The more the strategy corresponds to cost leadership, the more likely it is that managers will support it with a functional structure. If the balance is towards differentiation, the more likely there will be a divisional, team or network structure.

Technology

Technology is the knowledge, equipment and activities used to transform inputs into outputs.

Technology includes the knowledge, tools and techniques used to transform organisational inputs into outputs. It includes buildings, machines, computer systems and the knowledge and procedures associated with them. Some technologies seem to be better supported by some structures than others.

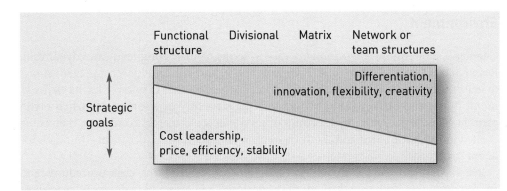

Figure 10.9

The relationship between strategies and structural types

Joan Woodward's study of organisations and their structure (1965) had a great influence on thinking about management. She gathered information from 100 British firms to establish whether structural features such as the span of control or the number of levels in the hierarchy varied between them. The researchers could see no pattern until they analysed the companies by their manufacturing process, which they grouped into 11 categories, of three broad types. These formed a scale of increasing technical complexity. The researchers then noticed a relationship between the degree of technical complexity and company structure.

- *Unit and small batch production* Firms in this group produce goods in small numbers, often to a customer's unique order. It is similar to craft work, as people and their skills are deeply involved in the process – custom-built cycles, designer furniture, Aston Martin sports cars or luxury yachts.
- *Large batch and mass production* This form is typified by the production of large quantities of standard products. The physical products move along an assembly line, with people complementing the machinery – mobile phones, Ford cars or Electrolux washing machines.
- *Continuous process* Here the entire workflow is mechanised, in a sophisticated and complex production technology. The machinery does the production work, with operators monitoring it, fixing faults and generally overseeing the process – a Guinness Brewery, a Shell oil refinery or a Mittal steel plant.

Woodward concluded that the different technologies impose different demands on people. Unit production requires close supervision to ensure that staff meet the customer's unique requirements. Supervisors can communicate directly with those working on different parts of the task and so manage the uncertainties and changes involved in producing 'one-off' items. On an assembly line the work is routine and predictable, so a supervisor can monitor more staff: there is a wide span of control. Commercially successful firms were those where the structure provided the right kind of support to the technology.

Technology also helps to deliver services, and managers create structures to shape the way staff interact with customers. Staff at banks used to handle many cash transactions, and sat behind secure glass screens that made them seem remote and unwelcoming. Technology means that little cash is now handled in branches – which have been redesigned to bring staff and customers closer together. The Part 4 Case – Royal Bank of Scotland – traces structural changes in that service business, including its centralised manufacturing division.

Environment

Chapter 3 showed how environments vary in terms of their complexity and dynamism. Research by Hage and Aiken (1967), Gerwin (1979) and Hill and Pickering (1986) shows that a firm's performance depends on having a structure that is suitable for its environment. Burns and Stalker (1961) compared the structure of a long-established rayon plant in Manchester with the structures of several new electronics companies then being created in the east of Scotland. Both types of organisation were successful – but had different structures.

The rayon plant had clearly set out rules, tight job descriptions, clear procedures, and coordination was primarily through the hierarchy. There was a high degree of specialisation, with tasks divided into small parts. Managers had defined responsibilities clearly and discouraged people from acting outside of their remit. They had centralised decisions, with information flowing up the hierarchy, and instructions down.

The small companies in the newly created electronics industry had few job descriptions, while procedures were ambiguous and imprecise. Staff were expected to use their initiative to decide priorities and to work together to solve problems. Communication was horizontal, rather than vertical (see Table 10.3).

Burns and Stalker (1961) concluded that both forms were appropriate for their circumstances. The rayon plant had a stable environment, as it was the production unit of a larger business, and its sole purpose was to supply a steady flow of rayon to the company's spinning factories. Delivery schedules rarely changed, the technology of rayon manufacture was well known and fully documented. In contrast, the electronics companies were in direct contact with their customers, mainly the Ministry of Defence. The demand for commercial and military products was volatile, with frequent changes in delivery requirements. The technology was new, often applying the results of recent research. Contracts were often taken in which neither the customer nor the company knew what the end product would be: it was likely to change during the course of the work.

Oticon – the case continues – communication and technology www.oticon.com

CASE STUDY

Lars Kolind knew that the dramatic change in structure he proposed would not be achieved without pain: he was attacking the established culture, privileges tied to seniority and titles, and on work processes. In moving to an organisation in which there would be only project members, project leaders and project owners, many would not easily accept losing the power they derived from controlling information. He used his power to drive the change, announcing:

I am 100 per cent sure that we will try this. There's enough time so that you can make a choice – whether you are going to try it with us or whether ... you find another job (quoted in Rivard *et al.*, 2004, p. 174).

While the company used advanced information systems (IS) for many functions Kolind believed that dialogue is better than e-mail, and designed the build-ing to support face-to-face dialogue between staff. The problem owner will usually use e-mail or personal contact to bring two or three people together and have a stand-up meeting. Decisions are noted in the computer (accessible by everyone).

By 1994 the company had halved product development time and more than doubled sales. It employed half as many administrative staff as in 1990, but double the number on product development. Financial performance improved dramatically in the years following the change. Lars Kolind said, 'Hardware companies have organisations that look like machines: a company that produces knowledge needs an organisation that looks like a brain, i.e. which looks chaotic and is unhierarchical.'

Source: Based on Bjorn-Andersen and Turner (1994); Rivard *et al.* (2004).

Case questions 10.3

- Oticon has had both mechanistic and organic structures: what prompted the change?
- Why has the new structure improved business performance?

Burns and Stalker (1961) concluded that neither mechanistic nor organic structures were appropriate in all situations. Stable, predictable environments were likely to encourage a mechanistic structure. Volatile, unpredictable environments were likely to encourage an organic structure. This recognition that environmental conditions place different demands upon organisations was a major step in understanding why companies adopt contrasting structures – an idea illustrated in Figure 10.10.

Environment / **Structure**	*Mechanistic*	*Organic*
Uncertain (unstable)	**Incorrect Fit:** Mechanistic structure in uncertain environment Structure too tight	**Correct Fit:** Organic structure in uncertain environment
Certain (stable)	**Correct Fit:** Mechanistic structure in certain environment	**Incorrect Fit:** Organic structure in certain environment Structure too loose

Figure 10.10 The relationship between environment and structure

Activity 10.5 Comparing mechanistic and organic forms

Think of a department you have worked in, or about which you can gather information.

- Was it broadly mechanistic or organic?
- Why has that form evolved, and is it suitable?
- How does it compare to other departments in the organisation?

Organic problem solving in a mechanistic structure

The organisation I work for has just come through a short-term cash-flow crisis. The problem arose because, while expenditures on contracts are relatively predictable and even, the income flow was disrupted by a series of contractual disputes.

The role culture permeates the head office, and at first the problem was pushed ever upwards. But faced with this crisis all departments were asked for ideas on how to improve performance. Some have been turned into new methods of working, and others are still being considered by the 'ideas team', drawn from all grades of personnel and departments. This was a totally new perspective, of a task culture operating within a role culture – that is, we developed an organic approach. What could be more simple than asking people who do the job how they could be more efficient?

To maintain the change in the long run is difficult, and some parts have now started to drift back to the role culture.

Source: Private communication.

Differentiation The state of segmentation of the organisation into subsystems, each of which tends to develop particular attributes in response to the particular demands posed by its relevant external environment.

Integration is the process of achieving unity of effort amongst the various subsystems in the accomplishment of the organisation's task.

Organisations do not face a single environment. People in each department try to meet the expectations of players in the wider environment, and gradually develop structures that help them to do that. A payroll section has to meet strict legal requirements on, amongst other things, salary entitlements, taxation and pensions records. Staff must follow strict rules, with little scope for using their initiative: they work in a mechanistic structure. The product development or advertising departments face quite different requirements – and so will have evolved a structure that encourages creativity and innovation: they work in an organic structure.

An important implication of this is that coordination between such departments will be difficult, as they will work in different ways. Paul Lawrence and Jay Lorsch explored this issue, and their contribution is in the Key Ideas feature.

Lawrence and Lorsch: differentiation and integration

Two American scholars, Paul Lawrence and Jay Lorsch, developed Burns and Stalker's work. They observed that departments doing different tasks face a separate segment of the environment – some relatively stable, others unstable. Lawrence and Lorsch predicted that to cope with these varying conditions departments will develop different structures and ways of working. Those in stable environments would move towards mechanistic forms, those in unstable environments would move towards organic.

Empirical research in six organisations enabled Lawrence and Lorsch to show that departments did indeed differ from each other, and in ways they had predicted. Those facing unstable environments (research and development) had less formal structures than those facing stable ones (production). The greater the **differentiation** between departments the more effort was needed to integrate their work. Successful firms achieved more **integration** between units by using a variety of integrating devices such as task forces and project managers with the required interpersonal skills. The less effective companies in the uncertain environment used rules and procedures.

Source: Lawrence and Lorsch (1967).

Size and life cycle

Small organisations tend to be less formal with less division of labour – people take part in a wide range of tasks and coordination is achieved informally by face-to-face contact or direct supervision. Weber (1947) noted that larger organisations tended to have more formal, bureaucratic structures, and research by Blau (1970) and Pugh and Hickson (1976) showed that as organisations grow they develop more formal structures, hierarchies and specialised units. Like the head of Multi-show Events, as managers divide a growing business into separate units they need more controls such as job descriptions and reporting relationships.

Growth and structure in a housing association

management in practice

A manager in a housing association, which was created to provide affordable housing for those on low incomes, describes how its structure changed as it grew.

Housing associations have to give tenants and their representatives the opportunity to influence policy. In the early days it had few staff, no clear division of labour and few rules and procedures. It was successful in providing housing, which attracted more government funds, and the association grew. Managing more houses required a more formal structure to support the work. The association no longer served a single community, but several geographical areas. Staff numbers grew significantly and worked in specialised departments. The changes led to concerns amongst both staff and committee that the organisation was no longer responsive to community needs and that it had become distant and bureaucratic.

Source: Private communication from the manager.

This implies that organisations go through stages, with structures adapting to suit. The entrepreneur creates the business alone, or with a few partners or employees. They operate informally with little division of labour – tasks overlap (for a discussion of the unique structural issues facing entrepreneurs in high technology industries, see Alvarez and Barney (2005)). There are few rules or systems for planning and coordination. The owner makes the decisions, so they have a centralised structure. If the business succeeds it will need to raise more capital to finance growth. The owner no longer has sole control, but shares decisions with members of the growing management team. Tasks become divided by function or product, creating separate departments and more formal controls to ensure coordination. Many small companies fail when they expand rapidly but fail to impose controls and systems for managing risks – as an executive of a publishing company that got into difficulties recalled: 'We were editors and designers running a large show, and we were completely overstretched. Our systems were simply not up to speed with our creative ambitions.' This observation is consistent with a study by Sine *et al.* (2006), which shows how successful Internet companies were those that were able to balance the essential creative spirit of their companies with a degree of formalisation, specialisation and administrative intensity. They survived, while those that lacked even the most rudimentary structures failed.

If a business continues to grow it takes on more of the features of a bureaucracy. There is more division of responsibilities and more rules to ensure coordination. There are more professional and specialist staff in areas such as finance or human resources, with systems for budgeting, financial control and rewards. Mature, established firms tend to become mechanistic, with a strong vertical system and well-developed controls.

More decisions are made at the centre – bringing the danger of slow response to new conditions. To overcome these barriers to innovation and to encourage cross-functional communication managers may change the structure. One approach is to decentralise the organisation by creating separate divisions with profit responsibility – as Microsoft did when it created seven business units with a high degree of autonomy.

Oticon – the case continues – limiting risks
www.oticon.com

CASE STUDY

While the changes at Oticon had spurred creativity, the board of the firm also became concerned about profitability in the early years, as the new structure was creating so many initiatives and new products that it was difficult to manage them all effectively. They therefore appointed Neils Jacobsen as co-chief executive in 1992, to place more emphasis on financial discipline and performance. Jacobsen took over from Kolind as chief executive in 1998.

In 1996 more controls were introduced, to balance some of the risks of the new form. A competence centre was established that took over some of the rights previously held by project managers. It alone now had the right to initiate projects and appoint project managers – thus restraining the earlier principle that anyone could start a project. It also took over the task of negotiating salaries that had initially been delegated to project managers.

These changes were intended to overcome some of the costs associated with the radical structure. When there was no limit to the number of projects, nor to the number of projects on which a person could work, it had become hard to ensure completion: the most capable staff were spread over too many projects. There was also some concern that staff and teams were not always sharing knowledge as fully as expected. Despite these adjustments, the company remains a radically different form of organisation.

Source: Based on Foss (2003).

Contingencies or managerial choice?

Contingency approaches to organisation structure propose that the most effective structure will depend (be contingent) upon the situation in which the organisation is operating:

> The organization is seen as existing in an environment that shapes its strategy, technology, size and innovation rate. These contingent factors in turn determine the required structure; that is, the structure that the organization needs to adopt if it is to operate effectively. (Donaldson, 1996, p. 2)

Effective management involves formulating an appropriate strategy and developing a structure which supports that strategy by encouraging appropriate behaviour. The emphasis is **determinist** (the form is determined by the environment) and functionalist (the form is intended to serve organisational effectiveness) (Donaldson, 1995). Management's role is to make suitable adjustments to the structure to improve performance as conditions change – such as by increasing formality as the company grows. Others, such as GSK, introduce greater divisional autonomy to encourage creativity or responsiveness to local conditions.

Determinism is the view that an organisation's structure is determined by its environment.

John Child (1972, 1984) disagreed with this view, arguing that contingency theorists ignore the degree of **structural choice** which managers have. The process of organisational design is not only a technical, rational matter but one shaped by political processes. These political considerations (reflecting the values and interests of influential groups) are able to influence the structure that emerges for these reasons:

Structural choice approaches emphasise the scope management has for deciding the form of structure, irrespective of external conditions.

- The standards of performance against which organisational performance is assessed are not always rigorous. Some degree of under-performance caused by an inappropriate structure may be tolerated if there is sufficient 'slack' within the system.
- To some extent structures will reflect the interests of powerful groups within the organisation. They will try to secure structures that protect or advance their positions, even if this reduces performance to some degree.

Overall, writers of this view argue that contingency theory reduces managers almost to automatons, or puppets, able to exercise little influence on their own actions. In practice, they argue, managers do have choice over the structure they design. The contrasting ways in which leading grocery companies have used the Internet seems to support that view.

Retailers' response to the Internet

The Internet makes it possible for supermarket chains to create a website on which customers can order their shopping, which the company then delivers to their home. Sainsbury's responded by creating a new division to handle this business, with a separate management structure, warehouses and distribution system. Tesco chose to integrate its Internet shopping business with existing stores – staff pick the customer's Internet order from the shelves of a conventional store. Other chains, such as Somerfield and Morrisons do not (in 2007) offer an online service. So while the technology is available to all, only some have chosen to use it and they manage it with different structures.

Activity 10.6 Critical reflection – contingency or choice?

Recall some significant changes in the structure of your organisation. Try to establish the reasons for them, and whether they had the intended effects. Do those reasons tend to support the contingency or management choice perspectives?

Case questions 10.4

- Does the Oticon example support contingency or management choice approaches?
- Gather specific examples of management actions in the case which illustrate each theory.

Another consideration is that the direction of causality is not necessarily from strategy to structure. It is also possible that an organisation with a given structure finds that that makes it easier to embark on a particular strategy.

10.7 Learning organisations

Innovation is the main reason why many advocate the development of 'learning organisations', since organisations that operate in complex and dynamic environments can only be successful innovators if they develop the capacity to learn and respond quickly to changing circumstances. The term 'learning organisation' is used to describe an organisation that has developed the capacity to continuously learn, adapt and change. In a learning organisation the focus is on acquiring, sharing and using knowledge to encourage innovation.

According to Nonaka and Tageuchi (1995) the ability to create knowledge and solve problems has become a core competence in many businesses. In their view, everyone is a knowledge worker – someone dealing with customers, for example, quickly finds out about their likes and dislikes, and their view of the service. Because they are typically in low-paid jobs far from corporate headquarters, this valuable intelligence is overlooked.

Table 10.4

Features of a learning organisation

Feature	Explanation
A learning approach to strategy	The use of trials and experiments to improve understanding and generate improvements, and to modify strategic direction
Participative policy making	All members are involved in strategy formation, influencing decisions and values and addressing conflict
Informative	Information technology is used to make information available to everyone and to enable front-line staff to use their initiative
Formative accounting and control	Accounting, budgeting and reporting systems are designed to help people understand the operations of organisational finance
Internal exchange	Sections and departments think of themselves as customers and suppliers in an internal 'supply chain', learning from each other
Reward flexibility	A flexible and creative reward policy, with financial and non-financial rewards to meet individual needs and performance
Enabling structures	Organisation charts, structures and procedures are seen as temporary, and can be changed to meet task requirements
Boundary workers as environmental scanners	Everyone who has contact with customers, suppliers, clients and business partners is treated as a valuable information source
Inter-company learning	The organisation learns from other organisations through joint ventures, alliances and other information exchanges
A learning climate	The manager's primary task is to facilitate experimentation and learning in others, through questioning, feedback and support
Self-development opportunities for all	People are expected to take responsibility for their own learning, and facilities are made available, especially to 'front-line' staff

Source: Based on Pedler *et al.* (1997).

Table 10.4 (based on Pedler *et al.*, 1997) presents a view of the features of an ideal learning organisation – features to which managers can aspire. These features cluster under five headings, shown in Figure 10.11.

In a learning organisation members share information and collaborate on work activities wherever required – including across functional and hierarchical boundaries. Boundaries between units are either eliminated (as at Oticon) or are made as porous as possible to ensure that they do not block the flow of ideas and information. Learning organisations tend to emphasise team working, and employees operate with a high degree of autonomy to work as they think will best enhance performance. Rather than directing and controlling, managers act as facilitators, supporters and advocates – enabling their staff to work and learn to the greatest degree possible.

Learning depends on information, so there is an emphasis on sharing information amongst employees in a timely and open manner. This too depends on managers creat-

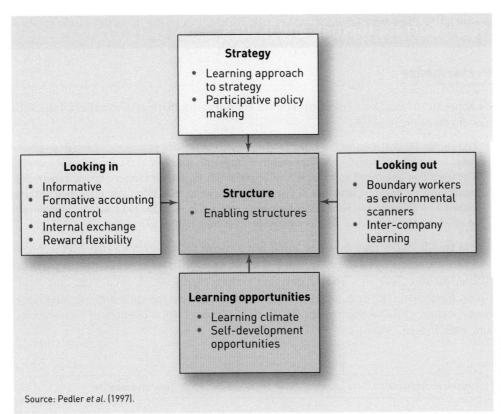

Figure 10.11

Clusters of learning organisation features

Source: Pedler *et al.* (1997).

ing a structure that encourages people to pass information in this way. Leadership is also important in the sense that one of their primary roles is to facilitate the creation of a shared vision for the business, and ensuring employees are enabled to work continually towards that. Finally the culture is one in which all agree on a shared vision and understand how all aspects of the organisation – its processes, activities, environment – are related to each other. There is a strong sense of community and mutual trust. People feel free to share ideas and communicate, share and experiment – able to learn without fear of criticism or punishment.

Argyris (1999) distinguished between single-loop and double-loop learning. The classic example of single-loop learning is the domestic thermostat which, by detecting temperature variations, takes action to correct deviations from a predetermined level. In single-loop learning, the system maintains performance at the set level, but is unable to learn that the temperature is set too high or too low. Learning how to learn involves double-loop learning – challenging assumptions, beliefs and norms, rather than accepting them and working within their limitations. In single-loop learning, the question is 'How can we better achieve that standard of performance?' In double-loop learning the question becomes: 'Is that an appropriate target in the first place?' In the context of developing the skills to cope more effectively with change, the aim is to enhance the ability of members to engage in double-loop learning.

10.8 Current themes and issues

Performance

Changes in the business environment are encouraging managers to experiment with new forms of organisation:

> During the 1990s the transition from an economy based on the processing of materials to one based on flows of information became ever more apparent, especially in the developed economies. The transition unfettered many aspects of organization from their former physical constraints, permitting, for example, activities in dispersed locations to be as effectively integrated as those gathered on the same site. Increased information intensity is today the fundamental development to which new organizational designs must respond. (Child, 2005, p. 27)

These trends encourage many to advocate a move from bureaucratic, hierarchical, mechanistic structures to smaller, more organic units with more emphasis on personal discretion and creativity. They argue that arrangements which encourage empowerment, flexibility, learning, innovation and teamwork are the only ways to survive in many sectors of the economy, and Table 10.5 contrasts some features of conventional and 'new' forms.

Table 10.5

Contrasts between conventional and new forms of organisation

Structural elements	Conventional organisation	New organisation
Initiative and authority	Centralised	Distributed
Control	Centralised, rule based	Decentralised, cultural
Basis of reward	Individual's position	Group performance
Roles	Specialised, defined	Fuzzy, loosely defined
Systems	To reduce uncertainty	To signal need for change
Coordination	By rules and procedures	By direct contact and IS
Networking	Only major stakeholders	Integral to the value chain
Outsourcing	Little	Much (non-core activities)
Alliances	Avoided	Extensive

The Oticon case in this chapter, and the examples of Semco (Chapter 14) and W.L. Gore (the Part 5 Case) illustrate how some managements have responded to these conditions.

However, these decentralised structures also expose the organisation to the danger that actions by managers in the autonomous units damages the business as a whole. BP has suffered because staff in its US subsidiary were careless about safety, and Siemens has exposed cases of bribery in one of its divisions. In both cases, the companies have decentralised decision making to local managers.

Responsibility

Many companies respond to competitive pressures by granting significant autonomy to local subsidiaries, or joining a network structure of suppliers contributing to the final product. This often enables them to outsource the production of many goods and services to poor regions of the world, which in turn is one of the main drivers of globalisation. These structural choices add to local incomes, and many governments compete for this work.

However many criticise the policies and behaviour of subsidiaries and suppliers – especially when they adopt labour and/or environmental standards that would be unacceptable in the companies' home country. The structural changes do not, in the view of their critics, absolve the organisation from responsibility for what happens in their suppliers. Nike suffered bad publicity for years after the conditions experienced by staff producing Nike products in Indonesia were revealed. The company responded by further structural measures, such as a requirement that all suppliers would be regularly monitored and inspected to ensure they met adequate labour standards. Coca-Cola is currently receiving similar criticism over the practices of some of its overseas joint ventures.

Reconciling demands for greater accountability and control with the performance benefits of decentralisation is a challenge for those shaping organisational structure.

Internationalisation

Internationalisation makes it possible for a firm to extend its operations into many other countries, and so be able to produce more cheaply by spreading costs over a larger volume. At the same time it may face pressure to vary the design of its products and services to suit local tastes. So managers may need to create a structure that is able to achieve both more standardisation and more flexibility within the same organisational structure.

The same process exposes a firm to greater external complexity, by expanding the number of organisations – customers, competitors, suppliers, governments, non-governmental organisations (NGOs) and many more – whose actions may be relevant to it. Many more events in the external world are relevant to the global firm, which needs to enter into more intensive dialogue with external parties. This greater external complexity has to be matched by suitable structural arrangements – more specialists in relevant fields, and more attempts to influence a wider constituency of stakeholders.

Summary

1 **Outline why the structure of an organisation affects performance**
   - People create structures to signify people's tasks and responsibilities towards the current objectives, and to provide incentives for work that supports them. The structure signals what people are expected to do within the organisation, and is intended to support actions that are in line with performance goals.

2 **Give examples of management choices about dividing and coordinating work, with their likely advantages and disadvantages**
   - Managers divide work to enable individuals and groups to specialise on a limited aspect of the whole, and then combine the work into related areas of activity. Task division needs to be accompanied by suitable methods of coordination.
   - Centralisation brings consistency and efficiency, but also the danger of being slow and out of touch with local conditions. People in decentralised units can respond quickly to local conditions but risk acting inconsistently.

- Functional forms allow people to specialise and develop expertise and are efficient; but they may be inward looking and prone to conflicting demands.

- Divisional forms allow focus on particular markets of customer groups, but can duplicate facilities thus adding to cost.

- Matrix forms try to balance the benefits of functional and divisional forms, but can again lead to conflicting priorities over resources.

- Networks of organisations enable companies to draw upon a wide range of expertise, but may involve additional management and coordination costs.

3 Compare the features of mechanistic and organic structures

- Mechanistic – people perform specialised tasks, hierarchical structure of control, knowledge located at top of hierarchy, vertical communication, loyalty and obedience valued.

- Organic – people contribute experience to common tasks, network structure of contacts, knowledge widely spread, horizontal communication, commitment to task goals more important than to superiors

4 Use the 'contingencies' believed to influence choice of structure to evaluate the suitability of a form for a given unit

- Strategy, environment, technology, age/size and political contingencies are believed to indicate the most suitable form, and the manager's role is to interpret these in relation to their circumstances.

5 Summarise the work of Woodward, Burns and Stalker, Lawrence and Lorsch and John Child, showing how they contributed to this area of management theory

- Woodward: appropriate structure depends on the type of production system ('technology') – unit, small batch, process.

- Burns and Stalker: appropriate structure depends on uncertainty of the organisation's environment – mechanistic in stable, organic in unstable.

- Lawrence and Lorsch: units within an organisation face different environmental demands, which implies that there will be both mechanistic and organic forms within the same organisation, raising new problems of coordination.

- John Child: contingency theory implies too great a degree of determinism – managers have greater degree of choice over structure than contingency theories implied.

6 Explain and illustrate the features of a learning organisation

- Learning organisations are those that have developed the capacity to continuously learn, adapt and change. This depends, according to Pedler *et al.* (1997), on evolving learning-friendly processes for looking in, looking out, learning opportunities, strategy and structure.

Review questions

1 Draw the organisation chart of a company or department that you know. From discussing it with people in one or more of the positions shown, compare their account of the structure with that shown on the chart.

2 What factors are encouraging companies to (a) centralise, (b) decentralise organisational functions?

3 Several forms of coordination are described. Select two that you have seen in operation and describe in detail how they work – and how well they work.

4 How does the structure of an organisation support or hinder its strategy?

5 Explain the difference between a mechanistic and an organic form of organisation.

6 Explain the term 'contingency approach' and give an example of each of the factors that influence the choice between mechanistic and organic structures.

7 If contingency approaches stress the influence of external factors on organisational structures, what is the role of management in designing organisational structures?

8 What is the main criticism of the contingency approach to organisation structure?

9 What examples can you find of organisational activities that correspond to some of the features of a learning organisation identified by Pedler *et al.* (1997)?

Concluding critical reflection

Think about the structure and culture of your company, or one with which you are familiar. Review the material in the chapter, and perhaps visit some of the websites identified. Then make notes on these questions:

● What examples of the themes discussed in this chapter are currently relevant to your company? What type of structure do you have – centralised or decentralised; functional or divisional, etc? Which of the methods of coordination identified do you typically use? What structural issues arise that are not mentioned here?

● In responding to issues of structure, what **assumptions** about the nature of organisations appear to guide your approach? If the business seems too centralised or too formal, why do managers take that approach? What are their assumptions, and are they correct?

● What factors in the **context** of the company appear to shape your approach to organising – what kind of environment are you working in, for example? To what extent does your structure involve networking with people from other organisations – and why is that?

● Have you seriously considered whether the present structure is right for the business? Do you regularly compare your structure with that in other companies to look for **alternatives**? How do they do it?

● What **limitations** can you identify in any of the ideas and theories presented here? For example how helpful is contingency theory to someone deciding whether to make the organisation more or less mechanistic?

Further reading

Woodward, J. (1965), *Industrial Organization: Theory and practice*, Oxford University Press, Oxford. Second edition 1980.

Burns, T. and Stalker, G.M. (1961), *The Management of Innovation*, Tavistock, London.

Lawrence, P. and Lorsch, J.W. (1967), *Organization and Environment*, Harvard Business School Press, Boston, MA.

These influential books are short and accessible accounts of the research process, and it would add to your understanding to read at least one of them in the original. The second edition of Woodward's book (1980) is even more useful, as it includes a commentary on her work by two later scholars.

Donaldson, L. (2001), *The Contingency Theory of Organizations*, Sage, London.

A comprehensive and up-to-date account by one of the leading scholars of contingency theory. Outlines the underlying principles of the theory and the controversies surrounding it, as well as offering valuable guidance on emerging research possibilities.

Rivard, S., Benoit, A.A., Patry, M., Pare, G. and Smith, H.A. (2004), *Information Technology and Organizational Transformation*, Elsevier/Butterworth-Heinemann, Oxford.

As well as being the source of some information on the Oticon case, this book includes other examples of the way in which information technology is enabling managers to develop new forms of organisation. A coherent theoretical structure makes the book a useful addition to this area.

Weblinks

These websites have appeared in the chapter:

www.oticon.com
www.baesystems.com
www.cadburyschweppes.com
www.philips.com
www.jnj.com
www.toyota.com
www.unilever.com
www.siemens.com
www.gsk.com

Visit two of the business sites in the list, and navigate to the pages dealing with corporate news, investor relations or 'our company'.

● What organisational structure issues can you identify that managers in the company are likely to be dealing with? Can you find any information about their likely culture from the website?

● What kind of environment are they likely to be working in, and how may that affect their structure and culture?

Annotated weblinks, multiple choice questions and other useful resources can be found on **www.pearsoned.co.uk/boddy**

Chapter 11
Human resource management

BMW, whose headquarters are in Munich, was established in 1916. By the late 1980s it employed some 54,000 people, was the seventh largest automobile manufacturing company in the world, and had subsidiaries in many European countries, New Zealand, South Africa, the United States, Canada and Japan. The company has continued to grow strongly, and by 2006 had 22 production sites in 12 countries on four continents. Management has chosen to focus on three premium segments of the international car market, with each of its three brands – BMW, Mini and Rolls-Royce – being the market leader in its segment.

In 2006 it delivered 1,138,000 automobiles to customers, an increase of 3.5 per cent over the previous year, and at the end of that year BMW employed 106,000 people. Western Europe is its major market, accounting for 59 per cent of all BMW cars sold (though China is an increasingly important market for luxury Rolls-Royce vehicles). BMW also manufactures motorcycles and has a joint venture with Rolls-Royce to produce aircraft jet engines.

BMW needs to be placed in the larger context of competitiveness in the German motor industry. A 1996 report by the German Motor Industry Association identified increased wage costs, higher non-wage labour costs, shorter agreed working time than many competitor countries and the continuing strength of the Deutschmark as factors undermining German competitiveness. These had lowered employment in the industry, stimulated investments abroad and encouraged companies to give high priority to improving labour productivity.

The strategy of focusing on the premium end of the car market is supported by its approach to HRM, which derives from, and is highly consistent with, the company's 'six inner values': communication, ethical behaviour to its staff, achievement and remuneration, independence, self-fulfilment and the pursuit of new

© BMW Group.

goals. This value-oriented policy dates back to the early 1980s, arising out of a scenario-planning exercise among senior managers. This underlying philosophy is important in shaping the design of any new BMW plant ('an open design' that advances the visual management of the process) and the process of introducing any new or reformed HRM practices. The company emphasises extensive consultation, information sharing and seeking to establish positive interrelationships between individual changes.

Source: *European Industrial Relations Review*, issue 27 (1996), pp. 32–34.

Case questions 11.1

- What issues concerning the management of people are likely to be raised in a group such as BMW that has rapidly expanded its production and distribution facilities?

- How have these issues been affected by domestic developments in Germany?

- How is increased competition likely to affect the people who work for BMW?

| Activity 11.1 | Defining HRM |

Before reading on, note down how you would define human resource management. What topics and issues do you think it deals with, and how does it relate to management as a whole? Keep your notes by you and compare them with the topics covered in the chapter as you work through it.

11.1   Introduction

BMW is a large and successful business in a growing area of the world economy – automobile production. Yet it faces competitive problems stemming in part from high employment costs in its German operations, and competition from new sources. Management is attempting to retain the company's position by diversifying the product range and the number of countries in which it manufactures. The company believes that its business strategy has to be matched by its HRM strategy – and is adapting this to bring about a better-trained and more flexible workforce suited to the new conditions.

Such activities are part of a wider change taking place in many western companies, as managers try to align the way they deal with people with broader company strategies. Management influences other people through both personal and institutionalised practices. It seeks to be less reactive, less focused on grievances and the routine aspects of personnel administration. Instead it wants to be more proactive in developing a labour force at all levels that will support the organisation's strategy. It also seeks greater coherence between the main aspects of HRM – especially in the areas of selection, development, appraisal and rewards.

Human resource management is the effective use of human resources in order to enhance organisational performance.

This chapter focuses on some institutionalised practices intended to influence the attitudes and actions of employees. These practices are commonly referred to as **human resource management** (HRM). HRM covers four main areas (Beer *et al.*, 1984):

1 employee influence (employee involvement in decision making);
2 work systems (work design, supervisory style);
3 human resource flow (recruitment, selection, training, development and deployment);
4 reward management (pay and other benefits).

Employee influence and work systems are discussed in Chapters 14 and 15. Consequently this chapter focuses on human resource flow and reward management. Human resource flow is concerned with the flow of individuals into and through the organisation – human resource planning, job analysis, employee recruitment and selection. Management designs these practices to help ensure that the organisation has the right people available to help it achieve its larger strategic objectives. Reward management aims to attract, retain and acknowledge employees.

The chapter begins by discussing the basic purpose and objectives of HRM, and the reasons for its greater prominence in management discussions. It then presents a range of current practices in the areas of human resource flow and reward management. HRM is more than a sum of policies and it is important to see how these fit together within a company's broad approach to HRM.

11.2 Emergence and meaning of HRM

HRM refers to all aspects of managing people in the workplace: this section outlines why the function has become an essential component in organisational success.

Historical development of HRM

The term 'human resource management' is relatively new, gaining prominence in US companies and business schools from about 1980 (Brewster, 1994). Traditionally, managers had tried to institutionalise the way they managed staff by creating personnel departments. Partly stimulated by the human relations model (Chapter 2), they believed they could ensure a committed staff by paying attention to employee grievances and looking after their welfare. Growing trade union power also led management to create departments that specialised in conducting negotiations and monitoring the agreements.

Such personnel management departments had limited power, and found it difficult to show that they contributed to organisational performance (Legge, 1978; Tyson and Fell, 1985). Senior management saw them as reactive, self-contained and obsessed with procedures, concerned with employee grievances, discipline and relations with trade unions. Their aim was to minimise costs and avoid disrupting production – they typically had little influence on strategic issues.

Changes in the business world led some observers to propose that issues concerned with managing people should have a higher profile, and especially that line managers should take more interest (Fombrun *et al.*, 1984). Guest (1987) attributes this change to:

- The emergence of more globally integrated markets in which competition is more extensive and severe. Product life cycles are shorter, with innovation, flexibility and quality often replacing price as the basis of competitive advantage.
- The economic success during the 1980s of countries that had given employee management a relatively high priority, such as Japan and (West) Germany.
- The highly publicised 'companies of excellence' literature (Peters and Waterman, 1982) which suggested that high-performance organisations were characterised by a strong commitment to HRM.
- Changes in the composition of the workforce, particularly the growth of a more educated staff.
- Declining trade union membership and collective bargaining in many economies.

Early advocates of HRM proposed that key themes would be integration, planning, a long-run orientation, proactive and strategic – believing that managing people more effectively would improve organisational performance. This reflected theories of sustained competitive advantage that emphasise the importance of firm-specific resources and competences that are difficult to imitate (Pfeffer, 1994). Table 11.1 highlights the policies that are likely to affect HRM and organisational outcomes.

Case questions 11.2

- When did HRM policies begin to be seriously developed at BMW?
- What led management to take this initiative?

Table 11.1

Policies for supporting HRM and organisational outcomes

Policies	Human resource outcomes	Organisational outcomes
Organisational and job design		High job performance
Managing change	Strategic planning and integration	High problem solving
Recruitment, selection and socialising	Commitment	Successful change
Appraisal, training and development	Flexibility/adaptability	Low turnover
Manpower flows through the organisation		Low absence
Reward systems	Quality	Low grievance level

Source: Guest (1987, p. 503).

Activity 11.2 **Assessing the changes needed**

An organisation has decided to pursue a quality-enhancement strategy in which team-working arrangements will be a central feature. It recognises the need to enhance its level of workforce training and to replace its individual performance-related pay arrangements. Are there any other changes in the HRM area that it needs to consider? (Use Table 11.1 to assist you.)

key ideas **Features of an organisation committed to HRM**

- The firm competes on the basis of quality and differentiation as well as price.
- Human resource considerations weigh heavily in corporate strategic decision making and governance processes. Employee interests are represented through the voice of human resource staff and/or senior executives consult with employee representatives on decisions that affect HRM policies and employee interests. In either case, employees are treated as legitimate stakeholders in the organisation.
- Investments in new hardware or physical technology are combined with the investments in human resources and changes in organisational practices required to realise the full potential benefits of these investments.
- The firm sustains a high level of investment in training, skills development and education, and personnel practices are designed to use these skills fully.
- Compensation and reward systems are internally equitable, competitive and linked to the long-term performance of the firm.
- Employment continuity and security are important priorities and values to be considered in all corporate decisions and policies.
- Workplace relations encourage flexibility in the organisation of work, empowerment of employees to solve problems, and high levels of trust amongst workers, supervisors and managers.
- Workers' rights to representation are acknowledged and respected. Union or other employee representatives are treated as joint partners in designing and overseeing innovations in labour and human resource practices.

Source: Kochan (1992).

The philosophy of HRM

HRM adopts a strategic perspective and contributes to organisational performance by managing staff effectively. The philosophy through which this is pursued aims for a win–win situation for both employer and employee; the organisation gains profitability and employees gain not only economically but also intrinsically through having a satisfying and challenging job. This assumes that employees and employer share the same goal – the long-term success of the organisation. This unitary view (see Chapter 2) is widely held by the management community (Geare *et al.*, 2006) and can be contrasted with the pluralist view, which recognises the legitimacy of different views – between trade unions, between managerial functions, and between managers and trade unions.

A distinction within HRM itself is between 'hard' and 'soft' approaches (Storey, 1992, pp. 26–28; Legge, 1995, pp. 66–67). The former takes a business-led perspective, while the latter sees people as valuable assets whose motivation, involvement and development should have priority. Another theme is that if HRM is to support performance, management needs to balance external and internal fit (Beer and Spector, 1985).

External fit

External fit refers to the link between business strategy and HRM strategy, whereby managers try to establish a close and consistent link between the two so that HRM practices encourage people to act in ways that support competitive strategy. Chapter 8 distinguished low-cost and differentiation strategies. These require different employee attitudes and behaviours, which HRM policies can encourage. Extensive training, team working and shop-floor problem-solving arrangements are likely in an organisation committed to a differentiation strategy.

External fit is when there is a close and consistent relationship between an organisation's competitive strategy and its HRM strategy.

Such HRM practices are unlikely in an organisation that follows a low-cost strategy, paying low wages to a casual labour force. A review by Greer (2001) suggested that there is a greater performance impact when HRM policy matches strategy. The study also showed that some HRM practices (cognitive tests in selection, staffing selectivity and training) increase performance in almost any setting.

Case questions 11.3

- What is your image of BMW cars? What words would you use to describe them?
- In order to meet the image you expect, what kind of behaviour would you expect of employees?
- What HRM practices will encourage/discourage that behaviour?

Activity 11.3 Comparing HRM policies

List the major differences in HRM policies that you would expect to observe between two organisations, one pursuing a low-cost strategy and the other a quality enhancement strategy. (Use the Key Ideas on p. 356 to assist you.)

Internal fit

Organisations also benefit if their HRM policies are internally consistent, in the sense that individual measures complement and reinforce each other by sending *consistent* signals to the workforce. An organisation that encourages team working can support this through the payment system. It is likely to fail if this rewards people for their individual contribution, as this will encourage competition rather than cooperation. Achieving **internal fit** requires HRM professionals to be familiar with both HRM and business issues. Research at the University of Michigan highlighted five such HRM competency domains (Becker *et al.*, 2001, pp. 158–161):

Internal fit is when the various components of the HRM strategy support each other and consistently encourage certain attitudes and behaviour.

1 knowledge of the business
2 delivery of HR practices
3 management of change
4 management of culture
5 personal credibility.

This section has introduced and defined the field of HRM and highlighted the strategic nature of this discipline and ways in which it contributes to wider organisational performance. The next deals with human resource planning.

11.3 Human resource planning

Human resource planning focuses on the size and nature of the workforce required to fulfil the strategy. It typically begins with a broad forecast of the number and type of employees necessary, followed by a more precise analysis to ascertain skills and competencies required of recruits. That informs recruitment and selection.

Forecasting

In the 1960s and 1970s (at a time of labour shortage) researchers developed techniques for forecasting the demand and supply of labour, and practitioners still value workforce planning (HR Focus, 2006). Planners expected the demand for labour to follow from the organisation's business plan, as an estimate of the numbers and types of employees needed to meet financial and output objectives. The ability to have the staff likely to be required in each category depends on staff in post at the beginning of the planning period adjusted for (a) the outflow of staff over the planning period (e.g. retirements, dismissal, resignations), (b) the inflow of staff during the planning period (i.e. new recruits), and (c) the internal movement of staff between job categories (e.g. promotions). The two strands are:

1 *Forecasting human resource demands:* refers to the number of staff required to meet expected needs.
2 *Forecasting human resource supplies:* examines skills required for the portfolio of jobs and analyses whether current staff can meet these demands.

Table 11.2 presents some forecasting techniques.

Table 11.2

Forecasting techniques

Forecasting human resource demands		
Judgemental forecasting	Delphi technique	Involves obtaining independent estimates of future staffing needs through successive distribution of questionnaires to various levels of management. The expectation is that four or five iterations should produce a convergence in the estimates.
Statistical projection	Simple linear regression	A statistical calculation in which projected future demand is based on a past relationship between the organisation's employment level and a variable such as the level of sales.
Forecasting human resource supplies		
Judgemental forecasting	**Succession planning**	This involves developing charts indicating present jobholders and the names of possible replacements.
Statistical projection	Markov matrix analysis	This approach can model or simulate human resource flows by examining the rates of movement between job categories over time.

Succession planning is the use of a deliberate process to ensure that staff are developed who are able to replace senior management as required.

A major limitation of such planning models is the uncertainty of the business environment that, paradoxically, limits the usefulness of comprehensive planning, since forecasts will be inaccurate and of limited value. This has led to changes in the practice of human resource planning, namely reduced planning horizons, more line management involvement, more qualitative forecasting techniques and more attention to the process, as opposed to the outcomes, of planning.

Monitoring human resource planning

management in practice

Staff in a health board drew up a strategic HRM plan to ensure an adequate supply of suitably trained and qualified technical support staff to fill a new role within an acute hospital. Unfortunately, a failure to monitor the implementation of the plan resulted in the board being unaware of changes in external training provision for these staff. The result was that the staff being trained were unable to assume their responsibilities at the planned time, which obliged other staff to provide cover. That led to temporary staff shortages in their areas.

Source: Interview with manager.

11.4 Job analysis

Job analysis identifies the principal constituents of a role, including skills and level of responsibility. It typically leads to a written job description that guides selection, training and performance appraisal.

Issues to consider in job analysis include:

Job analysis is the process of determining the characteristics of an area of work according to a prescribed set of dimensions.

- How is the data for the job description collected? Possibilities include interviewing the job incumbent, observing people doing the job, and distributing questionnaires.
- Who should collect this information or data? Should it be the job incumbent, the supervisor or an internal or external specialist?
- How should the job information be structured and laid out?

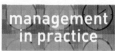
management in practice The elements of a job description

A consultancy firm recently advised a financial services business on how to devise job descriptions. Their job description form had ten sections:

- job title
- job purpose
- job dimensions (e.g. responsibilities for managing budgets or staff
- organisation chart (who reports to you and who you report to)
- role of your department
- key result areas (end results of your job)
- assignment and review of work (process of work allocation and monitoring)
- communication and working relationships (internal and external)
- most challenging part of your job
- sign off by job holder and immediate boss.

Source: Interview with manager.

The process aims to describe the purpose of a job, its major duties and activities, the conditions under which it is performed and the necessary knowledge, skills and abilities. Jobs are broken into *elements* (such as those in the Management in Practice feature) that can then be rated on dimensions such as extent of use, importance, amount of time involved and frequency. Job analysis is made difficult by the volume and complexity of data (McEntire *et al.*, 2006) and web-based job analysis programmes have been created to solve this (Reiter-Palmon *et al.*, 2006).

management in practice Job analysis in financial services

The job description in the previous box was created through a job analysis that covered three areas:

1 job know-how (technical knowledge/skills/experience required for fully acceptable job performance);
2 range of problem-solving activity (with/without direct supervision);
3 accountability (answerable for actions and consequences of actions).

The consultants used these areas to analyse all jobs in the organisation – from the CEO downwards.

Source: Interview with manager.

Competencies

Competencies refer to knowledge, skills, ability and other personal characteristics for good performance of a specific job.

Rather than thinking about jobs as a set of tasks HRM practitioners now aim to identify and develop the **competencies** an individual requires to meet the job requirements (Kalb *et al.*, 2006). The subtle change reflects the perceived need for organisations to be flexible and responsive. The use of competencies enables the flexible use of employee skills, in that they can adapt to new requirements rather than only being able to perform a prescribed set of tasks.

Competencies for a senior team

Consultants developed a competency framework for the senior team of a large public sector organisation. The main competencies identified were:

- people leadership (e.g. influences others to gain commitment);
- personal style (e.g. deals with people in an open, honest and ethical manner);
- strategic management and thinking (e.g. makes a decision and takes action); and
- action oriented (e.g. thinks about business opportunities in a positive manner).

These competencies were assessed by performance criteria in the formal appraisal system (ranking each manager on a scale from 'exceptional' to 'weak').

Source: Interview with manager.

Team working and job analysis

Moves towards team working also have implications for job analysis:

> [In] a team situation individual tasks may be quite fluid. Further, team effectiveness often asks for team members to develop a wide variety of skills so that they are capable of providing an assortment of inputs. Thus cross-training is becoming more common and narrow job descriptions are giving way to individual contributions being driven by dynamic relationships within the team. The fluidity of tasks and the flux of individual inputs as a function of interdependency on the inputs of other team members means that a snapshot of the work activities for individual employees may be difficult to take and would likely soon be limiting and out of date in a team environment. Thus, the traditional job analysis assumption of continuing tasks for individuals appears to be incorrect when in team situations. (Academy of Management, 1996, p. 11)

The BMW case illustrates the introduction of team working.

BMW – the case continues – new work structures   www.bmwgroup.com

CASE STUDY

In response to increased competition, market over capacity and lower working hours in Germany (a 35-hour week in the metal industries was agreed from October 1995), BMW sought more efficient working practices. In 1995 it introduced new forms of work organisation, arranging employees into self-managing groups (each with 8–15 workers), with a high degree of autonomy but with clearly defined tasks. Members of the group decide upon each individual's responsibility and the rotation of jobs, as well as making suggestions and decisions about product improvement.

Each group elects a spokesperson to coordinate activities and to represent them, though they have no power to give orders or take disciplinary action.

Supervisors remain as the group's immediate superior in technical and disciplinary matters, but play more of an advisory/facilitating role. The supervisor is responsible for proposing and agreeing objectives, presenting progress figures, helping progress continuous improvements and ensuring that group members improve their qualifications. The company has to ensure that adequate training is available, goals are agreed upon and results circulated. Improved product quality and job satisfaction are the aims, leading in turn to greater productivity. BMW was hoping for a 4 per cent annual increase in productivity, compared with 2 per cent previously.

Source: *European Industrial Relations Review*, issue 271 (1996), pp. 23–24. ▶

Case questions 11.4

● How would the introduction of team working have helped to improve the external fit between HRM and broader strategy?

● To achieve internal fit, what other changes will BMW need to make to support team working?

Job analysis aims to produce a comprehensive and accurate job description, to inform recruitment and selection.

11.5 Recruitment and selection

The goal of recruitment is to produce a good pool of applicants and select the best of these to fit the job. The selection process aims to minimise (a) *false positive errors*, whereby the selection process predicts success in the job for an applicant, who is therefore hired, but who fails and (b) *false negative errors*, whereby an applicant who would have succeeded in the job is rejected because the process predicted failure. As the costs of the latter are not directly experienced by the organisation managers are more concerned about the former. Selecting the wrong person can cost the organisation dearly and create serious long-term problems (Geerlings and van Veen, 2006).

Studies of the selection process have mainly centred on the **validity** of the process, in the sense of its ability to predict future performance, though additional criteria include fairness and cost. The three most commonly used techniques are interviews, selection tests and assessment centres.

Validity occurs when there is a statistically significant relationship between a predictor (such as a selection test score) and measures of on-the-job performance.

Interviews

Management traditionally relies on application forms, references and interviews for selecting employees. The interview remains popular as it has low direct costs and can be used for most jobs, despite research showing it has low validity (Robertson, 1996; Newell and Tansley, 2001), especially in group interviews (Tran and Blackman, 2006). Interviewer ratings correlate poorly with measures of subsequent performance of the candidates hired (i.e. they generate too many false positive errors). Many interviewers are not good at seeking, receiving and processing the amount and quality of information needed for an informed decision. Problems with the interview as a selection device are:

● decisions are made too quickly;
● information obtained early in the interview has a disproportionate influence;
● interviewers compare applicants with an idealised stereotype;
● appearance and non-verbal behaviour strongly shape decisions;
● interviewers are poorly prepared and ask too many questions of limited value.

Aware of these difficulties, organisations are systematically training people in interview techniques. Others use standard schedules in which all applicants are asked the same questions in roughly the same order. There is evidence that structured interviews, such as 'situational' or 'behavioural' approaches, have a higher predictive validity than

Activity 11.4 Interviewing interviewees

Arrange to talk to some friends or colleagues who have recently been interviewed for jobs. Ask them to describe the overall process and to identify any features or aspects of the experience that they particularly liked or disliked. Ideally you should talk to at least one person who was offered the job and to one who was not.

As background work for this exercise, compile a checklist of the key features of 'good practice' interviews that should help inform the way you ask questions. A useful reference here is Rebecca Corfield's (1999) *Successful Interview Skills*. As well as practising your own interviewing skills you should compare the experience of the interviewees with best practice techniques.

unstructured ones (Heffcutt and Arthur, 1994). The membership of interview panels is also changing – organisations using teamwork often include team members in the process.

Selection tests

The weaknesses of the interview method and the changing nature of jobs has encouraged the use of more formal methods – especially personality tests. Some organisational psychologists question their accuracy and value on the grounds that:

- they should only be used and interpreted by qualified and approved experts;
- candidates can give the answers they think the tester is looking for;
- an individual's personality may vary with circumstances;
- good performers in the same job may have different personalities.

Table 11.3 illustrates this technique with the profile of a service manager.

> A **selection test** is a sample of attributes obtained under standardised conditions that applies specific scoring rules to obtain quantitative information for those attributes which the test is designed to measure.

Table 11.3

Selected items from the personality profile of a service manager

Scale description (1)	Score 1 to 10	Scale description (10)
Supportive	4	Dominant
Inconsiderate	9	Considerate
Diffident	6	Self-assured
Easygoing	5	Alert
Conventional	7	Open minded
Action oriented	4	Reflective
People minded	4	Technically minded
Detail averse	7	Precise
Content	7	Ambitious
Balanced	5	Determined
Hesitant	5	Decisive
Expressive	8	Resilient

There is some concern that the misuse of tests may breach equal opportunities legislation, and there is the potential problem of managing employee expectations. One long-standing criticism of the employee selection process is that the organisation is 'over-sold' to those hired. If employees' expectations are then not met on the job they are likely to leave. There is a danger of creating a sense of an elite labour force that will be well looked after when 2000 applicants are reduced to fewer than 300 who are offered a job. Extensive testing risks adding to the 'over-sell' problem.

Online psychometric testing has advantages of speed and cost, but also brings problems:

- People with less acute vision may find a small font difficult to read.
- Complexity of instructions may disadvantage those who rarely use the Internet.
- Timed tests may be unfair unless they take account of slow Internet servers.
- Cheating is possible if the test is delivered online and unsupervised (Florance, 2006).

Assessment centres

Assessment centres are multi-exercise programmes designed to identify the recruitment and promotion potential of personnel.

Assessment centres use many systematic tests and several assessors to create a comprehensive picture of a candidate's abilities and potential (Melancon and Williams, 2006; Newell, 2006). They appear to have higher validity than interviews, since using many tests and several assessors simulates more closely what the job will involve. Other commentators offer a more critical explanation of their relatively high validity, namely that they represent a self-fulfilling prophecy. Knowing that someone has succeeded in an assessment centre, their managers and colleagues ensure that the person does well. Other concerns include:

- their high cost;
- their tendency to generate a huge amount of paper;
- the ethical and practical problems of providing feedback to individuals whose performance was not impressive;
- the possibility of producing 'clones' who are very similar to the present job incumbents, which may not be appropriate in rapidly changing circumstances.

Online recruitment can save time and money in the first stages of shortlisting and interviewing candidates: in one survey two-thirds of the sample used e-recruitment in 2005 with 84 per cent saying that they have made greater use of it in the last three years (CIPD, 2006).

Do individuals fit the organisation?

This essentially narrow, technical task of achieving an 'individual employee/individual job fit' has been questioned by some who stress the strategic nature of HRM. For instance, some studies of culture change programmes have emphasised the need to select employees who fit the larger direction of change in the organisation. A specific instance of change along these lines is the attempt to identify the competencies required of people who will work well in multi-disciplinary teams (West and Allen, 1997). One view is that individuals should be hired for the organisation, not the job. Bowen *et al.* (1996) write:

> Diverse firms ... are using the approach to build cultures that rely heavily on self-motivated, committed people for corporate success. New, often expensive, hiring practices are changing the traditional selection model. An organisational analysis supplements a job analysis, and personality attributes are screened in addition to skills, knowledge and abilities. (p. 139)

The *organisational* analysis mentioned here is concerned with the leading components of the larger work *context*, such as the longer-term goals and values of the organisation, rather than simply the content of the individual job.

Hiring for the organisation rather than the job

Potential benefits
- more favourable employee attitudes (e.g. greater organisational commitment)
- more desirable individual behaviours (e.g. lower absence and turnover)
- reinforcement of organisational design (e.g. support for desired organisational culture).

Potential problems
- greater investment of resources in the hiring process
- relatively undeveloped and unproven supporting selection technology
- individual stress
- may be difficult to use the full model where pay-offs are greatest
- lack of organisational adaptation.

Source: Bowen *et al.* (1996, p.146).

Case questions 11.5
- In what ways are developments in BMW already encouraging a 'hire for the organisation, not for the job' approach?
- What implications will that have for achieving internal fit in the company's HRM policies?

11.6   Reward management

Table 11.4 summarises some common methods of reward management.

Table 11.4

Approaches to reward management

Type of system	Explanation
Time rate	Reward is related to the number of hours worked
Payment by results	Reward is related to quantity of output
Skill-based pay	Reward is based on the level of knowledge and skills an employee has
Performance-related pay	Reward is based upon individual performance in relation to agreed objectives
Flexible benefits packages	Reward is based upon selection of benefits (for example, health care or company car) to suit individuals' preferences and lifestyles.

Changes in reward management aim to align employer and employee objectives, by influencing action in line with organisational goals (Daniels *et al.*, 2006). There has also been a shift towards flexible and variable reward systems, driven by the search for greater employment flexibility. Trends include:

● a shift from collectively bargained pay towards more individual performance or skills-driven systems;
● linking pay systems more directly to business strategy and organisational goals;
● emphasising non-pay items, such as life assurance and childcare vouchers;
● flexible pay components and individualised reward packages.

Developments in pay policies are also linked to changes in work organisation, and the BMW case illustrates both.

BMW – the case continues – changes to reward structures www.bmwgroup.com

CASE STUDY

The new work structures, with their emphasis on multi-skilled workers, quality objectives and the individual's contribution to group performance, were accompanied by new payment arrangements. A bonus system applied to all 36,000 production employees who operated with defined performance targets.

Basic remuneration consists of the minimum pay rate agreed in the metalworking industry collective agreement plus a 10 per cent BMW supplement. The previous six wage groups were expanded to nine, allowing finer gradations based on the criteria of function, difficulty and variety of activities, and scope for decision making. If a worker regularly performed a higher value activity they could move to a higher group.

On top of the basic remuneration a 25 per cent *bonus* was paid to all employees for meeting prearranged production quotas. Employees in each group were consulted and invited to comment on whether the quotas were realistic and achievable.

Employees could also earn extra pay through a *personal supplement*, payable for an individual's contribution to group results. Expectations and goals were agreed between the employee and the supervisor. An individual's contribution to the group was discussed

every year and this assessment determined the personal supplement received.

In early 2001 new pay agreements emphasising flexible working arrangements and performance-related pay were introduced. In the new Hams Hall plant in the United Kingdom the two-year deal contains a performance bonus that will deliver up to 5 per cent of production workers' annual pay, calculated individually rather than on the site's performance. A similar deal was initially rejected by workers at the Cowley plant, as workers and unions opposed the flexible working arrangements that included an extended working week.

Source: *European Industrial Relations Review*, issue 271 (1996), p. 24; *Financial Times*, 26 January 2001; *The Times*, 8 February 2001.

Case questions 11.6

● What external factors may have prompted this review of the payment system at BMW?
● How would it affect the management of the appraisal system?
● What demands would it make on the management information system (see Chapter 12)?

Performance-related pay involves the explicit link of financial reward to performance and contributions to the achievement of organisational objectives.

Performance-related pay

Performance-related pay aims to link a human resource flow activity (performance appraisal) with reward, which brings the risk of expecting the appraisal process to achieve too many objectives. Some organisations have used such arrangements for many years and report positive effects on both individual and organisational performance. At others, the results of performance-related pay have been less impressive. Either there has been little positive impact on organisational performance or the arrangements have been counter-productive for other reasons (Beer and Cannon, 2004). Research by Lawson (2000) noted:

> the amount of work being undertaken in organisations to modify, change and improve individual performance pay schemes indicates a trend of unhappiness with them. In short, the record of performance-related pay arrangements has been highly variable (p. 315).

Possible reasons for these difficulties include:

- Introducing the new pay arrangements without adequate discussion, consultation and explanation.
- Performance-related pay fits the circumstances of some organisations better than others: it is unlikely to work where employees and managers do not trust each other.
- Performance-related pay has multiple goals, not all of which can be achieved by the one set of arrangements. It may demonstrate to staff that performance affects pay, but inhibit cooperation between them.

Performance-related pay: avoiding conflict

management in practice

In this voluntary organisation the annual appraisal system was used as the basis for determining a performance-related payment that could be quite substantial in size. In practice, however, managers were overwhelmingly concerned not to risk demotivating their staff, or to risk disrupting good working relationships. As a result the performance appraisal scores always tended to be 'on the overly generous side', which resulted in a substantial increase in the annual wage bill for the organisation with no obvious enhancement in terms of employee motivation, effort or resulting improvements in organisational performance.

Source: Interview with manager.

Activity 11.5 Deciding when performance-related pay is appropriate

Identify some of the key features of an organisation where performance-related pay arrangements are likely to be appropriate.

While many public sector organisations have begun to use performance-related pay, the initiatives have encountered difficulties including:

- a lack of differentiation in performance ratings;
- a clustering of staff at the top of the salary range in merit pay schemes where they are no longer eligible for merit increments;
- relatively low levels of funding that make schemes highly competitive;
- reductions in the size of bonuses paid.

Flexible reward systems

More flexible mechanisms for calculating pay have become popular, under labels such as cafeteria benefits, flexible benefits and package compensation. Essentially remuneration is calculated within an overall compensation package that may include life insurance, medical care or a company car.

Benefits for the employer include aligning reward strategy with both HRM and business strategies; ensuring benefits match the requirements of an increasingly diverse workforce; value for money; and the creation of an employer brand. This individualistic approach to remuneration can however be costly and complicated (Benders *et al.*, 2006). For the employee a choice of benefits means they can balance work–life issues more successfully.

BMW – the case continues – outcomes of team working www.bmwgroup.com

CASE STUDY

Unions at the Cowley plant had initially rejected proposals for flexible working, but in 2002 it won the CIPD People Management Award where it was reported:

with self-directed teamworking, they have managed to do what the British and Japanese could not do at Cowley. A decade ago, no one would have thought that they had a chance of delivering high performance, but it seems they've succeeded against all the odds. The judges were impressed with the emphasis on unlocking the creativity of shopfloor operators. We had the sense that teams were really shaping the self-directed teamwork, and this is changing the business from the inside out. (*People Management*, 6 November 2002, p. 29)

What had produced such a dramatic change in such a short period of time? Individual HR changes need to be seen in the context of more than £230 million invested since 2000 to refit and upgrade the plant, which has underpinned a sense of enhanced employment security (employee numbers had risen from 2500 to 4500 to allow a seven-day operation, although many are temporary workers). This major organisational change programme aimed to upgrade the site to world-class standards and to launch a new vehicle (the Mini).

One high-profile HRM initiative within this larger change was the establishment of hundreds of self-directed teams of 8–15 employees right across the site. These were extensively trained, given the authority to tackle production problems, and to rotate tasks among members. Management viewed this as a major instrument of cultural change, seeking to embed the following attributes into the culture: working in groups; management performance; strengthened identity; information/communication; integration of support functions; competence assessment training; standardised processes; reward management.

The second HRM initiative was to aim for continuous process improvement via an employee suggestion scheme in which individual bonus payments are given in return for cost savings and production improvement suggestions. Workers must come up with an average of three suggestions and save £800 each to qualify for the full £260 annual bonus.

How did these initiatives work in practice? Some statistics:

- In 2002, production targets were exceeded by more than 60 per cent.
- The programme of continuous process improvement saved £10.5 million in the two years 2002–2003.
- In 2003 there were 14,333 employee suggestions of which 11,064 (80 per cent) were implemented.

Source: *FT Intelligence*, 19 March 2003; *People Management*, 6 November 2003.

Case questions 11.7

- In light of the idea of internal fit, what would you conclude about these changes?
- What theories of motivation (Chapter 15) could explain these results?
- How might you investigate whether the 'Hawthorne effect' has influenced results?

11.7 Managing diversity

The workforce in advanced industrialised economies is diverse, and the management challenge is to match that diversity within their organisation. This is both for legal compliance and to gain possible business advantage from this environmental change – there is indeed a 'business case' for diversity.

Gender and ethnic origin are but two dimensions of diversity. Anti-discrimination legislation has largely concentrated on demographic or visible diversity spreading beyond the early locus of gender and race to increasingly embrace other dimensions such as disability, age and sexual orientation.

Gender segregation

Although the number of women in the workforce has increased, they do not have equal access to all occupations. Many tasks are still predominantly male or female occupations. For example, women are much more likely than men to work as teachers, nurses or librarians than as doctors, judges or chartered accountants. They often do routine office work and shop work, but rarely do what is defined as skilled manual work. The reverse is true for men.

Gender segregation is both horizontal and vertical. Horizontal segregation occurs where men and women are associated with different types of jobs. In the UK Labour Force Survey statistics relating to gender and occupation show that women provided 79 per cent of staff in health and social work, and 73 per cent of staff in education: but only 24 per cent in transport and 10 per cent in construction (Equal Opportunities Commission, 2006). Women in management roles also tend to be concentrated in certain areas – principally in HRM and other staff functions, rather than in line functions. In 2005 women in full-time work earned about 17 per cent less than men.

If women are confined to lower occupational positions and to less responsible work they will have fewer opportunities for professional growth and promotion. This in turn distances them from positions of power and the exercise of formal authority. This results in vertical segregation – men in the higher ranks of an organisation and women in the lower. A study of the proportion of women in senior management positions in large UK companies showed that of the 1048 directors of the 100 largest UK companies by market value, only 58, less than 7 per cent, were women (Linstead *et al.*, 2004, p. 59). Alvesson and Billing (2000) concluded that in Sweden gender division of labour was as pronounced as in most western countries – 'in most high-level jobs male over-representation is very strong. Only about 10–15 per cent of higher middle and senior managers and seven per cent of all professors are women' (p. 4).

Gender in management

Another question is whether men and women differ in the way they interpret and perform the management role. Researchers have focused on identifying distinctive characteristics of 'masculine' and 'feminine' management styles. Rosener (1997) found that male managers tended to adopt what she termed a transactional style. This uses the principle of exchange as the dominant way of managing – giving rewards for things done well, and punishing failure. Male respondents tended to rely mainly on their positional authority – the status conferred on them by their formal role to influence others. Women tended to use a relational style, motivating staff by persuasion, encouragement and using personal qualities rather than position: they generally try to make staff feel good about themselves. She believes that this female model of leadership is more suited to modern, turbulent conditions than the command and control styles typical of the male managers in her research.

Other studies have found similar differences in the styles of women – Helgesen (1995), for example, suggesting that women are better at developing cooperation, creativity and intuition than men. She also found that women prefer to manage through relationships rather than by their place in the hierarchy, and claims that they listen and empathise more than men. However, those in a position to make promotion decisions may see it differently, and use the supposedly masculine nature of organisational work to prevent women reaching senior positions (Knights and Murray, 1994). Managers who emphasise the value of hard analytical skills above soft interpersonal skills support, perhaps unwittingly, the progression of men and discourage that of women. Stressing competitiveness, tension and long unsocial working hours has a similar effect. It drives some women away from senior positions owing to domestic responsibilities that continue to be primarily theirs.

The business case for a diverse workforce

The increasing scope of anti-discrimination legislation may have reduced discrimination, but alongside that is a more proactive stance, which stresses the business case for diversity – that the business will gain from promoting diversity (Anderson and Metcalfe, 2003, p. lx) by:

● gaining access to a wider range of individual strengths, experiences and perspectives;
● a greater understanding of the diverse groups of potential and existing customers represented within a workforce;
● better communication with these diverse groups of potential and existing customers.

Kochan *et al.* (2003) state the business case as follows:

> Diversity is a reality in labour markets and customer markets today. To be successful in working with and gaining value from this diversity requires a sustained, systematic approach and long-term commitment. Success is facilitated by a perspective that considers diversity to be an opportunity for everyone in an organisation to learn from each other how better to accomplish their work and an occasion that requires a supportive and co-operative organisational culture as well as group leadership and process skills that can facilitate effective group functioning. Organisations that invest their resource are taking advantage of the opportunities that diversity offers and should outperform those that fail to make such investments. (p. 18)

 **Calls for more diversity in the Civil Service**

Diversity initiatives have been high on the agenda in the UK Civil Service; the chairman of the Inland Revenue (now HM Revenue and Customs), Sir Nicholas Montagu, commenting 'nothing less makes moral, business and social sense'. Diversity targets set in 2000 stated that by 2004–2005, 35 per cent of senior civil servant jobs should be held by women (from the current level of 26 per cent). In addition, the number of senior posts held by individuals from ethnic minorities should be increased from 2.8 per cent to 3.2 per cent and 1.7 per cent to 3 per cent for employees with disabilities. Nonetheless, inclusiveness goes beyond merely employment figures and 'diversity is about creating a culture change where people feel valued and where talents are going to be fully utilised'. As a consequence of this broader cultural challenge, the public sector has expended time, money and energy on training, for example on the topics of communication, leadership and effective networking.

Source: *Financial Times*, 10 May 2004.

BMW – the case continues – 'today for tomorrow'   C A S E   S T U D Y
www.bmwgroup.com

The BMW group are aware of demographic changes in the workforce where the birth rate in many western countries has consistently been lower than the number of deaths, while life expectancy has continued to rise. This ageing workforce affects nations' social security systems and businesses. BMW has formed a project, 'Today for Tomorrow', to help the group adapt to changing demographics, through five areas:

1 design of the working environment: ergonomically designed work stations in offices and manufacturing to help avoid physical strain;
2 health management and preventive health care: gyms and fitness courses at all plant locations;
3 needs-based retirement models: flexible retirement packages that allow individuals to retire early or continue after the age of 65;
4 qualifications and skills: the increasing importance of lifelong learning;

5 communications: increase awareness of social and corporate changes amongst managers and associates.

Source: Company website.

Case questions 11.8
- What benefits might BMW gain from a higher proportion of older workers?
- What do you think are the problems associated with an older workforce?
- How might human resource practices change as a result of an older workforce?

Current themes and issues

Performance

A frequent challenge which those advocating HRM practices lay down is whether they support organisational performance. Some argue that the quantity and quality of evidence supporting a strong, positive relationship between HRM and organisational performance is weak and ambiguous (Legge, 1995; Zheng *et al.*, 2006).

Others point to more positive studies, such as that by Huselid (1995). This survey of around 1000 firms in the United States reported a strong relationship between a set of HRM practices and measures of performance such as employee turnover, productivity and financial performance. Similarly, Boselie and Dietz's (2003) review concluded that practices related to employee development and training, empowerment, information sharing and reward systems yielded tangible returns for employers, a view supported by West *et al.* (2006).

However, a common theme in all reviews is that organisations can only obtain strategically important benefits if they take a strategic orientation towards HRM, in the sense of ensuring a high degree of external and internal fit.

Responsibility

Winstanley and Woodall (2000) point out that,

> until very recently, the field of business ethics was not preoccupied with issues relating to the ethical management of employees ... The main debates in business ethics have centred round the social responsibility of business in relations with clients and the environment. (p. 5)

They suggest that raising ethical awareness and sensitivity in relation to HRM is a legitimate reference point alongside perspectives which stress the business case for HRM, together with notions of strategic fit and best practice. They point out that the Harvard analytical framework for HRM (Beer *et al.*, 1984) was one of the earliest to suggest that HRM ought to be concerned with individual and social well-being as well as organisational well-being. They claim that most HRM research and practice has focused on the business case, and has almost wholly ignored the ethical dimension. Reasons for redressing the balance include:

● enlightened self-interest – the view that business will be more successful if it pays attention to ethical issues as this will enhance its reputation with customers and improve employee motivation;

● the Friedmanite view (see Chapter 5) is not dominant in not-for-profit organisations, which includes much of the public sector, social business, NGOs and the voluntary sector;

● the view that business organisations exist to serve human and social needs, not the other way round.

Several themes associated with HRM practices have an ethical dimension. Flexibility in pay systems and employment contracts, together with high performance work practices, raise ethical questions through their effect on employee working hours, stress, and work–life balance. Performance measurement systems incorporating stretch targets and close surveillance and control raise questions about an employer's duty of care, and about individual rights to autonomy, privacy and self-esteem (Francis and Keegan, 2006).

Internationalisation

Both Sparrow *et al.* (2004) and Tayeb (2005) examine the significance of internationalisation for HRM since, as with domestic firms, there is a close connection between strategy and HRM. An international strategy needs to be supported by HRM practices that take account of the international dimensions of employee influence, work systems, human resource flows and reward management.

Companies operating internationally face the dilemma of balancing a desire for closer regional or global integration of HRM practices with the need to make these responsive to probably contradictory local demands. Their workforce will include different national cultures, working physically distant from each other. They will also be working in different management systems, which, as Chapter 4 showed, have implications not only for the overall structure and management of business enterprises, but for the rights and responsibilities of employees.

How a company chooses to go international will affect the issues that arise – internationalising through a joint venture with a local business raises different HRM issues from creating a wholly owned subsidiary. A company that seeks to achieve a tight integration between its global businesses, including HRM policies, will face different issues from one which adopts a looser approach, leaving more autonomy to globally dispersed units. Sparrow *et al.* (2004) identify four areas that have attracted the attention of researchers and practitioners:

1 the structures adopted by international companies;
2 differences between domestic and international HRM – with the latter being of greater complexity;
3 how MNCs approach the staffing and management of their subsidiaries; and
4 factors that influence the choice consistency of HRM practice and adapting it to suit local conditions.

Summary

1 **Understand the contribution of HRM to organisational performance**
   - The rise of HRM can be explained by issues such as more globally integrated markets, highly publicised 'companies of excellence', changing composition of the workforce and the decline of trade unions.

2 **Understand the potential links between strategy and HRM**
   - The importance of external fit by linking the wider business strategy and HRM strategy.
   - Internal coherence of HRM policies is crucial.

3 **Describe the HRM practices concerned with the flow of people into and through the organisation**
   - In recent years, due to the need for flexibility, there has been a move away from viewing jobs as a set of tasks to thinking about the set of competencies a person requires to accomplish a job successfully.

4 **Describe the HRM practices concerned with reward management**
   - Reward management aims to align employer and employee objectives, and practices to achieve this include:
     - performance-related pay
     - flexible reward systems.

5 **As a potential job seeker, recognise some of the important issues that will face you at the recruitment/selection stage**
   - Each technique has a number of strengths and weaknesses and it is important to be aware of these.

Review questions

1 What do the terms internal and external fit mean in an HRM context?

2 What are the arguments put forward in favour of an organisation adopting a deliberate HRM strategy?

3 Summarise the criticism of HRM that it is based on a unitary perspective (see Chapter 2) of organisations.

4 There is little evidence that HRM has achieved the business objectives claimed for it. What evidence would you look for, and how would you show the link between cause and effect?

5 How can the concept of organisational analysis support the recruitment process?

6 What are the main criticisms of personality testing?

7 What are the advantages and disadvantages of performance-related pay?

8 What lessons can you draw from the way BMW has used the payment system to support other aspects of the HRM policy? More generally, summarise the lessons you would draw from the BMW case.

Concluding critical reflection

Think about the way your company, or one with which you are familiar, deals with HRM. Review the material in the chapter, and make notes on these questions:

● Which of the issues discussed in this chapter are most relevant to your approach to HRM? Is there a clear and conscious attempt to link HRM with wider strategy? Can you give examples of issues where the two support, or do not support, each other? How did those arise, and what have been the effects?

● What **assumptions** do people make in your business about the role of HRM? Is it, for example, seen as mainly a topic for the specialist, or as part of every manager's responsibility? Does the workforce as a whole buy in enthusiastically to the policies adopted, or do they perceive a gap between the rhetoric and the reality?

● What is the dominant view about how changes in the business **context** will affect staff commitment, and the need for new HRM policies to cope with this? Why do they think that? Do people have different interpretations?

● Can you compare your organisation's approach to HRM with that of colleagues on your course, especially those in similar industries, to see what **alternatives** others use?

● If there are differences in approach, can you establish the likely reasons, and does this suggest any possible **limitations** in the present approach? How open is your organisation to innovation in this area?

Further reading

Bratton, J. and Gold, J. (2007) *Human Resource Management* (4th edn) Palgrave, London.

A comprehensive coverage of the field and specifically connects HRM and the business context.

Redman, T. and Wilkinson, A. (2006), *Contemporary Human Resource Management: Text and cases* (2nd edn) Prentice Hall, London.

An up-to-date collection of texts and case studies in human resource management covering key practice areas.

Legge, K. (2005), *Human Resource Management: Rhetorics and realities* (anniversary edn) Macmillan, London.

A highly critical examination of many of the leading, individual themes in HRM; emphasises the gap between the theory and practice of HRM.

Scullion, H. and Lineham, M. (2005), *International Human Resource Management: A critical text*, Palgrave Macmillan, London.

An explicitly international perspective on the topic.

Annotated weblinks, multiple choice questions and other useful resources can be found on **www.pearsoned.co.uk/boddy**

Chapter 12

Information technology and e-business

To examine why managers need information and how they can use technology to make the most of this resource.

By the end of your work on this chapter you should be able to outline the concepts below in your own terms and:

1 Explain how developments in information technology make its effective management critical to performance

2 Give examples of the difference between data, information and knowledge

3 Distinguish between information systems in terms of their type, scope and function

4 Explain four major types of information system – enterprise, knowledge management, customer relations and Internet based (e-business)

5 Understand how information systems affect the tasks and roles of management

6 Explain how the Internet enables radical changes in organisations and their management.

This chapter introduces the following ideas:

data
information
knowledge
information system
information systems management
Internet
intranet
extranet
enterprise resource planning (ERP)
knowledge management (KM)
customer relationship management (CRM)
e-commerce
e-business
disintermediation
reintermediation

Each is a term defined within the text, as well as in the Glossary at the end of the book.

Sergey Brin and Larry Page founded Google in 1999 and by 2007 it was the world's largest search engine.

Its mission is 'to organise the world's information and make it universally accessible and useful'. The need for search services arose as the World Wide Web expanded, making it progressively more difficult for users to find relevant information. The company's initial success was built on the founders' new approach to online searching: their PageRank algorithm (with 500 million variables and 3 billion terms) identifies material relevant to a search by favouring pages that have been linked to other pages. These links were called 'votes', because they signalled that another page's webmaster had decided that the focal page deserved attention. The importance of the focal page is determined by counting the number of votes it has received.

As a business Google generates revenue by providing advertisers with the opportunity to deliver online advertising that is relevant to the search results on a page. The advertisements are displayed as sponsored links, with the message appearing alongside search results for appropriate keywords. They are priced on a cost-per-impression basis, whereby advertisers pay a fixed amount each time their ad is viewed. The charge depends on what the advertiser has bid for the keywords, and the more they bid the nearer the top of the page their advertisement will be.

A feature of Google is the speed with which it returns search results – usually within a second. From the start its focus has been on developing 'the perfect search engine', defined by Page as something that 'understands what you mean and gives you back what you want'. Rather than use a small number of large servers that tend to run slowly at peak times, Google invested in thousands of linked PCs which quickly find the answer to each query.

The software behind the search technology conducts a series of simultaneous equations in a fraction of a second. It uses PageRank to determine which web pages are most important, and then analyses their content to decide which are relevant to the current search. By combining overall importance and query-specific relevance, Google claims to be able to put the most relevant results first. That enhances its value to advertisers who have bid for the relevant keywords. In October 2006 it took 31 per cent of US online advertising revenue.

When the company offered shares to the public in 2004, Page warned potential investors that Google was

Photo courtesy Google UK.

not a conventional company and did not intend to become one. In the interests of long-term stability the share ownership structure was such that the founders owned roughly one-third of the shares, but controlled over 80 per cent of the votes. The company had also, in its short existence, developed a distinctive culture.

Source: Based on Harvard Business School case 9-806-105, *Google Inc.*, prepared by Thomas R. Eisenmann and Kerry Herman; company website; *Business Week*, 9 April 2007.

Photo courtesy Google UK.

Case questions 12.1

- What are the inputs and the outputs of the Google business?
- What are the distinctive features of the Google story set out here?
- How would you expect it to have organised the business to secure such a rapid and profitable growth?

12.1 Introduction

Google is an organisation founded on information – it relies on gathering, processing and disseminating information from and to a range of people and organisations. All have different requirements and work in different ways, yet Google has developed a search engine that works at astonishing speed to meet their different needs. Since the search is free, it can only survive by securing income from advertisements – which depends on the quality of the search systems.

Google (like eBay, lastminute or YouTube) is an example of a company created to use the Internet – it is a pure 'e-business' company, whose managers have built it around information technology. In that sense it differs from companies that were created long before the Internet, but which now use it to support many of their activities. Long-established banks such as ABN-AMRO and Barclays were early users of computer-based information systems, as they offered an efficient way of handling huge volumes of routine transactions. They still perform that function – but now enable the banks to offer new services through alternative distribution channels, such as online banking, mortgages and investment services. They also enable joint ventures with, for example, Tesco, whereby the retailer offers customers the services of Tesco Financial Services – through a joint venture with The Royal Bank of Scotland.

People managing activities of all kinds depend on information. As you manage your work on an assignment you need information – what your teacher requires, the due date, advice from previous assignments and which theories and evidence you should use. People at all levels of an organisation need information about each stage of the process:

inputs – the cost and availability of materials, staff and equipment;
transformation – delivery schedules, capacity utilisation, efficiency, quality and costs;
outputs – prices, market share and customer satisfaction.

The information system (IS) gathers data about inputs, transformation processes and outputs, and feeds information to those working throughout the organisation. Figure 12.1 shows how information systems support these fundamental management processes.

As well as enabling significant changes to internal activities, they also bring changes to the way services are created and delivered:

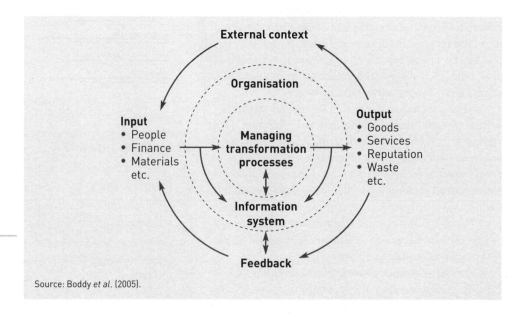

Figure 12.1

The role of information systems in organisations

Source: Boddy *et al.* (2005).

- delivering films, music or sports events over the Internet to computers or mobile phones as well as to TV sets;
- setting up blogs in which users can share their views of a company;
- satellite freight tracking systems that allow companies to monitor continually the exact location and expected time of arrival of their vehicles;
- social networking websites in which users share photos, blogs or chat – and with which established media business and advertisers are trying to forge links.

These and countless other applications of IS can affect the strategy and competitiveness of an organisation. The challenge managers face is to ensure that their organisation uses, rather than squanders, the potential of such systems. This responsibility has become more widespread as IS has come to be used not just in background activities (such as accounting and stock control) but also in foreground activities (such as an online banking website) that directly affect customers. So while the design of information systems depends on the skills of IS experts, managers are responsible for ensuring that IS staff develop systems that suit the business.

Jean-Pierre Corniou – Renault's CIO www.renault.com

management in practice

Frankly my job [as chief information officer] consists of being a bilingual guy: I speak both the language of business and the language of technology. Renault, like other companies, started investing in information technology [IT] in the middle 1960s. It was pioneering work – there were just a few people in IT, working on large systems of great complexity. People inside still have that pioneering attitude, of an era when IT was seen as secret, and complex ... but we need to open up, to build transparency, to build the confidence and trust of all stakeholders in the company.

We have invested a lot of money in [advanced applications] and websites, and when we analysed the level of utilisation of these products and tools, we were very surprised to see how much money had been spent on products that people were not using.

I spend a lot of time in plants, in discussions with foremen in the field, trying to understand how they use technology to increase their efficiency. I spend lots of time in commercial departments too, to understand the key business processes. Bringing IT to the business community means the CIO has to be embedded in the day-to-day life of the organisation, and of course to have a seat on the board. I consider myself more a business guy than an IT guy.

FT

Source: *Financial Times*, 17 September 2003.

The chapter begins by outlining how managers depend on information and knowledge, and the different types of IS they use. The evolution of such systems from background to foreground applications is illustrated, leading to sections that summarise four major applications. Final sections trace their effects on the tasks of managing and raise some current themes and issues.

Activity 12.1 Applying the open systems model

Apply the open systems model in Figure 12.1 to an organisation that you know.

- What are the inputs and outputs?
- Describe the transformation process.
- List examples of information systems that provide information about inputs, outputs and transformations.

12.2 Managing depends on information and knowledge

Data, information and knowledge

The terms 'data', 'information' and 'knowledge' are sometimes confused with each other.

> **Data** are raw, unanalysed facts, figures and events.

- **Data** refers to recorded descriptions of things, events, activities and transactions – their size, colour, cost, weight, date and so on. It may be a number, a piece of text, a drawing or photograph, or a sound. In itself it may or may not convey information to a person.

> **Information** comes from data that has been processed so that it has meaning for the person receiving it.

- **Information** is a subset of data that means something to the person receiving it, which they judge to be useful, significant or urgent. It comes from data that has been processed (by people or with the aid of technology) so that it has meaning and value – by linking it to other pieces of data to show a comparison, a sequence of events, or a trend. The output is subjective since what one person sees as valuable information another may see as insignificant data – their interpretation reflects diverse backgrounds and interests.

> **Knowledge** builds on information and embodies a person's prior understanding, experience and learning.

- '**Knowledge** builds on information that is extracted from data' (Boisot, 1998, p. 12). While data is a property of things (size, price, etc.) knowledge is a property of people, which predisposes them to act in a particular way. Knowledge embodies prior understanding, experience and learning, and is either confirmed or modified as people receive new information.

The significance of the distinction is that people use knowledge to economise on the use of resources. Accurate knowledge enables them to react more intelligently to information and data than those without that experience and learning. Someone with good knowledge of a market will use it to interpret information about current sales. They can identify significant patterns or trends, and so attach a different meaning to the information than someone without that knowledge. They can act in ways that add more value to the resources they use.

The data that is the basis of this system is of many kinds and from many sources. It could be the manager's informal system (such as a conversation with a colleague) or a formal company system that collects data regularly. In itself, data is of little value – information systems convert it into information or knowledge that people can use. Figure 12.2 shows the relation between data, information, knowledge and IS.

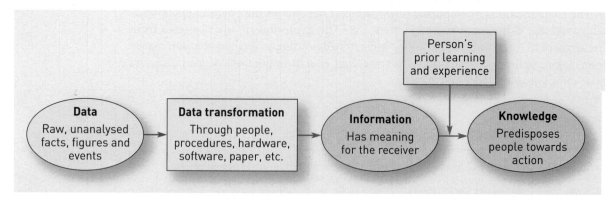

Figure 12.2 The links between data, information and knowledge
Source: Boddy *et al.* (2005).

12.3 Types of information system

Information systems

An **information system** is a set of people, procedures and technology that collects data which it transforms and disseminates. Human societies have developed successively more powerful ways of communicating with one another over space and time. This has *not* meant that all communication has become electronic. For all the power of computer systems to handle internal and external data, organisations have infinite networks of informal communication. People use these to pass gossip, rumour and useful information between colleagues with often astonishing speed. These informal systems exist in parallel with formal, computer-based IS.

> An **information system** is a set of people, procedures and resources that collects and transforms data into information and disseminates this information.

Human information systems

The earliest humans communicated through sign language, painting and drawing, and speech. These are informal information systems. Everyone uses sense organs to receive impulses from the environment; the brain interprets these impulses that lead to decisions on how to respond. From this perspective, everyone is an information system. For managers, this means observing events in the organisation and in the environment and using this information to help manage their area of responsibility. Direct observations by managers and discussions with other people are effective ways of collecting information. Studying is a human information process. The study material is data, but the student has to transform that data and present it as information which is relevant to tutorial discussions and examination questions.

Paper-based IS

The development of writing and numeric symbols, and especially the development of printing technology, greatly extended the capacity of people to communicate information to people in distant places. They could now record data on paper, transform it into information and present it on paper. People still use many paper-based systems as they are cheap to implement and easy to understand. Paper has some virtues and the genuinely paperless office is rare. Companies often define their procedures on paper, and staff are confident with information on paper. They can file a hard (paper) copy and use it easily for audit purposes. Staff use paper systems when traceability is important and responsibility is high. The format of paper information systems is often a piece of A4 paper with printed instructions or boxes to complete. It may be a label attached to a part being routed through a shop floor with instructions on what work to do. A manual, paper-based attendance list kept by a lecturer is another example, as is an address book or diary.

Activity 12.2 Evaluating information systems

Identify two formal but paper-based information systems that you use, or that affect you. What are the advantages and disadvantages of a paper-based system?

Computer-based IS

Computer-based systems, which transform other symbols into digital form, dramatically lower the cost of processing and disseminating information. Most IS beyond the smallest now use electronic means to collect and record data and to transform it into information. Electronic devices can collect the initial data, such as the barcodes and scanners that capture product details in shops. Electronic systems then process, manipulate, distribute and record the data. The systems can provide paper output if required at various stages – such as a till receipt for the customer or a sales report for managers.

Activity 12.3   **Evaluating computer-based systems**

List three computer-based information systems you use or that affect you.

- What are the objectives of these systems?
- Could you process that information without using computers?
- What advantages and disadvantages have you experienced with these systems? Are computer-based systems always better?

Figure 12.3 shows the elements of a computer-based IS. It shows that as well as hardware and software, it also includes people and procedures. It is also part of a wider system – the organisational context, which affects its performance. **Information systems management** includes the planning, acquisition, development and use of IS to ensure that information meets certain quality standards, affecting its value to managers.

Information systems management is the planning, acquisition, development and use of these systems.

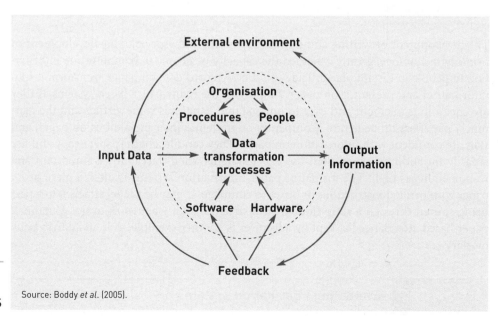

Figure 12.3

The elements and context of a computer-based IS

Source: Boddy *et al.* (2005).

Information systems are about organisations

An IS project is not a matter of managing a technical project, but an organisational one. Promoters need to be able to change both the technology and the organisation. They design an IS to meet what they understand to be the requirements of senior managers. They must also take account of the elements in the context. How other people (users, managers, etc.) react to the resulting system will be influenced by their view of the system entering the context. Will it increase or decrease their power? Is it consistent with the prevailing culture? Will they be better off in some way? These are the areas to which promoters and project managers need to give attention. As well as investing in the technology, they need to reconstruct other aspects of the organisational context in which people are working. The outcomes of the project (success, embarrassing failure or something in between) will depend on how they manage these contextual elements.

Source: Boddy *et al.* (2005), pp. 17–18.

A computer-based student record system

This description of part of a university IS illustrates the elements in Figure 12.3. The system requires people (e.g. administrative staff) to enter data (about students and their results) following certain rules – such as that only employees may enter data on student results into the system. Another rule is that a student cannot graduate unless the system confirms that the student has paid their fees and library fines.

The hardware consists of computers and peripherals such as printers, monitors and keyboards. This runs the student record system, using software to manipulate the data in a particular way and to print the results for each student. Another procedure sends results to each student – for whom it is information. The staff in the department and the faculty want to compare the pass rates of all the courses – so the results system then becomes an element of the university's management information. Staff will use their knowledge (based on learning and experience) to interpret trends and evaluate the significance of any patterns.

12.4 The evolution of information systems

From background to foreground

Between 1965 and 1975 organisations concentrated on automating those administrative functions where they could make large efficiency gains – often referred to as back-office functions. Typical targets were those that processed many routine transactions, such as payrolls, inventory and financial transactions. Department managers often delegated responsibility for information management to their IS department. These became very skilled at running large, routine and usually centralised systems. The IS function also became influential, and line managers were rarely involved in discussions on IS strategy and development. The technologies had little effect on smaller organisations. The objective of most applications was to process routine transactions more efficiently.

In the following decade technical developments made smaller systems possible and more useful to managers in other parts of the organisation such as planning, manufacturing and distribution. More managers discovered the possibilities of computer-based IS and became familiar with issues of budgeting for hardware, requesting support, defining requirements and setting priorities. Suppliers developed systems that were suitable for smaller organisations.

Since the mid-1980s the IS environment has again changed significantly. Systems that support the background functions continue to develop and employ more modern technology. Rapid technical developments have brought IS to the foreground of organisations, changing the way the company deals with customers by offering new channels across which to communicate or to deliver services. IS supports managers and professional staff directly through decision support systems or video conferencing. People in most types of organisation depend on computer-based IS.

Convergence of voice, vision and data

The most dramatic changes in managing data, information and knowledge come from the rapid convergence of three technologies that developed independently during their long histories:

> the telephone was invented in 1876, the first television transmission occurred in 1926, and the electronic computer goes back to 1946, if not earlier. For much of that time the pace of change was slow, but began to gather pace in the late 1980s. (Cairncross, 2001, p. 27)

Major developments include:

- *The telephone* The ability to send signals along glass fibre-optic cables has increased capacity, and reduced cost, dramatically. The cost of carrying additional calls is virtually zero, irrespective of distance. This has encouraged people to use the telephone not only for speech, but for passing data and pictures between fixed computers *and* between them and the growing range of mobile devices. The cost of long-distance communication continues to fall, with major implications for managing businesses around the world.
- *The television* Although consumers rapidly adopted television after the launch of the first commercial station in 1947, the technology changed little for many years. A breakthrough came with the development of communications satellites, which enabled viewers to see that they were in some respects part of a global community. The other big change was when broadcasters began to transmit programmes in digital form, increasing the capacity of available channels, and foreshadowing the convergence of televisions and computers.
- *The networked computer* By fitting more power into the microchips that are at the heart of a computer, engineers are able to roughly double computing power every two years. As the power of each microchip multiplies so the price of computing falls, leading to smaller computers and greater capacity. From being stand-alone calculators, computers are now embedded in many other gadgets – such as games and video cameras.
- *The Internet* The invention of the Transmission Control Protocol/Internet Protocol (TCP/IP) provides a common language and a set of rules that enable computers all over the world to talk to each other. TCP/IP does this by specifying the format in which data sent over the **Internet** must be packaged – enabling telephone, television and computer networks to connect with each other as a single network. Linking mobile phones to the Internet has led to the explosive growth of the 'Wireless Internet', which in effect liberates the computer from the desktop, enabling information to pass readily between people wherever they are.

The Internet is a web of hundreds of thousands of computer networks linked together by telephone lines and satellite links through which data can be carried.

Figure 12.4 shows the widening role of information systems. The early stages featured single, unconnected systems for separate business functions. In stages 3 and 4 managers are linking systems together and using them to make radical changes to previously separate processes. In stage 5 they are using common information systems based on the Internet to move information between organisations, often having direct electronic links with their customers.

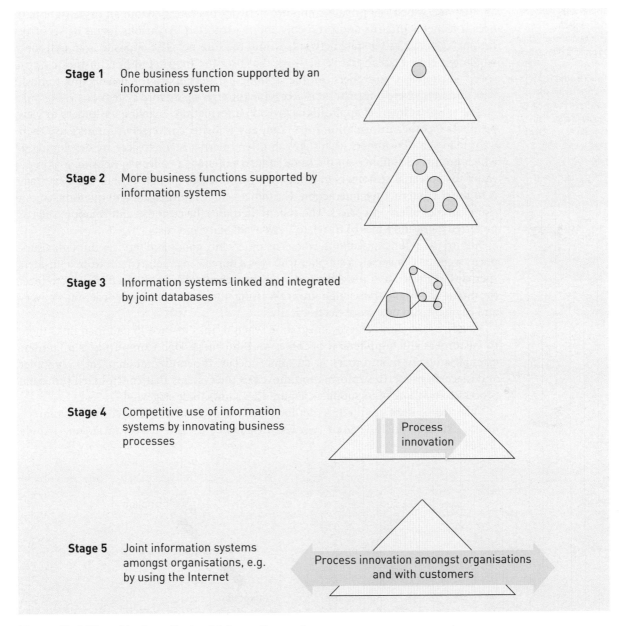

Figure 12.4 The widening effects of information systems

Managing over the Internet

The significance of the Internet for everyone who works in organisations cannot be overstated. It affects all aspects of organisational activity, enabling new forms of organisation and new ways of doing business (Cairncross, 2001). This includes selling a product or service over the Internet and using the Internet to integrate all the required processes, from suppliers through to delivery to the customers. Another relevant term is an **intranet**, which is a private computer network operating within an organisation. It uses Internet standards and protocols and is protected by various forms of security. Intranets operate as separate networks within the Internet. The opposite is an **extranet**, which is a closed collaborative network that uses the Internet to link businesses with specified suppliers, customers or other trading partners. Extranets usually link to business intranets where information is accessible through a password system.

The simplest Internet applications provide information, enabling customers to view products or other information on a company website; conversely suppliers use their website to show customers what they can offer. Internet marketplaces are developing in which groups of suppliers in the same industry operate a collective website, making it easier for potential customers to compare terms through a single portal. The next stage is to use the Internet for interaction. Customers enter information and questions about (for example) offers and prices. The system then uses the customer information, such as preferred dates and times of travel, to show availability and costs.

A third use is for transactions, when customers buy goods and services through a supplier's website. Conversely a supplier who sees a purchasing requirement from a business (perhaps expressed as a purchase order on the website) can agree electronically to meet the order. The whole transaction, from accessing information through ordering, delivery and payment, can take place electronically.

Finally, a company achieves integration when it links its own IS and then links them to customers and suppliers: it becomes an e-business. Dell Computing is a familiar example amongst many others. As customers decide the configuration of their computer and place an order, this information moves to the systems that control Dell's internal processes and those of its suppliers. Figure 12.5 shows these stages.

Other companies use the Internet to create and orchestrate active customer communities. Examples include Kraft (**www.kraftfoods.com**), Intel (**www.intel.com**), Apple

An **intranet** is a version of the Internet that only specified people within an organisation can use.

An **extranet** is a version of the Internet that is restricted to specified people in specified companies – such as major customers or suppliers.

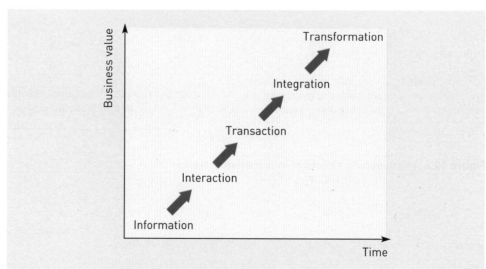

Figure 12.5

Stages in using the Internet

(www.apple.com) and Harley-Davidson (www.harley-davidson.com). These communities enable the companies to become close to their customers, and to learn how best to improve a product or service much more quickly than is possible through conventional market research techniques.

easyGroup www.easygroup.com

From the day that Stelios Haji-Ioannou launched easyJet as a low-cost airline, the company had a strategy centred on meeting customer needs efficiently, using technology wherever possible and adapting processes to suit market conditions. When it began to operate it took reservations on the telephone, so paid no commissions to travel agents. The company's emphasis on technology meant that as the Internet became available easyJet rapidly adapted its business model to offer online reservations. easyJet took its first online reservation in April 1998. By April 2001 over 85 per cent of reservations were made online – probably the highest proportion of total sales for any established business. Soon that became the only way to book with the airline – making huge savings in the cost of printing and distributing tickets.

Its success in using the Internet led to the launch of a further range of online services, such as easyCar (car rental) and easyMoney (financial services). Stelios then created easyGroup as a private holding company that creates new ventures based around the easyJet model of efficient, low-cost ventures. In late 2004 it reached an agreement with Deutsche Telekom's T-Mobile business to launch a low-cost mobile service – renting air-space from T-Mobile.

Source: *Financial Times*, 24 November 2004; published information and company websites.

The Internet is evidently challenging many established ways of doing business. Combined with political changes, this is creating a wider, often global, market for many goods and services. The challenge for managers is to make profitable use of these possibilities. This includes looking beyond technology – which receives most attention – to the wider organisation. A manager who played a major role in guiding Internet-based changes at his company commented:

> The Internet is not a technology challenge. It's a people challenge – all about getting structures, attitudes and skills aligned.

12.5 Classifying information systems

Understanding the management implications of different types of IS depends on some system for classifying them. To be useful, a classification needs to reflect empirically based differences between systems – such as the complementarities they require and the intended users.

Classifying IS by their complementarities

McAfee (2006) classifies information systems according to the extent of the complementary organisational changes that they require. Some information technologies can deliver results without the complements being in place; others allow the complements to emerge over time; and still others impose the complements they need as soon as companies deploy the technologies. The significance of this is that it helps managers to understand the scale of the organisational changes they are likely to need to make to benefit from the investment. It can also indicate which projects will be relatively easy to implement.

Functional systems include technologies that make the execution of stand-alone tasks more efficient. Word processors and spreadsheets are the most common examples of this category. Designers, accountants, doctors and many other specialists use these technologies in the normal course of their work. As they often work individually with a high degree of professional independence, they often use the technology as a stand-alone system, with few if any complementary changes required elsewhere in the organisation.

> For instance, an R&D engineer can use a computer-aided design (CAD) program to improve the way he does his work without making any changes in how the rest of the department functions. Furthermore, [functional systems] don't bring their complements with them. CAD software, for example, doesn't specify the processes that make the most of its power. Companies must identify the complements that [functional systems need]. (McAfee, 2006, p. 144).

Network systems help people to communicate with each other. They include e-mail, instant messaging, blogs, and groupware such as Lotus Notes. These allow people to interact, but do not define how they should do so: people can experiment. These systems bring some complements with them, but allow users to implement them gradually, and to modify them. They allow people to work together, but do not specify who should send or receive messages. Their effective use will probably depend on some complementarities – such as rules on who can access which parts of the system, or who is responsible for responding to customer comments on a blog: but these can be modified by users in the light of experience.

Enterprise systems allow companies to restructure interactions amongst groups of employees or with business partners. Applications that structure entire business processes, or enable data to pass between organisations, fall into this category.

> Unlike network technologies, which percolate from the bottom, enterprise technologies are very much top-down; they are purchased and imposed on organisations by senior management. Companies can't adopt enterprise systems without introducing new interdependencies, processes, and decision rights. Moreover, companies can't slowly create the complements to enterprise systems; changes become necessary as soon as the new systems go live. (McAfee, p. 145)

Enterprise systems allow companies to redesign business processes, and to ensure that employees follow the correct procedures. They also enable companies, once they have identified complementary business processes, to implement them widely and reliably throughout the organisation. They also enable close monitoring of what is happening around the enterprise, bringing a high degree of almost instant control.

The value of McAfee's analysis is that it alerts managers to the organisational implications of different systems. The organisational issues raised by functional systems will be quite limited, as it is mainly up to the professional to decide if and how to use them. Network systems will require attention to complementarities to ensure effective use, but these can emerge with experience. Enterprise systems require very significant organisational changes if the company is to gain a benefit, and will be correspondingly difficult to implement.

Classifying IS by their reach

Another way to analyse systems is by their geographic reach.

Individual

Many people use word-processing systems, spreadsheet programs and database systems to manage their work. They can download data from company-wide systems to use on their tasks. The main advantage is that users decide what to use the system for and are able to control the way they work. The disadvantage is that the quality of the software varies greatly. The data extracted from the corporate database may no longer be current or the systems may not link easily with other systems.

Local or departmental

If separate units or departments in companies have a distinct task to perform, it may be worthwhile for them to have their own IS. Management often creates these as separate systems, though many are now being integrated into the systems network of the whole company. A university may use a system that provides information about courses and assessments on the local departmental network which students can access.

Organisational

These systems integrate departments and people throughout the organisation. In hospitals many units use centralised patient data to retrieve or update information about a patient. Such systems make it much easier for staff from various departments to treat a patient in a consistent way. If managers want to implement a hospital-wide system they will discourage the continued use of stand-alone systems, such as a doctor's list of patients held on a spreadsheet that she or he considers the definitive list.

Inter-organisational systems

Many systems link organisations electronically by using networks that transcend company boundaries. These inter-organisational systems (IOS) enable firms to incorporate buyers, suppliers and partners in the redesign of their key business processes, thereby enhancing productivity, quality, speed and flexibility. New distribution channels can be created, and new information-based products and services can be delivered. In addition, many IOS radically alter the balance of power in buyer–supplier relationships, raise barriers to entry and exit and, in many instances, shift the competitive position of industry participants.

Community systems

Social network sites such as MySpace or YouTube that people use to exchange information, ideas or videos, independently of an organisation, are growing very quickly. Blogging is one major use, as are websites through which people with particular interests exchange information. Although not related to an organisation (apart from those that own the site) they are significant for managers, since customers can use them to exchange positive or negative information about the company.

Combining the complementarities of systems with their reach leads to Figure 12.6, which gives a systematic way of distinguishing information systems. A spreadsheet application in Excel developed and used by one employee would fit in box F1 while a computer-aided design system used by engineers in a company and in their suppliers' would probably fit boxes F3 and F4. Systems such as e-mail or groupware extend beyond the company, so they would be N4 or N5 if, for example, it was a corporate blog that supported communication with customers. Customer relationship management systems (CRM) would be in areas E3 to E5.

The significance of this is that the organisational implications of systems vary across the figure. Those in the top left-hand area – largely individual, functional – will be easy to implement and affect few staff. Those towards the lower right-hand of the figure raise increasingly complex technical and organisational issues.

		Reach				
		Individual	Local/ departmental/ team	Organisation	Inter-organisational	Community
Complementarities	Functional	F1	F2	F3	F4	F5
	Network	N1	N2	N3	N4	N5
	Enterprise	–	–	E3	E4	E5

Figure 12.6 Complementarities and reach of IS combined

Google – the case continues www.google.com   CASE STUDY

The company has rapidly extended the range of services it offers, while remaining rigorously focused on search. Although the headquarters is in California Google's mission is to facilitate access to information across the world – more than half of its searches are delivered to users living outside the United States, in more than 35 languages. The company offers volunteers the opportunity to help in translating the site into additional languages.

While a principle within Google has been that it did not interfere with the results of a search (not favouring one advertiser over another, once they had bid for keywords) it faced criticism when it agreed to place certain restrictions on the site in China.

The company acquired YouTube, the video-sharing site, in 2006, as a further extension of its services. In 2007 Viacom, a major entertainment producer, sued YouTube and Google, contending that 160,000 unauthorised clips of Viacom programmes were available on YouTube, and that this infringed the company's copyright over the material.

Such acquisitions can be seen as a way of growing the business in a way that stays focused on Google's distinctive competence: that of developing superior search solutions, and earning a revenue from these through targeted advertising. One alternative direction would be to aggregate the content into thematic channels, similar to Yahoo!. Another could be to extend its service beyond the search process (which helps buyers to identify suitable sellers) and into the transaction process – by developing systems (such as eBay) that would facilitate the actual transactions.

Source: Based on information provided by the company and the company website.

Case questions 12.2

- Referring to Chapter 8 (Strategic management), what kind of strategy is Google following?
- What 'strategic direction' (Section 8.4) does the purchase of YouTube represent?
- Visit the website to identify recent strategic developments, and consider what they reveal about the company's strategy for growth.

Activity 12.4 **Collecting examples of applications**

The media regularly report new applications of computer software. Collect examples over the next week of new inter-organisational systems. Identify what they are likely to mean for the way people will work and manage in organisations adopting such systems. Compare notes with others and decide which of the systems you have found is likely to be of greatest organisational significance over the next two years.

12.6 Enterprise resource planning systems

Fulfilling a customer order requires that people in sales, accounting, production, purchasing and so on cooperate with each other to exchange information. However the IS on which they depend were often designed to meet the needs of a single function. They were built independently and cannot automatically exchange information. Manufacturing will not automatically know the number and types of product to make because their systems are not linked to the systems that process orders. A common solution is to use **enterprise resource planning** (ERP) systems, which aim to coordinate activities and decisions across many functions by creating an integrated platform that integrates them into company-wide business processes. Information flows between the functions and levels, as shown in Figure 12.7.

Enterprise resource planning (ERP) An integrated process of planning and managing all resources and their use in the enterprise. It includes contacts with business partners.

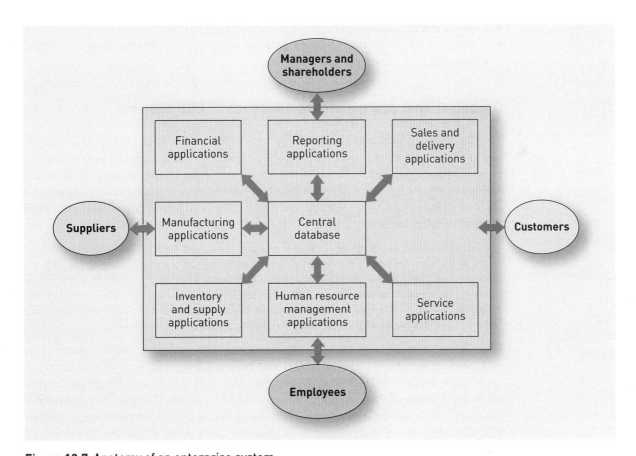

Figure 12.7 Anatomy of an enterprise system

At the heart of an enterprise system is a central database that draws data from and feeds data into a series of applications throughout the company. Using a single database streamlines the flow of information. Table 12.1 shows examples of business processes and functions that enterprise systems support. These 'modules' can be implemented separately, but promise much greater benefits when they are linked to exchange information continuously through the central database.

Table 12.1

Examples of business processes supported by enterprise systems

Financial	Accounts receivable and payable, cash management and forecasting, management information, cost accounting, profitability analysis, profit-centre accounting, financial reporting
Human resources	Payroll, personnel planning, travel expenses, benefits accounting, applicant tracking
Operations and logistics	Inventory management, maintenance, production planning, purchasing, quality management, vendor evaluation, shipping
Sales and marketing	Order management, pricing, sales management, sales planning, billing

ERP systems give management direct access to current operating information and so enable companies to, amongst other things:

- integrate customer and financial information
- standardise manufacturing processes and reduce inventory
- improve information for management decisions across sites
- enable online connections with systems of suppliers and customers with internal information processing.

Organisational and management issues of ERP systems

There is controversy about whether adopting an ERP system gives a competitive advantage (McKeen and Smith, 2003). A company may not benefit if using the generic models provided by standard ERP software prevents it from using unique business models that had given it a competitive edge. ERP systems promote centralised coordination and decision making, which may not suit a particular firm, and some companies do not need the level of integration they provide:

> Enterprise systems are basically generic solutions. The design reflects a series of assumptions about the way companies operate in general. Vendors of ES try to structure the systems to reflect best practices, but it is the vendor that is defining what 'best' means. Of course, some degree of ES customisation is possible, but major modifications are very expensive and impracticable. As a result, most companies installing ES will have to adapt or rework their processes to reach a fit with the system. (Davenport, 1998, p. 125)

Some believe that ERP systems lock companies into rigid processes, which makes it difficult to adapt to market changes (Hagel and Brown, 2001). This may help explain the results of a study by Wieder *et al.* (2006) that found no significant differences in performance between adopters and non-adopters of ERP systems. Bozarth (2006) illustrates the complexities of implementing such systems, and contrasts alternative approaches. The Management in Practice feature illustrates these issues from the experience of Nestlé.

Nestlé struggles with enterprise systems www.nestle.com

Nestlé is a food and pharmaceuticals company that operates all over the world. Traditionally it allowed local units to operate as they saw fit, taking into account local conditions and business cultures. The company had many purchasing systems and no information on how much business they did with each supplier: each factory made independent arrangements. Nestlé's management concluded that these local differences were inefficient and costly. They wanted to integrate the systems to act as a single entity, using the company's world wide buying power to lower prices.

Managers therefore started a programme to standardise and coordinate Nestlé's processes and information systems. The project team decided to install financial, purchasing, sales and distribution modules throughout every Nestlé US division. The new system would standardise and coordinate the company's information systems and processes. A year after the project started, a stock market analyst in London doubted its success: 'it touches the corporate culture, which is decentralised and tries to centralise it. That's risky. It's always a risk when you touch the corporate culture'. Jeri Dunn from Nestlé later agreed: at a US plant most of the key stakeholders failed to realise how much the project would change their business processes. Dunn said: 'they still thought it was just software'. A rebellion had taken place when the plant moved to install the manufacturing modules. The lower-level workers did not understand how to use the new system and did not understand the changes. Their only hope was to call the project help desk, which received 300 calls a day. Turnover increased and no one seemed motivated to learn and use the system. The project team stopped the project and removed the project leader. This person had put too much pressure on the project and the technology. By doing so the team had lost sight of the bigger picture.

Sources: Laudon and Laudon, (2004a).

12.7 Knowledge management systems

Developments in IS are of great interest to those who want to improve their organisation's ability to create and mobilise knowledge. Many businesses depend on the skill with which they are able to create and acquire knowledge, and ensure that people use it throughout the organisation. Knowledge is vital to innovation and many see it as the primary source of wealth in modern economies. People in large organisations often believe the knowledge they need to improve performance is available within the business – but that they cannot find it. **Knowledge management** (KM) refers to attempts to improve the way organisations create, acquire, capture, store, share and use knowledge. This will usually relate to customers, markets, products, services and internal processes, but may also refer to knowledge about relevant external developments.

Managing knowledge is not new – the Industrial Revolution occurred when people applied new knowledge to manufacturing processes. What *is* new is the degree to which developments in IS make it easier for people to share data, information and knowledge irrespective of physical distance. This growing technological capacity has encouraged many managers to believe that implementing knowledge management or similar systems to make better use of knowledge assets will enhance performance – and some studies, such as that by Feng *et al.* (2004) find that companies adopting a KM system perform better than non-adopters. Voelpel *et al.* (2005) shows the benefits of such a system at Siemens. Three common purposes of KM systems are to:

> **Knowledge management** systems are a type of IS intended to support people as they create, store, transfer and apply knowledge.

- code and share best practices
- create corporate knowledge directories
- create knowledge networks.

Table 12.2 illustrates how IS can potentially support each element of KM – these subdivisions are arbitrary, and many systems will support several processes.

Table 12.2 Knowledge management processes and the potential role of IS

Knowledge management processes	Knowledge creation	Knowledge storage/ retrieval	Knowledge transfer	Knowledge application
Supporting information technologies	Data mining Learning tools	Electronic bulletin boards Knowledge repositories Databases	Discussion forums Knowledge directories	Expert systems Workflow systems
IT enables	Combining new sources of knowledge Just-in-time learning	Support of individual and organisational memory Inter-group knowledge access	More extensive internal network More communication channels Faster access to sources	Knowledge can be applied in many locations More rapid application of new knowledge through workflow automation
Platform technologies	Groupware and communication technologies Intranets and sometimes extranets			

Source: Based on Alavi and Leidner (2002), p. 125.

Echikson (2001) outlined how the oil company BP uses advanced information systems to enable staff in the huge global business (including those in recently acquired companies) to share and use information and knowledge. These include a web-based employee directory (an intranet) called 'Connect', which contains a home page for almost every BP employee. Clicking on someone's name brings up a picture, contact details, interests (useful for breaking the ice between people who have not met) and areas of expertise. When a manager in a BP business needed to translate their safety video into French, he used 'Connect' to identify French-speaking employees who could do the work, rather than an external translation service. At the core of the business, decisions on where to

---

management in practice **Buckman Labs – successful KM** www.buckman.com

Buckman Labs is a science-based company, operating around the world. The founder realised that the company needed to become more effective in managing the knowledge of their 1300 scientific staff. Buckman has steadily developed systems that connect codified databases around the world – containing information on current global best-practice methods, ideas and current problems. This enables scientists throughout the company to keep in touch with each other and to share knowledge electronically amongst themselves and with customers: 'This single knowledge network aims to encompass all of the company's knowledge and experience, empowering Buckman representatives to focus all of their company's capabilities on customer challenges' (Pan, 1999, p. 77).

A notable feature of the company's approach has been the extent to which it has supported technological innovation with organisational change. Initial attempts at knowledge sharing were unsuccessful, with little activity on the system. Managers then instituted a series of changes to encourage greater use. These included producing weekly statistics showing which staff had used the system. Non-users were penalised, frequent contributors rewarded. Processes were also changed to ensure the immediate capture of information during projects.

Source: Pan (1999).

drill are now informed by an Internet system that brings geological data to one of several high-tech facilities. Engineers view the images and make decisions in hours that used to take weeks – and help reduce the danger of expensive drilling mistakes.

It is important to recall the distinction between data, information and knowledge – knowledge being the expertise, understanding and experience that comes from learning. Many systems that people refer to as 'knowledge' management systems appear on closer examination to deal with data and information rather than knowledge. While computer-based systems are effective at dealing with (structured) data and information, they are much less effective at dealing with (unstructured) knowledge. As Hinds and Pfeffer (2003) observe

> systems (to facilitate the sharing of expertise) generally capture *information or data*, rather than *knowledge or expertise*. Information and information systems are extremely useful but do not replace expertise or the learning that takes place through interpersonal contact. (p. 21)

This point was developed by Scarbrough and Swan (1999), who propose that while technological systems deal well with explicit data and information they are much less use when dealing with tacit knowledge, which develops amongst people as they learn to work together. Tacit knowledge reflects the shared understanding and meaning that is unique to a situation. While a 'cognitive' model of KM is an appropriate way to deal with explicit knowledge, a 'community' model is more suitable for tacit knowledge. Table 12.3 contrasts these views.

Cognitive model	Community model
Knowledge is objectively defined concepts and facts	Knowledge is socially constructed and based on experience
Knowledge is transferred through text, and information systems have a crucial role	Knowledge is transferred through participation in social networks including occupational groups and teams
Gains from KM include recycling knowledge and standardising systems	Gains from KM include greater awareness of internal and external sources of knowledge
The primary function of KM is to codify and capture knowledge	The primary function of KM is to encourage individuals and groups to share knowledge
The dominant metaphor is human memory	The dominant metaphor is human community
The critical success factor is technology.	The critical success factor is trust.

Source: Scarbrough and Swan (1999).

Table 12.3

Two views of the knowledge management process

Organisational and management issues of KM systems

Presenting the community model alongside the cognitive model helps to identify the issues in the success or failure of knowledge management projects:

> whilst it might be relatively easy to share knowledge across a group that is homogeneous, it is extremely difficult to share knowledge where the group is heterogeneous. Yet it is precisely the sharing of knowledge across functional or organisational boundaries ... that is seen as the key to the effective exploitation of knowledge. (Scarbrough and Swan, 1999, p. 11)

Systems with a technical, cognitive perspective do not take account of structures and cultures, which represent people's beliefs and values about what to do and how to reward it. These contexts may inhibit people from sharing knowledge in the way intended.

Emerging technical possibilities provide an infrastructure that enables global access to data, information and knowledge. KM tools can exploit explicit knowledge about previous projects, technical discoveries or useful techniques. But reusing existing knowledge may do less for business performance than using it to create new knowledge that suits the situation. This creative process depends more on human interaction than on technology. Since most managers receive too much information it does not follow that pushing more information across such boundaries will improve performance. That depends not just on knowledge, but on insight and judgement. Gupta and Govindarajan (2000) observed:

> effective knowledge management depends not merely on information-technology platforms but ... on the social ecology of an organisation – the social system in which people operate [made up of] culture, structure, information systems, reward systems, processes, people and leadership. (p. 72)

People will be more likely to use a KM system if the culture recognises and rewards knowledge sharing – lively communities of practice will be more effective than technology (Thompson and Walsham, 2004).

management in practice   Problems with KM in a consultancy

The company is one of the leading global management consultancies, with over 75,000 consultants in over 40 countries. As do most such firms it considers the knowledge of its staff to be a core capability for achieving competitive advantage. To ensure that this knowledge is widely shared it has spent large sums on KM systems, especially Knowledge Exchange (KX) – a repository of internally generated knowledge about clients, topics, best practices and so on – to which consultants were expected to contribute ideas as they completed projects for clients.

Paik and Choi (2005) found that few East Asian consultants contributed, and identified three reasons:

1 a perception amongst East Asian consultants that others did not appreciate their regional knowledge;
2 a requirement to provide ideas in English; East Asian consultants were conversant in English, but found it difficult and time consuming to translate documents into English before submitting them;
3 cultural differences; staff in some countries were not motivated to contribute if there was no direct personal incentive – which the global reward system did not take into account.

They conclude that their study shows that global companies seeking a common approach to knowledge management need to make allowances for local cultural differences.

Source: Paik and Choi (2005).

Activity 12.5   What knowledge do you need for a task?

Identify for an employee (perhaps yourself) what knowledge is created, acquired, captured, shared and used while doing a particular task.

- Identify examples of explicit and tacit knowledge in this example.
- Discuss to what extent a computerised knowledge system could be useful in managing that knowledge.
- Also discuss whether such a system would be in your interests or those of the organisation.

12.8 Customer relationship management systems

Customer relationship management (CRM) systems are intended to build and sustain long-term business with customers. They represent a move from mass markets and mass production to customisation and focused production. CRM software tries to align business processes with customer strategies to recruit, satisfy and retain profitable customers (Ryals, 2005; Kumar *et al.*, 2006). Figure 12.8 shows three approaches. The first treats all customers in the same way by sending impersonal messages in one direction. The second sends one-way, but different messages to customers, depending on their profile. The third personalises the messages, which may lead to real interaction, in the hope of increasing customer loyalty.

Customer relationship management (CRM)
The process of maximising the value proposition to the customer through all interactions, both online and traditional. Effective CRM advocates developing one-to-one relationships with valuable customers.

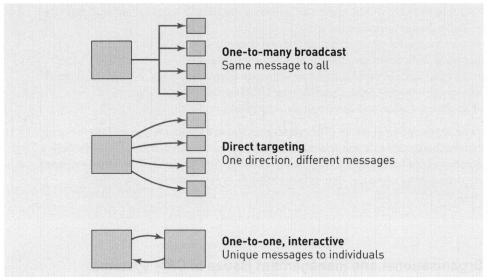

One-to-many broadcast
Same message to all

Direct targeting
One direction, different messages

One-to-one, interactive
Unique messages to individuals

Figure 12.8

Communications methods and message

In many businesses the key to increasing profitability is to focus on recruiting and retaining high lifetime value customers. So the promise of CRM is to:

- gather customer data swiftly
- identify and capture valuable customers while discouraging less valuable ones
- increase customer loyalty and retention by providing customised products
- reduce costs of serving customers
- make it easier to acquire similar customers.

Some CRM systems consolidate customer data from many sources to answer questions such as:

- Who are our most loyal customers?
- Who are our most profitable customers?
- What do these profitable customers want to buy?

Others focus on managing customer communications – as when Merck-Medco (a US pharmaceutical firm) redesigned its customer contact centres (Torkzadeh *et al.*, 2006), or when IBM redesigned the way customers interacted with the company (see Management in Practice).

CRM at IBM www.ibm.com

Managers at IBM became aware in the late 1990s that sustained changes in technology and markets required it to rethink they way it engaged with customers. These were expressing dissatisfaction with the company on several grounds, such as how to get consistent information on products to confusion about the right person to deal with a query. The company therefore undertook a major research project in conjunction with its customers to develop a CRM system. Extensive consultation with customers enabled the project team to design a new CRM process and electronic system, called *Inside IBM*. This would use IT, the Internet and IBM's intranet to support the customer relationship.

Inside IBM was designed to:

1. Provide a *common and single interface*, or point-of-contact, for the customer.
2. Be *flexible in use*, allowing customers to control as much of the interaction as possible according to their needs. Multiple sources of information should be accessible in a consistent way, but customisable to reflect individual customer needs.
3. Be *intuitive and user friendly* for all external and internal audiences who interface with it.
4. Provide *easy access to IBM's* organisational knowledge-based resources.
5. Provide a *learning opportunity* by facilitating knowledge exchange in the areas of business, technology and marketing, i.e., integrate product development, CRM and the supply chain.
6. *Improve back-end communication* and *cross-functional coordination*.

This information guided the design of a pilot CRM project that was evaluated after six months in operation. This indicated that *Inside IBM* had had positive effects on customer satisfaction, especially from a much closer integration of the customer and the many units within IBM. The project was then extended as a standard system across the company, with further enhancements constantly being added.

Source: Massey *et al.* (2001).

Organisational and management issues of CRM systems

The paper by Massey *et al.* (2001) shows how implementing successful CRM depends more on strategy than on technology, and also that even when a customer strategy *is* established other dimensions such as business processes, other systems, structures and people need to change to support it. If a company wants to develop better relationships with its customers it needs first to rethink the key business processes that relate to customers, from customer service to order fulfilment. If consumers have a choice of channels – such as e-mail, web and telephone, marketing, sales and service can no longer be treated separately. A customer may place an order by phone, use the web page to check the status of the order, and send a complaint by e-mail. Multi-channel interactions pose considerable challenge if the company is to maintain a single comprehensive and real-time view of each customer.

For companies focused on products or services this means realigning around the customer – which can be a radical change in a company's culture. All employees, but especially those in marketing, sales, service and any other customer contact functions, have to think in a customer-oriented way. Much of the time and cost of CRM projects has to be spent on organisational issues. Successful CRM depends on coordinated actions by all departments within a company rather than being driven by a single department (Boulding *et al.*, 2005).

12.9 | e-commerce and e-business

Networked IS allow companies to coordinate joint processes with other organisations across great distances. Transactions such as payments and orders can be exchanged electronically, thereby reducing the cost of obtaining products and services. Many such systems use web technology, with labels such as extra-organisational systems, e-commerce systems, e-business systems and supply chain management systems. Since they cross organisational borders they are widely called inter-organisational systems (IOS).

IOS can create new relationships between an organisation, its customers, suppliers and business partners, redefining organisational boundaries. Firms are using these systems to work jointly with suppliers and other business partners on product design and development and to schedule work in manufacturing, procurement and distribution. IOS includes two commonly used terms – **e-commerce** and **e-business.**

e-commerce refers to the activity of selling goods or services over the Internet.

Many businesses use the Internet to support their distribution, by offering goods and services through a website – which is defined here as e-commerce. A more radical way to use the Internet is for what is here called e-business, when companies use a website to manage information about sales, capacity, inventory, payment and so on – and to exchange that information with their suppliers or business customers. They use the Internet to connect all the links in their supply chain, so creating an integrated process to meet customer needs – see Management in Practice.

e-business refers to the integration, through the Internet, of all an organisation's processes, from its suppliers through to its customers.

Using the Internet at Siemens   www.siemens.com

management in practice

Siemens' plan to do much of their business over the Internet includes:

- Knowledge management – using a company-wide system to capture and share knowledge about scientific and technical developments throughout the business.
- Online purchasing (or e-procurement). Large savings are expected from pooling the demands of buying departments through a company-wide system called click2procure.
- Online sales. Most of Siemens' customers are other companies who can click on 'buy from Siemens' on the website and place orders for most Siemens products.
- Internal administrative processes – such as handling 30,000 job applications a year online, or expecting employees to book their business travel arrangements over the Internet.

If you want to transform a company to an e-business company, the problem is not so much e-procurement and the face to the customer. All this can be done rather fast. What is truly difficult is to reorganise all the internal processes. That is what we see as our main task and where the main positive results will come from.

Source: Boddy *et al.* (2005) and company website.

The relationship between a company and its channel partners can be changed by the Internet or by other applications of inter-organisational systems, because electronic networks can help to bypass channel partners, also called **disintermediation**. Figure 12.9 shows how a manufacturer and a wholesaler can bypass other partners and reach customers directly.

The benefits of disintermediation are that transaction costs are reduced and that it enables direct contact with customers. This also makes it possible to increase the reach of companies, e.g. from a local presence to a national or international presence.

Disintermediation Removing intermediaries such as distributors or brokers that formerly linked a company to its customers.

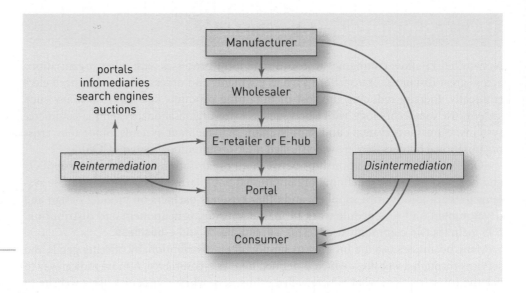

Figure 12.9

Reinventing the supply chain

Reintermediation
Creating intermediaries between customers and suppliers, providing services such as supplier search and product evaluation.

Reintermediation is the creation of new intermediaries between customers and suppliers by providing (new) services such as supplier search and product evaluation (Chaffey, 2002). Examples are portals such as Yahoo.com, Amazon.com and Moneyfacts.co.uk, which help customers to compare offers and link them to suppliers.

Organisational and management issues of e-commerce and e-business

A major concern of companies moving towards e-commerce or e-business has been to ensure they can handle the associated physical processes. These include handling orders, arranging shipment, receiving payment, and dealing with after-sales service. This gives an advantage to traditional retailers who can support their website with existing fulfilment processes. Given the negative effects of failure once processes are supported by IOS, it seems advisable to delay connecting existing systems to the new system until robust and repeatable processes are in place.

Kanter (2001) found that the move to e-business for established companies involves a deep change. She found that top management absence, shortsightedness of marketing people and other internal barriers are common obstacles. Based on interviews with more than 80 companies on their move to e-business, her research provides 'deadly mistakes' as well as some lessons, including:

- Create experiments and act simply and quickly to convert the sceptics.
- Create dedicated teams, and give them autonomy. Sponsor them from the wider organisation.
- Recognise that e-business requires systemic changes in many ways of working.

12.10 IS and the tasks of managing

Chapter 1 presented the management job as being to add value through the tasks of planning, organising, leading and controlling the use of resources. Whatever their level, managers perform these tasks in a fluid, interactive way, and through their relations with other people. Modern IS have considerable implications for how they do so.

Planning

This deals with the overall direction of the business, and includes forecasting trends, assessing resources and developing objectives. Chapter 3 introduced Porter's five forces, widely used as a tool for identifying the competitive forces affecting a business. Figure 12.10 shows that IS can become a source of competitive advantage if a company can use them to strengthen one or more of these forces. They can equally represent a competitive threat if others use them more effectively: Table 12.4 illustrates some possibilities.

Managers also use IS to support their chosen strategy – such as a differentiation or cost leadership. IS can support a cost leadership strategy when companies substitute robotics for labour, use stock control systems to reduce inventory, use online order entry to cut processing costs, or use systems to identify faults that are about to occur to reduce downtime and scrap.

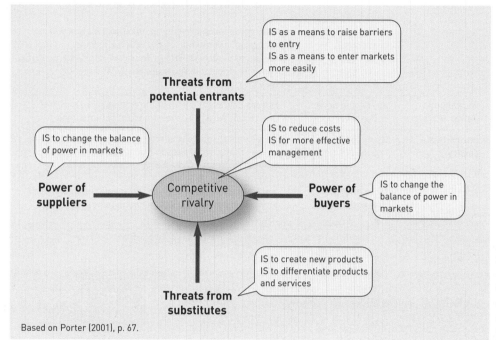

Based on Porter (2001), p. 67.

Figure 12.10

How information systems can change competitive forces: Porter's model

A differentiation strategy tries to create uniqueness in the eyes of the customer. Managers can support this by, for example, using the flexibility of computer-aided manufacturing and inventory control systems to meet customers' unique requirements economically. CRM systems can have similar effects in differentiating one company's services from others.

Organising

This is the activity of moving abstract plans closer to reality, by deciding how to allocate time and effort. It is about creating a structure to divide and coordinate work. IS enable changes in structure – perhaps centralising some functions and decentralising others. Telephone sales can be centralised to single call centres, which reduces the cost of sales and allows the companies to compete with new entrants. A Management in Practice feature in Chapter 10 (p. 332) showed how Siemens had used the Internet to bring more central control.

Table 12.4

Using information systems to affect the five forces

Porter's five forces		Examples of information systems support
Threat of potential entrants	Raise entry barriers	Electronic links with customers make it more costly for them to move to competitors. Supermarkets use electronic links to banks and suppliers, and so gain a cost advantage over small retailers
	Entering markets more easily	Bertelsmann, a German media group, entered book retailing by setting up an online store. Virgin offers financial services by using online systems
Threat of substitutes	Creating new products	Telephone banking (a threat to branch banking) has only been possible with modern information systems
	Differentiating their products	Using database technology and CRM systems to identify precise customer needs and then create unique offers and incentives
Bargaining power of suppliers	Increasing power of suppliers	Airlines use yield management systems to track actual reservations against capacity on each flight, and then adjust prices for the remaining seats to maximise revenue
	Decreasing power of suppliers	Auto companies have set up electronic marketplaces that suppliers must use, and which allow the customers (such as Ford or General Motors) to compare prices offered more easily, and identify new suppliers
Bargaining power of buyers	Increasing power of buyers	Buyers can use the Internet to access more suppliers, and to compare prices for standard commodities
Intensity of rivalry	Using IS to reduce costs	Enterprise resource planning systems make it possible to make radical changes in manufacturing systems, leading to greater consistency in planning and lower costs
	More effective management	Information systems provide more detailed information on trading patterns, enabling management to make more informed decisions

Google – the case continues   www.google.com   CASE STUDY

Early in the company's history Page and Brin instilled some distinctive corporate values, which observers say still influence the way people work. They include:

- **Don't be evil** – centred on the value of never compromising search results: 'We never manipulate rankings to put [advertisers] higher in our search results. No one can buy better page rank. Our users trust Google's objectivity and no short-term gain could ever justify breaching that trust.
- **Technology matters** – evident in continuing research to improve the search algorithms and in software to support advertisers. The company invests heavily in the infrastructure to support very fast returns to search queries.

- **Make own rules** – such as refusing to provide earnings guidance to financial analysts, and a tendency to be secretive with outsiders.
- **Managing innovation** – staff are encouraged to spend 20 per cent of their time on projects of their own choosing, a policy that has spawned many commercial innovations. Brin maintains that all Google's new product ideas have emerged from employee ideas, rather than from a top-down planning process. To encourage rapid implementation, Google engineers typically work in teams of three to five people.

Source: Based on Harvard Business School case 9-806-105, *Google Inc.*, prepared by Thomas R. Eisenmann and Kerry Herman; company website; and published information.

Case questions 12.3

Google appears to seek innovation both by encouraging staff to generate ideas and by acquiring other companies.

- Visit its website or other sources to identify recent innovations.
- Which have come from internal development and which from acquisition?
- What are the advantages and disadvantages of each approach?

Other companies have used the power of IS to decentralise – Oticon in Chapter 10 is an example.

Leading

This is the activity of generating effort and commitment towards meeting objectives. It includes influencing and motivating other people to work in support of the plans. Computer-based IS can have significant effects on work motivation, by changing the tasks and the skills required. Research into many computer-based information systems (Boddy *et al.*, 2005) shows that some managers use them in a way which reduces the intrinsic quality of work (see Chapter 15) while others use them to enhance it. This has little to do with the nature of the technology itself, but with how managers choose to design and implement it.

Computer systems in an ambulance service

The organisation transports patients to and from hospitals for routine treatment at a clinic. The Patient Transport Service work involves ambulance crews transporting patients between their homes and clinics within a hospital. The manual procedures that the service used to plan drivers' routes were flexible but labour intensive. To reduce costs the service invested heavily in computer systems, including a route-planning system.

Planning officers received orders and keyed them into a computer that stored them until the day before the appointment. It then sorted them by area and allocated them to an available ambulance crew. The list was then printed, checked for feasibility and issued to the crew. Two years after implementing the system a control manager said:

> The basic system has not changed but we have made some changes in how we use it. We used to tell the crew how to do the run: what we do now is put all the patients in a geographic area on to a log sheet, with their appointment times. We have devolved responsibility to the crew members to decide how best they should schedule that journey to meet the appointments. Initially we told them in much more detail, manually intervening with the computer data. But it was very labour intensive, and we did not see the traffic jams. We hand out the work in the morning, and we only want to hear if the crews are having operational problems.
>
> The planning officer's role has developed into a liaison role with the hospitals, building up a relationship with them. The planner becomes a crucial personality, not just a worker. Someone coming into the job now could take two years to build up those working relationships. The machine does the routine bits. At first the planning officer did that: now we have pushed it down.

Source: Based on a case in Boddy and Gunson (1996).

Business becomes more dependent on skilled and committed people as technology increases. Since the business world is dynamic and uncertain there will be changes, errors and uncertainty to cope with. Staff need to be able and willing to use their initiative to deal with that, to exploit the hidden potential of the system, and generally to contribute imaginatively to the work.

Controlling

Computer-based monitoring systems can constantly check the performance of an operation, whether the factor being monitored is financial, quality, departmental output or personal performance. Being attentive to changes or trends gives the business an advantage as it can act promptly to change a plan to suit new conditions. Universities in The Netherlands use student trail systems that monitor the academic progress of students. These systems link to the national institution that provides scholarships. This information enables the institution to stop or reduce the scholarship when results are below the required standard.

Information systems allow management at head office to control subsidiaries or branch offices much more tightly. Head office can gather information much more frequently and measure branch performance almost as it happens rather than by weekly or monthly reports. It is a matter of management judgement whether that is a wise or unwise move.

12.11 Current themes and issues

Performance

Developments in information technology have had, and will continue to have, profound implications for organisations and those who work in them. The effects are greatest in those sectors able to benefit from the dramatically lower cost of communication that the Internet enables – finance, media, entertainment and direct retailing. The Internet also brings organisations closer, enabling some to transfer activities to partners in a network of suppliers, often in distant locations. Many companies have significantly enhanced their competitive performance by using modern IT.

Yet investing in IT alone does not ensure competitive success. Research consistently shows that that depends on making equally significant changes to the organisation. Taking the examples developed in the earlier sections, ERP systems promote centralised coordination and decision making, which may not suit a particular firm. They may also be inflexible, locking companies into rigid processes that make it harder to change. Knowledge management systems need to fit the context in which they are used, since people are more likely to use them in a culture that recognises and rewards the benefits of sharing knowledge. Those running CRM projects need to align them with deeper customer strategy; to adapt business processes to support new ways of interacting with customers; and to ensure all employees think in a customer oriented way. E-business ventures raise issues of handling the associated physical processes and other internal changes required.

In all cases, managers need to make changes in their organisation if they are to secure competitive advantage.

Responsibility

Advances in IS that can improve performance can also be used to damage the interests of others. Managing information systems also includes being aware of the issues of individual ethics they raise, and considering how to include such issues in discussions of corporate responsibility. Table 12.5 shows how trends in technology raise ethical issues.

Table 12.5

Technology trends that raise ethical issues

Trend	Impact
Computing power doubling every 18 months	More organisations depend on computer systems for critical operations
Rapidly declining data storage costs	Organisations can easily maintain detailed databases on individuals
Datamining advances	Organisations can analyse vast quantities of data on individuals to develop detailed profiles of individual behaviour
Networking advances and the Internet	Copying data from one location to another and accessing personal data from remote locations is much easier

Source: Based on Laudon and Laudon (2002), p. 470.

Most people value privacy, the right to be left alone without fearing surveillance or interference from others – at the workplace and in social life. Developments in IS threaten this by making the invasion of privacy cheap, effective and often profitable. Most transactions an individual has with an organisation generate an administrative record. In themselves these are usually uncontroversial, and when held as pieces of paper were probably harmless, as it was almost impossible to link them together for any purpose. Modern technology makes it easy not only to store that data and process it into useful information – but also to link it with other data records to build up a very detailed profile of an individual.

The European Union has reacted by issuing a Directive on Data Protection that requires companies to inform people if they hold information about them, and to disclose how it will be stored and used. Customers must also give their consent before a company can legally use data about them, and they have the right to check the accuracy of any information held. The Internet raises new challenges for this approach, as information may pass through many computers, in different jurisdictions, before it reaches its destination. Retailers selling online can use software to observe people's behaviour while they are visiting a website and making purchases.

This technical ability raises ethical issues such as the conditions under which it is right to use such systems to invade a person's privacy, what makes it legitimate to intrude on others through unobtrusive surveillance or market research. Is a company acting responsibly if it uses information about, say, their credit history when it is considering them for employment?

Internationalisation

New technologies are enabling the processes of international business, since firms can disperse their operations round the globe, and manage them economically from a distance. The technology enables managers to keep in close touch with dispersed operations – though at the same time raising the dilemma between central control and local autonomy: the fact that technology enables tight supervision from the centre does not necessarily mean that it is wise to do so.

It also makes it possible to work interdependently with other organisations: previously this was constrained by physical distance and the limited amount of information that was available about the relationship. As technology has advanced, interdependent operations become more cost effective – most obviously through outsourcing and other forms of joint ventures. Companies can routinely exchange vast amounts of information with suppliers, customers, regulators and many other elements of the value chain.

This implies that managers need to develop the skills of managing these links. As Child (2005) comments:

> Whereas [technology] renders greater interdependence feasible in terms of information processing, to operate effectively it also requires new organizational supports in the form of practices designed to foster coordination and trust between network members. (p. 36)

The cultural and other differences discussed in Chapter 4 also need to be taken into account in developing an information system that crosses national boundaries.

Summary

1 **Explain how developments in information technology make its effective management critical to performance**

- People at all levels depend on information about inputs, outputs and transformation processes to help them add value to the resources they use.

- The significance of IS has increased as it is now widely applied to support direct interaction with customers.

2 **Give examples of the difference between data, information and knowledge**

- Data is the recorded description of things, events or activities – such as their size or cost.

- Information is processed data that has meaning for the person receiving it – they judge it to be useful.

- Knowledge builds on information by using experience to evaluate its significance.

3 **Distinguish between information systems in terms of their complementarities and reach**

- Complementarities – functional, network and enterprise.

- Scope – individual, departmental, organisational, inter-organisational and community.

4 **Explain four major types of information system – enterprise, knowledge management, customer relations and Internet based (e-business)**

- Enterprise systems use a central database to integrate data about many aspects of the business as an aid to planning.

- Knowledge management systems attempt to improve the ability of an organisation to use the information it possesses.

● Customer relations systems aim to capture and process information about each customer, so that products and services can be tailored more closely to individual needs.

● Internet-based systems (e-business) are systems that operate across organisational boundaries, enabling new relationships with business partners and customers.

5 Understand how information systems affect the tasks and roles of management

● Computer-based IS can potentially affect all tasks of managing:

  – *Planning* – e.g. modern IS can affect all of the forces in Porter's model;
  – *Organising* – e.g. IS can enable the removal of routine tasks, break down barriers between departments and functions, and enable work to be more centralised or more decentralised;
  – *Leading* – e.g. IS can enable changes in the design of work, and can increase or decrease the motivational potential of jobs;
  – *Controlling* – e.g. IS can greatly increase the frequency and detail with which activities can be monitored, irrespective of distance.

6 Explain how the Internet enables radical changes in organisations and their management

● The Internet enables management to erode the boundaries between companies, through the use of inter-organisational systems. They can then develop systems for e-commerce and e-business, ultimately connecting all stages in their supply chain.

Review questions

1 Give some examples of data and of information you have at this moment. Use these to explain the difference between the two.

2 What information do you lack that harms your work or study performance? How could this information be generated?

3 Give examples of the use of information systems in a business you know. How are they helping or hindering the managers in performing their tasks? Compare the needs of senior and lower-level managers if possible.

4 What are the advantages of human and paper-based information systems over computer-based ones, and vice versa?

5 Give an example of each type of IS identified by McAffee (2006).

6 Give examples of how an information system can affect at least two of the forces in Porter's model, and so affect the competitiveness of a business.

7 Describe how an IS can support either a cost leadership or a differentiation strategy, with an example of each.

8 How do information systems affect the other functions of management – such as leading or controlling?

9 How are companies in an industry of your choice (e.g. finance, music, news, manufacturing) using the Internet, and how is this affecting the structure of the industry and the power of the different players?

Concluding critical reflection

Think about the main computer-based information systems you use in your company, or that feature in one with which you are familiar. Review the material in the chapter, and perhaps visit some of the websites identified. Then make notes on these questions:

● What examples of the themes discussed in this chapter are currently relevant to your company? How have information systems helped or hindered managers' performance? How well have the social as well as the technological aspects of new systems been managed? How, if at all, have they altered the tasks and roles of managers, staff or professionals? What stage have you reached in using the Internet?

● If the business seems to pay too much attention to the technical aspects of IS projects, and not enough to the social and organisational aspects, why is that? What **assumptions** appear to have shaped managers' approach?

● How have changes in the business **context** shaped the applications being implemented? Do they seem well suited to their organisational (structural, cultural, etc. factors) and external contexts?

● Have managers considered any **alternatives** to the way IS projects are managed differently to improve their return on investment – for example by greater user involvement in the projects?

● Do they regularly and systematically review IS projects after implementation to identify any **limitations** in their approaches? Do the presentations on ERP and CRM systems match experience in your organisation with such systems?

Further reading

Applegate, L.M., McFarlan, F.W. and McKenney, J.L. (2000), *Corporate Information Systems Management: Text and cases* (5th edn), Irwin, Chicago, IL.

Provides a broad perspective on the management implications of the rise of information systems. The book is organised around a management audit of the information services activity.

Laudon, K.C. and Laudon, J.P. (2004b), *Management Information Systems: Organization and technology in the networked enterprise*, Prentice Hall, Harlow.

This text, written from a management perspective, focuses on the opportunities and pitfalls of computer and communications technologies.

Phillips, P. (2003), *E-Business Strategy: Text and cases*, McGraw-Hill, Maidenhead.

A comprehensive European perspective on Internet developments relevant to business and strategy.

Boulding, W., Staelin, R. and Ehret, M. (2005), 'A customer relationship management roadmap: what is known, potential pitfalls, and where to go', *Journal of Marketing*, vol. 69, no. 4, pp. 155–166.

Bozarth, C. (2006), 'ERP implementation efforts at three firms', *International Journal of Operations & Production Management*, vol. 26, no. 11, pp. 1223–1239.

McAfee, A. (2006), 'Mastering the three worlds of information technology', *Harvard Business Review*, vol. 84, no. 11, pp. 141–149.

Three recent empirical studies of the management issues involved in managing information systems.

Weblinks

These websites have appeared in the chapter:

www.google.com
www.renault.com
www.kraftfoods.com
www.intel.com
www.apple.com
www.harley-davidson.com
www.easygroup.com
www.nestle.com
www.buckman.com
www.ibm.com
www.siemens.com

Visit two of the business sites in the list, and answer these questions:

● If you were a potential employee, how well does it present information about the company and the career opportunities available? Could you apply for a job online?

● Evaluate the sites on these criteria, which are based on those used in an annual survey of corporate websites:

  – Does it give the current share price on the front page?

  – How many languages is it available in?

  – Is it possible to e-mail key people or functions from the site?

  – Does it give a diagram of the main structural units in the business?

  – Does it set out the main mission or business idea of the company?

  – Are there any other positive or negative features?

Annotated weblinks, multiple choice questions and other useful resources can be found on **www.pearsoned.co.uk/boddy**

Chapter 13

Managing change and innovation

To outline theories of change in organisations and show how these relate to practice.

By the end of your work on this chapter you should be able to outline the concepts below in your own terms and:

1 Explain the meaning of organisational change and give examples
2 Explain what the links between change and context imply for those managing a change
3 Compare life cycle, emergent, participative and political theories of change
4 Evaluate systematically the possible sources of resistance to change
5 Explain the meanings of organisational development and the learning organisation
6 Illustrate the factors believed to support innovation.

This chapter introduces the following ideas:

external context
perceived performance gap
performance imperatives
organisational change
interaction model
receptive contexts
non-receptive contexts
life cycle
emergent model
participative model

political model
counterimplementation
organisation development
sensitivity training
process consultation
survey feedback
creativity
innovation
idea champions

Each is a term defined within the text, as well as in the Glossary at the end of the book.

In 2007 Vodafone offered mobile services to subscribers in 28 countries and was the world's largest mobile network operator, with about one-quarter of the market. Ericsson was the world's largest supplier of mobile network infrastructure, and Vodafone its largest customer. Vodafone has achieved its strong market position partly by internal growth and by acquiring other operators – such as AirTouch (USA) in 1998 and Mannesmann (Germany) in 2000. Many of these acquisitions also had shareholdings in other mobile operators, meaning that in some countries Vodafone operates through partially rather than wholly owned subsidiaries.

As demand for mobile services grew, Vodafone extended the network on a country-by-country basis, with local management teams running the business. They usually ordered network equipment from Ericsson, negotiating terms with Ericsson staff in their country. Although Vodafone's in-country managers communicated with their counterparts in other countries, Vodafone did not attempt to coordinate the way they operated. Ericsson operated in a more centralised fashion, though with some scope for local managers to establish terms of business that reflected their market or competitive environment.

This had the following consequences:

© Vodafone 2007.

- Terms and conditions for purchasing network equipment varied between countries.
- Communication between the two companies in each country was direct, through meetings, telephones, letters, fax and e-mail.
- Communication about Ericsson products between Vodafone operators in different countries was *ad hoc*.
- Sharing of product information between Ericsson and Vodafone was in-country, mainly through written documents.
- Ordering and order tracking was done by local systems in each country.
- Configuration of network equipment varied between countries, as did service and support arrangements.

Before the merger with AirTouch, Vodafone management had begun to assess what synergies it could gain from the merger, especially in the supply of network equipment. The company expected to make big savings if it could aggregate its worldwide requirements for net-

work equipment, and source this from common global suppliers. The later acquisition of Mannesmann increased the scope for synergy – and claims about the potential savings in this area were made to shareholders and the financial markets.

Vodafone therefore began a project with Ericsson to develop new ways of managing the relationship. The intention was to find ways of aggregating Vodafone's global requirements so that the companies would manage their relationship in a unified way. They realised that managing a change of this scale would raise difficult issues about the:

- degree of planning to undertake
- scale and value of the synergies from a new global relationship
- attitudes of those managing Vodafone operations in the various countries
- resources that would be needed to manage the change.

Source: Based on material from Ibbott and O'Keefe (2004).

Case questions 13.1

- How may the structure of Vodafone's in-country operations affect the project?
- Will a new global relationship mean a more centralised or a more decentralised company?
- Should the two companies put significant resources into planning the change in advance?

13.1 Introduction

The manager whom Vodafone appointed to manage this change faces a problem that is familiar to many managers. The chief executive has put him in charge of implementing a major change that will affect many people, some of whom will be uneasy about how it will affect them. Changing from a country to a global structure will have implications for the way they run the business in their country, and change their relationship with their main equipment supplier.

Managers initiate or experience change so regularly that in many organisations change is seen as the normal state of affairs, interrupted by occasional periods of relative stability. In the most innovative areas of the economy some senior managers see one of their primary tasks as being to challenge current practices, hoping to foster a climate of exploration and innovation. They want people to see change as the norm – merely one further intervention in a continuing flow of events rather than something that will be followed by a return to stability. At BP, for example, the challenge to successive senior managers has been to continue transforming the business from a relatively small (for that industry), diversified business into the world's second-largest oil company. Mergers, such as that between Chrysler (USA) and Daimler (Germany), are usually followed by internal changes. Small businesses make radical changes too – as when Hindle Power, an engineering company with 30 employees, faced the loss of a valuable distribution contract unless it changed the way it worked. It embarked on a radical programme of change that returned the company to profit, and grew the business (*People Management*, 3 February 2000, p. 52).

The external environment described in Chapter 3 is the main source of change. The evolving PESTEL factors change what people expect of a business – which may encourage managers to alter their strategy or operations. Research by the Institute of Personnel and Development (IPD) into 151 large organisations found that major reasons for change were a need to create closer customer relationships, significant financial pressure to improve performance, or intensifying competition (IPD, 1999). Anecdotal evidence is that while most managers accept the need for change, many are critical of the way their organisations introduce it. Managers still experience great difficulty in implementing major organisational changes successfully.

This chapter presents theories about the nature of change in organisations. It begins by explaining current external pressures for change, and how these prompt internal change to one or more elements of the organisation. The chapter then outlines a model that shows how change depends on the interaction between the external and internal environments of the organisation. It then presents four complementary perspectives on

---

Activity 13.1 Recording a major change

From discussion with colleagues or managers, identify a major attempt at change in an organisation. Make notes on the following questions and use them as a point of reference throughout the chapter.

- What was the change?
- Why did management introduce it?
- What were the objectives?
- How did management plan and implement it?
- How well did it meet the objectives?
- What lessons have those involved taken from the experience?

how people try to manage that interaction, each with different management implications. Further sections deal with diagnosing the characteristics of a change, managing resistance, skills and structures, and organisation development.

13.2 Initiating change

Chapter 1 introduced the idea that managers work within a context that shapes what they do, and which they may also change. This chapter explains the interactive nature of that process, and Figure 13.1 illustrates the themes it will cover. A particular episode of change begins when enough people perceive a gap between desired and actual performance – usually because the internal context of the organisation is unable to meet the external demands upon it. Using their implicit or explicit theory of change, they initiate a project to change one or more aspects of the internal context in the hope of closing the performance gap. The outcomes of the change effort will be affected by practical issues of design and implementation – but whatever the outcomes they will in turn affect the subsequent shape of the external and internal contexts, providing the starting point for future changes.

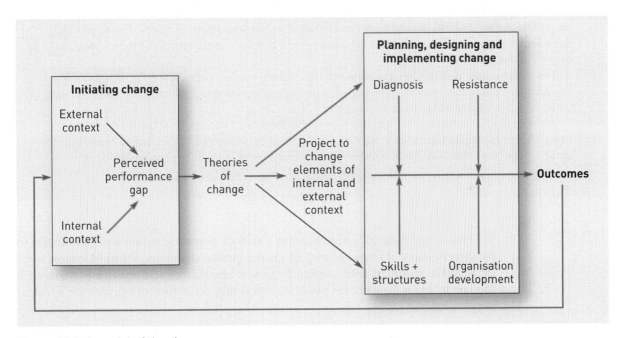

Figure 13.1 A model of the change process

The external context

Chapter 3 described the **external context** of business and successive chapters have illustrated the changes taking place, such as internationalisation, information technology and expectations about corporate responsibility. Together with deregulation and the privatisation of former state businesses these are transforming the competitive landscape in which firms operate. They face competition from unexpected quarters, threatening their prosperity or even their survival. Managers at British Airways and KLM have had to respond to the pressure of new competition from low-cost airlines such as Ryanair and

The **external context** consists of elements beyond the organisation such as competitors, or the wider PESTEL factors.

easyJet. Established banks face competition from new entrants such as retailers (Sainsbury's) or conglomerates (Virgin) offering financial services. The growth of the Internet has enabled companies offering high-value/low-weight products to open new distribution channels and invade previously protected markets.

---

management in practice   **Successful change at GKN**   www.gknplc.com

GKN is a leading global supplier to automotive, aerospace and off-highway manufacturers, employing 40,000 people in GKN companies and joint ventures. It was created by a series of mergers at the start of the twentieth century, creating Guest, Keen and Nettlefolds – then one of the largest manufacturing businesses in the world. It was involved in iron and coal mining, steel production and finished products such as nuts, bolts and fasteners.

Its present form reflects a small number of successful decisions made in the 1980s. The first was to abandon any thought of re-entering the steel industry (its interests there had been nationalised in the 1960s), and to focus instead on seeking growth in the motor components business. This decision was shaped by a piece of luck, in that in 1966 it had bought a UK engineering company and in doing so acquired a share in a German business which had worldwide patents for a unique constant velocity joint system for powering front-wheel drive cars.

A second decision was to cut back sharply on non-vehicle activities, into which the group had diversified in the 1970s. At that time unrelated diversification was a popular management strategy, but it soon became clear that unrelated businesses were best run independently: GKN soon disposed of most of that portfolio.

The third decision was to purchase Westland Helicopters – mainly because it gave GKN entry into the rapidly growing business of manufacturing aerospace components, which complemented the automotive business (Westland was sold in 2004).

In his book *Change Without Pain* Abrahamson (2004) identifies GKN as one of the most successful companies at managing significant strategic changes – not by disposing of skills, but by recombining them in ways that create even greater value – see Section 13.9 for more on Abrahamson's ideas.

Sources: *Financial Times*, 6 January 2004, 28 February 2007; *Independent*, 15 March 2007; company website.

These forces have collectively meant a shift of economic power from producers to consumers, many of whom now enjoy greater quality, choice and value. Managers wishing to retain customers need continually to seek new ways of adding value to resources if they are to retain their market position. Unless they do so they will experience a widening performance gap.

Perceived performance gap

A **perceived performance gap** arises when people believe that the actual performance of a unit or business is out of line with the level they desire. If those responsible for transforming resources into outputs do so in a way that does not meet customer expectations, there is a performance gap. Cumulatively this will lead to other performance gaps emerging – such as revenue from sales being below the level needed to secure further resources. If uncorrected this will eventually cause the business to fail.

In the current business climate, two aspects of performance dominate discussion – what Prastacos *et al.* (2002) call '**performance imperatives**': the need for flexibility and the need for innovation. In a very uncertain business world the scope for long-term

A **perceived performance gap** arises when people believe that the actual performance of a unit or business is out of line with the level they desire.

Performance imperatives are aspects of performance that are especially important for an organisation to do well, such as flexibility and innovation.

planning is seriously limited. Successful businesses are likely to be those that develop a high degree of strategic and organisational flexibility, while also (Volberda, 1997) maintaining efficient and stable processes. This apparent paradox (combining flexibility and stability) reflects the fact that while companies need to respond rapidly they also need to respond efficiently. This usually depends on having developed a degree of stability and predictability in the way they transform resources into goods and services.

The other imperative identified by Prastacos *et al.* (2002) is innovation:

> to generate a variety of successful new products or services (embedding technological innovation), and to continuously innovate in all aspects of the business (p. 58).

In many areas of business, customers expect a constant flow of new products, embodying the latest scientific and technological developments: companies that fail to meet these expectations will experience a performance gap. Selling, say, an advanced mobile phone profitably depends not only on the quality of the applied research which goes into a better screen display, but also on turning that research into a desirable product *and* delivering the devices at a price which customers will pay. This depends on the organisation – the internal context of management.

The internal context

Chapter 1 introduced the internal context (Figure 1.3, repeated here as Figure 13.2) as the set of elements within an organisation that shape behaviour. Change begins to happen when sufficient influential people believe, for example, that outdated technology or a confusing structure is causing a performance gap, by inhibiting flexibility or innovation. They notice external or internal events and interpret them as threatening the performance that influential stakeholders expect. This interpretation, and their implicit theory of change, encourages them to propose a change to one or more aspects of the organisation, shown in Figure 13.2.

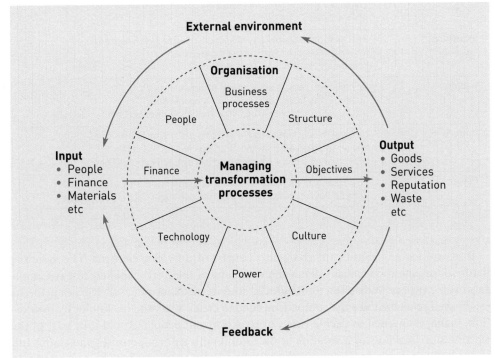

Figure 13.2

Elements of the internal context of management

They then have to persuade enough other people that the matter is serious enough to earn a place on the management agenda. People in some organisations are open to proposals for change, others tend to ignore them – BP faced new competitive pressures throughout the 1980s, but it was only around 1990 that sufficient senior people took the threats seriously enough to initiate a period of rapid change.

People initiate organisational change for reasons other than a conscious awareness of a performance gap – fashion, empire building or a powerful player's personal whim can all play a part. Employees or trade unions can propose changes in the way things are done to improve working conditions. The need for change is subjective – what some see as urgent others will leave until later. People can affect that process by managing external information – magnifying customer complaints to make the case for change, or minimising them if they wish to avoid change.

Organisational change is a deliberate attempt to improve organisational performance by changing one or more aspects of the organisation, such as its technology, structure or business processes.

Whatever the underlying motivations, **organisational change** is an attempt to change one or more of the elements shown in Figure 13.2. Table 13.1 illustrates specific types of change that people initiate under each element, including some which appear elsewhere in this book.

Table 13.1

Examples of change in each element of the organisation

Element	Example of change to this element
Objectives	Developing a new product or service Changing the overall mission or direction Oticon's new strategic objectives as a service business (Chapter 10 Case)
Technology	Building a new factory Creating a website on the Internet Pensco implementing a new computer system (see Section 13.4)
Business processes	Improving the way maintenance and repair services are delivered Redesigning systems to handle the flow of cash and funds Benetton's new system for passing goods to retailers (Chapter 20 Case)
Financial resources	A set of changes, such as closing a facility, to reduce costs New financial reporting requirements to ensure consistency The Royal Bank of Scotland reducing costs after the NatWest merger (Part 4 Case)
Structure	Reallocating functions and responsibilities between departments Redesigning work to increase empowerment Vodafone/Ericsson moving to a global structure (Chapter 13 Case)
People	Designing a training programme to enhance skills Changing the tasks of staff to offer a new service IKEA's policies to encourage high staff commitment (Chapter 15 Case)
Culture	Unifying the culture between two or more merged businesses Encouraging greater emphasis on quality and reliability GSK creating a more entrepreneurial research culture (Chapter 10)
Power	An empowerment programme giving greater authority to junior staff Centralising decisions to increase the control of HQ over operations

It is rare for any significant change to consist of only one element. The systemic nature of organisations means that a change in any of these areas is likely to have implications for others. When Tesco introduced its Internet shopping service alongside its established retail business the company needed to create a website (technology). In addition, managers needed to decide issues of structure and people (would it be part of the existing store business or a separate business unit with its own premises and staff?) and about business processes (how exactly would an order on the website be converted to a box of groceries delivered to the customer's door?). They had to manage these ripples initiated by the main decision. Managers who ignore these consequential changes achieve less than they expect.

Once they have perceived a need for change, those promoting it then use their implicit or explicit theory of change (Sections 13.3 and 13.4) to set up and implement change (Sections 13.5–13.8) in the relevant organisational unit. How well people manage the steps in this process determines the effect on the performance gap, which in turn feeds back to the context.

Case questions 13.2

Identify the possible ripple effects that may need to be managed in the Vodafone/Ericsson change, using the elements in Figure 13.2 as a guide.

- How may the move to a global relationship affect the structure area?
- What implications may that change have for other elements?
- Which of these are likely to cause most difficulty?

These begin to form the management agenda for this project. If possible compare your answers with others on the course, to see how many *alternative* possibilities you have identified.

13.3 The interaction of context and change

How managers implement change depends on their theory about its nature. This section presents an '**interaction model**', a theory of how a change interacts with its context. The following section outlines four complementary perspectives on managing that interaction.

> The **interaction model** is a theory of change that stresses the continuing interaction between the internal and external contexts of an organisation, making the outcomes of change hard to predict.

People introduce change to alter the context

Management attempts to change elements of its context to encourage behaviours that close the performance gap. Vodafone wanted to change the context within which it worked with Ericsson. By moving from country relationships with Ericsson to a more unified global structure, management hoped to create a structure that enabled people in both companies to reduce the cost to Vodafone of expanding the network. When Tesco introduced online shopping management needed (at least) to change technology, structure, people and business processes to enable staff to deliver the new service. When people plan and implement a change they are creating new 'rules' (Walsham, 1993) that they hope will guide the behaviour of people involved in the activity.

People do not necessarily accept the new arrangements without question, or without adapting them in some way: in doing so they make further changes to the context. As people begin to work in new circumstances – with a new technology or a new structure – they make small adjustments to the original plan. As they use a new information system or website they decide which aspects to ignore, use or adapt.

As people become used to working with the new system their behaviours become routine and taken for granted. They become part of the context that staff have created informally. These new contextual elements may add to, or replace, the context that those formally responsible for planning the change created. These informally created aspects of the context may or may not support the original intentions of those who initiated the project. The interaction between people and context continues into the future.

Sun Microsystems and a supplier   www.sun.com

Boddy *et al.* (2000) studied Sun Microsystems and one of their suppliers as they moved towards a more cooperative supply chain relationship. Managers in both companies introduced changes to the context of work – technology, processes and roles. These were designed to create a context that encouraged more cooperation, and closer interpersonal links, between people in the two companies. For example, the supplier's sales coordinator:

> There is a close relationship with my opposite number in Sun. We speak several times a day, and he tries to give me as much information as he possibly can.

Sun staff echoed this:

> What makes them different is that you're talking to them daily . . . The relationships are a bit different – it is a bit closer than an ordinary supplier where you don't have that bond. Dealings are more direct. People are becoming more open with each other.

Both groups came to appreciate the other's requirements and tried to make things easier for them. Sun staff learned about the supplier, and vice versa. Both spoke of 'harmonising expectations'.

Source: Boddy *et al.* (2000).

The context affects the ability to change

While people managing a project aim to change the context, the context within which they work will itself help or hinder that attempt. All of the elements of Figure 13.2 will be present as the project begins, and some of these will influence how people react. Managers who occupy influential positions in an existing structure will review a proposal to change it from the perspective of their careers, as well as of the organisation. At Tesco the existing technology (stores, distribution systems, information systems) and business processes would influence managers' decisions about how to implement the Internet shopping strategy.

The prevailing culture (Chapter 3) – shared values, ideals and beliefs – influences how people view change. Members are likely to welcome a project that they believe fits their culture or subculture, and to resist one that threatens it.

Culture and change at a European bank

While teaching a course to managers at a European bank, the author invited members to identify which of the four cultural types identified in Chapter 2 best described their unit within the bank. They were then asked to describe the reaction of these units to an Internet banking venture that the company was introducing.

Course members observed that colleagues in a unit that had an internal process culture (routine back-office data processing) were hostile to the Internet venture. They appeared to be 'stuck with their own systems', which were so large and interlinked that any change was threatening. Staff in new business areas of the company (open systems) were much more positive, seeing the Internet as a way towards new business opportunities.

Source: Data collected by the author.

Culture is a powerful influence on the success or failure of innovation – see Jones *et al.* (2005) for evidence of how it affected the acceptance of a new computer system. Some cultures support change: a manager in Sun Microsystems commented on that fast-moving business:

> A very dynamic organisation, it's incredibly fast and the change thing is just a constant that you live with. They really promote flexibility and adaptability in their employees. Change is just a constant, there's change happening all of the time and people have become very acclimatised to that, it's part of the job. The attitude to change, certainly within the organisation, is very positive at the moment.

At Sun (and many other companies such as Google or eBay) the culture encourages change, while elsewhere it encourages caution. Cultural beliefs are hard to change, yet shape how people respond:

> Managers learn to be guided by these beliefs because they have worked successfully in the past (Lorsch, 1986, p. 97).

Receptive contexts are those where features of the organisation (such as culture or technology) appear likely to help change.

Non-receptive contexts are those where the combined effects of features of the organisation (such as culture or technology) appear likely to hinder change.

Receptive and non-receptive contexts

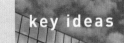
key ideas

Pettigrew *et al.* (1992) sought to explain why managers in some organisations were able to introduce change successfully, while others in the same sector (the UK National Health Service) found it very hard to move away from established practices. Their comparative research programme identified the influence of context on ability to change: **receptive contexts** are those where features of the context 'seem to be favourably associated with forward movement. On the other hand, in **non-receptive contexts** there is a configuration of features that may be associated with blocks on change' (p. 268).

Their research identified seven such contextual factors, which provide a linked set of conditions that are likely to provide the energy around change. These are:

1 quality and coherence of policy
2 availability of key people leading change
3 long-term environmental pressure – intensity and scale
4 a supportive organisational culture
5 effective managerial–clinical relations
6 cooperative interorganisational networks
7 the fit between the district's change agenda and its locale.

While some of these factors are specific to the health sector, they can easily be adapted to other settings. Together these factors give a widely applicable model of how the context affects ability to change.

Source: Pettigrew *et al.* (1992).

The distribution of power also affects receptiveness to change. Change threatens the status quo, and is likely to be resisted by stakeholders who benefit from the prevailing arrangements. Innovation depends on those behind the change developing political will and expertise that they can only attempt within the prevailing pattern of power.

The context has a history, and several levels

The present context is the result of past decisions and events: Balogun *et al.* (2005) show how internal change agents adapted practice to suit aspects of their context, such as the degree of local autonomy, senior management preferences, rewards systems and financial reporting systems. Management implements change against a background of previous events that shaped the context. The promoter of a major project in a multinational experienced this in his colleagues' attitudes:

> They were a little sceptical and wary of whether it was actually going to enhance our processes. Major pan-European redesign work had been attempted in the past and had failed miserably. The solutions had not been appropriate and had not been accepted by the divisions. Europe-wide programmes therefore had a bad name. (Boddy, 2002, p. 38)

Beliefs about the future also affect how people react. Optimists are more open to change than those who feel threatened and vulnerable.

Vodafone/Ericsson – the case continues
www.vodafone.com, www.ericsson.com

CASE STUDY

Vodafone conducted business in each country in partnership with other operators, with Vodafone often having a minority shareholding in the company. For example, in the United Kingdom it owned 100 per cent of the equity, in Germany 99 per cent and in Australia 91 per cent. In The Netherlands, Portugal and Spain this fell to 70, 50 and 22 per cent respectively.

This meant that

considerable political skill and discussion was required to handle the attitudes of the various operating companies with regard to Ericsson's local in-country operations. Some countries had acquired very favourable terms and conditions that would not necessarily be matched by the global agreements, while others had key skills that would now be 'given up' to the global effort.

Source: Ibbott and O'Keefe (2004), p. 226.

The context represented by Figure 13.2 occurs at (say) operating, divisional and corporate levels. People at any of these will be acting to change their context – which may help or hinder those managing change elsewhere. A project at one level may depend on decisions at another about resources, as this manager leading an oil refinery project discovered:

> One of the main drawbacks was that commissioning staff could have been supplemented by skilled professionals from within the company, but this was denied to me as project manager. This threw a heavy strain and responsibility on myself and my assistant. It put me in a position of high stress, as I knew that the future of the company rested upon the successful outcome of this project. One disappointment (and, I believe, a significant factor in the project) was that just before commissioning, the manager of the pilot plant development team was transferred to another job. He had been promised to me at the project inception, and I had designed him into the working operation. (Boddy, 2002, pp. 38–39)

Acting to change an element at one level will have effects at this and other levels, and elements may change independently. The manager's job is to create a coherent context that encourages desired behaviour, by using their preferred model of change.

Activity 13.2   Critical reflection on reactions to context

- What aspects of the contemporary context, shown in Figure 13.2, have had most effect on a project you are familiar with?
- How have historical factors affected people's reactions?
- Were the effects positive or negative for the project?
- To what extent is the context receptive or non-receptive to change?

13.4 Four models of change

There are four complementary models of change, each with different implications for managers – life cycle, emergent, participative and political.

Life cycle models

Much advice given to those responsible for managing projects uses the idea of the project **life cycle**. Projects go through successive stages, and results depend on managing each one in an orderly and controlled way. The labels vary, but common themes are:

1 Define objectives.
2 Allocate responsibilities.
3 Fix deadlines and milestones.
4 Set budgets.
5 Monitor and control.

Life cycle models of change are those that view change as an activity which follows a logical, orderly sequence of activities that can be planned in advance.

This approach (sometimes called a 'rational–linear' approach) reflects the idea that a change can be broken down into smaller tasks, and that these can be done in some preferred, if overlapping, sequence. It predicts that people can make reasonably accurate estimates of the time required to complete each task and when it will be feasible to start work on later ones. People can use tools such as bar charts (sometimes called Gantt charts after the American industrial engineer Henry Gantt, who worked with Frederick Taylor), to show all the tasks required for a project, and their likely duration. These help to visualise the work required and to plan the likely sequence of events – as illustrated in Figure 13.3.

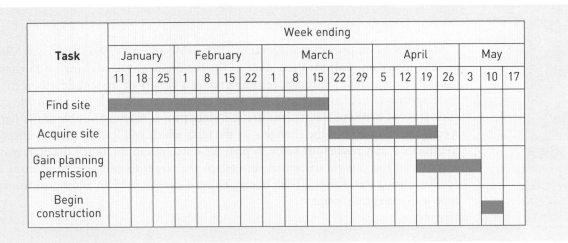

Figure 13.3 A simple bar chart

In the life cycle model successfully managing change depends on specifying these elements at the start and then monitoring them tightly to ensure the project stays on target. Ineffective implementation is due to managers failing to do this. Figure 13.4 shows the stages of a manufacturing project (Lock, 2003). He advises project managers to ensure that the stages are passed through in turn, 'until the project arrives back to the customer as a completed work package'. He emphasises the iterative, cyclical nature of the method:

> Clockwise rotation around the cycle only reveals the main stream. Within this flow many small tributaries, cross-currents and even whirlpools are generated before the project is finished (p. 26).

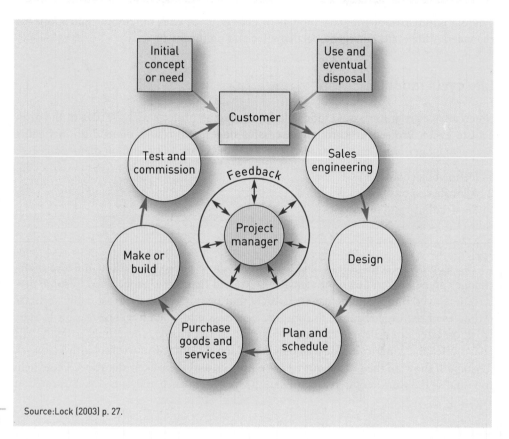

Figure 13.4

A project life cycle

Source: Lock (2003) p. 27.

Many books on project management, such as Woodward (1997) and Lock (2003), present advice on tools for each stage of the life cycle. Those advising on IS changes usually take a similar approach, recommending a variety of 'system development life cycle' approaches (Chaffey, 2003). For some changes the life cycle gives valuable guidance. It is not necessarily sufficient in itself, since people may not be able at the start to specify the end point of the change – or the tasks which will lead to that. In uncertain conditions it may make little sense to plan the outcomes in too much detail. It may be wiser to set the general direction, and adapt the target to suit new conditions that develop during the change. Those managing such change need an additional theory to cope with emergent change.

| Activity 13.3 | Critical reflection on the project life cycle |

You may be able to gain some insight into the project life cycle by using it on a practical task. For example:

- If you have a piece of work to do that is connected with your studies, such as an assignment or project, sketch out the steps to be followed by adapting Figure 13.4; alternatively do the same for some domestic, social or management project.
- If you work in an organisation, try to find examples of projects that use this approach, and ask those involved when the method is most useful, and when least useful.
- Make notes summarising how the life cycle approach helps, and when it is most likely to be useful.

Emergent models

In Chapter 8 (Section 8.6) Barthélemy (2006) offers an insight into the strategy process at IKEA (Chapter 15 case), showing how many of its strategies have emerged from chance events or external conditions, rather than from a formal planning process. Evidence such as this led Quinn (1980) and Mintzberg (1994a, 1994b) to see strategy as an *emergent* or adaptive process. These ideas apply to change projects as much as they do to strategy. Projects are the means through which organisations deliver strategy. They take place in the same volatile, uncertain environment in which the organisation operates. People with different interests and priorities influence the means and ends of a project. So while the planning techniques associated with the life cycle approach can help, their value will be limited if the change is closer to the **emergent model**.

Emergent models of change emphasise that in uncertain conditions a project will be affected by unknown factors, and that planning has little effect on the outcome.

Vodafone/Ericsson – the case continues
www.vodafone.com, www.ericsson.com

CASE STUDY

The globalisation strategy was developed and implemented through the Global Supply Chain Management (GSCM) forum that first met in 1999. Initially it was attended by representatives from both companies in those countries where Vodafone had a majority shareholding in the local operating company, though membership gradually expanded to include most countries in which Vodafone operated. The initial meeting resolved that all joint activities should be conducted in an open and transparent way: 'It would be a process of learning through experience; there would be no requirement to produce plans that formed a rigid basis of change control' (Ibbott and O'Keefe, 2004, p. 224).

The members believed that a planned project approach would not have worked, as it was important to be able to cope with rapid change.

Both the end point and direction were uncertain, and fundamental process changes had to be agreed within and between companies. The acquisition of Mannesmann of Germany, unplanned at the start of the transformation, provided an opportunity for further benefits (p. 229).

The forum also recognised that the two sides would benefit in different ways, but there was no attempt to plan how to share the benefits – either party would retain whatever benefits they secured. Vodafone's equity-based structure in the different countries meant that those leading the project had to sell the concept of the global endeavour to the management teams of each entity. Ericsson's more unified structure of wholly owned subsidiaries gave them less scope for resisting proposals.

GSCM meetings set up several work streams that would move the relationship towards global collabora- ▶

tion. The leadership of each work stream was assigned to one or other of the participating countries. The teams leading them had to secure resources for the project from within their country operations, working as they saw fit. Examples of work streams were:

- creating a global price book for all products bought from Ericsson (UK team)
- agreeing a standard base station design (UK team)
- agreeing a common procedure for software design and testing (Australia)
- developing a computer-based information system linking the parties for information sharing – initially called groupware (The Netherlands).

While the groupware project was at first intended to support communications between the teams working on the globalisation project, it later evolved into a system through which both parties conducted routine transactions – such as ordering products. The simple communication system emerged, without any formal plan, into a system for handling all orders from Vodafone to Ericsson that had a global price.

Source: Ibbott and O'Keefe (2004).

Boddy *et al.* (2000) show how this emergent process occurred when Sun Microsystems began the partnering project described earlier. Sun's initial intention was to secure a UK source for the bulky plastic enclosures that contain their products, while the supplier was seeking ways to widen its customer base. There were few discussions about a long-term plan. As Sun became more confident of its supplier's ability it gave them more complex work. Both gained from this emerging relationship. They acknowledge that at first they did not foresee the amount and type of business they would eventually be undertaking. A sales coordinator:

> It's something we've learnt by being with Sun – we didn't imagine that at the time. Also at the time we wouldn't have imagined we would be dealing with America the way we do now – it was far beyond our thoughts. (Boddy *et al.*, 2000, p. 1010)

Mintzberg's point is that managers should not expect rigid adherence to 'the plan'. Some departure from it is inevitable, due to unforeseeable changes in the external environment, the emergence of new opportunities, and other unanticipated events. A flexible approach to change is one which recognises that

> the real world inevitably involves some thinking ahead of time as well as some adaptation en route (Mintzberg, 1994a, p. 24).

Case questions 13.4

- Were those leading the change taking a life cycle or an emergent view?
- Which of those views does the evidence of later events seem to support?

Participative models

The **participative model** is the belief that if people are able to take part in planning a change they will be more willing to accept and implement the change.

Those advocating **participative models** stress the benefits of personal involvement in, and contribution to, events and outcomes. The underlying belief is that if people can say 'I helped to build this', they will be more willing to live and work with it, whatever it is. It is also possible that since participation allows a wider range of views to be expressed the outcome will be of higher quality than if it takes account of a limited range of views. Empirical support for this was provided by the study by Ketokivi and Castañer (2004), cited in Chapter 6 (Section 6.4). They found that when employees participated in planning strategic change, they were more likely to view the issues from the perspective of the organisation, rather than their own position or function. Participation can be good for the organisation, as well as the individual.

Enid Mumford and participation

key ideas

A leading advocate and practitioner of participative approaches to change was Edith Mumford, who applied the principles of socio-technical systems in her work. This theory was outlined in Chapter 2 (Section 2.7) and is based on the idea that an organisation has both technical and social components. Mumford and her colleagues focused on change based on the introduction of computer systems, noting that IS development projects typically overemphasised the technical, and underestimated the social aspects. She sought, through the development of the ETHICS method (Mumford and Weir, 1979), to enable developers to give adequate attention to both. Advocates claimed that this approach would lead to systems that not only worked (from a technical perspective) but were also more attractive from a human point of view, enhancing motivation and job satisfaction.

The approach required a high degree of participation by users in the design, to ensure as much compatibility with the social system in which the technology would be set. This participative approach typically involved people in decisions about the design of the system, and in making decisions within a work team about its operation. Reflecting on the limited acceptance of participative systems in recent years, she concludes that a major barrier has been that of the cultural context. With many organisations retaining a hierarchical form, those in higher positions are frequently reluctant to give up power to the degree implied by participative approaches to change (Mumford, 1997, 2006).

Source: Mumford (1997, 2006).

Staff participation in planning the CGU merger

management in practice

One of the UK's biggest mergers in 1998 was that of Commercial Union and General Accident to form CGU. The merger involved many changes, and management decided to involve employees in planning these, mainly through three large meetings of hundreds of staff, nominated by their colleagues:

1 Two hundred staff conducted a culture survey of the two companies. They were paired, one from each company, and escorted each other into the other's company, where they used a set format to build a culture map – how the firms were similar and how they differed.
2 Five hundred managers and technical specialists attended a two-day conference to work in teams on the results of the culture survey and other data. Their task was to form a view about what would make CGU the 'best place to work'. Video cameras captured the action and displayed it overhead on giant television screens around the hall, giving the two days the feel of a vibrant sporting event. Amongst the priorities the delegates agreed were clear boundaries of authority, freedom to take decisions within those boundaries, clear expectations, feedback, access to opportunity, and support for development.
3 Eighty people attended a four-day structured design workshop. Their task was to start designing a new organisation to meet the needs of shareholders, customers, employees and business partners. They produced a design that included principles of access (ensuring all would have easy entrance to their new offices), size of business units (30 to 50 people), and size of teams (between 10 and 12).

▶

Tony Clarry commented:

> The roll-out in the 51 locations so far has been smooth, which we attribute to the degree of commitment to the integration teams and to the conscientiousness of our people. Of course, there has been pain ... but involving people in decision making continues to be at the heart of what we do. We believe our approach has proved the value of real consultation.

Source: Based on an article by Tony Clarry, who led the integration of the two companies, in *People Management*, 2 September 1999.

While the approach is consistent with democratic values, it is not free. It takes time and effort, and may raise unrealistic expectations. It may be inappropriate when:

- there is already agreement on how to proceed;
- the scope for change is limited, because of decisions made elsewhere;
- those taking part in the exercise have little knowledge of the topic;
- decisions are needed urgently to meet deadlines set elsewhere;
- management has decided what to do and will do so whatever views people express;
- there is fundamental disagreement and inflexible opposition to a change.

Participative approaches assume that a sensitive approach by reasonable people will result in the willing acceptance and implementation of change. Other situations contain conflicts that participation alone cannot solve.

Activity 13.4 Critical reflection on participation

Have you been involved in, or affected by, a change in your work or studies?

If so

- What evidence was there that those managing the change agreed with the participative approach?
- In what way, if any, were you able to participate?
- How did that affect your reaction to the change?

If not:

- Identify three advantages and three disadvantages for the project manager in adopting a participative approach.
- Suggest how managers should decide when to use the approach.

Political models

The models described so far offer little guidance where a change challenges established interests, or where powerful players have opposing views. Change often involves people from several levels and functions who will pull in different directions, pursuing personal as well as organisational goals:

> Strategic processes of change are ... widely accepted as multi-level activities and not just as the province of a ... single general manager. Outcomes of decisions are no longer assumed to be a product of rational ... debates but are also shaped by the interests and commitments of individuals and groups, forces of bureaucratic momentum, and the manipulation of the structural context around decisions and changes. (Whipp *et al.*, 1988, p. 51)

Several analyses of organisational change emphasise a **political model** (Pettigrew, 1985, 1987; Pfeffer, 1992a; Pinto, 1998; Buchanan and Badham, 1999). Pettigrew (1985) was an early advocate of the view that change requires political as well as rational (life cycle) skills. Successful change managers create a climate in which people accept the change as legitimate – often by manipulating apparently rational information to build support for their ideas.

Political models reflect the view that organisations are made up of groups with separate interests, goals and values, and that these affect how they respond to change.

Tom Burns on politics and language   key ideas

Tom Burns (1961) observed that political behaviour in the organisation is invariably concealed or made acceptable by subtle shifts in the language that people use:

> Normally, either side in any conflict called political by observers claims to speak in the interests of the corporation as a whole. In fact, the only recognised, indeed feasible, way of advancing political interests is to present them in terms of improved welfare or efficiency, as contributing to the organisation's capacity to meet its task and to prosper. In managerial and academic, as in other legislatures, both sides to any debate claim to speak in the interests of the community as a whole; this is the only permissible mode of expression. (p. 260)

Pfeffer (1992a) also argues that power is essential to get things done, since decisions in themselves change nothing. It is only when someone implements them that anyone notices a difference. He proposes that projects require more than people able to solve technical problems. Projects frequently threaten the status quo: people who have done well in the past are likely to resist them. Innovators also need to ensure the project is on the agenda, and that senior managers support and resource it. Innovators also need to develop a political will, and to build and use their power. Buchanan and Badham (1999) consider why political behaviour occurs, and conclude that:

> Its roots lie in personal ambition, in organisation structures that create roles and departments which compete with each other, and in major decisions that cannot be resolved by reason and logic alone but which rely on the values and preferences of the key actors.
>
> Power politics and change are inextricably linked. Change creates uncertainty and ambiguity. People wonder how their jobs will change, how their workload will be affected, how their relationships with colleagues will be damaged or enhanced. (p. 11)

Reasonable people may disagree about means and ends, and fight for the action they prefer. This implies that successful project managers understand that their job requires more than technical competence, and are able and willing to engage in political actions.

Henry Kissinger on politics in politics   key ideas

In another work Pfeffer (1992b) quotes Henry Kissinger:

> Before I served as a consultant to Kennedy, I had believed, like most academics, that the process of decision-making was largely intellectual and all one had to do was to walk into the President's office and convince him of the correctness of one's view. This perspective I soon realised is as dangerously immature as it is widely held. (p. 31)

Source: Pfeffer (1992b).

Politics and change in the public sector

These views of change as a fluid process find support in a contemporary account of project management in the public sector, based on research amongst a group of managers implementing major change projects:

The powerful influence of the political process on organisational and cultural change is transparent for local authorities, but this may also be relevant in other non-elected organisations. Competing values and interests between different stakeholders are often less overt but none the less powerful factors championing or blocking processes of change.

Source: Hartley *et al.* (1997) p. 71.

The political perspective recognises the messy realities of organisational life. Major changes will be technically complex and challenge established interests. These will pull in different directions and pursue personal as well as organisational goals. To manage these tensions managers need political skills as well as those implied by life cycle, emergent and participative perspectives.

They need to be sensitive to the power and influence of key individuals, aware of how the change may alter those, and able to negotiate and sell ideas to indifferent or sceptical colleagues. They may have to filter information to change perceptions, and do things that make the change seem legitimate within the organisation.

Political action in hospital re-engineering

Managers in a hospital responded to a persistent performance gap (especially unacceptably long waiting times) by 're-engineering' the way patients moved through and between the different clinical areas. This included creating multi-functional teams responsible for all aspects of the flow of the patient through a clinic, rather than dealing with narrow functional tasks. The programme was successful, but was also controversial. One of those leading the change recalled:

I don't like to use the word manipulate, but ... you do need to manipulate people. It's about playing the game. I remember being accosted by a very cross consultant who had heard something about one of the changes and he really wasn't very happy with it. And it was about how am I going to deal with this now? And it is about being able to think quickly. So I put it over to him in a way that he then accepted, and he was quite happy with. And it wasn't a lie and it wasn't totally the truth. But he was happy with it and it has gone on.

Source: Buchanan (2001), p. 13.

Pensco

Pensco was a life insurance business. Changes to legislation brought new opportunities in the market for personal and group pensions, and also more competition. The board appointed a new general manager who began to change the organisation towards a market-led, sales-maximising approach. He recruited a colleague from his previous company as head of information systems (IS), who had a reputation as an autocratic and aggressive manager. Changing the pensions products depended on new IS to process the new business.

The actuarial department (AD) proposed some new pension products. Staff in sales and marketing (S&M) interpreted the market differently, were dismissive of the AD proposals, and actively lobbied for their alternative ideas. S&M also believed that the IS department had

> too much power in the organisation ... We are working to change that. S&M should drive the organisation ... But I can't get away from the view that IS still dictate what the company can and can't do. (Knights and Murray, 1994, p. 187)

For their part, IS had trouble identifying the business requirements – partly because of unresolved conflicts between AD and S&M over the product range. The head of IS was seen to be seeking favour with the general manager by accepting all requests for systems developments – which staff were unable to deliver.

The company presented the project as a success. The authors of the case reported different views from the clerical staff who were processing new proposals (without adequate IS support). As a team leader commented:

> They [the managers] don't have a grasp of what's going on. They just want the figures. They don't appreciate our problems. I wish they'd acknowledge there is one. (p. 162).

Source: Based on Knights and Murray (1994).

These perspectives (life cycle, emergent, participative and political) are complementary in that successful large-scale change, such as that at Vodafone/Ericsson, is likely to require elements of each. Table 13.2 illustrates how each perspective links to management practice.

Table 13.2

Perspectives on change and examples of management practice

Perspective	Themes	Example of management practices
Life cycle	Rational, linear, single agreed aim, technical focus	Measurable objectives; planning and control devices such as Gantt charts and critical path analysis
Emergent	Objectives change as learning occurs during the project, and new possibilities appear	Open to new ideas about scope and direction, and willing to add new resources if needed
Participative	Ownership, commitment, shared goals, people focus	Inviting ideas and comments on proposals, ensuring agreement before action, seeking consensus
Political	Oppositional, influence, conflicting goals, power focus	Building allies and coalitions, securing support from powerful players, managing information

13.5 Driving and restraining forces – Kurt Lewin

Lewin (1947) observed that any social system is in a state of temporary equilibrium. Driving forces are trying to change the situation in directions they favour. Restraining forces push the other way to prevent change, or to move it in another direction. This equilibrium 'can be changed either by adding forces in the desired direction, or by diminishing the opposing forces' (p. 26). Figure 13.5 illustrates the idea: see Burnes (2004) for an appraisal of the influence and continued relevance of Lewin's ideas.

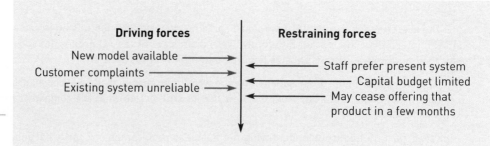

Figure 13.5

Driving and restraining forces

Driving forces encourage change from the present position. They encourage people and groups to give up past practice and to act in ways that support the change. They take many forms – such as a newly available technology, an inadequate business process or the support of a powerful player. Conversely factors such as the already-installed technology, shortage of finance, the opposition of powerful players or the company culture can be restraining forces. In many small companies, managers are said to be so absorbed in day-to-day matters that they are unable to put time and energy into major changes that would help the business to grow. They become committed to maintaining existing practice.

Those advocating a change can, in Lewin's terms, 'add forces in the desired direction' by stressing the advantages of the change, emphasising the threat from competitors or making the benefits seem more attractive. Mr Yun Jong-yon, chief executive of Samsung Electronics, was credited with transforming the company from a struggling producer of cheap electronics into one of the world's best-performing and most respected IT companies. He explained part of his approach:

> I'm the chaos-maker. I have tried to encourage a sense of crisis to drive change. We instilled in management a sense that we could go bankrupt any day. (*Financial Times*, 13 March 2003, p. 15)

Alternatively they can seek to 'diminish the opposing forces' by showing that the problems will not be as great as people fear, or pointing out that difficulties will be temporary.

Lewin observed that while increasing the driving forces could produce change in the desired direction, it could also increase tension amongst those 'forced' to change. The change may then be short-lived, or offset by the negative effects of the tension. Since these secondary effects may go against the interests of those promoting change, he suggested that trying to reduce the forces restraining change is usually the wiser route. The Management in Practice feature shows an alternative view – namely that increasing the driving forces can also work.

management in practice **The power of the visual image**

Kotter and Cohen (2002) give several examples of the use of dramatic visual images to overcome inertia. In one case, showing a video of an angry customer to employees sparked a sense of urgency that helped to overcome long-standing resistance to improving the product. Another explains how a taskforce handling poor investment planning made a light-hearted video with spoof characters who mimicked the damaging behaviour of senior executives. The video apparently shocked the executives into changing their behaviour. Kotter believes that the main reason why change efforts of any size fail is that there is not a great enough sense of urgency about the need to change – and that visual shocks can help break that barrier.

Source: Kotter and Cohen (2002).

External events can trigger and drive change: new competition, a change in legislation, the activities of a pressure group, a chance conversation. Information from any of these sources can trigger change. People with sufficient power can use these and countless other external signs to justify a proposal.

In the same way, forces within the organisation – changing management priorities, the availability of funds, opposition from groups who see their privileges threatened – can drive change, or restrain it. The degree and direction of change in an organisation reflect the shifting balance and direction of the driving and restraining forces.

13.6 Forms and sources of resistance to change

Most managers are expected to implement change in the context in which they work. In doing so they use their power to influence others to act in a particular way. Chapter 14 outlines theories of power and influence, so this and the following sections examine just three aspects of this activity – understanding resistance to change, using front-stage and back-stage tactics, and supporting individual activity with formal structures.

Much of the management literature presents resistance to change in pejorative terms as something to be overcome, but this discussion takes a more neutral stance. There is anecdotal evidence of managers introducing change to further personal interests – to build a reputation or extend departmental influence. Since organisations comprise political and career systems as well as working systems, this is inevitable. Even when people intend to support organisational interests they may misinterpret the situation and propose misguided changes.

For all these reasons people at all levels will sometimes resist change, either as a threat to their interests or because they believe it will damage the organisation. Many change programmes fade from view – unless someone is able to make the change stick by creating a favourable context (Roberto and Levesque, 2005).

Forms of resistance

Overt and public resistance is often unnecessary. There are many other ways in which those opposed to a change can delay it, including:

- making no effort to learn
- using older systems whenever possible
- not attending meetings to discuss the project
- excessive fault finding and criticism
- deliberate misuse
- saying it has been tried before and did not work then
- protracted discussion and requests for more information
- linking the issue with pay or other industrial relations matters
- not releasing staff for training.

These delaying tactics come from anywhere in the organisation – they are as likely to come from managers who see a change as a threat to their interests as they are to come from more junior staff. Change creates winners and losers, and potential losers are apt to engage in what Keen (1981) termed the tactics of **counterimplementation**.

Counterimplementation refers to attempts to block change without displaying overt opposition.

key ideas   Peter Keen on counterimplementation

Keen (1981) suggested that overt resistance to change is often risky, and may not in practice be necessary. He identified several ways in which those wanting to block a change can do so – even while appearing to support it. They include such tactics as:

- **Divert resources** Split the budget across other projects; give key staff other priorities and allocate them to other assignments; arrange for equipment to be moved or shared.
- **Exploit inertia** Suggest that everyone wait until a key player has taken action or read the report or made an appropriate response; suggest that the results from some other project should be monitored and assessed first.
- **Keep goals vague and complex** It is harder to initiate appropriate action in pursuit of aims that are multidimensional and specified in generalised, grandiose or abstract terms.
- **Encourage and exploit lack of organisational awareness** Insist that 'we can deal with the people issues later', knowing that these will delay or kill the project.
- **'Great idea – let's do it properly'** And let's bring in representatives from this function and that section, until we have so many different views and conflicting interests that it will take for ever to sort them out.
- **Dissipate energies** Have people conduct surveys, collect data, prepare analyses, write reports, make overseas trips, hold special meetings ...
- **Reduce the champion's influence and credibility** Spread damaging rumours, particularly amongst the champion's friends and supporters.
- **Keep a low profile** It is not effective openly to declare resistance to change because that gives those driving change a clear target.

Source: Based on Keen (1981).

Activity 13.5   **Critical reflection on resistance**

Discuss with someone who has tried to introduce change in an organisation what evidence there was of resistance.

- Which of the forms listed by Keen (in Key Ideas above) were in evidence?
- Can they identify any other forms?

Then consider these questions:

- Have you ever resisted a proposed change?
- What form did your resistance take?

Sources of resistance

Kotter and Schlesinger (1979) identified that sources of resistance included self-interest, misunderstanding and lack of trust: 'people also resist change when they do not understand its implications and perceive that it might cost them much more than they will gain' (p. 108). Employees assess the situation differently from their managers and may see more costs than benefits for both themselves and the company. Recardo (1991) made similar points from a study of new manufacturing systems. Change requires learning and exposure to uncertainty, insecurity and new social interactions, yet communication about the changes is often poor. Additional factors that Recardo identified as causing resistance were reward systems that did not reward the desired behaviour and a poor fit between the change and the existing culture.

These views can be enlarged by using the elements of the organisation shown in Figure 13.2. People can base their resistance on any of these contextual elements, as shown in Table 13.3.

Table 13.3

Sources of resistance to change

Element	Source of resistance
Objectives	Lack of clarity or understanding of objectives, or disagreement with those proposed
People	Change may threaten important values, preferences, skills, needs and interests
Technology	May be poorly designed, hard to use, incompatible with existing equipment, or require more work than is worthwhile
Business processes	As for technology, and may require unwelcome changes to the way people deal with colleagues and customers
Financial resources	Scepticism about whether the change will be financially worthwhile, or less so than other competing changes; lack of money
Structure	New reporting relationships or means of control may disrupt working relationships and patterns of authority
Culture	People likely to resist a change that challenges core values and beliefs, especially if they have worked well before
Power	If change affects ownership of and access to information, those who see they will lose autonomy will resist

In addition to these substantive or content reasons for resisting change, people may also resist because of the way others manage the change. They object to the process of change, irrespective of the specific change being made. Change is disturbing, and people are likely to resist if they do not feel they have been able to participate in discussions about the form it should take.

13.7 Organisation development

Organisation development (OD) is a comprehensive and widely used approach to managing change. It embodies a clear set of values about people and work, many of which relate to ideas on organisation culture (Chapter 3), human resource management (Chapter 11), and work design (Chapter 15).

A common theme in managing is how to balance the needs of the individual with the behaviour required for high organisational performance. OD practitioners believe that

> with appropriate interventions based on social scientific understanding, the conflicting interests of organizations and their members can be diagnosed and reconciled. (Huczynski and Buchanan, 2007, p. 560)

Organisation development is a systematic process in which applied behavioural science principles and practices are introduced with the goal of increasing individual and organisational performance.

Practitioners use OD to resolve conflicts within a single business unit or for the organisation as a whole, aiming for both individual development and organisational effectiveness. They try to achieve these mutually supporting goals through deliberate and systematic interventions, using knowledge from the social and behavioural sciences.

Robbins (2001, p. 553) outlines the values that underlie most OD activities:

- The individual should be treated with respect and dignity.
- The organisation climate should be characterised by trust, openness and support.

- Hierarchical authority and control are de-emphasised.
- Problems and conflicts should be confronted, not disguised or avoided.
- People affected by change should be involved in its implementation.

Some practitioners believe that this agenda is worth pursuing in its own right, though others stress that implementing practices based on these values will make a business more efficient and effective.

A common theme in OD is that bureaucracy is an obstacle to performance, and that an organisation in which staff have more freedom and flexibility in the way they work will also show a better financial performance. Table 13.4 summarises how OD practitioners tackle these problems in both private and public sector organisations (Bate, 2000).

Table 13.4

Bureaucratic diseases and OD cures

Bureaucratic disease	Symptoms	OD cures
Rigid functional boundaries	Conflict between sections, poor communications	Team building, job rotation, structural change
Fixed hierarchies	Frustration, boredom, narrow specialist thinking	Training, job enrichment, career development
Information only flows down	Lack of innovation, minor problems escalate	Process consultation, management development
Routine jobs, tight control	Boredom, absenteeism, conflict with supervisors	Job enrichment, job rotation, supervisory training

Source: Buchanan and Huczynski (2007), p. 563.

Common OD techniques are listed below, and more detail on each is contained in Huczynski and Buchanan (2007, pp. 568–572).

Sensitivity training is a technique for enhancing self-awareness and changing behaviour through unstructured group discussion.

- **Sensitivity training** Conducted in small groups, the aim of **sensitivity training** is to allow participants to discuss themselves, to observe and discuss how the members interact with each other and to exchange feedback on each other. The intention is that through such discussions participants become more sensitive to their behaviour, the effects they have on others, and how others see and relate to them.
- **Changing structure** OD projects often include efforts to decentralise organisations by giving more decision-making power to local units, or changing the horizontal structure of the organisation through business process redesign. Structural changes signify which areas of the organisation are becoming more significant, and which are in decline.

Process consultation is an OD intervention in which an external consultant facilitates improvements in an organisation's diagnostic, conceptual and action planning skills.

- **Process consultation** A consultant undertakes **process consultation** to help members of the organisation to develop a clearer insight into the problems facing the organisation, as distinct from an external consultant doing the analysis. It is consistent with core OD values that people are ultimately responsible for their development.
- **Survey feedback** This refers to the technique of conducting a survey of employee attitudes, and providing managers or supervisors with anonymous analyses of the results – hence the term **survey feedback**. Respondents may be invited to suggest themes or questions to include in the survey, and to take part in group discussions of the results.

Survey feedback is an OD intervention in which the results of an opinion survey are fed back to respondents to trigger problem solving on the issues the survey identifies.

- **Team building** Attempts to develop more effective teams using a wide variety of methods, such as that developed by Meredith Belbin (1993) in which members identify the distinctive team roles they play, and how different combinations affect performance (Chapter 17).

- **Intergroup development** This helps overcome the boundaries which can arise between groups that are expected to work together. Functional boundaries and diverse experiences lead groups to develop a strong internal identity – and possibly strong negative feelings towards other groups. Intergroup development helps to break down assumptions, and encourage more cooperative working across boundaries.
- **Grid organisation development** This is an application of Blake and Mouton's (1979) managerial grid, described in Chapter 14. The grid assumes that leadership styles vary on two dimensions – concern for production and concern for people. Managers can be assessed on the extent to which they are high, medium or low on each dimension. The prescription is that ideally they should be high on both, and the technique is intended to help managers reflect on their style, and move closer to the ideal type.

13.8 Stimulating innovation

An increasingly common aspect of managers' jobs is the pressure to stimulate innovation in the areas for which they are responsible. This covers being innovative in creating new products and services, and in the processes that deliver them. Some organisations have developed a reputation for being better able than others at sensing and satisfying consumer trends.

Lorne and Agnes Campbell and TravelCo

management in practice

TravelCo is an entrepreneurial travel company that specialises in delivering customised, luxurious holidays to US visitors interested in Scottish heritage. Employees must follow highly specified routines and systems in matters such as ticketing and scheduling: this is essential to ensure error-free reservations and other arrangements for their customers. However the same employees must be able to devise creative solutions to meet customers' individual requirements for their visit to Scotland – from where their ancestors often came. The company encourages employees to think laterally and creatively for this aspect of the work.

It does this by allowing them wide decision-making powers to come up with imaginative holiday ideas. An example was a US customer who wanted his itinerary to include an opportunity to meet some of his Clan Campbell ancestors. His guide, Abigail Forbes, was able to arrange for him to lunch with Lorne and Agnes Campbell, her 80-something grandparents in the ancient Scottish town of Inverary – which delighted the visitor as an imaginative and innovative way of achieving exactly what he wanted.

Source: Private communication.

Creativity and innovation

Creativity refers to the ability to combine ideas in a new way, or to make unusual associations between ideas. This helps people and organisations to generate imaginative ideas or ways of working: but that in itself does not ensure added value. That only comes when people turn the creative process into products or services that meet a demand, which they can meet profitably. In the public sector **innovation** is reflected in new ways of delivering services (such as the growing provision of online services); in the charities sector it could be a new way of raising funds, such as the RED brand associated with leading pop stars, which devotes a proportion of its profits to designated charities.

Creativity is the ability to combine ideas in a unique way, or to make unusual associations between ideas.

Innovation is the process of taking a creative idea and turning it into a useful product, service or method of operation.

Stimulating innovation

The systems model introduced in Chapter 1 helps to understand how organisations can become more innovative. Figure 13.6 shows that getting the desired outputs (more innovative products or work methods) depends on both the inputs and the transformation of those inputs.

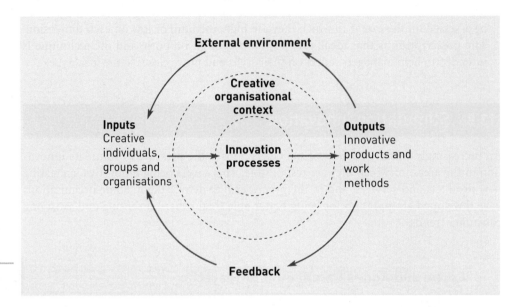

Figure 13.6

Systems view of innovation

Inputs include having creative people and groups who are able to generate novel ideas and methods, but creative people can only sustain their creativity in a favourable context. Figure 13.7 shows three significant elements of that context – cultures, HR policies and structures.

Cultures for innovation

Innovative organisations tend to have cultures that encourage experimentation, reward success and accept that some failures are inevitable – a source of learning rather than shame. Robbins and Coulter (2005, p. 329) suggest that an innovative culture is likely to have these features:

● *Acceptance of ambiguity* Too much emphasis on objective analysis and detailed planning constrains creativity.
● *Tolerance of the impractical* Individuals who offer impractical, even foolish, answers to speculative questions are not ridiculed. What at first seems impractical may lead to innovative solutions.
● *Low external controls* Rules, regulations and procedures are kept to a minimum.
● *Tolerance of risk* Employees are encouraged to experiment without fear of the consequence if they fail. Mistakes become opportunities for learning.
● *Tolerance of conflict* Diversity of opinions is encouraged. Harmony and agreement between people and sub-units is not taken as a sign of high performance.
● *Focus on end rather than means* Goals are clear, but individuals choose how to achieve them.
● *Open system focus* People are encouraged to monitor the business environment and to be ready to respond to change as it occurs.

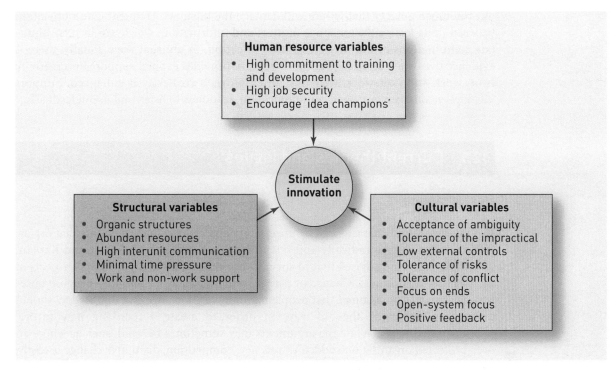

Figure 13.7 Innovation variables

- *Positive feedback* Managers provide positive feedback, encouragement and support so employees feel their creativity will receive attention.

HR policies for innovation

Innovative organisations actively promote the training and development of their members so that their knowledge remains current, offer job security to overcome the fear of making mistakes, and encourage people to become 'champions of change'. Such **idea champions** actively and enthusiastically support new ideas, build support, overcome resistance, and ensure that ideas are implemented. Idea champions tend to have similar personalities – high self-confidence, persistence, energy and a tendency to take risks. They also inspire and energise others with their vision of the potential of an innovation, and through their strong personal commitment to its success. They also need to be good at gaining the support of others – especially those at more senior levels of the organisation – which helps them overcome doubts elsewhere.

Idea champions are individuals who actively and enthusiastically support new ideas, build support, overcome resistance, and ensure that ideas are implemented.

Structures for innovation

Research into innovation has identified structural factors that encourage it, such as having an organic structure, encouraging horizontal communication, encouraging people to contribute ideas outside their loosely designed roles, having abundant resources, and frequent communication between units. Organic structures help because they have little formality, work in a decentralised way and encourage people to apply skills and knowledge to a wide range of tasks: this creates an atmosphere of cross-fertilisation and adaptability that in turn fosters innovation. Abundant resources help since they enable managers to purchase required expertise that may have developed in other companies, and also enables them to take risks by investing in new projects without too much anxiety that failure will damage the business. Frequent communication between units fosters the exchange of ideas and information, which can in turn stimulate combinations of knowledge, or its application, in unusual ways. Finally, there is evidence that when an organisation's structure provides explicit support for creativity from work and non-work activities, an employee's creativity is enhanced. Support includes encouragement, open communication, readiness to listen and useful feedback.

13.9 Current themes and issues

Performance

In a business world characterised by uncertainty and change, many advocate that organisations must change radically and relentlessly (see for example Foster and Kaplan, 2000). Managers are advised that to survive they must continually review all aspects of the way they do business. 'Change or perish' is the rationale of those who propose unrelenting change, who assume: 'that people naturally resist change and that leaders should destroy or cast aside the old ways in order to create a spanking new future' (Abrahamson, 2004). While the arguments may sometimes be valid, such as where an over-protected organisation suddenly faces new competition, disruptive change is costly, and does not necessarily improve performance (Barnet and Freeman, 2001).

Abrahamson (2004) identifies three symptoms of organisations suffering from excessive change – initiative overload, change related chaos and employee cynicism.

Initiative overload

An organisation in which managers become convinced of the need for radical change is likely to require more change than even they anticipate. Figure 13.2 reflects the systemic nature of organisations – a change in one area is likely to require complementary changes in others. An investment in IS may lead to further changes affecting, say, structures, people and business processes. They may or may not succeed – and if they fail then further changes follow. People experience 'initiative overload' and become dispirited and disinterested in whatever is proposed. Someone attempting to introduce a change in one area of a large business observed:

> There are so many changes taking place, they are more or less numb, and this is simply another change which they are just going to have to take on board. The result is that they are somewhat passive and neutral, and when I ask what their requirements might be, the response is usually 'you tell me'. (Boddy, 2002, p. 38)

Change related chaos

Major change inevitably means a period of overlap between old arrangements and the new, during which time there will be more than the usual scope for chaos. Abrahamson (2004) quotes the example of a bank that changed its cheque processing systems. Managers closed the previous system one Friday, opening the new one the following Monday. Things began to go badly wrong, as paper accumulated at all points in the system, which eventually collapsed:

> Why did the change fail so spectacularly? Because ... the new processes had not been fully tested and implemented. In the end, it became apparent to everyone that the change process had wreaked such chaos that it was almost destined to fail. (p. 17)

Employee cynicism

A succession of initiatives leading to change related chaos makes staff anxious and insecure. Communication failure will make this worse, leading to progressive alienation and dissatisfaction. Abrahamson (2004) refers to one senior banker he interviewed soon after a merger of the bank with a rival who told him that she was the only person left of the 60 people who had worked in her unit.

An alternative approach – change without pain?

Having taken a critical view of 'creative destruction', Abrahamson (2004) develops an alternative approach based on what he calls recombination. This takes the view that change will be a great deal less painful if managers take more time to analyse the positive aspects of the existing elements in the organisation. Taking these as the starting point, and basing change as far as possible on small adaptations to familiar arrangements will be much more acceptable to staff, and likely to produce better performance improvements than the radical alternatives.

Responsibility

The biggest challenge facing those implementing major change is that stakeholders will take different views of an organisation's problems, and will have varying degrees of commitment to changes intended to deal with them. Chapter 3 also quoted research by Nutt (2002) that half of the changes he studied produced poor results – in large part because decision makers failed to attend to interests and information held by key stakeholders.

An important step in influencing stakeholders is to assess their relative power and interest (Eden and Ackerman, 1998), which can be prepared to analyse the relative position of the stakeholders in an issue or project on two dimensions:

● their interest in the issue or activity being proposed, and
● their power to influence the outcomes of the issue or activity.

Those with both a high level of interest in the issue and high power to influence the outcome are the key players whom the organisation must seek to satisfy. Conversely those with low interest and power may require only minimal attention to ensure their acquiescence in a proposal.

A dilemma facing anyone with responsibility for implementing a change is how much attention they pay to different stakeholders. An instrumental approach would be to put most time and effort into meeting the needs of powerful stakeholders, as these are the ones who could cause most trouble if their needs are unmet. An alternative view would suggest that a responsible approach would take more account of the interests of those with less evident power – such as the disadvantaged, inarticulate or under-represented communities. Considerations of enlightened self-interest, as discussed in Chapter 5, could lead to a different approach to change management than one that only looked after the interests of the powerful.

International

The growing internationalisation of business has implications for the way international or global firms manage change. The issue here reflects one of the central themes within Chapter 4, namely the balance between a unified, global approach seeking to establish a common identity across all operations, or an approach that adapts the way the company operates to local conditions. Managers of local business units will have local priorities, and are likely to be unreceptive to change that the centre, or even another unit, appears to be imposing. The issues managers can face is illustrated by the experience of one who tried to introduce a new order processing system that would require compatible changes across seven European plants: see the Management in Practice feature.

---

management in practice · A Europe-wide change project

An individual needs to go out on a limb with an idea and be able to articulate that idea to a wider audience before they can get any interest, support and investment to go forward. In our company where the products and the business plan change very quickly it is enormously difficult to get people to focus on what is important rather than on what is urgent. We have seven sites all at different stages of development. We have in some way to make sure that each of them is positioned both in terms of resources, energy and commitment to support an integrated European programme. It is because we have a business which is fairly complex and so diverse that we have adopted the approach that basically says – generate a common level of understanding of what needs to be done, then allow each area to specify their unique requirements within this overall framework. It also allows each individual location to move at their own pace as long as they don't get too far out of line.

The team member from Valbonne wrote to me two weeks ago indicating that he's now been asked to do another European programme. Therefore because his particular group in Valbonne are very short of resources he will not be able to support this team. From my point of view as a programme manager that is totally unacceptable as his plant is a very big part of the order-fulfilment process. So without a representative from there any solution that we devise will only be partially successful.

Source: Boddy (2002), p. 172.

In this case, the manager was able to secure support for his role from European senior management, and was able to exert some influence over the individual plants. However, that influence was limited, meaning that the change introduced was less comprehensive, and less integrated, than would have been possible with a more centrally controlled structure. This balancing act faces all companies operating internationally.

Summary

1 **Explain the meaning of organisational change and give examples**
   - Organisational change refers to deliberate attempts to change one or more elements of the internal environment, such as technology or structure. Change in one element usually stimulates change in other areas.

2 **Explain what the links between change and context imply for those managing a change**
   - A change programme is an attempt to change one or more aspects of the internal context, which then provides the context of future actions. The prevailing context can itself help or hinder change efforts.

3 **Compare life cycle, emergent, participative and political theories of change**
   - Life cycle: change projects can be planned, monitored and controlled towards achieving their objectives.

- Emergent: reflecting the uncertainties of the environment, change is hard to plan in detail, but emerges incrementally from events and actions.

- Participative: successful change depends on human commitment, which is best obtained by involving participants in planning and implementation.

- Political: change threatens some of those affected, who will use their power to block progress, or to direct the change in ways that suit local objectives.

4 Evaluate systematically the possible sources of resistance to change

- Reasons can be assessed using the internal context model, as each element (objectives, people, power, etc.) is a potential source of resistance. Analysing these indicates potential ways of overcoming resistance.

- The force field analysis model allows players to identify the forces driving and restraining a change, and implies that reducing the restraining forces will help change more than increasing the driving forces.

5 Explain the meaning of organisational development and the learning organisation

- OD refers to a set of techniques that practitioners use to reconcile the conflicting interests of people and organisations, both to satisfy human needs and to improve organisational performance. Typical values include treating individuals with respect, a trusting, open and supportive climate, flat rather than hierarchical structures, confronting conflict, and involving those affected by change in implementation.

6 Illustrate the factors believed to support innovation:

- Structural – organic form, abundant resources, high communication between units, and work and non-work support;

- Cultural – acceptance of ambiguity, low external controls, tolerance of risks, open systems focus, and positive feedback;

- Human resource policies – high commitment to training and development, high job security, and creative people.

Review questions

1 What does the term 'performance gap' mean, and what is its significance for change?

2 Explain what is meant by the inner context of management, and give examples of attempts to change one or more elements.

3 What are the implications for management of the systemic nature of major change?

4 Review the change that you identified in Activity 13.1 and compare its critical dimensions (Table 13.1) with those at the Royal Bank of Scotland.

5 Can managers alter the receptiveness of an organisation to change? Would doing so be an example of an interaction approach?

6 Outline the life cycle perspective on change and explain when it is most likely to be useful.

7 How does it differ from the 'emergent' perspective?

8 What are the distinctive characteristics of a participative approach, and when is it likely to be least successful?

9   What skills are used by those employing a political model?

10 Is resistance to change necessarily something to be overcome? How would you advise someone to resist a change to which he or she was opposed?

11 What are likely to be the benefits and disadvantages of using an OD approach to a major change project?

12 To what extent does the evidence from Google (Chapter 12) support the innovation theory implied by Figure 13.7?

Concluding critical reflection

Think about the way people handle major change in your company, or one with which you are familiar. Review the material in the chapter, and perhaps visit some of the websites identified. Then make notes on these questions:

● What examples of the themes discussed in this chapter are currently relevant to your company? What performance imperatives are dominant, and to what extent do people see a performance gap? What perspective do people have on the change process – life cycle, emergent, participative or political?

● In implementing change, what **assumptions** about the nature of change in organisations appear to guide the approach? Is one perspective dominant, or do people typically use several methods in combination?

● What factors in the **context** of the company appear to shape your approach to managing change – is your organisation seen as being receptive or non-receptive to change, for example, and what lies behind that?

● Has there been any serious attempt to find **alternative** ways to manage major change in your organisation – for example by comparing your methods systematically with those of other companies, or with the theories set out here?

● Does the approach typically used generally work? If not, do managers recognise the **limitations** of their approach, and question their assumptions?

Further reading

Pettigrew, A.M. and Whipp, R. (1991), *Managing Change for Competitive Success*, Blackwell, Oxford.

Pettigrew, A., Ferlie, E. and McKee, L. (1992), *Shaping Strategic Change*, Sage, London.

> Both of these books provide detailed, long-term analyses of major changes – the first in four commercial businesses and the second in several units within the UK National Health Service. The theoretical approach of these works has informed the development of this chapter, emphasising the interaction of change and context. Although the cases are old, they still provide useful empirical insights into the task of managing change.

Lock, D. (2003), *Project Management* (8th edn), Gower, Aldershot.

> An excellent source of information on conventional project management techniques.

Buchanan, D. and Badham, R. (1999), *Power, Politics and Organizational Change: Winning the turf game*, Sage, London.

> A modern approach to politics in organisations, offering a theoretical and practical guide, based on extensive primary research.

Balogun, J., Gleadle, P., Hailey, V.H. and Willmott, H. (2005), 'Managing change across boundaries: boundary-shaking practices', *British Journal of Management*, vol. 16, no. 4, pp. 261–278.

> An empirical study of the practices that change agents used to introduce major boundary-shaking changes in large companies, and how the context shaped their use. Many insights into practice in this valuable research.

Roberto, M.A. and Levesque, L.C. (2005), 'The art of making change initiatives stick', *MIT Sloan Management Review*, vol. 46, no. 4, pp. 53–60.

> Another empirical study, this time in a single organisation, of how the context affected the willingness of people to change, and how senior managers needed to create a supportive context.

Weblinks

These websites have appeared in this and other chapters:

www.vodafone.com
www.ericsson.com
ww.gknplc.com
www.sun.com
www.siemens.com
www.ikea.com

Visit two of the business sites in the list, and navigate to the pages dealing with corporate news, investor relations or 'our company'.

- What signs of major changes taking place in the organisation can you find?
- Does the site give you a sense of an organisation that is receptive or non-receptive to change?
- What kind of environment are they likely to be working in, and how may that affect their approach to change?

Annotated weblinks, multiple choice questions and other useful resources can be found on **www.pearsoned.co.uk/boddy**

The Royal Bank of Scotland

www.rbs.co.uk

The Royal Bank of Scotland Group, founded in 1727, is one of Europe's leading financial services groups. During the economic recession of the early 1990s the bank was in trouble, as it had made heavy provisions for bad debts and was losing customers to the new competitors following deregulation of the financial services industry. The share price of just over £1 in 1992 reflected investors' critical view of recent performance. The cost:income ratio (a key measure of bank performance) was over 70 per cent.

In 2007 observers regarded RBS as one of the most innovative and best-performing banks in the United Kingdom. It was by then (on market capitalisation) the UK's seventh largest company, and the fifth largest bank in the world. In 2006 pre-tax profits rose 16 per cent to over £9 billion. In the United Kingdom alone RBS has more than 15 million customers and 2200 branches. At 31 December 2006 the Group had assets of £871 billion, over 135,000 staff worldwide and a cost:income ratio of 42 per cent.

What happened to bring about this change? Much of the credit is due to a series of major internal changes during the 1990s, followed by some successful acquisitions. The early internal changes took place between 1992 and 1997 during what was called Project Columbus. This drove a series of radical changes throughout the retail division, including:

- segmenting customers into three new streams – retail, commercial and corporate
- creating new management roles and organisation structures

© The Royal Bank of Scotland Group PLC.

- new human resource policies to base appointment and promotion on achievement and ability.

This transformed the bank's business, and provided the base for further acquisitions.

Over the years the bank has become more centralised. Initially banks were decentralised, as branch managers had considerable autonomy. With the first wave of IT in the 1960s many functions were centralised. Now the balance may be switching again, as customers complain they cannot get decisions from remote regional offices. Control brings more centralised decisions over products, margins, risk management, etc. Against that, the customer relationship managers press for more local flexibility to override the system.

The Manufacturing Division, which deals with routine functions such as clearing cheques, account opening and various other paper processes, is a very mechanistic structure. The bank created the Manufacturing

Division in 1999 by transferring most administrative tasks from the branches to a central location. To select staff for the new division from those working in the branches, they used psychometric tests to draw out those more comfortable with processes and systems. Those who were more interested in people remained in the branches. The chief executive of the division said:

The word manufacturing has a strong symbolism – we use this as a sign that this is not banking as you know it. People think of banking as relatively small scale, with lots of little branches. But our typical operating centre employs 500 people and handles huge volumes. We don't just pay lip service to economies of scale. (*Financial Times*, 20 June 2005, p. 9)

With many brands, RBS uses different sales and marketing channels to reach its customers. However, it aims to make the underlying processes of banking as uniform as possible, whether for customers of NatWest, the retail bank, or a corporate client.

The branches themselves had been mechanistic, with staff working on strictly defined tasks. Now the branches are more organic, with staff trying to interest customers in other products within a more open physical layout. The bank tries to be organic at the customer-facing areas, with customer relationship managers trying to improve service quality.

The bank was quick to exploit the opportunities that new technology offers. It was an early innovator when it launched Direct Line as one of the first examples of delivering financial services by telephone, and now one of the United Kingdom's largest private motor insurers. It has launched an online bank (**www.rbsdigital.com**), complementing the services offered by the traditional bank.

The formal structure in 2007 was that it had eight 'customer-facing' divisions:

- Retail (RBS and Natwest – two divisions)
- Wealth management (including Coutts Bank)
- Retail direct
- Corporate banking and financial markets
- RBS Insurance
- Ulster Bank Group
- Citizens (United States).

These were supported by six Group divisions – Manufacturing, Legal, Strategy, Finance, Risk and Internal Audit, Communications, and Human Resources.

It has a joint venture with Tesco – Tesco Personal Finance, one of the main supermarket banking brands in the United Kingdom, but most of its joint ventures are overseas. It has a strategic alliance with BSCH of Spain, which provides scope to develop financial service activities across Europe. In 2005 it purchased a 5 per cent stake in the Bank of China as leader of a consortium of banks, the bank's first step into Asian banking. In 2007 it reached a cooperation agreement with Renaissance Capital, a Moscow-based investment bank. This will enable it to offer sophisticated lending and risk management services to Russian companies.

RBS has developed a reputation for acquiring other financial institutions and integrating them profitably. Most notable was the acquisition of NatWest Bank in 2000, not least because NatWest was three times the size of RBS at the time. To win the bank RBS had to demonstrate its ability to extract major cost savings from the combined operations, and to drive greater income from the combination of brands, customers, products and skills. The RBS bid promised to deliver a 'new force in banking' with the scale and strength to exploit new opportunities in the United Kingdom, Europe and the United States. Some industry analysts doubted the ability of RBS to deliver on its bid promises, so the company was under pressure to complete the integration process on time and to meet the cost savings and income benefits quoted during the bid.

The integration programme was quickly established following the takeover, dividing the task into 154 integration initiatives to be completed in three years. These were expected to yield £1.1 billion in annual cost savings and reduce staff by 18,000. Programme management teams were established in each affected business and technology area, and control and reporting procedures were set up. The key elements of the integration strategy were agreed and widely communicated:

- to use RBS information systems as the single platform for operations across the merged bank;
- to migrate customer-facing systems such as credit cards, ATMs and Internet screens to RBS systems early;
- to transfer the NatWest customer and accounting data to the RBS systems in a single weekend.

The early stages of the integration programme involved some challenging decisions about the structure of the programme teams.

- *Centralised versus decentralised control* Once the initial programme strategy had been devised, the individual parts of the integration programme were allocated to local business areas to deliver. However, management maintained close central control of the change, as this would increase efficiency by developing a standard set of control procedures to be used by all areas. These simplify the process of compiling progress updates for the whole programme, and develop a common level of rigour to be applied by all areas. This ensures that progress updates and issues are communicated effectively to the senior executive, and that appropriate levels of prioritisation are applied across the whole programme.

- *Business versus technology control* While much of the work of the integration programme was IT related (i.e. the transfer of NatWest data to the RBS systems platform), it was critical for the business areas to have a strong say in what could be done when. Programme steering groups therefore contained a mix of representatives from the affected business areas and the appropriate technology teams. Project plans were required to contain an appropriate selection of both business and technology activities and milestones.

The programme had well-developed control procedures. A monthly reporting process compared the achievement of actual costs and benefits against budget, summarising the progress made so far and the main achievements and difficulties being encountered. Processes for controlling the programme and reporting on progress were put in place. In particular, procedures for tracking the financial performance were established, requiring regular financial reports on each project. The overall baseline figures for the whole programme were broken down into monthly figures to be achieved by each business area. As well as financial reporting, other controls included:

- *High-level plans* These consisted of a set of milestones covering the most important steps towards the completion of the initiatives. High-level plans were expected to contain approximately one milestone per month in order that progress could be assessed with sufficient regularity.
- *Project 'RAG' status* Project teams were required to report the status of their work using a 'traffic light' system of red, amber or green (RAG): green – satisfactory; amber – difficulties that may affect time, quality or costs; red – serious problems requiring changes to the agreed deliverables.
- *Change control* Once the initial plans and financial targets were established, they were fixed and could only be changed through a formal process at a defined level of seniority.

- *Dependencies* When one project depends on another, both parties must agree what is to be delivered and when. A dependency management process recorded and monitored these.

Monthly reports were presented to senior management, giving a clear view on progress being made against plans. The monthly reports were therefore designed to include a view of the progress planned for the next three months, with an indication of confidence in achieving this progress.

The largest integration task was that of moving all NatWest data on to the RBS computer systems and shutting down the NatWest systems. This was an enormous programme in itself, involving the migration of 18 million customer accounts worth £158 billion and with huge daily transaction volumes. The preparation work took over two years, which paid off when all the accounts were transferred over one weekend in October 2002. The integration programme was completed in early 2003 – within three years of the acquisition date as originally planned and promised.

Having made 23 acquisitions since 2000, and although not ruling out further ones if the opportunity arose, such as the Dutch bank ABN-AMRO, the Group has recently focused on growing 'organically', by building up existing businesses. Some markets are mature and competitive – such as the UK retail market and the Direct Line insurance business. It will therefore be hard to achieve significant growth in these areas.

To counter that, RBS has identified North America as its main growth opportunity, and aims to become the fourth largest bank in the United States. It aims to invest heavily in its corporate banking operations to offer financial advice and services to medium-sized companies that are not served by the major US investment banks. Corporate banking is dominated by JPMorgan Chase, Citigroup and Bank of America – and RBS believes there is a gap in the market for another large player.

It is also targeting the world's wealthiest people through the Coutts subsidiary. These are mainly entrepreneurs, media and entertainment stars. In 2007 it announced a joint venture with Bank of China to launch a private banking business for rich Chinese with more than $1 million to invest.

Sources: Kennedy *et al.* (2006); company website: other published sources.

Part case questions

- Is RBS becoming more centralised or more decentralised?
- What form(s) of structure has the bank used to divide the business? Since it is also necessarily a geographically dispersed organisation, what methods of coordination is it likely to use?
- What are the main issues of an HRM nature that are likely to be topical within RBS?
- From your understanding of the material in Chapter 11, what aspects of HRM should RBS be focusing its efforts upon?
- How will the merger with NatWest have affected this?
- Does RBS have a mechanistic or an organic structure?
- What contingency factors have probably shaped that structure?
- Visit the RBS website: in what ways is it using the Internet?
- What are the main features of the way in which RBS managed the NatWest integration programme?
- Which model(s) of change did RBS management use to implement its new policies? What management practices did it use?

Part 4   Skills development

To help you develop your skills, as well as knowledge, this section includes tasks that relate the key themes covered in the Part to your daily life. Working through these will help you to deepen your understanding of the topic, and develop skills and insights that you can use in many situations.

Task 4.1   Analysing a department or organisation

While every organisation is unique, all are made up of the elements shown in Figure 1.3. These form the internal context within which managers operate, and shape the demands the manager faces. A useful skill is that of being able to use this model to identify and analyse significant features of an organisation or business unit. This exercise invites you to analyse just four of the elements – select more if they seem relevant to the situation.

Analyse a department or organisation with which you are familiar by making a few notes in response to these questions:

- What is the main objective or mission of the department or organisation?
- What is the structure?
- What are the main characteristics of the people?
- What technologies (and in what layout) do people use to meet the objectives? This includes all kinds of physical facilities, including computer systems.

Consider a recent large change. What were the direct and indirect effects on each of these components? What difficulties, if any, had to be managed?

Compare your answers with those prepared by another student, to further increase your skills of analysis, and of identifying key organisational features.

Task 4.2   Distinguishing mechanistic from organic structures

Chapter 10 distinguished between mechanistic and organic forms. Since these greatly affect how people work, a manager needs to be able to identify each type, and the practices that can, whether intended or not, lead an organisation towards one or the other.

Analyse a department or organisation with which you are familiar by making a few notes in response to these questions:

- Identify a department that is mainly mechanistic, and indicate the features or practices which illustrate that.
- Identify a department that is mainly organic, and indicate the features or practices which illustrate that.
- Why do you think each takes the form it does?
- Is that form the appropriate one for the work being done?

- If not, what specific features or practices would you recommend that management change to move towards the form you think most suitable?
- Are there any examples of problems in the working relationships between units that may be due to their mechanistic and organic characteristics?

Task 4.3 Analysing information systems

Choose an organisation of which you have some direct knowledge – one you work in, or in which you are studying. Write a short report analysing the organisation's main information systems using themes from Chapter 12, and from other relevant chapters in the book, such as:

- What types of IS do different people in the organisation use – perhaps locating them on the grid provided in Figure 12.6?
- Do the information systems provide users with information that meets their needs? If not, is the problem mainly technical or mainly organisational?
- How do the information systems affect the ability of the organisation to compete in terms of innovation, quality, delivery or cost?
- Use Figures 12.4 and 12.5 to analyse the organisation's stage of development in using IS.
- Review the Sections 12.6–12.8. Has the organisation used one or more of these systems, and what have been the effects?
- To what extent are managers using the Internet to help manage the business?

Task 4.4 Analysing stakeholders

A valuable skill in managing any kind of organisational change (such as in strategy, structure or technology) is that of managing those with a stake in the project, and who can affect its success. This exercise enables you to practise using a tool that helps to understand and manage stakeholders constructively.

Select a major organisational change project with which you are familiar, or which you can ask someone about. Write the name of the project in a circle at the centre of a sheet of paper. Draw other circles around the sheet, each identifying an individual or group with a stake in the project. Place the most significant near the centre, and others around the edge.

Use a scale such as that shown below to assess the 'present' (X) and 'hoped for' (Y) level of commitment of each stakeholder to the project.

Key stakeholder	Vigorous opposition	Some opposition	Indifferent towards it	Will let it happen	Will help it happen	Will make it happen
				X		Y
				X	Y	
			X		Y	
				X		Y
		X			Y	

Rate each stakeholder on whether their power to affect the project is high or low.

Use a grid similar to that shown below to note your answers to these questions for the main (powerful) stakeholders:

Stakeholder	Their goals	Current relationship	What is expected of them?	Positive or negative to them?	Likely reaction?	Ideas for action

- What are their priorities, goals and interests?
- What is the general tone of our present relationship with them?
- What specific behaviour is expected of them, in relation to this project?
- Are they likely to see this as positive or negative for them?
- What is their likely action to defend their interests?
- What actions can we consider to influence them?

Compare your answers with those prepared by another student for their project, to further increase your skills of analysis, and of identifying ideas for managing stakeholders.

Part 5

LEADING

Introduction

Generating the effort and commitment to work towards objectives is central to managing any human activity. One person working alone, be it in private life or in business, has only him or herself to motivate. As an organisation grows management activities become, in varying degrees, separated from the core work activities. The problem of generating effort changes its nature: now one person, or one occupational group, has to secure the willing cooperation of other people and their commitment to the task. Those other people may be subordinates, peers or superiors whose support, and perhaps approval, needs to be generated and mobilised.

The quality of that commitment is as important as whether or not it is secured. Staff are often in direct contact with customers. They are aware of their unique and changing requirements, and have an immense effect on the view the customer forms of the organisation. Others are in creative roles, with a direct impact on the quality of the service delivered to the final customer, whether they are contributing to a core R&D project or a TV programme. Others need to work reliably and flexibly in order to meet changing external or internal customer needs.

Throughout a business, customers' expectations of service quality and efficiency translate into expectations of all those working in the business. Unwilling or grudging commitment damages the service offered and eventually the business itself. How does management secure the motivation it needs from others? Part Five offers several perspectives on the dilemma. Chapter 14 examines ideas on influencing others, while Chapter 15 presents a range of theories about what those others may want from work. Communication is central to most management functions and activities, and Chapter 16 examines this topic. Finally, teams are an increasingly prominent aspect of organisations, and the motivation and commitment generated within them is often central to performance – so they are the subject of Chapter 17.

The Part Case is W.L. Gore and Associates, an organisation renowned for its use of teams.

Chapter 14

Influence and power

Aim

To examine how people influence others by using personal skills and/or power.

Objectives

By the end of your work on this chapter you should be able to outline the concepts below in your own terms and:

1 Distinguish leading from managing, and explain why each is essential to performance

2 Explain why leading and managing both depend on being able to influence others

3 Compare trait, behavioural and contingency perspectives on influencing

4 Outline theories that focus on power (both personal and organisational) as the source of influence

5 Contrast the style and power perspectives, and explain why sharing power may increase it

6 Outline a model of the tactics people use to influence others, including the use of cooperative networks.

Key terms

This chapter introduces the following ideas:

influence
leadership
traits
the big five
transactional leaders
transformational leaders
behaviour
initiating structure
consideration
situational models
power
political behaviour
networking

Each is a term defined within the text, as well as in the Glossary at the end of the book.

Semco is a Brazilian company that in 2007 employed about 2500 people in three countries, working in manufacturing, professional services and software. The main offices are in São Paolo, where Antonio Semler founded the company in 1953 to make industrial equipment such as pumps and centrifuges. He ran it in a traditional way, but in 1982 his son Ricardo Semler took over as chief executive. The company has survived a turbulent Brazilian economy, and the annual revenue of what is in effect a federation of about ten companies exceeds $200 million.

Ricardo Semler has unusual ideas about business and has gradually dismantled the management structure he inherited, moving Semco towards a very flexible form with profit sharing, employee participation and a free flow of information. Under the profit-sharing plan employees (known as associates) receive one-quarter of the profits of their respective division. The scheme is run by an elected committee, which reflects Semler's trust in his employees' abilities to make decisions.

Employees are free to agree their working hours with their co-workers – coming in and leaving work at times to suit their domestic or other commitments. Many were sceptical of this innovation – but Semler argues that provided people are committed to their job and the company, they will (and do) manage their time responsibly –

they're the best judges of the amount of time and the proper place necessary to get the work done . . . do we really believe that responsible adults . . . would simply not show up after promising to do so? That a journalist who understands the urgency of deadlines would go to the movies while the presses are standing still, waiting for his submission? (Semler, 2003, pp. 27–28)

The Brazilian economy was in poor shape during the early 1990s, with many companies going bankrupt. Semco survived, though only by cutting costs sharply. The workers themselves proposed the solutions, such as having people do several jobs rather than one. This developed a workforce that was cross-trained in several skills, and with a deep knowledge of the business. Most work is now done by units that perform all the necessary support functions such as marketing and finance themselves. For many years the company has organised work in self-managed teams, whereby

Corbis: James Leynse.

groups of six to eight manufacturing employees take responsibility for all aspects of a production task. They set their targets and production goals, and decide what they should be paid. The teams vote on hiring and firing members and managers.

The management structure is like three concentric circles. The inner core has six counsellors who determine general policy and strategy, each acting as CEO for six months. Two seats at meetings are reserved for employees – the first there take the seats. The second circle consists of partners – the leaders of each division. All remaining associates make up the outer circle. Team leaders are within this outer circle – such as engineers, marketers and production supervisors. Associates are encouraged to openly oppose and reject proposals by upper management.

Sources: Based on material from Thunderbird, The American School of International Management, Case A15-98-0024, *Ricardo Semler and Semco S.A.*; Semler (2003); and other published material.

Case questions 14.1

● What examples are there of senior managers influencing associates?

● What examples are there of associates influencing senior managers?

● What assumptions about people lie behind Semler's management style?

14.1 Introduction

When Ricardo Semler took over Semco from his father he faced challenges typical of many managers today. The Brazilian economy was in trouble, and employee morale was threatened by the danger of losing their jobs or of not earning an adequate wage. While he could have used conventional means of authority and control to influence his staff, he took a radically different approach of delegating increasing amounts of power to employees, later commenting that:

> Semco managers are concerned with the essence of what employees do for the company, nothing more. (Semler, 2003, pp. 28–29)

All managers face this challenge of influencing others – such as when Sari Baldauf became head of Nokia's network division, and built it up to become one of the world's leading suppliers of network equipment. When the market collapsed in 2000, she had simultaneously to cut back that division (reducing staff by 7500 in three years) while still influencing the company and its staff to invest for future growth in other areas. Willie Walsh at British Airways faces these issues as he seeks to change the way people work, to reduce the company's costs in the face of competition from low-cost airlines.

management in practice **Deanna Oppenheimer of Barclays and Carlos Ghosn of Renault**

Deanna Oppenheimer became chief executive of retail banking at Barclays in 2005 after a successful banking career in the United States. She was instrumental in growing the insurance business for which she worked from a relatively small player to the seventh largest insurer in the United States.

Carlos Ghosn, now CEO of Renault (see Chapter 16), faced the challenge of influencing staff at Nissan (which is part-owned by Renault) to make unprecedented changes in the way they worked – changes that transformed it from a loss-making to a profitable business. He now faces a similar challenge at Renault.

Both have shown their ability to influence others (staff, unions, customers, colleagues or investors) of the wisdom of their policies.

Influence is the process by which one party attempts to modify the behaviour of others by mobilising power resources.

Whatever their role, people only add value to resources by influencing others. The tasks of planning, organising, leading and controlling depend on securing the cooperation of other people within a web of mutual **influence**. Everyone's performance depends on how well they do this, and the targets of their attempts at influence will often be in more senior positions.

In that sense the work of the manager is not that of the careful analyst, working out precisely the best solution to a problem. It is closer to that of an entrepreneur, determined to get things done in an often hostile, indifferent or political setting. Managers typically operate across established functional or departmental boundaries, working with many different people who have other priorities and interests.

This chapter explores the topics shown in Figure 14.1. It begins by clarifying what influence means in the context of managing and then presents three perspectives on the topic – traits, behavioural and contingency. It then examines theories on how people can use their power to influence others, power that can come from both personal and organisational sources. Finally it presents a model of the tactics people can use to influence, including that of networking. The figure also indicates that the outcomes of an influence attempt depend not only on the choice of method but on the circumstances in which it is used. Those outcomes in turn affect the influencer's power – a successful result is likely

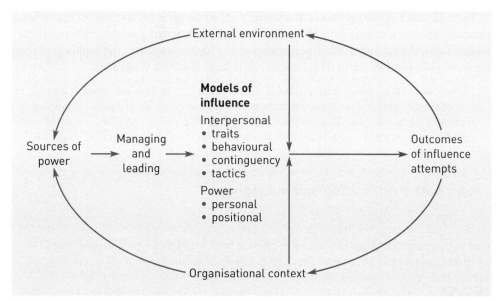

Figure 14.1

A model of the influencing process

to further increase it, and vice versa. The chapters on motivation, communication and teams are closely linked to influence and power.

14.2 Managing and leading

Research and commentary on influencing use the terms 'manager' and 'leader' (and their derivatives) interchangeably, as there is no definitive distinction. It is worth briefly clarifying the meanings that some attach to them.

Chapter 1 defined a manager as someone who gets things done with the support of others. Most commentators view an 'effective manager' as one who 'gets things done' to ensure order and continuity. They maintain the steady state – keeping established systems in good shape and making incremental improvements. People generally use the term 'effective leader' to denote someone who brings innovation, moves an activity out of trouble into success, makes a worthwhile difference. They see opportunities to do new things, take initiatives, inspire people.

Leif Beck Fallesen, chief executive of Borsen http://borsen.dk

Borsen is a Danish business newspaper, equivalent to the *Financial Times*. During the early 1990s circulation and profitability declined. In 1996 the board appointed Leif Beck Fallesen as chief executive, with a brief to improve the position. The paper's circulation has grown by about 15 per cent a year since 1997, while that of similar papers has remained static or declined. The leadership actions he took included creating:

● regular features aimed at growing market segments (such as small businesses, family-owned businesses and younger readers);
● a joint venture providing business content to Danish television;
● an innovative online version of the paper.

Source: Company presentation and other sources.

Leadership refers to the process of influencing the activities of others toward high levels of goal setting and achievement.

Peter Drucker (1999) writes of the leader's ability to generate unusual or exceptional commitment to a vision, and of **leadership** being 'the lifting of people's vision to a higher sight, the raising of their performance to a higher standard, the building of their personality beyond its normal limitations'. And Anita Roddick wrote that:

> [People] are looking for leadership that has vision ... You have to look at leadership through the eyes of the followers and you have to live the message. What I have learned is that people become motivated when you guide them to the source of their own power and when you make heroes out of employees who best personify what you want to see in the organization. (1991, p. 223)

key ideas John Kotter on leading and managing

Kotter (1990) distinguishes between the terms leadership and management – while stressing that organisations need both, and that one person will often provide both. He regards good management as bringing order and consistency to an activity – through the tasks of planning, organising and controlling. He observed that modern management developed to support the large companies which developed from the middle of the nineteenth century. These complex enterprises tended to become chaotic, unless they developed good management practices to bring order and consistency. The pioneers of management (such as Robert Owen, Chapter 2 Case) created the discipline

to help keep a complex organization on time and on budget. That has been, and still is, its primary function. Leadership is very different. It does not produce consistency and order . . . it produces movement.

Individuals whom people recognise as leaders have created change – whether for the better or not. Good leadership is that which

moves people to a place in which they and those who depend on them are genuinely better off, and when it does so without trampling on the rights of others.

Leaders succeed by establishing direction and strategy, communicating it to those whose cooperation is needed, and motivating and inspiring people. Managing and leading are closely related, but differ in their primary functions – the one to create order, the other to create change. Organisations need both if they are to prosper.

Source: Kotter (1990).

Many people work to create change and to create order in varying degrees, so there is no value in a sharp distinction between managing and leading (John Adair quotes a Chinese proverb: 'What does it matter if the cat is black or white, as long as it catches mice' (Adair, 1997, p. 2)). Managing and leading both depend on being able to influence others to put effort and commitment to the task – whether that is to create order or to create change.

People at all levels who want to get something done need to influence others. The effectiveness of senior managers in influencing others has the most visible effect on performance. They shape the overall direction of the business, moving it into new areas or changing the way it operates. Yet they depend on people lower down the organisation also being able and willing to exercise influence – whether to bring stability or to initiate change and creativity in their areas of responsibility.

Managers (and leaders) often influence people who are equally powerful – as the first woman to take the top management job at a leading City of London legal practice observed:

The hardest things in management ... are complicated people issues. Sometimes you realise you can't solve everything. Our assets are the brains and personalities of some highly intelligent people, so there are a huge number of relationship issues. Most of these 250 people are very driven. If you get it right, the commitment is already sorted out. But you've got to take a lot of people with you a lot of the time. (*Financial Times*, 15 February 2001, p. 17)

So managing and leading require people to influence colleagues on the same organisational level, those formally above them in the hierarchy and people outside the organisation. Figure 14.2 illustrates this.

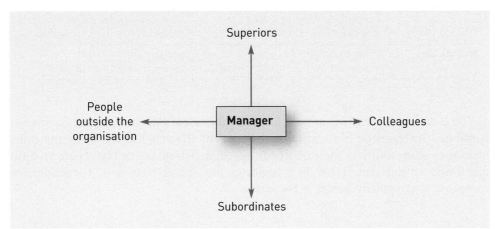

Figure 14.2

Influencing in four directions

How do managers and leaders try to ensure that others do what they want them to do? The following sections present answers to that question, beginning with trait theories.

14.3 Traits models

Many people have tried to identify the personal characteristics associated with effective leaders. They observed the personalities of prominent figures, and distinguished what they believed were enduring aspects of their personality, which they displayed in a variety of settings, and that appeared to influence them to behave in a particular way. Early work on personality and leadership identified numerous such **traits** – and this in itself hindered the development of a practically useful theory, as the lists of potentially valuable traits grew longer.

A **trait** is a relatively stable aspect of an individual's personality that influences behaviour in a particular direction.

The big five

A major advance in this area of study came when researchers noted that they could group the many observed traits into a much smaller number of clusters or 'super traits' (McCrae and John, 1992). These have become known as **the big five**: Table 14.1 shows the label for each cluster, and adjectives that describe the extreme positions on each.

McCrae and John (1992) show that each of the big five super traits contains six traits. Using these in personality assessments enables researchers to identify the pattern of traits an individual displays, which may then be linked to aspects of behaviour: in the present context the focus would be on which traits appear to affect the ability of people to influence others.

The big five refers to trait clusters that appear consistently to capture main personality traits: openness, conscientiousness, extraversion, agreeableness and neuroticism.

Table 14.1

The big five trait clusters

Openness	Explorer (O+): creative, open-minded, intellectual	Preserver (O–): unimaginative, disinterested, narrow-minded
Conscientiousness	Focused (C+): dutiful, achievement oriented, self-disciplined	Flexible (C–): frivolous, irresponsible, disorganised
Extraversion	Extravert (E+): gregarious, warm, positive	Introvert (E–): quiet, reserved, shy
Agreeableness	Adapter (A+): straightforward, compliant, sympathetic	Challenger (A–): quarrelsome, oppositional, unfeeling
Neuroticism	Reactive (N+): anxious, depressed, self-conscious	Resilient (N–): calm, contented, self-assured

The *Financial Times*/PwC annual survey of the world's most respected companies continues the tradition of identifying the traits of effective leaders. Common traits included vision, ability to forecast trends, speed, decisiveness, courage, tenacity, optimism and enthusiasm. Table 14.2 indicates the characteristics of the leaders of companies that regularly feature in the survey.

Table 14.2

Traits of those leading some of the world's most respected companies

Leader	Company	Traits
Jurgen Schremp	DaimlerChrysler	'daring behaviour'
Michael Dell	Dell Computers	'listening to customers and employees'
Richard Branson	Virgin	'a maverick, encouraging people to do things differently'
John Browne	BP (until 2007)	'taking lead on environment and social responsibility'

James Burns: transactional and transformational leaders

A **transactional leader** is one who treats leadership as an exchange, giving followers what they want if they do what the leader desires.

James Burns (1978) distinguished between **transactional** and **transformational leaders**. Transactional leaders influence subordinates' behaviour through a bargain. The leader enables followers to reach their goals, while at the same time contributing to the goals of the organisation. If subordinates behave in the way desired by the leader they receive rewards – transactional leaders tend to support the status quo by rewarding subordinates' efforts and commitment.

A **transformational leader** is a leader who treats leadership as a matter of motivation and commitment, inspiring followers by appealing to higher ideals and moral values.

Burns contrasted this approach with that of transformational (sometimes called charismatic) leaders. They are thought to change the status quo by infusing work with a meaning that encourages subordinates to change their goals, needs and aspirations. Transformational leaders raise the consciousness of followers by appealing to higher ideals and moral values. They energise people by, for example, articulating an attractive vision for the organisation, reinforcing the values in that vision, and empowering subordinates to come up with new and creative ideas. They also articulate

> transcendent goals, demonstration of self-confidence and confidence in others, setting a personal example for followers, showing high expectations of followers' performance, and the ability to communicate one's faith in one's goals. (Fiedler and House, 1994, p. 112)

What do charismatic leaders do to gain support? | key ideas

Conger and Kanungo (1994) note that people often use the terms 'charismatic' and 'transformational' leadership interchangeably, but go on to suggest that the first term directs attention to measurable leader behaviours, while the second focuses on the effects on followers: 'In essence the two formulations of charismatic and transformational are highly complementary, and study the same phenomenon only from different vantage points' (p. 442).

They then develop a set of behavioural scales to measure charismatic leadership, with 25 items in six groups:

1 vision and articulation e.g. 'consistently generates new ideas';
2 environmental sensitivity e.g. 'recognises barriers that may hinder progress';
3 unconventional behaviour e.g. 'uses non-traditional methods';
4 personal risk e.g. 'takes high personal risk for the sake of the organisation';
5 sensitivity to member needs e.g. 'shows sensitivity to needs and feelings of others';
6 not maintaining the status quo e.g. 'advocates unusual actions to achieve goals'.

The full scales have been validated and used widely in research on charismatic leadership (see for example Groves, 2005).

One limitation of the traits model is that a trait that is valuable in one situation is not necessarily valuable in another. Whatever traits Phillip Watts had that led to his appointment as head of exploration at Shell were still there when he resigned in 2004 after a scandal over the way the company reported their oil reserves. Having certain traits is probably necessary for effective leadership, but will not be sufficient – which may explain the inconclusive results of research that attempts to relate traits to performance (Bono and Judge, 2004). Their relative importance may depend on other factors in the situation. For example, De Hoog *et al.* (2005) found that while four of 'the big five' had a positive effect on both transactional and charismatic (transformational) leadership in a stable environment, they were negatively associated with charismatic leadership in a dynamic environment. Different conditions seem to need different traits.

Despite these limitations the traits model may help to explain why some people get to positions of great influence and others do not. Baum and Locke (2004) note a revival of interest in the personal characteristics of potential leaders, such as entrepreneurs creating new ventures. Management selection practices reflect this belief, and the criteria often include traits that are thought to be relevant for success. Table 14.3 lists the traits that the UK National Health Service Leadership Qualities Framework identifies as distinguishing 'effective and outstanding leaders'.

Table 14.3

NHS Leadership Qualities Framework

Personal qualities	Setting direction	Delivering the service
Self-belief	Seizing the future	Leading change through people
Self-awareness	Intellectual flexibility	Holding to account
Self-management	Broad scanning	Empowering others
Drive for improvement	Political astuteness	Effective and strategic influencing
Personal integrity	Drive for results	Collaborative working

Source: Based on Department of Health (2002), *NHS Leadership Qualities Framework*, NHS Leadership Centre, London.

As two of the foremost scholars of leadership concluded:

There is no one ideal leader personality. However, effective leaders tend to have a high need to influence others, to achieve; and they tend to be bright, competent and socially adept, rather than stupid, incompetent and social disasters. (Fiedler and House, 1994, p. 111)

Activity 14.1   Which traits do employers seek?

Collect some job advertisements and recruitment brochures. Make a list of the traits that the companies say they are looking for in those they recruit.

14.4   Behavioural models

Behaviour is something a person does that can be directly observed.

Another set of theories sought to identify the behavioural styles of effective managers. What did they do to influence subordinates that less effective managers did not? Scholars at the universities of Ohio State and Michigan respectively identified two categories of **behaviour**: one concerned with interpersonal relations, the other with accomplishing tasks.

Ohio State University model

Researchers at Ohio State University (Fleishman, 1953) developed questionnaires that subordinates used to describe the behaviour of their supervisor, and identified two dimensions – 'initiating structure' and 'consideration'.

Initiating structure is a pattern of leadership behaviour that emphasises the performance of the work in hand and the achievement of production or service goals.

Initiating structure refers to the degree to which a leader defines people's roles, focuses on goal attainment and establishes clear channels of communication. Those using this approach focused on getting the work done – they expected subordinates to follow the rules and made sure they were working to full capacity. Typical behaviours included:

- allocating subordinates to specific tasks
- establishing standards of job performance
- informing subordinates of the requirements of the job
- scheduling work to be done by subordinates
- encouraging the use of uniform procedures.

Consideration is a pattern of leadership behaviour that demonstrates sensitivity to relationships and to the social needs of employees.

Consideration refers to the degree to which a leader shows concern and respect for followers, looks after them and expresses appreciation (Judge *et al.*, 2004). Such leaders assume that subordinates want to work well and try to make it easier for them to do so. They place little reliance on their formal position and power, typical behaviours including:

- expressing appreciation for a job well done
- not expecting more from subordinates than they can reasonably do
- helping subordinates with personal problems
- being approachable and available for help
- rewarding high performance.

Surveys showed that supervisors displayed distinctive patterns – some scored high on initiating structure and low on consideration, while others were high on consideration and low on initiating structure. Some were high on both, others low on both. Research into the effects on performance were often inconclusive, but a recent review of over 130 such studies (Judge *et al.*, 2004) concluded that there was evidence that consideration tended to be more strongly related to follower satisfaction, while initiating structure was slightly more related to measures of leader performance.

University of Michigan model

Researchers at the University of Michigan (Likert, 1961, 1967) conducted similar studies and found that two types of behaviour distinguished effective from ineffective managers: job-centred and employee-centred behaviour.

- *Job-centred supervisors* ensured that they worked on different tasks from their subordinates, concentrating especially on planning, coordinating and supplying a range of support activities. These correspond to the initiating structure measures at Ohio.
- *Employee-centred supervisors* combined the task-oriented behaviour with human values. They were considerate, helpful and friendly to subordinates, and engaged in broad supervision rather than detailed observation. These behaviours were similar to what the Ohio group referred to as considerate.

From numerous studies, Likert (1961) concluded that:

> Supervisors with the best records of performance focus their primary attention on the human aspects of their subordinates' problems and on endeavouring to build effective work groups with high performance goals. (p. 7)

Managerial grid model

Blake and Mouton (1964, 1979) developed the managerial grid model to extend and apply the Ohio State research. Figure 14.3 shows various combinations of concern for production (initiating structure) and concern for people (consideration).

The horizontal scale relates to concern for production, which ranges from 1 (low concern) to 9 (high concern). The vertical scale relates to concern for people, also ranging from 1 (low concern) to 9 (high concern). At the lower left-hand corner (1,1) is the impoverished style: low concern for both production and people. The primary objective of such managers is to stay out of trouble. They merely pass instructions to subordinates, follow the established system, and make sure that no one can blame them if something goes wrong. They do only as much as is consistent with keeping their job.

At the upper left-hand corner (1,9) is the country club style: managers who use this style try to create a secure and comfortable family atmosphere. They assume that their subordinates will respond productively. Thoughtful attention to the need for satisfying relationships leads to a friendly atmosphere and work tempo.

High concern for production and low concern for people is found in the lower right-hand corner (9,1). This is the produce or perish style. These managers do not consider subordinates' personal needs. All that matters is achieving the organisation's objectives. They use their formal authority to pressure subordinates into meeting production quotas. They believe that efficiency comes from arranging the work so that employees merely have to follow instructions.

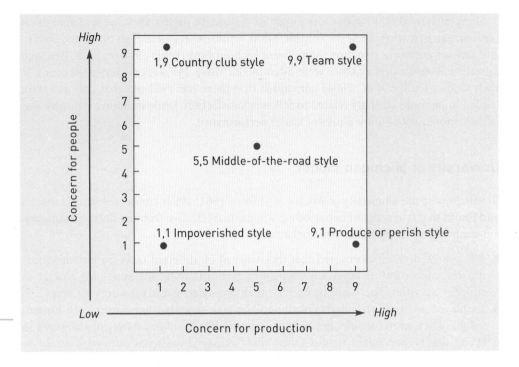

Figure 14.3

The managerial grid

In the centre (5,5) is the middle-of-the-road style. These managers obtain adequate performance by balancing the need to get the work done with reasonable attention to the interests of employees. In the upper right-hand corner (9,9) is the team style which, according to Blake and Mouton, is the most effective approach, aiming for both high performance and high job satisfaction. The manager fosters performance by building relationships of trust and respect.

Activity 14.2 Critical reflection on the managerial grid

- Reflect on two managers you have worked with, one effective and one ineffective from your point of view.
- Which of the positions in the Blake and Mouton grid most closely describe their style? Note some of their typical behaviours.
- What were they like to work for? Does your reflection support or contradict the model? If the latter, what may explain that?

 **Two leaders' styles**

Jeroen Van der Veer, CEO of Shell

Good leadership ... means being clear about what is weak and what is strong, and where you want to go in the longer term, and having the ability to put it into clear words. The best way for a leader to take a company forward is to have some very simple words about how you would like to change it and the culture of the company.

Source: *Financial Times*, 2 February 2007, p. 19.

David Michels, chief executive of Hilton Hotels

Argument is an essential part of the success of any business, he says:

> You have to talk to staff and you can't insulate yourself by getting in first-class limos all the time. You have to get on the Tube and you have to get people to argue with you. I argue so much with my staff I sometimes wonder who is in charge. I enjoy [life as chief executive], I really do. But sometimes I sit back and think 'bloody hell, this is difficult'.

Source: *Financial Times*, 6 June 2003.

Many trainers use the Blake and Mouton model to help managers develop towards the '9,9' style. Implicit in the approach is the idea of flexibility. Others question whether showing a high level of concern for both production and people is always the best approach. Sometimes a concern for production may be more important than concern for people – such as in a sudden crisis that requires swift action. Situational or contingency models offer a possible answer.

Semco – the case continues
http:///semco.locaweb.com.br/

CASE STUDY

Employees have gradually taken greater responsibility over everything from cafeteria menus to new product designs and plant relocations. They are always free to develop new skills in other areas of the business, and to transfer to different units if they are accepted by their new colleagues. Another innovation is that workers set their own production quotas and come in on their own time to meet them if necessary, without pressure from management and without overtime pay. Their managers have considerable autonomy over the strategy for their business unit, including setting levels of pay.

Employees can see all company financial information, and Semco developed a unique way of presenting financial information in a clear, simplified way. They also developed a course to teach everyone to read balance sheets and cash-flow statements. Employees in each business group use this financial information to develop their business plan for the next six months, deciding what staff they will need and fixing their salaries. There are 11 compensation options (such as fixed salaries, royalties or stock options), which employees can choose between.

Anyone who requests too large a salary . . . runs the risk of being rejected by their colleagues. So self-interest almost always prevents them from asking for excessive paycheques. We also encourage people to set their own salaries without creating a deficit in their departments. That's why monthly revenue reports, budgets, costs, salaries, profit sharing, and transparent numbers [publishing salaries] are so important at Semco. If workers understand the big picture, they'll know how their salaries fit. (Semler, 2003, p. 197)

All meetings, including those of the counsellors, are open to all employees who wish to attend. This gives staff the information they need to make informed decisions, and reinforces the democratic nature of the decision-making process.

Moving an organization or business ahead by virtue of what its people stand for means removing obstacles like official policies, procedural constraints and relentless milestones, all of which are set up in the pursuit of quarterly or otherwise temporary success. It means giving up control, and allowing employees to manage themselves. It means trusting workers implicitly, sharing power and information, and celebrating true democracy. (Semler, 2003, pp. 112–113)

Sources: Based on material from Thunderbird, The American School of International Management, Case A15-98-0024, *Ricardo Semler and Semco S.A.*; Semler (2003); and other published material.

▶

14.5 Situational (or contingency) models

Situational models of leadership attempt to identify the contextual factors that affect when one style will be more effective than another.

Situational (or contingency) **models** present the idea that managers influence others by adapting their style to the circumstances. Three such models are set out below (a fourth, developed by Vroom and Yetton (1973) featured in Chapter 7).

Tannenbaum and Schmidt's continuum of leader behaviour

Unlike the 'one best way' model implied by the behavioural models, Robert Tannenbaum and Warren Schmidt (1973) saw that leaders worked in different ways, which they presented as a continuum of styles, ranging from autocratic to democratic. Figure 14.4 illustrates these extremes and the positions in between. Which of these the leader uses should reflect three forces:

1 **forces in the manager:** personality, values, preferences, beliefs about participation and confidence in subordinates;
2 **forces in subordinates:** need for independence, tolerance of ambiguity, knowledge of the problem, expectations of involvement;
3 **forces in the situation:** organisational norms, size and location of work groups, effectiveness of team working, nature of the problem.

House's path–goal model

House (House and Mitchell, 1974; House, 1996) argued that effective leaders are those who clarify their subordinates' path to the rewards available, and ensure that rewards the subordinates value are available. They help subordinates to identify and learn behaviours that will help them complete the task and so secure the rewards for doing so. The model identifies four styles of leader behaviour:

1 **directive:** letting subordinates know what the leader expects; giving specific guidance; asking subordinates to follow rules and procedures; scheduling and coordinating their work;
2 **supportive:** treating them as equals; showing concern for their needs and welfare; creating a friendly climate in the work unit;
3 **achievement oriented:** setting challenging goals and targets; seeking performance improvements; emphasising excellence in performance; expecting subordinates to succeed;
4 **participative:** consulting subordinates; taking their opinions into account.

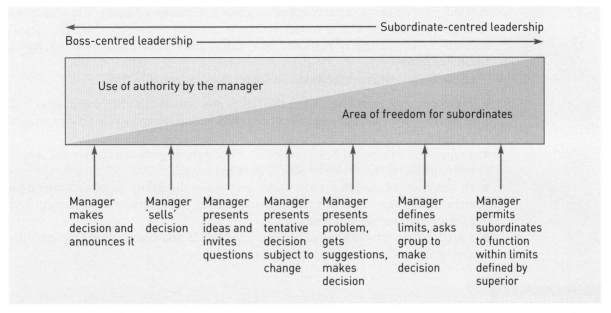

Figure 14.4 The Tannenbaum–Schmidt continuum of leadership behaviour

House suggested that the appropriate style would depend on the situation – the characteristics of the subordinate and the work environment. For example, if a subordinate has little confidence or skill then the leader needs to provide coaching and other support. If the subordinate likes clear direction they will respond best to a leader who gives it. Most skilled professionals expect to use their initiative and resent a directive style:

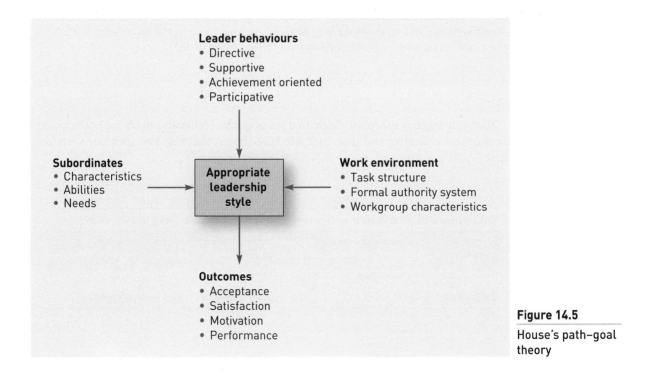

Figure 14.5

House's path–goal theory

they will respond best to a participative or achievement-oriented leader. The work environment includes the degree of task structure (routine or non-routine), the formal authority system (extent of rules and procedures) and the work group characteristics (quality of teamwork).

Figure 14.5 summarises the model which predicts, for example, that:

● a directive style works best when the task is ambiguous and the subordinates lack flexibility – the leader absorbs the uncertainty and shows the group how to achieve the task;

● a supportive style works best in repetitive frustrating or physically unpleasant tasks – subordinates respect the leader who joins in and helps;

● an achievement-oriented style works best when the group faces non-repetitive ambiguous tasks, which will challenge their ability – they need encouragement and pressure to raise their ambitions;

● a participative approach works best when the task is non-repetitive and the subordinate(s) are confident that they can do the work.

---

management in practice   **Helmut Panke, chief executive of BMW**   www.bmw.com

Helmut Panke became CEO of Bavarian Motor Works (BMW) in 2002, since when he has overseen a rapid expansion of the model range. Sales, and the company's share price, rose strongly after he took charge of the company. Panke demands top performance from staff, and from himself. He first demonstrated his skills at building BMW's global business as head of North American operations in the mid-1990s, during which time the United States became BMW's largest market.

> Panke's management style could be called Socratic. He loves to pose questions and lead debates with groups of managers – a practice that reflects his academic training (he has a doctorate in nuclear physics) and gets results . . . By encouraging debate, Panke has forged a performance-driven culture that isn't afraid to send tough questions up the ranks. 'Panke takes a huge amount of time to discuss with people, then he lets them manage on their own. That way he gets 120% from everyone', says a manager who has seen Panke rise up the ranks over 20 years . . . 'My biggest challenge is saying "no" to projects that are exciting but don't fit BMW's strategy', comments Panke (p. 48).

Source: *Business Week*, 7 June 2004.

Such contingency models indicate that participative leadership styles are not necessarily the most effective, and that, as Table 14.4 shows, there will be situations where a directive style is appropriate.

Table 14.4

Conditions favouring participative or directive styles

Participative style most likely to work when:	Directive style most likely to work when:
Subordinates' acceptance of the decision is important	Subordinates do not share the manager's objectives
The manager lacks information	Time is short
The problem is unclear	Subordinates accept top-down decisions

John Adair and Action Centred Leadership

key ideas

Over 2 million people worldwide have taken part in the Action Centred Leadership approach pioneered by John Adair. He proposes that people expect leaders to fulfil three obligations – to help them achieve the task, to build and maintain the team and to enable individuals to satisfy their needs. These three obligations overlap and influence each other – if the task is achieved that will help to sustain the group and satisfy individual needs. If the group lacks skill or cohesion it will neither achieve the task nor satisfy the members. Figure 14.6 represents the three needs as overlapping circles – almost a trademark for John Adair's work. To achieve these expectations the leader performs the eight tasks in the figure.

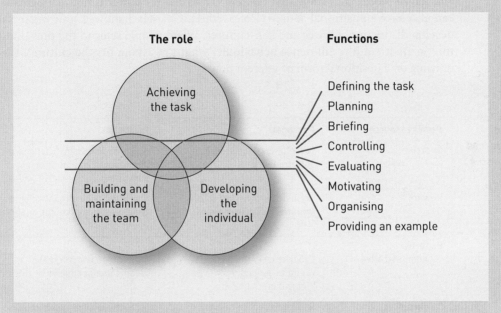

Figure 14.6 Adair's model of leadership functions

Source: Adair (1997, p. 21).

14.6 Sources of power to influence others

Earlier sections have centred on the personal skills that people can use to influence others, including their ability to adapt their methods to the situation in which they are working. Another perspective shows that people influence others by using **power**.

Power concerns 'the capacity of individuals to exert their will over others' (Buchanan and Badham, 1999).

Sources of power

What are the bases of one person's power over another? French and Raven's (1959) widely quoted classification identifies five sources of power:

1 **Legitimate power** flows from the person's formal position in the organisation. The job they hold gives them the power, for example, to make capital expenditures, offer overtime, choose a supplier or recruit staff.

2 **Reward power** is the ability to reward another if they comply with a request or instruction. The reward can take many forms – pay, time off or interesting work.

3 **Coercive power** is the ability to obtain compliance through fear of punishment or harm. It includes reprimands, demotions, threats, bullying language or a powerful physical presence.

4 **Referent power**, also called *charismatic* power, is when some characteristics in a person are attractive to others: they identify with them, which gives the charismatic person power.

5 **Expertise power** is when people acknowledge someone's knowledge and are therefore willing to follow their suggestions. This knowledge or skill may be *administrative* (how an organisation operates) or *technical* (how to do a task).

Table 14.5 develops the French and Raven list, by showing that each type of power can have both a personal and a positional source. The most significant change to the French and Raven model is to show that referent (charismatic) power is not just personal but can also have a positional source (Hales, 2001). Chapter 3 showed how organisations develop distinctive cultures and sub-cultures. When people refer to the prevailing culture in an attempt to influence behaviour ('what I'm asking fits the culture') they are drawing on a positional form of referent power.

Table 14.5

Personal and positional sources of power

Power resource	Personal	Positional
Coercive	Forcefulness, insistence, determination	Authority to give instructions, with the threat of sanctions or punishment available
Reward	Credit for previous or future favours in daily exchanges	Authority to use organisational resources, including the support of senior people
Expertise:		
Administrative	Experience of the business, whom to contact, how to get things done	Authority to use or create organisational policies or rules
Technical	Skill or expertise relevant to the task	Authority to access expertise, information and ideas across the business
Referent	Individual beliefs, values, ideas, personal qualities	Authority to invoke norms and values of the organisational culture

Source: Based on Hales (2001).

Someone who has little access to these sources of power will have less influence than someone with much access. People continually defend their power sources, and try to gain new ones.

Perceptions of power

Power is only effective if the target of an influence attempt recognises the power source as legitimate and acceptable. If they dispute the knowledge base of a manager, or challenge their positional authority over a matter, the influence attempt is likely to fail. Managers who are successful influencers ensure that their power sources are sustained, and take every opportunity to enhance them.

Marketing brand Me

Responses to the use of power

People respond to influence attempts in three ways – resistance, compliance and internalisation. Table 14.6 describes the alternatives. Resistant staff will have no commitment to the work. They do what is required grudgingly, and without enthusiasm or imagination. While it may be possible to overcome resistance by using threats or coercion, this may not be the most useful reaction in the longer term. Compliance too has limitations, especially if long-term success depends on further innovation. Only when staff are fully committed because they have internalised the influencer's goals, and see themselves as part of the creative process, is the influencing task complete.

Outcome	Description	Commentary
Resistance	Target is opposed to the request and actively tries to avoid carrying it out	Target may make excuses or try to dissuade the influencer from persisting. May also seek support from higher authority or undermine the influencer's efforts
Compliance	Target willing to do what is asked, but is apathetic, unenthusiastic and makes minimal effort	For a complex task, an unsatisfactory outcome. For routine tasks it may be enough for the influencer to accomplish their goals
Internalisation	Target internally agrees with a decision or request and makes a geat effort to meet it successfully	Usually the most successful outcome from the point of view of the influencer, especially on a difficult task

Table 14.6

Three outcomes of influence attempts

Grudging compliance is unlikely to lead to satisfactory performance. The complexities of work processes often require people to work with imagination and flexibility. In service industries employee behaviour directly influences customer perceptions, such as whether they see employees working responsibly and with concern for what they are doing. This is not likely to happen if managers have used their power in ways that have secured only compliance, not the commitment that comes from internalisation.

Activity 14.3 Critical reflection on sources of power

- Try to identify at least one example of each of the personal and positional power sources. Examples could come from observing a manager in action (including people in your university or college) or from your reading of current business affairs.
- Can you identify what the person concerned has done to develop their power?
- Have other events helped to build, or to undermine their power?

Case questions 14.3

- Which of the sources of power in Table 14.5 has Ricardo Semler used?
- What has he done to increase his power in the eyes of those he is trying to influence?
- What other forms of authority has he acquired?
- Which of the sources of power in Table 14.5 could the associates use?

14.7 Using positional power to influence others

Those who want to be effective influencers can increase their chances of doing so by building up those sources of power that come from their position within the organisation. Kanter (1979) observed that people are more likely to be influenced by strong and powerful managers than by weak and isolated ones. She identified many ways in which a manager's position in the organisation affects their power, such as:

- approvals needed for non-routine decisions (fewer approvals means more power)
- relation of job to current organisational priorities (central relation means more power)
- external contact (more opportunities for this means more power)
- senior contact (more opportunities for this means more power).

The nature of the job and the pattern of contacts that come with it give the manager access to three 'lines of power':

- **supply**: money and other resources that can be used to bestow status or rewards on others in return for their support;
- **information**: being in the know, aware of what is happening, familiar with plans and opportunities that are in the making;
- **support**: able to get senior or external backing for what he or she wants to do.

Political behaviour is 'the practical domain of power in action, worked out through the use of techniques of influence and other (more or less extreme) tactics' (Buchanan and Badham, 1999).

The more of these lines of power the manager has, the more will subordinates co-operate. They do so because they believe that the manager has the power to engage in **political behaviour** and make things happen: they have 'clout' – weight or political influence in the organisation. A person's position in the organisation gives them access to one or more of the sources of power shown in Table 14.5.

Coercive

This is the ability to give instructions or threaten penalties, derived from a person's formal position in the hierarchy. Kramer (2006) observed how many 'Great Intimidators' work – often achieving great success for their organisation, at other times failing badly. Their tactics included:

- getting up close and personal – being directly confrontational, often using aggressive behaviour and language;
- being angry – often using a calculated loss of temper to strike fear into their opponent;
- keeping them guessing – revealing as little as possible about their plans, to increase opponents' anxiety;
- know it all – extensive preparation to be able to dominate any discussion; this includes being aware of weaknesses in the opponent's history or character.

Reward

This is the ability that position gives to use the financial and other resources of the organisation in return for support. Managers with large budgets and valuable networks of contacts use these resources, or the promise of them, to exert influence. Managers who choose to be remote and isolated in back-room work will not have that power – and so will have little influence on people or events.

Expertise

Administrative expertise

This is the power that the holder of a position has to create formal policies which support their influence attempts. They can create rules, procedures or positions that sustain their power – especially if they can also appoint loyal supporters, or those in their debt, to those positions. In this way they encourage others to act in the way they prefer – as when the new chief executive of Centrica persuaded his staff to improve customer service.

Structures and rewards at Centrica   www.centrica.co.uk

Centrica inherited severe customer relations problems when it demerged from British Gas, so restoring customer trust was an important part of the new chief executive's job. He changed the structure of Centrica to influence other managers to give it priority. Customer service satisfaction targets were included in an executive bonus scheme covering its top 200 people. Also, a senior board executive was made responsible for all customer services.

Source: Based on *Financial Times*, 24 February 2001.

key ideas   Sir John Harvey-Jones's leadership at ICI

In a classic study of ICI under Sir John Harvey-Jones, Pettigrew traced the link between the leadership of the company and the change process. Sir John implemented fundamental changes in what was then a very large company, but Pettigrew shows he did not achieve this by a few dramatic acts or decisions. Rather it depended on actions he took over many years to change the structure of the organisation so that managers had more access to sources of power with which to influence others to make radical change. For example, greater power was given to divisional directors to reward staff according to their performance.

Pettigrew concluded that studies of leadership should not focus only on the actions of individuals, important though they are. Rather they should view leadership within a context. The leader exerts influence by shaping that context and providing others with positional power to initiate change.

Source: Pettigrew (1985, 1987).

management in practice   Too much internal focus

A department of a local authority consisted of a director, 2 senior officers, 3 officers and 14 staff. The director's style was to involve himself in operational matters, and he rarely worked with other senior managers. He normally met only the senior officers in his department and rarely involved others, believing that officers should not be involved in policy. He saw himself as the only competent person in the department and was comfortable in this operational role.

Staff consider themselves to be capable and professional. They expect to be involved more fully and are used to taking initiatives. The director's involvement in operational detail annoyed staff as it showed that he did not trust their abilities. They were even more annoyed at the low status of their department, due to the director not being active externally and so lacking influence outside the department.

Technical expertise

This is the power a person gains from holding a position that gives them access to information, of being in the know, aware of what is happening and of opportunities which are emerging. They can use their position, and the contacts that go with it, to build their image as a competent person. This credibility adds to their power to influence others. It is a contentious area, since people compete for access to information, and the power that goes with it.

Referent

This is where managers use their position to influence others by showing that what they propose is consistent with the accepted values and culture of the organisation. They invoke wider values in support of their proposal. The effectiveness of the influence attempt depends on the other people having a similar view of the culture.

The more of these sources of power the manager has, the more others will cooperate. They do so because they believe that the manager has the power to make things happen. Such a manager has weight or political influence, which encourages others to cooperate.

'To increase power, share it'

Kanter (1979) also proposed that managers can increase their power by, paradoxically, **delegating** some of it to subordinates. As subordinates carry out tasks previously done by the manager, he or she has more time to build the external and senior contacts – which further boost power. By delegating not only tasks but also lines of supply (giving subordinates a generous budget), lines of information (inviting them to high-level meetings) and lines of support (giving visible encouragement), managers develop subordinates' confidence, and at the same time enhance their own power. They can spend more time on external matters, making contacts, keeping in touch with what is happening and so building their visibility and reputation. A manager who fails to delegate, and who looks inward rather than outward, becomes increasingly isolated.

> **Delegation** occurs when one person gives another the authority to undertake specific activities or decisions.

Semco – the case continues
http:///semco.locaweb.com.br/

CASE STUDY

The offices are open plan (like those at Oticon – Chapter 10), and managers have none of the minor privileges often associated with the role, such as parking spaces, executive dining rooms or secretaries. There are very few rules, as Semler believes in treating employees like adults.

We have absolute trust in our employees . . . (and) we are proving that worker involvement doesn't mean that bosses lose power. What we do is strip away the blind, irrational authoritarianism that diminishes productivity. We're thrilled that our workers are self-governing and self-managing. It means that they care about their jobs and about their company, and that's good for all of us. (Semler, 1994, pp. 4–5)

A major innovation occurred when some engineers offered to develop new products and lines of business, working with Semco equipment and facilities in return for a share of the royalties or savings from their ideas. They would report to senior management after six months – who would extend or revoke the mandate. The group was successful, and senior managers have encouraged this 'satellite' system throughout the group. These have become highly innovative divisions within Semco, and some two-thirds of the company's new products come from satellites. Workers thrived on having complete accountability and responsibility, understanding that failure to perform would result in the unit being discontinued.

This way of growing the business has enabled it to develop from the original industrial machinery unit, which has evolved into high-tech mixing equipment used in, for example, the pharmaceutical industry. Another unit (SemcoBAC) makes cooling towers for commercial properties, and a third (Semco Johnson Controls) manages large properties such as hospitals and airports. Other units are in environmental consulting, inventory management, HRM outsourcing: in 2004 it entered a joint venture with Pitney-Bowes, the world leader in mail and document management solutions. The common theme is that they are all in markets in which the solutions are highly engineered (and therefore difficult) and in which Semco can be a market leader, able to charge a high price. Underlying all of the transformation that has taken place, Semler identifies a common core value:

If you ask people what Semco is, their answer will be the same as it was two decades ago . . . People will talk about shared ideas . . . and that comes from the freedom to ask, Why? (Semler, 2003, p. 8)

Sources: Based on material from Thunderbird, The American School of International Management, Case A15-98-0024, *Ricardo Semler and Semco S.A.*; Semler (2003); and other published material.

14.8 Choosing tactics to influence others

Another approach to the study of influence has been to identify directly how managers tried to influence others. An early example of this was work by Kipnis *et al.* (1980), who identified a set of influencing tactics that managers used in dealing with subordinates, bosses and co-workers. Yukl and Falbe (1990) replicated this work in a wider empirical study, and refined the categories – as shown in Table 14.7.

Table 14.7

Influence tactics and definitions

Tactic	Definition
Rational persuasion	The person uses logical arguments and factual evidence to persuade you that a proposal or request is viable and likely to result in the attainment of task objectives
Inspirational appeal	The person makes a request or proposal that arouses enthusiasm by appealing to your values, ideals and aspirations or by increasing your confidence that you can do it
Consultation	The person seeks your participation in planning a strategy, activity or change for which your support and assistance are desired, or the person is willing to modify a proposal to deal with your concerns and suggestions
Ingratiation	The person seeks to get you in a good mood or to think favourably of him or her before asking you to do something
Exchange	The person offers an exchange of favours, indicates a willingness to reciprocate at a later time, or promises you a share of the benefits if you help accomplish the task
Personal appeal	The person appeals to your feelings of loyalty and friendship towards him or her before asking you to do something
Coalition	The person seeks the aid of others to persuade you to do something, or uses the support of others as a reason for you to agree also
Legitimating	The person seeks to establish the legitimacy of a request by claiming the authority or right to make it or by verifying that it is consistent with organisational policies, rules, practices or traditions
Pressure	The person uses demands, threats or persistent reminders to influence you to do what he or she wants

Source: Based on Yukl and Falbe (1990).

The nine tactics cover a variety of behaviours that people can use as they try to influence others – whether subordinates, bosses or colleagues. Yukl and Tracey (1992) extended the work by examining which tactics managers used most frequently with different target groups. They concluded that managers were most likely to use:

● rational persuasion when trying to influence their boss
● inspirational appeal and pressure when trying to influence subordinates
● exchange, personal appeal and legitimating tactics when influencing colleagues.

Networking refers to 'individuals' attempts to develop and maintain relationships with others [who] have the potential to assist them in their work or career' (Huczynski, 2004, p. 305).

14.9 Influencing through networks

An important way to influence others is the ability to draw on a network of informal relationships. **Networking** refers to 'individuals' attempts to develop and maintain relationships with others [who] have the potential to assist them in their work or career' (Huczynski, 2004, p. 305). Table 14.8 shows several types of network.

Practitioners	Joined by people with a common training or professional interest, and may be formal or informal	
Privileged power	Joined by people in powerful positions (usually by invitation only)	
Ideological	Consisting of people keen to promote political objectives or values	
People oriented	Formed around shared feelings of personal warmth and familiarity – friendship groups that people join on the basis of identity with existing participants	
Strategic	Often built to help develop links with people in other organisations	

Table 14.8

Types of network

The ability to influence can be greatly enhanced by being connected to many such networks, giving access to contacts and information. They help people to know what is happening in their business and to extend their range of contacts in other organisations. Strong anecdotal evidence that networking influences career progression was supported by Luthans' (1988) research described in Chapter 1, which showed that people who spent a relatively large amount of time networking received more rapid promotion than those who did not. As Thomas (2003) observed:

> in management what you know and what you have achieved will seldom be sufficient for getting ahead. Knowing and being known in the networks of influence, both for what you have achieved and for who you are, may be essential (p. 141).

Art Kleiner and Core Groups

key ideas

Kleiner suggests that organisations, despite the rhetoric about customers and stakeholders, exist to serve the interests of what he calls their Core Group – 'the people who really matter'. The nature of the Core Group varies from place to place – sometimes concentrated amongst senior managers, at others widely dispersed – but every organisation is continually acting to fulfil the perceived needs and priorities of its Core Group – the organisation goes wherever people 'perceive the core group needs and wants to go' (p. 8). 'If we are going to act effectively in a society of organisations, we need a theory to help us see organisations clearly, as they are' (p. 6).

Source: Kleiner (2003).

Kotter (1982) observed that general managers rely heavily on informal networks of contacts to get things done. This is especially necessary to influence those in other organisations – to make a sale, to gain access to a country's market or to set up a joint venture – though as Anand and Conger (2007) found, few people have the abilities required to be fully effective networkers. Hillman (2005) showed how senior managers increase their influence over the business environment by appointing ex-politicians to their boards of directors. Government policy and regulations are a major source of uncertainty in some industries, and one way to reduce that is to build close links with politicians and others with access to or influence over the government process. Hillman proposed that the value of doing this would be more pronounced in heavily regulated industries such as telecommunications, biotechnology or tobacco, than in industries such as consumer electronics or retailing, which face little regulation. She found that firms in heavily regulated industries did indeed have more directors with political experience, and that firms with politicians on their board were associated with better financial performance, especially in the heavily regulated industries.

 **Influence in China and Taiwan**

Star TV (a subsidiary of Rupert Murdoch's News Corporation) developed close links with the Chinese authorities, in the hope of expanding the delivery of its entertainment channel on Chinese TV. This paid off in 2003, when it became the first foreign-owned company to receive permission for a limited nationwide service.

Everything in China is about relationships and mutual benefit,' said Jamie Davis, head of Star TV in China. 'I think Rupert Murdoch has a very good relationship with the Chinese Government . . . and we work hard at it

FT

Source: *Financial Times*, 9 January 2003.

The sudden elevation of Ho-chen Tan to the top job at Chunghwa Telecom last month was demonstration of the value of having friends in high places. He was in charge of transport in Taipei in the mid-1990s, when the Taiwanese President, Chen Shui-bian, was mayor of the city. Mr Ho-chen says his contacts in the administration will help Chunghwa to win a voice in how the government handles the company's privatisation: 'I hope our company can win the right to make suggestions. Perhaps my network in the current government and the faith put in me will help the company to get more opportunities.'

FT

Source: *Financial Times*, 21 February 2003.

Sparrowe and Liden (2005) note that informal networks are probably becoming more important as a means of influencing others:

> As traditional hierarchical structures have given way to flatter and more flexible forms, informal networks have become even more important in gaining access to valuable information, resources, and opportunities. The structure and composition of an individual's network allows him or her to identify strategic opportunities, marshal resources, assemble teams and win support for innovative projects ... Individuals who hold central positions in informal advice networks enjoy greater influence than those in peripheral positions (Brass, 1984) and receive more favorable performance ratings. (Sparrowe *et al.*, 2001, p. 505)

Whichever methods are used, the outcome of an influence attempt will depend not only on the tactics used but on how well the influencer is able to meet the needs of the person they are influencing – see Chapter 15.

14.10 Current themes and issues

Performance

The chapter has outlined what could be called interpersonal and structural ways of influencing others. The interpersonal methods include those based on trait and behavioural theories of influence, as well as those on tactics and networks. Structural approaches are those in which the influencer supplements their personal power sources with those that follow from their position within the organisation – the authority to promise promotion if a target is achieved, for example. While managers who develop high levels of interpersonal skills may be able to exert a great deal of influence, those who are able draw on structural sources of power are likely to be able to achieve much more.

Which of the many interpersonal and structural forms of influence are likely to be effective depends, as stressed in the chapter, on the situation in which the influence attempt is taking place. These can be distinguished on several dimensions, such as the people being influenced, the nature of the task, the dynamism or otherwise of the task environment, and the history of the relationships involved.

The essential influencing skill is that of being aware of the range of approaches, the conditions likely to favour the use of one approach rather than another, and the ability to diagnose to which of those conditions the current situation most closely corresponds. That enables the influencer to ensure that their attempts at influence enhance performance.

Responsibility

Influence is not an ethically neutral activity. The chapter has presented influencing as an essential element in the management task, being the means by which managers persuade others to act in ways that add value to resources. Both the content and the process of an influence attempt can reduce value for some stakeholders, at the same time as it may raise it for others.

Wealth can be created either by increasing the income from resources or reducing their costs. In either case it is possible that those responsible for an activity act in a way that others regard as irresponsible. This could include, for example:

- influencing customers to pay an unfairly high price because of an imbalance of power;
- influencing them to take a service or product that is inappropriate to their needs;
- influencing employees to accept less favourable or more stressful conditions to reduce costs;
- reducing costs by outsourcing or other means.

All of these could meet the criterion of adding value for the organisation, but destroying it for others.

The process by which someone influences others can also affect the distribution of wealth. Practices could include:

- using tactics that damage the target of influence, such as coercion or bullying;
- influencing through practices that may be illegal or unethical – such as bribery;
- deliberately using false or misleading information to support a case.

So although most discussion about corporate responsibility has focused on issues of customers or the environment, there are also issues about the processes of managing. Building a power base with which to influence others is an essential part of managing, but it may produce losers as well as winners. Awareness of this, and a willingness to act on it, is a mark of responsibility.

Internationalisation

The ability to manage internationally depends on being able to influence others in culturally mixed circumstances, where influence tactics that work in one place may be ineffective in another. Cross-cultural studies have found that cultural values (Chapter 4) affect the preferred influence tactics. For example Fu and Yukl (2000) found that Chinese managers rated coalition formation, giving gifts and favours, and personal appeals as more effective, and rational persuasion, consultation and exchange as less effective than did American managers. The authors noted that these preferences for influencing tactics were consistent with their respective cultural values: for the Chinese with their values of collectivism, feminism and a long-term orientation, and for the Americans with their values of equality, direct confrontation and pragmatism.

There is also evidence that styles of leadership vary between countries. Shao and Webber (2005) found that certain of 'the big five' personality traits associated with transformational leadership behaviour in North America are not evident in China. They attributed this to differences in the prevailing cultures:

> The Chinese culture, characterized as high power distance, high uncertainty avoidance and collectivism, fundamentally reinforces the hierarchical and conformist attributes of the top-down command structure. This structure emphasises a centralised authority and leadership, stability and predictability, which create barriers for the emergence of transformational leaders, who tend to challenge the status quo and raise performance expectations. (p. 943)

Summary

1 **Distinguish leading from managing, and explain why each is essential to performance**
   - Although both are essential and the difference can be overstated, leading is usually seen as referring to activities that bring change, whereas managing brings stability and order. Many people both lead and manage in the course of their work.

2 **Explain why leading and managing both depend on being able to influence others**
   - Achieving objectives usually depends on the willing commitment of other people. How management seeks to influence others affects people's reaction to being managed. Dominant use of power may ensure compliance, but such an approach is unlikely to produce the commitment required to meet innovative objectives.

3 **Compare trait, behavioural and contingency perspectives on styles of influence**
   - Trait theories seek to identify the personal characteristics associated with effective influencing.
   - Behavioural theories distinguish managers' behaviours on two dimensions, such as initiating structure and consideration.
   - Contingency perspectives argue that the traits or behaviours required for effective influence depend on factors in the situation, such as the characteristics of the employee, the boss and the task.

4 **Outline theories that focus on power (both personal and organisational) as the source of influence**
   - The more power a person has, the more they will be able to influence others. Table 14.5 identified sources of power as coercion, reward, expertise (administrative and technical) and referent – all of which can have both personal and organisational dimensions.

5 **Contrast the style and power perspectives, and explain why sharing power may increase it**
   - Sharing power with subordinates may not only enable them to have more satisfying and rewarding work, but by enabling the manager to have more time to develop senior and external contacts, he or she can then enhance their power more than if they focused on internal matters.

6 Outline a model of the tactics people use to influence others, including the use of cooperative networks

- Yukl and Falbe (1990) identified these tactics in attempts to influence others: rational persuasion, inspirational appeal, consultation, ingratiation, exchange, personal appeal, coalition, legitimating and pressure. They have also found that effective influencers vary their tactics depending on the person they are trying to influence. A further line of research identifies the value of building collaborative networks as part of effective influencing.

Review questions

1 Why is the ability to influence others so central to the management role?

2 What evidence is there that traits theories continue to influence management practice?

3 What are the strengths and weaknesses of the behavioural approaches to leadership?

4 What is meant by the phrase a '9,9 manager'?

5 Discuss with someone how he or she tries to influence people (or reflect on your own practice). Compare this experience with one of the contingency approaches.

6 Evaluate that theory in the light of the evidence acquired in review question 5 and other considerations.

7 Explain in your own words the main sources of power available to managers. Give examples of both personal and institutional forms of each.

8 List the lines of power that Kanter (1979) identifies and give an example of each.

9 What does the network perspective imply for someone wishing to be a successful influencer?

Concluding critical reflection

Think about the ways in which you typically seek to influence others, and about how others in your company try to exert influence. Review the material in the chapter, and then make notes on these questions:

- What examples of the issues discussed in this chapter struck you as being relevant to practice in your company?

- Thinking of the people you typically work with, who are effective and who are less effective influencers? What do the effective people do that enables them to get their way? What interpersonal skills do they use? What sources of power, or what networks, do they use? Do the prevailing **assumptions** fit with Kanter's view that 'to increase power, share it'? On balance, do their assumptions accurately reflect the reality you see?

- What factors in the **context** – including the history of the company or your personal experience – have shaped the way you manage your attempts at influencing? Does your current approach appear to be right for your present position and company – or would you use a different approach in other circumstances? (Perhaps refer to some of the Management in Practice features for how different managers exert influence.)

- Have people put forward **alternative** approaches to influencing, based on evidence about other companies? If you could find such evidence, how may it affect company practice?
- How do you and your colleagues react to the Semco approach, which appears to have helped create a successful, profitable business? What **limitations** can you see in it? Conversely what limitations does it expose in more conventional approaches to management?

Further reading

Yukl, G.A. (2004), *Leadership in Organizations* (6th edn), Prentice-Hall, Upper Saddle River, NJ.

Combines a comprehensive review of academic research on all aspects of organisational leadership with clear guidance on the implications for practitioners.

Buchanan, D. and Badham, R. (1999), *Power, Politics and Organizational Change: Winning the turf game*, Sage, London.

A modern approach to politics in organisations, offering a theoretical and practical guide, based on extensive primary research.

Huczynski, A.A. (2004), *Influencing Within Organizations* (2nd edn), Routledge, London.

Draws on a wide range of academic research to provide a practical guide to being an effective influencer – from how to conduct yourself at a job interview to coping with organisational politics.

Branson, R. (1999), *Losing My Virginity*, Virgin Books, London.

Roddick, A. (2000), *Business as Unusual*, Thorsons, London.

Semler, R. (2003), *The Seven Day Weekend: Finding the work/life balance*, Century, London.

Accounts of their approach to management by three charismatic leaders.

Kleiner, A. (2003), *Who Really Matters: The core group theory of power, privilege and success*, Doubleday, New York.

Absorbing perspective of the realities of corporate power, with many practical implications for career planning.

Adams, S. (1998), *The Dilbert Principle*, Boxtree, London.

Light relief from your studies.

Pedler, M., Burgoyne, J. and Boydell, T. (2004), *A Manager's Guide to Leadership*, McGraw-Hill, Maidenhead.

A highly practical book, based on the philosophy that leadership is defined by what people do when faced with challenging situations. The authors use their well-established self-development approach to encourage readers to act on situations requiring leadership, and then to reflect and learn from the experience.

Weblinks

Visit these websites (or others of similar companies of which you learn):

http://semco.locaweb.com.br/
http://borsen.dk
www.bmw.com
www.centrica.co.uk
www.thebodyshop.com
www.gore.com
www.oticon.com

Each of these organisations has tried to develop new approaches to managing and influencing staff, and have, despite periods of difficulty, survived and in most cases prospered. They are still quite rare, as relatively few entrepreneurs have successfully followed their example.

- Use the House model to analyse what conditions may explain their success.
- Why do you think so few others have adopted the same approach?

Annotated weblinks, multiple choice questions and other useful resources can be found on www.pearsoned.co.uk/boddy

Chapter 15

Motivation

Aim

To examine theories of behaviour at work and to connect them with management practice.

Objectives

By the end of your work on this chapter you should be able to outline the concepts below in your own terms and:

1 Understand the significance of work motivation, including the psychological contract, to the task of managing

2 Understand theories that focus on the content and process of motivation, and those which relate these ideas to issues of work design and empowerment

3 Explain the significance of understanding the assumptions managers use in motivating staff, and how these vary between national cultures

4 Use the models presented to diagnose motivational problems and recommend areas of possible action

5 Relate these ideas to current developments in the environment of managing.

Key terms

This chapter introduces the following ideas:

motivation
psychological contract
perceptions
behaviour modification
existence needs
relatedness needs
growth needs
motivator factors
hygiene factors
expectancy theory

subjective probability
instrumentality
valence
equity theory
goal-setting theory
self-efficacy
intrinsic rewards
extrinsic rewards
job enrichment model

Each is a term defined within the text, as well as in the Glossary at the end of the book.

At the end of 2006 there were 237 IKEA home furnishing stores in 35 countries: retail sales amounted to almost €18 billion. The company states that what it calls the IKEA Concept is founded on a low-price offer in home furnishings. It aims to offer a wide range of well-designed home furnishing products at prices so low that as many people as possible can afford them. The way IKEA products are designed, manufactured, transported, sold and assembled all contribute to transforming the Concept into reality.

The Concept began when Ingvar Kamprad, a Swedish entrepreneur, had the idea of offering well-designed furniture at low prices. He aimed to achieve this not by cutting quality, but by applying simple cost-cutting solutions to manufacture and distribution. IKEA's first showroom opened in 1953 and until 1963 all the stores were in Sweden. In that year the international expansion began with a store in Norway – it has entered one new country in almost every year since then – opening in Japan in 2006.

The objective of the parent company, Inter IKEA Systems BV, is to increase availability of IKEA products by the worldwide franchising of the IKEA Concept. It operates very large stores near to major cities. IKEA employs its own designers, though other companies manufacture most of the products. It is renowned for modern innovative design, and for supplying large products in a form that customers must assemble themselves. An example of its innovative approach is 'Children's IKEA', introduced in 1997. The company worked with child psychologists to develop products that would help children develop their motor skills, social development and creativity. Children helped to make the final selection of the range.

The company employs about 118,000 staff – whom it calls co-workers. In 1999 Ingvar Kamprad initiated the Big Thank You Event as a millennium reward for the co-workers. The total value of all sales on that day was divided equally amongst everyone in the company – for most it was more than a month's pay.

The company vision is to create a better everyday life for many people, and acknowledges that it is the co-

© Inter IKEA Systems BV 2006.

workers who make that possible. They aim to give people the possibility to grow both as individuals and in their professional roles: 'we are strongly committed to creating a better life for ourselves and our customers'. In its recruitment the company looks for people who share the company's values, which include togetherness, cost consciousness, respect and simplicity. The website explains that as well as being able to do the job IKEA seeks people with many other personal qualities, such as a strong desire to learn, the motivation to continually do things better, simplicity and common sense, the ability to lead by example, efficiency and cost consciousness:

These values are important to us because our way of working is less structured than at many other organisations.

Source: Edvardsson and Enquist (2002); company website.

Case questions 15.1

Growing a worldwide retail business implies a great deal of control to ensure common standards and a consistent brand image.

- How does the way IKEA aims to manage its co-workers support that need?
- What assumptions does the company make about the needs of its staff?

15.1 Introduction

Managers at IKEA understand that the continued success of their business depends on being able to attract and retain staff who are willing and committed to the business. The company cannot meet the expectations of their customers unless they maintain the **motivation** of employees. Employees who were disinterested or bored would not provide good service, would make mistakes, and damage IKEA's reputation.

Motivation refers to the forces within or beyond a person that arouse and sustain their commitment to a course of action.

All businesses need enthusiastic and committed employees who work in a way that supports organisational goals. When Centrica attempted to improve customer satisfaction and trust (see Chapter 14) management depended on staff being motivated to deliver better service. Microsoft and Dell depend on their engineers being motivated to develop a constant flow of innovative products. Hospitals depend on medical and nursing staff being willing to work there, and to work in a way that provides good patient care.

Yet motivation arises within people – so managers need to ensure that people can satisfy their needs through work. People have different motivations, so a reward that is attractive to one may be unimportant to another.

---

management in practice   **Terry Green of Debenhams**

'What is it you dream of when you're young?' Terry Green, chief executive of Debenhams, posed the question ... He is sitting in his shirt sleeves ... behind a massive desk in his rooftop office in London's West End.

'I'll tell you', says Green, before I have a chance to answer. 'Having a flash car, a sexy girlfriend and a house in the country. And this,' he continues, pulling out a book of photos of his new home, a 10-bedroomed mansion set in 22 acres of countryside, ... 'is my boyhood dream realised.'

If he has realised his dreams, will the hunger go? 'No,' he says, 'that's the brilliance of it.' Because since he took on [the new house] he's personally more in debt than he's ever been. He has to keep earning more money, making Debenhams a huge success, to pay off his mountainous mortgage.

Source: The Davidson Interview, *Management Today*, January 1999, p. 40.

Money is evidently a major motivator for Terry Green (who no longer works for Debenhams) – as it is for many on very low incomes too. Others find deep satisfaction in the work itself – like Theresa Marshall, who is a classroom assistant in a city primary school:

> I've found my niche and couldn't be happier – it's no exaggeration to say that I absolutely love my job. My favourite part is helping the children with their reading skills and seeing the pleasure that they can get out of books.

Some enjoy working with physical things or the challenge of designing an innovative product – while others enjoy working directly with other people.

With people having such diverse needs and interests, how can managers motivate them to work in ways that meet the manager's priorities? In small organisations the relationship between an owner-manager and a few employees is close and direct. Each can develop a good idea of what the other expects and adjust the pattern of work and the pattern of rewards to meet changing requirements. As the organisation grows the links become less personal. Motivation increasingly depends on more formal approaches, based on managers' theories of motivation – what they believe will influence employees.

They make working assumptions about how staff would respond to new policies. Staff evaluate what is on offer and respond according to how well it meets their needs.

This chapter outlines and illustrates the main theories of human needs, as shown in Figure 15.1. How managers interpret the wider context shapes what they expect from people – who also have needs and expectations of the organisation. The next section examines the psychological contract that expresses these mutual expectations. The following sections then present three groups of theories about motivation at work – content, process and work design. Content theories help explain why people work, by identifying human needs that work may satisfy. Process theories help explain how people decide which of several possible actions will best satisfy their needs. Work design theories connect the content and process approaches to workplace practice.

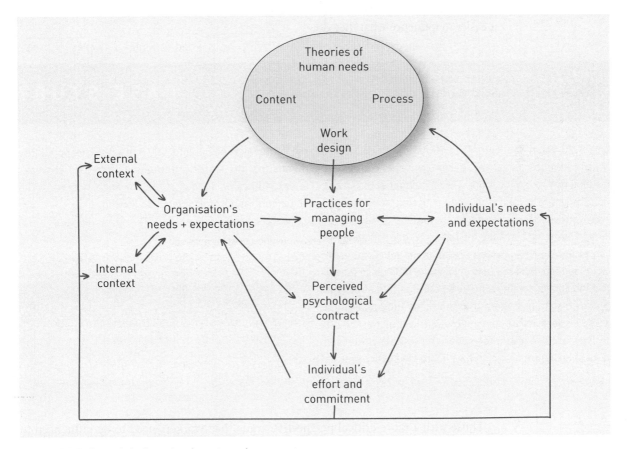

Figure 15.1 A model of motivation at work

15.2 Some constants in motivation

Much behaviour is routine, based on habit, precedent and unconscious scripts. This chapter is concerned with the larger, precedent-setting choices people make about behaviour at work. For some people work is an occasion for hard, enthusiastic and imaginative activity, a source of rich satisfaction. They are motivated, in the sense that they put effort (arousal) into their work (direction and persistence). For others it is something they do grudgingly – work does not arouse their enthusiasm, or merely passes the time until they find something more interesting. Managers try to understand why such differences occur, and seek to encourage the former rather than the latter. Theories of motivation, which try 'to explicate with increasing precision' (Steers *et al.*, 2004, p. 379) the factors that energise, channel and sustain behaviour, can inform that consideration.

Targets of attempts to motivate

Who are managers trying to motivate? Theories of motivation originally concentrated on how managers motivate subordinates, but they need to influence many other people: colleagues, their own senior managers, people in other organisations. They also try to influence consumers – marketers also use theories of human motivation. In all of these cases people try to understand human needs in the belief that doing so accurately makes it easier to influence what they do.

IKEA – the case continues   www.ikea.com   CASE STUDY

One of the distinctive features of IKEA is the store design, which often has a one way layout that leads customers the long way round the store. This ensures that they must visit the entire store, rather than choosing to go straight away to the section from which they intend to buy something. They must also take the flat-packed products home and assemble them, which is a frequent source of complaint as many find the instructions are difficult to follow. The instructions rely on pictures only, as this saves the cost of translating them into the many languages that would be necessary for an international company.

The only financial information the company releases is its sales figures – which have increased every year as the company expands into new markets. This popularity means that the stores are frequently crowded at weekends, with traffic queues at the entrance, queues at the checkouts, and traffic queues on leaving.

Source: Personal observation.

Case question 15.2
● What assumptions does the company make about the needs of its customers?

Those with a more critical perspective argue that 'workers need to be influenced to cooperate because of their essential alienation from the productive process' (Thompson and McHugh, 2002, p. 306). They also suggest that management typically uses motivation theories to maintain the established power relations between employer and employee. Management often imposes schemes on a relatively passive workforce to make work more interesting. The latter accept these in the absence of realistic alternatives. Staff may even express greater satisfaction with a new arrangement as a way of coming to terms with the inherent stability of the power structure. As always in management, people see the topic from different perspectives: motivation is not a neutral or value-free subject.

Figure 15.2 illustrates a simple model of human motivation. We all have needs for food, social contact or a sense of achievement, which motivate behaviour to satisfy that need. If the action leads to a satisfactory outcome we experience a sense of reward. The feedback loop shows that we then decide whether the behaviour was appropriate and worth repeating.

Individuals do not act in isolation, but within a social context that includes:

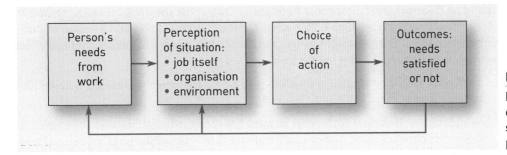

Figure 15.2

Human needs in context – the situational perspective

- the job – how interesting, varied or responsible it is;
- the organisation – supervision, career and promotion prospects, pay systems; and
- the environment – the chances of getting another job.

These contextual factors, some of which management can influence, affect the behaviours people choose to satisfy a need: they may put up with a boring job if there is little chance of getting another one. In considering this model, remember that:

- needs can only be inferred: we make assumptions about which needs a person values;
- needs change with age, experience and responsibilities;
- we face choices, when we can only satisfy one at the expense of another; and
- the effect of satisfying a need on the future strength of that need is uncertain.

The psychological contract

Managers have expectations of the people who work for them. At the same time employees have expectations of managers – not just on pay, but also on such things as fairness, trust and opportunities for self-development. This set of mutual expectations makes up the **psychological contract**.

A **psychological contract** is the set of understandings people have regarding the commitments made between themselves and their organisation.

> **Activity 15.1 Mutual expectations**
>
> Identify a time when you were working in an organisation, or think of your work as a student.
>
> - Describe what the organisation expected of you.
> - What policies or practices did the organisation use to encourage these?
> - What did you expect of the organisation?
> - How well did the organisation meet your expectations?
> - What was the effect of that on your behaviour?

The psychological contract expresses the idea that each side has expectations of the other regarding what they will give and what they will receive in return. Employers offer rewards in the hope of receiving certain types and levels of performance. Employees contribute effort in the expectation of reward. Rousseau and Schalk (2000) refer to psychological contracts as

> the belief systems of individual workers and their employers regarding their mutual obligations. (p. 1)

Some elements in the contract are written but most are tacit and informal. Its current state is the outcome of a process of mutual adjustment as the relationship evolves:

changing circumstances meant that both parties adjust the contract, filling in the blanks along the way (Rousseau, 1995). This adjustment is both inevitable and a source of difficulty, especially if the employer changes the contract in a way that makes employees feel worse off. As Kolb *et al.* (1991) remarked:

> a company staffed by 'cheated' individuals who expect far more than they get is headed for trouble. (p. 6)

While the psychological contract is enacted between the individual and the employer, this negotiation takes place within a national and then a global context (see Figure 15.3). Chapter 4 showed that nations develop distinct management systems that shape what people expect of the employment relationship. Some societies value a close and long-term relationship between employer and employee, while others see it as a temporary transaction that either party may break. The nature of an acceptable contract varies between countries, which has implications for those managing internationally (Rousseau and Schalk, 2000).

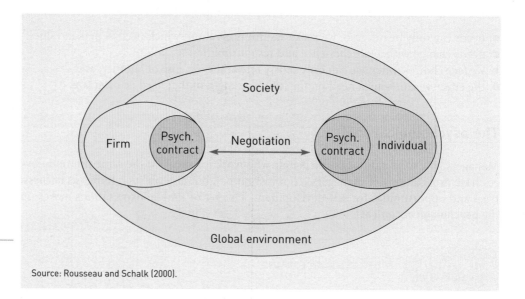

Figure 15.3

Key contexts for psychological contracting

Source: Rousseau and Schalk (2000).

Perception is the active psychological process in which stimuli are selected and organised into meaningful patterns.

In times of rapid economic change researchers have studied employees' **perceptions** of the state of the psychological contract with their employer, since competitive business conditions may lead employers to make changes that employees see as breaking the contract. If they do, what are the effects? Deery *et al.* (2006) studied employees in a call centre who perceived their employer had breached the contract by failing to deliver promises. Staff were committed to providing good customer service, but believed that 'Management are not interested in customer service – their only interest is statistics [on throughput] ... initiative is a dangerous quality in the "new" [organization]. Compliance is a virtue' (p. 172]. Staff perceived that the company had:

- failed to implement a pay-for-performance system;
- did not respect staff knowledge and skills; and
- did not ask for their opinions.

These breaches of the psychological contract led employees to have lower trust in management, to experience less cooperative employment relations, and to have higher rates of absence.

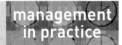

Best workplaces in Europe www.greatplacetowork.co.uk

The Great Place to Work Institute conducts an annual survey identifying the best workplaces in Europe and around the world. Table 15.1 indicates some of the top European firms in the 2006 survey.

Table 15.1 Some 'best places to work in Europe' 2006 (alphabetical)

Name, country and business	Comments
Bain & Company (Belgium, UK – consulting) www.bain.com	About 9% of total payroll costs spent on training and development, with other consultants honoured to be recognised as worthy trainers. 'They provide internal support to make the job fun.'
Colgate Palmolive (Greece, personal and household products) www.colgate.com.gr	Off-site team building retreats whenever a new manager is hired, and also team with colleagues in other European offices. To allow better use of free time, company offers on-site dry-cleaning, banking, travel and other services. Strong commitment to diversity.
ConSol* Software (Germany, IT consulting and software) www.consol.de	Two employees can attend each meeting of the board of directors on a first-come basis. Profit-sharing scheme. Supplementary pension scheme.
Danone (Spain, food and beverages) www.danone.com	Pioneering role in corporate responsibility, rapid growth in number of female managers, development opportunities for young professionals and managers; holds a free summer camp for staff children.
DuPuy (Ireland, orthopaedic joint replacements) www.depuy.com	Employees keep up with latest research through customised learning centre that allows access to the company's e-university at any time, at no cost. Exceptional contributions recognised; 'Management do listen to you if you have ideas.'

Source: www.greatplacetowork.co.uk.

'Employees leave managers, not companies'

From the employee's point of view, there is clear evidence that good management rests squarely on four foundations:

- having a manager who shows care, interest and concern for each of them
- knowing what is expected of them
- having a role that fits their abilities
- receiving positive feedback and recognition regularly for work well done.

In a Gallup study of performance at unit level, covering more than 200,000 employees across many industries, teams that rated managers highly on these four factors were more productive and more profitable. They also had lower staff turnover and higher customer satisfaction ratings.

Source: *People Management*, 17 February 2000, p. 45.

At a time of great change in the business world previously stable psychological contracts are easily broken. Technological changes and increased competition lead senior management to change employment policies and working conditions, or put staff under great pressure to meet demanding performance targets.

IKEA – the case continues   www.ikea.com   CASE STUDY

On the website the company explains that working for the company is a matter of give and take:

IKEA co-workers enjoy many advantages and opportunities from working in such a free and open environment – but all freedoms are counter-balanced with expectations. For example, the expectation that each co-worker is able to assume responsibility for his or her actions.

What do we expect from you?

- You have the ambition to do a good job and the desire to take on responsibility and to take the consequences that this entails.
- You do your best on the basis of your abilities and experience.
- You are service oriented and have the customers' best interests at heart.
- You are not status minded, but rather open in your approach to others.

What do we offer you?

- The chance to work in a growing company with a viable business idea.

- The opportunity to further develop your professional skills.
- The opportunity to choose between many different jobs in the company.
- A job with fair and reasonable conditions.
- The chance to assume responsibility following recognised good results, regardless of age.

Source: Company website.

Case questions 15.3

Visit the website to read a fuller account of the company's approach to co-workers. Read the stories of some of the co-workers.

- How does the psychological contract on offer at IKEA differ from that at companies you have worked for?
- In what ways is it more attractive, and in what ways less?

The next section outlines an early theory of motivation that some companies use to influence the actions of staff. Subsequent sections look at theories of human needs at work.

15.3   Behaviour modification

Behaviour modification is a general label for attempts to change behaviour by using appropriate and timely reinforcement.

Behaviour modification refers to a range of techniques developed to treat psychological conditions such as eating disorders and heavy smoking: managers have used them to deal with issues such as lateness and absenteeism. The techniques developed from Skinner's (1971) theory that people learn to see relationships between actions and their consequences, and that this learning guides behaviour. If we receive a reward for doing something, we tend to do it again: if the consequences are unpleasant, we do not.

Behaviour modification techniques focus on specific observable behaviours rather than on attitudes and feelings.

In promoting safety ... we did not dwell on accident-prone workers or probe for personality or demographic factors, none of which can be changed. Instead we focused on the organisation and what it can do to rearrange the work environment. (Komaki, 2003, p. 96)

This includes specifying what people should do, measuring actual behaviour and identifying the consequences that people experience. If the influencer sees the behaviour as undesirable, he or she tries to influence the person by changing the consequences – rewarding or punishing them.

Komaki (2003) explains how she and her colleagues used the method in a bakery to encourage safe working practices. They worked with management to design these steps:

- *Specify desired behaviour* This included defining very precisely the safe working practices that were required – such as walking round conveyor belts, how to sharpen knives, and using precise terms when giving instructions.
- *Measure desired performance* Trained observers visited the site and recorded whether workers were performing safely by following the specified behaviours.
- *Provide frequent, contingent, positive consequences* In this case, the positive consequence was feedback, in the form of charts showing current accident figures, which were much lower than previous levels.
- *Evaluate effectiveness* Collecting data on accident levels and comparing these with earlier data. In this case people were now working more safely, and the number of injuries had fallen from 53 a year to 10.

Practitioners emphasise that several principles must be used for the method to be effective (Komaki *et al.*, 2000):

- Pay-offs (benefits) must be given only when the desired behaviour occurs.
- Pay-offs must be given as soon as possible after the behaviour, to strengthen the link between behaviour and reward.
- Desirable behaviour is likely to be repeated if reinforced by rewards.
- Reinforcement is more effective than punishment, as punishment only temporarily suppresses behaviour.
- Repeated reinforcement can lead to permanent change in behaviour in the desired direction.

Behaviour modification in a call centre

In our call centre staff are rewarded when behaviour delivers results in line with business requirements. Each month staff performance is reviewed against a number of objectives such as average call length, sales of each product and attention to detail. This is known as Effective Level Review and agents can move through levels of effectiveness ranging from 1 to 4, and gain an increase in salary after six months of successful reviews. Moving through effective levels means that they have performed well and can mean being given other tasks instead of answering the phone. The role can become mundane and repetitive so the opportunity to do other tasks is seen as a reward for good performance. Thus it reinforces acceptable behaviour.

Conversely staff who display behaviour that is not desirable cannot move through these levels and repeated failure to do so can lead to disciplinary action. This can be seen as punishment rather than behaviour modification. People can become resentful at having their performance graded every month, particularly in those areas where it is their line manager's perception of whether or not they have achieved the desired results.

Source: Private communication from the call centre manager.

Above all, advocates stress the need to *reward* desirable behaviours rather than treat them with indifference. These rewards can result from individual action (a word of praise or thanks) or from organisational practices (shopping vouchers for consistently good timekeeping). Supporters believe the approach encourages management to look directly at what makes a particular person act in a desirable way, and to ensure those rewards are available. It depends on identifying rewards the person will value (or punishments they will try to avoid). Theories that attempt to understand these are known as content theories of motivation.

15.4 Content theories of motivation

Most writers on this topic have tried to identify human needs so that they can use this knowledge to influence their actions. Frederick Taylor (Chapter 2) believed that people worked for money and that they would follow strict working methods if management rewarded them financially. Chapter 2 also showed how Mary Parker Follett and Elton Mayo identified other human needs, such as being accepted by a group: if people value this more than the financial incentive, they will conform with what the group expects. Maslow developed a theory that incorporates these and other needs.

Activity 15.2   Was Taylor wrong?

Many managers believe that money is a powerful incentive.

- Find someone who works for an organisation where incentives or commissions make up a significant part of that person's pay and ask how that affects his or her behaviour.
- Are there are any negative effects?

Abraham Maslow – a hierarchy of needs

Maslow was a clinical psychologist who developed a theory of human motivation to help him understand the needs of his patients. He stressed the clinical sources of the theory and that it lacked experimental verification, though he was aware that Douglas McGregor (see Section 15.5) had used the theory to interpret his observations of people at work.

Maslow proposed that individuals experience a range of needs, and will be motivated to fulfil whichever need is most powerful at the time (Maslow, 1970). What he termed the lower-order needs are dominant until they are at least partially satisfied. Normal individuals would then turn their attention to satisfying needs at the next level, so that higher-order needs would gradually become dominant. He suggested these needs formed a hierarchy:

Self-actualisation
Esteem
Belongingness and love
Safety
Physiological

Physiological needs are those that must be satisfied to survive – food and water particularly. Maslow proposed that if all the needs in the hierarchy are unsatisfied then the physiological needs will dominate. People will concentrate on activities to obtain the necessities of life, and will not attempt to satisfy higher needs.

Once the physiological needs were sufficiently gratified a new set of needs would emerge, which he termed *safety needs* – the search for 'security; stability; dependency; protection; freedom from fear, anxiety and chaos; need for structure, order, law, limits ... and so on' (Maslow, 1970, p. 39). People concentrate on satisfying these to the exclusion of others. If this need is dominant for a person they can satisfy it by seeking a stable, regular job with secure working conditions and access to insurance for ill-health and retirement. They resent sudden or random changes in job prospects.

Belongingness needs would follow the satisfaction of safety needs:

> [If] both the physiological and the safety needs are fairly well gratified, there will emerge the love and affection and belongingness needs ... now the person will feel keenly the absence of friends ... and will hunger for affectionate relations with people in general. (p. 43)

These needs include a place in the group or family, and at work they would include wanting to be part of a congenial team. People object when management changes work patterns or locations if this disrupts established working relationships. They welcome change that brings them closer to people they know and like.

Maslow observed that most people have *esteem needs* – self-respect and the respect of others. Self-respect is the need for a sense of achievement, competence, adequacy and confidence. People also seek the respect of others, what he called a desire for reputation in the eyes of other people – prestige, status, recognition, attention. They can satisfy this by taking on challenging or difficult tasks to show they are good at their job and can accomplish something worthwhile. If others recognise this, they earn status and respect.

Research on organisation-based self-esteem

key ideas

Pierce and Gardner (2004) reviewed research on organisation-based self-esteem (OBSE) – that esteem which was influenced by a person's experience at their place of work. Earlier research had found that system-imposed controls through a division of labour, rigid hierarchy, centralisation, standardisation and formalisation carry with them assumptions about the inability of individuals to self-regulate and self-control. Conversely, systems that allowed higher levels of self-expression and personal control were likely to enhance OBSE. They reviewed over 50 studies and concluded that they: 'support the claim that an individual's self-esteem, formed around work and organizational experiences, may well play a significant role in shaping employee intrinsic motivation, attitudes ... and behaviors' (p. 613).

Structures that provide opportunities for the exercise of self-direction and self-control promote OBSE, as do signals to employees that they 'make a difference around here'. They also noted that 'adverse role conditions (such as role ambiguity), anticipated organizational change, job insecurity, discrimination and harassment ... undermine experiences of self-worth' (p. 613).

Source: Pierce and Gardner (2004).

Lastly, Maslow used the term *self-actualisation* needs to refer to the desire for self-fulfilment and for realising potential: 'At this level, individual differences are greatest. The clear emergence of these needs usually rests upon some prior satisfaction of the physiological, safety, love, and esteem needs' (pp. 46–47). People seeking to satisfy self-actualisation needs will look for personal relevance in their work. They may value new responsibilities that help them realise their potential or discover unknown talents.

To illustrate Maslow's hierarchy with a practical example, a member of staff in a government department summarised the ways in which the organisation satisfied the different needs (Table 15.2).

Table 15.2

How work in a government department enabled people to satisfy the needs identified by Maslow

Needs	How they were met
Self-actualisation	Promotion opportunities (steady and fast track) Funding and time off for further education
Esteem	Regarded in society as a good job Grade prestige Promotion
Belongingness and love	Sports and social clubs (local and national) Office parties/outings Permission for informal activities
Safety	Attractive non-contributory pension Safe working conditions 'No redundancy' policy Payment for absence due to illness
Physiological	Good working conditions Steady incremental salary

Maslow did *not* claim that the hierarchy was a fixed or rigid scheme. His clinical experience suggested that most people had these needs in about this order, but he had seen exceptions – people for whom self-esteem was more important than love. For others creativity took precedence, in that they did not seek self-actualisation *after* satisfying their basic needs, but in spite of them *not* being satisfied. Others had such permanently low aspirations that they experienced life at a very basic level.

Nor did he claim that as people satisfy one need completely, another emerges. Rather he proposed that most normal people are partially satisfied and partially unsatisfied in their needs. A more accurate description of the hierarchy would be in terms of decreasing percentages of satisfaction at successive levels. So a person could think of themselves as being, say, 85 per cent satisfied at the physiological level and 70 per cent at the safety level (the percentages are meaningless). A higher-level need did not emerge suddenly – a person would gradually become aware that they could now attain a higher need.

In summary, Maslow believed that people are motivated to satisfy needs that are important to them at that point in their life, and offered a description of those needs. The strength of a particular need would depend on the extent to which lower needs had been met. He believed that most people would seek to satisfy physiological needs first, before the others became operative. Self-actualisation was fulfilled last and least often, although he had observed exceptions.

How does Maslow's approach compare with Skinner's? Skinner believed that by providing positive reinforcement (or punishment) people would be motivated to act in a particular way. The rewards they obtained would satisfy their needs. Maslow took the slightly different position that people would seek to satisfy their needs by acting in a particular way. Both believed that to change behaviour it would be necessary to change the situation. Skinner emphasised that this would take the form of positive reinforcement to satisfy needs after an activity. Maslow implied that influencers should provide conditions which enable people to satisfy their needs from the activity.

A new manager at a nursing home

Jean Parker was appointed manager of a nursing home for the elderly. Recent reports by the Health Authority and Environmental Health inspectors had been so critical that they threatened to close the home. Jean recalls what she did in the first eight months:

> My task was to make sweeping changes, stabilise the workforce and improve the reputation of the home. I had no influence on pay, and low pay was one of the problems. To motivate staff I had to use other methods. Staff facilities were appalling – the dining areas were filthy, showers and some toilets were not working, there were no changing rooms and petty theft was rife. Given the lack of care and respect shown to staff it is little wonder that care given to residents was poor, and staff were demotivated. They turned up to work, carried out tasks and went home. There had been little communication between management and staff. My approach was to work alongside the staff, listen to their grievances, gain their trust and set out an action plan.
>
> The first steps were easy. The staff room was cleaned and decorated, changing rooms and working showers and toilets were provided. Refreshments were provided at meal breaks. Police advice was sought to combat petty theft and lockers were installed in each area. The effect of these changes on staff commitment was astounding. They felt somebody cared for them and listened. In turn, quality of care improved and staff started to take pride in the home, and bring in ornaments and plants to brighten it.
>
> I then started to hold monthly meetings to give management and staff an opportunity to discuss expectations. Policies and procedures were explained. Noticeboards displaying 'news and views' were put up. A monthly newsletter to residents and relations was issued. Staff took part enthusiastically in fund-raising activities to pay for outings and entertainment. This gave them the chance to get to know residents in a social setting, and was a break from routine. A training programme was introduced.
>
> Some staff did not respond and tried to undermine my intentions. Persistent unreported absence was quickly followed by disciplinary action. By the end of the year absenteesim was at a more acceptable level, many working problems were alleviated, and the business started to recover.

Source: Private communication and discussions with the manager.

Activity 15.3   Critical reflection on the theory

- Which of the needs identified by Maslow did Jean Parker's changes at the nursing home help staff to satisfy?
- Do your studies and related activities on your course satisfy needs identified by Maslow?
- What evidence can you gather from your colleagues on the relative importance to them of these needs?

Clayton Alderfer – ERG theory

Doubtful about the empirical support for the hierarchy of motives proposed by Maslow, Alderfer developed another approach (Alderfer, 1972). His work built on Maslow's ideas and presented an alternative. He developed and tested his theory by questionnaires and interviews in five organisations – a manufacturing firm, a bank, two colleges and a school. He aimed to identify the primary needs – those that an organism possesses by the nature of being the creature it is. Satisfaction refers to the internal state of someone who has obtained what he or she is seeking. Frustration is the opposite – when someone seeks something but does not find it.

Existence needs reflect a person's requirement for material and energy.

Relatedness needs involve a desire for relationships with significant other people.

Growth needs are those that impel people to be creative or to produce an effect on themselves or their environment.

Existence needs include all the physiological and material desires – hunger and thirst represent deficiencies in existence needs; pay and benefits represent ways of satisfying material requirements.

Relatedness needs involve relationships with significant other people – family members, colleagues, bosses, subordinates, team members or regular customers. People satisfy relatedness needs by sharing thoughts and feelings. Acceptance, confirmation and understanding help to satisfy relatedness needs.

Growth needs impel a person to be creative or to produce an effect on themselves and their environment. People satisfy them by engaging with problems that use their skills or require them to develop new ones. The greater sense of completeness this brings depends on having opportunities to exercise talents fully.

Figure 15.4 compares Alderfer's formulation of needs with Maslow's. Alderfer proposed that his three categories are active in everyone, although in varying degrees of strength. Unlike Maslow, he found no evidence of a hierarchy of needs, though he did find that if higher needs are frustrated, lower needs become prominent again, even if they have already been satisfied.

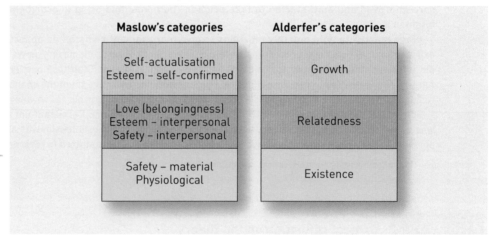

Figure 15.4

Comparison of the Maslow and Alderfer categories of needs

Both theories are hard to test empirically as it is difficult to establish whether a person has satisfied a need. One of the very few empirical tests (Arnolds and Boshoff, 2002) concluded that top managers were primarily motivated by growth needs, while front-line staff were primarily motivated by existence and relatedness needs. There was also some evidence that satisfying growth needs could also increase the motivation of front-line staff, by enhancing their self-esteem.

David McClelland

McClelland (1961) and his colleagues have examined how people think and react in a wide range of situations. This work led them to identify three categories of human need, which individuals possess in different amounts:

● need for affiliation – to develop and maintain interpersonal relationships
● need for power – to have control over one's environment
● need for achievement – to set and meet standards of excellence.

IKEA – the case continues   www.ikea.com

To ensure the success of the company, managers have placed great emphasis on developing a strong culture within IKEA, transmitting this to new employees and reinforcing it by events for existing ones. The belief is that if co-workers develop a strong sense of shared meaning of the IKEA concept they deliver good service wherever in the group they are. As Edvardsson and Enquist (2002) observe,

The strong culture ... can give IKEA an image as a religion. In this aspect the *Testament of a Furniture Dealer* [written by Kamprad and given to all co-workers] is the holy script. The preface reads: 'Once and for all we have decided to side with the many. What is good for our customers is also good for us in the long run.' After the preface the testament is divided into nine points: (1) The Product Range – Our Identity, (2) The IKEA Spirit. A Strong and Living Reality, (3) Profit Gives us Resources, (4) To Reach Good Results with Small Means, (5) Simplicity is a Virtue, (6) The Different Way, (7) Concentration of Energy – Important to Our Success, (8) To Assume Responsibility – A Privilege, (9) Most Things Still Remain to be Done. A Glorious Future! (p. 166)

Source: Edvardsson and Enquist (2002).

Case questions 15.4

- What human needs may this culture enable co-workers to satisfy?
- What does the international growth of the company suggest about differences in national cultures?

McClelland believed that, rather than being arranged in a hierarchy, individuals possess each of these possibly conflicting needs, which motivate their behaviour when activated. McClelland used the Thematic Apperception Test to assess how significant these categories were to people. The subjects of the research were shown pictures with a neutral subject and asked to write a story about it. The researchers coded the stories and claimed these indicated the relative importance to the person of the affiliation, power and achievement motives.

You can assess your scores on these motives by completing Activity 15.4.

Activity 15.4   Assessing your needs

- From each of the four sets of statements below choose the one that is most like you.

1 (a) I set myself difficult goals, which I attempt to reach.
   (b) I am happiest when I am with a group of people who enjoy life.
   (c) I like to organise the activities of a group or team.

2 (a) I only completely enjoy relaxation after the successful completion of exacting pieces of work.
   (b) I become attached to my friends.
   (c) I argue zealously against others for my point of view.

3 (a) I work hard until I am completely satisfied with the result I achieve.
   (b) I like to mix with a group of congenial people, talking about any subject that comes up.
   (c) I tend to influence others more than they influence me.

▶

4 (a) I enjoy working as much as I enjoy my leisure.
   (b) I go out of my way to be with my friends.
   (c) I am able to dominate a social situation.

● Now add your responses as follows:

The number of (a) responses ( ) Achievement
The number of (b) responses ( ) Affiliation
The number of (c) responses ( ) Power

This simple exercise will give you an insight both into the differences between McClelland's three types of motive and into your preference. The larger your score in an area, the more likely your preference is in that area. Compare your answers with others whom you know in the class. Discuss whether the results are in line with what you would have expected, given what you already know of each other.

Source: Based on Jackson (1993).

Frederick Herzberg – two-factor theory

While Maslow and McClelland focused on individual differences in motivation, Herzberg (1959) related motivation to the nature of a person's work. He developed his theory following interviews with 200 engineers and accountants about their experience of work. The researchers first asked them to recall a time when they had felt exceptionally good about their job, and then asked about the events that had preceded those feelings. The research team then asked respondents to recall a time when they had felt particularly bad about their work, and the background to that. Analysis showed that when respondents recalled good times they frequently mentioned one or more of these factors:

● achievement
● recognition
● work itself
● responsibility
● advancement.

They mentioned these much less frequently when describing the bad times. When talking about the bad times they most frequently recalled these factors:

Motivator factors are those aspects of the work itself that Herzberg found influenced people to superior performance and effort.

● company policy and administration
● supervision
● salary
● interpersonal relations
● working conditions.

Hygiene factors (or **maintenance factors**) are those aspects surrounding the task that can prevent discontent and dissatisfaction but will not in themselves contribute to psychological growth and hence motivation.

They mentioned these much less frequently when describing the good times.

Herzberg concluded that factors associated with satisfaction describe people's relationship to what they were doing – the nature of the task, the responsibility or recognition received. He named these '**motivator factors**', as they seemed to influence people to superior performance and effort. The factors associated with dissatisfaction described conditions surrounding the work – such as supervision or company policy. He named these '**hygiene**' or ('**maintenance**') factors as they served mainly to prevent dissatisfaction, not to encourage high performance. Figure 15.5 illustrates the results.

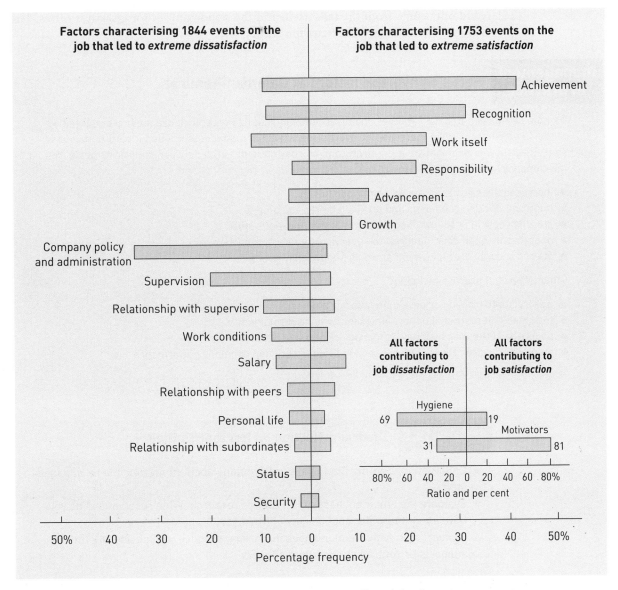

Figure 15.5 Herzberg's comparison of job satisfaction and job dissatisfaction scores

In summary, Herzberg concluded that the factors which produce job satisfaction are separate and distinct from those that lead to job dissatisfaction, hence the term 'two-factor' theory. He suggested that satisfaction and dissatisfaction are not opposites: they are separate dimensions influenced by different factors. The dissatisfiers (company policy and administration, supervision, salary, interpersonal relations and working conditions) contribute little to job satisfaction. The factors that lead to job satisfaction (achievement, recognition, work itself, responsibility and advancement) contribute little to job dissatisfaction if they are absent.

Herzberg explained this by his observation that when respondents were feeling dissatisfied this was because management had treated them unfairly. When they were satisfied it was because they were experiencing feelings of psychological growth and a sense of self-actualisation. So the hygiene factors can prevent discontent and dissatisfaction but will not in themselves contribute to psychological growth and hence satisfaction. These could only come from the task itself, and the opportunities for growth it offers. The Gamma Chemical story illustrates this theory.

management in practice   Focus on hygiene factors at Gamma Chemical

Gamma Chemical purchased another chemical company that had recently failed, and re-employed 30 of the 40 employees. While there was no overt dissatisfaction, management found it hard to motivate staff. They showed no initiative or creativity, and no commitment to the new company or its goals. Yet the company had:

- increased the salaries of the re-employed staff
- improved working conditions and provided better equipment
- placed people in positions of equal status to their previous jobs
- operated an 'open door' policy, with supervisors easily approachable
- offered security of employment and a no-redundancy policy.

Other aspects of practice included:

- no structured training or development programmes
- the small unit restricted opportunities for career advancement
- people had little responsibility as management made decisions
- there was no clear connection between individual work and company performance.

Source: Private communication and discussions with the manager.

Activity 15.5   Critical reflection on Herzberg's theory

- Comment on Gamma Chemical's assumptions about motivating the re-engaged staff.
- Evaluate the empirical base of Herzberg's research. What reservations do you have about the wider applicability of the theory?
- Gather other evidence of changes in working practice, and decide whether it supports or contradicts Herzberg's theory.

Herzberg believed that motivation depends heavily on whether a job is intrinsically challenging and provides opportunities for recognition and reinforcement. He linked thinking about motivation with ideas about job design, and especially the motivational effects of job enrichment. There are many examples where management has redesigned people's jobs with positive effects. Few if any of these experiments were the result of knowing about Herzberg's theory, but their effects are often consistent with its predictions. Section 15.8 has more on this.

15.5   Management assumptions – Theory X or Theory Y

As managers attempt to influence others they act on their assumptions about how people will react. Douglas McGregor (1960) developed this idea in his book *The Human Side of Enterprise:*

> every managerial act rests on assumptions, generalisations and hypotheses – that is to say, on theory. (p. 6)

Such assumptions are often implicit and unconscious – but nevertheless shape managers' predictions that if they do *a*, then *b* will occur. The theories may or may not be adequate but it is impossible to reach a managerial decision, or take a managerial action, uninfluenced by them:

> The insistence on being 'practical' really means 'Let's accept my theoretical assumptions without argument or test'. (p. 7).

McGregor presented two sets of assumptions underlying management practice. *Theory X*, which he called the traditional view of direction and control, expresses these assumptions:

- The average human being has an inherent dislike of work and will avoid it if at all possible.
- Because of this human characteristic, most people must be coerced, controlled, directed and/or threatened with punishment to get them to put forth adequate effort towards the achievement of organisational objectives.
- The average human being prefers to be directed, wishes to avoid responsibility, has relatively little ambition, and wants security above all.

McGregor believed that these assumptions led to a management strategy which ignored the full range of human needs. Theory X assumptions concentrated on the lower-level needs that Maslow had identified. Managers who acted on Theory X would fail to discover, let alone use, the potential of the average human being.

Recognising potential at 3M   www.3m.com

management in practice

Although you may not have heard of the company, you will have used some of its products such as sandpapers, 'Scotch' brand sticky tape, masking tape and Post-it notes. The company is regarded by many as one of the most innovative in the world, and the secret of their success over many years is attributed by Ghoshal and Bartlett (1998) to a 'deep, genuine and unshakeable belief in the ability of the average individual' (p. 43).

For over 80 years the company has nurtured unconventional people, creating a climate that stimulated ordinary people to produce extraordinary performances. It was a management philosophy that focused more on recognising the potential of each individual than on harnessing the power of structures and systems.

Source: Ghoshal and Bartlett (1998).

He then pointed out that accumulating knowledge about human behaviour made it possible to suggest an alternative, *Theory Y*, which expressed a different set of assumptions:

- The expenditure of physical and mental effort in work is as natural as play or rest.
- External control and the threat of punishment are not the only means of bringing about effort towards organisational objectives. People will exercise self-direction and self-control in the service of objectives to which they are committed.
- Commitment to objectives is a function of the rewards associated with their achievement.
- The average human being learns, under proper conditions, not only to accept, but also to seek, responsibility.
- The capacity to exercise a relatively high degree of imagination, ingenuity and creativity in the solution of organisational problems is widely, not narrowly, distributed in the population.
- Under the conditions of modern industrial life the intellectual potentialities of the average human being are only partially utilised.

The practical implications of the two sets of assumptions are clear. Those who hold Theory X will use time-recording systems, close supervision, external quality checks, narrowly defined jobs and precise job descriptions. The central principle of Theory X is that of external control by systems, procedures or supervision.

The central principle of Theory Y is integration. It advocates creating 'conditions such that the members of the organisation can achieve their own goals *best* by directing their efforts towards the success of the enterprise' (McGregor, 1960, p. 49). Managers who hold to Theory Y create conditions in which people accept responsibility, and apply imagination, ingenuity and creativity to organisational problems. Kevin Smith became chief executive of GKN, a successful engineering business in 2003. He recalled his first job in a mill:

> [The people there] were held back by an environment ill-suited to helping them reach their potential. I learned about the pent-up capabilities of people inside organisations. If you can unleash those capabilities, and give people the possibility to realise their hopes and dreams in their work, then you can create enormous power. (*Financial Times*, 20 December 2002)

McGregor argued that the modern organisation does not tap the creative ability of its staff. To take advantage of these hidden assets managers should be more willing to provide employees with scope to use their talents. They should be less prescriptive and directive and create the conditions that integrate individual and organisational goals.

management in practice   Motivating sales teams

I work as a sales manager for a medium-sized pharmaceutical company with a team of six. My role is to achieve maximum sales using the resources available. The company sets activity targets – 'more calls mean more sales' is a favourite slogan. This produces a problem, as there are doctors who are readily available but who are unlikely to produce business: others are less available but have more potential. Do we follow the company strategy or do things the way our experience tells us will work better?

Management has structured the company on Theory X assumptions. We are told what we are expected to achieve, and how we are expected to achieve them. There are few opportunities for us to express a view. We meet the senior people about twice a year. The meetings usually have a rushed agenda, and seem to be a way of telling us what will happen rather than encouraging discussion on what should happen. They ask us to write two-monthly reports, but the points we raise seldom get a reply.

Another company in the industry is now taking a different approach. This involves each salesperson developing his or her business plan. They have considerably more autonomy to use their ideas. The trade-off is that the consequences of failure are more severe, and this will not suit everyone – it is a different psychological contract with which they are working. The curious thing is that that company had been very successful with an earlier approach, which was like ours. But the market is experiencing its biggest ever change, and shifting responsibility to salespeople who are in constant contact with customers has a considerable advantage.

Source: Private communication and discussions with the manager.

Activity 15.6   Critical reflection on Theory X and Theory Y

- Write down the Theory X assumptions demonstrated in the first company in the 'Motivating sales teams' Management in Practice, and the Theory Y ones in the second.
- Make a list of management practices that you have experienced which reflect the assumptions of Theory X and Theory Y respectively. What were their effects?
- Can you identify someone who behaves in a way consistent with Theory X, and someone else who behaves according to Theory Y? Did this reflect the way they themselves were managed, or some other reason?

Although McGregor expressed the view that Theory Y assumptions were the most appropriate ones for effective management, others have challenged this. They argue that Theory Y assumptions may be as inappropriate in some circumstances as Theory X assumptions are in others. Morse and Lorsch (1970) first raised this prospect following their comparative study of management practices in four companies. Two were in routine operations, at which one was successful and one was not. The other two were in highly creative businesses, and again one was successful, the other not. They concluded that the successful company in the routine business used a consistent Theory X style. The successful company in the creative business used a consistent Theory Y style. This is an example of a contingency approach to managing, which is at odds with McGregor's emphasis on moral values – see Key Ideas.

Douglas McGregor, revisited   key ideas

Reviewing a book published to commemorate McGregor's work (Heil *et al.*, 2000), Jacobs (2004) reflects on the continued relevance of McGregor's ideas, while also noting that the moral core of the book is widely ignored. McGregor's views on management were shaped by his deeply held belief that it is a responsibility of management to make it possible for people to recognise and develop their capacity for decision making. He criticised Theory X because of the harm it would do to those subjected to practices based upon it, and challenged practices that ignored the personal and financial rights of employees. His preference for participatory approaches was rooted in his moral outlook and concern for the underdog, *not* because they would improve performance.

Jacobs (2004) is critical of contingency approaches that seek to adapt McGregor's ideas (of which Morse and Lorsch is an example) on the grounds that they diminish their moral emphasis. McGregor's advocacy of Theory Y was

> clearly shaped by the cardinal value he assigned to the improved treatment of workers. Contingency theorists seek analytical rigor in a narrowly instrumental context [by seeking to identify techniques that will enhance performance]. Enhancing the personal growth of employees is not ordinarily an explicit objective. (pp. 294–295)

Source: Jacobs (2004).

15.6   Process theories of motivation

Process theories try to explain why people choose one course of action towards satisfying a need rather than another. A person who needs a higher income could satisfy it by, say, moving to another company, applying for promotion or investing in training. What factors will influence their choice?

Expectancy theory

Vroom (1964) developed one attempt to answer that question with what he termed the **expectancy theory** of motivation. It focuses on the thinking processes people use to achieve rewards. Stuart Roberts is studying a degree course in Chemistry and has to submit a last assignment. He wants an A for the course, and so far has an average of B+. His motivation to put effort into the assignment will be affected by (a) his expectation that hard work will produce a good piece of work, and (b) his expectation that it will

Expectancy theory argues that motivation depends on a person's belief in the probability that effort will lead to good performance, and that good performance will lead to them receiving an outcome they value (valence).

receive a grade of at least an A. If he believes he cannot do a good job, or that the grading system is unclear, then his motivation will be low.

The theory assumes that individuals:

● have different needs and so value outcomes differently
● make conscious choices about which course of action to follow
● choose between alternative actions based on the likelihood of an action resulting in an outcome they value.

There are, then, three main components in expectancy theory. First, the person's expectation (or **subjective probability**) that effort (E) will result in some level of performance (P):

$$(E \rightarrow P)$$

Subjective probability (in expectancy theory) is a person's estimate of the likelihood that a certain level of effort (E) will produce a level of performance (P) which will then lead to an expected outcome (O).

This will be affected by how clear they are about their roles, the training available, whether the necessary support will be provided and similar factors. If Stuart Roberts understands what the assignment requires and is confident in his ability to do a good job, his (E → P) expectancy will be high.

The second component is the person's expectation that performance will be **instrumental** in leading to a particular outcome (O):

$$(P \rightarrow O)$$

Instrumentality is the perceived probability that good performance will lead to valued rewards, measured on a scale from 0 (no chance) to 1 (certainty).

This will be affected by how confident the person is that achieving a target will produce a reward. This reflects factors such as the clarity of the organisation's appraisal and payment systems and previous experience of them. A clear grading system, which Stuart understands and knows that staff apply consistently, will mean he has a high (P → O) expectancy. If he has found the system unpredictable this expectancy would be lower.

The third component is the **valence** that the individual attaches to a particular outcome:

$$(V)$$

Valence is the perceived value or preference that an individual has for a particular outcome.

This term is best understood as the power of the outcome to motivate that individual – how keen Roberts is to get a good degree. It introduces the belief that people differ in the value they place on different kinds of reward. So the value of V varies between individuals, reflecting their unique pattern of motivational needs (as suggested by the content theories). Someone who values money and achievement would place a high valence on an outcome that was a promotion to a distant head office. He or she would try to work in a way which led to that. Such an outcome would be much less welcome (have a much lower valence) to a manager who values an established pattern of relationships or quality of life in the present location.

In summary:

$$F = (E \rightarrow P) \times (P \rightarrow O) \times V$$

in which F represents the force exerted, or degree of motivation a person has towards an activity. Two beliefs will influence that motivation, namely the expectation that:

● making the effort will lead to performance (E → P)
● that level of performance will lead to an outcome they value (P → O).

Adjusting these beliefs for valence – how desirable the outcome is to the person – gives a measure of their motivation. The beliefs that people hold reflect their personality and their experience of organisational practices, as shown in Figure 15.6.

The use of the multiplication sign in the equation signifies that both beliefs influence motivation. If a person believes that however hard they try they will be unable to perform to a required standard then they will not be motivated to do so (so E → P = 0). The same applies for (P → O). A low score in either of these two parts of the equation, or in V, will lead to low effort, regardless of beliefs about the other part.

A criticism of the theory is that it implies a high level of rational calculation, as people weigh the probabilities of various courses of action. It also implies that managers estimate what each employee values, and try to ensure that motivational practices meet them. Neither calculation is likely to be made that rationally, which may diminish the model's practical value.

However, the model is useful in recognising that people vary in their beliefs (or probabilities) about the components in the equation. It shows that managers can affect these beliefs by redesigning the factors in Figure 15.6. If people are unclear about their role, or receive weak feedback, the theory predicts that this will reduce their motivation.

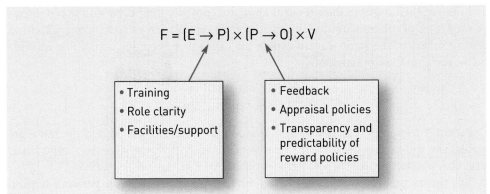

$$F = (E \rightarrow P) \times (P \rightarrow O) \times V$$

- Training
- Role clarity
- Facilities/support

- Feedback
- Appraisal policies
- Transparency and predictability of reward policies

Figure 15.6

Organisational practices affecting subjective probabilities

management in practice

Hindle Power

In 2000 this family-owned engineering company employed 50 people, selling and servicing Perkins engines in the east of England. In 1996 Perkins had told all its distributors that they would need to meet tougher customer service targets, or lose their contracts. Graham Hughes, Hindle's general manager, realised that long-term change would not occur unless people were trained to do their jobs better. Staff were given considerable scope in setting their own training needs. A new appraisal system was designed to help people clarify their career goals and request training to achieve them. The company's training manager Steve Widdrington believes the appraisal system encourages people to stretch themselves, rather than looking back and focusing on past results: 'People are taking more responsibility. I believe that works when you give staff the chance to develop.'

In 1996 the company was losing money on a turnover of £6 million. In 1999 it was profitable and hoped to turn over £15 million in 2000: 'Rarely has the link between training and the bottom line been so clear.'

Source: *People Management*, 3 February 2000, pp. 52–53.

As at Hindle Power, managers can influence motivation by practical actions such as:

● establishing the rewards people value
● identifying and communicating performance requirements

- ensuring that reasonable effort can meet those requirements
- providing facilities to support the person's effort
- ensuring a clear link between performance and reward
- providing feedback to staff on how well they are meeting performance requirements.

The theory links insights from the content theories of motivation with organisational practice.

Equity theory – J. Stacey Adams

Equity theory argues that perception of unfairness leads to tension, which then motivates the individual to resolve that unfairness.

Equity theory is usually associated with J. Stacey Adams (a behavioural scientist working at the General Electric Company) who put forward the first systematic account (Adams, 1963) of the idea that fairness in comparison with others influences motivation. People like to be treated fairly and compare what they put into a job (effort, skill, knowledge, etc.) with the rewards they receive (pay, recognition, satisfaction, etc.). They express this as a ratio of their input to their reward. They also compare their ratio with the input-to-reward ratio of others whom they consider their equals. They expect management to reward others in the same way, so expect the ratios to be roughly equal. The formula below sums up the comparison:

$$\frac{\text{Input (A)}}{\text{Reward (A)}} : \frac{\text{Input (B)}}{\text{Reward (B)}}$$

Person A compares the ratio of her input to her reward to that of B. If the ratios are similar she will be satisfied with the treatment received. If she believes the ratio is lower than that of other people she will feel inequitably treated and be dissatisfied.

The theory predicts that if people feel unfairly treated they will experience tension and dissatisfaction. They will try to reduce this by one or more of these means:

- reducing their inputs, by putting in less effort or withholding good ideas and suggestions;
- attempting to increase their outcomes, by pressing for increased pay or other benefits;
- attempting to decrease other people's outcomes by generating conflict or withholding information and help;
- changing the basis of their comparison, by making it against someone else where the inequity is less pronounced;
- increasing their evaluation of the other person's output so the ratios are in balance.

As individuals differ, so will their way of reducing inequity. Some will try to rationalise the situation, suggesting that their efforts were greater or lesser than they originally thought them to be, or that the rewards are reasonable. For example, a person denied a promotion may decide that the previously desired job would not have been so advantageous after all. Members may put pressure on other members of the team whom they feel are not pulling their weight. Some may choose to do less, thus bringing their ratio into line with that of other staff.

Clearly the focus and the components of the comparisons are highly subjective, although the theory has an intuitive appeal. The subjective nature of the comparison makes it difficult to test empirically, and there has been little formal research on the theory in recent years (though see Mowday and Colwell, 2003). There is, however, abundant anecdotal evidence that people compare their effort/reward ratio with that of other people or groups.

IKEA – the case continues www.ikea.com CASE STUDY

The founders of IKEA have created an ownership structure for the company intended to ensure its long-term independence and security from takeover. *The Economist* magazine reported that the ultimate owner of the company is Stichting Ingka Foundation, a Dutch-registered, tax exempt, non-profit-making legal entity ('stichting' are a common form of charitable body in The Netherlands). A five-person executive committee, chaired by Mr Kamprad, runs the Foundation. Its main asset is the Ingka Holding group, which operates most of the IKEA stores. Stichting Ingka Foundation channels the income it receives from the group to another Dutch-registered entity – Stichting IKEA Foundation. This funds projects dedicated to 'innovation in the field of architecture and interior design', though it does not issue details of its assets or awards.

While IKEA does not comment on the financial accounts of a private group of companies, *The Economist* concluded that

the overall set-up of IKEA minimises tax and disclosure, handsomely rewards the founding Kamprad family, and makes IKEA immune to a takeover.

Source: *Economist*, 11 May 2006.

Case questions 15.5

● Consider what this approach implies about the motivation of the IKEA founder.

● What assumptions does it imply about the company's co-workers?

Goal-setting theory – Edwin A. Locke

Goal-setting theory refers to a series of propositions designed to help explain and predict work behaviour. Its best-known advocate is Edwin Locke (Locke, 1968; Locke and Latham, 1990, 2002) and the theory has four main propositions:

Goal-setting theory argues that motivation is influenced by goal difficulty, goal specificity, participation in setting goals and knowledge of results.

● *Challenging goals* lead to higher levels of performance than simple or unchallenging goals. Difficult goals are sometimes called 'stretch' goals because they encourage us to try harder, to stretch ourselves. However, beyond a point this effect fades – if people see a goal as being impossible, their motivation declines.
● *Specific goals* lead to higher levels of performance than vague goals (such as 'do your best'). We find it easier to adjust behaviour when we know exactly what the objective is, and what is expected of us.
● *Participation* in goal setting can improve commitment to those goals, since people have a sense of ownership and are motivated to achieve the goals. However, if management explains and justifies the goals, without inviting participation, that can also increase motivation.
● *Knowledge of results* of past performance – receiving feedback – is necessary to motivation. It is motivational in itself, and contains information that may help people attain the goals.

The main attraction of goal theory is the directness of the practical implications, including:

● *Goal difficulty*: set goals that are hard enough to stretch employees, but not so difficult as to be impossible to achieve.
● *Goal specificity*: set goals in clear, precise and if possible quantifiable terms.
● *Participation*: allow employees to take part in setting goals, to increase ownership and commitment.

- *Acceptance*: if goals are set by management, ensure they are adequately explained and justified, so that people understand and accept them.
- *Feedback*: provide information on past performance to allow employees to use it in adjusting their performance.

While goal theory has many implications for appraisal schemes and other performance management techniques, several variables have been shown to moderate the relationship between goal difficulty and performance – such as ability, task complexity and situational constraints. Another major question is whether personality traits also moderate the relationship – someone with a high need for achievement may be more likely to respond positively to a challenging goal than someone with a lower need for achievement.

Fried and Slowik (2004) suggest that the value of goal-setting theory could be increased by taking into account the role of time, since how people perceive and interpret time affects their decisions. We can see time as either objective or subjective. Objective, or clock, time moves from past to present to future at a constant rate, and any two observers will agree on how much has passed. This view of time informs many organisational practices, such as estimating how long a task will take, and using that to set deadlines for that and other activities within a plan. An alternative view notes the subjective experience of time. Days associated with some activities feel different from other days, and in some activities time appears to pass very quickly, while on others it drags. Individuals and professions differ in what they mean by 'soon' or 'late', some thinking in terms of hours and days, others in months and years. These subjective views of time raise the possibility that incorporating time into goal-setting theory may increase the insights to be gained from it.

One aspect of the theory which does take time into account is the prediction that performance goals should be both challenging and achievable: this specifically includes the amount of time available for completion. Other aspects of time however have not yet been fully incorporated. The motivational quality of challenging goals may not always apply: in some careers entry to, or advancement within, the high status aspects of the job may depend on spending time, perhaps months or years, on less challenging assignments. People may be willing to work diligently at less challenging tasks if they see them as a stepping stone to more challenging work in future times. The motivational effect of challenging tasks may also be affected by a person's career stage – by late career, people may be less inclined to seek challenge than they were when young.

Self-efficacy

Self-efficacy is an individual's belief that he or she is capable of performing a task.

A contingency that influences the effects of goal theory is a person's self-confidence. **Self-efficacy** refers to a person's belief in their ability to perform a task: the higher your level of self-efficacy, the more confident you are that you will succeed in a task. In difficult situations or where goals are challenging people with low self-efficacy are likely to reduce or abandon their efforts, while those with high self-efficacy will welcome the challenge of a demanding goal. Those with high self-efficacy respond to negative feedback with increased effort and motivation, whereas those with low self-efficacy reduce their efforts. Bandura (1997) observed: 'substandard performances diminish effort in individuals who doubt their capacity but lead self-assured individuals to redouble their efforts to succeed' (p. 461). The same principles apply to teams and organisations – a high sense of collective efficacy improves team performance. Having studied the performance of schools Bandura (1997) concluded that:

> Schools in which the staff members have a strong sense of collective efficacy flourish academically. Schools in which the staff members have serious doubts about their collective efficacy achieve little progress or decline academically. (p. 469)

15.7 Motivation as a form of social influence

People value both **extrinsic** and **intrinsic rewards**. Extrinsic rewards are those that are separate from the task, such as pay, security and promotion. Intrinsic rewards are those that people receive as they do the task itself – using skills, sensing achievement, doing satisfying work. Recall that a central element in scientific management was the careful design of the 'one best way' of doing a piece of manual work. Experts analysed how people did the job and identified the most efficient method, usually breaking the job into many small parts. Such work provided few if any intrinsic rewards – and Taylor's system concentrated on providing clear extrinsic rewards.

Working on a small element of a task is boring to many people, making them dissatisfied, careless and frequently absent. As these limitations became clear managers looked for ways to make jobs more intrinsically rewarding – so that the work itself brought a reward of interest or challenge. The ideas from Maslow, Herzberg and McGregor prompted attempts to increase the opportunity for people to satisfy higher-level needs at work. The assumption was that staff would work more productively if management offered intrinsic rewards (motivators in Herzberg's terms) as well as extrinsic ones (Herzberg's hygiene factors), leading to the job enrichment model.

Intrinsic rewards are valued outcomes or benefits that come from the individual, such as feelings of satisfaction, achievement and competence.

Extrinsic rewards are valued outcomes or benefits provided by others, such as promotion, a pay increase or a bigger car.

Job enrichment model

The **job enrichment model** formulated by Hackman and Oldham (1980) proposed that managers could change the design of a job to satisfy more of their employees' higher-level needs.

The model identifies three *psychological states* that must be present to achieve high motivation. If any are low, motivation will be low. The three states are:

A **job enrichment model** represents the idea that managers can change specific job characteristics to promote job satisfaction and so motivate employees.

- *Experienced meaningfulness*: the degree to which employees perceive their work as valuable and worthwhile. If workers regard a job as trivial and pointless, their motivation will be low.
- *Experienced responsibility*: how responsible people feel for the quantity and quality of work performed.
- *Knowledge of results*: the amount of feedback employees receive about how well they are doing. Those who do not receive feedback will care less about the quality of their performance.

These psychological states are influenced by five *job characteristics* that contribute to experienced meaningfulness of work:

- *Skill variety*: the extent to which a job makes use of a range of skills and experience. A routine administrative job is low in variety, whereas that of a marketing analyst may require a wide variety of statistical and interpersonal skills.
- *Task identity*: whether a job involves a complete operation, with a recognisable beginning and end. A nurse who organises and oversees all the treatments for a hospital patient will have more task identity than one who provides a single treatment to many different patients.
- *Task significance*: how much the job matters to others in the organisation or to the wider society. People who can see that their job contributes directly to performance, or that it is a major help to others, will feel they have a significant task.
- *Autonomy*: how much freedom and independence a person has in deciding how to go about doing the work. A sales agent in a call centre following a tightly scripted (and recorded) conversation has less autonomy than a sales agent talking face to face to a customer.

● *Feedback*: the extent to which a person receives feedback on relevant dimensions of performance. Modern manufacturing systems can provide operators with very rapid information on quality, scrap, material use and costs. Operators can then receive a high level of feedback on the results of their work.

The extent to which a job contains these elements can be calculated using a tested instrument, and then using the scores to calculate the *motivating potential* score for the job. Figure 15.7 presents the model schematically.

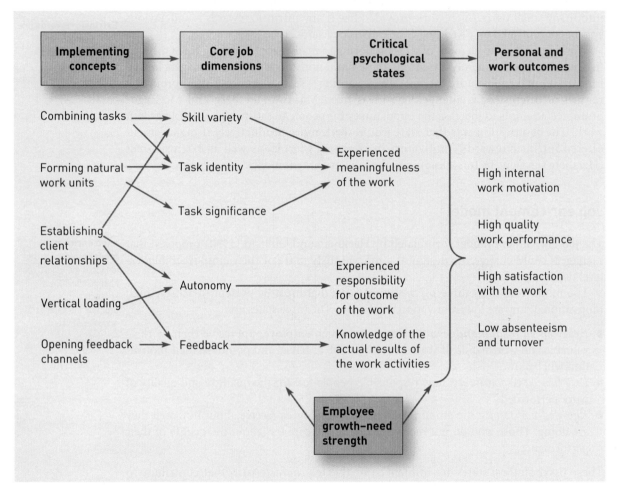

Figure 15.7 The job characteristics model

Source: Adapted from Hackman and Oldham (1975).

The model also shows how management (or staff) can increase the motivating potential of jobs by using five implementing concepts:

● **Combine tasks** Rather than divide the work into small pieces, as Taylor recommended, staff can combine them so they use more skills and complete more of the whole task. An order clerk could receive orders from a customer and arrange transport and invoicing instead of having these done by different people.

● **Form natural workgroups** In order to give more responsibility and enable sharing of skills, groups could be created that carry out a complete operation. Instead of a product passing down an assembly line, with each worker performing one operation, a group may assemble the whole product, sharing out the tasks amongst themselves.

- **Establish customer relations** This would bring home to employees the expectations of the people to whom their work goes, whether inside or outside the organisation, enabling them to see how their job fits into the larger picture. Instead of people doing part of the job for all customers, they can look after all the requirements of some customers. They establish closer relationships and gain a better understanding of their customers' needs.
- **Vertical loading** This involves workers taking on some responsibilities of supervisors to solve problems and develop workable solutions, thus adding to their autonomy. Operators may be given responsibility for checking the quantity and quality of incoming materials and reporting any problems. They may use more discretion over the order in which they arrange a week's work.
- **Open feedback channels** This would ensure that people receive feedback on their performance from internal or external customers. Operators can attend meetings at which customers give their views on the service provided as a basis for improving performance and building client relationships.

The last feature of the Hackman–Oldham model is growth–need strength – the extent to which an individual desires personal challenges, accomplishment and learning on the job. Some may want jobs that satisfy only their lower-level needs but others want more. Individuals with high needs for challenge, growth and creativity are likely to respond positively to job enrichment programmes. If an individual's growth needs are low, attempts at job enrichment may cause stress. The model takes this into account by showing that the strength of a person's need for growth moderates the relationship of job characteristics to performance and/or satisfaction.

Many managers, such as those at Gamma Chemical (see Management in Practice), have changed the kind of work they expect employees to do. This has not usually been to provide more interesting jobs, but as a response to business conditions. Nevertheless the results of such changes often support what the theory predicts. Another approach is to give staff more responsibility for decisions, without referring to supervisors above them in the hierarchy. This is usually called empowerment.

Changing work at Gamma Chemical

management in practice

Some two years after taking control, Gamma Chemical had made these changes to working arrangements:

- They introduced a cross-training programme to improve job diversity and individual growth.
- They created problem-solving teams from natural work units to give operators a sense of ownership and achievement.
- They expected operators to make more decisions, increasing individual authority and accountability.
- They introduced an appraisal system that shows operators how their function affects company performance.

Management believed these changes had resulted in 20 per cent more output and 50 per cent less wastage.

Source: Private communication and discussions with the manager.

15.8 Empowerment

People use the term 'empowerment' to refer to a range of practices that give more responsibility to less senior staff. They aim to help people take more control of their working environment, and so provide opportunities for personal growth and self-fulfilment. Advocates of empowerment claim the advantages include:

● quicker responses, since staff decide on issues previously passed to a more senior manager;
● more job satisfaction from doing more responsible work and developing skills;
● employees welcome greater customer contact, which in turn is a source of ideas for service improvement;
● building customer loyalty and repeat business.

Bowen and Lawler (1992) define empowerment in terms of the degree to which four ingredients of the organisation are shared with front-line employees:

● information about the organisation's performance;
● rewards based on the organisation's performance;
● knowledge that enables employees to contribute to organisational performance; and
● power to make decisions that influence organisational direction and performance.

If these elements remain at the top, management still exercises fairly direct control. If they are passed down so that front-line employees have more information and more power to make decisions, management is trying to empower. The more that staff exercise self-control and self-direction, the more they are empowered.

 **management in practice**   **Empowering nurses at Western General Hospital**

A nurse manager at the Western General Hospital in a large city commented on the empowerment of nurses at the hospital:

> The service has been trying to be more responsive to the needs of patients by delegating power and responsibility to local level. Nurses have recognised the benefits to patients if nurses carry out their work by patient allocation rather than by task allocation. This has developed into the 'named-nurse' concept, which intriguingly incorporates four of the five core dimensions of the job characteristics model. The nurse assesses needs, plans, implements and evaluates the care of his or her patients, so having skill variety, task identity, task significance and autonomy.
>
> Perhaps even the feedback element is provided from the evaluation stage of each patient's care. The empowerment approach fits with the organisation's unpredictable environment, the individualised service relationship and staff needs and characteristics. The recently appointed nurse managers are enthusiastic, and this has filtered down to staff. They are gradually becoming aware of the move from Theory X to Theory Y style of management. They appreciate that at last their skills and experience are being recognised and used.
>
> Information flows more freely and openly. Decisions are made only after discussion with the staff who will be affected by the outcome. Nurses in the wards are aware of their allocated budgets and what they are spending. Recruitment of staff is now done by existing staff on the ward, where previously managers decided whom to appoint.

Source: Private communication from a senior nurse in the hospital.

Figure 15.8 summarises a range of empowerment options, ranging from a control orientation at one extreme to an involvement orientation at the other. The options are:

- *Suggestion involvement*: staff are encouraged to submit ideas to improve ways of working and are rewarded for doing so. Control remains with management, which chooses whether or not to accept an idea.
- *Job involvement*: staff are able to develop and use more skills, have greater autonomy and receive more feedback. Supervisors' jobs change from direction to support.
- *High involvement*: occurs when organisations give their lowest-level employees a sense of involvement in the total organisation's performance. All of the four ingredients listed above are designed to support that condition.

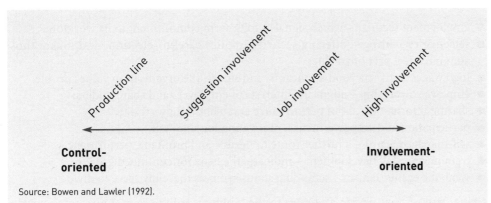

Source: Bowen and Lawler (1992).

Figure 15.8

Levels of empowerment

Air Asia: allowing people to think   www.airasia.com

management in practice

Air Asia is a rapidly growing discount airline based in Malaysia and run by CEO Tony Fernandes. It keeps costs down by selling tickets only over the Internet and offering no free meals. Fernandes grills ground crews on how to shorten turnround times between landing and take off, and confers with mechanics on how to coddle spare parts so they last longer. His chief engineer, Wan Hasmar, once told Fernandes that the tyres on the landing gear, which cost $6000 a set, would last longer if pilots took a shallow approach on landing. Fernandes immediately issued orders for pilots to sweep in low, short-circuiting the airline's chain of command. 'We allow people to think', says Fernandes – and the tyres now last 180 landings, up from 70 before the change.

Source: *Business Week*, 1 September 2003.

Increasing empowerment can be difficult, with some initiatives experiencing:

- the usual problems of introducing any significant change (see Chapter 13);
- resistance from some staff who value familiar ways;
- resistance from middle managers who fear losing parts of their role (Ezzamel *et al.* 1994);
- the risks of losing control (Simons, 1995a).

Empowerment can increase if senior managers redistribute power from the centre, or if they remove the constraints that prevent people using the power they already have – such as their knowledge of customers or processes.

15.9 Current themes and issues

Performance

Jeffrey Pfeffer (2005) drew upon his extensive experience to outline ways of achieving a high-performance organisation by working with people, not by replacing them or limiting the scope of their activities. He regards the workforce as a source of strategic advantage, not as a cost to be minimised or avoided. Most successful companies owe their sustained (*not* temporary) success to the collection of practices through which they manage people. This becomes a strategic capability (Chapter 8) that cannot easily be copied, because the practices fit together, and reinforce each other. They include:

- employment security – which signals a long-term commitment to its workforce;
- selective recruiting – offering security implies careful selection, and makes those appointed feel part of an elite;
- high wages – attracts good applicants, and signals the organisation values people;
- employee ownership – aligns the interests of employees and shareholders;
- sharing information about performance and plans – shows trust;
- participation and empowerment – motivating for able staff;
- self-managed teams – a further route to flexible and profitable performance;
- training and skill development – indicates the need for continued growth;
- symbolic egalitarianism – scrapping status symbols that only serve to divide.

Pfeffer stresses that paying attention to these human aspects cannot guarantee survival and success – financial downturn, a misguided strategy or bad luck can destroy the healthiest of organisations. But the examples of Innocent Drinks (Part 1), Semco (Chapter 14) or W.L. Gore and Associates (Part 5 Case) show what is possible.

Corporate responsibility

Practitioners' interest in theories of motivation is understandably instrumental – they seek to understand what motivates workers as this may guide their efforts to enhance individual and group productivity. They can develop policies that meet the needs of staff for work which is fulfilling and at the same time contributes to organisational performance. Managers can, for example, use theories of goal setting or achievement motivation to develop practices that shape the direction and intensity of individual efforts.

This raises two aspects of corporate responsibility. An immediate issue concerns corporate responsibility for the overall health and well-being of their staff, and specifically the danger of managers unintentionally using the theories in a way that damages staff. Goal-setting theory, for example, makes the case for goals that are difficult but achievable: but if goals are set too high staff may experience excessive and unhealthy stress in achieving them. Some corporate scandals have been linked to company policies that encouraged staff to meet demanding targets, irrespective of what rules or codes of ethical behaviour they were breaking.

The emphasis in other theories on the benefits of autonomy, responsibility and challenge can also, if misapplied, lead to stress, domestic pressure and family breakdown. Needs differ significantly between people, and between people at different stages of their lives. People also experience conflict between needs – a need for security because of family circumstances may challenge a need for recognition that could imply a risky job change or a move to another town.

The broader question is whether motivational theories can only be used instrumentally. An alternative approach would focus on identifying people's needs from work and trying to meet them as ends in themselves, not because of their supposed effects on productivity. Managers taking that approach would still be performing their fundamental role of adding value to resources, but the value so added would be distributed differently, and in less tangible ways. Some of the companies identified as among the 'Best workplaces in Europe' gain that reputation for their attention to, and care for, the wider context of staff members, seeing them not as isolated individuals but as people with a range of external commitments. Placing those external commitments higher in the list of a company's responsibilities does not necessarily damage economic performance.

Internationalisation

The growing significance of managing internationally sits uncomfortably with the fact that the theories outlined were developed in the United States. Do they apply to people working in other countries? Hofstede (1989) articulated the 'unspoken cultural assumptions' present in both Theory X and Theory Y. He writes:

> in a comparative study of US values versus those dominant in ASEAN countries, I found the following common assumptions on the US side and underlying both X and Y:
>
> 1 Work is good for people.
> 2 People's capacities should be maximally utilised.
> 3 There are 'organisational objectives' that exist apart from people.
> 4 People in organisations behave as unattached individuals.
>
> These assumptions reflect value positions in McGregor's US society; most would be accepted in other western countries. None of them, however, applies in ASEAN countries. Southeast Asian assumptions would be:
>
> 1 Work is a necessity but not a goal in itself.
> 2 People should find their rightful place in peace and harmony with their environment.
> 3 Absolute objectives exist only with God. In the world, persons in authority positions represent God so their objectives should be followed.
> 4 People behave as members of a family and/or group. Those who do not are rejected by society.
>
> Because of these different culturally determined assumptions, McGregor's Theory X and Theory Y distinction becomes irrelevant in Southeast Asia. (p. 5)

Hofstede's work in Chapter 4 showed marked differences in national cultures. These are likely to influence the relative importance that people in those countries attach to the various motivational factors. People in Anglo-Saxon countries tend to display a relatively high need for achievement, strong masculinity scores and low uncertainty avoidance. This is not the norm in other cultures.

Summary

1 Understand the significance of work motivation, including the psychological contract, to the task of managing

- People depend on others within and beyond the organisation to act in a particular way, and understanding what motivates them is critical to this. Motivation includes understanding the goals people pursue (content), the choices they make to secure them (process) and how this knowledge can be applied to influence others (including through work design).

- The relationship between employer and employee is expressed in the psychological contract, which needs to be in acceptable balance for effective performance.

2 Understand theories that focus on the content and process of motivation, and those which relate these ideas to issues of work design and empowerment

- Content theories seek to understand the needs that human beings may seek to satisfy at work and include the work of Maslow, Alderfer and Herzberg as well as of earlier observers such as Taylor and Mayo.

- Expectancy theory explains motivation in terms of valued outcomes and the subjective probability of achieving those outcomes.

- Equity theory explains motivation in terms of perceptions of fairness by comparison with others.

- Goal-setting theory believes that motivation depends on the degree of difficulty and specificity of goals.

- Self-efficacy theory may moderate the predictions of goal-setting theory, by suggesting that how people respond depends on their level of personal confidence in being able to complete a task successfully.

3 Explain the significance of understanding the assumptions managers use in motivating staff, and how these vary between national cultures

- McGregor's Theory X and Theory Y set out different assumptions managers have about their staff, which has implications for how they seek to motivate them. These appear to vary between nations and cultures.

4 Use the models presented to diagnose motivational problems and recommend areas of possible action

- Most of the models can be used to analyse the likely effects of organisational practices on motivation, and to indicate areas for possible management action.

- People are only motivated if the job meets a need that they value – providing appropriate content factors leads to satisfaction and performance.

- Herzberg suggests that motivation depends on paying attention to motivating as well as hygiene factors.

- Jobs can be enriched by increasing skill variety, task identity, task significance, autonomy and feedback.

- Expectancy theory predicts that rewards motivate high performance when the organisational practices support performance, and when the links between performance and rewards are clear – provided that individuals have strong growth needs.

- Setting high and specific goals will enhance performance, provided that employees have high levels of confidence in their abilities to do the task.

5 Relate these ideas to current developments in the environment of managing

- As educational levels rise and staff become more informed, they expect to have more opportunities to meet higher-level needs at work, in addition to lower-level needs.

- Changing competitive conditions mean that critical performance indicators for many organisations stress responsiveness, creativity and innovation – which can only be encouraged by motivational policies that encourage these behaviours. Economic and predictable performance also remain important for many organisational functions, which raises possible dilemmas for organisation-wide motivational policies.

Review questions

1 Outline the idea of the psychological contract. What are you expecting (a) from a future employer in your career; (b) from an employer who provides you with part-time work while you are studying?

2 What are the three things that are pinpointed when using behaviour modification?

3 How does Maslow's theory of human needs relate to the ideas of (a) Frederick Taylor and (b) Elton Mayo and the human relations movement?

4 How does Alderfer's theory differ from Maslow's? What research lay behind the two theories?

5 How did you score on the McClelland test? How did your scores compare with those of your fellow students?

6 Explain the difference between Herzberg's hygiene and motivating factors. Give at least three examples of each.

7 Explain the difference between E → P and P → O in expectancy theory.

8 Outline the basic assumptions of Theories X and Y that Douglas McGregor used to characterise alternative ways in which managements view their workers. List three management practices associated with each.

9 What are the five job design elements that are expected to affect people's satisfaction with their work?

10 Give an example of an implementing concept associated with each element.

Concluding critical reflection

Think about the ways in which you typically seek to motivate other people (staff, colleagues or those in other organisations) and about your company's approach to motivation. Review the material in the chapter, and then make notes on these questions:

● What examples of the issues discussed in this chapter struck you as being relevant to motivational practice in your company?

● Thinking of the people you typically work with, who are effective and who are less effective motivators? What do the effective people do that enables them to motivate others? Do they seem to take a mainly Theory X or mainly Theory Y approach? Do their **assumptions** seem to be broadly correct, or not? To what extent does the work people do have a high Motivational Potential Score?

● What factors in the **context**, such as the history of the company or your experience, have shaped the way you motivate others, and your organisation's approach to motivation? Do these approaches appear to be right for your present position and company – or would you use a different approach in another context? (Perhaps refer to some of the Management in Practice features for how different managers motivate others.)

● Have people put forward **alternative** approaches to motivating, based on evidence about other companies? If you could find such evidence, how may it affect company practice?

● What **limitations** can you identify in any of these motivational theories? For example you could consider their usefulness in hi-tech working environments, or how well they apply in non-western economies.

Further reading

Roethlisberger, F.J. and Dickson, W.J. (1939), *Management and the Worker*, Harvard University Press, Cambridge, MA.

Herzberg, F. (1959), *The Motivation to Work*, Wiley, New York.

McGregor, D. (1960), *The Human Side of Enterprise*, McGraw-Hill, New York.

Maslow, A. (1970), *Motivation and Personality* (2nd edn), Harper & Row, New York.

> The original accounts of these influential works are unusually readable books showing organisations and research in action. Roethlisberger and Dickson's account of the Hawthorne experiments is long, but the others are short and accessible.

Heil, G., Bennis, W. and Stephens, D.C. (2000), *Douglas McGregor Revisited*, Wiley, New York.

> A review of McGregor's ideas, which the authors argue are more in tune with modern organisational needs than when he wrote *The Human Side of Enterprise* in 1960.

Rousseau, D.M. and Schalk, R. (2000), *Psychological Contracts in Employment: Cross-national perspectives*, Sage, London.

> A collection of essays by experts from 13 countries, providing a rich insight into the varying national circumstances within which individuals and firms develop acceptable contracts.

Deery, S., Iverson, R.D. and Walsh, J.T. (2006), 'Towards a better understanding of psychological contract breach: a study of customer service employees', *Journal of Applied Psychology*, vol. 91, no. 1, pp. 166–175.

> Empirical study of the consequences of not meeting staff expectations.

Locke, E.A. and Latham, G.P. (2002), 'Building a practically useful theory of goal setting and task motivation: a 35-year odyssey', *American Psychologist*, vol. 57, no. 9, pp. 705–717.

> Valuable and clear review by the founders of goal-setting theory, including the results of many empirical studies.

Beirne, M. (2006), *Empowerment and Innovation: Managers, principles and reflective practice*, Edward Elgar, Cheltenham.

> Excellent review of empowerment and its potential from a balanced, critical perspective, drawing on experience in both commercial and voluntary activities.

Weblinks

Visit the websites of companies that interest you, perhaps as possible places to work. Or you could visit the websites of some of those that appeared in the Management in Practice feature, 'Best workplaces in Europe', included along with other websites mentioned in the chapter.

www.ikea.com
www.greatplacetowork.co.uk
www.bain.com
www.colgate.com.gr
www.consol.de
www.danone.com
www.depuy.com
www.timpson.co.uk
www.3m.com
www.airasia.com

Navigate to the pages dealing with 'about the company' or 'careers'.

● What do they tell you about working there? What seem to be the most prominent features?

● What needs do they seem to be aiming to meet? Would they meet your needs?

Annotated weblinks, multiple choice questions and other useful resources can be found on www.pearsoned.co.uk/boddy

Chapter 16

Communication

Aim

To describe and illustrate the main aspects of communication in organisations, and how these can help or hinder performance.

Objectives

By the end of your work on this chapter you should be able to outline the concepts below in your own terms and:

1 Explain the role of communication in managing
2 Identify and illustrate the elements and stages in the communication process
3 Use the concept of information richness to select a communication channel
4 Compare the benefits of different communication networks
5 Describe how new technologies support communication
6 Outline some essential interpersonal communication skills
7 Consider how aspects of the wider context affect communication.

Key terms

This chapter introduces the following ideas:

communication
message
coding
decoding
noise
feedback
non-verbal communication
selective attention
stereotyping
channel
information richness
information overload
blogging
blogs
groupware

Each is a term defined within the text, as well as in the Glossary at the end of the book.

In 1999 Renault bought a controlling stake in the struggling Japanese car maker Nissan. The Renault board immediately sent one of their senior managers, Carlos Ghosn, to Japan as head of the newly acquired business. The company was deeply in debt and losing market share in both Japan and the United States and was doing little product development. On taking over as boss, Ghosn promised that if Nissan was not profitable by 2000, he and his entire management team would quit.

In 2004 the company reported that sales had risen by 8 per cent over the previous year, and that profits had also risen strongly. Nissan had overtaken Honda within Japan, had the highest operating profit of any of the world's auto companies and was no longer in debt.

This rapid improvement in company performance was even more remarkable because it involved a westerner operating in Japan's closed, tradition-bound business environment. Ghosn rapidly transformed a traditional Japanese company, whose business culture valued a slow, methodical search for consensus before taking decisions. His cost cutting was controversial as it meant closing surplus plants, making 23,000 employees redundant and ending long-established purchasing contracts. He reorganised the company and replaced a promotion system based on seniority with one based on performance. As well as cutting costs, Ghosn revived the company's design, innovation and quality processes, and initiated the design and launch of an ambitious range of new vehicles.

Carlos Ghosn was born in Brazil of Lebanese parents, though raised as a French citizen. He speaks five languages fluently, and has transformed ailing companies in the United States, South America, France and now Japan. In an interview he said:

The basic objective of management is to create value. It's very important never to forget why we're here, and the higher you are in management, the more obvious it has to be. At the heart of all this is how you get the attention of people and how you get people motivated to what you are doing. How do you get people thrilled in a certain way

PA Photos: Paul Sancya/AP

about what's going on in the company? There's a lot of doubts and a lot of scepticism. But you know it's a competition and if you do better than your competition you're going to get better results. Motivation is the ultimate weapon. My management style is inspired by this.

His approach to management stresses:

● the importance of transparency in all business dealings
● extensive use of cross-functional teams
● breaking cultural barriers between employees
● sparking innovation through empowerment.

In April 2005 he became CEO of Renault, which owns 44 per cent of Nissan, as well as retaining his position as CEO at Nissan. That alliance was now the fourth largest car producer, after General Motors, Toyota and Ford, but to improve its profitability in the face of new competition from Asia would be another severe challenge.

Sources: *Business Week*, 4 October 2004 and 25 April 2005, and other published sources.

Case questions 16.1

● What examples can you find in the case of potential areas of communication difficulty?
● What clues can you find about Ghosn's beliefs about communicating?

16.1   Introduction

When Carlos Ghosn began the task of saving Nissan there were many who doubted whether he could succeed. While he had succeeded in vigorously and quickly rebuilding several companies, these had been in western economies and cultures. Would his methods be acceptable in Japan, where the business culture has been more secretive, slow-moving and consultative? How would he convince managers and staff at Nissan of the need to change established practices? How could he bridge the gap between what his directors at Renault expected him to do and the interests of the Japanese employees? How would it be possible to communicate his vision and reach a mutual understanding about the future of the company?

Most managers experience similar communication issues, though in less challenging circumstances. Those in companies such as W.L. Gore and Associates and Oticon want research teams to communicate ideas and results within and between research projects. Those in service organisations such as Forté Hotels want staff to communicate ideas and suggestions – and to understand company policy. The final assembly of the Airbus A380 at Toulouse depends on intense communication between staff at hundreds of suppliers around the world.

Even with the technologies now available, people continue to experience ineffective communication. Computer-based systems provide useful tools, but do not replace the need for human communication. Company-wide information systems make it easy for geographically separated people to exchange messages – but how they interpret those messages depends on their relationship:

> Technology won't make messages more useful unless we build personal relationships first. The message will get through more easily if the recipient has some pre-existing relationship with the sender. (Rosen, 1998)

Until people meet they cannot develop the mutual trust and shared knowledge essential for true communication.

Some managers underestimate the communication problems. Someone who works with a major utility business wrote to the author:

> The majority of managers within [the business] consider themselves to be effective communicators. Staff have a different perspective, and a recent staff survey rated communications as being very poor, with information being top down, no form of two-way communications and managers only hearing what they want to hear.

This chapter begins by showing how communication is essential to the management role of adding value to resources. Securing the mutual understanding that is the aim of communication involves navigating the stages of a generic communication process. People send and receive messages through one or more distinct channels (or media), passing along formal and informal organisational networks. While technology can help, communication is still a human endeavour that depends on identifiable interpersonal skills. People exercise these within an organisational context, which affects the choice of communication methods and whether communication leads to mutual understanding. Figure 16.1 provides an overview.

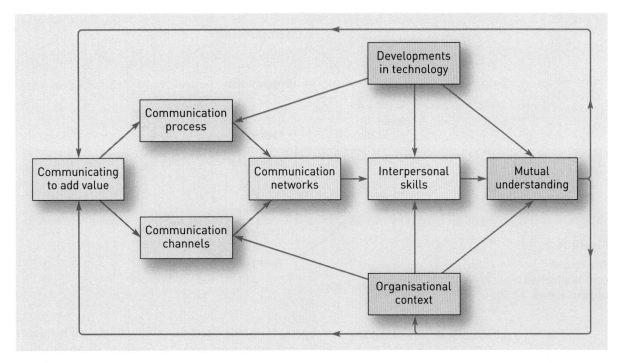

Figure 16.1 An overview of communication in organisations

16.2 Communicating to add value

We base our understanding of the world on information and feelings that we receive and send. People at all levels of an organisation need to communicate with others about:

inputs – e.g. the availability of materials or equipment
transformation – e.g. about capacity or quality
outputs – e.g. customer complaints or advertising policy.

Information about an order needs to flow accurately to all the departments that will help to satisfy it – and then between departments as the task progresses. People communicate information up and down the vertical hierarchy, and horizontally between functions, departments and other organisations. Figure 16.2 shows how communication supports these value-adding processes.

Stewart (1967) and Mintzberg (1973) showed that both formal and informal communication was central to the management job. This is most evident in the informational role – but equally managers can only perform their interpersonal and decisional roles by communicating with other people. Computer-based information systems are clearly part of the communication system – but only part. They deal very efficiently with structured, explicit data and information – but much less so with the unstructured, tacit information and knowledge.

What is communication?

Communication happens when people share information to reach a common understanding. Managing depends on conveying and interpreting messages clearly so that people can work together. Speaking and writing are easy: achieving a common under-

> **Communication** is the exchange of information through written or spoken words, symbols and actions to reach a common understanding.

525

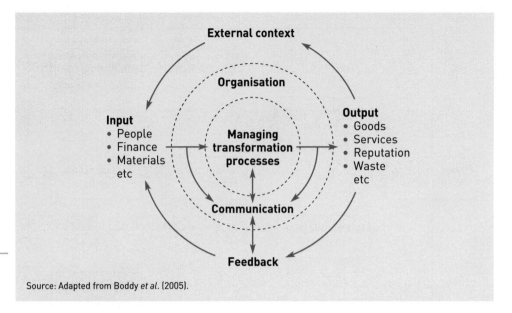

Figure 16.2

The role of communication in organisations

Source: Adapted from Boddy *et al.* (2005).

standing is not. Background and personal needs affect our ability to absorb messages from those with different histories, but until people reach a common understanding, communication has not taken place.

Activity 16.1 Collecting symbols and actions

The definition of communication refers to words, symbols and actions. Try to identify examples of symbols and actions that intentionally or unintentionally communicate a message to you. Some clues:

- *Symbols*: someone's style of dress or manner, or the appearance of the entrance to your college or university.
- *Actions*: someone taking time to offer directions to a visitor or looking bored during a meeting; interrupting someone.

How communicating adds value

Communication features in some way in every chapter – influencing others, working in teams, giving marketing information to senior management, interpreting financial data or posting a job vacancy on the company website. It is through communication that people add value in innovation, quality, delivery and cost. *Innovation* depends on good information about customer needs and relevant discoveries – which comes from communication with the scientific community. Embodying ideas in usable products requires communication within cross-functional project teams and with suppliers and customers. Efforts to enhance *quality* depend on everyone involved understanding what quality means to the customer. Without communication there is no quality.

Another measure of performance is *delivery* – supplying the customer with what they expect, when they expect it. That is only possible if people are communicating accurate, reliable and timely information up and down the supply chain. Competition adds to pressure to continually reduce the *cost* of goods and services – so people need information about current performance and ways of removing waste.

Communication failure in a small Dutch company

The company was founded in 1881 and the present owner is one of the fourth generation of the family. The company trades and manufactures packaging machines and employs 16 people. Someone who has recently joined the company said:

> Last year was difficult. Five people left the company and took with them much knowledge and experience. The company really consists of one person – the owner. He does not delegate much and there is little communication between him and the rest of the organisation. The only part of the company that interests him is the game of selling machines. He describes the rest of his tasks as annoying. The result is that, for example:
>
> - When we sell a machine, Operations do not know exactly what Sales has promised a customer. The customer expects the machine they specified, but do not always get it.
> - There is lack of internal communication – people in the company do not know their precise responsibilities or who is responsible for which tasks.
> - There is no time planning for ordered machines. No one knows the delivery date that we have promised a customer.
> - There is no budget system for a machine project. When we sell a machine we do not know if we will make a profit or a loss.
>
> All together, the company faces serious problems because of a lack of policy, management, information and communication.

Source: Private communication from the manager.

Forté's Commitment to Excellence Programme

In 1999 Forté launched a pilot Commitment to Excellence Programme at 26 of its hotels, which transformed communication between managers and staff. One junior employee commented that she was full of ideas, but until recently few members of staff, especially those in the 'back of house' jobs, would have dared to make suggestions. There was a culture of fear, in which people were afraid to make decisions, or make mistakes. James Stewart was a regional general manager whose territory included one of the hotels chosen to pilot the programme. He recalled that in the past there was 'no communication with head office, which was seen as being there not to help, but to find people out'.

When Granada took over Forté, the directors of customer services and human resources commissioned research by MORI (a market research consultancy) into customer and staff perceptions. Interviews with more than 500 customers and 300 employees in seven countries revealed inconsistencies in service standards across and within the hotel brands. There was more focus on completing tasks than on looking after customers, while weak internal communication meant that hotels did not work effectively with head office. The research also drew attention to low staff morale: 'We knew that a key to improving staff satisfaction, which then clearly triggers customer satisfaction, was to address that [communication] issue.'

Source: *People Management*, 14 October 1999.

16.3 The communication process

The **message** is what the sender communicates.

We communicate whenever we send a **message** to someone and as we think about what he or she says in return. This is a subtle and complex process, through which people easily send and receive the wrong message. Whenever someone says: 'That's not what I meant' or 'I explained it clearly, and they still got it wrong' there has been a communication failure. We waste time when we misunderstand directions, or cause offence by saying something that the listener misinterprets.

We infer meaning from words and gestures and then from the person's reply to our message. We continually interpret their messages and create our own. As colleagues have a conversation, each listens to the other's words, sees their gestures, reads the relevant documents or looks over the equipment to understand what the other means. When they achieve a mutual understanding about what to do they have communicated effectively. To understand why communication problems occur we need a model of the process, shown in Figure 16.3.

Communication requires at least two people – a sender and a receiver. The *sender* initiates the communication when they try to transfer ideas, facts or feelings to the *receiver* – the person to whom they send the message. The sender **codes** the idea they wish to convey into a message by using symbols such as words, actions or expressions. Deciding how to code the message is an important choice, and depends in part on the purpose:

Coding is translating information into symbols for communication.

- Is it to convey specific and unambiguous information?
- Is it to raise an open and unfamiliar problem, and a request for creative ideas?
- Is it to pass on routine data, or to inspire people?

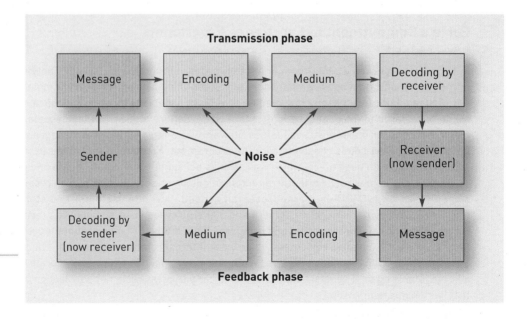

Figure 16.3

The communication process

Decoding is the interpretation of a message into a form with meaning.

The message is the tangible expression of the sender's idea. The sender chooses one or more channels (the communication medium) – such as an e-mail, a face-to-face meeting or a letter – to transmit the coded message. The receiver **decodes** the symbols contained in the message, and tries to reconstruct the sender's original thought. Coding and decoding are sources of communication failure as the sender and receiver have different knowledge, experience and interests. Receivers also evaluate a message by their knowledge of the sender, which affects whether they regard the information received as valuable.

These 'filters' interfere with the conversion of meaning to symbols and vice versa and, along with other distractions and interruptions, are referred to as **noise**, which

> arise within individuals (psychological filters), within the message (semantic filters) and within the context (mechanical filters). (Dimbleby and Burton, 1992, p. 221)

Noise is anything that confuses, diminishes or interferes with communication.

The final stage in the episode is when the receiver responds to the message by giving **feedback** to the sender. This turns one-way communication into two-way. Without feedback the sender cannot know whether the receiver has the message or whether they have interpreted it as the sender intended. The flow of information between parties is continuous and reciprocal, each responding by giving feedback to the other, and is only completed when the sender knows that the receiver has received and understood the message as intended.

Feedback (in communication) occurs as the receiver expresses his or her reaction to the sender's message.

Effective communicators understand it is a two-way process, and positively check for feedback. They do not rely only on making their message as clear as possible, but also encourage the receiver to provide feedback. Without some response – a nod, a question that implies understanding, a quick e-mail acknowledgement – the sender has not communicated successfully.

Assume that communication is going to fail, and then put time and effort into preventing that.

Non-verbal communication

Non-verbal communication is the process of coding meaning through behaviours such as facial expression, gestures and body posture.

An important type of interpersonal communication is **non-verbal communication**, sometimes called body language. Experts in the field claim that the words in a message have less impact on the receiver than the accompanying non-verbal signals. These include the tone of voice, facial expression, posture and appearance, and provide most of the impact in face-to-face communication (Knapp and Hall, 2002; Beall, 2004).

Small changes in eye contact, such as raising eyebrows or a directed glance while making a statement, add to the meaning that the sender conveys. A stifled yawn, an eager nod, a thoughtful flicker of anxiety gives the sender a signal about the receiver's reaction. Gestures and body position give equally vivid signals – leaning forward attentively, moving about in a chair, hands moving nervously, gathering papers or looking at the clock – all send a message.

Positive non-verbal feedback helps to build relations within a team. A smile or wave to someone at least acknowledges that they exist. Related to a task it indicates approval in an informal, rapid way that sustains confidence. Negative feedback can be correspondingly damaging. A boss who looks irritated by what the staff member sees as a reasonable enquiry is giving a negative signal, as is one who looks bored during a presentation.

management in practice

Virtual teams at Cisco www.cisco.com

Cisco Systems supplies much of the physical equipment that supports the Internet, and most of its design teams are formed of staff who work in different facilities throughout the world. Says a member of one such team:

> It means you have to be a bit more careful when it comes to communication. Most of the time you have to use e-mail and instant messaging to discuss issues, which means there can be misunderstandings if you're not careful. When you interact in person you use things like facial expression and hand gestures – none of these are available when e-mailing so you have to state your arguments more clearly.

Source: Chapter 17 Case.

As with any interpersonal skill, some people are better at interpreting non-verbal behaviour than others. The sender of a spoken message can benefit by noting the non-verbal responses to what they say. If they do not seem appropriate (raised eyebrows, an anxious look), the speaker should pause and check that the receiver has received the message that the sender intended.

Perception

Selective attention is the ability, often unconscious, to choose from the stream of signals in the environment, concentrating on some and ignoring others.

Perception is the process by which individuals make sense of their environment by selecting and interpreting information. We receive a stream of information beyond our capacity to absorb, and a process called **selective attention** helps us to remain sane. We actively notice and attend to only a small fraction of the available information, filtering out what we do not need. Factors such as the strength of the signal and the reputation of the sender influence what we select.

Even when people observe a common piece of information they interpret it, and react to it, in different ways. This 'perceptual organisation' arranges incoming signals into patterns that give some meaning to the data – relating it to our interest, the status of the sender or the benefits of attending to it. Experience, social class and education influence this perceptual organisation, which leads people to attach different meanings to the same information. Effective communicators understand this, and know it affects how the receiver reacts.

A common form of perceptual organisation is **stereotyping**. 'They always complain' or 'You would expect people from marketing to say that' are signs that someone is judging a message not by its content but by the group to which the sender belongs. An inaccurate stereotype means that we misinterpret the meaning because we are making inaccurate assumptions about the sender.

Perceptual differences are natural, but interfere with communication. Our unique personalities and perceptual styles affect how we interpret a message, so senders cannot assume that receivers attach the same meaning to a message as they intended.

> **Stereotyping** is the practice of consigning a person to a category or personality type on the basis of their membership of some known group.

Case questions 16.2

- As Carlos Ghosn began work at Nissan, he would have needed to secure common understandings on, amongst other things, issues of innovation, quality, delivery and cost.
- Review the model of the communication process and identify how each of the steps could have been a source of difficulty in achieving common understanding on the action required. Also consider the possible effects of selective attention and stereotyping.

16.4 Selecting communication channels

The model of communication in Figure 16.3 shows the steps that people need to take to communicate effectively. The process fails if either sender or receiver does not encode or decode the symbols of the message in the same way. Selecting the wrong communication **channel** can also lead to difficulty – for example, sending a sensitive message that requires subtle interpretation as a written instruction with no chance for feedback.

> A **channel** is the medium of communication between a sender and a receiver.

Activity 16.2 Understanding communication practices

- Think of an example where communication between two or more people failed. Note down why you think that happened, using the model in Figure 16.3.
- E-mail is widely used in business: list the advantages and disadvantages of that medium compared with face-to-face communication.

Lengel and Daft (1988) developed a model using the idea of **information richness** to compare the capacity of channels to promote common understanding between sender and receiver, shown in Figure 16.4.

The richness of a medium (or channel) depends on its ability to:

- handle many cues at the same time
- support rapid two-way feedback
- establish a personal focus for the communication.

> **Information richness** refers to the amount of information that a communication channel can carry, and the extent to which it enables sender and receiver to achieve common understanding.

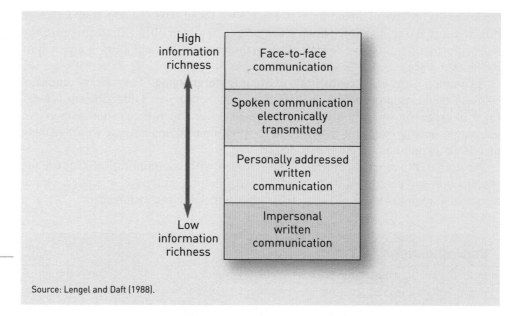

Figure 16.4

The Lengel–Daft media richness hierarchy

Face-to-face communication

Face-to-face discussion is the richest medium, as both parties can pick up many information cues (concentration, eye contact, body movements, facial expression) in addition to the spoken words. This enables them to gain a deep understanding of the nuances of meaning.

Most managers prefer to talk than write, and spend most of their time in face-to-face contact with others. Oral communication is quick, spontaneous and enriched by non-verbal signals. It takes place in one-to-one conversation (face to face), through meetings of several people or when someone communicates to many people at a conference. Management by wandering around is a widely used and effective communication technique. Rather than having formal meetings, managers go into the work areas and talk to employees about the issues that concern them. They gain insights into what is happening, which reports from supervisors may filter.

Despite the benefits, few managers rely entirely on this method. It takes time and becomes less practical as managers and staff become geographically dispersed. There is also no written record, so some prefer to combine face-to-face communication with a written communication confirming what was agreed.

Advances in technology are helping in this area. Videoconferencing is a technology that allows people to communicate face to face (and so see each others' facial expressions and gestures) without the time and cost of travel.

Spoken communication electronically transmitted

This is the second highest form of communication in terms of media richness. Although when we speak over the telephone we cannot see the non-verbal signals of expression or body language, we can pick up the tone of voice, the sense of urgency or the general manner of the message, as well as the words themselves. It is also easy to get quick feedback, as both sides can check that the other has understood what has been said.

Voicemail systems and answering machines can supplement telephone systems, by allowing people to record messages by both the sender and the intended receiver. Many

Videoconferencing at W.R. Grace www.grace.com

W.R. Grace manufactures speciality chemicals and has facilities in 40 countries. To improve communications between its staff, and with customers, it installed videoconferencing for both training and meetings in its larger premises around the world. It uses the system to integrate audio, video, telephone calls and interactive web access to documents. A third of calls now involve customers who typically have their own dedicated facilities.

Electronic collaboration is used to present new products and to answer technical support issues. In one case the engineers diagnosed the cause of a fault at a South American refinery from still pictures uploaded into the web conferencing facility. This saved the customer vital time and saved Grace the expense of flying an engineer to the site.

The company's manager of global collaborative services said:

> With a video call you can tell much more about the person by their gestures and body language than by what they are saying over a telephone. You can tell if you are going in the right direction or if you are coming to an agreement.

Electronic collaboration allows people to work as a more integrated team. In the past managers used to fly to headquarters for discussions and take the results back to their staff:

> We now get input from more junior staff who would never be able to fly to a meeting. They have a valuable contribution because they are dealing with the issue every day. This gives them a vested interest, so they take ownership and move it forward.

Source: *Financial Times*, 21 January 2004.

FT

companies now use message recording systems to pass customers to the right department, by offering options to which they respond by pressing the buttons on their keypads. These undoubtedly reduce costs but are usually badly designed, causing an irritating communication failure.

Personally addressed written communication

Personally addressed written communication has the advantage of face-to-face communication in that, being addressed personally to the recipient, it tends to demand their attention. It also enables the sender to phrase the message in a way they think best suits the reader. If both parties express their meanings accurately and seek and offer feedback, a high level of mutual understanding can be reached, which is also recorded. Even if people reach their understanding by communicating face to face, they will often follow it up with a written e-mail, fax or letter.

E-mail has grown rapidly as a means of communication within and between organisations. It has the advantages of the letter, and the instant delivery allows an interchange to be completed in minutes that could have taken days. People use it to send written messages quickly from wherever they have access to a computer, enabling more to work from home for at least part of the time. Mobile phones that receive e-mails and text messages make it easier for people to exchange personally addressed written communication. Disadvantages include:

- lack of body language
- adding many recipients to the 'copy' box, leading to e-mail overload
- using the technology to send unsolicited messages.

Impersonal written communication

This is the medium with the lowest amount of information richness – but it is suitable for sending messages to large numbers of people. Newsletters and routine computer reports are lean media because they provide a single cue, are impersonal and do not encourage response.

Managers often use them to send a simple message about the company and developments in it to widely dispersed employees and customers. They also use them to disseminate rules, procedures, product information and news about the company, such as new appointments. The medium also ensures that instructions are communicated in a standard form to people in different places, and that a record of the message is available. Electronic means such as e-mails and company websites supplement paper as a way of transmitting impersonal information. The ease with which electronic messages can be sent to large numbers of people leads to **information overload**, when people receive more information than they can read, let alone deal with adequately.

Information overload arises when the amount of information a person has to deal with exceeds their capacity to process it.

Each channel has advantages and disadvantages. If the message is to go to many people and there is a significant possibility of misunderstanding, some relatively structured written or electronic medium is likely to work best. If it is an unusual problem that needs the opinion of several other people, then a face-to-face discussion will be more effective.

In a study of 95 executives in a petrochemical company Lengel and Daft (1988) found that the preferred medium depended on how routine the topic was:

> Managers used face-to-face [communication] 88 per cent of the time for non-routine communication. The reverse was true for written media. When they considered the topics routine and well understood, 68 per cent of the managers preferred ... written modes. (p. 227)

Carlos Ghosn – the case continues www.renault.com CASE STUDY

Five years after arriving from France's Renault to run Nissan, CEO Ghosn is still ... mobbed for autographs during plant tours, and generally heaped with national adulation for saving a car company once given up for dead. At glitzy auto shows from Paris to Beijing, his cosmopolitan air ... and sterling track record make him a star attraction. He's as smooth as Thai silk in public, and his colleagues marvel at his personal magnetism, his 24/7 work ethic, and his rigorous attachment to benchmarks and targets. But ... there is another side ... if you miss a number or blindside the boss with a nasty development, watch out. 'To people who don't accept that performance is what is at stake, he can be ruthless', says Dominique Thormann, a senior vice-president with Nissan Europe.

Ghosn explains his approach:

I'm very demanding on myself, and I'm very demanding on the people around me. But I know that to be able to be demanding you have to empower people. You can't be demanding of someone who isn't empowered, it isn't fair. If you would put two words around the management style, I would say value and motivation. If you show the pain, but not the vision, you're not going to get what you want from anybody.

One of his early visions was simply expressed – 1 million cars sold, top level of profitability in the industry, and no debt. He explained: 'When people see this, they say: "Yeah, I'm ready to fight for this." If you eliminate the benefit, why will people want to work 14 hours a day?'

He reaches deep into the organisation by constant – and often unannounced – visits to dealerships, test tracks, assembly plants and parts suppliers. On a recent visit to Nissan's Iwaki engine plant, 180 km north of Tokyo, he was mobbed by eager factory hands. He doubtless enjoyed the attention, but at each stop it was evident he was looking for nuggets that would help him squeeze yet another ounce of productivity from the plant. He worked the floor, chatting to assembly workers, drilling foremen, all to get that extra fact which would edge the company forward. The visit clearly paid off for Ghosn, who knows he is nothing without an inspired workforce. 'The only power that a CEO has is to motivate', he says. Speaking of his approach he advises: 'Be transparent and explain yourself in clear, lucid terms. Do as you say you are going to do. Listen first: then think.' An experienced industry observer: 'He's not a superman, only a human being, but he gets results. He sets goals and holds people accountable.'

Another interviewer wrote:

Today he is focused on the global competition. 'There is no doubt they will be coming to the US,' says Ghosn, leaning towards his listener to make a point. He is referring to the Chinese and Indian vehicle manufacturers that will soon hit the US market.

Sources: *Business Week*, 4 October 2004; *Fortune*, 30 November 2006.

Case questions 16.3

- What evidence is there in the case about the communication channels which Ghosn prefers to use?
- What are their advantages and disadvantages in the circumstances at Nissan, and what other methods could the company use?

Activity 16.4   Assessing university communications

List the communications channels that your university or college uses to send you information about these aspects of your course:

- changes to rooms, timetables, or dates
- reading lists and other study materials
- ideas and information intended to stimulate your thinking and to encourage discussion and debate
- your performance so far and advice on what courses to take.

Were the methods appropriate or not? What general lessons can you draw?

Blogs and blogging

Blogging is a form of two-way communication characterised by an informal tone, timely updates and frank discussion. Weblogs, or **blogs**, initially took the form of online diaries in which people recorded (logged) features of their personal lives, thoughts and opinions on either their personal website or a common one. Others could respond, add comments or provide links to other sources. The scope of the activity rapidly extended as bloggers developed sites for those wishing to comment on current events, politics, sport – or any other topic. Bloggers began to provide almost instant commentary on current events, often supplementing established media. News services such as the BBC and political candidates now use blogs to reach new audiences, to interact with present audiences and to try to gather and form opinion.

During 2005 the management implications of blogging began to become clear. If customers complain about a company or its products on a community blog, it attracts much wider attention than if they had complained to the company in the traditional way. Conversely, positive stories would benefit the company. Former or current employees could do the same – airing grievances or making statements that were immediately and widely available.

A blog is a frequently updated, interactive website through which people can communicate with anyone who has access to the medium. Dearstyne (2005) distinguishes five types of blog:

- individual/personal – set up by individuals to share personal and family news and ideas;
- news/commentary – report, comment and interpret current events;
- advertising/promotional/customer service – communicate with potential customers;
- business/professional – insight and commentary on business and professional issues, including company practices;
- internal/knowledge management – used within companies to share information about products and projects.

While some companies are cautious about blogging, others have established a blog on an internal website (their intranet). Sun Microsystems is a prominent example, where employees are encouraged to share information and ideas about current projects or marketing ideas as well as to chat socially. They can also highlight articles or other information, enabling instant sharing across the company. Others have sites for customers and the public. Examples from companies featured in this book are:

www.bp.com
www.innocentdrinks.com
www.tesco.com

As with any technological innovation, using blogs effectively depends on dealing with organisational issues (Chapter 12).

16.5 Communication networks

Communicating in groups and teams

To understand how people in a group communicate members need to have some tools to analyse the patterns of interaction. Shaw (1978) conducted a laboratory experiment to identify the range of communication processes used, and how they helped or hindered the groups in their task. Figure 16.5 shows the communication patterns used. Autocratic leadership was associated with the wheel, and a democratic style with the all channel structure. Shaw noted that in centralised networks (chain, wheel and 'Y') groups had to go through a person located at the centre of the network to communicate with others, which led to unequal access to information. In the decentralised networks (circle and all channel) information flowed freely and equally between members.

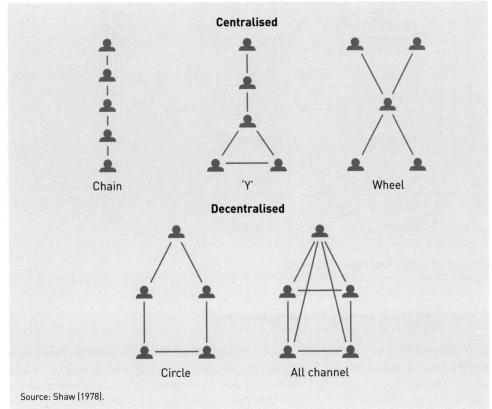

Source: Shaw (1978).

Figure 16.5

Centralised and decentralised communication networks in groups

Different tasks require different forms of interpersonal communication. Figure 16.6 illustrates this with two communication patterns. In a centralised network information flows to and from the person at the centre, while in the decentralised pattern more of the messages pass between those in the network. If the task is simple, the centralised pattern will work adequately. An example would be to prepare next year's staff budget for the library when there are to be no major changes. The person at the centre can give and receive familiar, structured information from section heads.

However, if the task is uncertain the centralised structure will obstruct performance. An example would be a team developing a new product rapidly in conjunction with suppliers and customers. Because of the novelty of the task, unfamiliar questions or situations will arise. Group members can deal with these only by exchanging information rapidly amongst each other. If all information has to pass through a person at the centre they will not be able to handle the volume of queries, which will lead to unacceptable delays while those in the network wait for replies.

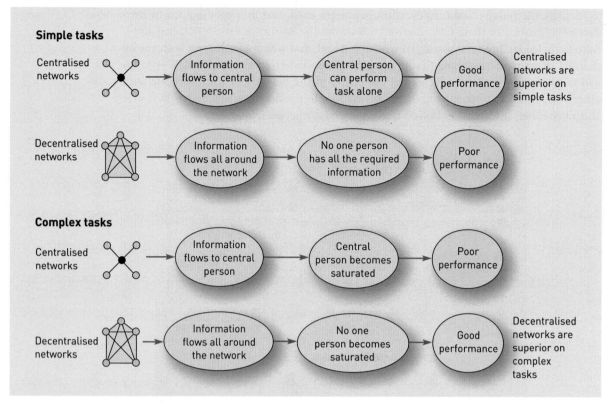

Figure 16.6 Communication structure and type of task

Source: Based on Baron and Greenberg (1997).

Communicating across the organisation

As organisations grow they need to supplement informal communication methods with more formal arrangements. At first these are quite simple, such as a list of current orders and what stage they have reached. Then there may be a system for setting budgets for the different parts of the activity and for collecting information on what they cost. Later people probably develop some rules or guidelines about passing information to other departments so that they know about changes that affect them. These systems are the basis of the formal or institutionalised communication system. As Figure 16.7 shows, they pass information downward, upward or horizontally.

Downward communication

Management uses downward communication when they try to ensure coordination by issuing a plan and expect those lower in the hierarchy to follow it. Examples include information about:

- new policies, products or services
- orders received, as a signal to relevant departments to start planning their part
- budget changes or any changes in financial reporting and control systems
- new systems and procedures
- new appointments and reorganisations
- changes to roles or job descriptions.

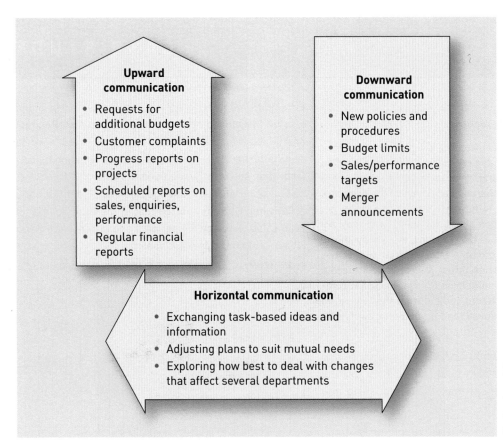

Figure 16.7

Directions of formal communications in organisations

If the downward communication inhibits comments or responses, the sender will be unclear how receivers reacted to the message. If downward communication is rare, so that subordinates are unclear about policy or changes, it usually indicates that managers do not trust subordinates to understand the information or use it responsibly.

Team briefings

Team briefings are a popular way of passing information rapidly and consistently throughout the organisation – Blakstad and Cooper (1995) quote the results of a survey of 915 companies in which 57 per cent of respondents rated team briefings as the most common method of communicating with employees. Under this method senior management provides a standard message and format, and briefs the next level in the hierarchy. Those managers then brief their subordinates following the same standard format, and this process continues down the organisation. Team briefings are a way of communicating company issues to all staff through line managers. Addressing small groups with a common structure enables management to:

- deliver a consistent message
- involve line managers personally in delivering the message
- deliver the message to many people quickly
- reduce the possible distortions by 'the grapevine'
- enable staff to ask questions.

Asked to summarise his approach to turning round an ailing company, Ghosn replied:

The key factors are three: Number one, you have to establish with the people of the company a very simple vision about where you're going, what's the destination; where we're going has to be shared at all levels of the company. Number two, you have to have a strategy, how do we get there, what are the action plans, and make sure they are deployed at every level of the company, everybody knows what is the contribution that is expected from him or her for the company. Number three, people have to feel a strong commitment coming from the top, personal commitment, team commitment coming from the top, we're here to revive the company, and if you don't do it, well we're out of here.

As CEO of both Renault and Nissan, his abilities to turn companies round would be further tested. Japanese and Korean car makers were pushing into

Europe, threatening Renault's core products. He would also be threatened by a new alliance between Peugeot and Toyota. To met this challenge he would need to secure further cost-saving synergies by stepping up collaboration between Renault and Nissan.

The scale of this challenge became evident in early 2007, when Nissan reported that in the third quarter of 2006 sales were down 4 per cent and profits were down 22 per cent on the previous year.

Sources: *CNN.com*, 6 June 2005; *Business Week*, 25 April 2005; and other published sources.

Case questions 16.4
● What does the latest episode suggest about the role of communication in managing?

Upward communication

Upward communication refers to systematic methods of helping employees to pass on their views and ideas to management. Managers try to ensure coordination by encouraging feedback. In small organisations this is usually fairly easy. The owner-manager is likely to be in close touch with what employees are thinking, so information and ideas reach the boss quickly. As the business grows the layers of the hierarchy can easily break the flow. Unless they create mechanisms to allow information to move upwards, their boards may be acting on the wrong information.

 **key ideas** **Why businesses ignore vital information**

Sidney Finkelstein has studied the causes of corporate failure – one of which is when managers fail to recognise and act on vital information. He found that this was not usually due to incompetence or idleness, but to a combination of circumstances that made them unreceptive to information that mattered. These included:

● **Undirected information** – when staff are slow to recognise the importance of new information, because they have not been shown that they need to take the implied danger seriously. It may also be that there is no one who is able to act on the information.
● **Missing communication channels** – when companies cannot act on vital information because there are no communication channels between people receiving the information and those who need to act on it. This also happens if channels are blocked – a subordinate reports a problem to a boss, but cannot pass it elsewhere if the boss takes no action.

- **Missing motives** – when employees are reluctant to share vital information because there is no incentive – such as fearing ridicule or displeasure if they bring bad news. If the payment system encourages competition between divisions there will be no incentive to share information between them.
- **Missing oversight** – when senior managers assume that the information they receive is correct, without checking that this is the case. It is easy to accept good news unquestioningly, but that carries the danger that someone may be deliberately hiding news of severe problems.

Source: Finkelstein (2003).

Communication failures at BP   www.BP.com

In March 2005 an explosion at BP's Texas City refinery killed 15 and injured 500 people. A US Chemical Safety Board report showed that the oil group was so intent on improving the big picture on safety – its statistics – that it missed the pointers to deeper problems. The company focused on improving compliance with procedures and reducing occupational injury rates, while leaving 'unsafe and antiquated equipment designs and unacceptable deficiencies in preventive maintenance'. Supervisors knew that key instruments did not work, or were unreliable.

Yet Don Holmstrom, the CSB investigator leading the investigation, said the poor state of the refinery was hidden in the statistics. Indeed, in 2004 the refinery had the lowest injury rate in its history, but that did not take account of catastrophic hazards or distinguish between injuries and fatalities. 'When personal safety statistics improved, the refinery leadership thought it had turned the corner', he said. 'However, existing process safety metrics and the results of a safety culture survey indicated continuing problems with safety systems and concerns about another major accident'.

Source: *Financial Times*, 31 October 2006. See also Part 2 Case.

Employee opinion surveys

Some companies conduct regular surveys amongst their employees to gauge their attitudes and feelings towards company policy and practice. They may also seek views on current issues, or about possible changes in policy or practice. The surveys can be valuable both as a general indicator of attitudes and as a way of highlighting particular issues that need attention, such as a growing demand for childcare facilities.

Suggestion schemes

These are devices by which companies encourage employees to suggest improvements to their job or other aspects of the organisation. Employees usually receive a cash reward if management accepts their idea.

Activity 16.5   Researching opinion surveys

Gather some evidence from a company about its experience of using employee opinion surveys or suggestion schemes. What are their purposes? Who designs them and interprets the results? What have the benefits been?

Formal appeal or grievance procedures

These set out the steps to be followed when an individual or group is in dispute with the company. For example, an employee who has been penalised by a supervisor for poor timekeeping may disagree with the facts as presented or with the penalty imposed. The grievance procedure states how the employee should set about pursuing a claim for a review of the case. Similar procedures now exist in colleges and universities, setting out how a student with a grievance about their assessment can appeal against their results to successively higher levels of the institution.

Horizontal communication

Horizontal communication crosses departmental or functional boundaries, usually connecting people at broadly similar levels within the organisation. Computer-based information systems have greatly increased the speed and accuracy with which routine information can pass between departments. As a customer places an order, modern systems can quickly pass the relevant information to all the departments that will play a part in meeting it, making production a much smoother and predictable process.

Much horizontal communication is about less routine, less structured problems: when different parts of the organisation cooperate on projects to introduce new products or systems, people communicate frequently. They need to pass information to each other on the current state of affairs so that each distinct unit can be ready to contribute to the project as required.

As management creates a structure for the organisation it influences how much horizontal communication will take place. In a hierarchical, mechanistic organisation (see Chapter 10) most information passes vertically between managers and subordinates. In organic structures, where managers delegate more decisions to lower levels, there is more horizontal communication. Instead of referring problems up the hierarchy to a common boss, staff in the respective departments sort out problems themselves.

 **Managing knowledge at Ebank**

Ebank is a large European bank that was created by merging two separate banks. It has grown by acquiring other banks, and now operates in 70 countries. Separate divisions deal with different types of business, such as domestic, international and investment banking. It received a shock when a major global client left the bank because it was not providing an integrated service across countries. Despite Ebank calling itself a 'global bank' the reality was different. Each country and department operated independently and had its own systems and processes. While the vision from the top was to create a truly networked global bank there was little knowledge sharing between business units.

Members of the corporate business strategy group wrote a paper recommending that Ebank develop a worldwide communication network connecting all the businesses, using intranet technology. The paper recognised that the true competitive advantage of the bank was not in financial transactions but in providing knowledge to customers. For example, it may be able to advise a client (a European supermarket chain) to buy a similar business in China based on its global knowledge of economic trends and financial conditions. However, to offer such advice the bank needed to integrate knowledge from a range of departments and countries. At the time this was not possible because staff did not share such knowledge. So the vision was to develop a global communication system – a knowledge management system – to integrate the knowledge within the bank.

Source: Based on Newell (1999).

Informal communication

The grapevine is the spontaneous, informal system through which people pass information and gossip. It happens throughout the organisation and across all hierarchical levels as people meet in the corridor, by the photocopier, at lunch, on the way home. The information that passes along the grapevine is usually well ahead of the information in the formal system. It is about who said what at a meeting, who has applied for another job, who has been summoned to explain their poor results to the directors, or what orders the company has won.

The grapevine does not replace the formal system, but passes a different kind of information around – qualitative rather than quantitative, current ideas and proposals rather than agreed policies. As it is uncensored and reflects the views of people as a whole rather than of those in charge of the formal communications media it probably gives a truer picture of the diversity of opinions within the company than the formal policies do. Nevertheless, the rumours and information on the grapevine might be wrong or incomplete. Those passing gossip and good stories of spectacular disasters in department X may also have their own interests and agendas, such as promoting the interests of department Y. The grapevine is as likely to be a vehicle for political intrigue as any of the formal systems.

The grapevine can be a source of early information about what is happening elsewhere in the organisation. This allows those affected but not yet formally consulted to begin preparing their position. Put the other way round, someone preparing proposals or plans can be quite sure that information about them will be travelling round the grapevine sooner than they expect. Sometimes it is useful to deliberately let the matter slip out and begin circulating information to be able to gauge reaction before going too far with a plan.

16.6 Developments in communication technology

Chapter 12 (Section 12.4) describes how the convergence of three communication technologies that developed independently of each other – telephone, television and computers – has radically transformed the potential of digital communication. It shows how these have led to the development of the Internet (and associated intranets and extranets) and how linking mobile phones to the Internet has led to the explosive growth of the 'Wireless Internet', liberating much computing from the desktop and enabling people to communicate wherever they are.

These developments have clearly transformed many aspects of communication between people in organisations, and between them and their customers. Using computer technologies to transmit data automatically between different stages of a production or service process generally ensures that it is transmitted more accurately, consistently and quickly than was possible with manual methods. Computer networks with multimedia capabilities enable people to transmit messages, documents, video images and sound around the world. **Groupware** systems support the work of people who are physically remote but who need to work together. Customers and employees routinely expect information technology to function smoothly and the information it manages to be reliable. Sound decisions and competitive advantage depend on such accuracy.

Groupware systems provide electronic communication between members of geographically dispersed teams.

However, as Whetten and Cameron (2007) point out,

> comparable progress has not occurred in the interpersonal aspects of communication. People still become offended at one another, make insulting statements and communicate clumsily. The interpersonal aspects of communication involve the nature of the relationship between the communicators. (p. 219)

Using groupware at PwC www.pwc.com

PricewaterhouseCoopers (PwC) is one of the world's leading advisory organisations whose member firms employ 122,000 people in over 140 countries. The company, founded 150 years ago, traditionally operated as a collection of national or regional groups, further divided into functions. These worked in relative isolation from colleagues, especially those in other countries.

PwC realised that clients (especially large multinationals) required it to handle bigger and more complex jobs. Staff would have to offer a wider range of experience – which was largely available in the collective but unorganised experience of the consultants. How could management gather and communicate this valuable information quickly? The solution was to install a groupware system incorporating database management, e-mail, spreadsheets and other functions.

The system enables staff to share information quickly worldwide. They use their PCs to communicate and work on the same electronic files. The company has invested heavily in knowledge databases, containing details on

> all the projects we've done in particular industries and topics. So I can find out from my desk where our knowledge base is. I can have a set of case studies on our client's desk in a few hours. Other databases contain what the company has learned from those projects. Consultants on a project use the database as a source of ideas and information. The system is central to communications between offices and consultants across time zones. This is essential in a global business and the system allows much easier internal communication, irrespective of location.

A senior manager in the company reflected on their experience with the groupware product:

> The ability to manage globally in a people-business depends on good communications. Our groupware has helped us to move as quickly as we have. We've been able to respond to opportunities partly because we had the systems in place. Virtually everyone in the practice is now a groupware user.

Source: Private communication from a manager in the company.

Although modern communication technologies greatly aid the transmission of data and information between people, they do not in themselves ensure communication which, as the definition states, requires the parties to achieve mutual understanding. That depends on people combining appropriate communication technologies with interpersonal communication skills.

Activity 16.6 **Critical reflection on Internet systems**

Review the relevant parts of Chapter 12 from a communication perspective. Discuss the implementation of an Internet, intranet or extranet system with someone who has experienced it in a working organisation. Ask them about matters such as:

(a) the advantages and disadvantages compared with previous communication methods

(b) how it affected the way people communicate with each other

(c) whether it was a satisfactory substitute for face to face or spoken communication.

16.7 Interpersonal communication skills

If communication was perfect the receiver would always understand the message as the sender intended. That rarely happens, as people interpret information from their perspectives, and their words fail to express feelings or emotions adequately. Power games affect how people send and receive information, so we can never be sure that the message sent is the message received. Breakdowns and barriers can disrupt any communication chain.

Communication skills for senders

The ideas presented in this section suggest some practices that are likely to help improve anyone's interpersonal communication skill.

Send clear and complete messages

The subject, and how the sender views it, is as much part of the communication process as the message itself. The sender needs to compose a message that will be clear to the receiver, and complete enough to enable both to reach a mutual understanding. This implies anticipating how others will interpret the message, and eliminating potential sources of confusion.

Encode messages in symbols the receiver understands

Senders need to compose messages in terms that the receiver will understand – such as avoiding the specialised language (or jargon) of a professional group when writing to an outsider. Similarly, something that may be read by someone whose native language is different should be written in commonplace language, and avoid the clichés or local sayings that mean nothing to a non-native speaker.

Select a medium appropriate for the message

The sender should consider how much information richness a message requires, and then choose the most appropriate of the alternatives (such as face to face, telephone, individual letter or newsletter), taking into account any time constraints. The main factor in making that choice is the nature of the message, such as how personal it is or how likely it is to be misunderstood.

Select a medium that the receiver monitors

The medium we use greatly affects what we convey. Receivers prefer certain media and pay more attention to messages that come by a preferred route. Some dislike over-formal language, while others dislike using casual terms in written documents. Putting a message in writing may help understanding, but others may see it as a sign of distrust. Some communicate readily by e-mail, others are reluctant to switch on their system.

Avoid noise

Noise refers to anything that interferes with the intended flow of communication, which includes multiple – sometimes conflicting – messages being sent and received at the same time. If non-verbal signals are inconsistent with the words, the receiver may see a different meaning in your message from what was intended. Noise also refers to the inclusion in a message of distracting or minor information that diverts attention from the main business. Communication suffers from interruptions that distract both parties and prevent the concentration essential to mutual understanding.

Communication skills for receivers

Pay attention

Busy people are often overloaded and have to think about several things at once. Thinking about their next meting or a forthcoming visit from a customer, they become distracted and do not attend to messages they receive. In face to face communication the sender will probably notice this, and that in turn will affect their further actions.

Be a good listener

Communication experts stress the importance of listening. While the person sending the message is responsible for expressing the ideas they want to convey as accurately as they can, the receiver also has responsibilities for the success of the exchange. Listening involves the active skill of attending to what is said, and gaining as accurate a picture as possible of the meaning the sender wished to convey.

Many people are poor listeners. They concentrate not on what the speaker is saying but on what they will say as soon as there is a pause.

key ideas　Six practices for effective listening

1　**Stop talking**, especially that internal, mental, silent chatter. Let the speaker finish. Hear them out. It is tempting in a familiar situation to complete the speaker's sentence and work out a reply. This assumes you know what they are going to say: you should instead listen to what they are actually saying.
2　**Put the speaker at ease** by showing that you are listening. The good listener does not look over someone's shoulder or write while the speaker is talking. If you must take notes, explain what you are doing. Take care, because the speaker will be put off if you look away or concentrate on your notes instead of nodding reassuringly.
3　Remember that your **aim is to understand** what the speaker is saying, not to win an argument.
4　Be aware of your **personal prejudices** and make a conscious effort to stop them influencing your judgement.
5　Be alert to **what the speaker is not saying** as well as what they are. Very often what is missing is more important than what is there.
6　**Ask questions.** This shows that you have been listening and encourages the speaker to develop the points you have raised. It is an active process, never more important than when you are meeting someone for the first time – when your objective should be to say as little and learn as much as possible in the shortest time.

Be empathetic

Receivers are empathetic when they try to understand how the sender feels, and try to interpret the message from the sender's perspective, rather from their own position. A junior member of staff may raise a problem with a more senior colleague, which perhaps reflects their inexperience. The senior could be dismissive of the request, indicating that the subordinate ought to know how to deal with the situation. An empathetic response would take account of the inexperience, and treat the request with a greater understanding.

Supportive communication

Whetten and Cameron (2002) argue that ineffective communication leads people to dislike each other, and to become defensive, mistrustful and suspicious. That in turn leads to a further decline in the quality of communication, and a further decline in relationships: a cycle that harms personal satisfaction and organisational performance. To break out of this cycle they advocate the use of supportive communication – communication that seeks to preserve a positive relationship between the communicators while still dealing with the business issues. There are eight principles in the model, illustrated in Key Ideas.

Whetten and Cameron – supportive communication

key ideas

1 **Problem oriented, not person oriented**
A focus on problems and issues that can be changed rather than people and their characteristics.

Example: 'How can we solve this problem?'   Not: 'Because of you there is a problem.'

2 **Congruent, not incongruent**
A focus on honest messages in which verbal messages match thoughts and feelings.

Example: 'Your behaviour really upsets me.'   Not: 'Do I seem upset? No, everything's fine.'

3 **Descriptive, not evaluative**
A focus on describing an objective occurrence, your reaction to it, and offering an alternative.

Example: 'Here is what happened, here is my   Not: 'You are wrong for doing what you did.'
reaction, here is a suggestion that
would be more acceptable.'

4 **Validating, not invalidating**
A focus on statements that communicate respect, flexibility and areas of agreement.

Example: 'I have some ideas, but do you   Not: 'You wouldn't understand, so we'll do it
have any suggestions?'   my way.'

5 **Specific, not global**
A focus on specific events or behaviours, avoiding general, extreme or vague statements.

Example: 'You interrupted me three times   Not: 'You're always trying to get my attention.'
during the meeting.'

6 **Conjunctive, not disjunctive**
A focus on statements that flow from what has been said and facilitating interaction.

Example: 'Relating to what you've just said,   Not: 'I want to say something (regardless of
I suggest ...'   what you have just said).'

7 **Owned, not disowned**
A focus on taking responsibility for your statements by using personal ('I') words.

Example: 'I have decided to turn down your   Not: 'Your suggestion is good, but it wouldn't
request because ...'   get approved.'

▶

8 **Supportive listening, not one-way listening**
A focus on using a variety of responses, with a bias towards reflective responses.

Example: 'What do you think are the obstacles   Not: 'As I said before, you make too many
standing in the way of improvement?'   mistakes: you're just not performing.'

Source: Whetten, David A. and Cameron, Kim S., *Developing Management Skills*, 7th edition (2007), © 2007. Reprinted by permission of Pearson Education, Inc., Upper Saddle River, NJ.

They argue that following these principles ensures greater clarity and understanding of messages, while at the same time making the other person feel accepted and valued. As such they can be effective tools for achieving the mutual understanding, as well as the accuracy, of whatever is being communicated.

16.8 The organisational context of communication

While good interpersonal skills will improve communication, their effect on achieving mutual understanding will be affected by factors in the context – such as cultures, structures and power.

Culture

Differences in culture (as well as differences in language skills) can clearly impede efforts to communicate in multinational teams – though another view is to stress the learning benefits of such teams, as the Carlos Ghosn case study indicates.

Structure

Organisations are typically divided into separate units, focusing on their part of the total task. This often leads people to focus too much on their interests and priorities and not enough on other players. They forget that others will have an interest in what they are doing, or will be affected by it – and fail to communicate information that would be relevant to both parties. Finkelstein (2003) quotes the example of Nissan's US operation:

> Nissan, for example, operated for years with a rigid bureaucratic culture that required its sales, manufacturing and R&D divisions in the US to report separately to Japan, and not interact with each other. In effect all the corporate communication channels led only to Tokyo. To make matters worse, there was no direct interaction between regional managers in America and top corporate executives in Japan. This meant that if the Nissan sales people discovered customers were rejecting an automobile because of a small but irritating design feature, the design department was unlikely ever to hear about it. (p. 197)

Conversely, people in a structure that encourages and rewards cooperation and teamwork (such as those at Oticon or W.L. Gore) will experience freer communication.

Power

Information has great value. Those who possess it have something others do not have and may need or want. Sole ownership of information can also be used to boost or protect a person's status or the significance of his or her role. Chapter 14 showed that access to information and the means of communicating it to others is a source of power. People may hoard it rather than share it, and use it at the most opportune moment. Those with access to inside information have both prestige and power.

A further look at PwC www.pwc.com

management in practice

The manager also made the following comment, which illustrates how information can be seen as 'currency', and how the company dealt with it.

> We had to overcome a number of issues to encourage [groupware] use because some of the consultant managers think they're competing with each other. The competition still exists in practice units. So we've 'incentivised' them to share. If they're not meeting the culture, not sharing, that's not going to help them. We have a peer recognition system and an upward appraisal system. So if a consultant thinks a manager is not applying the culture, that will show up. And the peer recognition system allows people who have been sharing and helping others to be acknowledged and rewarded. We apply peer recognition throughout the business. It also needs certain disciplines – people must see it as part of their job to maintain information and record details of their projects. It's part of how they manage a client.

Source: Private communication from a manager in the company.

16.9   Current themes and issues

Performance

Argenti *et al.* (2005) show how managers can apply the themes of this chapter to strategic performance. They suggest that while there are adequate models for developing strategies, less attention has been paid to communicating. Citing examples of corporate disasters which show the damage that poor communication of strategy can do to a company's reputation, they propose that managers ensure a close link between communication practices and strategy, quoting Michael Dell:

> I communicate to customers, groups of employees and others, while working on strategy. A key part of strategy is communicating it. Communication is key to operations and an integral part of the process. (2005, p. 84)

Their research enabled them to develop a framework for strategic communication shown in Figure 16.8, comprising a variety of iterative loops between elements of a strategy and the constituencies likely to be affected.

They claim that putting the approach into practice requires an integrated, multilevel approach, linking communication functions with relevant stakeholder groups and the channels most likely to be suitable for each topic and group. They stress that while the approaches shown in Table 16.1 can be tailored to each stakeholder group, the messages need to be consistent with each other and with the intended strategy.

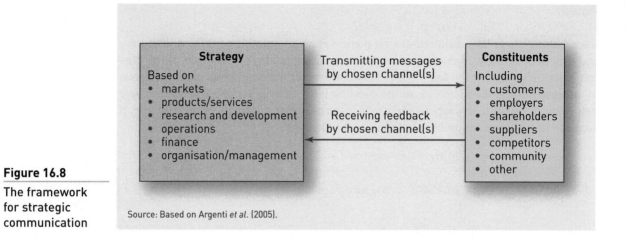

Figure 16.8

The framework for strategic communication

Table 16.1 Elements of a strategic approach to communications

Communication functions	Objectives	Constituencies		Channels
		Primary	**Secondary**	
Media relations	Public relations, crisis management	All constituents	Media	Press releases, interviews
Employee communications	Internal consensus building	Employees	Customers, families	Public meetings, memos, newsletters
Financial communications	Transparency, meeting financial expectations	Investors	Analysts, media	Conference calls, CEO, CFO
Community relations	Image building	Communities	NGOs, media	Events, speeches, philanthropy
Government relations	Regulatory compliance, meeting social expectations	Regulators	Media customers	Lobbying efforts, one-to-one meetings
Marketing communications	Driving sales, building image	Customers	All key constituencies	Advertising, promotions

Source: Based on Argenti *et al.* (2005).

Responsibility

Information is not neutral, as people can use it to legitimise particular sets of values and to exclude discussion of others. Those with power can try to maintain it by managing what is communicated, encouraging some types of information or discussion and suppressing others. Alvesson and Wilmott (1996) argue that most official company language uses terms that legitimise the idea of organisations as models of rationality and especially of instrumental rationality. Arguments presented as supporting a rational analysis or solution often hide the self-interest of those presenting the information.

However, what is communicated as 'rational' may be highly contentious or 'irrational'. Management may propose to concentrate production in larger factories on the rational grounds of lower costs. Opponents may argue that this ignores other costs such as extra traffic pollution or the effects on communities if plants are closed. If these criteria are used, the decision to concentrate production may be irrational. At the root of the issue is whether communication is used instrumentally to reach particular ends (low costs to one company) or to encourage critical reflection (the possibility that company goals could include avoiding pollution and supporting smaller communities).

Internationalisation

Many managers who develop their companies into international operations find that communicating across cultures makes the process even more hazardous than communicating within a single culture. Insights into the obstacles to such communication, and into a way of resolving them, are in the continuation of the chapter case study.

Carlos Ghosn – the case continues   www.renault.com   CASE STUDY

Ghosn has created many cross-company teams to study urgent problems such as product planning, vehicle engineering, power trains and purchasing – even when two companies with such different values have to work together. Asked about his experience of managing Nissan's largely Japanese workforce, he said:

It's interesting to see how human beings handle difference. People have always had problems with what is different from them. Different religion, race, sex, age, training – human beings have always had a challenge confronting what is different.

You feel more comfortable, more secure, with somebody who is like you. You feel insecure with someone who is different from you – younger, or a foreigner. But I recognise that even if someone is different, I'm going to learn a lot. We have a tendency to reject what is different – and yet we need what is different. Because what is different is the only way we can grow by confronting ourselves.

I have no doubt that cultural influences can affect the outcomes of discussions among multi-cultural teams, contributing much richer solutions than those teams' members would have developed on their own.

Generally speaking, my impression is that Japanese people are naturally process-oriented thinkers. French people are conceptual, ingenious and innovative. Americans are direct, get-to-the-point, bottom-line driven. The mix of those traits can be a tremendous asset during problem-solving or brainstorming sessions.

Sources: *Business Week*, 4 October 2004; and other published sources.

Summary

1 Explain the role of communication in managing

- People at all levels of an organisation need to add value to the resources they use, and to do that they need to communicate with others – about inputs, the transformation process and the outputs. It enables the tasks of planning, organising, leading and controlling.

- It also enables managers to perform their informational, decisional and interpersonal roles.

2 Identify and illustrate the elements and stages in the communication process

- Sender, message, encoding, medium, decoding receiver and noise.

3 Use the concept of information richness to select a communication channel

- In descending order of information richness, the channels are
  - face to face communication
  - spoken communication electronically transmitted
  - personally addressed written communication
  - impersonal written communication.

4 Compare the benefits of different communication networks

- Centralised networks work well on structured, simple tasks, but are less suitable for complex tasks as the centre becomes overloaded.

- Decentralised networks work well on complex tasks, as information flows between those best able to contribute. On simple tasks this is likely to cause confusion.

5 Describe how new technologies support communication

- The convergence of vision, voice and data technologies has greatly enhanced the ability to communicate data and information with little regard to distance, especially of structured, explicit data.

- However, mutual understanding of information and knowledge depends on senders and receivers having a shared context. Using information systems to support mutual understanding still depends on dealing with the human context of the process.

6 Outline some essential interpersonal communication skills

- Send clear and complete messages.

- Encode messages in symbols the receiver understands.

- Select a medium appropriate for the message.

- Include a feedback mechanism in the message.

- Pay attention.

- Be a good listener.

7 Consider how aspects of the wider context affect communication

- However good the interpersonal skills, mutual understanding will also be affected by cultural, structural and political factors in the situation.

Review questions

1 Explain why communication is central to managing.

2 Draw a diagram of the communication process, showing each of the stages and elements. Then illustrate it with a communication episode you have experienced.

3 How does feedback help or hinder communication?

4 What is non-verbal communication, and why is it important to effective communication?

5 What do you understand by the term 'information richness', and how does it affect the choice of communication method?

6 What is team briefing?

7 Name three practices that can improve interpersonal communication skill.

8 What limits the ability of computer-based systems to solve communication problems?

9 Give examples of the way that the context of an organisation can affect communication.

Concluding critical reflection

Think about the ways in which you typically communicate with others, and about communication in your company. Review the material in the chapter, and then make notes on these questions:

● What examples of the issues discussed in this chapter struck you as being relevant to practice in your company?

● Thinking of the people you typically work with, who are effective and who are less effective communicators? What do the effective communicators do? What interpersonal communication skills do they use? How have modern communications systems supported communication in your company? On balance, have **assumptions** about their value been supported? Can you see examples of structural, cultural and political factors affecting the degree of mutual understanding?

● What factors such as the history of the company or your personal experience have shaped communication practices? Does your current approach appear to be right for your present **context** – or would you use a different approach in other circumstances? (Perhaps refer to some of the Management in Practice features for how different managers communicate.)

● Have people put forward **alternative** approaches to communicating, based on evidence about other companies? If you could find such evidence, how may it affect company practice?

● What **limitations** can you identify in any of these communication theories? For example do you find the Lengle-Daft model a helpful way of choosing a channel?

Further reading

Goffman, E. (1959), *The Presentation of Self in Everyday Life*, Doubleday, New York.

A classic (and short) work that gives many insights into interpersonal communications.

Whetten, D.A. and Cameron, K.S. (2007), *Developing Management Skills*, Prentice-Hall International, Upper Saddle River, NJ.

Extended discussion of interpersonal communication skills, with useful exercises.

Hargie, O.D.W. (1997), *Handbook of Communication Skills*, Routledge, London.

A collection of papers covering all aspects of interpersonal communications skills, including non-verbal behaviour, explaining, listening, humour, and the selection interview.

Beall, A.E. (2004), 'Body language speaks: reading and responding more effectively to hidden communication', *Communication World*, vol. 21, no. 2, pp. 18–20.

A well-illustrated article about body language, which also lists some further resources.

Finkelstein, S. (2003), *Why Smart Executives Fail: And what you can learn from their mistakes*, Penguin, New York.

Fascinating account of the sources of communication failure in public and private organisations.

Weblinks

These websites have appeared in the chapter:

www.renault.com
www.cisco.com
www.grace.com
www.bp.com
www.innocentdrinks.com
www.tesco.com
www.pwc.com

Visit two of the business sites in the list, or others that interest you, and navigate to the pages dealing with recent news, press or investor relations.

● In what ways is the company using the website to communicate information about inputs, outputs and transformation processes?

● Is it providing a one-way or a two-way communication process?

Annotated weblinks, multiple choice questions and other useful resources can be found on **www.pearsoned.co.uk/boddy**

Chapter 17

Teams

To outline the significance of teams and how they develop.

By the end of your work on this chapter you should be able to outline the concepts below in your own terms and:

1 Explain why organisations use teams for a wide range of tasks

2 Distinguish the stages of development through which groups pass

3 Explain Belbin's theory of team roles

4 Evaluate the effectiveness of a team and identify possible reasons for variations in performance

5 Outline the organisational factors that influence team performance

6 Describe the meaning of 'groupthink', and give some examples of its symptoms.

This chapter introduces the following ideas:

structure
working groups
team
formal teams
informal groups
self-managing team
virtual teams
team-based rewards
preferred team role
observation
content
concertive control

*Each is a term defined within the text, as well as
in the Glossary at the end of the book.*

Cisco Systems is a company at the heart of the Internet. It is a leading developer and supplier of the physical equipment and software that allow digital data to travel around the world over the Internet, and also provides various support services that enable companies to improve their use of the network. It was founded in 1984 by a group of scientists from Stanford University, and its engineers have focused on developing Internet Protocol (IP)-based networking technologies. The core areas of the business remain the supply of routing and switching equipment, but it is also working in areas such as home networking, network security and storage networking.

The company employs 34,000 staff working from 70 offices around the world, developing new systems and working with customers to implement and enhance their network infrastructure. Most projects are implemented by staff from several sites working as virtual teams, in the sense that they are responsible for a collective product but work in physically separate places.

The company created a team to coordinate the testing and release of a new version of Cisco's Element Management Framework (EMF), a highly complex piece of software that monitors the performance of large numbers of elements in a network. When the product was released a few months later, the members of the team were free to work on other projects. The team had eight members, drawn from four sites and three countries:

Name	Location	Role
Steve	Raleigh, North Carolina	Project coordinator
Richard	Cumbernauld, Scotland	Development manager
Graham	Cumbernauld, Scotland	Development engineer
Eddie	Cumbernauld, Scotland	Development engineer
Rai	Austin, Texas	Test engineer
Silvio	Austin, Texas	Test engineer
Jim	Raleigh, North Carolina	Network architect
Gunzal	Bangalore, India	Release support engineer

The role of the coordinator was to ensure the smooth operation of the team and to monitor actual progress against the challenging delivery schedule. The software was developed in Cumbernauld, by engineers writing the code and revising it as necessary after testing by the test engineers. They were responsible for rigorously testing all software and reporting all problems concisely and accurately to the development engineers.

The network architect has extensive knowledge of the network hardware that the software would manage, and supervised the development and testing of the software to ensure that it worked as efficiently as possible with the hardware. The release support engineer dealt with the logistics of software release, such as defining each version and ensuring deliverables are available to the manufacturing departments at the appropriate times.

Each member worked full-time on the project, though they never met physically during its lifetime. All members took part in a weekly conference call, and also a daily call attended by the coordinator, development manager and a member of the test team. Communication throughout the team was mainly by electronic mail, together with instant messaging.

Source: Communication from members of the project team.

Case questions 17.1

● What challenges would you expect a team that never meets will face during its work?

● In what ways may it need to work differently from a conventional team?

17.1 Introduction

Cisco is an organisation where management uses teams extensively to deliver its products and services to customers. The people with the skills it needs for a particular project will be widely dispersed around the organisation but need to work together to meet customer needs. Teams are a way of bringing them together for the duration of a project – they then disperse and re-form in different combinations to work on other projects. The company also uses teams for internal development projects, where staff from a variety of functions and geographical areas work together on a part-time basis to deal with a pressing management problem, such as improving a financial or marketing system.

People at work have always developed loyalties amongst small groups of fellow workers and there are well-documented examples of industries where work was formally organised in small, self-managing teams (Trist and Bamforth, 1951). This is now happening much more widely, with teams rather than individuals becoming the basic building block of many organisations. This is most evident in research-based organisations such as Microsoft (Cusumano, 1997), W.L. Gore and Associates or GlaxoSmithKline, where scientists or engineers from different disciplines come together to work on a common project and then disband when the work is complete. There are many cross-organisational teams – such as when Sun Microsystems and one of their major suppliers created a range of teams to manage the flow of components between the two businesses (Boddy *et al.*, 2000, and see Management in Practice in Section 13.3). Teams bring together people with different ideas and perspectives to solve difficult problems. Most economic and social problems require the contribution of several disciplines or organisations. Creating a team draws people from these areas together to work on the problem.

However, putting people together as a group does not in itself ensure either performance or satisfaction. Some teams, such as that at Cisco, work to very high standards and levels of achievement. They are conspicuously successful and achieve more than was expected. Others fail, wasting both time and opportunity. The differences in performance – in meeting business goals or in satisfying members – reflect how the members managed the team.

The diversity of backgrounds that makes a team worthwhile also makes it harder for the team to work. Creating a team (or 'group', 'section', 'task force' or 'working party') is only the start. Members then need to learn to work together collaboratively to reach a target. The greater the diversity, the greater the challenge it will be to make the team work.

This chapter examines the use of teams in organisations, and the management issues that they raise, as shown in Figure 17.1. The chapter begins by outlining why more organisations now use teams and introduces a way of evaluating how well a team performs. It then discusses the different types of teams and the stages through which an effective team must pass. This leads to a theory about the sources of team effectiveness, which forms the structure for the rest of the chapter – the motivation, composition and working methods of teams. For all their potential advantages, teams have costs as well as benefits, and are not appropriate for all kinds of work. Deciding to invest in teams should reflect a conscious evaluation of their potential costs as well as their potential benfits.

17.2 Benefits of teams

Those who decide to create a team probably do so in the hope that the members and the organisation will benefit.

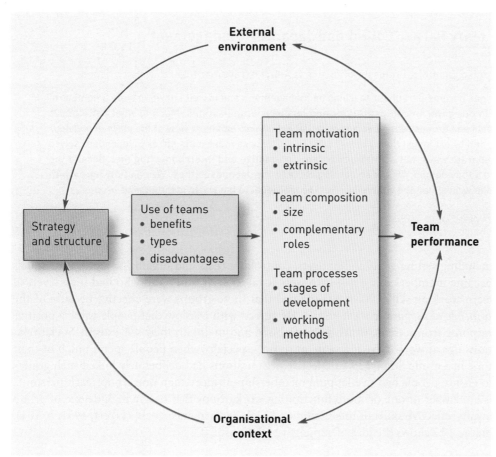

Figure 17.1

A model of team performance

Benefits to members

The Hawthorne studies described in Chapter 2 showed that a supportive work group had more influence on performance than physical conditions. People have social needs that they seek to satisfy by being acknowledged and accepted by other people. This can be done person to person (mutual acknowledgement or courteous small-talk on the train), but most people are also members of several relatively permanent cooperative groups. These provide an opportunity to express and receive ideas and to reshape one's views by interacting with others. Acceptance by a group meets a widely held human need.

Mary Parker Follett observed the social nature of people and the benefits of cooperative action. She saw the group as an intermediate institution between the solitary individual and the abstract society, and believed that it was through the group that people organised cooperative action. In 1926 Follett wrote:

> Early psychology was based on the study of the individual; early sociology was based on the study of society. But there is no such thing as the 'individual', there is no such thing as 'society'; there is only the group and the group-unit – the social individual. Social psychology must begin with an intensive study of the group, of the selective processes which go on within it, the differentiated reactions, the likenesses and the unlikenesses, and the spiritual energy which unites them. (Quoted in Graham, 1995, p. 230)

Likert (1961) developed this theme of organising work in groups. He observed that effective managers encouraged participation by group members in all aspects of the job,

key ideas　Mary Parker Follett and Japanese management

According to Tokihiko Enomoto, Professor of Business Administration at Tokai University, Japan:

Follett's work has become part of our teaching on management, and is well known to quite a number of ... managers in our government institutions and business organisations. Much of what Follett says about individuals and groups reflects to a substantial extent our Japanese view of the place of individuals in groups, and by extension their place in society ... She sees individuals not as independent selves going their separate ways, but as interdependent, interactive and interconnecting members of the groups to which they belong. This is something close to the Japanese ethos. We can fully agree with Follett when she writes that 'the vital relation of the individual to the world is through his groups'.

Source: Quoted in Graham (1995), pp. 242–243.

including setting goals and budgets, controlling costs and organising work. Individuals became members of a team who were loyal to each other and who had high levels of team-working skills. Likert maintained that these groups were effective because of the *principle of supportive relationships*. He agreed with Maslow that people value a positive response from others, which helps to build and maintain their self-esteem. Social relationships at work serve the same purpose, especially when people spend much of their time in a group. Managers in effective organisations had deliberately linked such groups to ensure people had overlapping membership of more than one group: 'each person ... is a member of one or more functioning workgroups that have a high degree of group loyalty, effective skills of interaction and high performance goals' (Likert, 1961, p. 104). Figure 17.2 shows the idea of supportive relationships.

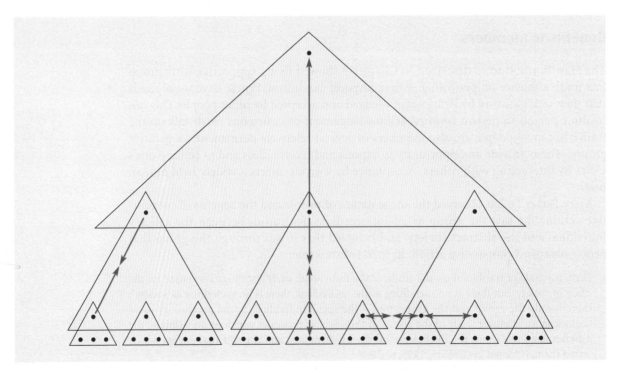

Figure 17.2 Likert's principle of supporting relationships

Note: The arrows indicate the linking pin-functions, both vertical and horizontal – as in cross-functional teams.
Source: Adapted from Likert (1967), p. 50.

These ideas continue to influence practice. Katzenbach and Smith (1993) observed that members of a team who surmount problems together build trust and confidence in each other. They benefit from the buzz of being in a team, and of 'being part of something bigger than myself'.

Benefits to performance

Scientific and technical knowledge is created by different professional groups, so solving many technical, production, social, health and other types of problem involve several disciplines working together. Even if staff remain within their separate hierarchical structures, managers create multidisciplinary teams to deliver a service or resolve some common problem. Teams can bring complementary skills beyond those of any individual.

In health care there is a growing interest in team working amongst those delivering care. One reason is the suffering caused when members of one group fail to pass information to others. Many also believe that encouraging different professions to work as multi-professional teams improves care and uses resources more effectively. Teams can also reduce costs and blur professional boundaries.

Other organisations seek similar benefits:

> When representatives from all of the relevant areas of expertise are brought together, team decisions and actions are more likely to encompass the full range of perspectives and issues that might affect the success of a collective venture. Multidisciplinary teams are therefore an attractive option when individuals possess different information, knowledge, and expertise that bear on a complex problem. (Van Der Vegt and Bunderson, 2005, p. 532)

The snag is that managers find it difficult to secure the benefits of multidisciplinary teams. The idea that diversity leads to performance is being replaced by one that examines how, and under what conditions this happens. For example, a team with a professionally diverse membership is more likely to bring performance benefits when the task is non-routine, and when there is a high degree of information sharing and sense of collective identity within the team (Van Der Vegt and Bunderson, 2005). Creating a team with appropriate authority gets talent working on organisational problems much more quickly than hierarchical structures could (Druskat and Wheeler, 2004).

Teamwork pays off at Louis Vuitton www.vuitton.com

The French company Louis Vuitton is the world's most profitable luxury brand. The success of the company is attributed to a relentless focus on quality, a rigidly controlled distribution system and ever-increasing productivity in design and manufacture. Eleven of the 13 Vuitton factories are in France: although they could move to cheaper locations, management feels more confident about quality control in France.

Employees in all Vuitton factories work in teams of between 20 and 30 people. Each team, such as the ones at the Ducey plant in Normandy, works on one product, and members are encouraged to suggest improvements in manufacturing. They are also briefed on the product, such as its retail price and how well it is selling, says Stephane Fallon, a former manager for Michelin who runs the Ducey factory. 'Our goal is to make everyone as multi-skilled and autonomous as possible', says team leader Thierry Nogues.

The teamwork pays off. When the Boulogne Multicolour (a new shoulder bag) prototype arrived at Ducey, workers who were asked to make a production run discovered that the decorative metal studs were causing the zipper to bunch up, adding time and effort to assembly. The team alerted factory managers, and technicians quickly moved the studs a few millimetres away from the zipper. Problem solved.

Source: *Business Week*, 22 March 2004.

Teams can also cut costs, as the Management in Practice feature on Coats Ltd shows.

 **Teams at Coats**

Coats Ltd (a textile company) decided to introduce self-managed work teams into its manufacturing operations to improve quality and efficiency. The aim was to replace the traditional manufacturing set-up with teams of highly trained employees fully capable of managing themselves and completing a whole piece of work. The members of each team would be able to perform a wide variety of tasks, have more decision-making power and access to more information. They would perform roles traditionally performed by supervisors such as scheduling, setting priorities and monitoring quality. A manager:

> We started with some pilot groups, and after some initial difficulties they are working well. The performance of the teams has reached, and in some cases exceeded, expectations, especially in three key performance measures of machine efficiency, wastage and absence.
>
> The role of individuals has also evolved. They are more flexible, committed and also willing to act in different team roles. A survey after six months showed that 85 per cent of staff prefer working in teams.

Source: Communication from a manager in the plant.

Teams do not always work, and the next Management in Practice feature is a cautionary tale.

 **A community mental health team**

The management of a health care unit decided to reduce the number of hospital places and increase resources for community care. As part of the change a resource centre was established containing multidisciplinary teams, each with about 30 staff, to provide a 24-hour service for the severely mentally ill in the community. The service would use a team approach with a flattened hierarchy and greater mutual accountability, and this was supported by many team building and similar activities.

It soon became clear that many staff could not cope with the extra responsibility and shared decision making. The job is difficult and sometimes dangerous, since people's lives are at stake. Management therefore changed the system to clarify the role of each member of staff and to give a clearer structure of authority and management. It also recognised that, while team working may be an ideal, it needs to be supported by broader management structures and practices.

Source: Communication from a manager in the service.

Case questions 17.2

- What were the business reasons that led Cisco to use teams, especially virtual ones?
- On the information you have on the case so far, does the team meet the definition of a 'real team'? (See Table 17.1, p. 565.)

Why effective teams contribute to business performance

Teams can be a way of reaching a synthesis between high efficiency and high-quality jobs, since they can:

- provide a structure within which people with a range of skills and perspectives work together;
- provide a forum in which issues can be raised and dealt with – rather than being ignored;
- enable people to extend their roles, so possibly improving responsiveness and reducing costs;
- encourage acceptance and understanding by staff of a problem and the solution proposed;
- promote wider learning by encouraging reflection, and spreading lessons widely.

Activity 17.1 Gathering data on teams

Gather some original information on how at least two organisations have used teams to get work done, or where an organisation has abandoned teamwork. Use the questions below as a starting point for your enquiry. The data you collect may be useful in one of your tutorials, as well as adding to your knowledge of teams.

- What is the main task of the organisation or department?
- How are the staff in the area grouped into teams?
- Use the definition of a 'real team' (see Table 17.1) to describe the team.
- What type of team is it? (Use the ideas in Section 17.4 as a guide.)
- What do management and team members see as the advantages and disadvantages of team working in this situation?
- Have there been any recent changes in the organisation of the teams, such as members taking on new tasks? If so, why?

17.3 Crowds, groups and teams

A group (or team) is not just any collection of people. A crowd in the street is not usually a group: they are there by chance, and will have little if any further contact. Are 150 students in a lecture theatre a team? What about the staff in a supermarket? In a takeaway restaurant? In the same section of a factory? They are not a crowd: they have some things in common, and people may refer to them as a group. Compare them with five people designing some software for a bank, each of whom brings distinct professional skills to their collective discussions of the most suitable design, or with seven students working together on a group assignment. They have a **structure** to handle the whole process, work largely on their initiative, and move easily between all the tasks, helping each other as needed.

Structure is the regularity in the way a unit or group is organised, such as the roles that are specified.

Activity 17.2 Crowds, groups and teams

Note down a few words that express the differences between the examples given. Do some sound more like a group than others?

One difference is in the extent to which they share a common purpose. Groups or teams aim to produce some outcome to which all members have contributed, and for which they share some collective responsibility. A second difference is in the extent to which members share ideas and activities to get the job done. Teams can add value to individual work by exchanging ideas, information and effort. There is some continuing interdependence, which leads to a sense of membership, and of being (temporarily) distinct from outsiders.

Activity 17.3 Teams or not?

Consider a Davis Cup tennis or Ryder Cup golf team, in which most of the action takes place between individual participants from either side. No significant coordination occurs between the members during each of the matches.

- In what ways would such teams meet the above definition?
- Can you think of other examples of people who work largely on their own but are commonly referred to as a team?

In normal conversation people typically use the words 'group' and 'team' interchangeably – they mean the same thing. This book follows that common usage, but it is essential to be aware that the words can mean different things. Some work effectively and others do not. Becoming an effective group or team costs time and effort. That cost is not necessary if the task could be done by well-motivated and cooperative individuals. It is worth taking a few sentences to clarify the meaning behind the terms.

Katzenbach and Smith (1993) define a team as: 'A small number of people with complementary skills who are committed to a common purpose, performance goals, and working approach for which they hold themselves mutually accountable' (p. 45). A group of people that works together is not necessarily a team on this definition. The essential point is that groups (or teams) differ in what they produce.

Katzenbach and Smith use the 'team performance curve' shown in Figure 17.3 to make the point clear. While many groups call themselves teams, most do not clarify their shared purpose or common approach, and so do not achieve as much as they could. They rely on the contributions and expertise of the individual members. Members engage in normal social courtesies and interactions, and perhaps exchange some task advice and information. But they are accountable for their work as individuals. In many situations such '**working groups**' (see Table 17.1) are all that is needed, provided individuals do their job competently. **Teams** use collective discussion, debate and decision to deliver 'collective work products' – something more than the sum of individual effort. Figure 17.3 shows this difference, with working groups delivering individual work products, while teams produce collective work products. Table 17.1 describes the five points on the curve.

Having, for the purpose of their argument, distinguished between working groups and teams, Katzenbach and Smith emphasise that they do not advocate particular labels. They recommend (and this author agrees) that people should use the terms with which they are comfortable. It is what groups and teams *do* that matter, not what they are called.

A **working group** is a collection of individuals who work mainly on their own but interact socially and share information and best practices.

A **team** is 'a small number of people with complementary skills who are committed to a common purpose, performance goals, and approach for which they hold themselves mutually accountable' (Katzenbach and Smith, 1993).

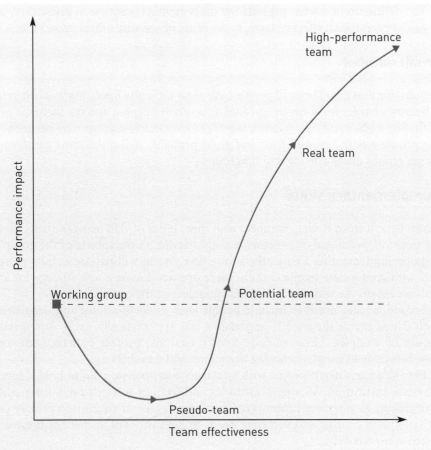

Figure 17.3

The team performance curve

Table 17.1

Description of the points on the team performance curve

Point	Description
Working group	There is no significant need to become a team. The focus is on individual effort. Members interact mainly to share information and best practices. They help each other to perform within their area of responsibility. There is no strong common purpose or joint work product for which they are all accountable
Pseudo-team	There are opportunities for collective performance, but members have not focused on trying to achieve it. No interest in shaping a common purpose or set of performance goals, though it may call itself a team. Time in meetings detracts from individual performance, without any joint benefits. Whole is less than potential sum of parts
Potential team	There are opportunities for collective performance, and members are trying to achieve this. They still need to develop clarity over purpose, goals or joint work products. They may require more discipline in working out a common approach or to establish collective accountability
Real team	A small number of people with complementary skills who are equally committed to a common purpose, performance goals and working approach for which they hold themselves mutually accountable
High-performance team	Meets all the tests of a real team, and in addition members are deeply committed to one another's personal growth and success

The definition of a team suggests the tools members can use to assess their progress towards becoming an effective team, in the sense of meeting others' expectations.

Small number

Groups of more than about 12 people have great difficulty operating as a coherent team. It becomes harder for them to agree on a common purpose and the logistical problems of finding a place and time to work together increase. Most teams have between two and ten people – with between four and eight probably being the most common range. Larger groups usually divide into subgroups.

Complementary skills

Teams benefit from having members with three types of skill between them. First, there are *technical, functional* or *professional skills*, relevant to the subject of the group's work. A group implementing a networked computer system will require at least some members with appropriate technical skills, while one developing a new strategy for a retailer will contain people with strategic or business development skills.

Second, a team needs to include people with *problem-solving* and *decision-making skills*. These enable the team to approach a task systematically, using appropriate techniques of analysis. These include SWOT analysis, project management methods, cost–benefit analysis, diagramming techniques and flowcharting.

Finally, a team needs people with adequate *interpersonal skills* to hold it together as a human institution. Members' attitudes and feelings towards each other and to the task change as work continues. The changing degree of commitment may generate irritation and conflict and someone needs to have the skill to manage these disagreements constructively.

Common purpose

Teams cannot work to a common purpose unless members spend time and effort clarifying that purpose. They need to express it in clear performance goals. These focus members' energy on activities that support their achievement. A common purpose helps communication between members, since they can interpret and understand their contributions more easily.

Common approach

Teams need to decide how they will work together to accomplish their common purpose. This includes deciding who does which jobs, what skills members need to develop, and how the group should make and modify decisions. The common approach includes supporting and integrating new or reticent members into the team. Working together on these tasks helps to promote the mutual trust and constructive conflict necessary to team success.

Mutual accountability

A team cannot work as one until its members willingly hold themselves to be collectively and mutually accountable for the results of the work. As members do real work together towards a common objective, commitment and trust usually follow. If one or more members are unwilling to accept this collective responsibility, the team will not become fully effective.

17.4 Types of team

Teams have to cope with different issues, depending on their function, formality, autonomy and location.

Function

Hackman (1990) distinguished seven types of team in terms of the functions they perform, and the risks and opportunities associated with each. Table 17.2 summarises these.

Table 17.2

Hackman's classification of team types and their associated risks and opportunities

Type	Risks	Opportunities
Top management teams – to set organisational directions	Underbounded; absence of organisational context	Self-designing; influence over key organisational conditions
Task forces – for a single unique project	Team and work both new	Clear purpose and deadline
Professional support groups – providing expert assistance	Dependency on others for work	Using and honing professional expertise
Performing groups – playing to audiences	Skimpy organisational supports	Play that is fuelled by competition and/or audiences
Human service teams – taking care of people	Emotional drain; struggle for control	Inherent significance of helping people
Customer service teams – selling products and services	Loss of involvement with parent organisation	Bridging between parent organisation and customers
Production teams – turning out the product	Retreat into technology; insulation from end users	Continuity of work; able to hone team design and product

Source: Hackman (1990), p. 489.

Case questions 17.3

- What kinds of team does Cisco use, in Hackman's typology?
- What other kinds of team from the list have you experienced?

Formality

Formal teams

Formal teams are created by the organisation as part of the business's basic structure. There are both vertical and horizontal teams, as shown in Figure 17.4.

Vertical teams consist of a manager and his or her subordinates within a single department or function. The manager and staff in the treasury department of a bank, and the senior nurse, nursing staff and support staff in a unit of the Western General Hospital, are formally constituted vertical teams. So is a team leader and his or her staff in an ING Bank call centre in The Netherlands. In each case senior managers created them to support their goals.

A **formal team** is one that management has deliberately created to perform specific tasks to help meet organisational goals.

567

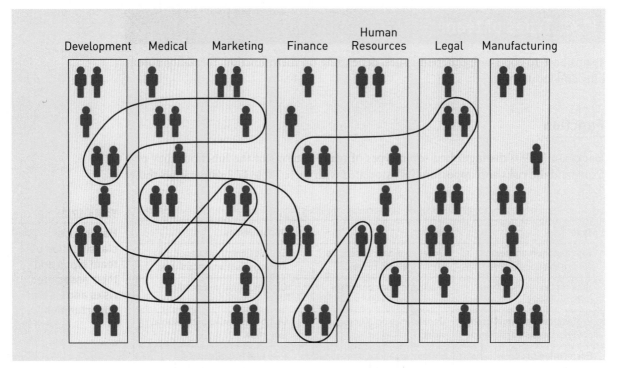

Figure 17.4 Horizontal and vertical teams within Eli Lilley (a pharmaceutical company)

Source: *Business Structures* (video), TV Choice Productions, Bromley, Kent, UK (2004).

Horizontal teams consist of staff from roughly the same level, but from different functions. The Cisco EMF team is an example, being brought together to release the new software. In Hackman's typology, task forces would be an example: often called cross-functional teams, these deal with non-routine problems that require several types of professional knowledge, such as how to develop a new product or process.

Informal groups

An **informal group** is one that emerges when people come together and interact regularly.

Although not created by management, **informal groups** are a powerful feature of organisational life. They develop as day-to-day activities bring people into contact with each other – who then discover common sporting or social interests. Work-related informal groups arise when people in different formal groups exchange information and ideas: staff using a software package may begin to pass around problems or tips. Staff in separate departments dealing with a customer may start passing information to each other to avoid misunderstandings, even though this is not part of the specified job. Informal groups may also develop in opposition to management – as when people believe they are being unfairly treated, and come together from across groups to express a common dissatisfaction with a management policy.

Autonomy

A **self-managing team** operates without an internal manager and is responsible for a complete area of work.

Another type of team that is commonly used is the **self-managing team**, a group of employees who operate without the close supervision of a manager and are responsible for a complete area of work. They reflect in part theories of motivation that advocate doing more to satisfy workers' higher-order needs. Members are responsible for getting

Informal networks: the company behind the chart — key ideas

According to Krackhardt and Hanson (1993):

> If the formal organization is the skeleton of the company, the informal is the central nervous system. This drives the collective thought processes, actions and reactions of the business units. Designed to facilitate standard modes of production, management create the formal organization to handle easily anticipated problems. When unexpected problems arise, the informal organization becomes active. Its complex web of social ties form every time colleagues communicate and solidifies over time into surprisingly stable networks. Highly adaptive, informal networks move diagonally and elliptically, skipping entire functions to get work done.

The authors argue that these informal networks can either foster or disrupt communication processes. They recommend that managers try to understand them in order to make use of their strengths, or even adjust aspects of the formal organisation to complement the informal.

Source: Krackhardt and Hanson (1993), p. 104.

the work done but have a high degree of autonomy in how they do it: they manage themselves, including planning and scheduling tasks, and assigning tasks amongst the members. They are also likely to establish the pace of work, make operating decisions, work out how to overcome problems and manage quality. They are also likely to have a considerable influence over selecting new employees.

Druskat and Wheeler (2004) examined the apparent paradox of the leadership of such teams – although referred to as self-managing, in practice they manage within constraints. A team that manages its work activities works within targets and expectations set by those in the wider organisation – receiving directions and reporting back to them. A manager external to the team will be responsible for its performance – and faces the dilemma of how best to carry out that role. From an empirical study of 300 self-managing teams in a single organisation they concluded that successful leaders of such teams had developed a distinctive set of skills, primarily those of managing the boundary between the team and the larger organisation.

Location

Modern communications technologies enable and encourage people to create teams in which the members are physically distant for most of the time, even though they are expected to deliver high-quality collective outcome. Many of the teams in Cisco are like this. The growing internationalisation of management means that people frequently work in **virtual teams** drawn from different nations and cultures, as well as working remotely, raising new teamwork challenges (Govindarajan and Gupta, 2001; Robey *et al.*, 2003).

Virtual teams are those in which the members are physically separated, using communications technologies to collaborate across space and time to accomplish their common task.

Virtual teams use computer technology to link members together, communicating via technologies such as e-mail, videoconferencing and online discussion through a website. They can perform all the functions of a team that is located in the same place, but lack the face-to-face interaction and discussion which helps to smooth working relationships. While virtual teams can sometimes use the fact that they are in different time zones to their advantage, Saunders *et al.* (2004) examine some of the challenges. At a superficial level differences of time zone create problems of managing different working hours, lunch breaks and holiday cycles. More fundamental difficulties arise from contrasting visions of time between cultures and nations – such as whether it is an objective or subjective notion, or differences in the meaning of words such as 'soon' or 'urgent'.

While virtual teams bring expertise together without the expense of travel, they require careful management to ensure the benefits of team working are retained. Practices include ensuring that some regular (or at least initial) face-to-face contact occurs, and that members resolve issues of roles, working methods and conflict management (Maruca, 1998).

17.5 Stages of group development

Putting people into a group does not mean they perform well immediately, as teams need to go through stages of growth. Some never perform well. Tuckman and Jensen (1977) developed a theory that groups can potentially pass through five fairly clearly defined stages of development. Figure 17.5 shows these.

Teams need to have the chance to grow up and to develop trust amongst the members. As the work makes progress people learn about each other, and how they can work well together. The closer they get, the easier it becomes to develop mutual trust.

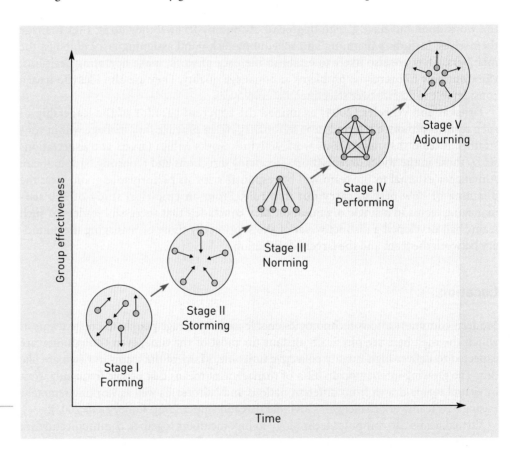

Figure 17.5

Stages of group development

Forming

Forming is the stage at which members choose, or are told, to join a team. Managers may select them for their functional and technical expertise or for some other skill. They come together and begin to find out who the other members are, exchanging fairly superficial information about themselves, and beginning to offer ideas about what the group should do. People are trying to make an impression on the group and to establish their identity with the other members.

Storming

Conflicts may occur at the storming stage, so it can be an uncomfortable time for the group. As the group begins the actual work members begin to express differences of interest that they withheld, or did not recognise, at the forming stage. People realise that others want different things from the group, have other priorities and, perhaps, have hidden agendas. Different personalities emerge, with contrasting attitudes towards the group and how it should work. Some experience conflicts between the time they are spending with the group and other duties. Differences in values and norms emerge.

Some groups never pass this stage. There may be little open conflict and members may believe the group is performing well – but may be deluding themselves. If the group does not confront disagreements it will remain at the forming or storming stage and will do no significant work. Performance depends on someone doing or saying something to move the group to the next stage.

Norming

Here the members are beginning to accommodate differences constructively and to establish adequate ways of working together. They develop a set of shared norms – expected ways of behaving – about how they should interact with each other, how they should approach the task, how they should deal with differences. People create or accept roles so that responsibilities are clear. The leader may set those roles formally or members may accept them implicitly during early meetings. Members may establish a common language to guide the group and allow members to work together effectively.

Performing

Here the group is working well, gets on with the job to the required standard and achieves its objectives. Not all groups get this far.

Adjourning

The group completes its task and disbands. Members may reflect on how the group performed and identify lessons for future tasks. Some groups disband because they are clearly not able to do the job, and agree to stop meeting.

A team that survives will go through these stages many times. As new members join, as others leave, as circumstances or the task change, new tensions arise that take the group back to an earlier stage. A new member implies that the team needs to revisit, however briefly, the forming and norming stages. This ensures the new member is brought psychologically into the team and understands how they are expected to behave. A change in task or a conflict over priorities can take a group back to the storming stage, from which it needs to work forward again. The process will be more like Figure 17.6 than the linear progression implied by the original theory.

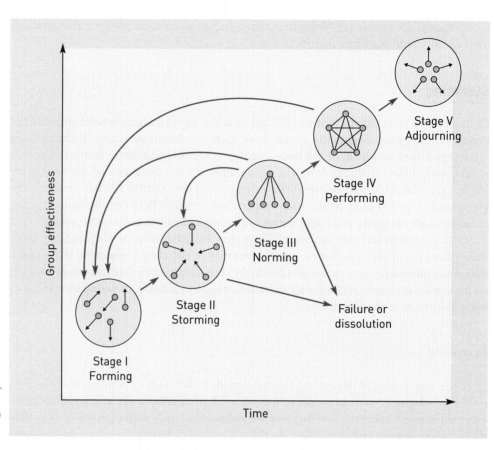

Figure 17.6

Modified model of the stages of group development

---

key ideas **Managing the virtual team life cycle**

Furst *et al.* (2004) noted the benefits of virtual teams in eliminating boundaries of time and space, but also found that they more often fail than succeed. To explain this they tracked the evolution of six virtual teams in a company, using the Tuckman and Jensen model. They found that virtual teams faced additional problems at each stage of the model, compared to those working in the same place.

Forming is more difficult, and takes longer, as there is less frequent communication, especially the informal chat between workers who meet regularly. This reduces the speed at which people make friendships and increases the risk of forming false impressions or stereotypes about other team members.

Storming can also be more fraught, as the absence of frequent non-verbal clues increases the risks of misunderstanding. Disagreements can be exacerbated or prolonged if people do not respond quickly to electronic communication – even if caused by differences in working times or poor technology.

Norming in virtual teams needs to clarify how to coordinate work, how to communicate, and how quickly to respond to requests. The process of norming itself is made more complex with electronic communication, as it is harder to try out ideas tentatively and to gauge reactions.

Performing depends on sharing information, integrating ideas and seeking creative solutions. The challenges of virtual working at this stage include competing pressure from local assignments, losing focus, and the fear of a failure that would damage a career.

Furst *et al.* use their analysis to suggest what those managing a virtual team could do at each stage to increase the chances of virtual teams reliably adding value.

Source: Furst *et al.* (2004).

Cisco – the case continues   www.cisco.com   **CASE STUDY**

Members of the team commented on the way the team developed. A common issue was the problem of scheduling meetings:

I've always found in virtual teams that when the team is first formed it isn't really getting any serious work done (unless we're under severe time pressure), it's about getting everyone together so they at least have some knowledge of the others in the team. (Steve)

Another said:

It was strange when we first started working together, because we didn't push on and get any testing or fixing done straight away. Steve was really pushing for us all to spend a few hours in conference calls getting to know each other and how we were all going to work together. We took our time to get into the actual work that was required. (Graham)

Other reflections included:

I had a few discussions with Steve . . . he wanted us to spend most of our time in conference meetings with the rest of the team, while my engineers already had a good understanding of the work that was needed and just wanted to get on with it. But Steve is the team lead so we had to go along with his approach. (Richard)

It's weird having to form such a close relationship with someone [when] you don't even know what they look like. But as we're using IM [Instant Messenger] just about every day you get used to it. I think you sometimes have to make an extra effort to talk directly to people, just to keep the relationship going. Sometimes it'd be easier for me to e-mail Rai, but I phone him, just so we can have a bit of a chat. (Eddie)

It means you have to be a bit more careful when it comes to communication. Most of the time you have to use e-mail and IM to discuss issues, which means there can be misunderstandings if you're not careful. When you interact in person you use things like facial expression and hand gestures – none of these are available when e-mailing so you have to state your arguments more clearly. (Jim)

Source: Communication from members of the project team.

Case questions 17.4

- Relate these accounts to the stages of team development.
- What examples of forming, storming and norming does it contain?

Evaluating team effectiveness

Hackman (1990) suggested three ways of evaluating team effectiveness, summarised in Table 17.3. These are subjective, and a team may succeed on some and fail on others. Judgement must also reflect the conditions in which the team is working.

Criteria	Description
Has it met performance expectations?	Is the group completing the task managers gave to it – not only the project performance criteria, but also measures of cost and timeliness?
Have members experienced an effective team?	Is it enhancing their ability to work together as a group? Have they created such a winning team that it represents a valuable resource for future projects?
Have members developed transferable teamwork skills?	Are members developing teamwork skills that they will take to future projects? This indicates a team meeting the needs of the business and the team members

Source: Based on Hackman (1990).

Table 17.3

Criteria for evaluating team effectiveness

Research with 27 teams of different types led Hackman to propose that to perform well a group must surmount three hurdles. Members must:

● be willing to exert sufficient effort to accomplish the task to an acceptable level;
● bring adequate knowledge and skill to the task;
● use group processes that are appropriate to the work and the setting.

These hurdles (see Figure 17.7) show how well a group is doing and where difficulties are arising.

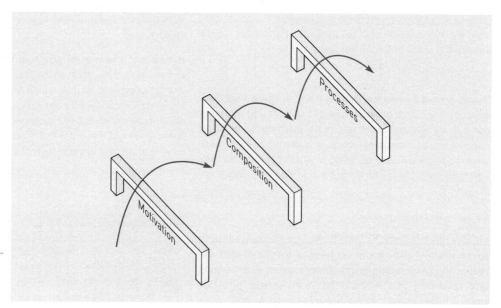

Figure 17.7

Hurdles in the way of team effectiveness

Team-based rewards are payments or non-financial incentives provided to members of a formally established team and linked to the performance of the group.

To overcome them, Hackman suggested that a team needs both internal and external support, as the manager cannot rely only on internal team practices or personal enthusiasm. He or she should also attend to wider organisational conditions such as the availability of **team-based rewards**. If both are in place it is more likely that the group will put in the effort, have the skill and use good team processes. Table 17.4 summarises these points.

Table 17.4

Points of leverage for enhancing group performance

Requirements for effectiveness	Internal conditions	Organisational context
Effort (see Chapter 15)	Motivational structure of task	Remedying coordination problems and rewarding team commitment
Knowledge and skill	Team composition	Available education and training, including coaching and guidance
Performance strategies	Working processes that foster review and learning	Information system to support task and provide feedback on progress

Source: Based on Hackman (1990), p. 13.

Securing adequate effort is essentially a matter of motivation and so draws on the ideas in Chapter 15 – such as the intrinsic nature of the task and whether adequate extrinsic rewards are available. The present chapter deals with the other two hurdles – team composition and team processes.

17.6 Team composition

In a mechanical sense, team composition includes questions of size and membership. Is there an acceptable balance of part-time and full-time members? Are the relevant functions represented? Equally important is whether members have the right skills and ways of working to form an effective team – Uhl-Bien and Graen (1998) warn:

> Although cross-functional teams may be highly effective if implemented correctly (for instance, staffed with strong team players), if implemented incorrectly (staffed with independently focused self-managing professionals) they may ... harm organizational functioning. (p. 348)

As people work in a team they behave in ways that reflect diverse perspectives, skills and interests, which lead them to take on distinctive roles. A group needs a balance of these, so a task for the team leader is to do what they can to shape its composition. Two useful ideas are the distinction between task and maintenance roles, and Belbin's research on team roles.

Task and maintenance roles

Some people focus on the task, on getting the job done, on meeting deadlines. Others put their energy into keeping the peace and holding the group together. Table 17.5 summarises the two.

Emphasis on task	Emphasis on maintenance
initiator	encourager
information seeker	compromiser
diagnoser	peacekeeper
opinion seeker	clarifier
evaluator	summariser
decision manager	standard setter

Table 17.5

Summary of task and maintenance roles

Teams need both roles, and skilful project managers try to ensure this happens.

Meredith Belbin – team roles

Meredith Belbin and his colleagues systematically observed several hundred small groups while they performed a task, and concluded that each person in a group tends to behave in a way that corresponds to one of nine distinct roles. The balance of these roles in a group affects how well or badly it performs.

Belbin's research method

Henley School of Management based much of their training on inviting managers to work in teams of up to ten on exercises or business simulations. The organisers had long observed that some teams achieved better financial results than others – irrespective of the abilities of the individual members as measured by standard personality and mental tests. The reasons for this were unclear. Why did some teams of individually able people perform less well than teams that appeared to contain less able people?

Belbin conducted a study in which observers, drawn from course members, used a standard procedure to record the types of contribution that members made. Team members voluntarily took psychometric tests, and team performance led to a quantifiable result. The researchers formed teams of members with above-average mental abilities, and compared their performance with the other teams. The 'intelligent' teams usually performed less well. Of 25 such teams only 3 were winners, and the most common position was sixth in a league of eight. The explanation lay in the way they behaved, typically spending time in debate, arguing for their point of view to the exclusion of others'. These highly intelligent people were good at spotting flaws in others' arguments, and became so engrossed in these that they neglected other tasks. Failure led to recrimination. The lesson was that behaviour (rather than measured intelligence) affected group performance.

Source: Belbin (1981).

The researchers identified different preferred team roles. Some people were creative, full of ideas and suggestions. Others were concerned with detail, ensuring that the team dealt with all aspects and that quality was right. Others spent their time keeping the group together. Table 17.6 lists the nine roles identified in Belbin (1993). Belbin observed that winning teams had members who fulfilled a balance of roles that was different from the less successful ones.

Table 17.6

Belbin's team roles

Role	Typical features
Implementer	Disciplined, reliable, conservative and efficient. Turns ideas into practical actions
Coordinator	Mature, confident, a good chairperson. Clarifies goals, promotes decision making, delegates well
Shaper	Challenging, dynamic, thrives on pressure. Has the drive and courage to overcome obstacles – likes to win
Plant	Creative, imaginative, unorthodox – the 'ideas' person who solves difficult problems
Resource investigator	Extrovert, enthusiastic, communicative – explores opportunities, develops contacts, a natural networker
Monitor–evaluator	Sober, strategic and discerning. Sees all options, judges accurately – the inspector
Teamworker	Cooperative, mild, perceptive and diplomatic. Listens, builds, averts friction, calms things – sensitive to people and situations
Completer	Painstaking, conscientious, anxious. Searches out errors and omissions. Delivers on time
Specialist	Single-minded, self-starting, dedicated. Provides scarce knowledge and skill

Source: Based on Belbin (1993).

Winning teams had an appropriate balance, such as:

- a capable coordinator
- a strong plant – a creative and clever source of ideas
- at least one other clever person to act as a stimulus to the plant
- a monitor–evaluator – someone to find flaws in proposals before it was too late.

Ineffective teams usually had a severe imbalance, such as:

- a coordinator with two dominant shapers – since the coordinator will almost certainly not be allowed to take that role;
- two resource investigators and two plants – since no one listens or turns ideas into action;
- a completer with monitor–evaluators and implementers – probably slow to progress, and stuck in detail.

Belbin did *not* suggest that all teams should have nine people, each with a different **preferred team role**. His point was that team composition should reflect the task:

> The useful people to have in a team are those who possess strengths or characteristics that serve a need without duplicating those that are already there. Teams are a question of balance; what is needed is not well-balanced individuals but individuals who balance well with one another. In that way human frailties can be underpinned and strengths used to full advantage. (Belbin, 1981, p. 77)

Preferred team roles are the types of behaviour that people display relatively frequently when they are part of a team.

Trainers use the model widely to enable members to evaluate their preferred roles. They also consider how the balance of roles within a team affects performance. Some managers use it when filling vacancies. A personnel director joined a new organisation and concluded that it employed few 'completer–finishers'. Management started initiatives and programmes but left them unfinished as they switched to something else. She resolved that in recruiting new staff she would try to bring at least one more 'completer–finisher' to the senior team.

Using Belbin's roles in film-making teams

management in practice

Hollywood had experienced a shift from long-term jobs to short-term project teams. With their highly skilled freelance staff who come together for a brief period to carry out specific tasks and then disband, film making offers a model for the future of work in the wider world. Angus Strachan has been using Belbin's model to help film directors manage expensive production teams more effectively:

> Managing film teams requires a mature coordinator who can handle creative people with delicate egos and strong opinions ... A good unit production manager is a strong monitor–evaluator, someone who can carefully analyse the overall situation and make the big calls. The second assistant director needs to be a strong completer–finisher, passing on accurate information that enables the unit production manager to keep abreast of the situation ... A successful assistant director also needs to be a good communicator and organizer who has the flexibility to adjust schedules – in Belbin's terms to take on the resource investigator role.

Source: Angus Strachan, 'Lights, camera, action', *Personnel Management*, 16 September 2004, pp. 44–46.

However, there is little evidence that companies deliberately use the model when forming teams from existing staff. Managers typically form teams on criteria of technical expertise, departmental representation, or who is available. How the team processes will work is a secondary consideration. This is understandable, but in doing so managers make the implicit assumption that people will be able and willing to cover roles if one seems to be lacking.

Whether the theory is widely used or not, it implies that a manager responsible for a team may find the work goes better if they put effort into securing the most suitable mix of members.

Cisco – the case continues   www.cisco.com   CASE STUDY

Recalling the roles within the team, Steve said:

My job was mainly to ensure that everything in the virtual team runs smoothly – often just a matter of arranging and coordinating meetings, but also encouraging some kind of creative spark that'll help discussion along. Gunzal takes his time to make decisions, but when he does, he's usually correct. Eddie is very systematic in his work, and very hard working.

Another commented:

I'd say Graham is often the one who comes up with original ideas, while Jim has an incredible range of contacts within the company, and can usually find the right person to go to. Rai is very precise in everything he does and it's very

important that he receives the correct information from the engineers. If they don't explain something properly he's good at going back to ask for more information.

Source: Communication from members of the project team.

Case questions 17.5

- Which of the Belbin roles can you identify amongst the members of the team?
- Are any of the roles missing, and how may that have affected team performance?

Activity 17.4   Critical reflection on team composition

Evaluate a team you have worked with using Belbin's team roles.

- Which roles are well represented, and which are missing?
- Has that affected the way the team has worked?
- Which of the roles most closely matches your own preferred role?
- What are the strengths and weaknesses of Belbin's model to the manager?
- Have you any evidence of managers using it to help them manage teams? If so, in what way was it used, and with what effect?

17.7   Team processes

Effective teams, often with the help of skilled team coaches (Hackman and Wageman, 2005), develop processes that help them work together to accomplish their common purpose. These include developing a common approach, attending to the dominant type of communication, and observing team practices.

Common approach

A primary outcome of an effective 'norming' stage is that members agree both the administrative and social aspects of working together. This includes deciding who does which jobs, what skills members need to develop, and how the group should make and modify decisions. In other words the group needs to agree the work required and how it will fit together. It needs to decide how to integrate the skills of the group and use them cooperatively to advance performance.

The common approach includes supporting and integrating new members into the team. It also includes practices of remembering and summarising agreements. Working together on these tasks helps to promote the mutual trust and constructive conflict necessary to team success. Groups need to spend as much time on developing a common approach as they do on developing a shared purpose.

Team members need to control their meetings effectively – whether face to face or at a distance. That involves ensuring they are conducted in a way that suits the purpose of the task, without participants feeling they are being manipulated. Table 17.7 is an example of the advice widely available to managers about effective and ineffective meetings.

Table 17.7

Five tips for effective meetings

Meetings are likely to succeed if:	Meetings are likely to fail if:
• they are scheduled well in advance	• they are fixed at short notice (absentees)
• they have an agenda, with relevant papers distributed in advance and invite additions at the start	• they have no agenda or papers (no preparation, lack of focus, discussion longer)
• they have a starting and finishing time and follow prearranged time limits on each item	• they are of indefinite length (discussion drifts), time is lost and important items are not dealt with (delay, and require a further meeting)
• decisions and responsibilities for action are recorded and circulated within 24 hours	• decisions lack clarity (misunderstanding what was agreed, delay, reopening issues)
• they keep subgroups or members of related teams informed of progress	• the team is not aware of work going on in other teams that is relevant to its work

Categories of communication

Group members depend on information and ideas from others to help them perform the group task; a useful skill is to be able to identify the kind of contribution that people make (Chapter 16 illustrated patterns of group communication), and whether this helps the group to manage the task. To study and learn how people behave in groups we need a precise and reliable way to describe events. There are many such models, each suited to a purpose: Table 17.8 illustrates one such list of behaviours. The significance of this is the evidence that how a group uses its time between these categories of communication will affect performance. A group that devotes most of its time to proposing ideas and disagreeing with them will not progress far. A more effective group will spend more time proposing and building, which of course implies developing better listening skills.

Table 17.8

Categories of communication within a group

Category	Explanation
Proposing	Putting forward a suggestion, idea or course of action
Supporting	Declaring agreement or support for an individual or their idea
Building	Developing or extending an idea or suggestion from someone else
Disagreeing	Criticising another person's statement
Giving information	Giving or clarifying facts, ideas or opinions
Seeking information	Seeking facts, ideas or opinions from others

Observing the team

Observation is the activity of concentrating on how a team works rather than taking part in the activity itself.

Content is the specific substantive task that the group is undertaking.

Members can develop the skill of assessing how well a team is performing a task. There are many guides to help them do this, and anyone can develop their ability to **observe** groups by concentrating on this aspect rather than on the **content** of the immediate task. They work slightly apart from the team for a short time and keep a careful record of what members say or do. They also note how other members react, and how that affects the performance of the team. At the very least, members can reflect on these questions at the end of a task:

● What did people do or say that helped or hindered the group's performance?
● What went well during that task, which we should try to repeat?
● What did not go well, which we could improve?

With practice skilled members of a team are able to observe what is happening at the same time as they work on the task itself. They can do this more easily and powerfully if they focus their observations on certain behaviour categories, such as those shown in Table 17.8 – but suited to the purpose of the observation.

17.8 The disadvantages of teams

For all the undoubted benefits of teams, they have disadvantages and costs.

Take on their own purpose

Some groups take on a life of their own, and become too independent of the organisation that created them. As members learn to work together they generate enthusiasm and commitment – and become harder to control. The team may divert the project to meet goals that they value, rather than those of the sponsor. As experts in the particular issue they can exert great influence over management, by controlling or filtering the flow of information to the organisation as a whole, so that their goals become increasingly hard to challenge. Their work becomes relatively isolated from other parts of the organisation, and they focus on what they see to be key issues.

Use too much time

The benefit of wider perspectives comes from discussion. This inevitably takes longer than if an individual made the decision. Time spent in discussion may encourage participation and acceptance – but only if the group manages this well. If discussion strays over unrelated issues, or goes over matters that they have already dealt with, the team loses time. This can also be an opportunity for members opposed to the project to prolong group discussion and to use the search for agreement as a blocking tactic. Some members will complain about the time spent. In fast-moving situations they may simply not be able to afford the time and so withdraw their support.

Allow an individual to dominate

Some teams allow one member to dominate. This may be the formal leader of the group in a hierarchical organisation, where people do not challenge those in a position of authority. It may be a technical expert who takes over, when others hesitate to show their lack of knowledge or to ask for explanations. In either case the group will not draw on the experience available, and it will probably be a dissatisfying and unproductive experience. It may produce a worse result, and be more costly, than if one person had dealt with the issue.

Succumb to groupthink

Chapter 7 (Section 7.7) examined the concept of groupthink, which occurs when members become so attached to a group that they suppress dissenting views so as not to jeopardise their acceptance by the other members. This can lead the group to reach dangerously wrong decisions. Groupthink is an important aspect of team working, so you should check that section now.

Activity 17.5   Critical reflection on teams

Recall some teams of which you have been a member.

- Which of the advantages and disadvantages have you observed?
- When teams have performed well, or badly, can you relate that to ideas in this chapter, such as the stages of group development, or to Belbin's team roles?

17.9   Current themes and issues

Performance

While in many circumstances a well-designed and skilled team can produce exceptional performance, they are not always necessary. Individuals can handle many tasks as well as a group – and perhaps better. An example is where a task requires people to use their expertise on a narrowly defined technical issue with no wider implications. For such purposes an effective working group (in terms of Table 17.1) can meet the performance required and there is no need to invest the extra effort needed for team performance –

which could indeed be counter-productive. Off-site team development activities can be exciting and motivating. If members then find that the task to be done involves little real interaction beyond normal interpersonal cooperation they will feel let down by the effort to build a real, or high-performance, team.

If the task clearly does require people to work together to create joint work products besides individual contributions, then the risk and cost of creating a real, or high-performance, team will be worthwhile.

Responsibility

Many organisations use self-managed teams to secure business benefits and also to bring benefits associated with a greater degree of autonomy and self-control to staff. These are valuable benefits, but Barker (1993) raises the possibility that self-managing teams may in some cases exert a much tighter control over the actions of members than traditional bureaucratic structures. He showed how three teams in an electronics company developed a system of rules about how members should behave that controlled their actions more powerfully and completely than the former system. This system of **concertive control** arose as workers negotiated a consensus amongst themselves.

Concertive control is when workers reach a negotiated consensus on how to shape their behaviour according to a set of core values.

The components company that Barker studied was struggling to survive in an newly competitive market. One of the founders decided to organise the 90 manufacturing staff (two-thirds of whom were women) into self-managing teams. The factory was rearranged to form three distinct and self-sufficient work areas, with each team being responsible for part of the product range. The teams themselves had considerable responsibility, and had to work out for themselves how they would work together.

An example of how concertive control developed occurred when the late delivery of components meant that a team would miss a customer deadline. They were committed to meeting targets, so agreed to work late and also to accommodate the external commitments some members had. This agreement set a strong precedent for the way the team would behave in future. A member later described the continuing power of the team's internally agreed consensus about personal responsibility:

> I work my best at trying to help our team to get stuff out the door. If it requires overtime, coming in at five o'clock and spending your weekend here, that's what I do. (Barker, 1993 p. 422)

New team members began to obey the norms agreed by the original members, as the team's concertive control began to penetrate their attitudes and actions. A temporary employee at the time explained how she tried to conform to the norms: 'When I first started I really didn't start off on the right foot, so I've been having to re-prove myself as a team player' (p. 425).

Members rewarded those who conformed by making them feel part of the team and a participant in their success. They punished those who had 'bad' attitudes.

The norms gradually evolved from a loose system that the workers 'knew' to a tighter system of objective rules. This transformation most often occurred when new members were not acting according to the team's work norms, such as coming to work on time. One explained:

> Well we had some disciplinary thing. We had a few certain people who didn't show up on time and made a habit of coming in late. So the team got together and kind a set some guidelines and we told them, you know, 'If you come in late the third time and you don't wanna do anything to correct it, you're gone.' That was a team decision that this was a guideline that we were gonna follow. (p. 426)

Barker concludes that creating autonomous or self-managed teams does not free workers from the obligation to follow rules. Instead:

The iron cage becomes stronger. The powerful combination of peer pressure and rational rules in the concertive system creates a new iron cage whose bars are almost invisible to the workers it incarcerates. They must invest a part of themselves in the team: they must identify strongly with their team's values and goals, its norms and rules. If they want to resist their team's control, they must be willing to risk their human dignity, being made to feel unworthy as a 'teammate'. Entrapment in the iron cage is the cost of concertive control. (pp. 435–436)

This research shows that for all the benefits of teams, especially self-managing teams, they are not without their negative sides. Peer-enforced concertive control can create constraining and even oppressive systems.

Internationalisation

A common feature of internationalisation is that companies create multinational or global teams to work on projects or regular activities. Such teams are often 'virtual', in the sense that although they are working on a common task they are physically separated and span different time zones. Their dominant means of communication is usually through computer-based systems such as e-mails and videoconferencing.

Virtual teams face all the challenges of team performance which face teams that are located in the same place, and in addition they need to overcome the difficulties of working with those from different cultures. Their transitory nature means that members may be part of several such teams simultaneously, limiting their ability to build close relationships with members of any particular one. Finally, virtual meetings lack the physical cues present in face-to-face meetings, which makes it more difficult for members to give and respond to the non-verbal cues that prevent misunderstanding.

Govindarajan and Gupta (2001) surveyed executives from European and US multinationals with experience of virtual teams, and concluding that they face unique challenges:

- **Cultivating trust amongst team members** Trust between members encourages cooperation and avoids conflict, and is highest when members share similarities, communicate frequently and operate in a common context of norms and values. By their nature, global teams suffer on all these dimensions.
- **Hindrances to communication** Distance hinders face-to-face communication, which technology can still only partially resolve. Language barriers are a further block to communication: even if people are speaking the same language, differences in meaning and usage can obstruct work. Cultural differences (Chapter 3) mean that members bring profound differences in values to the discussions. Those from collectivist cultures place a high value on achieving consensus, and are willing to prolong a meeting to achieve it: this can seem wasteful to those from individualist cultures who place less value on consensus.

Summary

1 **Explain why organisations use teams for a wide range of tasks**

- As management faces new expectations about cost and quality many see teams as a way of using the talents and experience of the organisation more fully to meet these tougher objectives.

- Teams also meet important motivational needs – for social contact and to be part of a collective achievement.

2 Distinguish the stages of development through which groups pass

- Forming, storming, norming, performing and adjourning. Note also that these stages occur iteratively as new members join or circumstances change.

3 Explain Belbin's theory of team roles

- Belbin identified nine distinct roles within a team and found that the balance of these roles within a team affected performance. The roles are: implementer, coordinator, shaper, plant, resource investigator, monitor–evaluator, teamworker, completer, specialist.

4 Evaluate the effectiveness of a team and identify possible reasons for variations in performance

- Criteria include meeting performance expectations, members having experienced an effective team, and members developing transferable teamwork skills.

- Team performance depends on effort, knowledge/skill and performance strategies – each of which can be affected by the team itself *and* by wider organisational factors.

5 Outline the organisational factors that influence team performance

- Effort can be encouraged by removing coordination problems and rewarding teamwork.

- Knowledge/skill can be fostered by education, training and coaching.

- Performance strategies can be encouraged by relevant technologies being available and by providing feedback.

6 Describe the meaning of 'groupthink', and give some examples of its symptoms

- When members become so committed to maintaining group cohesiveness, they may no longer look critically at alternatives. Symptoms include illusion of invulnerability, belief in the inherent morality of the group, rationalisation, stereotyping out-groups, self-censorship, direct pressure, mindguards, and an illusion of unanimity.

Review questions

1 What are the potential benefits of teamwork to people and performance?

2 Katzenbach and Smith (1993) distinguish between working groups and real teams. Describe the differences, and suggest when each form is appropriate to a task.

3 W.L. Gore and Associates (see Part Case) is beginning to form more distant teams. What management issues are likely to arise in this form of team?

4 How many stages of development do teams go through? Use this model to compare two teams.

5 List the main categories of behaviour that can be identified in observing a group.

6 Compare the meaning of the terms 'task' and 'maintenance' roles.

7 Evaluate Belbin's model of team roles. Which three or four roles are of most importance in an effective team? What is your preferred role?

8 Give examples of the external factors that affect group performance. Compare the model with your experience as a group member.

9 What are the potential disadvantages of teams?

Concluding critical reflection

Think about your experience of teams, and about the ways in which your organisation uses teams. Review the material in the chapter, and then make notes on these questions:

- Which of the issues discussed in this chapter struck you as being relevant to practice in your organisation?

- Thinking of the teams in which you have worked, which are effective and which ineffective? What happens in the effective teams that does not happen in the less effective ones? What team-building skills do people use, and to what extent are they supported or hindered by wider organisational factors? Are teams supported by specific coaching or guidance? What **assumptions** have people made when creating teams?

- What factors such as the history of the company or your personal experience have shaped the way you use teams? Does your current use of teams appear to be right for your present **context** position and company – or would you use a different approach in other circumstances?

- Have people put forward **alternative** working methods (such as introducing more self-managing teams), based on practice in other companies? If you could find such evidence, how may it affect company practice?

- What **limitations** can you identify in any of these team theories, or in your organisation's approach to using teams. Do people create too many teams, or too few?

Further reading

Belbin, R.M. (1993), *Team Roles at Work*, Butterworth/Heinemann, Oxford.

An account of the experiments that led Belbin to develop his model of team roles.

Hayes, N. (1997), *Successful Team Development*, International Thomson Business Press, London.

A lively and well-referenced account of many of the issues covered here.

Hackman, J.R. (1990), *Groups that Work (and Those that Don't)*, Jossey-Bass, San Francisco, CA.

Katzenbach, J.R. and Smith, D.K. (1993), *The Wisdom of Teams*, Harvard Business School Press, Boston, MA.

Both books contain many good examples of the use of teamwork.

Sandberg, A. (ed.) (1995), *Enriching Production*, Avebury, Aldershot.

A very wide range of perspectives on the use of teams at Volvo, and of the wider forces that affected the fate of the Volvo experiments.

Druskat, V.U. and Wheeler, J.V. (2004), 'How to lead a self-managing team', *MIT Sloan Management Review*, vol. 45, no. 4, pp. 65–71.

Govindarajan, V. and Gupta, A.K. (2001), 'Building an effective global business team', *MIT Sloan Management Review*, vol. 42, no. 4, pp. 63–72.

Two contemporary articles based on empirical research in a manufacturing plant and a series of global businesses respectively.

Hackman, J. R. and Wageman, R. (2005), 'A theory of team coaching', *Academy of Management Review*, vol. 30, no. 2, pp. 269–287.

Valuable overview of the development of interest in team processes, and of research into the skills of team development.

Weblinks

These websites have appeared in this and other chapters:

www.cisco.com
www.vuitton.com
www.microsoft.com
www.oticon.com
www.bmw.com
www.gore.com

Each has tried to develop new approaches to using teams – encouraging staff to share ideas and experience, as well as gaining personal satisfaction from them. Try to gain an impression from the site (perhaps under the careers/working for us section) of what it would be like to work in an organisation in which teams are a prominent feature of working.

Annotated weblinks, multiple choice questions and other useful resources can be found on **www.pearsoned.co.uk/boddy**

W.L. Gore and Associates in Europe www.gore.com

W.L. Gore and Associates is a remarkable example of a business organised around team principles. While working as a scientist at Dupont Corporation, Bill Gore became convinced of the potential value of polytetrafluoroethylene (PTFE), commonly known as Teflon, as an insulating material for wire. This led him and his wife Vieve to begin W.L. Gore and Associates in Newark, Delaware, in 1958. The company has plants around the world, including three in Scotland – two in Livingston and one in Dundee. In March 2007 it came first in *The Sunday Times* list of 'Britain's Best 100 Companies to Work For'. The company is owned by the Gore family and the associates (see below).

In 1969 Bill and Vieve Gore's son, Bob, discovered that PTFE could be stretched to form a strong porous material, which enabled the company to broaden the range of its electronics products to include new applications such as medical implants, high-performance fabrics and solutions to environmental pollution. The business is well known for the GORE-TEX® brand, under which many of its products are marketed. GORE-TEX® fabric works in a wide range of temperatures, does not age, is weather durable, porous and strong.

The focus of the business is the development, manufacture and engineering of products and technologies based on PTFE and other fluoroplastics for a wide range of applications. It has four product divisions:

1 *electronic products*: special cables and cable assemblies for the aviation, aerospace, automation, telecommunication, medical and IT industries;
2 *medical products*: vascular grafts, implants, patches and dental implants;
3 *fabrics*: branded high-performance fabrics for sportswear, leisurewear, work and protective wear;
4 *industrial products*: filter media and gaskets in environmental technologies, and in the food, fibre and textile industries.

The company has a tradition of valuing close and direct personal contact amongst people, which is seen as essential to the success of this kind of innovative business. There are no job titles in the company – all employees are known as 'associates'. Associates are hired for general work areas, and with the guidance of their sponsors, and a growing understanding of oppor-

Courtesy of W.L. Gore and Associates. © 2007 W.L. Gore & Associates.

tunities and team objectives, commit to projects that match their skills. Teams organise around opportunities and leaders emerge based on the needs and priorities of a particular business unit – some would provide technical leadership, others business leadership and so on. Leaders usually emerge naturally by demonstrating special knowledge, skill or experience that is in line with business objectives.

The company has avoided traditional hierachy, opting instead for a team-based environment that fosters personal initiative, encourages innovation and promotes direct communication. The business philosophy reflects the belief that given the right environment there are no limits to what people can accomplish, provided these are consistent with the business objectives and strategies.

Associates work to four principles:

1 fairness to each other and everyone with whom they come in contact;
2 freedom to encourage, help and allow other associates to grow in knowledge, skill and scope of responsibility;
3 the ability to make one's own commitments and keep them;
4 consultation with other associates before undertaking actions that could affect the reputation of the company – this is known as the waterline principle.

The last principle is intended to balance the risks of innovation: while associates are encouraged to be innovative they are not expected to make significant financial commitments without thorough review and participation by other associates and in line with business objectives.

Selection is rigorous. Would-be associates spend up to eight hours being interviewed, over three days. This careful selection appears to pay off, as more than half of the staff have worked at the company for at least ten years. A new associate is assigned one or more sponsors who help them become acquainted with the company and its ways of working, ensure they receive credit and recognition for their work, and ensure that they are fairly paid.

To ensure a fair and effective pay structure the company asks associates to rank their team members each year in order of contribution to the enterprise. This includes an associate's impact and effectiveness as well as past, present and future contributions. The company ensures that pay is competitive by regularly comparing the pay of Gore associates with their peers at other companies.

The benefit plan consists of core benefits and flexible benefits. Core benefits are provided to all eligible associates and include pay, holidays, sick pay, life insurance and the Associate Stock Option Plan (ASOP). The purpose of ASOP is to provide equity ownership in the company, and through that a degree of financial security in retirement. All associates can acquire a share in the company, in which the Gore family holds a major stake.

An associate from the United Kingdom commented:

Leadership probably happens in three different ways. We still have the concept of natural leaders emerging through followership. There are then some areas of the business where leaders are appointed, and we probably find that more in this plant where we have a large production operation. We need associates with operational expertise which meets our business needs.

Decisions to take on additional staff are made on a consultative basis. At the moment it's very much project driven in certain areas. So a group would be working on a specific new product development, and they'll look at the resources they require for that work – and if they haven't got the resources a decision will be taken to go outside. What therefore tends to happen is that people are brought into the business with a specific area of work in mind. Not necessarily a job description, but a role description. That would then settle that person into the business. Once that work commitment has finished they'll then try to seek an alternative role in the business, with another dedicated team.

We have about 140 associates in this plant, organised according to what we call the three-legged principle. The legs consist of sales, product management and manufacture, and these legs are bound together in areas such as marketing, administration, inside sales and vendor support. We also have a position called product specialist, and that person is typically someone with a technical background, who is perhaps working in sales. They are in effect sales people, developing very close links with our customers. They work very closely with our customers on current products, but also to identify customer requirements and move with them to research and develop new products. And we have a team of them in each plant. All of them take an industry sector. Say, for example, in the fabrics plant, we have a product specialist looking after the fire industry, one looking after police, one military, one ski. Each group covers customers throughout Europe.

Associates tend to be committed to one area of work. So, for example, here in industrial filtration we are working on products for office automation technology – basically photocopiers – and we then assemble a team to develop that product. There'd be some production people, engineers, admin support: somebody will have seen a need, researched the product, brought together a team.

The focus is very much on the R&D. One challenge is to retain the team-working ethos while working globally. There is a danger of duplication if the interests of separate teams in different parts of the world evolve in such a way that they are working on similar products. Yet at the same time we don't want to create structures or processes that stifle creativity. We don't want to say that people should focus on specific areas of research. We need to find ways of sharing expertise globally.

Freedom of choice is not total. People will be asked at some point to go on a work commitment by the leader of the business group. When there is a pressing business objective, someone leading a commitment will find the right person for the job, in a way that is best for them and the company. Leaders might be appointed because people recognise that they have exercised leadership within their function (say as a chief chemical engineer). It could also be that each plant has an overall business leader. We have a business leader for industrial filtration and, if there was a particular skill needed on an area of work, he may decide to ask somebody to commit to that.

Balance between procedures and guidelines, and human initiative

We do have standard procedures and rules and regulations. The underpinning principle is to keep them to the minimum, and it's about questioning why we need them. If there's a business reason why that is the best way to deal with it then we're not afraid to put in policies and procedures, for example ISO 9000. There is a mentality that people understand the need for processes when there's something tangible. So, in manufacturing, people accept that that is required. Less so in areas like HR, where there is a reluctance to do anything that people would see as a limiting structure. So if people can readily see the need, we put in procedures; but when it's not tangible we are very questioning about whether it's required. We are very flexible in the way we introduce things. If it increases profits, protects health and safety, and if people can see the tangible results, then there really isn't too much of a problem. The buy-in is absolutely essential.

How do you go about securing that buy-in?

You go and speak to key people and influence people, and you make a judgement as to who is key to get this project through, trying to see where opposition might come from, and trying to deal with it before you actually impose the procedure. You don't need everyone fully committed – apart from those who actually have to do something. Commitment in Gore is very much when you personally have to deliver something, so a commitment in Gore is when you commit to doing XYZ on a certain project. It's not in terms of 'you've got my support', it's 'I have to deliver for a certain project'. Buy-in is willingness to accept and to put the effort in on behalf of the team.

In a report accompanying the announcement of the 2007 'Britain's Best 100 Companies' award Karl Williamson, a member of the new product development team, said: 'It's nice to go to the shows and see the garment that you have had a hand in making.' He took a six-week job at the company to kill time after graduating 11 years ago and never left. 'There is something special about it,' he says. There must be – almost half (45 per cent) the workforce have been on the payroll for at least 10 years.

Carole-Anne Smith, the firm's European specialist for snow sports, admits that Gore was not initially an easy place to work. 'I hated it when I started,' she says. 'Gore challenges you as an individual more. I had come from a very structured organisation. Here you do not get a job specification, you get set the problem.'

This autonomy empowers workers at the firm, which gets top positive scores for staff believing they can make a difference (89 per cent), feeling fully involved (88 per cent) and finding work stimulating (85 per cent). Staff also say working at the firm is good for their personal growth, giving it a top score of 89 per cent.

Even though how you get the job done is up to you, workers are not left to go it alone. Asking for help is seen as a sign of strength. Each individual chooses a person to help them grow and develop, and people say colleagues go out of their way to help them and care a lot about each other (both 88 per cent) and are fun to work with (87 per cent).

After her initial reservations Smith is surprised she has been at Gore as long as she has: 'I never imagined I would stay longer than five years,' she says. Smith has travelled around the world with the firm and found it very accommodating when she requested reducing her working week to three days after having her children. 'I have no plans to leave,' she adds.

Sources: Company website; discussion with associates; *Sunday Times*, 11 March 2007. Copyrighted material reproduced with the permission of W.L. Gore and Associates. © 2005 W.L. Gore and Associates.

Part case questions

- How does W.L. Gore and Associates influence staff to work on vital projects?
- How do research staff influence each other? Compare the way that people at Gore and at Semco influence other members of the company.
- How is W.L. Gore and Associates balancing personal and institutional sources of power and influence?
- How does management ensure that associates are motivated to work on projects that are important to the company's future prosperity?
- If you were a talented research scientist, what would be the attractions and rewards of working for Gore?
- Which theories of human needs appear to be supported by the reported policies and attitudes at W.L. Gore and Associates?
- In what ways are the associates at Gore empowered?
- Why do teams seem to work so well for Gore? What benefits do you think they bring both to the business and to the individuals? What if teams compete, rather than cooperate?
- What, if any, differences are there between Gore's approach and that used by Cisco?

Part 5 Skills development

To help you develop your skills, as well as knowledge, this section includes tasks that relate the key themes covered in the Part to your daily life. Working through these will help you to deepen your understanding of the skills and insights that you can use in many situations.

Task 5.1 Acquiring power to influence others

Power is a feature of any group or organisation, and to work effectively people need to acquire and use power – the capacity of individuals to exert their will over others. Chapter 14 identified personal and organisational sources of power – coercive, reward, expertise and referent. It also showed that a person's position in the organisation can affect their access to power. Using some or all of these behaviours, based on the ideas in the book, will help you become more familiar with ways of increasing your power, and hence your ability to influence others.

1 Use tactics to influence others
Draw on the Yukl and Falbe (1990) research to select the right tactics to use when influencing others:

- Use rational persuasion – logical arguments backed up with convincing information – when influencing your boss.
- Use exchange, personal appeal and legitimating tactics (e.g. relating your request to organisational policy) when influencing colleagues.
- Use inspirational appeal and pressure when influencing subordinates.

2 Gain control over organisational resources
To use the power which comes from being able to offer something to others you want to influence, seek out opportunities that give you control over budgets, information, expertise, facilities – anything which others may value and that you can use in return. The investment and trouble in gaining that control will usually be worthwhile.

3 Manage your reputation – be visible
Try to understand what the culture of your organisation most values in successful staff, and what images it is best to avoid. Do they prefer those who are risk takers or those who play safe? Do the important things get agreed during social occasions or in formal meetings? How are people expected to behave with colleagues? Also:

- Ensure that your achievements are known about, and that people talk about them.
- Manage your boss – find out what is important to them, and try to help them achieve their goals – why irritate a person who can affect your career?

4 Build your network
Research clearly shows that networking pays – by giving contacts, sources of information, sources of rewards and so on. Networks take time to develop, so don't waste time before you start. They also need maintaining – do people favours that they will remember when you want something from them.

5 Develop your expertise

Ensure that the skills and knowledge you have are relevant to the organisation, and that you keep them up to date. Concentrating on significant new areas of technical or administrative knowledge will soon mean that you are acknowledged as the local expert, so that others seek out your views and opinions.

6 Be ready to share power with subordinates

They will probably be more committed to working for you, and more importantly, delegating will give you more time to cultivate the external and senior contacts you need to develop your power.

Task 5.2 | Motivating others

Being able to motivate others (colleagues as well as subordinates) will be one of the keys to your performance as a manager. While there is no single answer to this managerial challenge, the theories in Chapter 15 give some clues about the practices and skills you can use.

1 Recognise individual differences

Individuals have unique interests and needs, and all motivational theories need to be implemented with that in mind. They help to indicate likely motives and processes, but motivating people depends on recognising their diversity.

2 Enable people to pursue their goals through their work

If responsible, informed people are able to do work that satisfies their needs they will be more committed and motivated to it than if it does not satisfy them. People who seek challenge and achievement will thrive in jobs that enable them to set goals, have autonomy in how they do the work and receive feedback on performance.

3 Use goals imaginatively

Goal-setting theory includes some clear prescriptions about the motivational effects of goals – such as setting goals that are clear and challenging, but achievable; allow staff to participate in setting goals or explain the reasons for them convincingly; provide feedback on performance. Also try to build and maintain people's self-confidence in their abilities, as this affects how they react to challenging goals.

4 Ensure that effort will lead to performance

People will be more motivated if they see a predictable link between effort and performance – which can be done by ensuring they are clear about what is expected, have adequate training opportunities, have competent colleagues, and have adequate facilities and technologies.

5 Ensure that performance is clearly linked to rewards

People will also be more motivated if they are confident that performance will be rewarded – so ensure that appraisal and reward schemes are seen to be well designed and fairly administered.

6 Check for equity

While equity theory is hard to test empirically, strong anecdotal evidence shows the dangers of inadvertent management action leading to a sense of inequity and therefore a loss of motivation. Ensure that perceived differences in the ratio of inputs to rewards can be justified, and also that people are using appropriate bases of comparison.

7 Ensure extrinsic rewards are satisfied as well as intrinsic ones

People value extrinsic rewards as well as intrinsic ones. Money matters to most people, and ensuring that they see their pay is adequate, and fair for the work they do, provides an essential basis on which to build other motivational practices.

Task 5.3   Interpersonal communication

Interpersonal communication skills are a vital management skill. This activity helps you develop your awareness and understanding of listening.

Answer *True* or *False* to each of these statements:

1 People's thoughts can interfere with their listening.
2 People may resist listening to others who blame or get angry with them.
3 People are more likely to talk to those with whom they feel safe than to those with whom they do not.
4 People who have something they are keen to say are good at listening.
5 Some people listen too much because they are afraid of revealing themselves.
6 Talking is more important than listening.
7 People who feel very emotional about issues make good listeners.
8 People who are very angry are rarely good listeners.
9 People are less likely to hear messages that agree with their view than messages which challenge those views.
10 Fatigue never affects the quality of people's listening.

How did you score?

The correct answers to the good listening test are:

1 True	2 True	3 True	4 False	5 True
6 False	7 False	8 True	9 False	10 False

Give yourself two points for each correct answer. Most accomplished listeners will score 16 or more. A score under 10 suggests you can benefit by improving your listening skills, as you are probably missing a lot of useful information.

Task 5.4   Observing a group

A useful skill to develop is that of observing the processes within a group – that is, how the members work together. This can give you a new insight into the successful and unsuccessful group practices, which you can then use to improve future groups.

One method is to observe the behaviours within the group, noting how other members react and how that affects the performance of the team – perhaps using the list in Chapter 17:

Proposing	Putting forward a suggestion, idea or course of action
Supporting	Declaring agreement or support for an individual or their idea
Building	Developing or extending an idea or suggestion from someone else
Disagreeing	Criticising another person's statement
Giving information	Giving or clarifying facts, ideas or opinions
Seeking information	Seeking facts, ideas or opinions from others

Alternatively you could assess how well a team is performing a task by asking, at the end of a meeting:

- What did people do or say that helped or hindered the group's performance?
- What went well during that task that we should try to repeat?
- What did not go well, which we could improve?

Another idea is to rate the team using these scales – circle the number that best reflects your opinion of the discussion in a group.

1 How effectively did the group obtain and use necessary information?

1	2	3	4	5	6	7
Badly						Well

2 To what extent was the group's organisation suitable for the task?

1	2	3	4	5	6	7
Unsuitable						Suitable

3 To what extent did members really listen to each other?

1	2	3	4	5	6	7
Not at all						All the time

4 How fully were members involved in decision taking?

1	2	3	4	5	6	7
Low involvement					High involvement	

5 To what extent did you enjoy working with this group?

1	2	3	4	5	6	7
Not at all						Very much

6 How well was time used?

1	2	3	4	5	6	7
Badly						Well

Part 6

CONTROLLING

Introduction

Any purposeful human activity needs some degree of control if it is to achieve what is intended. From time to time you check where you are in relation to your destination. The sooner you do this, the more confident you are of being on track. Frequent checks ensure you take corrective action quickly to avoid wasting effort and resources.

An owner-manager can often exercise control by personal observation, reference to limited paperwork and then a decision about corrective action. As the organisation grows so does the complexity. It becomes increasingly difficult to know the current position as work goes on in many separate places at the same time. People in those separate places may differ about their precise objectives and targets.

To help them exercise control, management is able to use a range of systems and techniques. Chapter 18 introduces generic ideas on control – the nature of the process, tools for control and the human issues raised by control systems. Financial control is clearly one form so Chapter 19 introduces the main financial measures that people use to assess performance. Chapter 20 reviews the main concepts in operations management.

The Part Case is Tesco, Britain's largest retailer, which illustrates many approaches to controlling an ever-expanding business.

Chapter 18

Performance measurement and control

Aim

To show why control is one of the four tasks of managing, and how the design of control systems can support performance.

Objectives

By the end of your work on this chapter you should be able to outline the concepts below in your own terms and:

1 Define control and explain why it is an essential activity in managing

2 Describe and give examples of the generic control activities of setting objectives, measuring, comparing and correcting

3 Explain how the choice of suitable measures of performance can reflect an explicit theory, such as the competing values framework or the balanced scorecard

4 Compare the features of output, behavioural, cultural and concertive controls

5 Explain why those designing control systems need to take account of human reactions

6 Distinguish between mechanistic and organic strategies of control, and indicate when each is most suitable.

Key terms

This chapter introduces the following ideas:

control	balanced scorecard
control process	efficiency
control system	effectiveness
performance	feedforward control
range of variation	concurrent control
immediate corrective action	feedback control
basic corrective action	management by objectives
organisational performance	

Each is a term defined within the text, as well as in the Glossary at the end of the book.

AXA is a French insurance group that is now one of the world's largest companies. Founded in 1816 as a fire insurance company in Rouen, the original company extended its range of activities by growth and acquisition until, by 1982, it was the largest private sector insurer in France. In 1985 the Board decided to expand internationally, and changed the name to AXA, as this was easy for people from all over the world to pronounce. In 1991 Claude Bebear, the then chairman and CEO formulated a vision of becoming a global company:

To become a multinational an enterprise must outgrow the very notion of nationality: all its entities, whatever their market, all its employees, whatever their nationality, must be dealt with on equal terms and must pursue one single identical object: the considered interest of the whole enterprise. (p. 4)

The company expanded first in Europe by acquiring other insurance businesses, and in 1991 made its first purchase in the United States. This was followed by further acquisitions and growth in North America, Australasia, South-East Asia and China. While concentrating on acquisitions to grow, the company also constantly evaluated its portfolio to ensure that it continued to meet its business objectives: units that did not do so were sold, such as a health insurance business in Australia in 2002.

The strategy of growth by acquisition meant that AXA accumulated companies with a great variety of products, which worked under many different national rules and traditions. Bebear was determined to shape these into a truly global company rather than have AXA remain a French company with several international subsidiaries.

By 2006 AXA was focused on three lines of business:

life and savings – individual and group savings, life and health insurance
property and casualty – individual motor and household insurance, company insurance
asset management – investment management for individuals.

Life and savings was by far the biggest segment, accounting for 65 per cent of premium income, followed by property and casualty (29 per cent) and asset management (6 per cent).

Photolibrary.com

The company is ultimately managed by a supervisory board that is accountable to the shareholders, and which must approve major decisions such as large acquisitions, strategic partnerships and dividend payments. It also appoints the chairman and members of the management board, whose members are each responsible for defined functions such as 'brand and communications'. Below that are the CEOs of each of the company's ten business units, each of which is responsible for a geographic area (such as Asia Pacific).

By 2006 AXA had over 110,000 employees and over 50 million clients. In announcing its results for 2006 the chairman noted strong growth in each of its three businesses:

life and savings – income up 15 per cent
property and casualty – income up 4 per cent
asset management – income up 29 per cent.

In each case the growth exceeded the ambitious targets that had been set in the current strategy document, Ambition 2012.

Sources: Based on company annual reports; company website.

Case questions 18.1

- Why will control matter to AXA?
- What will be the main issues to consider in developing control systems in AXA?
- What examples of control systems can you see in the story so far?

18.1 Introduction

Control is the process of monitoring activities to ensure that results are in line with plan, and acting to correct significant deviations.

As AXA grew, its chairman realised that **control** would be critical to the success of the company. Insurance is about managing risks – ensuring that the insurer collects enough money in premiums to be able to meet the liabilities it owes to its policy holders – liabilities which may arise many years in the future. All insurance companies must have controls in place to manage this risk – but in AXA's case there are other control issues. These include ensuring that the separate lines of business are profitable, that strategic decisions enhance long-term value, and that people in the businesses around the world act in ways that enhance the AXA reputation. There are also strategic issues – how to balance central and local control, and whether to take a mechanistic or organic approach to control.

All managers exercise control as they try to add value by transforming resources into outputs of greater value. However thoroughly they plan their objectives and how to meet them, internal and external events intervene. So they need to supplement the activity of planning with that of controlling – checking that work is going to plan, and if necessary taking corrective action. The sooner they note deviations, the easier it is to bring performance into line with the plan. This applies at all levels – a supervisor responsible for the performance of a team in a customer service centre, a divisional manager responsible for delivering a product or service, a board member responsible for overall company performance. If a manager is considering an innovation, such as a move to team working, he or she may set up a pilot study in one department to see if it improves output. To do that they will have a target of the output they expect, which they can compare with actual output. That is a simple control process, showing how control is essential to an informed decision.

In this sense, control has many positive meanings – standing for order, predictability or reliability. If things are under control, suppliers know what to deliver and when, people know what they are expected to do, customers know when to expect a delivery, staff know they will be paid. In this sense, control is an essential part of organisational life: it helps to ensure that cooperative work by many people and units collectively adds value to resources. An absence of such control implies uncertainty, chaos, inefficiency and waste – an organisation that is destroying, rather than enhancing, value.

However, control depends on influencing people, so designing a control system is not a technical, rational process, but one that needs to take account of human factors and the context. Control also depends on power, and can alter the balance of power.

The chapter begins by outlining the generic steps in control, and its potential benefits. The sections that follow consider deciding what to measure, when to measure and how to do it, including the balanced scorecard. A section introduces a human perspective on control, which is followed by one on broader strategies that guide the design of controls.

18.2 The control process

The **control process** is the generic activity of setting performance standards, measuring actual performance, comparing actual performance with the standards, and acting to correct deviations or modify standards.

A **control system** is the way the elements in the control process are designed and combined in a specific situation.

The **control process** is intended to support the achievement of objectives at any level, from the individual to the enterprise, so it needs to reflect those objectives and set of beliefs about the behaviour required to meet them. Managers design specific **control systems** for different organisational activities. Although their degree of formality and explicitness varies, the control process incorporates the activities shown in Figure 18.1 – setting objectives or standards, measuring actual performance, comparing this against the standard, and taking action to correct any significant gap between the two.

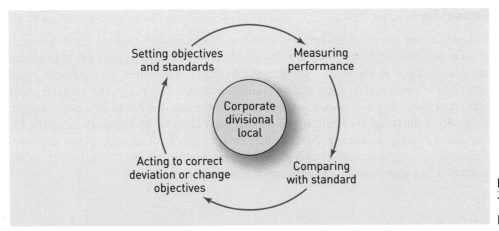

Figure 18.1

The control process

Setting objectives – what and when to measure

Objectives provide direction and a standard of **performance** to aim for. The standard will itself have an effect on its achievement – standards that are too high will be ignored as unattainable, while standards that are too low will artificially lower performance (see Chapter 15 on goal-setting theory). Some measures are generic – widely used and relevant to most management situations – such as employee satisfaction or absence; actual costs against budgeted costs; or actual sales against target sales. Managers will also use measures that are unique to their activity and area of responsibility – pages of advertising booked or students recruited.

Some aspects of performance can be measured in apparently objective and quantifiable terms – such as sales, profit or return on assets. Equally important aspects of performance (product innovation, flexibility, company reputation or service quality) are more open to subjective interpretations, and here managers look for acceptable qualitative measures. Even if relatively vague, they may be just as useful to the control function.

Performance is the result of an activity.

Measuring – the tools of control

Control requires that performance can be measured against a target. Table 18.1 shows the sources of information people can use to measure performance, and their advantages and disadvantages: combining them gives a more reliable picture of performance than relying on one alone.

Table 18.1

Common sources of information for measuring performance

	Advantages	**Disadvantages**
Personal observation	Gives first-hand knowledge Information is not filtered Indicates the manager is interested	Subject to personal bias Time consuming Obtrusive – people see what is happening
Oral reports	Quick way to get information Allows for verbal and non-verbal feedback	Information is filtered No permanent record
Written reports	Comprehensive, and can show trends and relationships Easy to store and retrieve	Time to prepare May ignore subjective factors
Online information systems	Rapid feedback, often during the process	Information overload May be stressful to staff

Comparing

This step shows the variation between actual and planned performance. There is bound to be some variation from the plan, so before taking action a manager needs to know the acceptable **range of variation** – the acceptable limits of variation between actual and planned performance. As long as the variation is within this range, the manager need take no action – but as it goes beyond that range, the case for action becomes stronger, especially if the trend is continuing to be adverse. This stage also implies searching for the causes of a significant variation, to increase the chances of an appropriate response. Failure to meet a standard set may have little to do with the efforts of the unit being measured, but a great deal to do with events elsewhere.

The **range of variation** sets the acceptable limits within which performance can vary from standard without requiring remedial action.

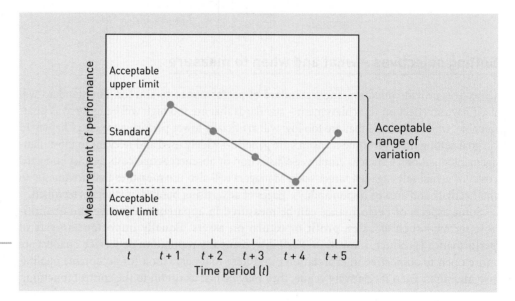

Figure 18.2

Defining the acceptable range of variation

Correcting

The final step is to act on significant variations from the plan – either to correct future performance or to revise the standard. Attempts to bring performance up to the required standard could involve any aspects of the transformation process within the manager's area of responsibility – such as taking on more or different staff, changing a manufacturing process or increasing prices. They may involve taking some **immediate corrective action** (such as cutting prices to sell excess stocks) or looking for initiating **basic corrective action** to identify the sources of failure. This could, for example, mean dealing with longer-term issues of product design or quality if these seem to be the reason for poor sales.

Immediate corrective action aims to correct problems at once to get performance back on track.

Basic corrective action aims to understand the deeper sources of performance failure, and tries to correct them.

Sometimes the variation may be the result of an unrealistic standard: changing conditions have made it unattainable or, conversely, it may have been set too low, making it too easy to achieve, and so it needs to be raised.

Figure 18.3 shows the relationship between these four steps in the control process.

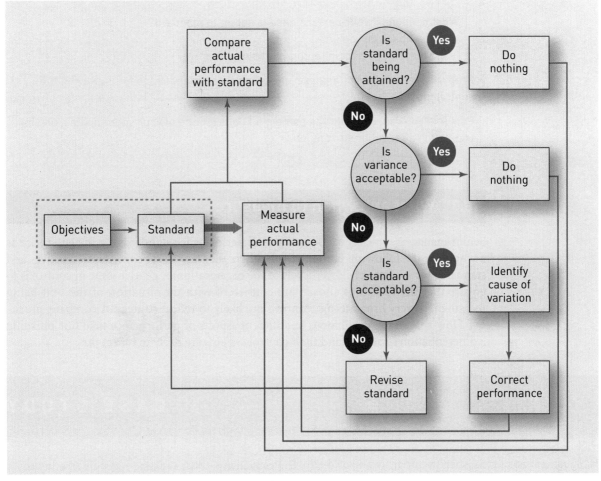

Figure 18.3 Managerial decisions in the control process
Source: Robbins and Coulter (2005, p. 464).

Activity 18.1   **Assessing control systems**

Part A Consider the course you are studying. With your fellow students, analyse how your performance on the course is controlled by answering these questions:

What standards of performance are you expected to achieve?
Who sets the standards?
Do you know what the standards are?
Are the standards clear or ambiguous? Too high or too low?

How is your performance measured?
Do you know what the criteria are? How often is performance measured?

Who compares your performance with the standard?
Is this done publicly or in secret? By one person or by several?
Is the comparison objective or subjective?

▶

What happens if your performance is not up to standard?
What feedback do you get?
Is the feedback useful in telling you how to improve?

Prepare a report on your analysis, including recommendations for improving the control process.

Part B If you can, consider the same questions for one of your subordinates, and for yourself in a recent or current job.

18.3 What and when to measure

Senior managers typically set objectives and performance standards for the enterprise as a whole for the following period, which others then use to set consistent objectives and standards for successively lower levels of the organisation. A generic issue in control is to ensure that the measures chosen are consistent with the situation of the unit being measured. In very broad terms, controls are likely to reflect strategy. A company pursuing a low-cost strategy will focus on different aspects of performance than one pursuing a differentiation strategy – and their control systems are likely to reflect this.

AXA – the case continues   www.axa.com   CASE STUDY

Management has established five priorities, known as 'cylinders of growth' to guide the company towards operational excellence:

1 **Product innovation** – a source of differentiation that reflects AXA's desire to offer added value every time it introduces a new product.
2 **Core business expertise** – aims to offer the best service at the best price.
3 **Distribution management** – the company aims to continually reduce the administrative burden on the agents upon whom it relies to sell its products.
4 **Quality of service** – all AXA employees are expected to follow the AXA way of continuous improvements in processes.

5 **Productivity** – AXA seeks to reduce operating costs and improve quality each year.

Case questions 18.2

- For each of these general objectives, identify at least one measurable standard of performance
- For each of those, explain what information you would require to be able to measure performance against that standard.

Measures that are compatible with a situation are more likely to be accepted as valid than measures which are not. If managers use measures that staff see as inappropriate they will resent them, and the control system is unlikely to have the intended effects on behaviour. Choosing control measures reflects the manager's theory about those that are most suitable for the circumstances: the competing values framework and the balanced scorecard offer ways of thinking systematically about this choice.

Competing values framework

The competing values framework of Quinn *et al.* (2003) used in Chapter 2 provides one tool for considering what measures to use. It sets out four models of management, which represent different ways of analysing effectiveness. Although presented as 'competing' Quinn *et al.* also point out that they are parts of a larger whole, in the sense that they focus on different criteria of effectiveness – implying different measures to judge performance. Table 18.2 lists the alternative values, and illustrates performance measures (drawing on Harrison, 2005) consistent with each.

Table 18.2

Performance standards based on the competing values framework

Value	Criteria of effectiveness	Examples of performance measures
Rational goal	Attaining goals	Achievement of objectives, task completion, profits
	Output quantity	Sales, profits, productivity, efficiency
	Output quality	Reliability, service, responsiveness, reputation, recognition
Internal process	Efficiency and costs	Operating costs, productivity, efficiency
	Continuity, smooth workflow	Work coordination; adequacy, quality and distribution of information
Human relations	Employee satisfaction	Quality of working life, absenteeism, turnover, health and safety
	Interpersonal relations	Trust, diversity and community relations, conflict resolution
	Involvement	Participation in decision making, empowerment
Open systems	Resources: quantity	Financial resources, physical assets, grants and budgets secured
	Resources: quality	Skills and reputation of staff, knowledge base; quality of clients (student admission grades)
	Proactiveness	Impact on environment – clients, competitors, regulators, suppliers, entry into new markets
	Competitive position	Standing compared to competitors; reputation for leadership
	Adaptation	Capacity to cope with external change and uncertainty; flexibility in handling crises, surprises
	Innovativeness	Technological and administrative innovation; implementation of new technologies and practices

Sources: Based on Quinn *et al.* (2003) and Harrison (2005).

Such measures of **organisational performance** show how well managers have conducted their role of adding value to the resources they have used in their unit or area of responsibility.

Organisational performance is the accumulated results of all the organisation's work processes and activities.

The balanced scorecard

Kaplan and Norton (1992, p. 71) noted that while 'traditional financial performance measures worked well for the industrial era ... they are out of step with the skills and competencies companies are trying to master today'. Financial measures are still essential, but carry the hazard that short-term targets may be met by practices that damage long-run performance – for example by postponing investment in equipment or customer service. They found that senior executives recognised that no single measure could provide a clear performance target or focus attention on the critical areas of the

The **balanced scorecard** is a performance measure that looks at four areas: financial, customer, internal processes and innovation which contribute to organisational performance.

business. Rather, they wanted a balanced presentation of both financial and operational measures. Their research enabled them to devise a **balanced scorecard** – a set of measures that gives managers a fast but comprehensive view of the business. It includes financial measures that tell the results of actions already taken, and complements these with operational measures on customer satisfaction, internal processes and innovation – measures which drive future financial performance.

It allows managers to view performance in several areas simultaneously, by providing answers to four questions:

1 How do customers see us? (customer perspective);
2 What must we excel at? (internal perspective);
3 Can we continue to improve and create value? (innovation and learning perspective);
4 How do we look to shareholders? (financial perspective).

The scorecard illustrated in Figure 18.4 brings together in a single management report many elements of a company's agenda, such as the need to be customer oriented, to shorten response time, improve quality or cut the time taken to launch a new product. It also guards against the dangers of working in isolation, as it requires senior managers to consider all the important operational measures together. They can then judge whether improvement in one area may have been achieved at the expense of another.

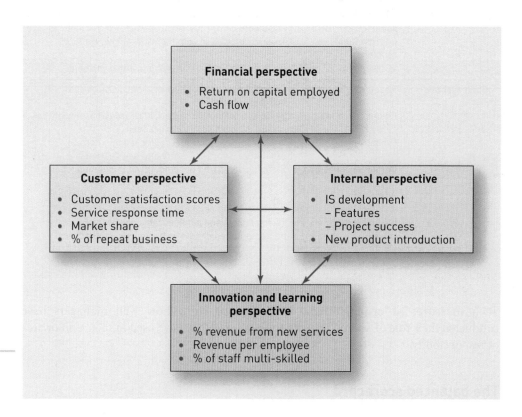

Figure 18.4

The balanced scorecard – an example

Kaplan and Norton (1993) advocate that companies spend time identifying, for each of the four measures, the external and internal factors which are important to them, and developing suitable measures of performance for these. For example, under the customer heading, they may believe that customers are concerned about time, quality, performance, service and cost. They should therefore articulate goals for each factor, and then translate these goals into specific measures.

The approach has been widely adopted (Neely and Najjar, 2006) – Tesco, the Part Case uses it, and there is an illustration of their scorecard on p. 684. Despite its popularity, Akkermanns and Oorschot (2005) point out that it should be applied critically by asking:

- Are the selected measures the right ones?
- Should there be more, or fewer?
- At what levels should performance targets be set?

Moreover, if the measures are to reflect the different perspectives within a business, should people from those perspectives help to set the measures? They go on to describe how they sought to overcome these difficulties in developing a balanced scorecard for a Dutch insurance company, while McAdam and Walker (2003) describe its application in UK local government, illustrating the process with four case studies.

Activity 18.2 Starting a balanced scorecard

Begin to develop a balanced scorecard for your unit.

- Note possible goals and measures under each of the four headings.
- Compare your results with a colleague working on a different unit.

Comment on the strengths and weaknesses of the balanced scorecard for performance measurement.

Efficiency or effectiveness?

Performance can also be measured in terms of efficiency or effectiveness.

Efficiency

Efficiency ('doing things right') is a measure of output divided by the inputs needed to produce the output. It is widely used to show how productive a unit is, and how well people have managed it – the more output for the fewer inputs, the better, since that implies that value is being added to the resources. A simple measure of output would be sales revenue (number sold × price), while input can be measured by the cost of acquiring and transforming resources into the output. An increase in the ratio of output to input indicates an increase in efficiency. Many are under constant pressure from competitors or their shareholders to produce their output more efficiently, by using fewer resources.

> **Efficiency** is a measure of the inputs required for each unit of output.

Effectiveness

Effectiveness ('doing the right things') is a measure of how well the outcomes of an activity relate to the broader objectives of the unit – that is, how well it supports the achievement of broader goals. A library can measure the efficiency of its cataloguers by recording the number of volumes catalogued by each employee. That would not measure effectiveness, which would require measures of accuracy, consistency, timeliness or maintenance of the catalogue. A delivery service can measure efficiency (cost of the service) or effectiveness (predictability, frequency of collections, or accuracy of deliveries).

> **Effectiveness** is a measure of how well an activity contributes to achieving organisational goals.

Measuring performance in public or not-for-profit enterprises

Public and not-for-profit enterprises need control as much as any other – but the measures will often be different. Historically attention often focused on inputs (number of nurses recruited or hospital beds closed), but governments are increasingly attempting to move the focus of control towards measuring outcomes, such as quality of service (waiting times or mortality rates).

The choice of measure is often contentious, since stakeholders in the enterprise will favour different measures – and there may be uncertainty about which activities will contribute most to performance – see the Management in Practice feature.

---

management in practice — **Performance indicators in child protection**

Munro (2004) points out that the broad objective of protecting children from abuse can be linked to performance indicators such as:

- re-registration on the child protection register
- reviews of child protection cases
- duration on the child protection register
- relative spend on family support

and these in turn can be measured against standards of achievement such as 'by year 2000, reduce by 10 per cent the proportion of children who are re-registered, compared to 1997'.

She notes there is a distinction between service outcomes (removing a child from a protection register) and user outcomes (ensuring the child is safe from abuse): 'Since the ultimate goal is to make a difference to the user, user outcomes are the most accurate measure' (p.1085) but observes that service outcomes are more widely used.

Setting performance indicators implies that focusing on these areas will have most effect on meeting goals, but in many areas of social work setting indicators has 'involved theoretical assumptions that have no clear authority from empirical research or empirical consensus' (p. 1084).

Source: Munro (2004).

Activity 18.3 — **Collecting examples of effectiveness criteria**

- Which criteria are used to measure performance in your area of work?
- Select a business, and go to its website. What criteria are used to measure performance?

Timing

Managers can use control systems before, during and after an activity.

Feedforward control

Feedforward control focuses on preventing problems as it takes place before the work activity.

Feedforward control is a form of control that anticipates problems before an activity, the aim being to prevent problems rather than having to correct them after the damage has been done. They include preventive maintenance programmes, in which equipment parts are inspected or replaced before they wear out, so reducing the risk of costly delays when a part breaks unexpectedly.

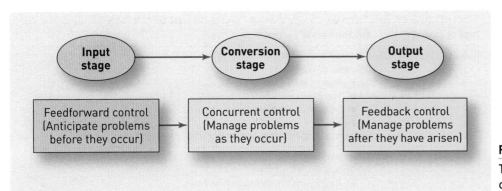

Figure 18.5

Three types of control

Concurrent control

If a manager uses **concurrent control**, this means he or she is exercising control during an activity, detecting and correcting problems with the least possible delay. The best-known example would be a manager directly supervising an operation – by walking around the work area, seeing staff, perhaps meeting customers. They can then see directly what is going on, and obtain feedback from employees and customers about recent and current performance. Many computer systems build in this form of control, by alerting the user to faults or errors (your computer's spell-checker, for example, or an engine diagnostic system in a car) during the performance of a task.

Concurrent control takes place while an activity is in progress.

Feedback control

Under a system of **feedback control** information about performance is gathered after the activity is completed. This has the disadvantage that any problems of quality or cost have now occurred, and action can only be aimed at preventing a recurrence. But for many controls this is the only form that is possible – financial statements, for example, are inevitably prepared after an activity, and any problems they identify have already happened – they are a form of feedback control.

Feedback control takes place after an activity is complete.

Feedback control is when information about performance is gathered when an activity is complete.

Tools of control

Research into performance management and control has identified many ways in which managers aim to measure and control performance. These are often grouped into the categories of output, behavioural and cultural. Table 18.3 summarises these, and the following sections explain them.

18.4 Output control

This is the activity of measuring the quantity of output for a definable area of work – whether for a unit or the business as a whole. If meeting these targets is linked to rewards (and failing to meet them is linked to punishments) then they are a major aspect of the control system, as they will have a clear and direct influence on behaviour. Individuals and departments can be given financial targets, performance standards and budgets that are expected to guide their performance – and against which it can be measured.

Table 18.3

Types of organisational control

Type of control	Mechanisms of control
Output	Financial measures Operational measures • Productivity • Waste • Customer satisfaction • Etc. Operating budgets – expressing targets for the operational measures
Behavioural	Direct personal control Organisational structure • Defining tasks and responsibilities • Decision-making limits • Reporting requirements Rules and procedures Technology
Cultural	HRM control • Selection procedures • Appraisal and rewards • Values and beliefs • Socialisation • Reinforcement

Financial measures

These are widely used to measure the overall performance of the organisation, common ones being profit ratios, liquidity and activity ratios.

Profit ratios measure how much profit the organisation has made from the assets used. The return on investment (RoI) measure is very widely used, as it shows the firm's net income before taxes, divided by its total assets. Gross profit margin shows the difference between the revenue received from sales and the cost of making and delivering the product or service. The greater these measures are, the more value managers are adding to the resources they use.

Liquidity ratios enable senior managers or investors to judge the ability of the business to meet short-term obligations. The ratio of current assets to current liabilities (assets divided by liabilities) indicates how easily it can meet its debts: an organisation may be trading profitably, but delays in customers paying their bills will reduce current assets, and move the ratio in an unfavourable direction. This would eventually threaten the firm with bankruptcy, so this is an important control measure, giving an early warning of potential difficulties.

Activity ratios show how effective managers are at using the assets available to them. For example the inventory (stock) ratio takes the cost of goods sold and divides it by the value of the inventory. The higher this ratio is, the more efficiently managers are using inventory – they are managing in a way that uses stock quickly, so that it costs less to hold and there is less risk of having to discard obsolete stocks of materials or components.

Financial measures appear objective and unambiguous, and so are widely used by managers and analysts to assess the performance of a company. Senior managers will normally set targets for each of these across the business for the following financial year, and managers' performance will then be measured against them. That exerts a powerful influence on behaviour. Financial measures show the results of past activities, but do not in themselves show what activities a manager should focus on to ensure good financial results in future. To encourage that behaviour, senior managers need to set more specific organisational goals, for each unit.

Examples of output controls

This activity invites you to gather examples of financial control measures. Go to the AXA website (or that of any other organisation which interests you) and find their recent financial report (usually under 'investor relations' or similar).

- What financial controls do they use?
- Do they show performance has improved, or not?

If you want further guidance, consult Chapter 19 – especially the Chapter Case (BASF) and Section 19.3.

Operational measures

Once the higher-level financial targets have been set, senior managers can then set performance standards for functions and divisions. These will include financial targets derived from the higher-level ones, but also non-financial targets relevant to the division or function. Production managers may be given targets for output, waste reduction, energy use, labour costs and many more. Transport managers, sales managers, marketing managers and all the others will be given specific goals to meet, which are expected to contribute to overall performance.

AXA – the case continues www.axa.com   CASE STUDY

The executive committee consists of the CEOs of each of the ten business units and members of the management board. The executive committee conducts quarterly business reviews to evaluate performance and monitor the progress of key projects.

The CEO of each business unit (such as Asia Pacific or United Kingdom and Ireland) provides the management board with quarterly reports on performance and operational issues, and the meetings then compare the performance of the unit with the established target. At the same time, economic and market trends, and the competitive environment, are examined.

Key performance indicators that are measured include:

Customers	market share
	income from premium payments
	customer satisfaction measures
Employees	satisfaction with AXA (measured by a regular survey)
Shareholders	profit ratios
	cost:income ratios
	present value of future profits in the life business

Source: Company website and annual reports.

Case questions 18.3

AXA appears to be using a range of measures similar to the balanced scorecard.

- Go to its website and consult the annual report, to identify the performance measures it uses.
- Group these under the headings of Figure 18.4.
- Use information from the annual report to gather information on recent performance.

Operating budgets

The final step in creating an output control system is to set operating budgets for each manager in charge of some resources – typically a manager at one level setting budgets for those immediately below them in the hierarchy, usually with some negotiation between them. A budget is simply a numerical plan for allocating resources between activities. They can cover financial matters such as revenue, current expenditure and perhaps an allowance for larger capital items, such as equipment.

They can also include non-financial items such as hours worked, space or equipment utilisation, quality or customer satisfaction. They offer a quite direct way of measuring performance and comparing it with the plan to see if managers need to take corrective action. It can be a way of delegating other aspects of control to people in the unit concerned: once the output targets are agreed, they can be left with a degree of autonomy over how they achieve them, without management interference. At the end of the period for which the budget is set, managers can be assessed on whether or not they have met the budget – and as such it is expected to influence their behaviour.

 **Standards of comparison**

In designing a control system managers must also decide what time periods and comparison standards to use. They can compare:

● current and past performance
● performance of units within their organisation
● performance of their organisation relative to others
● performance in relation to some minimum, or ideal, standard.

The time period for comparison varies from hours to years, and will affect the results of, and reactions to, the control process.

Financial measures, operational goals and budgets are the key components in a system of output control. Most organisations develop such systems to enable managers to track performance throughout the year, so that they can act quickly if actual performance is deviating from that which was expected.

18.5 Behaviour control

While output controls provide one way of influencing behaviour, they can be supplemented by a set of practices that encourage their achievement – direct supervision, structures, rules and procedures, management by objectives and control through machinery.

Direct personal control

In small organisations most control is of this type, in the sense that the owner or the small management team can see directly what is happening. They can personally inspect and report on progress, quickly see if it is in line with the plan, and if necessary take remedial action. Done with enthusiasm, sensitivity and good humour this method is very effective – done clumsily and staff will see it as intrusive and overbearing.

Organisation structure

Most organisations set out what people are expected to do by giving them job descriptions that record the person's tasks and responsibilities. These can be very narrowly and specifically defined, or they can be broad and defined in very general terms. They may also establish with whom the job holder is expected to communicate, and the boundaries of their decision-making responsibility. In these ways they are a form of control, as they constrain people by specifying what they can or cannot do, and what output standards they are expected to achieve. Similarly organisations can be very centralised, with control being held at the top, or the opposite.

Rules and procedures

As organisations become too large to depend on personal control, they can develop rules and procedures to control what the growing number of people in the organisation do, and alert more senior people if there are significant deviations. Rules establish acceptable behaviour and levels of performance and as such are a way of controlling behaviour. They can guide people on how to conduct the business – how to perform the tasks, how to apply for a new piece of equipment, what to do in the event of a customer complaint, what to do when a customer places an order.

Management by objectives

Some organisations use a system called management by objectives, in which managers and their staff, at all levels in the hierarchy, agree their goals for the following period. The approach is partly based on goal-setting theory (Chapter 15), which predicts that the level of difficulty of a goal will affect the effort people put into achieving it. The Management in Practice feature illustrates the method.

Management by objectives is a system in which managers and staff agree their objectives, and then measure progress towards them periodically.

Management by objectives in a consultancy

Dirsmith *et al.* (1997) report on the evolution of control in a major consultancy. During the 1990s it grew rapidly from local offices offering a range of services to companies in the area, to a major international firm organised as a centralised, international business. This greater centralisation was driven by a desire to deal with major international clients, and to do so the consultancy sought to harmonise audit practices across the firm, centralise authority and formalise management control systems.

A major formal control tool which it used was that of management by objectives, in which senior managers establish operating objectives, usually in quantitative terms such as the monetary value of fees collected from clients. These were set for the firm as a whole, and then broken down into smaller objectives for local offices and the professional staff within them. Senior partners in the firm regularly visited regional offices to ensure that they were meeting the plan. ▶

This formal system was reinforced by a system of mentoring, which was intended to focus on the professional development of individuals. This was intended to be an informal social process, in which experienced partners offered regular and informal advice to junior staff on how to behave and appear like a partner. This covered not only dress and appearance, but also how to conduct their relationships with clients and partners, and how to focus on business objectives.

The research concluded that while the two systems of control were created separately, and with different aims (one focused on the firm, the other on the individual) they gradually came to reinforce each other, moving the process towards more uniform and centrally controlled practices.

Source: Dirsmith *et al.* (1997).

Control through machinery

This is when machines or information systems are designed to control, directly or indirectly, what people do. Direct technological controls occur where the machine directs what people do or say. Assembly lines move the object being made along a moving conveyor, with operators performing a short task to add another piece to the product, with almost no scope to alter the way they work. The scripts in a call centre that specify the speed with which calls are answered, the questions to ask, how to respond to customer questions, how to close the conversation, have a similar controlling effect on the way a person works. The speed of work is paced by the machine, the time spent on the task is very short, and there is limited scope for interaction with fellow workers. Video surveillance is sometimes used to monitor aspects of a worker's performance. In process industries such as oil refining or brewing, computer sensors capture information on process performance, compare it with set criteria and, if needed, automatically adjust the equipment to keep the process in line with the plan. Airport design controls very tightly the way passengers move through them.

 **Using technology to control staff**

A travel company introduced a networked computer system linking all of its branches to head office. Many benefits were expected and achieved, one of which was that, having sold a holiday, staff should work in a more disciplined routine to complete the transaction. The IT director:

> We are finding that paper is never a standard system – there are always different ways you can handle paper. You can always choose to fill in a form or not, choose to complete a box or not. We expect that automation will finally provide the disciplined system that people must adhere to.

Source: Boddy and Gunson (1996).

Indirectly machinery enables managers to control by giving them accurate and timely information about performance, which can guide their corrective action if required.

Using a dashboard to see the big picture

A 'dashboard' is software that presents corporate information, such as sales data or customer service requests, on a PC in colour graphics, just like the speedometer of a car. Lawrence Ellison, founder of Oracle Corporation, is one of a rapidly growing number of keen users of the technology. It lets him identify latest sales information in seconds:

> Like the instrument panel in a car [it] displays critical information in easy-to-read graphics, assembled from data pulled in real time from corporate software programs.

Another user said:

> The dashboard puts us in real time touch with the business. The more eyes that see the results we're obtaining every day, the higher the quality of the decisions we take.

Managers can see key changes in their business almost simultaneously and take quick corrective action.

Source: *Business Week*, 13 February 2006, pp. 48–51.

18.6 Cultural control

Human resource management control

The processes of HRM discussed in Chapter 11 can be tools to support the control process. Selection and training procedures ensure that the number and types of recruits fit the profile of attitudes, social skills and technical competence that support wider objectives, and that new staff are trained to follow the company's ways of working. The appraisal and reward system can encourage behaviour that supports business objectives, and discourage that which does not. The behaviour of employees can be controlled by offers to provide valued rewards if people comply with management policies, and to withdraw them if they do not.

Barker on concertive control

Barker (1993) draws attention to three broad strategies that have evolved as organisations seek to control members' activities. The first is 'simple control', the direct, authoritarian and personal control of work and workers by the company's owner or hired bosses, best seen in nineteenth-century factories and in small family-owned companies today. The second is 'technological control', in which control emerges from the physical technology, such as in the assembly line found in traditional manufacturing. Third and most familiar is bureaucratic control, in which control derives from the hierarchically based social relations of the organisation and the rules that reward compliance and punish non-compliance.

Technological and bureaucratic control represent adaptations to the forms that preceded them, intended to counter the disadvantages of the previous form. Technological control resulted not only from technological advances but also from worker alienation and dissatisfaction with the despotism too often possible in simple control. But technological control via the assembly line also led to worker protests, slow-downs, and worker alienation. Bureaucratic control, with its emphasis on ▶

615

rational–legal rules, hierarchical monitoring and rewards for compliance was developed to counter the problems of technological control.

Bureaucracy too has problems, especially of being unable to respond quickly to changing conditions. Many companies have sought to overcome these by introducing a greater degree of self-control, such as the wide use of self-managing teams.

Barker's research (see Chapter 17, Section 17.9) in one company showed how team members developed values and norms about good team behaviour, and put great pressure on members, especially new members, to follow them. This form of concertive control was not only stronger than many bureaucratic controls, but was also less visible, as team members accepted it as the normal way of doing things.

Source: Barker (1993).

Values and beliefs

Another approach to control aims to ensure that members of the organisation meet management requirements by encouraging internal compliance rather than relying on external constraint. To the extent that a unit develops a strong culture with which staff identify, then that will help to control their actions. Extensive socialisation and other practices encourage them to act in ways that are consistent with the dominant values and beliefs. It may be unobtrusive and invisible, but can have a powerful effect on behaviour. This may be positive, but can sometimes be oppressive and constraining.

Activity 18.5 **Examples of control tools**

- Identify at least one example from your work of each of these approaches to control.
- What are their advantages and disadvantages in the situation where they are used?
- If possible, compare your information with colleagues on your course, and draw some conclusions.

18.7 Human perspectives on control

Control systems are intended to influence people to act in ways that support the objectives – and so reflect the assumptions that those who designed the systems have about the people they are trying to control. The more accurate these assumptions are, the more likely the control system will support business objectives.

People have personal and local objectives that they seek to achieve, in addition to, or perhaps in place of, the stated objectives of the organisation or unit. People seek to satisfy human needs at work (Chapter 15), and will evaluate a control system in part by asking whether it helps them or hinders them in that goal. How they react will reflect their interests and their interpretation of the situation – which may be different from the interests of those establishing the controls.

Control is also a political process in which powerful individuals and groups seek to dominate others. People may oppose a control system not for its intrinsic features, but for what it implies about their loss of power relative to another group, or because they feel it will restrict their ability to use their initiative and experience. So while there is a clear functional perspective on control – a neutral idea of keeping actions in line with goals – it is closely tied to ideas about motivation, influence and power.

While effective control depends on suitable control systems, these in turn depend on how people see them. Control is only effective when it influences people to act in the way intended by those designing the system, who therefore need to take into account the likely reactions of those being controlled.

Lawler on the problems of formal control

Lawler (1976) identified three potential problems with formal control systems – rigid bureaucratic behaviour, inaccurate data and motivational effects.

First, management controls lead to what Lawler describes as 'rigid bureaucratic behaviour'. Most people prefer to act in ways that make them look good to others, so we tend to concentrate on activities that are measured. If the consequences of a poor assessment are severe, then people will tend to focus their efforts on those parts of the job that are assessed, and ignore those which are not (Kerr, 1975). The standards tell people what they have to do to perform well and perhaps to gain promotion: these behaviours may not necessarily be in the best interests of the business as a whole. Sales staff in a store who are paid an bonus on the volume of sales may focus on generating sales, perhaps using high-pressure tactics that secure a sale, but discourage the customer from coming again. Or they may focus on sales at the expense of checking stock or maintaining the display areas – especially if these are not assessed as part of the control system. Other examples could be reluctance to work outside one's own area of responsibility, concentrating on meeting sub-unit goals rather than those of the enterprise as a whole, or accepting minimum standards as long as they exceed the target.

Second, controls may encourage people to supply inaccurate information. The more important the measure, the more likely it becomes that people will distort information to enhance recorded performance. The bargaining that surrounds payment by results or a commission payment system is an example. Line managers and employees will have different views about the fairness of a particular piece rate, and the latter will often give invalid data on the complexity of the work or the time it requires to overcome a difficulty, to ensure a more favourable rate.

Third, people may resist a system that they feel threatens their satisfaction or in some way undermines their ability to meet their psychological needs from work. Table 18.4 illustrates this by showing how a control system can have either positive or negative effects on a person's ability to satisfy each of the human needs identified by Maslow (1970), discussed in Chapter 15.

More generally, controls may:

- automate human skill and expertise – since skill is often a source of identity and self-esteem, an inability to use valued skills may be resisted;
- measure performance accurately and comprehensively; some may welcome this, but others fear their performance being immediately visible to supervisors;
- create competition and suspicion between groups that are being measured, so damaging social relationships and friendships;
- reduce autonomy by specifying more precisely how people should work, thus reducing their ability to satisfy intrinsic needs.

Controls can encourage both positive and negative behaviour – positive by encouraging commitment, enthusiasm and higher ambition, negative if they lead people to be fearful and defensive.

Table 18.4

Possible effects of control systems on human needs

Maslow's categories of human needs	Controls may support satisfaction	Controls may hinder satisfaction
Self-actualisation	Feedback encourages higher performance, accepting new challenges	Controls may limit initiative, autonomy, ability to experiment and discover
Esteem	Publishing successes builds recognition, self-confidence; reputation with colleagues and senior managers	Publishing failure damages esteem, undermines reputation; inaccurate information also damaging
Belongingness	Team-based assessments can support bonding and team development	Individual rewards may breed competition and damage cooperation
Security	Knowledge of how performance is assessed gives certainty	Controls that leave expectations unclear undermine security; information seen as threat
Physiological	Help focus effort and meet performance requirements	Controls highlight poor performance and threaten job

---

Activity 18.6 **Assessing the human effects of a control system**

Consider a control system at work, or where you are studying.

- Have they had any effects similar to those that Lawler identified?
- How did that affect the way people reacted to the system?
- How could management have redesigned the controls to avoid those effects?

Simons' four levers of control

Another contribution to the human aspects of control systems was made by Robert Simons (1995), who examined the dilemma between control and empowerment:

> How do senior managers protect their companies from control failures when empowered employees are encouraged to redefine how they [do] their jobs? How do [they] ensure that subordinates with an entrepreneurial flair do not put the business at risk? (p. 80)

Simons argued that most managers define control narrowly – as measuring progress against plans to help achieve goals. Such diagnostic control systems are, however, only one ingredient of control. Three other levers are equally important: beliefs systems, boundary systems and interactive control systems. Each has a distinct purpose for managers attempting to harness the creativity of employees. Diagnostic control systems allow managers to ensure that important goals are being achieved efficiently and effectively. Beliefs systems communicate core values and inspire all participants to commit to the organisation's purpose. Boundary systems establish the rules of the game. Interactive control systems enable top-level managers to learn about new threats and opportunities.

Diagnostic controls

These enable managers to monitor performance and to keep critical variables within preset limits. Most businesses rely on them to help managers track the progress of individuals or units toward targets such as revenue growth and market share, by periodically measuring output and comparing it with preset standards. They are not in themselves enough to ensure performance, since employees pursuing a goal may act in ways that endanger the company. This risk can be reduced by considering three other essential levers of control.

Beliefs systems

These are concise statements of the core beliefs of the business: how it creates value ('A better type of banking'); the level of performance it strives for ('Pursuit of Excellence'); and how individuals are expected to manage relationships ('Respect for the Individual'). Their main purpose is to inspire and promote commitment to the business – in the hope that they will not put personal or local interests above those of the whole. They can be supported by another control – boundary systems.

Boundary systems

These tell people what activities are off-limits – what not to do. Unlike diagnostic controls (which monitor performance) or beliefs systems (which communicate core values), boundary systems are stated in negative terms or as minimum standards. Pressures to achieve superior results can encourage people to bend the rules, and boundary systems counter this by making it clear what actions are unacceptable – such as not seeking business in certain industries, not disclosing information to people outside the firm or not making improper payments.

Interactive control systems

As organisations grow larger, senior managers have less personal contact with staff, they need to create systems to share emerging information and encourage creativity. They need sensing systems that expose them to new information and help identify patterns of change. Interactive controls are the formal systems that managers use to involve themselves regularly and personally with subordinates, to focus attention on key issues. Simons quotes the example of a major drinks company where senior managers schedule weekly meetings to discuss the latest market and sales information, to challenge subordinates to explain the trends and to review their action plans:

> Interactive control systems track the strategic uncertainties that keep senior managers awake at night – the shocks to the business that could undermine their assumptions about the future and the way they have chosen to compete. (p. 87)

Collectively, these four levers of control set in motion powerful forces that reinforce one another. By using the control levers effectively managers can be confident that the benefits of innovation and creativity are not achieved at the expense of control.

Activity 18.7   **Examples of Simons' four levers**

- List examples from your experience or your reading of each of Simons' four control levers.
- Note the benefits and disadvantages of each.

18.8 Strategies for control – mechanistic or organic?

The tools of control described in earlier sections can be designed on different assumptions about their effects on behaviour. Rules and procedures can be designed to give people precise and unambiguous directions on how to perform tasks, and how to deal with unusual events. Alternatively they can be written in broad and relatively ambiguous terms, leaving discretion to staff. Procedures may cover all aspects of the work, or only a small number of critically important activities. Another contrast could be between cultural controls that emphasise conformity and those which encourage creativity.

Mechanistic or organic?

If such decisions are made consistently and coherently, this suggests that managers are taking a strategic approach to control, in the sense that they have a clear sense of the purposes of control, and designed all the elements to support them. A simple contrast is between mechanistic and organic controls (Chapter 10).

Mechanistic control involves the extensive use of rules and procedures, top-down authority, written job descriptions and other formal methods of influencing people to act in desirable rather than undesirable ways. They represent a distinct approach to management, which is effective in certain circumstances. In contrast, organic control involves the use of flexible authority, relatively loose job descriptions, a greater reliance on self-control and other informal methods of correcting deviations from desired objectives. This too is a distinct approach, effective in certain conditions. Table 18.5 compares the two strategies.

Table 18.5

Examples of mechanistic and organic controls

Tools	Mechanistic control methods	Organic control methods
Output	Focus on outputs that can be measured by objective, quantitative methods	Include outputs that can be measured by subjective, qualitative method
Direct	Stress on following procedures, sticking to plan	Stress on encouraging learning and creativity
Organisation structure	Top-down authority, emphasis on position power Job descriptions focus on prescribing work methods	Dispersed authority, emphasis on expert power Job descriptions focus on results to be achieved
Rules and procedures	Detailed, on many topics	Broad, on as few topics as practicable
Machinery	Information on performance used by supervisors to check on staff	Information on performance used by staff to learn and improve
HRM	Emphasis on individual extrinsic rewards	Emphasis on extrinsic and intrinsic rewards, linked to teamwork
Cultural	Encourages conformity, rules Focus on controlling individuals	Encourages creativity and innovation Encourages self-managing teams

Which strategy to choose?

Chapter 10 contrasted mechanistic and organic structures, and introduced the theory that choice of form reflects one or more contingencies. It also pointed out that organisations often combine both approaches, using mechanistic forms in stable, predictable operations, and organic for more volatile, uncertain parts of the business. The same thinking can be used in considering the choice of control systems. John Child (2005) proposed contingency factors that could affect the choice of control strategy – such as competitive strategy, importance of innovation and employee expertise. Table 18.6 compares these to suggest whether a mechanistic or organic approach would be appropriate.

Contingency	When	Control strategy likely to be appropriate
Competitive strategy	Cost leadership	Mechanistic, with use of rules and procedures, and machinery to measure quantitative output
	Differentiation	Organic, with use of HRM and cultural controls stressing self-managing teams, and qualitative output measures
Importance of innovation	Low	Mechanistic, with use of rules and procedures, and machinery to measure quantitative output
	High	Organic, with use of HRM and cultural controls stressing self-managing teams, and qualitative output measures
Employee expertise	Low	Mechanistic, with use of rules and procedures, and machinery to measure quantitative output
	High	Organic, with use of HRM and cultural controls stressing self-managing teams, and qualitative output measures

Table 18.6

Contingencies and choice of control strategies

Being aware of these alternative approaches enables managers to choose an approach to control that is suitable for the context.

18.9 Current themes and issues

Performance

Richard Walton (1985) has pointed out that managers have to choose between a strategy based on imposing control and one based on eliciting commitment. He argues that the latter is consistent with recognising employees as stakeholders in the organisation, and is likely to lead to higher performance, especially in situations requiring them to use imagination and creativity in an uncertain business environment. He concludes that organisations must develop a culture of commitment if they are to meet customer expectations with respect to quality, delivery and market changes. Table 18.7 contrasts the approaches.

Workforce strategy	Control	Commitment
Job design	Deskilled, fragmented, fixed	Emphasis on whole task, flexible, use of teams
Performance expectations	Minimum standards defined	Emphasis on 'stretch' goals
Management structure	Many layers with rules and procedures	Flat structure with shared goals and values
Rewards	Individual incentives linked to job evaluation	Group incentives with gain sharing, linked to skills
Employee participation	Narrow, with information given on a 'need to know' basis	Encouraged, with widely shared business information

Source: Walton (1985).

Table 18.7

Elements of control and commitment strategies

> **Activity 18.8** **Using Walton's model**
>
> - Review your organisation's practices in relation to Walton's model.
> - Indicate specifically which are consistent with a control orientation, and which with one of eliciting commitment.

Responsibility

Control systems are developed to influence people to act in ways that support organisational objectives. They draw on motivational theories to develop measurement and reward systems that encourage workers to act in a way which meets their needs and at the same time contributes to organisational performance. Managers can use theories of goal setting or achievement motivation to develop practices that shape the direction and intensity of individual efforts.

This raises the issue of responsibility for the overall health and well-being of staff, and specifically whether managers use the theories in a way that can damage staff. Goal-setting theory, for example, makes the case for goals that are difficult but achievable: this may tempt managers to set goals so high that staff experience considerable stress in achieving them, leading to sickness of various degrees. Some corporate scandals have been linked to company policies that encouraged staff to meet demanding targets, irrespective of what rules or codes of ethical behaviour they were breaking.

Internationalisation

Developments in information technology make it technically possible to set targets and measure performance against them irrespective of the geographical spread of a company. This should enable the smooth and controlled performance of international businesses. The discussion in this chapter suggests several other considerations to take into account in reaching such decisions. These include:

Central or local control. There is a strategic issue about how much central control to impose, and how much to encourage local autonomy and responsiveness. If part of the reason for success has been the ability of local companies to act entrepreneurially, then implementing a control system that imposed greater central control would be counterproductive.

Reliance on technology. Sections 18.4 to 18.6 showed several means of control, all of which can be part of a comprehensive control system. For reasons of remoteness, head office has comparatively few opportunities to use direct control and supervision, which is often a very effective means. Instead it has to rely more on rules and procedures, and a range of formal financial and output controls. An alternative is to try to develop strong cultural controls, which influence people to act in ways that align with corporate aims, irrespective of their location.

National and cultural differences. As Chapter 4 showed, countries have developed substantially different management systems, as well as differences of national culture. These factors will affect very significantly how people respond to control systems, as well as raising difficult issues of comparability between the reports for different countries, and the interpretations to be placed upon them.

Summary

1 Define control and explain why it is an essential activity in managing

- Control is the counterpart of planning, helping to ensure that actions add value, and enabling corrective action.

2 Describe and give examples of the generic control activities of setting objectives, measuring, comparing and correcting

- Setting objectives gives direction to an activity and sets standards of acceptable performance.

- Measuring involves deciding what measures to use, and how frequently.

- Comparing involves selecting suitable objects for comparison, and the time period over which to do it.

- Correcting aims to correct a deviation from plan either by altering activities or changing the objectives.

3 Explain how the choice of suitable measures of performance can reflect an explicit theory, such as the competing values framework or the balanced scorecard

- Control should reflect the situation of the unit being measured: people resent unsuitable measures, which are therefore unlikely to have the effect intended.

- The competing values framework distinguishes between open systems, rational goal, internal process and human relations cultures, and indicates control measures suitable for each.

- The balanced scorecard supplements measures of financial performance with those of customer satisfaction, internal process and innovation: all play a part in an overall assessment of performance.

4 Compare the features of output, behavioural, and cultural controls

- Output control measures a unit performance by using financial measures, and measures based on operational goals and performance against budgets.

- Behavioural control attempts to influence behaviour by direct supervision, structures, rules and procedures, and technology.

- Cultural control attempts to influence behaviour by the design of the rewards system, and by encouraging internal compliance through the values and beliefs of the organisation.

5 Explain why those designing control systems need to take account of human reactions

- Control depends on influencing people, so is only effective if it takes account of human needs. Lawler identified three persistent control problems:

  1 Controls can encourage behaviour that is not in the best interests of the organisation.

  2 Controls can encourage people to supply the system with inaccurate information.

  3 People will resist controls that they feel threaten their ability to satisfy their needs from work.

6 Distinguish between mechanistic and organic strategies of control, and indicate when each is most suitable

- The accumulation of decisions in the control process produces a control system that is more or less mechanistic or organic.

- Mechanistic approaches are likely to be suitable in stable environments or in support of cost leadership strategies.

- Organic approaches are likely to be suitable in unstable environments or in support of differentiation strategies.

Review questions

1 Explain why control is important.

2 Is planning part of the control process?

3 Describe the four steps in the control process.

4 Give an example of a performance standard based on each part of the competing values framework.

5 Give an original example of a measure in each quadrant of the balanced scorecard.

6 Explain how feedforward, concurrent and feedback control can be used to control inputs, transformation and outputs.

7 Identify examples of output, behavioural and cultural control.

8 What are the implications for those designing a control system of Lawler's work on control?

Concluding critical reflection

Think about the way your company, or one with which you are familiar, seeks to control performance. Review the material in the chapter, and perhaps visit some of the websites identified. Then make notes on these questions:

- What examples of the themes discussed in this chapter are currently relevant to your company? What types of controls are you most closely involved with? Which of the techniques suggested do you and your colleagues typically use, and why? What techniques do you use that are not mentioned here?

- In responding to these issues, what **assumptions** about the nature of control appear to guide your approach? Do the assumptions take account of, say, the competing values framework, or the balanced scorecard?

- What factors in the **context** of the company appear to shape your approach to control – is the balance towards a mechanistic or an organic approach, and is that choice suitable for the environment in which you are working?

- What **alternative** approaches to planning have you identified in your work on this chapter? Would any of them possibly make a useful contribution to your organisation?

- Has the chapter highlighted any possible **limitations** in the control systems used in your organisation? Have you considered, for example, if there is too much control, or too little? Have you compared your control processes with those in other companies?

Further reading

Kerr, S. (1975), 'On the Folly of Rewarding A, while hoping for B', *Academy of Management Journal*, vol. 18, no. 4, pp. 769–783.

A classic study of the unintended consequences of control systems.

Simons, R. (1995a), 'Control in an age of empowerment', *Harvard Business Review*, vol. 73, no. 2, pp. 80–88.

A review of the range of control strategies which managers can use, showing the range of alternatives.

van Veen-Dirks, P. and Wijn, M. (2002), 'Strategic control: meshing critical success factors with the balanced scorecard', *Long Range Planning*, vol. 35, no. 4, pp. 407–427.

Compares two approaches to control at a strategic level, using several of the concepts introduced in this chapter.

Weblinks

These websites illustrate the themes of the chapter, and in the Part Case:

www.axa.com
www.oracle.com
www.ba.com
www.tesco.com

Visit two of the business sites in the list, and go to the section in which the company reports on its performance:

- What financial measures do they report on most prominently?
- From the chairman's and/or chief executive's reports, what other measures have they been using to assess their performance?
- Sketch the heading of a balanced scorecard which would represent an appropriate set of performance measures for that company.

Annotated weblinks, multiple choice questions and other useful resources can be found on **www.pearsoned.co.uk/boddy**

Chapter 19

Finance and budgetary control

Aim

To show why organisations need finance, where it comes from, how its use should be controlled and why financial measures are critical indicators of performance.

Objectives

By the end of your work on this chapter you should be able to outline the concepts below in your own terms and:

1 Understand the role of the finance function in management

2 Be able to interpret basic financial reports

3 Know the difference between profit and cash

4 Know what a simple financial plan contains and its purpose

5 Understand the importance of financial results to evaluate performance

6 Know the basic steps in calculating the financial consequences of a management decision

7 Be able to explain how budgets aim to ensure internal activities are directed at meeting external financial requirements.

Key terms

This chapter introduces the following ideas:

capital market
limited liability company
shareholders
cash flow statement
assets
profit and loss statement
balance sheet
fixed assets
current assets
shareholders' funds
liabilities

*Each is a term defined within the text, as well as
in the Glossary at the end of the book.*

BASF is one of the world's leading chemical companies, with production sites in 41 countries and customers spread across the world. The head office and main chemical processing complex is located at Lugwigshafen, Germany. The group comprises more than 160 subsidiaries and affiliates. Its main product groups are chemicals, plastics, products for the agricultural industry, 'performance products' designed in conjunction with customers to meet specific needs. It also engages in oil and gas exploration and production.

A main objective of the company is to earn a premium on its cost of capital in order to ensure profitable growth, thereby giving it a competitive advantage in gaining access to international capital markets. The pursuit of profit has to be achieved while recognising the importance of the principles of sustainable development, combining economic success with environmental protection and social responsibility. BASF's shares are listed in the Dow Jones Sustainability Index. Research and development has to be at the heart of the group's efforts to retain its competitive position.

BASF has successfully developed highly integrated processing plants to use resources and materials to maximum advantage. Waste and by-products are fed directly into other processes where they are important materials. Pipe networks facilitate efficient, safe and environmentally friendly transfer of resources. They describe this integration as 'Verbund'.

The hazardous nature of the industry demands the highest safety standards amongst employees. Risk identification, measurement and control are most important. The Verbund system minimises undesirable emissions, but also benefits BASF customers. The group maintains close relationships with its customers to find mutually beneficial solutions to their problems. Reward systems for employees are as closely related to corporate objectives as possible, especially by using a measure known as earnings before interest on capital and taxation (EBIT).

© BASF Aktiengesellschaft.

A summary of the BASF operating (profit) report for year ended 31 December 2006 is:

		€ millions
Sales		52,610
Less Cost of sales		37,698
Gross profit on sales		14,912
Selling expenses	4,996	
General and administrative expenses	893	
Research and development expenses	1,276	
Other items	1,220	8,385
Operating profit before tax (EBIT)		6,527
Less Taxation		3,061
Minority interests		251
Net income		3,215

Source: Company *Annual Report*, 2005–2006.

Case questions 19.1

- What was the company's profit in the year to 31 December 2006?
- What proportion of its sales revenue was spent on research and development?
- What questions does the information in the summary financial report raise for you?

19.1 Introduction

In the financial year that ended on 31 December 2006 BASF made a profit of €3215 million from its activities. This 'headline' figure is a very crude measure of the effectiveness with which the managers have run the company over the year. The problem for investors is how to assess this performance. How does it compare with other firms in similar businesses? Is it consistent with the stated targets of the company? Does the way it has been achieved bode well for the future by, for example, investing in research that will bring returns in later years? Investors will also want to know how these broad summary figures relate to the work of managers and staff within the firm – are they motivated and organised in ways that encourage them to produce good returns in the future?

Similar questions arise about the annual report of any public firm – you can read commentaries on these every day in the financial pages of your newspaper. Investors and financial analysts continually evaluate a company's financial performance against its objectives and against comparable businesses. They try to judge its prospects, and how effectively managers are doing their jobs. Much of the information is qualitative and subjective, designed to create a favourable impression and to create positive expectations. Responsible retailing in M&S may well have adverse cost implications in the short term, but it is intended to appeal to their customers' sense of environmental and social responsibility. Unless it is successful in expanding its sales profitably, all the best intentions will not save a failing organisation. Profit has to be earned, otherwise the organisation will fail.

Chapter 1 described organisations as aiming to add value to the resources they used. It is crucial to the success of an organisation that it has the appropriate resources and that these are managed to achieve the results that stakeholders expect. Whatever the nature of the organisation or its line of business, it will need financial resources to operate. It needs to manage these well if it is to prosper. Most companies depend on people in the external environment for the funds they need to grow the business. The main source of information for people outside the business who wish to assess its performance and prospects is the company's annual report to shareholders. This contains a great deal of financial and other data – but is more subjective than at first appears. It is important to know how financial performance is measured, and the assumptions that people make in constructing the figures. It is also important to know how these financial measures relate to the performance of those working within the firm.

The chapter begins by explaining why companies need the capital market and how they communicate with it. A major link in that process is the annual report, so the chapter then explains important parts of that document. The chapter goes on to show how these figures, which are intended mainly for investors outside the organisation, influence and are themselves influenced by processes of internal planning and control.

19.2 The pressures on companies to perform

Many people reading this book will be expecting to start a career that they hope will provide an income to support an attractive lifestyle. Few will be thinking about retirement or the need to support themselves after their working lives have ended. This may be a sombre subject to introduce, but it is fundamentally important to understanding the financial environment in which organisations operate. Governments are increasingly concerned about the ability of traditional public pension schemes to support people in their old age. Furthermore individuals are expected to take more responsibility for their own pension.

Obtain a copy of the annual report and accounts for Marks & Spencer plc and Mothercare plc for the year ended 1 April 2006. What can you discover about the shareholders in the companies?

Pension funds and life assurance companies expect to pay their investors an acceptable income or lump sum when they retire. The funds can only do this if they invest contributions successfully, and investors naturally expect their premiums to be invested profitably by pension fund managers. These pension fund and life assurance companies compete with each other, and the rewards for success, and consequent growth in contributions from investors, are high. There is pressure on the fund managers to perform well by identifying good investment opportunities, which is also in the investors' best interests as eventual pensioners. The fund managers will be looking for good investment opportunities in companies that are profitable and well managed.

This is where the discussion comes full circle, back to the investor. In order to attract money into its business to enable it to expand, management needs to demonstrate to the capital market that it is a profitable and successful business.

The fund managers in the **capital market** expect management to operate their businesses profitably. So this pressure from the external capital market directly affects the organisation and all employees. There may be bad years or periods of low or negative profitability (losses) and the capital markets know that. But continual losses will eventually lead to failure. The business will simply run out of money and not be able to meet its financial obligations. So the pressures to perform that managers and employees feel originate outside the organisation. However, as future pensioners, dependent on the performance of fund managers, those pressures serve their long-term interests (Coggan, 2002).

Within an organisation it is unlikely that managers, apart from those at the top, will feel the direct pressure from outside. Yet, as the chapter shows, this external pressure does affect the expectations that top managers have of those below them. These expectations are gradually transmitted down the organisation, so that all staff experience them in some way, even if indirectly. The pressures can be considerable as the senior managers expect to be rewarded with the opportunity to purchase shares in the company at a favourable price at some future time (share or stock options). Sometimes this pressure leads to dubious practices and alleged fraud designed to enhance the share price, as in the recent cases of Enron and Parmalat. This has brought considerable pressure from regulators to improve corporate governance and the quality of financial reporting.

The **capital market** comprises all the individuals and institutions that have money to invest, including banks, life assurance companies and pension funds and, as users of capital, business organisations, individuals and governments.

19.3   The world outside the organisation

Raising capital

If you have looked at the annual report of M&S or Mothercare you will have discovered that life assurance companies and pension funds are major shareholders. Most reports do not show such detail, and it is often difficult to discover because the shares are not necessarily ultimately owned by the company named in the share register. They are just one of the many sources from which large organisations raise capital.

A large public company can raise money by issuing shares to people and institutions that respond to a share issue. The main benefit is to enable companies to finance large-scale activities. The shareholders appoint the directors who are ultimately responsible for managing the company. A shareholder is entitled to vote at general meetings in accordance with the number of shares owned. Once the shareholders have paid for their shares in full they cannot generally be required to pay more money into the company, even if it fails.

The affairs of companies are governed by company law, in some countries administered by a government body such as the Securities and Exchange Commission in the United States, and by the body governing the share market, such as the Bourse in France and the Stock Exchange in the United Kingdom. Before a company can invite the public to subscribe for shares it has to be registered with the national financial regulators and fulfil a number of requirements. The first step after registration in order to raise money is to issue a prospectus. Again there are many rules and legal matters that have to be satisfied. In essence, the prospectus explains the history of the company, what it plans to do as a business, and what it plans to do with the money raised.

If the business is small it will not invite the public to buy shares. The promoters will contribute their own money, most likely in sufficient amount to ensure that they have control (more than 50 per cent of the shares). The amount of capital available to the company in these circumstances will be limited by the money the founders can afford to contribute. They may go to a bank to seek finance, but the willingness of a bank to lend will also depend on the amount subscribed by the shareholders.

Banks, fund managers and investors at large will contribute only if they believe that there is a good, sound, well-managed business that is likely to make a profit. The investors have many investment opportunities. They will not invest in a company that will not reward them, as by investing they are taking a risk. The amount of return they expect will be related to the risk – the greater the risk the greater the required return.

Activity 19.2 Borrowing money

Find out the interest rate at which you could borrow money to (a) buy a car, (b) buy a house, (c) spend on your credit card. Can you explain what you discover?

A **limited liability company** has an identity and existence in its own right as distinct from its owners (shareholders in Europe, stockholders in North America). A shareholder has an ownership right in the company in which the shares are held.

Shareholders are the principal risk takers in a company. They contribute the long-term capital for which they expect to be rewarded in the form of dividends – a distribution from the profit of the business.

A **limited liability company** gives a business access to large amounts of capital, but at the same time allows some protection to the **shareholders**, as they cannot be held liable for the debts of the business in the event of its financial failure. This limited liability means that investors can contribute capital knowing that their private and personal assets are not at risk. Of course they could lose all their investment in the shares. This is the risk they take, and is why they expect a higher return than they would receive if they put their money in a bank or in government securities, where the risk of default is virtually zero.

Because a company has access to capital in this form there has to be regulation. The Companies Act is the principal instrument of control, with the addition of the Stock Exchange for those listed as public companies within the United Kingdom. A most important requirement is to provide information about the performance of the business from time to time (Elliott and Elliott, 2006). This is done most comprehensively in the company's annual report. Amongst other things the annual report includes detailed financial information of three distinct types. There is a profit and loss (or income) statement, a cash flow statement and a balance sheet.

Cash flow statement

The easiest to understand of the three types of statement is the cash flow, as it states just that. It shows where cash has come from and how it has been spent. The following is a simplified summary of the **cash flow statement** for M&S for the year ended 1 April 2006.

	£ millions
Net cash inflow from operating activities	1,197
Payment of taxation	(101)
Net cash inflow from operating activities	1,096
Cash flows from investing activities	
Capital expenditure and financial investment	(266)
Interest received	13
Net cash (outflow) on investing activities	(253)
Cash flows from financing activities	
Interest paid	(143)
Other debt financing	(420)
Equity dividends paid	(204)
Other equity financing	56
Net cash outflow from financing activities	(711)
Net cash inflow from all activities (above)	132
Effect of exchange rate changes	1
Opening net cash	149
Net closing cash	282

A **cash flow statement** shows the sources from which cash has been generated and how it has been spent during a period of time.

In the ordinary course of successful business it might be expected that the cash received from trading (selling products or services) should be greater than the cash spent to purchase components, supplies, labour, energy and all the other resources combined to make, promote, distribute and secure the sales. The cash surplus could then be reinvested to help finance expansion and some of it paid to the shareholders by way of a dividend to recompense them for their investment. Their original contribution remains in the company, however, as part of the continuing capital base. In the case of M&S there was an increase in cash of £132 million after paying dividends and investing in some new **assets** including store refurbishing.

The idea of a cash surplus being the essential requirement from operations is appealing but unfortunately too simplistic. Taking as an example a motor vehicle manufacturer, a car has to be designed and tested, components sourced from suppliers, production lines prepared, cars distributed to dealers, and motoring journalists and publicity agents organised in preparation for a major launch promotion. All of this

Assets are the property, plant and equipment, vehicles, stocks of goods for trading, money owed by customers and cash: in other words, the physical resources of the business.

631

before any of the cars can be sold – so there will be very heavy cash outflows before cash starts to come in. This process may take a couple of years. In the pharmaceutical industry there is a large investment in continuing research and development that may take ten years or longer before cash begins to flow back, and then only if the research is successful. Heavy investment in product development in the electronics industry has to be made before any products emerge.

Much the same thing occurs in new technology-based service companies such as eBay.com or lastminute.com. They, like all new dotcom companies, have to invest heavily in building their website and in advertising to make people aware that they exist before cash begins to flow in. It would be highly unlikely in these conditions for the business to show a cash surplus in periods when it is making such heavy investment. Indeed it may be necessary to raise additional capital from shareholders or banks to finance the investment in equipment and in training the people who will operate it.

Activity 19.4 | **Measuring R&D expenditure**

Look at the annual report for BASF (**www.basf.com**), Siemens (**www.siemens.com**), Solvay (**www.solvay.com**) or any large manufacturing business, and find out what it tells you about research and development. List the projects that the report mentions. What does the report say about the length of time before the projects will be profitable?

It is impossible to draw sensible conclusions about the company's financial performance on the basis of cash flow alone. Not only is the annual surplus or deficit influenced by major investment, but other infrequent events, such as a major restructuring exercise following a new strategy, could also distort the impression.

The profit and loss statement

A **profit and loss statement** reflects the benefits derived from the trading activities of the business during a period of time.

The **profit and loss statement** (or income statement) is designed to overcome the limitations of a cash flow statement, although cash has the important characteristic of complete objectivity. Cash flows can be observed, measured and verified. Profit measures are subjective.

The profit after taxation and the profit retained in the business are quite different from the cash surplus reported in the cash flow statement. This is because the profit statement is not based on cash but on business transactions that (a) may result in cash transactions in the future, or (b) reflect cash transactions from previous periods.

Sales may be credit sales that approved customers may pay for later. Cost of goods sold may include the purchase of goods that will be paid for in the next financial year. Operating expenses will include depreciation which, with other terms, is explained below.

Case questions 19.2

Refer to the summary income statement for BASF.

● Calculate the gross profit as a percentage of sales.

● Calculate the operating profit before tax as a percentage of sales.

Activity 19.5   Calculating and comparing profit

Look at the annual report of a company in a similar line of business to BASF, such as DSM or ICI.

- Calculate the gross profit in a recent year as a percentage of sales.
- Calculate the profit before tax as a percentage of sales.
- How does the company compare on these measures against BASF?
- Is there a major difference in the items in the profit statements of the two companies?

Depreciation

Depreciation is a major cause of the difference between cash flow and profit. Think about the investments mentioned in relation to motor vehicle production. Apart from occasional modifications, the same basic model may be produced and sold for several years, perhaps as many as ten for a small-volume producer. So the initial investment to develop the design and make the cars should be spread over the life of the investment and will be subtracted from sales revenue in each year. This process is called depreciation. The idea is simple, but there are several estimates required before the annual amount can be measured. Depreciation is based on the original cost of the investment, including set-up and training, less the expected scrap value at the end of its life. It may also be necessary to add the expected cost of decommissioning: think about a nuclear power generator in this respect. Hence an estimation must be made of the life of the investment, the residual value and the initial cost, which itself is open to conjecture. To make matters worse there are at least four methods of spreading the cost over the life span. The simplest is to allocate an equal amount each year. Assets may also be periodically revalued to take account of changes in their fair value that then becomes the base for calculating depreciation. In both circumstances, if the fair value (the present value of expected future cash flows, or the expected market price less selling costs if it were to be sold) is less than the amount already allowed for depreciation, then the difference must be charged as an expense and subtracted from revenue. This diminution in value is described as impairment.

Credit

Most products are not sold for cash but on credit, sometimes for an extended period of time, possibly many months. A retail store might offer generous credit terms in order to promote sales – 'nothing to pay for six months' or 'easy terms over nine months' are familiar promotional devices. Creditworthiness will be checked before the customer is given credit. However, even the most careful checks cannot ensure that the customer may not become redundant or fall ill and not be able to work. As an example, suppose that the company's financial year ends on 31 December and that a customer is buying a personal computer at the end of October on nine months' credit of equal monthly payments. Should the company report the full value of the sale, the three instalments that the customer has paid, or nothing until the PC has been paid for in full? It is usual practice to report the full amount, as the business has a legal contract to force the customer to pay. The idea is fine, but experience shows that not all customers will pay in full. There will be bad debts. An estimate of doubtful debts has to be made before arriving at profit.

Warranty claims

If a problem arises with a product sold under warranty it will be replaced or fixed, but at a cost to the manufacturer. The cost of repairing under warranty has to be estimated because warranty claims may not be made within the same financial year as the sale.

These are simple examples of subjectivity in profit measurement. There are many more, but these suffice to illustrate the point that the measure of profit cannot be said to be accurate. It is an approximation. Nevertheless, it is the main indication of trading performance measured in financial terms. The question remains, how well does profit reflect good performance? To evaluate this, profit needs to be related to the amount of investment in the business.

19.4   Measuring periodic performance

Both the cash flow and the profit statements relate to a period of time – conventionally to a financial or trading year. It is usual for large organisations also to produce brief reports on their performance quarterly or half-yearly.

Just how much profit is desirable has to be considered in relation to the investment in a business. Therefore a measure of investment is needed with which to compare periodic profit. When you think that an investor (fund manager) could invest in risk-free government securities for a guaranteed minimum return known in advance, an investment in a risky company that did not offer at least the same expectation of reward would not be contemplated. So the return, or ratio of profit to investment, would be expected to be higher for a risky investment than for a risk-free opportunity. The rate of return required for a particular investment has to be assessed by comparing alternative investment opportunities and their rates of return.

Measuring the investment base

How can the investment base be measured? The obvious base is the amount of the initial investment. If you deposit money in a bank deposit account it will attract interest. At the end of the year you can measure the rate of return by expressing the interest earned for the year as a percentage of the initial investment. If you leave the interest in the account the following year, the investment base would be increased by the amount of interest reinvested. The initial investment plus the interest you earned in the first year now becomes a part of the capital base, as you chose not to withdraw it. The investment base can grow over time. Much the same happens in a business. Profit is generated, some is distributed as a cash dividend and the balance, usually the larger proportion, is retained in the business to finance expansion.

A simple measure of the capital base with which to compare profit appears to be the amount of capital originally contributed plus profit that is retained and added each year to the base.

Another way to look at it, for companies listed on the Stock Exchange, is to relate the profit or earnings per share to the share price. This approach recognises that a successful business will grow and develop a good reputation and image that will reflect the results of good, professional management and reliable, high-quality products and service. If you own shares in such a company you would expect the value of those shares to increase to reflect the success of the business, for example from customer loyalty, brand reputation and reliability, loyal relationships with suppliers of components and services, and good design. You would continue to hold the shares only as long as the return based on the price at which you could sell the shares in the market is at least equal to that from an alternative investment with similar risk. This topic is revisited later in the chapter.

19.5 The balance sheet

The report that shows the capital base of a business is the **balance sheet**. The BASF balance sheet at 31 December 2006 is shown in the next instalment of the case study.

A **balance sheet** shows the assets of the business and the sources from which finance has been raised.

BASF Group – the case continues   www.basf.com   C A S E   S T U D Y

Group balance sheet as at 31 December 2006

Assets		€ millions
Intangible (patents, licences, goodwill)		8,922
Property, plant and equipment (at cost after depreciation deducted)		14,902
Financial assets		3,075
		26,899
Current assets		
Inventories	6,672	
Accounts receivable from customers and others	10,830	
Liquid assets (including cash)	890	18,392
		45,291
Shareholders' equity		
Issued shares and retained profit		18,578
Long term liabilities	12,733	
Accounts payable and other short-term liabilities	13,980	26,713
		45,291

The balance sheet reveals two separate but related aspects of the business. First it shows the **fixed** and **current assets** of the business. These include the physical resources such as property, buildings, machinery, computers, stocks (or inventories) of raw materials, work in progress and completed products, money owed by customers, and cash. The other dimension is the sources of the finance that have enabled the business to acquire its assets. Finance (or capital) comes from shareholders by way of contributions for shares when they are first issued, together with retained profits from successful operations as previously explained. This is the shareholders' capital (or **shareholders' funds**). In addition there will usually be money borrowed from a bank and possibly from other sources as well. These are the **liabilities** of the organisation. The sum total of the shareholders' funds and liabilities will equal the amount of assets. The former represents the source from which the finance has been raised. The latter shows the destination or the physical resources in which the capital has been invested. Assets and liabilities are divided into two categories: current, applying to those that are expected to be traded within a year, and non-current, expected to remain in the business longer than a year.

Fixed assets are the physical properties that the company possesses – such as land, buildings, production equipment and vehicles – and which are likely to have a useful life of more than one year. There may also be intangible assets such as patent rights or copyrights.

Current assets can be expected to be cash or to be converted to cash within a year.

Shareholders' funds are the capital contributed by the shareholders plus profits that have not been distributed to the shareholders.

Liabilities of a business as reported in the balance sheet are the debts and financial obligations of the business to all those people and institutions that are not shareholders, e.g. a bank, suppliers.

The shareholders are the main risk takers and the profit is attributable to them. Therefore, to measure the efficiency with which the funds are used, it is usual to measure the *rate of return on equity*, that is profit after tax divided by shareholders' funds. However, there are many imperfections in the measure, one of which is the fact that goodwill will not usually be included as an asset unless it appears following the purchase of another business. Brands and names such as the title of a newspaper or the name of a consumer product can only be included if they were purchased. They may not be included if internally generated. This apparent inconsistency may be surprising. Accountants argue that newspaper mastheads, or brand names, could be sold separately from the business, whereas goodwill can only be sold with the business as a whole. Goodwill arises when one company is taken over by another for a price greater than the value of the tangible and separately identified intangible assets such as brand names, minus the liabilities (net worth). Further difficulties in measuring a rate of return arise from problems in measuring depreciation and, consequently, asset values, changes in price levels and share values.

Case question 19.3

- Refer to the summary financial information for BASF. Calculate the rate of return (after tax) on equity (shareholders' funds).

The discussion of the profit statement explained that depreciation in particular was an expense item that was difficult to measure. It represents an attempt to estimate the proportion of the cost of using long-term assets that is attributable to a particular accounting period. Any of the cost that has not already been subtracted in the profit statements remains to be subtracted in the future.

Measuring depreciation at Marks & Spencer
www.marksandspencer.com

In the M&S annual report for 2006 the assets fixtures and fittings were shown in note 14 at a cost of £3162 million at the beginning of the year. The accumulated depreciation up to 2 April 2005 was £1927 million which when subtracted from the cost gave a book value of £1235 million. This figure was adjusted for additions and disposals during the year and to the remaining amount was applied the rate of depreciation applicable to each type of asset as indicated in note 1C (Accounting Policies) to generate a charge of £257 million which was a part of the depreciation charge for the year that appeared in the income statement as an expense.

When added to depreciation charged in earlier years, and allowing for the sale of some assets, and subtracted from the cost, the book value in the balance sheet as at 1 April 2006 was £1225 million. This represents the amount to be subtracted from sales revenue as an expense as the assets are used in future years. This remaining balance is part of the total value that appears in the balance sheet for long-term assets (fixed or non-current assets) of £3576 million.

The estimate of doubtful debts subtracted from customers' outstanding accounts (debtors or accounts receivable), estimated warranty claim costs (in a manufacturing company), estimated pension fund liabilities, the value of goodwill, brands or other intangible assets are all highly subjective measures. Furthermore, the accounting policies may well differ between companies even though they are in the same industry. So the aggregate amount shown in the balance sheet for assets is not necessarily a reflection of market values.

> **Activity 19.6** **Comparing accounting policies**
>
> Look at the annual reports for two or three companies in the same industry, or in similar industries, and read the section called accounting policies. Make a list of practices that seem to be different.

Changes in price levels

There is a further complication to measuring performance, especially in periods of unstable prices. An asset is recorded at its original cost less depreciation. Suppose there are two companies involved in much the same business with similar assets, but one company purchased its equipment when prices were much lower than was the case for the second company. Although they may have similar physical assets, the costs showing for one may be quite different from those for the other. Traditionally accountants do not make allowances for differences in price levels through time. Money amounts at different times are added together as though they represented the same values, which is clearly nonsense. Consequently, during a period of changing prices it is difficult to compare the rate of return on equity between companies based on the profit statement and balance sheet. These days in most western economies the rate of inflation is very low, so this is not a problem, although the prices of some commodities, components and products will frequently change.

Share values

There is another way of approaching the question of performance measurement. If you were thinking of buying shares in the market through the Stock Exchange, you would consider the likely future returns in relation to the price you would have to pay for the shares. You will therefore be comparing different investment opportunities and will attempt to choose the one that offers the best return for whatever degree of risk you are prepared to accept. The return you expect would be an estimate of future dividends plus the likely growth in the share price, and you would relate this to the price you would have to pay to buy the shares. If the potential investment offered a greater expected return than shares you already hold (assuming the same degree of risk), not only would you be interested in buying the new shares, but you would also be inclined to sell your existing shares to buy more new ones to increase your return. It would be rational for all investors in this position to behave in the same way. The consequence of this action should be clear. Selling pressure for the shares of one company would drive the price down to the point at which investors would be indifferent as to which company's shares they purchased, as they would tend to offer the same expected return. This process, known as arbitraging, is likely to happen in a well-organised and efficient market (Ross *et al.*, 2005).

So the measure of performance that shareholders are likely to adopt will not be directly related to the company's financial reports, but more to the financial markets. They will be comparing expected returns with the prices of securities (shares) in the market. This does not mean that financial reports from companies do not serve any useful purpose. They do, because they provide some of the information that helps the traders in shares to assess the likely returns from these companies in the future and, above all, provide information about past performance and recent financial position. While share prices in the market are directly influenced by buying and selling pressure, the expectations that give rise to those pressures come in part from the financial reports.

Companies whose shares do not offer returns consistent with those of competitors are likely to become takeover targets with bids from stronger, more efficient performers. Figure 19.1 shows the comparative changes in the share price for two companies in the banking business – Bank of Scotland and Halifax – at the time they were merging. The graph shows clearly how the share price for the Bank of Scotland had performed better than that for the Halifax. This may have enhanced the bargaining power of the Bank of Scotland.

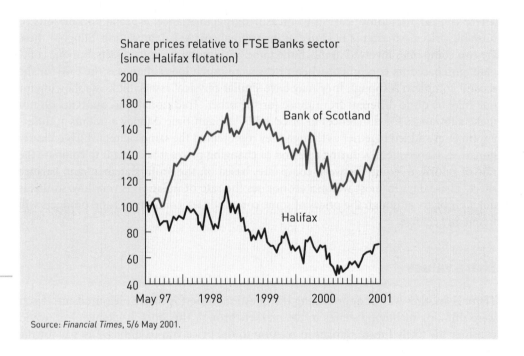

Figure 19.1

Pre-tax profits compared: Halifax/Bank of Scotland

Company directors have to watch share price movements. Unexpected movements might signal activity in the market that they ought to know about. For example, if another company is actively buying shares in the market and so raising the price, this might indicate they are planning a takeover bid. If a large shareholder is selling shares, thus pushing the price down, has performance in the company fallen short of expectations? In both circumstances the directors need to find out what they can about the market activities in order to take defensive action.

Case question 19.4

● Look at the balance sheet of BASF. Calculate the proportion of the finance for the company that is attributable to the shareholders, and the proportion attributable to the liabilities.

The directors and senior managers of a company cannot ignore what is going on in the markets outside their business. They operate in markets, some specific to their own activities, and some general – the capital and labour markets. Their performance is being evaluated all the time and they need to know what the buyers and sellers in the financial markets are thinking. Financial managers will be watching the share price. They have to convert external pressures from the market into pressure for internal action. This is what financial management is about.

19.6 Internal control

Most managers and employees can do little themselves to influence the share price directly. Nevertheless much of what they do has financial implications and eventually all their decisions will indirectly affect the share price. So management needs systems and procedures to ensure that the financial consequences of decisions are understood and that the action proposed is acceptable. An organisation cannot wait until the accountant prepares a financial report at the end of the year to see whether the operation has been profitable or not. It is too late to do anything. Profit does not just happen. It has to be planned (Horngren *et al.*, 2005). At least once a year management must prepare a financial plan, commonly known as a budget.

Activity 19.7 Preparing a budget

Prepare a simple cash budget for your own finances for next month. You will need to consider the cash you have available from savings in the past, how much cash you expect to receive during the month and what you plan to spend.

The budgeting process usually begins at the top level when the directors set a target or goal for the growth in shareholder value that will keep the business performing as well as, if not better than, its competitors. From this assessment they derive a profit target for the whole organisation. It may be expressed as a rate of return on invested capital (shareholders' funds) or as an absolute amount, but either way it will need to be translated into objectives that have meaning at lower operating levels within the business.

Controlling elements within an organisation

A large organisation will have a variety of products, markets and locations in which it operates. An international business may have highly independent operating divisions in a variety of locations, each expected to achieve a given rate of return.

In contrast, a smaller business may have just one location, but within it a range of functions such as purchasing, design, production, assembly, inspection, dispatch and accounts receivable. Each may be independently managed yet coordinated to ensure that they are all operating to achieve the required corporate objective. None of these divisions could be set a required rate of return or even a profit target because none of them has independent control over its activities. The volume of production will depend on sales, purchases will depend on production and accounts receivable on sales. However, each has control over certain aspects of the business. Purchasing must negotiate prices and specifications for supplies of material or components, but it has little control over volume. Based on the sales and production plan it will have a reasonable idea of volume, but it will be subject to change as the year progresses in light of actual sales and production. Similarly, the performance of the dispatch and shipping operation will depend on sales and customers' delivery requirements. They can base plans on the sales projections but, as with all plans in business, the actual activities will inevitably be different.

All parts of the organisation, then, have to be flexible and adaptable in response to market opportunities and customers' requirements. For this reason it is vital to establish and maintain good relationships with other organisations that the firm deals with. It is not unusual in smaller organisations to hear managers complain that the process of planning and budgeting is a waste of time because events always turn out differently. They certainly do, but this is no reason not to plan. As circumstances change plans should also change. Since desktop computers can easily perform the mechanics of budget preparation, budgets should always be up to date and reflect contemporary operating and market conditions.

management in practice   Earnings per share at M&S

The earnings per share (profit after tax divided by the number of shares issued) for M&S increased from 29.1 pence in 2005 to earnings of 31.4 pence in 2006. The jump from 24.2 pence in 2004 may have been partly attributable to the change in accounting from GAAP (generally accepted accounting principles) to IFRS (international financial reporting standards). It cannot be known what plans the directors have for the future. The annual report does not include forecasts or plans. However, it can be seen from the executive chairman's and chief executive's letter that the improvement in the rate of profit was probably attributable to expansion and consolidation.

Plans consistent with the future strategic direction outlined in the letter will have been incorporated into the 2006/2007 budget, although we cannot know the details. The achievable earnings per share will have been planned.

Without a plan there is no sense of direction or clarity of purpose at operating levels. The process of budget preparation in itself is a useful exercise: not only does it enable the various parts of an organisation to relate their activities to others, but it is also a valuable coordination device to help the various parts of the organisation focus on the same objective. The starting point for planning at operational level is generally the sales plan in a profit-oriented organisation. In not-for-profit organisations it may be the desired level of service to its constituency, for example the number of units of blood to be collected by the transfusion service.

In all cases the capacity to achieve the desired volume will depend on the resources available – especially people, equipment and finance. If added resources are needed management can anticipate both what is required and when. For example, if more people are required they have to be recruited and trained so that they will be ready to contribute to productive activity at the appropriate time. If more cash is needed to pay for added supplies of raw materials, it is important to have a financial plan to present to the bank manager well in advance of the time that a cash crisis begins to occur. Crises often arise because there has been insufficient care and attention with planning – and failure to update plans as circumstances change. Plans need to be changed as activity grows for the simple reason that growth requires added finance. Labour, supplies of materials and services will have to be paid for before cash begins to flow back from customers.

Case question 19.5

You have read aspects of the annual report of BASF. Now use your imagination to think through the process that might have been adopted in the construction of the budget for the year ended 31 December 2007. To help you, think about the following:

● Where did the process begin? How were the various elements or product groups brought together into a coherent plan?

● What steps might have been involved in arriving at an agreed budget?

Planning growth and improved performance

The length of the planning cycle depends on the kind of product or service. It may be no more than a couple of months or it could be much longer. Companies can fail as they grow simply because the rate of growth outpaces the ability to generate cash or because they have not anticipated the need for cash and made the necessary plans. Coordination of the various aspects has to be supervised centrally in the organisation to ensure that the overall objectives are achievable in the plan.

Much of the detail has to come from the operating units, especially performance targets related to work activity. It is here that there is likely to be a process of negotiation with central coordinators. Their activity is to improve productivity, whereas the objectives at the lower level may be to ensure that the performance targets do not put excessive pressures on employees. A process of genuine negotiation and cooperation may well lead to a budget that is acceptable both to operating divisions and to the central organisation. However, a budget cast in conditions of fear and apprehension can lead to attempts to create budget slack. This is exemplified by the readiness or otherwise of employees to introduce improved working methods. It is conceivable that more efficient working methods can be discovered through experience. Staff and management may choose not to disclose or introduce them at the earliest opportunity. Instead they may keep them in reserve to cushion the effects of a tight budget at some future time. Such behaviour is not in the best interests of the business as a whole, but it shows how budget preparation can lead to conflicts. The subject of participation in the process of budget preparation has been a topic for extensive research in recent years (Drury, 2004).

Typically a corporate budget will include:

● *sales budget* – showing expected revenue for each product in each market;
● *materials budget* – showing purchases for each component, from each supplier;
● *labour budget* – showing deployment of employees and staff to each activity;
● *overhead budget* – showing the consumption of resources that cannot be identified with particular products, e.g. advertising, directors' fees, energy;
● *capital budget* – showing planned spending on new equipment, buildings and acquisitions of other companies;
● *research and development budget* – showing planned spending on particular projects;
● *cash budget* – showing the cash receipts and payments;
● *budget balance sheet*.

Once the budget is negotiated and agreed, it becomes an operating plan that reflects expectations about the conditions in which the organisation is operating. Each budget will be identified with a responsibility centre, i.e. with managers responsible for achieving the budget expectations. Sometimes alternative budgets are prepared for different purposes. For example, the performance targets incorporated for operating divisions may have been negotiated at a tighter level than past achievements with the objective of improving productivity. Although these targets may be achieved during the period of the budget, the process may take some months. If the cash or profit forecast given to the bank is based on these targets, it is likely that the cash or profit projections will not be achieved. So the cash budget may be based on looser performance. Similarly, a sales budget might reflect a higher sales level than that incorporated in the profit plan. The risk of having different budgets is the possibility that they will lose credibility within the organisation.

Performance measurement

Another favourite research topic has been the way in which budgets are used to judge performance. The behaviour of managers can be seriously influenced by the budget style in an organisation. If this is authoritarian and unthinking in manner, in which achieving the budget is the primary objective of management, it may lead to suboptimal performance. The pressure may be translated into action that is against long-term interests. For example, a salesperson might threaten customers with a price increase in the coming month to boost current sales and achieve a sales target.

In some organisations the immediate reaction to employees who fail to achieve budget is to presume that they are to blame. Any idea that the budget itself may be inappropriate or unachievable is not entertained. If this style is carried forward to performance evaluation it can be very destructive. In contrast, a budget can be prepared after discussion with those who know the area. It can then be used as a guide for judging performance after allowing for changing circumstances. This approach is more likely to achieve employee support.

Consistent failure to achieve budget should first lead to a review of the budget to ensure that the targets are fair and achievable. Only then should there be an attempt to take remedial action to improve an activity. The successful use of budgets depends on those affected, managers and staff alike, developing a sense of ownership towards them. As conditions change, the budget should be revised so that it continues to be credible.

A budget is, in essence, short term – usually for no more than one year. Nevertheless it has to be set in a longer-term context and be consistent with the strategy for the future development of the organisation. Long-term investments in research and development, product and market development, new plant and equipment or even the acquisition of other businesses have to be included in the short-term budget, and cash requirements in the cash budget.

If, in the longer term, a product is going to be phased out, it would be senseless to mount a major promotion campaign to strengthen its market position. It may make sense to promote it at a discount in stores in order to clear inventories. This further illustrates coordination, but, in particular, it shows a link between short-term action and longer-term strategy.

This conventional approach to budgeting is being challenged as businesses operate in rapidly changing conditions. More authority has to be delegated, with faster response times. So the emphasis is shifting towards value creation and benchmarking with other organisations rather than mere cost control.

19.7 Decision making

The one certainty in any organisation is that conditions will change. The budget cannot be revised every time minor changes occur or fresh opportunities arise. An organisation has to be flexible and responsive. Frequently opportunities arise that require prompt action – for example, a special order for a normal product or service, but to be sold at a low promotional price into a new market. In these circumstances the normal measurement of the average cost of producing and delivering the service may be an inappropriate starting point for computing potential profit. Many of the costs will not change as a result of accepting this opportunity: there will be no further research and development, no requirement to increase productive capacity (assuming that capacity is available) and, possibly, no added labour cost. In these conditions consideration need only be given to the costs that will increase directly as a result of choosing to accept this order: delivery, materials or additional resources consumed. Depreciation can be ignored and, in the very short term, so too can the labour cost since the employees will already have been paid for their time.

Let us suppose that Osram has an opportunity to make and sell electric light bulbs to a retailer. The bulbs will be packaged especially for the retailer and not identified with Osram. How will the costs be estimated?

- Is there enough manufacturing capacity without having to reduce normal production? If so, there is no need to take account of any additional capital costs.
- Are additional employees required or will existing employees have to work longer? If so, the extra costs will be attributable to this order; otherwise there are no added labour costs.
- Materials will be required according to the retailer's specification.
- Are there packaging costs? In this case there may be design and printing costs as well as costs of packaging material. The set-up costs will have to be included.
- Will the retailer collect the bulbs, or do they need to be delivered? Will there be added costs, or will existing transport arrangements be adequate?

The important issue is to identify costs that are directly traceable and attributable to this opportunity. The normal average cost of producing light bulbs may be irrelevant, since that includes research and development, capital equipment costs and administrative overheads which will not necessarily increase with this order.

Undoubtedly the retailer is looking for a special price, lower than that which Osram might normally charge. If this price exceeds the identified cost it may be an attractive opportunity. The critical issue for Osram to decide is whether or not this might damage its own long-term market position. Against this is the threat that the retailer will probably also be negotiating with a competitor to supply the light bulbs.

Suppose that the normal selling price is 80 cents and that the usual cost is made up (per unit) as follows:

	Cents
Labour	10
Materials	20
Packaging	5
Delivery	3
Overheads	25
	63
Contribution to profit	17
	80

The retailer wants to buy lamps at a price of 60 cents. If we establish that Osram's overheads will not increase, that labour costs will be 8 cents, materials 20 cents and packaging 10 cents, then the appropriate cost per unit will be 38 cents. If additional delivery is $100 per journey for up to 10,000 light bulbs, the design and set-up costs for printing the packaging are $10,000 and the order is for 100,000 bulbs, is it acceptable to sell at 60 cents?

			Cents
Unit costs:	labour		8
	material		20
	packaging		10
			38
			$
Cost for 100,000			38,000
Delivery cost			1,000
Design, set-up			10,000
Relevant cost			49,000
Revenue			60,000
Contribution to profit			11,000

This appears to be an acceptable sales opportunity as long as it does not erode Osram's normal market and as long as the existing customers do not expect the normal price to be lowered.

It is the job of the cost or management accountant to process financial information quickly in order to assist managers to take decisions of the kind described above. It is not usual for the information to be directly available from the financial records. The accountant will have to find out the alternative courses of action, extract the appropriate financial data from the system, process it and report in a coherent and understandable way to those responsible for taking the decision. Accountants are more likely to be useful if they understand the processes of service or product delivery. They also need to appreciate that they are providing a service to other managers.

Routine information for managers

Another aspect of internal financial measurement is more routine. Unlike the system of financial reporting for the organisation as a whole, which is geared to the needs of the capital market, internal information has to be related to the needs of the managers. They will be interested in financial measurements related to their own area of responsibility. For example, a marketing manager will need information about groups of products, brands, customers, regions and marketing areas. In research and development, costs accumulating for each project might be compared with research progress to date. This approach runs right through the value chain, recognising that value can be added from research, development and design, through to distribution and customer service. It is not just the manufacturing process or service delivery process that adds value and requires measurement.

As organisations develop stronger alliances and cooperative arrangements, at both the strategic and operational levels, the role of the accountant is expanded beyond the limits of the organisation within which he or she works. Cooperation in the supply chain can result in improved performance for both organisations involved. To achieve benefits of cost reduction and/or improved profitability through quality improvement, there has to be an open relationship and trust between the organisations. Accountants play a role in this cooperation by advising on the financial consequences for both organisations (Atkinson *et al.*, 2006).

19.8 Current themes and issues

Performance

Traditionally financial measures were taken as the main test of how well an organisation was performing. Kaplan and Norton (1992, 1996) argued that while this was clearly an essential aspect of performance, it was not the only one. They therefore developed what is known as the balanced scorecard, which attempts to link business strategy to performance by defining not one but several measures of performance. These include:

- operational measures of performance; financial, production, and customer satisfaction related;
- development of the organisation (learning and growth);
- alignment of operational performance measures, and hence operating system design, with strategic management targets.

The core of the balanced scorecard approach is to develop and specify operational measures of performance under the headings of: finance, customers, internal business processes, and learning and growth – all in support of the vision and strategy of the business unit. Under each of these headings, managers identify aspects that affect performance. For each aspect, they then identify objectives, measures and targets. Finally, they identify initiatives to create improvements.

When developing a scorecard for each of the four headings, managers are expected to draw on existing concepts and techniques such as activity-based costing, total quality management, managing change, and business process re-engineering. In essence, these links represent causal relationships, a virtuous cycle, and the value chain of the business. The final stage of the business scorecard process is to re-evaluate the scorecards and their value in the context of evolving strategy.

The balanced scorecard is used by many organisations to supplement financial measures of performance, but of course not to replace them.

Responsibility

One consequence of competitive conditions is that managers at the top of the organisation feel under great pressure to meet the expectations of stakeholders, especially shareholders in the main financial institutions. These external pressures affect the expectations that top managers have of those below them, and these are gradually transmitted down the organisation, so that all staff experience them in some way, even if indirectly. The pressures can be considerable as the senior managers expect to be rewarded with the opportunity to purchase shares in the company at a favourable price.

Sometimes this pressure leads to dubious practices and alleged fraud designed to enhance the share price, as in the cases of Enron and Parmalat (Chapter 5). This has brought considerable pressure from regulators to improve corporate governance and the quality of financial reporting.

Internationalisation

Different legal systems, industry financing, taxation systems, structure of the accounting profession, language and traditions mean that financial reporting varies between countries. France, Germany, Portugal, Spain and Japan have historically required compliance with a rigid framework for financial reporting (Alexander and Nobes, 2004). This is now changing as international financial reporting standards (IFRS) are being introduced in more than 90 countries, having started the process in 2005.

IFRS should help to overcome the difficulties of comparing the financial performance of companies in different countries and promote their access to international capital markets. The Accounting Standards Board in the United States will not adopt IFRS, and the EU will not apply them all. The US system has been much more prescriptive than the standards previously applied in the United Kingdom. For example, it generally requires all research and development costs to be subtracted from revenue as incurred and not carried forward in the balance sheet. The prescriptive approach in the United States has encouraged adherence to the letter of the standards rather than the spirit, and this has enabled some companies to construct dubious, and allegedly fraudulent, arrangements to enhance reported earnings.

Summary

1 **Understand the role of the finance function in management**

- Management needs funds, along with other resources, to help achieve the objectives of the business.

- It must choose between investment opportunities.

- Shareholders expect management to invest in projects to add shareholder value.

- Management requires adequate financial information.

- The finance function offers a system for assessing the financial consequences of decisions in a relatively objective way.

- Management is required to communicate financial information about the company to actual and prospective shareholders through the financial reports.

2 **Be able to interpret basic financial reports**

- Operating profit, EBIT, and net profit as a proportion of sales is a useful basis for comparing firms in the same industry and for each firm through time.

- Net profit as a proportion of shareholders' funds appears to be a measure of overall performance.

- All measures of performance based on accounting numbers are subject to the opinions of those who prepare them.

3 **Know the difference between profit and cash**

- Profit is based on accounting interpretation of financial data.

- Cash flow measures actual cash transactions and is less subject to opinion than profit.

4 Know what a simple financial plan contains and its purpose

- A financial plan sets out the financial implications of anticipated actions for a future period.

- In most businesses a plan will show expected sales, costs, resources needed to fulfil the plan, a cash forecast and an expected balance sheet.

- The plan sets out a course of action for the future.

5 Understand the importance of financial results to evaluate performance

- Owners and shareholders, and the capital market generally, exercise significant influence over managers.

- The capital markets' reaction to reports of financial performance affects the ability of the company to raise capital.

- Top management will experience this external pressure and transmit it internally.

- Financial information also helps to measure management performance internally – actual revenue and expenditure can be compared with the budget.

- Financial information can help control the management of projects, to ensure that what is spent corresponds to what has been planned.

6 Know the basic steps in calculating the financial consequences of a management decision

- Understanding the objectives of an organisation is essential in order to discriminate between alternative opportunities.

- Increments to profit may not require the recovery of all costs so long as incremental revenue exceeds incremental costs.

- Costs and revenue for decision purposes are estimates that reflect expected future operating conditions.

7 Be able to explain how budgets aim to ensure internal activities are directed at meeting external financial requirements

- Budgets give focus and direction to the plans that management makes to achieve objectives.

- Budgets help to coordinate the activities of different functions and activities.

- The levels at which budgets are set have effects on motivation – impossible or very slack budgets have little beneficial effect. Those that are challenging but achievable have a positive effect on commitment.

- Organisations normally have a regular cycle of budgeting activity, conducted between those at the centre and those in the operating units.

- In some companies line managers are heavily involved in decisions about budgets; in others the budgets are imposed from the centre in an authoritarian manner, which affects the degree to which employees and managers accept ownership of the budgets.

Review questions

1 Why do companies have to make a profit? Check the website for Marks & Spencer plc (**www.marksandspencer.com**). What do the directors have to say about profit and recent performance?

2 How is profit measured?

3 Explain why profit is different from cash. Look up any company report on **www.carol.co.uk** and see if you can explain the main difference between profit and cash for the company.

4 What does a balance sheet tell us about an organisation? What can you discover about the activities of BASF (**www.basf.com**) from the balance sheet?

5 Can you explain how the external pressures on a company to generate a profit are translated into internal planning systems? Explain how this occurs in M&S. What is the purpose of a budget?

6 How does a budget operate as a control mechanism?

7 Explain why the financial information prepared for external purposes is not necessarily appropriate for managers.

8 Explain the notion of contribution to the profit of a business. What do the directors of M&S and Morrisons (**www.morrisons.co.uk**) have to say in the 2006 annual reports about sources of profit?

9 What are international financial reporting standards of accounting? Explain how they differ from requirements that applied in your country prior to their introduction.

Concluding critical reflection

Think about the ways in which your company, or one with which you are familiar, deals with financial reporting and management accounting matters. Then make notes on these questions:

● What examples of the issues discussed in this chapter struck you as being relevant to practice in your company?

● To what extent do you experience the external pressures from the financial markets for high performance and for frequent and positive financial statements? To what extent do you feel the financial community has a realistic understanding of your business? Has the need to meet short-term financial targets affected long-term performance (e.g. by affecting investment decisions)?

● Is the budget setting process conducted fairly, and in a reasonably participative way? What **assumptions** about the effects of budgets on motivation appear to guide those who set them? Are those who must meet the budgets adequately involved in setting them?

● What factors such as the history or current **context** of the company appear to influence the way the company handles these financial and budgeting processes? Does the current approach appear to be right for the company in its context – or would a different view of the context lead to a more effective approach?

- Have people put forward **alternative** approaches to budget systems, based on evidence about other companies? If you could find such evidence, how may it affect company practice?
- To what extent are people in your organisation aware of the **limitations** of financial measures of performance? Have they acted to take account of this by, for example, considering some kind of balanced scorecard approach?

Further reading

Coggan, P. (2002), *The Money Machine*, Penguin, Harmondsworth.

A useful introduction to the mechanisms that management can use to raise capital and the expectations they have to satisfy.

Elliott, B. J. and Elliott, J., (2006), *Financial Accounting and Reporting* (11th edn), Financial Times/Prentice Hall, Harlow.

Alexander, D. and Nobes, C. (2007), *Financial Accounting: An International Introduction* (3rd edn), Financial Times/Prentice Hall, Harlow.

Provides a European perspective on the topic.

Horngren, C.T., Datar, S.M. and Foster, G. (2007), *Cost Accounting* (12th edn), Financial Times/Prentice Hall, Harlow.

A standard text that covers all areas of the topic in great detail.

Drury, C. (2004), *Management and Cost Accounting*, Thomson Learning, London.

A useful concentration on behavioural aspects of management accounting.

Atkinson, A., Kaplan, R., Matsumura, E.M. and Young, S. (2006), *Management Accounting* (5th edn), Financial Times/Prentice Hall, Harlow.

A pioneering text introducing modern concepts of cost accounting.

Ross, S., Westerfield, R. and Jordan, B. (2005), *Fundamentals of Corporate Finance* (7th edn) McGraw-Hill/Irwin, New York.

A sound introduction to principles of corporate finance.

Henry, D. (2004), 'Fuzzy numbers', *Business Week*, 4 October, pp. 79–87.

A critical review of the ways in which financial reports can be manipulated.

You should also visit company websites to access financial reports. As well as illustrating the financial issues covered in this chapter, they usually provide a lot of information that relates to other chapters.

Weblinks

These websites contain material relevant to the chapter:

www.basf.com	www.morrisons.co.uk
www.siemens.com	www.carol.co.uk
www.solvay.com	www.mothercare.com
www.marksandspencer.com	www.jsainsbury.co.uk

Visit the websites in the list, or any other company that interests you, and navigate to the pages which include their annual report or investor relations (see also 'recent trading statements'). Sometimes they may include 'presentations to analysts' (who advise fund managers on investment decisions).

- What kind of information do they include in these pages, and what messages are they trying to present to the financial markets? If performance has been poor, what reasons do they give, and what do they promise to do about it? What implications might that have for people working in the company?

- You could keep the most recent trading statement, and then compare it with the next one, which will be issued in a few months.

- Gather information from the media websites (such as **www.ft.com**) that relate to the companies you have chosen. What stories can you find that indicate something about the financial performance of those companies?

Annotated weblinks, multiple choice questions and other useful resources can be found on **www.pearsoned.co.uk/boddy**

Chapter 20

Managing operations and quality

Aim

To set the operations function in its historical context and show how it supports business performance.

Objectives

By the end of your work on this chapter you should be able to outline the concepts below in your own terms and:

1 Understand how the operations function can support performance in manufacturing and service organisations

2 Describe four types of transformation and their physical layout.

3 Compare the process approach to operations with the functional approach

4 Recognise the need to manage operations across an extended supply chain

5 Explain how the idea of 'order winners' and 'order qualifiers' links operations to the strategic process of delivering customer satisfaction, and making a profit.

Key terms

This chapter introduces the following ideas:

craft producers
factory production
inventory
line layout
functional layout
quality
total quality management
SERVQUAL (Service Quality Model)
delivery
demand lead time
supply lead time
cost
partnering
order winner
order qualifier

Each is a term defined within the text, as well as in the Glossary at the end of the book.

There are many aspects to the success of Benetton. One of these is undoubtedly its unusual operations management system.

With a radical approach to knitted goods, the Benettons in effect created a knitted pullover as a seasonal fashion good rather than a garment for comfort intended for years of service. Their bold colours brought a youthful image and created a need for dedicated retail outlets working to a closely defined and controlled specification. As a two-person business there was little need for systems. Giuliano designed and produced while Luciano sold. Their early success encouraged them to buy new machines and recruit local staff to produce a small range of goods in greater volume.

Where production was in Benetton factories, employees' suggestions for improvement were encouraged and acted upon while, early on, the company used subcontractors as producers. Initially these were outworkers to whom part-made garments would be delivered in their homes for completion and later collected. Larger groups of such workers formed a subcontractor network around the main Benetton factories. These grew up at a time when Benetton could not raise its own capital to build capacity internally. Instead, Luciano devised a partnership agreement with them such that, in return for providing a steady stream of work, the suppliers would invest in fixed assets.

The nature of the relationship with the retailers also impacts on Benetton's operations systems. The retail outlets are separate businesses (that do not pay royalties to their parent company).

The product line has increased each year with new garments and materials being used, but the essence of the Benetton system remains in operation terms dependent on a large number of independent entrepreneur suppliers working very closely in partnership with Benetton, growing and developing with them.

United Colors of Benetton, Autumn/Winter 2007/2008 collection (ph.: David Sims)

Benetton thus demonstrates many of the characteristics of the Japanese auto companies in their supply system relationships: tiers of subcontractors collaborate to make their supply chains effective against Benetton's competitors. All of this is done without compromising the core of the Benetton belief system that customers deserve choice, variety, value for money and a guaranteed level of quality and service.

Source: Based on *Building the Benetton System*, European Case Clearing House, No. 390-042-1.

> ## Case questions 20.1
>
> - What business practices did Benetton introduce that seem unusual to you?
> - What particular issues do you think would arise in managing an organisation with so many independent suppliers and shop owners?
> - What contrasts and similarities are there between Benetton and Tesco from a management point of view?

20.1 Introduction

This chapter sets the operations function in its historical context and shows how this function supports other manufacturing or service activities. It then considers the current state of development of the management approaches inside the function and the increasingly cross-boundary aspects being demonstrated in the best organisations. The boundaries being crossed include those between departments of the same organisation. The role of the operations function often incorporates the management of the whole integrated supply chain. This begins with the supplier of raw material and ends with the delivery of the product or service to the customer. Thus the function has a major strategic dimension where it can hinder or help the achievement of corporate goals.

The first section introduces the historical ideas and techniques that have shaped our understanding of how operations and quality add value to activities. The chapter then describes four types of operations system, and the five activities that together deliver a product or service. It outlines how operations contributes to quality in both manufacturing and services, and the benefits of taking a business process view of an organisation. It concludes by showing the link to marketing, and thus to the strategic position of operations in management.

20.2 Historical development

The operations function developed in manufacturing, and it was only in the second half of the twentieth century that academics and practitioners began to apply operations theories in the service sector, and to develop theory specifically for that sector. A major difference between the two is that in manufacture output (goods) can be produced and stored until the customer requires them, but in services output and consumption is simultaneous – so the customer is often present during the production process.

Craft production

The operations activity has existed for as long as there have been intelligent beings working with tools to transform base material into something different and desirable. In this regard, management created the specialism earlier than marketing, information systems and human resources. These latter depend more on size and complexity to justify separate status.

Craft production refers to a system in which the craft producers do everything. With or without customer involvement they design, source materials, make, display, sell, perhaps service and do the accounts.

From the beginnings of trade, **craft producers** have embodied their ideas and skills in a product or service, and usually some elements of both. Craft producers do everything themselves. With or without customer involvement they design, source materials, make, display, sell, perhaps service and do the accounts. Once they generate income they re-invest and often train apprentices to continue the skills.

Craft producers conduct each stage of the complete product life cycle. Their output is unique and very variable. Sometimes batch production is possible – see Management in Practice box.

The range of skills employed by a craft worker is a microcosm of the operations function. The flexibility that craft producers can achieve, and their ability to modify ideas to suit customer requirements, are now sought by large producers. Craft workers also gain a personal satisfaction from completing the whole set of tasks that is often absent in factories.

The Belgravia Gallery   www.belgraviagallery.com

The Belgravia Gallery in London is a family-run business that stocks the work of many well-known artists. As well as individual works of sculpture and painting it also sells limited editions of etchings, silkscreen prints, and lithographs. Visit the website and link to ArtForm for a description of how artists make small batches of these types of work.

Activity 20.1   Visit a craft worker

Visit a craft fair and talk to one or two of the craft workers about the way they work, how they sell, if they design to order or according only to their ideas, and how they organise the production of goods and the supply of materials.

Alternatively go to a craft show website, for example **www.craft-shows.co.uk**.

Factory production

Factory production made it possible to increase the supply of goods to rapidly growing populations. It broke down the integrated nature of the craft worker's approach. Management realised that dividing work into smaller units allowed workers to concentrate on developing a narrow range of specialised skills. In turn this allowed managers to employ less-skilled people and to increase production.

The division of labour was between different tasks and also between the thinking and doing tasks of manager and worker. This division began the evolution towards narrow, functionally defined boundaries with jealously guarded 'territory'. These would become the focus of conflict across the organisation.

> **Factory production** broke down the integrated nature of the craft worker's approach and made it possible to increase the supply of goods by dividing tasks into simple and repetitive sequences.

Activity 20.2   Visit a factory

Many large manufacturers offer visiting facilities. Try to visit several to see if you can understand the way they work. Alternatively you can visit the Cameron Balloons virtual factory at **www.bized.ac.uk/virtual/cb/welcome.htm**. This site is structured to give a broad view of many of the issues covered in this chapter.

Managers found that they needed two other techniques to enable high-volume production – standardisation and interchangeability. If several people are producing sets of parts that must fit together at some stage, they must work to a standard specification. Moreover, each part must be completely interchangeable with its equivalent produced by someone else. This was not an issue for the craft worker as he or she could work on only one product at a time, and had the skill to shape the parts to ensure a good fit.

Management in the developing factory system wanted to avoid this 'fitting' effort, so they designed both processes and machines to be regular and repeatable. This also influenced the nature of capital investment. At first, factory owners used this mainly to provide motive power for essentially human-based machines – they invested largely to supplement human muscle power. By removing variable human effort and increasing machine power, the machines themselves worked more precisely, so it became easier to make interchangeable parts.

Case questions 20.2

- Is Benetton a craft or a factory system?
- Review the information about the system Benetton uses and list its advantages and disadvantages.

Twentieth-century developments in manufacture

The aim of Frederick Taylor (1917) and the Gilbreths (1911, 1914) in creating a 'scientific' approach to management was to move away from methods that were variable and dependent on individual abilities and motivation (see Chapter 2). Some commentators criticise Taylor's approaches to work measurement. Yet people who are performing a sequence of related activities need to know how long to allow for each stage and what resources they need. The method study approaches that the Gilbreths pioneered as they searched for the 'one best way of working' have much to offer. What has changed is that management often expects operators themselves to look for improved ways of working as part of a continuous improvement effort.

A disadvantage of scientific management was the concentration on finely divided tasks that a worker would repeat thousands of times in a working life. This process was deskilling and dehumanising, permitting no variation or individuality.

This reached its peak with Henry Ford's automobile assembly plants. Ford brought high levels of interchangeability to moving production lines, highly 'scientific' management and vertical integration along the lines of supply (Ford, 1922). That is to say, Ford owned all the stages of production from raw materials through to final distribution to customers. In the 1920s his system could transform iron ore into a finished car in 81 hours, of which only about 5 hours were taken up by manufacturing and assembly. It was economically very efficient and reduced the real cost of producing a car over many years of continuous improvement. Over an 18-year period the retail price of the Model T Ford decreased from just over $3000 to less than $900. Ford's was a single model system, but General Motors later offered more varied products. They used different organisational principles, and created severe competition for Ford.

At the height of Ford's capability one of the many visitors was Taichi Ohno, who was the production engineer at the fledgling Toyota car company in Japan. While some of the Ford system impressed Ohno he learnt more from US supermarkets. He noted in particular how stores satisfied the needs of customers with minimal shelf space in the store. As customers took products away staff restocked the shelves. This is the logic behind what many observers regard as the world's best manufacturing company. It was also an early example of the two-way technology transfer (of managerial technologies) between west and east.

It was around this time that engineers developed a statistical approach to control quality. The method used control charts and sampling plans. Control charts tried to prevent people creating defects. Sampling plans ensured that any defects did not pass beyond the sampling stage. This statistical process control was instrumental in supporting production effort in the Second World War. Another development at that time was operational research (OR) (Chapter 2), which attempted to create mathematical models of management situations. Staff could then manipulate these models to develop optimum results that management could use to inform their decisions. The assumptions needed to make problems feasible for mathematical models sometimes appeared unrealistic to managers, though some OR techniques are still valuable. A prime example is critical path analysis, which helps people to manage complex projects.

During the 1960s the availability of relatively cheap computing power encouraged people to develop techniques for managing production and **inventory**, known as material requirements planning (MRP) systems (Orlicky, 1975). These aimed to manage the production activity by controlling every part at every stage, and seemed to offer the complete computer integration of the manufacturing process. The reality was often less than ideal. Nevertheless it caused managers in the western world to look to computers to solve the problems of managing increasingly complex production systems.

Management in resource-starved Japan followed a different approach. Ford's model of mass production had not made sense to Toyota. Ohno began to build a system that used the supermarket model of simplicity and customer-driven operations. This approach did not need computers, but did need dedicated and capable people working together.

> **Inventory** consists of materials and part or finished goods that are held in anticipation of need by customers along a chain of supply from raw materials through to final consumption (and recycling?).

Activity 20.3 Visit McDonald's

- Visit a McDonald's or similar fast-food outlet and try to discover the material inventories that are used. What non-material inventories will there be? Given their attempt to meet the 'healthy living' agenda by introducing new salads and lower-fat meals, what impact will this have on their inventories?
- Consider a hospital accident and emergency unit. What inventories are normally stored in such units? Remember that inventories are not just about products or things: other resources can be stored in some ways.

Modern thinking: service, systems and models

Any operation can be represented as a system that takes inputs of various kinds and transforms them into some kind of desired output. Inputs may include materials, equipment, finance and people. Outputs include products, services, reputation and waste. The aim of systems thinking is to use an abstract view of the total system and then to operate each subsystem according to the defined 'best way' for the complete system. This can be drawn as a simple systems diagram. A control mechanism is included to ensure that the outputs expected are delivered and that they meet customers' needs. A feedback control loop measures, analyses and modifies the inputs, as shown in Figure 20.1.

The transformation stage can take many forms, only one of which is production. Service-oriented types are more numerous, although the history of the subject concentrates on production.

Case questions 20.3

Draw a systems diagram that represents the Benetton production system.

- What are the main sources of feedback?
- How critical are they to input activities?

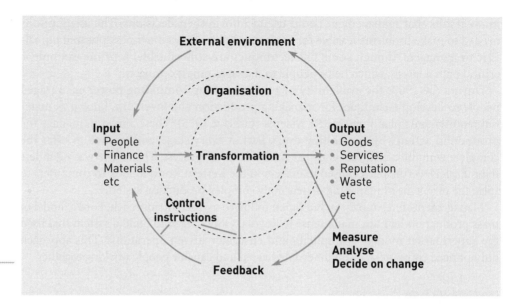

Figure 20.1

A basic systems diagram

Table 20.1 lists the transformation types. Operations systems need to deal with two distinguishing features. The first is whether the system results in a tangible 'product' that can be stored. If not, either someone consumes the output immediately or the system has wasted the capability. If nobody occupies a hotel room or an airline seat it creates no output. The companies cannot store the capacity and have lost for ever the opportunity to sell it. A car, on the other hand, embodies its value in a less time-dependent form.

The second distinguishing feature is that in a pure service transformation (such as a visit to the hairdresser) the customer must be present throughout the transformation and largely defines the details of the transformation. In making a physical product both design and transformation can be done without contact with the customer. In services the people with whom the customer interacts *are* the service.

Table 20.1

Transformation types

Transformation type	Commonly called	Applications, variations and customer relationship	
Form	Manufacture	Additive (several inputs, one output. e.g. auto assembly)	Outputs can be stored until required by customers
		Subtractive (one input, several outputs, e.g. chemical distillation)	
Possession	Retail	Goods	
Place	Transport/ Distribution	Goods	
	Extraction	Natural resources	Customer presence is not needed at the point of production, except in last case
	Transport	People	
Personal attribute	Service	Education	Production and consumption of output is simultaneous
		Entertainment	
		Appearance	Customer needs to be present at point of production
		Health	

Some service businesses are becoming like factories, especially in back-office areas that have no contact with customers (see the Part 4 Case – The Royal Bank of Scotland – for a description of its manufacturing division, which is deliberately modelled on factory methods). Another example is the cash dispenser system providing cash and sometimes other transactions with customers without direct contact between bank staff and customers. Conversely, many factories are trying to become closer to their customers to satisfy needs more precisely.

The objectives of operations managers are to select and manage the best mix of resources and transformation process to meet customer requirements. They must also do this in a way that permits the organisation to add value. The customer requirements will cover aspects of product or service design, delivery, reliability, speed and quality. All must be at an acceptable cost.

Characteristics that differentiate operational systems — key ideas

- **output volume**;
- **nature of processing** (continuous or intermittent);
- **outputs are continuous or discrete** (e.g. electricity or cars);
- **specificity to actual customer requirements** (degree to which the output and the flexibility of the system's response are specific to or specified by the customer);
- **physical layout** of transformation equipment.

Volume ranges from unique items such as a dam or fine art picture (jobbing production), through multiple copies or batches of similar items, to mass production. The latter can be continuous (e.g. cement) or discrete (e.g. video recorders). The design of the production system is related to the variety and quantity of demand, which ranges from unique single items to high-volume standard products.

For high-volume situations specialised linear flow lines, termed **line layouts**, can be constructed to benefit from efficiencies of scale. Such systems are said to have a *product focus*, as the system is designed around the generic nature of the product. However, in one-of-a kind situations processing equipment must be shared between products to use it efficiently, and this results in jumbled flows of materials and people. These systems are said to have a *process focus*, as attempts are made to gain benefits of similarities in the equipment and skills of the production processes. The resulting layouts are called **functional layouts**.

> A **line layout** is completely specified by the sequence of activities needed to transform materials into a product, or a natural sequence of treatments to provide a service.
>
> A **functional layout** groups similar physical processes together and brings materials and/or customers to these areas.

Most systems fall between the two extremes, and organisations typically use several types. A restaurant might have a functionally organised kitchen producing batches of meals for parties of diners. The waiter is a pure service person interacting to create a uniquely specified meal for a single diner. If there is a buffet or carvery area this may be in a line with customers moving along and being part of the transformation process. Figure 20.2 shows these systems with examples of each in the art, clothing, catering, and health sectors.

Activity 20.4   Defining transformation types

Define the transformation type and possible layout form of the following: (a) university matriculation or enrolment process, (b) a motorway fast-food servery, (c) a hospital accident and emergency unit, (d) a Benetton customer sales and service area.

Work/Customer flow	Product/volume: 1 One of a kind or very low volumes	Product/volume: 2 Mix of custom and standard products or services with moderate volumes	Product/volume: 3 High volumes for a few standard products or services
1 Jumbled flows 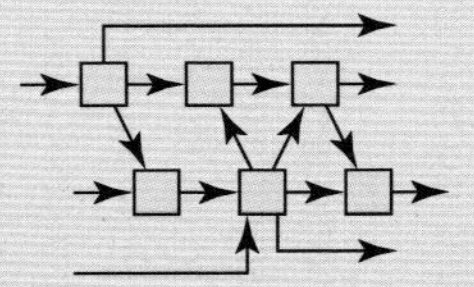	**Process focus – job shop:** • Individual painted portrait • Individual wedding dress • Private chef • Own doctor consultation		
2 Jumbled, but with some dominant flows 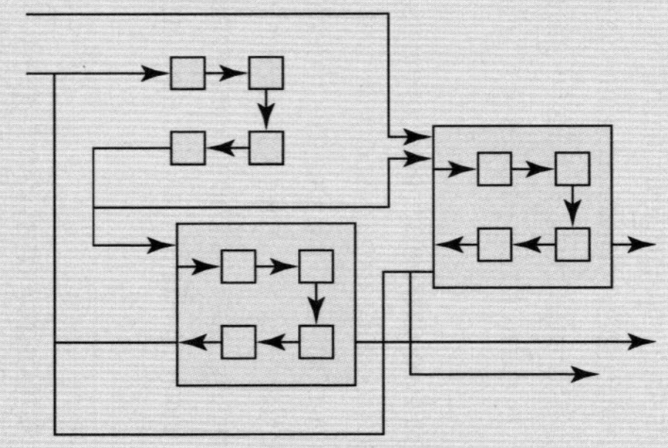		**Intermediate focus** • Limited edition art prints • Haute couture clothes • A la carte restaurant • Health clinic	
3 Line flows 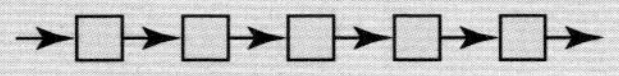			**Product focus – assembly/ service line** • Art shop prints • Department store clothes • Fast food restaurant • Specialist laser eye surgery

Figure 20.2 A process choice matrix

One of the dangers of diagrams such as Figure 20.2 is that they may imply that there are limited choices. Certainly there is a tendency to fit these categories together. The idea of the trade-off suggests that people can design systems to do certain things well – but they will then do other things less well (Skinner, 1969). When this is true, that original decision is very important, especially since the time and cost to make major changes of system structure will be significant. Nevertheless it may be possible to reduce these trade-offs in some way. If customer satisfaction is improved then this will be an important aspect of competitive advantage. This is what the best organisations try to do. They challenge the assumptions underlying the trade-offs and continually strive to do more with less while ensuring continuing and expanding customer support.

20.3 A framework for analysing operations

Providing goods and services to a customer depends on five key operations activities, and these provide a useful way of describing and analysing an organisation's operations system (Sprague, 1990). Figure 20.3 shows these activities of

● capacity
● standards
● materials
● scheduling
● control

and that each of these activities is connected to the others.

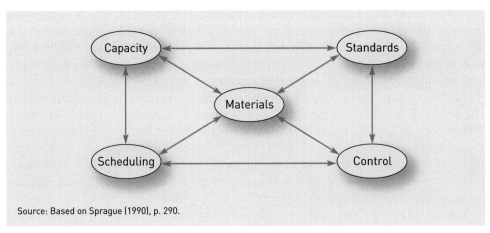

Source: Based on Sprague (1990), p. 290.

Figure 20.3

A framework for analysing operations management

Capacity

Capacity is the ability to yield an output – it is a statement of the ability of the numerous resources within an organisation to deliver to the customer: it indicates the limitations of a system. Defining capacity depends on identifying the main resources required to deliver a saleable output – staff, machinery, materials and finance. Capacity is limited by whichever resource is in shortest supply – a hospital's capacity to conduct an operation will be determined by some minimum number of specifically competent surgeons, nurses, technicians and related professionals, as well as more transferable staff such as catering and domestic staff. In service organisations all aspects of capacity may be visible to the customer – they can see the quality of staff, and the state of the physical equipment and resources.

Technology may sound as if it relates only to the physical facilities available, but experience suggests otherwise. Technology depends on people who are able and willing to use it to best effect. If managers in a government service dealing with pensions or other benefits aim to increase capacity by installing a new computer system, they also need to ensure that staff are willing and able to use the system, otherwise capacity will not increase (Chapter 12):

> It is the mix of physical technology – machines, equipment, buildings, the physical assets – and labor-embodied technology that establishes the organization's capacity. (Sprague, 1990, p. 273)

Standards

Standards relate to either quality or work performance. Quality standards are embedded in the specification of the product or service delivered to the customer (Section 20.4). Work performance standards enable managers to estimate and plan capacity by providing information on the time it takes to make or do something. One of the advantages which low-cost airlines have established is that the time it takes them to turn round an aircraft between landing and take-off is much lower than for conventional airlines. This enables them to fly more journeys with each aircraft – significantly increasing capacity at little cost.

Materials

A vital aspect of the operations function is to ensure an adequate supply of the many material resources needed to deliver an output: in late 2004 Nissan announced that it was halting car production for five days because it was unable to obtain adequate supplies of steel in a world market suddenly experiencing shortages. One of the dilemmas is that holding stocks of materials, otherwise known as inventory, is expensive – it ties up finance and incurs storage costs, and there is a risk, in rapidly changing markets, that stocks of components become out of date because of a change in model. Too much material can be as costly as too little. Materials management is particularly important in manufacturing systems where all labour costs are invested in the product itself. Hence the costs of material in the system, and in particular work-in-progress materials, are much greater than that in service situations, where most material is simple and is usually consumed by the customer in the service process.

Traditionally people saw inventory as an asset, representing the money value of stocks of raw materials. From a sales point of view, it enables an immediate sale, turning goods into cash. Those close to the customers stress the benefits of large stocks to solve manufacturing and distribution problems. They value being able to smooth demand and cover unexpected production difficulties – it was useful to have, 'just in case'. A modern view is fundamentally different, stressing the high cost of holding inventory and seeing it as something to be avoided. This approach focuses on solving the underlying manufacturing problems that inventory could avoid, rather than relying on expensive inventory to cover them up.

Scheduling

This is the function of coordinating the available resources by time or place – specifying which resources need to be available and when in order to meet demand. It begins with incoming information about demand and its likely impact on capacity. Service, productivity and profitability depend on matching supply with demand. Capacity management generates supply; scheduling links demand with that capacity. It can be carried out over several time periods. *Aggregate scheduling* is done for the medium term, and is closely associated with planned levels of capacity: as airlines plan their future fleets, which they need to do several years ahead, they make judgements about both their capacity and the likely demand (translated into frequency of flights on particular routes). *Master scheduling* deals with likely demand (firm or prospective orders) over the next few months, while *dispatching* is concerned with immediate decisions, for example about which rooms to allocate to which guests in a hotel.

Control

Control is intended to check whether the plans for capacity, scheduling and inventory are actually working. Without control, there is little point in planning, as there is no mechanism then to learn from the experience. Chapter 18 identified four steps in the control process:

- setting objectives – setting direction and standards
- measuring – seeing what is happening
- comparing – relating what is happening to what was expected to happen
- acting – taking short-term or long-term actions to correct significant deviations.

Only through control can immediate operations be kept moving towards objectives, and lessons learned for future improvements.

20.4 The operations function and its contribution

To add value, those in operations need to work closely with other managers, especially those concerned with strategy, design, marketing, HRM and finance: operations can help people throughout the business to make decisions that add value. The distinctive contribution of operations is in the areas of innovation, quality, delivery and cost.

Innovation

In products, the impetus for change comes from two sources. Market pull occurs when customers make new demands or when competitors try to change the strategic balance in some way. Such innovations are low risk as it is likely there will be a demand and since the product is based on what is known it should be easy to estimate costs. The danger is that while such innovations are safe, they do not advance quickly enough to gain a competitive advantage.

Technology push is the other main force for innovation. Here an expert with an idea proposes a new and often dramatic innovation in a product or service, or the process of producing it. The danger is that no customer has yet requested this item, and many will not be able to express a need for it. Such innovations are high risk. There are no forecasts

One famous innovation took place in 1972, at a time when the colours were still simple, i.e. one colour per garment and no complicated patterns. Traditionally, wool is dyed its final colour when it is still a yarn, i.e. a long time before being used in a garment and a long time ahead of actual customer demand. By designing a process to dye the completed garment Benetton incurred some increased production costs but greatly reduced the cost of carrying the inventory of coloured garments formerly needed to react to customers' demands. Instead, the decision about colour was moved much closer to customers' buying decision, thus removing much risk and complexity. It also meant that stocks that were selling well could be replenished, while stocks of less popular goods could be minimised.

As the company grew it continued to rely on a network of subcontractors – often created by internal groups being encouraged to become independent contractors to Benetton. By 1987 only 5 per cent of final garment sewing assembly was done internally by Benetton.

Source: Based on *Building the Benetton System*, European Case Clearing House, No. 390-042-1.

of market demand and no historical data for cost estimates. Many innovations of this type fail. Those that succeed, however, can change companies, industries and societies, as the Benetton case demonstrates. Think of the photocopier, jet engine or scanning electron microscope to realise the importance of major breakthrough innovations in product design. In reality management needs to consider both possibilities. It can seek incremental innovation continuously while the essentially intermittent nature of a breakthrough needs a different management approach.

Organisations need innovation in both products and processes – and not just those in the production area. Many office systems and most service businesses repay a serious effort to redesign them in more effective ways. Telephone-based and web-enabled insurance companies have dramatically increased their market share by innovations in the way they deliver the service. Banking is going in the same direction. Inditex shows the role of innovation in fashion retailing reaching new heights with Zara's attempts to remove 'seasons' from the business.

management in practice Inditex Group www.inditex.com

Inditex is one of the world's largest fashion distributors, including the Zara, Pull and Bear, Massimo Dutti, Berschka and Stradivarious formats. In 2007 it had over 3000 stores in 64 countries. Over 200 designers help meet the aim to be close to their customers and do away with seasons in fashions. They now introduce 20,000 new items a year – and to do this they need to be even more responsive than Benetton.

In effect they have redefined the interaction with the customers who now know that, because of the high rate of new product introduction, if they do not buy a product when it appears in the shops then they might miss the opportunity altogether since that same item may never appear again. This encourages customers to keep visiting the stores to catch the new ideas before someone beats them to it.

In a retail sector where many companies struggle, Inditex continues to expand. In 2007 it announced that it now has 29 stores in Russia, and had just opened its first store in China at a prestigious location in Beijing.

Source: Company website and other published information.

Quality

Theory and techniques concerned with product and service quality were developed first in the manufacturing sector, as were those of the operations function in general. Again, only in the second half of the twentieth century did academics and practitioners begin to apply them in the service sector, and to develop theory specifically applicable there.

When considering manufacture, in craft production the **quality** of output is crucial, for without it customers may not pay and will certainly not return. Craftspeople also tend to have pride in their work and continuously strive to improve their mastery of the craft. During the evolution of the factory system this ideal suffered as management subdivided the work process. Management separated quality approval from production. Even quality control charts were tools for quality inspectors, not production workers.

> The **quality** of a product or service is the (often imprecise) perception of a customer that what has been provided is at least what was expected for the price he or she paid.

Benetton – the case continues – response to new market trends www.benetton.com

CASE STUDY

Without giving up the strongest aspects of its networked model, Benetton is integrating and centralising, instituting direct control over key processes throughout the supply chain. Vertical integration has meant establishing state-of-the-art production poles in Benetton's foreign locations. The Castrette pole, near its headquarters, decides what each of the foreign poles should produce (on the basis of the skills and experience of the local population), and the foreign poles contract out production tasks.

Benetton has also increased its upstream vertical integration to exercise greater control over its supply of textiles and thread. At the retail end, the company is supplementing its network of small, independently owned shops with large, directly controlled megastores. To stay ahead of fashion's ever-changing whims, Benetton is streamlining its brands and collections, supplementing two basic collections with smaller, flash collections.

Source: Camuffo *et al.* (2001).

During the 1950s the Americans sent experts to Japan to help rebuild their manufacturing capability. The Japanese learned from Joseph Juran (Juran, 1974), W.E. Deming (Deming, 1988) and Armand Feigenbaum (Feigenbaum, 1993), and applied the lessons widely and conscientiously. They also recognised the fundamental truth of craft production – that the person who performs the transformation is the best person to ensure quality is correct. History has thus come full circle, with individuals taking pride in doing quality work and striving to make regular improvements.

Another realisation is that quality and customer satisfaction are responsibilities for all in the business and not simply the producer at the end of the chain. Each customer throughout the chain must receive top quality performance.

Principles of total quality management (TQM)

key ideas

- **philosophy**: waste reduction through continuous improvement
- **leadership**: committed and visible from top to bottom of the organisation
- **measurement**: costs involved in quality failures – the cost of quality
- **scope**: everyone, everywhere across whole supply chain
- **methods**: simple control and improvement techniques implemented by teams.

total quality management (TQM) is a philosophy of management that is driven by customer needs and expectations and focuses on continually improving work processes.

The philosophy underpinning **total quality management (TQM)** is that not having perfect quality wastes resources. Some of these wastes are obvious – scrapped material and lost time through equipment failure – but other wastes come through bad systems or poor communications and may be more difficult to find and measure. The philosophy advocates that a constant effort to remove waste adds value. Progressive, small improvements reduce costs as the system uses resources more effectively. It also avoids a tendency to consider delivery of any product as more important than the delivery of the correct product. Crosby introduced the idea that 'quality is free': it is getting it wrong that costs money (Crosby, 1979). Leadership of a visible and tangible type is needed to keep TQM efforts going.

In contrast to the scientific management approach, modern writers propose that quality inspection should not be separated from production. Everyone has to take responsibility for his or her proportion of the quality effort. This includes those people outside the organisation – the whole supply chain must function as a total quality system. Methods used include simple descriptive statistics, brainstorming techniques and simple statistical process controls (Oakland, 1994). The people performing the transformation are the ones trained and encouraged to use these tools and they will often display the results in their work area to spur further improvement. In this they will work as a team, calling on different people to support them as required.

Company teams can take part in Quality Award schemes. The Deming prize in Japan set the tone, with the winners enjoying high prestige. In the United States, the Baldrige Quality Award (**www.baldrige.com**) has set a pattern of very wide-ranging definitions of quality, and this has influenced the equivalent European Quality Awards (see the European Foundation for Quality Management website at **www.efqm.org**). National quality standards are often demanded of organisations to qualify as approved providers of goods or services (see **www.iso.ch**). The key is not the award but the thought processes of all the people in the organisation and their commitment to the total quality ideals.

Thinking about quality at the design stage brings important benefits. Choices here should incorporate ideas and information from as many insiders, customers and suppliers as is sensible. Such processes capture the prevention and 'right first time' ideals and create opportunities to save cost and time. Waste minimisation is the goal. Waste is any use of resources that does not add value for the customer. Note that customers are not the only stakeholders. Management may be able to justify an activity not directly related to the requirements of a direct customer. Environmental considerations fall into this category, as do those based on legislation.

The service sector has successfully adopted many of the quality theories and techniques developed in the manufacturing sector. However, the fundamental differences between manufacture and service make it more difficult to specify quality of a service than quality of a product. As a result individual preferences affect the assessments of service quality, which is created when the customer compares the quality delivered to that which they expected. These expectations are created by personal needs, past experience, word-of-mouth communication, and communications from the organisation.

SERVQUAL (service quality model) is a generic framework for analysing and delivering service quality to customers.

The service quality 'five-gap' model, known as **SERVQUAL** (Zeithaml *et al.*, 1990) identified five dimensions of service quality, following analysis of hundreds of customers' ratings:

1 **Tangibles** – appearance of physical facilities, equipment, personnel and communication materials;
2 **Reliability** – ability to perform the promised service dependably and accurately;
3 **Responsiveness** – willingness to help customers and provide prompt service;

4 **Assurance** – knowledge and courtesy of employees and their ability to convey trust and confidence;

5 **Empathy** – caring, individualised attention the firm provides its customers.

Customers will assess an organisation's performance on each of these five dimensions. It is relatively easy to define operational measures and performance standards for tangibles and reliability, usually in terms of physical parameters and time. However it is far more difficult to do this for responsiveness, assurance and empathy, which rely much more on the interpersonal skills and culture of people in the organisation.

In the SERVQUAL model a five-gap framework is defined to assist service organisations in managing service quality delivery. The gaps are described in Table 20.2, and although 'quality is the responsibility of everybody' an indication is given of who is primarily responsible for each gap and the question they must address.

Gap	Description	Responsibility of
1	Difference between what the customer expects, and what the organisation believes the customer expects.	Marketing: Do we know what the customer expects?
2	Difference between what the organisation thinks the customer expects, and the standards/specifications we set to deliver those expectations.	Marketing and Operations: Do we measure the right things, and are we setting correct levels of delivery?
3	Difference between the standards/specifications we set, and the levels we deliver.	Operations: Do we meet the quality specifications (levels) we set ourselves?
4	Difference between the standards/specification levels the organisation delivers and what it tells the customer it delivers.	Marketing: Are we honest with customers?
5	Difference between what the customer expects, and what the organisation delivers. This is the perceived quality created at the point of delivery, the aggregation of the other 4 gaps.	All: Have we delivered to expectations?

Table 20.2
The five gaps of the SERVQUAL service quality framework

Sources of quality cost

key ideas

- **prevention**: getting the systems right
- **appraisal**: measuring how the systems are performing
- **internal failure**: faults found during checks inside the operation
- **external failure**: faults found by users – the worst kind.

Quality is never completely free because of the investment in prevention. It is clear, however, that switching proportionately more resources into prevention cuts other costs such that the total reduces.

Happy   www.happycomputers.co.uk

In 2006 Happy (formerly known as Happy Computers) was named as the small business with the most impact on society in the United Kingdom. It had earlier been the overall winner of the *Management Today* Service Excellence Award. Happy is an IT training company which believes that learning should be fun. It was established to combine technical expertise and excellent training skills with an enjoyable learning environment. All their training is based around the age-old principle:

- Tell me and I will forget.
- Show me and I will remember.
- Involve me and I will understand.

There are no lectures at Happy. All their courses are designed to involve delegates to the full, ensuring active learning and enabling people to reach their potential. Happy is not the largest IT training company, although they are in the top 50 by size. Happy – with only 48 employees – is the only training company in the United Kingdom to be rated in the top three by the Institute of IT Training in each of the past three years.

Source: *Management Today*, October 2003, Service Excellence Awards Supplement; company website.

Dell Computing   www.dell.com

By redesigning their whole supply chain Dell has made a virtue out of speed and response to customers in a way that repays the company by efficient use of money. Customers buy online and pay for their product in advance. Dell also tries to manage the elective choices customers make by offering discounts for inventory that is moving too slowly. Its operational control system is such that a customer can call into Dell to check progress in the manufacture of their order. By then Dell has the use of their money and some time later will pay its suppliers' bills for the materials they have provided. This system is so responsive that Dell is able to change its pricing structure daily to take advantage of material price fluctuations and to price aggressively for certain markets in ways that its less flexible competitors find difficult to match.

Activity 20.5   Defining quality

Define what quality means in the following: (a) a fast-food hamburger restaurant, (b) a five-star hotel, (c) an executive automobile, (d) a travel agency, (e) the products sold by Zara, (f) the service provided by Zara sales staff.

Delivery

Speedy and on-time delivery is of fundamental importance in creating a perception of quality in both the service and manufacturing sectors. In manufacture each link in the chain of supply from raw material to final consumer is formed between an individual or group acting as a customer to a supplier. The customer is in turn the supplier to another. Thus the next customer along the chain immediately feels any failure in quality, unless large amounts of inventory hide the failure. This is a direct benefit of reducing inventory: it exposes quality problems so that people can deal with them permanently.

Benetton – the case continues – innovations in ordering www.benetton.com

CASE STUDY

The fashion cycle for the important spring/summer season begins in February with selection of around 500 items. During May–July small samples are produced to allow retailers a chance to place orders for the season seven months ahead. As the first orders roll in, production plans are made and subcontractors informed. The shop owners are then obliged to buy the goods produced as Benetton does not accept any returned goods unsold at the end of the season. Most of the shop orders are delivered between November and the following May as the Basic collection in readiness for the new season.

The balance of the orders fall into two categories: 'Flash' consists of reactions to new trends or competitor offerings while 'Reassortment' allows for individual choice of product mix in a particular store, and possibly for those late-dyed popular colours.

Thus the operations system has to cope with fairly stable production runs of the 'standard order' for 80–90 per cent and 'specials' on a much faster response time for the late variations.

Source: Based on *Building the Benetton System*, European Case Clearing House, No. 390-042-1.

As with quality, so with **delivery**. Any failure to supply the customer when expected causes the wastes of delay, remedial action and extra effort. The first step in delivery performance is total reliability. Every downstream customer is dependent on every upstream supplier fulfilling his or her delivery promise, otherwise there is more waste. Every chain needs reliability, but sometimes it also needs speedy delivery. Speed is crucial when a company is bringing a new product (or service) to the market. It wants to make sales to early adopters before competitors can produce alternatives that will drive the price down. In competitive situations speed of response may be the distinguishing factor that wins the order. Figure 20.4 captures the relative timescales on the supply and demand side.

Figure 20.4 illustrates a manufactured product for which the customer is prepared to wait some time between placing and receiving the order – the **demand lead time**. In some markets, such as retailing and service, this time is zero. That is, supply has to be

Delivery relates to the achievement of all promises made by any supplier to a customer.

Demand lead time is the elapsed time that a customer is prepared to allow between placing an order for a product or service and actually receiving it; in certain situations this time is effectively zero.

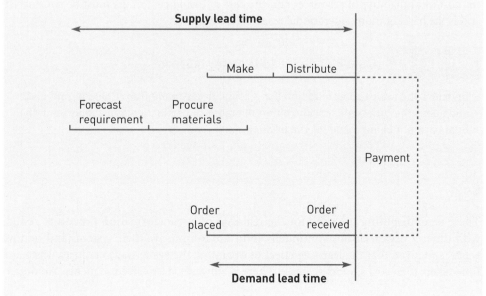

Figure 20.4

Manufacturing supply/demand lead time balance

Supply lead time is the total elapsed time between the decision to obtain the basic input resources to the final delivery of the product or service to the customer.

instantaneous (off the shelf) or the buyer goes elsewhere. In most manufacturing situations the addition of all the supply-side activities that constitute the **supply lead time** far exceeds the demand lead time. The critical fact is that all of the investment tied up in decisions to the left of the order placement point are at risk. In these areas there is no guarantee that a customer will place an order. So there is continual pressure to reduce the time needed on the supply side of the balance. Ideally the supply total would be less than the demand total. That would guarantee sales success, but only markets producing customised products to order are like this.

One of the most effective ways to reduce the supply lead time in the linked manufacturing supply chain is to consider the flow of materials through to the final customer as the real challenge. The task then is to synchronise all of the tributary flows into the main stream to maximise the main flow and minimise waste. Such synchronisation of flow calls for coordinated effort in scheduling deliveries from internal and external suppliers according to an integrated master plan and reinforces the need for absolute control of quality and delivery performance. In manufacture materials should flow continuously downstream to satisfy all the intermediate customer requirements before passing from the chain to the final consumer. In service the customer should pass through the system smoothly without interruption, experiencing additional value at each stage.

The concept of flow is a useful one. It is implied in the concept that Michael Porter describes as a value chain. Here the horizontal flow consists of the five stages of inbound logistics, transformation, outbound logistics, sales and service, and the generation of a financial margin (see Chapter 8). Porter extends the value system idea to include the output from one organisation's value chain being the input to another one. It is then similar to the supply chain model described above (Porter, 1980b). This concept also lies behind the just-in-time system of production where the total quality management and synchronised flow approaches are coupled with a cross-trained and committed workforce to produce very effectively (Schonberger, 1983).

In service businesses the situation is different since the customer must be present during the service. If instant service is expected then all resources, people, equipment and materials must be on standby when the customer arrives. In most service situations customers do not expect instant service, but will be willing to wait for some time, either in a queue or appointment system (though there are some obvious exceptions). The customer perception of what is an acceptable service time can produce difficulties for the supply system if the system cannot match expectations effectively. The trade-off between the cost of availability of resources and the cost of losing customers must be considered, and is the basis of many operational research techniques.

Activity 20.6 **Consider the lead time for a dress**

Consider the total supply lead time for a bridal dress made from Chinese silk. List and guess the timescales for the different stages of production and supply up to the final garment being made for the bride.

Cost expresses in money units the effect of activating or consuming resources. It is an internal control process of the producing organisation and is not visible to outside parties.

Cost

There is no disputing the need for the real **cost** of a transformation process to reduce with time. If organisations continually innovate to improve their systems and remove waste, and given that the learning effect of operating the systems also reduces waste and time taken, then cost should decrease. There is, however, a preferred sequence. An organisation must first build a solid base of quality performance and reinforce it with careful control over delivery. Doing these things correctly will lead to lower cost. If, on the other hand, the organisation tries to reduce costs and simply takes resources away, this is likely to lower overall quality and delivery performance.

Cost is also an internal factor that customers do not always need to know. What they need to understand is what pricing possibilities the organisation can offer as a result of its performance on cost reduction. It is also important that an organisation does not concentrate solely on the direct money aspect of the business transaction, since many of the factors that go towards creating a satisfied customer will not necessarily be reflected in the unit price quoted for the good or service. The operations function has an important role to play as part of the supply chain team that delivers the goods and/or services in the most effective manner.

Case question 20.4

Consider the supply lead time for the Benetton Basic collection and for the Flash or Reassortment goods. What is the demand lead time for each of these categories?

Chester Royal Hospital

management in practice

The Chester Royal Hospital is part of a UK National Health Service (NHS) trust. Some time ago a problem arose in the Day Clinic as patients' case notes were often not available when they arrived for their appointment. This meant that the hospital was not meeting a target of treating a patient within 30 minutes.

The notes were stored in a central Medical Records office, and when needed in a department (such as the Day Clinic), they were requested and delivered by hospital porters through the internal mail system, which covered several sites. When a record was taken from Medical Records a 'tracer' note was left in its space indicating where it had been taken.

To tackle this problem a team from several functions and departments, in effect a Quality Circle, was formed, working under the guidance of a facilitator. They spent two days gathering information to identify why records were not available when the patient arrived, and identified these reasons:

- Consultants, or their secretaries, were keeping the case notes 'just in case' they would be needed again, ignoring the possibility of need elsewhere.
- Sometimes a department would pass the record to another department without passing it back through Medical Records or amending the tracer note. In fact records were often taken to other geographical sites.
- The mail system did not deliver in time for early morning appointments.
- Records were lost in the mail system.
- Porters had difficulty in finding records because of poor signage and storage in medical departments.

The suggested actions were:

- an amnesty for lost records and asking all medical departments to return them;
- enforcing the existing record-tracking system better;
- improving signage in medical departments, identifying the assistants of consultants;
- improving signage on internal mail bags to prevent misdirection of internal mail;
- revising internal mail transport systems to fit scheduling of patient appointments.

The exercise rapidly reduced the number of missing records. Some consultants' secretaries and junior managers resisted the changes, feeling they were losing authority over records or their staff.

Relating the experience at Chester Royal to the theory in this chapter shows that:

● the SERVQUAL model is a way of setting service quality standards that relate to customer expectations;
● total quality management and continuous improvement has an important role in satisfying these expectations by meeting the quality standards specified;
● the internal supply chain is an important link in satisfying expectations of customers, in this case by synchronising medical record flow with patient appointments.

This form of system awareness is important when possible cost reductions and quality improvements are considered. Each unit has an interest in supporting both the immediate and the final customer, and also has to look good as measured by current performance. The difficulty is that sometimes the best supply chain solution means that one part operates less efficiently (from a local perspective) to improve overall chain performance.

key ideas   Conflicting performance targets

The classic description of the problem of each part trying to maximise its own performance relates to the ideal specifications for the production area and the sales area. The manufacturing stereotype is a preference for long runs of a standard product. The sales stereotype is a preference for providing unique products that meet particular customer requirements. There has to be a balance. It is possible for an organisation to become bankrupt satisfying customer requirements that it is not designed to satisfy, so the maxim cannot be 'customer satisfaction at all costs' since some costs are unacceptable.

Thus cost reduction is a continuing necessity but needs to be done with care. Suppliers can reduce some costs without any impact on the customer simply by doing things more smartly. One waste worth challenging is the amount of material held in the various categories of stock. By re-examining where to hold protection stocks and eliminating all others a supplier can make large savings at no risk to customer service.

Case question 20.5

Examine the points in the Benetton supply chain where inventory is stored and identify why it is likely to be held there.

The major leverage point for cost reduction is, however, at the initial design stage. Staff make decisions here that incur costs later. By thinking through both quality and operational logistics issues at this stage people can avoid creating unnecessary costs at the source.

20.5 The business process view

The concept of flow as horizontal through the organisation is opposed to the vertical orientation of traditional organisational principles based around functions. This is in accord with a greater focus on customers and their satisfaction. The functional (process focused) structure reflects the same thought patterns that lead to the functional (jumbled flow) layout discussed earlier. Both optimise internally regardless of the effect on the customer.

To escape from this mindset, organisations are trying to restructure their activities around basic business processes that all organisations will use to meet their customers' requirements. By defining these in generic terms they hope to create new insights. The essence of flow also means removing the waste from the interfaces between the traditional functions. Since organisations are unique there are no universal definitions of these core processes. They will vary between organisations, but it is possible to identify some relatively common ones: generating orders, fulfilling orders, managing money, and keeping customers afterwards.

Direct Line Insurance www.directline.com

Re-engineering business processes has been critical for this company, which redefined the insurance business in the United Kingdom. Most other providers were then forced to copy this model just to remain in the same marketplace.

Each of Direct Line's products is designed with the same basic philosophy: to offer consumers *clear*, *straightforward*, *good value* alternatives to products that are sold through traditional distribution channels. This is especially so where those channels involve a 'middleman' that can be cut out to reduce costs.

As the company conducts most of its business by telephone, customer service is at the core of the Direct Line proposition. It introduced new levels of service to the financial services sector, putting customer needs and considerations first in everything that it does.

To ensure that standards are maintained the company provides all staff with extensive customer care training and re-engineers sales processes to cut out complicated forms and jargon. In one of its first revolutionary moves Direct Line removed the need for 'cover notes' by arranging for all documents such as policy and insurance certificates to be laser printed immediately and forwarded by first-class post to customers – usually in time for the following day.

Innovative technology helps Direct Line keep down costs that, in turn, helps to reduce premiums. For example, most Direct Line products are paid for using credit cards or direct debits so that all payments are processed electronically. This keeps staffing levels and overheads to a minimum. Automated call handling systems also ensure that the company's 15 million customer calls each year are quickly and effortlessly rerouted between Direct Line's six call centres to ensure the minimum wait for an available operator.

Of course, the option to provide such call centre activity from outsourced and off-shored providers in, for example, India is one that many such companies are now considering.

Source: Company website and other published sources.

Generating orders: creating and capturing intention to buy

This process recognises the two sources of innovation – technology push and market pull – and uses either or both to define new product or service packages to bring to the customer market. Defined as a business process, this will cover activities often associated in the past with marketing, product design, prototype production, trial marketing, and product advertising and launch. The creative process is intended to bring together all of the interests associated with a forward look at customers. The aim is to fully define their requirements. In the case of truly innovative ideas the intention is to specify the product or service in a way that determines what the operations systems have to do to support these new market requirements.

Fulfilling orders: delivering to the customer

Having created the intention to buy, this process does everything necessary to deliver the product or service to the customer. It aims to do this in such a way that the transaction satisfies both the customer and the supply system.

The process starts with capturing a customer order. From here it will cover all of the planning stages that allocate resources to produce and deliver the order. It also recognises the need to source resources from other suppliers in the chain. Thus the traditional functions of sales processing and forecasting, production planning and control, manufacture or service provision and resource procurement (buying) can all be included. So too can those concerned with the physical movement of materials and ensuring people are available to do the work. The flows in this process are clearly two-way: from customers to supply system about demand, and from supply system to customers with the order. The flow returns again with money to pay for the exchange. There are many interfaces between activities in this business process, often acting in very short timescales, and clearly this is one of the major (direct) value-adding sets of activities in the organisation.

management in practice   e-government

In a different context of delivering services rather than products, the EU Commission is coordinating member states as they move towards e-government that is believed to be capable of delivering

better, more efficient public services and improve the relationship between citisens and their governments. The resulting benefits to the quality of life, industrial competitiveness and society will only be realised, however, if administrations change the way they operate.

Expected benefits include:

cost for both businesses and governments can be reduced, cutting the tax burden and boosting competitiveness; the public sector can be made more open and transparent, delivering governments which are more comprehensible and accountable to citizens, improving civic involvement in policy making and reinforcing democracy at every level across Europe; administrations can be made more user-centred and inclusive, providing 24/7 personalised services to everyone, no matter their circumstances or special needs.

Depending on the nature of the demand (a forecast or a firm customer order) the planning process can be aimed either at building inventory or at meeting the customer order. Speed is not always necessary, although delivery reliability is. In building for inventory, management strikes a balance between the costs of making a large and economical batch now and the costs of holding stocks of finished goods. If it produces too much for immediate requirements it has to store and care for the product until it is sold. The economic order quantity can be calculated by making assumptions about actual cost patterns. Management can then establish and manage stockholding policies.

Computerised planning approaches are appropriate when demand is known or can be calculated. Every order for a family car will generate an order for five wheels. Planners then add to this how long they believe it will take to produce or purchase the wheels. They can then decide when they need to place an order for the earlier parts of the supply system.

The just-in-time approach omits the computer calculations. It replaces them with a simple 'pull' signal sent when a customer removes some material from the end of the previous stage of the supply chain. This action sends a replenishment signal (a *kanban*) upstream telling the supplier to produce replacement parts. The signal can then ripple its way upstream and, ideally, the supply chain then operates quickly and with a much reduced level of inventory compared with both of the other ways described.

Pure service operations concentrate on scheduling service staff to ensure that they are available to deal with the customers as they arrive.

Managing money: making and receiving payments, and keeping records

Transactions to transfer the ownership of goods or to pay for services must be properly accounted for. It is also necessary to create an audit trail to establish that the activities have been done legally. This process also provides the funds with which the organisation pays its own bills. More businesses fail through mismanaging their cash flow than fail for lack of customers. This is another reason to look for speed through the business processes in order to convert customer interest into cash.

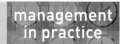

Cash handling process in supermarkets

management in practice

Supermarkets have a very profitable cash handling process. They receive cash or credit transfers almost instantaneously but pay their suppliers as long as 30 days from the date of the invoice. Meanwhile they can earn interest on both sets of money in the short-term financial marketplace. It is perhaps not surprising that the larger retail chains are providing their own banking opportunities for their customers. In some ways they have been behaving as banks for years. At the same time they have been highly efficient at converting shelf space to sales with minimum in-store inventory. Remember the Toyota story and its production system that was inspired by the supermarkets.

New ways of working eliminate many paper-based and costly transaction-processing activities. They use simplified techniques and place greater responsibility on the suppliers to do what they have contracted to do without the customer checking. In the car wheel example, all cars leaving the assembler's premises must have five wheels. Rather than arrange a transaction for each delivery of wheels, common practice now is to record the number of cars leaving the system (which is done anyway). The system multiplies that number by five and regularly pays the supplier for that number of wheels. As an alternative, for low-value items all purchasers can be issued with the equivalent of a plastic bank card so that orders can be sent in, deliveries made and a fully detailed statement sent to the purchasing organisation at the end of the month for one payment.

These are well-established examples of what has come to be called electronic or e-commerce. The speed of web-based electronic communications allows for more efficient markets to be established. Whole industries are trying to move in this direction and companies are creating business opportunities where previously none were possible.

Retaining customers: providing service

In many product areas management has come to realise that it is much cheaper to retain a customer than to find a new one (a common estimate of the ratio is 1:10). This has caused them to re-examine the nature of the customer relationship and to support valued customers well beyond any contractual or warranty requirement. In service areas the degree of direct involvement with the client or customer changes the nature of the considerations again. The arguments about customer retention are even more important in this environment and often there will be a need to keep in regular contact (special newsletters, magazines, offers) to try to keep the relationship going.

In all cases current customers have great value in evaluating new product or service ideas at the trial market stage. They also help secure new customers through recommendations and contact names. This will be the case particularly where the price for a single transaction is not the most important factor in the buying decision.

20.6   Current themes and issues

Performance

Two themes have become prominent in considering how the operations function contributes to performance. The first stresses the value of looking at the need to manage across boundaries – both (upstream) suppliers and (downstream) customers. Those in the value chain need to manage the relationships so that the chain as a whole meets the needs of the final customer through smooth coordination between independent but cooperating organisations. It is also about encouraging, recognising and implementing innovation throughout the chain to benefit the ultimate customer, and hence all members of the chain.

Partnering describes a business relationship based on taking a long-term view that the partners wish to work together to enhance customers' satisfaction.

When separate organisations use this approach they often refer to it as **partnering** (Macbeth and Ferguson, 1994). The logic applies to all management activities that cross boundaries, not only those with different ownership. The essence is to recognise complementary capabilities, look for ways to coordinate informational and logistical flows, and invest for the long term in a jointly planned way.

The second theme relates operations to strategy and marketing. Chapter 8 distinguished between low-cost and differentiation strategies, and clearly the successful pursuit of either depends on adequate interaction with operations. There needs to be an iterative process involving all interested parties deciding what the company must do well to succeed in the market. The concepts of order winners and order qualifiers can help to frame the discussion and bridge the language gap between the marketing and the operations staff (Hill, 2004).

An **order winner** is some feature of the product or service that so positively differentiates it that customers want to buy it in preference to competing products.

An **order qualifier** is a necessary but not sufficient requirement to be considered by a customer.

An **order winner** is some feature or combination of features of the product or service that differentiates it from others, and which makes customers want to buy it – ideally something unique that competitors cannot replicate. An **order qualifier** is the ticket to the game. It is a feature that is a necessary but not a sufficient requirement for purchase. Customers will not consider you without it. Qualifiers get the seller into the race but do not guarantee that it will win the prize. Some qualifiers are so critical that any deviation from the expected standard means instant disqualification. Customers will ignore otherwise attractive features if the seller does not meet this basic requirement.

These concepts are useful in the debate between marketing and operations personnel since they can be defined in terms that both can understand. The operations staff can convert them into system specifications for process design once the parties agree them. It is also possible to rein in the wilder flights of fancy from marketers who see a new opportunity that the operations system has no prospect of satisfying in a sensible time. It is better to recognise this and to modify the target market than to risk everything to make a total change of operating system.

Thus the discussion of order winners and qualifiers needs to be a regular part of the chain process. Often it is a service-related feature that distinguishes qualified products. It is these aspects that are most likely to occur at the boundaries between traditional organisations. An integrated view of the whole supply chain helps management to improve them.

Activity 20.7 **Defining order winners and qualifiers**

- Define the order winners and qualifiers for the following: (a) a music, food and drink club catering for students; (b) a personal computer.
- Highlight those features most likely to change and comment on the implications for the operations system design needed to support them.

Responsibility

A major theme in many companies is how best to combat climate change, and many have announced ambitious targets for reducing waste and emissions. Chapter 6 illustrated this with Marks & Spencer's Plan A, a business-wide 'eco-plan' that will affect every part of the business over the next five years. The 100-point plan means that by 2012 the company will:

become carbon neutral
send no waste to landfill
extend sustainable sourcing
set new standards in ethical trading
help customers and employees live a healthier lifestyle.

The plan sets targets in each area, and specifies about 20 more specific plans in each. While presented as a part of the company's overall strategy, implementing the plan will depend on how well those in the operations function can change the way the company currently conducts the transformation process. It will cover all forms of transformation, and will also involve close relations with those in the supply chain.

Internationalisation

Tightening performance requirements often depend on firms rearranging their supply chain, especially by outsourcing some aspect of the production or service delivery overseas. This inevitably puts additional demands on the operations function, who have to manage an ever more extended, and complex, network of relationships with suppliers and logistics providers.

At the same time companies come under pressure from NGOs and other lobbying bodies about working conditions overseas. So while the growing range of international suppliers helps meet performance targets, it can at the same time raise dilemmas within the responsibility agenda.

This extends the role of operations, since not only do they need to manage increasingly complex physical aspects of the supply chain, but also ensure that the practices of suppliers are consistent with the company's policies on corporate responsibility with regard to suppliers.

Summary

1 Understand how the operations function can support performance in manufacturing and service organisations

- By improving the capabilities of the organisation to achieve high standards of innovation, quality, delivery, cost and flow.

- Operations developed in factories but now applies to service areas as well as products. It needs to be seen as part of an integrated approach to business connected with other functions internally and externally to customers and suppliers.

2 Describe four types of transformation and their physical layout

- Transformation types are:
  - form (manufacture)
  - possession (retail)
  - place (transport, distribution, extraction)
  - personal attribute (service – education, entertainment, appearance, health).

- Layout options range from
  - line layouts (product focus, line flow) to
  - functional layouts (process focus, jumbled flow).

  Between these the intermediate focus mixes aspects of the two extremes.

3 Compare the process approach to operations with the functional approach

- The functional approach organises activities 'vertically' within distinct functional specialisations, between which communication can be difficult. An alternative is to focus on horizontal flows of business processes that are directed at meeting customer needs. Such processes vary between businesses, but commonly important ones are those aimed at:
  - generating orders: creating and capturing a customer's intent to buy the product or service;
  - fulfilling orders: delivering the product or service to the customer;
  - managing money: getting and giving payments, and keeping transaction records for reporting;
  - keeping customers afterwards: maintaining service.

4 Recognise the need to manage operations across an extended supply chain

- Each stage in a supply chain has particular expertise, and the relations across the chain should be managed to maximise the scope for each player to do what they do best – recognising complementary capabilities. Further benefits come if the players in the chain coordinate their activities and invest for the long term in a jointly planned way.

5 Explain how the idea of 'order winners' and 'order qualifiers' links operations to the strategic process of meeting customer needs profitably

- While order qualifiers are an essential ticket to offer a product or service, order winners are those combinations of features that positively discriminate a company from its competitors. This concept is familiar to both marketing and operations: operations' contribution is through being able to specify the implications for process design of particular order winners.

Review questions

1 Describe systems concepts as they apply to an operating system.

2 What are the major categories of operations system and their associated physical layout types?

3 Why is control over quality at source so important?

4 How does service quality differ from manufacturing quality?

5 Why is delivery reliability more important than delivery speed?

6 Describe and discuss the importance of the demand/supply balance.

7 In what ways is the business processes approach different from traditional approaches?

8 List and discuss the main features of a partnering approach to business relationships. (See **www.scmg.co.uk** or **www.pslcbi.com** for ideas.)

9 Discuss the concepts of order winners and order qualifiers.

Concluding critical reflection

Think about the ways in which your company, or one with which you are familiar, deals with operational issues – such as innovation, quality or cost. Then make notes on these questions:

- What examples of the issues discussed in this chapter struck you as being relevant to practice in your company?

- To what extent do you experience external pressures from customers for rapid and sustained operating improvements? Which of the areas to which operations can make a contribution (innovation, flow, etc.) are most relevant to your situation?

- How much attention is paid to identifying order qualifiers and order winners, and to ensuring that internal processes are redesigned to support order-winning features of your services or products? How are the **assumptions** about winners and qualifiers checked for accuracy?

- What factors such as the history or current **context** of the company appear to influence the way the company handles operations issues, and the relation between operations and other functions? Does the current approach appear to be right for the company in its context – or would a different view of the context lead to a more effective approach?

- Have people suggested a greater or more prominent role for operations, based on the **alternative** approaches used in other companies? If you could find such evidence, how may it affect company practice?

- What, if any, **limitations** are there in the way your organisation deals with operations? How has it affected performance?

Further reading

Bicheno, J. (1998), *The Quality 60: A guide for service and manufacturing*, Picsie Books, Buckingham.

A simply presented collection of many of the quality approaches you are likely to need.

Brown, S. (1996), *Strategic Manufacturing for Competitive Advantage*, Prentice Hall International, Hemel Hempstead.

Provides much detail about operations management in a product environment and offers extra material about many of the concepts covered in this chapter.

Womack, J.P. and Jones, D. (1996), *Lean Thinking*, Simon & Schuster, New York.

Develops the theme established in *The Machine that Changed the World* (Womack *et al.*, 1990), which first comprehensively described the Toyota production system as clearly superior to other car assemblers' systems by means of a benchmarking study. It sets JIT, TQM and supply chain thinking in an integrated framework. The latest book uses a number of case examples.

Heller, R. (2001), 'Inside Zara', *Forbes Global*, 28 May, pp. 24–25, 28–29.

Comments on the development of this fashion brand and the company founder behind it.

Kay, J. (1993), *Foundations of Corporate Success*, Oxford University Press, Oxford.

A highly rated text on strategy that, interestingly, also emphasises a number of key capabilities that are related to operations and the supply chain view as described here.

Krajewski, L.J. and Ritzman, L.P. (2004), *Operations Management: Strategy and analysis* (7th edn), Pearson Education, London.

This is a US textbook that provides a wealth of extra materials including useful website exercises.

Slack, N. and Lewis, M. (2002), *Operations Strategy*, Financial Times/Prentice Hall, Harlow.

This UK book has a wealth of good material about most of the issues covered in this chapter.

http://bized.ac.uk/virtual/cb/

This is an excellent interactive learning site based on the successful real company that built the round-the-world balloon Brietling Orbiter 3, which was the first to circumnavigate the globe.

Weblinks

These are some of the websites that have appeared in the chapter:

www.benetton.com
www.inditex.com
www.happycomputers.co.uk
www.dell.com
www.directline.co.uk

- Visit two of the websites in the list (or any other company that interests you) and navigate to the pages dealing with the products and services they offer. This is usually the first one you see, but in some it may be further back.

● What messages do they give about the nature of the goods and services they offer? What challenges are they likely to raise for operations in terms of their emphasis on, for example, innovation, quality, delivery or cost? What implications might that have for people working in the company?

● See if you can find any information on the site about the operating systems, or how they link with their suppliers.

● Gather information from the media websites (such as www.ft.com) which relate to the companies you have chosen. What stories can you find that indicate something about the performance of those companies?

Annotated weblinks, multiple choice questions and other useful resources can be found on **www.pearsoned.co.uk/boddy**

Jack Cohen founded Tesco in 1919 as a grocery stall, opening the first store in 1929. He was aware that supermarkets had been successful in the United States and tried to introduce the idea to the United Kingdom. He opened small self-service stores in 1948, followed by his first self-service supermarket in 1956. The company grew rapidly by acquisition during the 1960s, taking advantage of the ending of the Retail Price Maintenance Act. This prohibited retailers from selling goods at prices below the levels agreed with suppliers, and served to prevent the growth of large, efficient stores.

The Act was abolished in 1964, opening the way for Tesco and similar chains to compete with established retailers (mainly small, family-owned local businesses) on price. Tesco's growth enabled it to buy products from food manufacturers much more cheaply than its smaller rivals.

The business continued to grow, but as consumers grew wealthier they became less attracted by the cheapness Tesco offered. In 1985 Ian MacLaurin became the first CEO from outside the Cohen family, and began to reshape the group's operations. He closed many smaller stores, concentrating instead on larger, suburban outlets. He also centralised the distribution system, offered fresh foods, and own-label brands. By 1992 the company was the second largest supermarket chain in the United Kingdom, behind Sainsbury's but ahead of Asda and Safeway.

Terry Leahy became CEO in 1997, having previously been marketing director. The core UK business accounted for 80 per cent of total sales, employing over 250,000 people in 1800 stores in 2007. It had four formats:

1 Tesco Express – local stores selling fresh food, wines, beers and spirits;
2 Tesco Metro – larger stores in city centres offering a range of food, including sandwiches and ready-meals;
3 Tesco Superstore – even larger stores offering a wide range of food and non-food products;
4 Tesco Extra – very large, edge-of-town stores offering the widest range of food and non-food items.

© Tesco PLC.

To continue growth, increasing emphasis was put on developing the range of non-food items, such as clothes, furnishings, entertainment and health products. Tesco Personal Finance (a joint venture with The Royal Bank of Scotland – see Part 4 Case) offers loans, credit cards, mortgages and many other financial products to retail customers.

The company responded to the Internet by creating an online shopping division, Tesco.com, which rapidly established a leading position in that segment of the market. One factor in the rapid success may have been the way it was established. While some competitors set up online operations as separate business units, with their own warehouses and staff, Tesco integrated the online business with the physical stores, with orders being assembled from stock in the store. This reduced the investment cost and enabled the company to launch the new business quickly.

Since the mid-1990s the company has been investing in markets overseas, and by 2007 was active in 12 countries outside of the United Kingdom. Over half of the group's space is now overseas, and its strategy reflects the lessons learned in developing that business, including:

● Be flexible – each market is unique and requires a different approach.
● Act local – local customers, cultures and suppliers require a local approach: very few members of the Tesco International team are expatriates.
● Keep focus – to be the leading local brand takes years to achieve.

In the year to the end of February 2006 the main financial indicators of performance were as shown in the table.

	2006	2005
Group revenue (£m)	38,259	33,866
Group profit before tax (£m)	2,251	1,925
Earnings per share (p)	20.06	18.58
Dividend per share (p)	8.63	7.56
Group enterprise value (£M)	30,841	27,910
Return on capital employed	12.7%	11.8%

Leahy implemented the concept of the balanced scorecard to help manage the business, adapting the idea and calling it the steering wheel. He said:

If we are to meet our objectives, the Tesco team needs to work together. Because we need to focus on every aspect of what Tesco does, we use a management tool we call the steering wheel to bring together our work in all areas and measure our performance. It helps us manage Tesco in a balanced way, by covering everything we do, and allows us to plan for the future by setting targets for years to come. The steering wheel literally guides us through our daily running of the company, while allowing us to change to meet customers' demands.

The table shows the balanced scorecard quadrants, with the key performance indicators upon which Tesco focuses.

Tesco steering wheel

Customer	Operations
Earn lifetime loyalty	Shopping is better for customers
The aisles are clear	Working is simpler for staff
I can get what I want	The way we operate is cheaper for Tesco
The processes are good	The way we operate is responsible and safe
I don't queue	
The staff are great	
People	**Finance**
We trust and respect each other	Grow sales
My manager supports me to do a good job	Maximise profit
My job is interesting	Maximise our investment
I have the opportunity to get on	

Responsibility for delivering the KPIs was delegated to the relevant business unit. Every Tesco store had its own steering wheel with specific deliverables ranging from strategy to day-to-day work. The KPIs were measured regularly and quarterly reports were sent to the board for review, so that it was clear whether or not the business was on track. The summary report for the company was sent to all store managers, and shared with staff. At the end of each year every KPI is reviewed to determine if that aspect of the objectives has been met. The pay of senior management depends on the achievement of these indicators.

The steering wheel is used to communicate strategy across all levels, to align goals and also to manage overall company performance. There is a high-level corporate steering wheel, functional ones, and one for each store. It shapes the objectives of all employees so that each works towards achieving the corporate goals. According to one member of Tesco staff: 'The wheel sets the staff targets for areas like customer relations, people, operations and finance. It lets everyone know exactly what we're working on.'

In 1994 Tesco launched its Clubcard scheme, which has over 11 million active holders. Shoppers join the scheme by completing a simple form with some personal information about their age and where they live. Their purchases earn vouchers based on the amount they spend. Every purchase they make at Tesco is electronically recorded, and the data analysed to identify their shopping preferences. This is then used to design a package of special offers which are most likely to appeal to that customer, based on an analysis of what they have bought. These offers are mailed to customers with their quarterly vouchers, and each mailing brings a large increase in business.

More broadly, the data is analysed to identify the kind of person the Clubcard holder is – whether they have a new baby, young children, whether they like cooking, and so on. Each product is also ascribed a set of attributes – expensive or cheap? An ethnic recipe or a traditional dish? Tesco own-label or an upmarket brand? The information on customers, shopping habits and product attributes is used to support all aspects of the business – identifying possible gaps in the product range, assessing the effect of promotional offers, noting variations in taste in different parts of the country.

The information is also sold to suppliers, who use it when planning to launch new products. Within hours of a product going on sale, or of launching a promotional offer, brand managers can track who is buying their products or responding to promotions. The company is keen to stress that no data on individuals is ever released – the analysis is based on categories of consumers, not individuals. The database is believed to be the largest holding of personal information about named individuals within the United Kingdom.

It has also shaped a series of strategic decisions, such as the move into smaller store formats, and the launch of the Internet shopping site. It also shaped the development and sale of Tesco mobile phones, pet insurance and the Finest food range.

To its over 250,000 employees in the United Kingdom, Tesco offers a flexible range of pay and benefits, including the opportunity to buy shares in the company at a discounted rate. Staff can also join a pension scheme. The company states that its core purpose is 'to create value for customers and earn their lifetime loyalty'. It goes on to say that if staff enjoy their work, they are more likely to make extra effort to please the customers.

Source: Published information and company website.

Part case questions

- What are the main problems of control in a company of this sort?
- What benefits do you expect the company will have gained from using the steering wheel?
- What other forms of control can you see being used in this account of the company?
- How will information systems help management to exercise control over current operations, and to support its competitive strategy?
- What can you discover about the movement of the Tesco share price over the past year and the reasons for this?
- What are the main operational problems that Tesco management have to deal with in running the UK business?
- What are the main business processes in Tesco that are crucial to satisfying customer requirements?

Part 6　Skills development

To help you develop your skills, as well as knowledge, this section includes tasks that relate the key themes covered in the Part to your daily life. Working through these will help you to deepen your understanding of the topic, and develop skills and insights that you can use in many situations.

Task 6.1　Budgeting

Managers typically have fewer resources than they would like, so need to work with budgets – a tool to help them allocate resources between the various tasks they need to carry out. As a planning tool, budgets help identify what activities are important to the wider task, and how much resource to devote to each. Then as a control tool they help people to compare how the resources they have actually used compare with what they planned to use. Managers can then take corrective action if needed.

You can develop your skills of budgeting by working on this task.

1. Identify a project that you need to work on over the next few weeks. It could be a major study assignment or dissertation, a piece of research, a charity or student union activity you are taking part in, or an activity at work. The main criterion is that the job is one that matters to you, and will involve using scarce resources, probably of time and money. It could even be a simple personal budget for the next month.
2. List the resources you will need – your time, other people's time, materials, money, information. Think widely, as the more requirements you can anticipate now, the easier it can be to arrange for them to be available in good time. Also think how much of each you will need, being as realistic as possible: it is probably safer to overestimate what you need than to underestimate.
3. Map out when you will need these resources to be available. Do this by listing the tasks down the left-hand side of a sheet, and time (in weeks) across the top. Then work out when you will start and finish each part of the task, to show when you will need a resource. Along the bottom of the sheet you could include a row for money, indicating the total cost, if any, you will be incurring in each week. Alternatively, use that space to summarise the non-financial resources you will be needing that week (such as time).
4. As you work through the task, note regularly what activities you have completed. This is using the budget as a control tool. Compare the resources you planned to use for that with the resources you have actually used.
5. You may also have to act to ensure the budget is in line with what you planned, or take some other action such as trying to secure more resources or changing the objective.
6. Use any deviations as a basis for learning from the experience. If there is a gap, consider why that is, and whether there are any lessons to draw from it (such as being too optimistic or pessimistic, the power of unexpected events, or the influence of other people having different priorities). Use the results and lessons from this task as a starting point for future budgeting activities.

Task 6.2   Analysing a factory operation

Go to the website for the Cameron Balloons virtual factory, at **www.bized.ac.uk/ virtual/cb/**. Do not confuse it with Cameron Balloons' own commercial website (**www.cameronballoons.co.uk**).

The Cameron Balloons virtual factory site contains background theory and concepts, as well as information about the company's operations.

Write a two-page report analysing the company by using the ideas in Chapter 20, such as:

- What is the business, and what are the main factors upon which the company competes?
- Which represent order winners and which represent order qualifiers?
- What affects the demand for Cameron Balloons' products and services? How variable is the demand likely to be? How can it be forecast?
- What is the main transformation performed in Cameron Balloons?
- Draw a system diagram for the company.
- What workflow systems do you think will be appropriate for the company – line, cell, functional or concentric?
- How do you think Cameron Balloons should manage resources (human, equipment and materials) to deal with variation in demand?
- What quality management philosophies and techniques are appropriate to use in Cameron Balloons?

You could then use the same framework to analyse another company with which you are familiar, or about which you would like to find out more.

Administrative management is the use of institutions and order rather than relying on personal qualities to get things.

The **administrative model of decision making** describes how people make decisions in uncertain, ambiguous situations.

Ambiguity is when people are uncertain about their goals and how best to achieve them.

Applied ethics is the application of moral philosophy to actual problems, including those in management.

Arbitrariness (of corruption) is the degree of ambiguity associated with corrupt transactions.

Assessment centres are multi-exercise programmes designed to identify the recruitment and promotion potential of personnel.

Assets are the property, plant and equipment, vehicles, stocks of goods for trading, money owned by customers and cash: in other words, the physical resources of the business.

A **balance sheet** shows the assets of the business and the sources from which finance has been raised.

The **balanced scorecard** is a performance measure that looks at four areas: financial, customer, internal processes and people/innovation/growth which contribute to organisational performance.

Basic corrective action aims to understand the deeper sources of performance failure, and tries to correct them.

Behaviour is something a person does that can be directly observed.

Behaviour modification is a general label for attempts to change behaviour by using appropriate and timely reinforcement.

The **big five** refers to trait clusters that appear consistently to capture main personality traits: openness, conscientiousness, extraversion, agreeableness, and neuroticism.

A **blog** is a frequently updated, interactive website through which people can communicate with anyone who has access to the medium.

Blogging is a form of two-way communication characterised by an informal tone and frank discussion.

Bounded rationality is behaviour that is rational within a decision process which is limited (bounded) by an individual's ability to process information.

Bureaucracy is a system in which people are expected to follow precisely defined rules and procedures rather than to use personal judgement.

A **business plan** is a document that sets out the markets the business intends to serve, how it will do so and what finance they require.

The **capital market** comprises all the individuals and institutions that have money to invest, including banks, life assurance companies and pension funds and, as users of capital, business organisations, individuals and governments.

A **cash flow statement** shows the sources from which cash has been generated and how it has been spent during a period of time.

Centralisation is when a relatively large number of decisions are taken by management at the top of the organisation.

Certainty describes the situation when all the information the decision maker needs is available.

A **channel** is the medium of communication between a sender and a receiver.

Coding is translating information into symbols for communication.

Collectivism 'describes societies in which people, from birth onwards, are integrated into strong, cohesive in-groups which ... protect them in exchange for unquestioning loyalty' (Hofstede, 1991, p. 51).

Communication is the exchange of information through written or spoken words, symbols and actions to reach a common understanding.

Competences (organisational) are the activities and processes through which an organisation deploys resources effectively.

Competencies (personal) refer to knowledge, skills, ability and other personal characteristics for good performance of a specific job.

A **competitive environment (or context)** is the industry-specific environment comprising the organisation's customers, suppliers and competitors.

Competitive strategy is concerned with the basis on which an organisation (or unit within it) might achieve competitive advantage in its market.

Concertive control is when workers reach a negotiated consensus on how to shape their behaviour according to a set of core values.

Concurrent control takes place while an activity is in progress.

Consideration is a pattern of leadership behaviour that demonstrates sensitivity to relationships and to the social needs of employees.

A **consumer-centred organisation** is focused upon, and structured around, identifying and satisfying the demands of its consumers.

Consumers are individuals, households, organisations, institutions, resellers and governments that purchase the products offered by other organisations.

Content is the specific substantive task that the group is undertaking.

Contingencies are factors such as uncertainty, interdependence and size that reflect the situation of the organisation.

Contingency approaches to organisational structure are those based on the idea that the performance of an organisation depends on having a structure that is appropriate to its environment.

Control is the process of monitoring activities to ensure that results are in line with plan, and acting to correct significant deviations.

The **control process** is the generic activity of setting performance standards, measuring actual performance, comparing actual performance with the standards, and acting to correct deviations or modify standards.

A **control system** is the way the elements in the control process are designed and combined in a specific situation.

Core competences are the activities and processes through which resources are deployed to achieve competitive advantage in ways that others cannot imitate or obtain.

Corporate responsibility is the awareness, acceptance and management of the wider implications of corporate decisions.

Corporate strategy 'is concerned with the firm's choice of business, markets and activities' (Kay, 1996), and thus it defines the overall scope and direction of the business.

Cost expresses in money units the effect of activating or consuming resources. It is an internal control process of the producing organisation and is not visible to outside parties.

A **cost leadership strategy** is one in which a firm uses low price as the main competitive weapon.

Counterimplementation refers to attempts to block change without displaying overt opposition.

Craft production refers to a system in which the craft producers do everything. With or without customer involvement they design, source materials, make, display, sell, perhaps service and do the accounts.

Creativity is the ability to combine ideas in a unique way or to make unusual associations between ideas.

Critical success factors are those aspects of a strategy that must be achieved to secure competitive advantage.

Critical thinking identifies the assumptions behind ideas, relates them to their context, imagines alternatives and recognises limitations.

Culture is a pattern of shared basic assumptions that was learned by a group as it solved its problems of external adaptation and internal integration, which has worked well enough to be considered valid and transmitted to new members (Schein 2004, p. 17).

Current assets can be expected to be cash or to be converted to cash within a year.

Customer relationship management (CRM) The process of maximising the value proposition to the customer through all interactions, both online and traditional. Effective CRM advocates developing one-to-one relationships with valuable customers.

Data are raw, unanalysed facts, figures and events.

Decentralisation is when a relatively large number of decisions are taken lower down the organisation in the operating units.

A **decision** is a specific commitment to action (usually a commitment of resources).

Decision criteria define the factors that are relevant in making a decision.

Decision making is the process of identifying problems and opportunities and then resolving them.

A **decision tree** helps someone to make a choice by progressively eliminating options as additional criteria or events are added to the tree.

Decoding is the interpretation of a message into a form with meaning.

Delegation occurs when one person gives another the authority to undertake specific activities or decisions.

Delivery relates to the achievement of all promises made by any supplier to a customer.

Demand lead time is the elapsed time that a customer is prepared to allow between placing an order for a product or service and actually receiving it; in certain situations this time is effectively zero.

Democracy is a system of government in which the people, either directly or through elected officials, decide what is to be done.

Determinism is the view that an organisation's structure is determined by its environment.

Differentiation The state of segmentation of the organisation into subsystems, each of which tends to develop particular attributes in response to the particular demands posed by its relevant external environment.

A **differentiation strategy** consists of offering a product or service that is perceived as unique or distinctive on a basis other than price.

Disintermediation Removing intermediaries such as distributors or brokers that formerly linked a company to its customers.

A **divisional structure** is when tasks are grouped in relation to their outputs, such as products or the needs of different types of customer.

E-business refers to the integration, through the Internet, of all an organisation's processes from its suppliers through to its customers.

E-commerce refers to the activity of selling goods or services over the Internet.

Effectiveness is a measure of how well an activity contributes to achieving organisational goals.

Efficiency is a measure of the inputs required for each unit of output.

Emergent models of change emphasise that in uncertain conditions it is likely that the results of a project will be affected by unknown factors, and that planning has only a limited effect on the outcome.

Emergent strategies are those that result from actions taken one by one which converge in time in some sort of consistency or pattern.

Enlightened self-interest is the practice of acting in a way that is costly or inconvenient at present, but which is believed to be in one's best interest in the long term.

Enterprise resource planning (ERP) is a computer-based planning system that links separate databases to plan the use of all resources within the enterprise.

An **entrepreneur** is someone with a new venture, project or activity, and is usually associated with creative thinking, driving innovation and championing change.

Equity theory argues that perception of unfairness leads to tension, which then motivates the individual to resolve that unfairness.

Escalating commitment is a bias that leads to increased commitment to a previous decision despite evidence that it may have been wrong.

Ethical audits are the practice of systematically reviewing the extent to which an organisation's actions are consistent with its stated ethical intentions.

Ethical consumers are those who take ethical issues into account in deciding what to purchase.

Ethical decision-making models examine the influence of individual characteristics and organisational policies on ethical decisions.

Ethical investors are people who only invest in businesses that meet specified criteria of ethical behaviour.

Ethical relativism is the principle that ethical judgements cannot be made independently of the culture in which the issue arises.

Existence needs reflect a person's requirement for material and energy.

Expectancy theory argues that motivation depends on a person's belief in the probability that effort will lead to good performance, and that good performance will lead to them receiving an outcome they value (valence).

The **external environment (or context)** consists of elements beyond the organisation – it combines the competitive and general environments.

External fit is when there is a close and consistent relationship between an organisation's competitive strategy and its HRM strategy.

An **extranet** is a version of the Internet that is restricted to specified people in specified companies – such as major customers or suppliers.

Extrinsic rewards are valued outcomes or benefits provided by others, such as promotion, a pay increase or a bigger car.

Factory production broke down the integrated nature of the craft worker's approach and made it possible to increase the supply of goods by dividing tasks into simple and repetitive sequences.

Feedback (in communication) occurs as the receiver expresses his or her reaction to the sender's message.

Feedback control is when information about performance is gathered when an activity is complete.

Feedback (in systems theory) refers to the provision of information about the effects of an activity.

Feedforward control focuses on preventing problems as it takes place before the work activity.

Femininity pertains to societies in which social gender roles overlap.

Five forces analysis is a technique for identifying and listing those aspects of the five forces most relevant to the profitability of an organisation at that time.

Fixed assets are the physical properties that the company possesses – such as land, buildings, production equipment and vehicles – and which are likely to have a useful life of more than one year. There may also be intangible assets such as patent rights or copyrights.

A **focus strategy** is when a company competes by targeting very specific segments of the market.

Formal authority is the right that a person in a specified role has to make decisions, allocate resources or give instructions.

Formal structure is the official guidelines, documents or procedures setting out how the organisation's activities are divided and coordinated.

A **formal team** is one that management has deliberately created to perform specific tasks to help meet organisational goals.

Formalisation is the practice of using written or electronic documents to direct and control employees.

Franchising is the practice of extending a business by giving other organisations, in return for a fee, the right to use your brand name, technology or product specifications.

A **functional layout** groups similar physical processes together and brings materials and/or customers to these areas.

Functional managers are responsible for the performance of an area of technical or professional work.

A **functional structure** is when tasks are grouped into departments based on similar skills and expertise.

The **general environment (or context)** (sometimes known as the macro-environment) includes political, economic, social technological, (natural) environmental and legal factors that affect all organisations.

General managers are responsible for the performance of a distinct unit of the organisation.

Global companies work in many countries, securing resources and finding markets in whichever country is most suitable.

Globalisation refers to the increasing integration of internationally dispersed economic activities.

A **goal** (or **objective**) is a desired future state for an activity or organisational unit.

Goal-setting theory argues that motivation is influenced by goal difficulty, goal specificity, participation in setting goals and knowledge of results.

Groupthink is 'a mode of thinking that people engage in when they are deeply involved in a cohesive in-group, when the members' striving for unanimity overrides their motivation to realistically appraise alternative courses of action' (Janis, 1972).

Groupware systems provide electronic communication between members of geographically dispersed teams.

Growth needs are those that impel people to be creative or to produce an effect on themselves or their environment.

Heuristics Simple rules or mental short cuts that simplify making decisions

High-context cultures are those in which information is implicit and can only be fully understood by those with shared experiences in the culture.

Horizontal specialisation is the degree to which tasks are divided among separate people or departments.

The **human relations approach** is a school of management that emphasises the importance of social processes at work.

Human resource management is the effective use of human resources in order to enhance organisational performance.

Hygiene factors (or **maintenance factors**) are those aspects surrounding the task that can prevent discontent and dissatisfaction but will not in themselves contribute to psychological growth and hence motivation.

Idea champions are individuals who actively and enthusiastically support new ideas, build support, overcome resistance, and ensure that ideas are implemented.

An **ideology** is a set of integrated beliefs, theories and doctrines that helps to direct the actions of a society.

The **illusion of control** is a source of bias resulting from the tendency to overestimate one's ability to control activities and events.

Immediate corrective action aims to correct problems at once to get performance back on track.

People use an **incremental model** of decision making when they are uncertain about the consequences. They search for a limited range of options, and policy unfolds from a series of cumulative small decisions.

Individualism pertains to societies in which the ties between individuals are loose.

Influence is the process by which one party attempts to modify the behaviour of others by mobilising power resources.

An **informal group** is one that emerges when people come together and interact regularly.

Informal structure is the undocumented relationships between members of the organisation that inevitably emerge as people adapt systems to new conditions and satisfy personal and group needs.

Information comes from data that has been processed so that it has meaning for the person receiving it.

Information overload arises when the amount of information a person has to deal with exceeds their capacity to process it.

Information richness refers to the amount of information that a communication channel can carry, and the extent to which it enables sender and receiver to achieve common understanding.

An **information system** is a set of people, procedures and resources that collects and transforms data into information and disseminates this information.

Information systems management is the planning, acquisition, development and use of these systems.

Initiating structure is a pattern of leadership that emphasises the performance of the work in hand and the achievement of production or service goals.

Innovation is the process of taking a creative idea and turning it into a useful product, service or method of operation.

Institutional advantage 'is when a not-for-profit body performs its tasks more effectively than comparable organisations' (Goold, 1997).

Instrumentality is the perceived probability that good performance will lead to valued rewards, measured on a scale from 0 (no chance) to 1 (certainty).

Intangible resources are non-physical assets such as reputation, knowledge or information.

Integration is the process of achieving unity of effort amongst the various subsystems in the accomplishment of the organisation's task.

The **interaction model** is a theory of change that stresses the continuing interaction between the internal and external contexts of an organisation, making the outcomes of change hard to predict.

The **internal environment (or context)** consists of elements within the organisation such as its technology, structure or business processes.

Internal fit is when the various components of the HRM strategy support each other and consistently encourage certain attitudes and behaviour.

International management is the practice of managing business operations in more than one country.

The **Internet** is a web of hundreds of thousands of computer networks linked together by telephone lines and satellite links through which data can be carried.

An **intranet** is a version of the Internet that only specified people within an organisation can use.

Intrinsic rewards are valued outcomes or benefits that come from the individual, such as feelings of satisfaction, achievement and competence.

Inventory consists of materials and part or finished goods that are held in anticipation of need by customers along a chain of supply from raw materials through to final consumption (and recycling?).

Job analysis is the process of determining the characteristics of an area of work according to a prescribed set of dimensions.

A **job enrichment model** represents the idea that managers can change specific job characteristics to promote job satisfaction and so motivate employees.

A **joint venture** is an alliance in which the partners agree to form a separate, independent organisation for a specific business purpose.

Knowledge builds on information and embodies a person's prior understanding, experience and learning.

Knowledge management systems are a type of IS intended to support people as they create, store, transfer and apply knowledge.

Leadership refers to the process of influencing the activities of others toward high levels of goal setting and achievement.

Liabilities of a business as reported in the balance sheet are the debts and financial obligations of the business to all those people and institutions that are not shareholders, e.g. a bank, suppliers.

Life cycle models of change are those that view change as an activity which follows a logical, orderly sequence of activities that can be planned in advance.

A **limited liability company** has an identity and existence in its own right as distinct from its owners (shareholders in Europe, stockholders in North America). A shareholder has an ownership right in the company in which the shares are held.

A **line layout** is completely specified by the sequence of activities needed to transform materials into a product, or a natural sequence of treatments to provide a service.

Line managers are responsible for the performance of activities that directly meet customers' needs.

Low-context cultures are those where people are more psychologically distant so that information needs to be explicit if members are to understand it.

Management is the activity of getting things done with the aid of people and other resources.

Management as a distinct role develops when activities previously embedded in the work itself become the responsibility not of the employee, but of owners or their agents.

Management as a universal human activity occurs whenever people take responsibility for an activity and consciously try to shape its progress and outcome.

Management by objectives is a system in which managers and staff agree their objectives, and then measure progress towards them periodically.

Management tasks are those of planning, organising, leading and controlling the use of resources to add value to them.

A **manager** is someone who gets things done with the aid of people and other resources.

Market segmentation is the process of dividing markets comprising the heterogeneous needs of many consumers into segments comprising the homogeneous needs of smaller groups.

Marketing is a management process that identifies, anticipates and supplies consumer requirements efficiently and effectively.

The **marketing environment** consists of the actors and forces outside marketing that affect the marketing manager's ability to develop and maintain successful relationships with its target consumers.

A **marketing information system** is the systematic process for the collection, analysis and distribution of marketing information.

The **marketing mix** is the mix of decisions about product features, prices, communications and distribution of products used by the marketing manager to position products competitively within the minds of consumers.

Marketing orientation is an organisational orientation that believes success is most effectively achieved by satisfying consumer demands.

Masculinity pertains to societies in which social gender roles are clearly distinct.

A **matrix structure** is when those doing a task report both to a functional and a project or divisional boss.

A **mechanistic structure** means there is a high degree of task specialisation, people's responsibility and authority are closely defined and decision making is centralised.

The **message** is what the sender communicates.

A **metaphor** is an image used to signify the essential characteristics of a phenomenon.

A **mission statement** is a broad statement of an organisation's scope and purpose, aiming to distinguish it from similar organisations.

A **model (or theory)** represents a complex phenomenon by identifying the major elements and relationships.

Motivation refers to the forces within or beyond a person that arouse and sustain their commitment to a course of action.

Motivator factors are those aspects of the work itself that Herzberg found influenced people to superior performance and effort.

Multinational companies are managed from one country, but have significant production and marketing operations in many others.

A **network structure** is when tasks required by one company are performed by other companies with expertise in those areas.

Networking refers to 'individuals' attempts to develop and maintain relationships with others [who] have the potential to assist them in their work or career' (Huczynski, 2004, p. 305).

Noise is anything that confuses, diminishes or interferes with communication.

Non-linear systems are those in which small changes are amplified through many interactions with other variables so that the eventual effect is unpredictable.

A **non-programmed decision** is a unique decision that requires a custom-made solution when information is lacking or unclear.

Non-receptive contexts are those where the combined effects of features of the organisation (such as culture or technology) appear likely to hinder change.

Non-verbal communication is the process of coding meaning through behaviours such as facial expression, gestures and body postures.

Observation is the activity of concentrating on how a team works rather than taking part in the activity itself.

An **open system** is one that interacts with its environment.

Operational plans detail how the overall objectives are to be achieved, by specifying what senior management expects from specific departments or functions.

Operational research is a scientific method of providing (managers) with a quantitative basis for decisions regarding the operations under their control.

An **opportunity** is the chance to do something not previously expected.

An **order qualifier** is a necessary but not sufficient requirement to be considered by a customer.

An **order winner** is some feature of the product or service that so positively differentiates it that customers want to buy it in preference to competing products.

An **organic structure** is one where people are expected to work together and to use their initiative to solve problems; job descriptions and rules are few and imprecise.

An **organisation** is a social arrangement for achieving controlled performance towards goals that create value.

An **organisation chart** shows the main departments and senior positions in an organisation and the reporting relations between them.

Organisation development is a systematic process in which applied behavioural science principles and practices are introduced with the goal of increasing individual and organisational performance.

Organisation structure 'The structure of an organisation [is] the sum total of the ways in which it divides its labour into distinct tasks and then achieves co-ordination among them' (Mintzberg, 1979).

Organisational change is a deliberate attempt to improve organisational performance by changing one or more aspects of the organisation, such as its technology, structure or business processes.

Organisational performance is the accumulated results of all the organisation's work processes and activities.

The **participative model** is the belief that if people are able to take part in planning a change, they will be more willing to accept and implement the change.

Partnering describes a business relationship based on taking a long-term view that the partners wish to work together to enhance customers' satisfaction.

A **perceived performance gap** arises when people believe that the actual performance of a unit or business is out of line with the level they desire.

Perception is the active psychological process in which stimuli are selected and organised into meaningful patterns.

Performance is the result of an activity.

Performance imperatives are aspects of performance that are especially important for an organisation to do well, such as flexibility and innovation.

Performance-related pay involves the explicit link of financial reward to performance and contributions to the achievement of organisational objectives.

A **person culture** is one in which activity is strongly influenced by the wishes of the individuals who are part of the organisation.

Pervasiveness (of corruption) represents the extent to which a firm is likely to encounter corruption in the course of normal transactions with state officials.

PESTEL analysis is a technique for identifying and listing the political, economic, social, technological, environmental and legal factors in the general environment most relevant to an organisation.

Philanthropy is the practice of contributing personal wealth to charitable or similar causes.

Planning is the task of setting objectives, specifying how to achieve them, implementing the plan and evaluating the results.

A **planning system** refers to the processes by which the members of an organisation produce plans, including their frequency and who takes part in the process.

A **policy** is a guideline that establishes some general principles for making a decision.

Political behaviour is 'the practical domain of power in action, worked out through the use of techniques of influence and other (more or less extreme) tactics' (Buchanan and Badham, 1999).

Political models reflect the view that organisations are made up of groups with separate interests, goals and values, and that these affect how they respond to change.

Power concerns 'the capacity of individuals to exert their will over others' (Buchanan and Badham, 1999).

A **power culture** is one in which people's activities are strongly influenced by a dominant central figure.

Power distance is the extent to which the less powerful members of organisations within a country expect and accept that power is distributed unevenly.

Preferred team roles are the types of behaviour that people display relatively frequently when they are part of a team.

Prior hypothesis bias results from a tendency to base decisions on strong prior beliefs, even if the evidence shows that they are wrong.

A **problem** is a gap between an existing and a desired state of affairs.

A **procedure** is a series of related steps to deal with a structured problem.

Process consultation is an OD intervention in which an external consultant facilitates improvements in an organisation's diagnostic, conceptual and action planning skills.

The **product life cycle** suggests that products pass through the stages of introduction, growth, maturity and decline.

A **profit and loss statement** reflects the benefits derived from the trading activities of the business during a period of time.

A **programmed decision** is a repetitive decision that can be handled by a routine approach.

Project managers are responsible for managing a project, usually intended to change some element of an organisation or its context.

A **psychological contract** is the set of understandings people have regarding the commitments made between themselves and their organisation.

The **quality** of a product or service is the (often imprecise) perception of a customer that what has been provided is at least what was expected for the price he or she paid.

The **range of variation** sets the acceptable limits within which performance can vary from standard without requiring remedial action.

The **rational model of decision making** assumes that people make consistent choices to maximise economic value within specified constraints.

Real goals are those to which people give most attention.

Receptive contexts are those where features of the organisation (such as culture or technology) appear likely to help change.

Reintermediation Creating intermediaries between customers and suppliers, providing services such as supplier search and product evaluation.

Relatedness needs involve a desire for relationships with significant other people.

Representativeness bias results from a tendency to generalise inappropriately from a small sample or a single vivid event.

Responsibility refers to a person's duty to meet the expectations others have of them.

Risk refers to situations in which the decision maker is able to estimate the likelihood of the alternative outcomes.

A **role** is the sum of the expectations that other people have of a person occupying a position.

A **role culture** is one in which people's activities are strongly influenced by clear and detailed job descriptions and other formal signals as to what is expected of them.

A **rule** sets out what someone can or cannot do in a given situation.

Satisficing is the acceptance by decision makers of the first solution that is 'good enough'.

Scenario planning is an attempt to create coherent and credible alternative stories about the future.

Scientific management The school of management called 'scientific' attempted to create a science of factory production.

A **selection test** is a sample of attributes obtained under standardised conditions that applies specific scoring rules to obtain quantitative information for those attributes which the test is designed to measure.

Selective attention is the ability, often unconscious, to choose from the stream of signals in the environment, concentrating on some and ignoring others.

Self-efficacy is an individual's belief that he or she is capable of performing a task.

A **self-managing team** operates without an internal manager and is responsible for a complete area of work.

A **sensitivity analysis** tests the effect on a plan of several alternative values of the key variables.

Sensitivity training is a technique for enhancing self-awareness and changing behaviour through unstructured group discussion.

SERVQUAL (service quality model) is a generic framework for analysing and delivering service quality to customers.

Shareholders are the principal risk takers in a company. They contribute the long-term capital for which they expect to be rewarded in the form of dividends – a distribution from the profit of the business.

Shareholders' funds are the capital contributed by the shareholders plus profits that have not been distributed to the shareholders.

Situational models of leadership attempt to identify the contextual factors that affect when one style will be more effective than another.

The **social contract** consists of the mutual obligations that society and business recognise they have to each other.

A **sociotechnical system** is one in which outcomes depend on the interaction of both the technical and social subsystems.

A **span of control** is the number of subordinates reporting directly to the person above them in the hierarchy.

Staff managers are responsible for the performance of activities that support line managers.

Stakeholder mapping is a means of identifying the views and influence of stakeholders, and the major issues that need to be managed.

Stakeholders are individuals, groups or organisations with an interest in, or who are affected by, what the organisation does.

Stated goals are those that are prominent in company publications and websites.

Stereotyping is the practice of consigning a person to a category or personality type on the basis of their membership of some known group.

A **strategic business unit** consists of a number of closely related products for which it is meaningful to formulate a separate strategy.

Strategic capability is the ability to perform at the level required to survive and prosper, and includes resources and competences.

Strategic management is the set of decisions and actions intended to improve the long-run performance of an organisation.

A **strategic plan** sets out the overall direction for the business, is broad in scope and covers all the major activities.

Strategy is concerned with deciding what business an organisation should be in, where it wants to be, and how it is going to get there.

Structural choice approaches emphasise the scope management has for deciding the form of structure, irrespective of external conditions.

Structure is the regularity in the way a unit or group is organised, such as the roles that are specified.

Subjective probability (in expectancy theory) is a person's estimate of the likelihood that a certain level of effort (E) will produce a level of performance (P) which will then lead to an expected outcome (O).

Subsystems are the separate but related parts that make up the total system.

Succession planning is the use of a deliberate process to ensure that staff are developed who are able to replace senior management as required.

Supply lead time is the total elapsed time between the decision to obtain the basic input resources to the final delivery of the product or service to the customer.

Survey feedback is an OD intervention in which the results of an opinion survey are fed back to respondents to trigger problem solving on the issues that the survey identifies.

A **SWOT analysis** is a way of summarising the organisation's strengths and weaknesses relative to external opportunities and threats.

A **system** is a set of interrelated parts designed to achieve a purpose.

A **system boundary** separates the system from its environment.

Tangible resources are physical assets such as buildings, equipment, people or finance.

A **target market** is the segment of the market selected by the organisation as the focus of its activities.

A **task culture** is one in which the focus of activity is towards completing a task or project using whatever means are appropriate.

A **team** is 'a small number of people with complementary skills who are committed to a common purpose, performance goals, and approach for which they hold themselves mutually accountable' (Katzenbach and Smith, 1993).

Team-based rewards are payments or non-financial incentives provided to members of a formally established team and linked to the performance of the group.

Technology is the knowledge, equipment and activities used to transform inputs into outputs.

Total quality management (TQM) is a philosophy of management that is driven by customer needs and expectations and focuses on continually improving work processes.

Totalitarianism is a system of government in which one individual or political party maintains complete control and either refuses to recognise other parties or suppresses them.

A **trait** is a relatively stable aspect of an individual's personality that influences behaviour in a particular direction.

A **transactional leader** is one who treats leadership as an exchange, giving followers what they want if they do what the leader desires.

A **transformational leader** is a leader who treats leadership as a matter of motivation and commitment, inspiring followers by appealing to higher ideals and moral values.

Transnational companies operate in many countries and delegate many decisions to local managers.

Uncertainty is when people are clear about their goals, but have little information about which course of action is most likely to succeed.

Uncertainty avoidance is the extent to which members of a culture feel threatened by uncertain or unknown situations.

Unique resources are resources that are vital to competitive advantage and which others cannot obtain.

Valence is the perceived value or preference that an individual has for a particular outcome.

Validity occurs when there is a statistically significant relationship between a predictor (such as a selection test score) and measures of on-the-job performance.

Value is added to resources when they are transformed into goods or services that are worth more than their original cost plus the cost of transformation.

A **value chain** 'divides a firm into the discrete activities it performs in designing, producing, marketing and distributing its product. It is the basic tool for diagnosing competitive advantage and finding ways to enhance it' (Porter, 1985).

A **value for money** service is one that is provided economically, efficiently and effectively.

Vertical specialisation refers to the extent to which responsibilities at different levels are defined.

Virtual teams are those in which the members are physically separated, using communications technologies to collaborate across space and time to accomplish their common task.

A **working group** is a collection of individuals who work mainly on their own but interact socially and share information and best practices.

References

Abrahamson, E. (2004), *Change Without Pain*, Harvard Business School Press, Boston, MA.

Academy of Management (1996), Human Resources Division, *News*, Summer.

Ackroyd, S. and Thompson, P. (1990), *Organizational Misbehaviour*, Sage, London.

Adair, J. (1997), *Leadership Skills*, Chartered Institute of Personnnel and Development, London.

Adams, J. S. (1963), 'Towards an understanding of inequity', *Journal of Abnormal and Social Psychology*, vol. 67, no. 4, pp. 422–436.

Adams, S. (1998), *The Dilbert Principle*, Boxtree, London.

Akkermanns, H.A. and van Oorschot, K.E. (2005), 'Relevance assumed: a case study of balanced scorecard development using system dynamics', *Journal of the Operational Research Society*, vol. 56, no. 8, pp. 931–941.

Alavi, M. and Leidner, D.E. (2001), 'Knowledge management and knowledge management systems: conceptual foundations and research issues', *MIS Quarterly*, vol. 25, no. 1, pp. 107–136.

Alderfer, C. (1972), *Existence, Relatedness and Growth: Human needs in organizational settings*, Free Press, New York.

Alexander, D. and Nobes, C. (2007), *Financial Accounting: An international introduction* (3rd edn), Financial Times/Prentice Hall, Harlow.

Alvarez, S.A. and Barney, J.B. (2005), 'How do entrepreneurs organize firms under conditions of uncertainty?', *Journal of Management*, vol. 31, no. 5, pp. 776–793.

Alvesson, M. and Billing, Y.D. (2000), 'Questioning the notion of feminine leadership: a critical perspective on the gender-labelling of leadership', *Gender, Work and Organization*, vol. 7, no. 3, pp. 144–157.

Alvesson, M. and Wilmott, H. (1996), *Making Sense of Management*, Sage, London.

Anand, N. and Conger, J.A. (2007), 'Capabilities of the consummate networker', *Organizational Dynamics*, vol. 36, no. 1, pp. 13–27.

Andersen, T.J. (2000), 'Strategic planning, autonomous actions and corporate performance', *Long Range Planning*, vol. 33, no. 2, pp. 184–200.

Anderson, L.W. and Krathwohl, D.R. (2001), *A Taxonomy for Learning, Teaching and Assessing: A revision of Bloom's taxonomy of educational objectives*, Longman, New York.

Ansoff, H.I. (1965), *Corporate Strategy*, Penguin, London.

Ansoff, H.I. (1991), 'Critique of Mintzberg's "Design School"', *Strategic Management Journal*, vol. 12, no. 6, pp. 449–461.

Applegate, L.M., McFarlan, F.W. and McKenney, J.L. (2000), *Corporate Information Systems Management: Text and cases* (5th edn), Irwin, Chicago, IL.

Aquiar, L.L.M. (2001), 'Doing cleaning work scientifically: the reorganization of work in the contract building cleaning industry', *Economic and Industrial Democracy*, vol. 22, no. 2, pp. 239–269.

Argenti, P.A. (2004), 'Collaborating with activists: how Starbucks works with NGOs', *California Management Review*, vol. 47, no. 1, pp. 91–116.

Argenti, P.A., Howell, R.A. and Beck, K. A. (2005), 'The strategic communication imperative', *MIT Sloan Management Review*, vol. 46, no. 3, pp. 83–89.

Argyris, C. (1999), *On Organizational Learning* (2nd edn) Blackwell, Oxford.

Armstrong, G. and Kotler, P. (2006), *Marketing: An introduction* (7th edn), Financial Times/Prentice Hall, Harlow.

Armstrong, J. (1982), 'Value of formal planning for strategic decisions', *Strategic Management Journal*, vol. 3, no. 3, pp. 197–211.

Arnolds, C.A. and Boshoff, C. (2002), 'Compensation, esteem valence and job performance: an empirical assessment of Alderfer's ERG theory', *International Journal of Human Resource Management*, vol. 13, no. 4, pp. 697–719.

Aslani, A. and Luthans, F. (2003), 'What knowledge managers really do: an empirical and comparative analysis', *Journal of Knowledge Management*, vol. 7, no. 3, pp. 53–66.

Atkinson, A., Kaplan, R. and Young, S. (2006), *Management Accounting* (5th edn), Financial Times/Prentice Hall, Harlow.

Babbage, C. (1835), *On the Economy of Machinery and Manufactures*, Charles Knight, London. Reprinted in 1986 by Augustus Kelly, Fairfield, NJ.

Baker, M. (2002), *The Marketing Book* (5th edn), Butterworth/Heinemann, London.

Balogun, J., Gleadle, P., Hailey, V.H. and Willmott, H. (2005), 'Managing change across boundaries: boundary-shaking practices', *British Journal of Management*, vol. 16, no. 4, pp. 261–278.

Bandura, A. (1997), *Self-efficacy: The exercise of control*, Freeman, New York.

Barker, J. R. (1993), 'Tightening the iron cage: concertive control in self-managing teams', *Administrative Science Quarterly*, vol. 38, no. 3, pp. 408–437.

Barnard, C. (1938), *The Functions of the Executive*, Harvard University Press, Cambridge, MA.

Barnett, W.P. and Freeman, J. (2001), 'Too much of a good thing: product proliferation and organizational failure', *Organizational Science*, vol. 12, no. 5, pp. 539–558.

Baron, R.A. and Greenberg, J. (1997) *Behaviour in Organizations*, Pearson Education, Upper Saddle River, NJ.

Barthélemy, J. (2006), 'The experimental roots of revolutionary vision', *MIT Sloan Management Review*, vol. 48, no. 1, pp. 81–84.

Bartlett, D. (2003), 'Management and business ethics: a critique and integration of ethical decision-making models', *British Journal of Management*, vol. 14, no. 3, pp. 223–235.

Bate, P. (2000), 'Changing the culture of a hospital: from hierarchy to networked community', *Public Administration*, vol. 78, no. 3, pp. 485–512.

Baum, J.R. and Locke, E.A. (2004), 'The relationship of entrepreneurial traits, skill and motivation to subsequent venture growth', *Journal of Applied Psychology*, vol. 89, no. 4, pp. 587–598.

Bazerman, M.H. (2005), *Judgment in Managerial Decision Making*, Wiley, New York.

Beall, A.E. (2004), 'Body language speaks: reading and responding more effectively to hidden communication', *Communication World*, vol. 21, no. 2, pp. 18–20.

Becker, B., Huselid, M.A. and Urich, D. (2001), *The HR Scorecard*, Harvard Business School Press, Boston, MA.

Beer, M. and Cannon, M.D. (2004), 'Promise and peril in implementing pay-for-performance', *Human Resource Management*, vol. 43, no. 1, pp. 3–48.

Beer, M. and Spector, B. (eds) (1985), *Readings in Human Resource Management*, Free Press, New York.

Beer, M., Spector, B., Lawrence, P.R., Quinn Mills, D. and Walton, R.E. (1984), *Managing Human Assets*, Macmillan, New York.

Beirne, M. (2006), *Empowerment and Innovation: Managers, prinicples and reflective practice*, Edward Elgar, Cheltenham.

Belbin, R.M. (1981), *Management Teams: Why they succeed or fail*, Butterworth/Heinemann, Oxford.

Belbin, R.M. (1993), *Team Roles at Work*, Butterworth/Heinemann, Oxford.

Benders, J., Delsen, L. and Smits, J. (2006), 'Bikes versus lease cars: the adoption, design and use of cafeteria systems in the Netherlands', *International Journal of Human Resource Management*, vol. 17, no. 6, pp. 1115–1128.

Bicheno, J. (1998), *The Quality of 60: A guide for service and manufacturing*, Picsie Books, Buckingham.

Biggs, L. (1996), *The Rational Factory*, The Johns Hopkins University Press, Baltimore, MD.

Bjorn-Andersen, N. and Turner, J. (1994), 'Creating the twenty-first century organization: the metamorphosis of Oticon', in R. Baskerville *et al.*, *Transforming Organizations with Information Technology*, Elsevier Science/North-Holland, Amsterdam.

Blackwell, E. (2004), *How to Prepare a Business Plan* (4th edn), Kogan Page, London.

Blake, R.R. and Mouton, J.S. (1979), *The New Managerial Grid*, Gulf Publishing, Houston, TX.

Blake, R.R. and Mouton, J.S. (1964), *The Managerial Grid*, Gulf Publishing, Houston, TX.

Blakstad, M. and Cooper, A. (1995), *The Communicating Organization*, Institute of Personnel and Development, London.

Blau, P.M. (1970), 'A formal theory of differentiation in organizations', *American Sociological Review*, vol. 35, no. 2, pp. 201–218.

Bloemhof, M., Haspeslagh, P. and Slagmulder, R. (2004), *Strategy and Performance at DSM*, INSEAD, Fontainebleau (Case 304-067-1, distributed by The European Case Clearing House).

Boddy, D. (2002), *Managing Projects: Building and leading the team*, Financial Times/Prentice Hall, Harlow.

Boddy, D., Boonstra, A. and Kennedy, G. (2005), *Managing Information Systems: An organisational perspective* (2nd edn), Financial Times/Prentice Hall, Harlow.

Boddy, D. and Gunson, N. (1996), *Organizations in the Network Age*, Routledge, London.

Boddy, D., Macbeth, D.K. and Wagner, B. (2000), 'Implementing collaboration between organisations: an empirical study of supply chain partnering', *Journal of Management Studies*, vol. 37, no. 7, pp. 1003–1017.

Boisot, M.H. (1998) *Knowledge Assets: Securing competitive advantage in the information economy*, Oxford University Press, Oxford.

Bono, J.E. and Judge, T.A. (2004), 'Personality and transformational and transactional leadership: a meta-analysis', *Journal of Applied Psychology*, vol. 89, no. 5, pp. 901–910.

Boselie, P. and Dietz, G. (2003), *Commonalities and contradictions in research on human resource management and performance*, paper presented at the Academy of Management Meeting in Seattle, WA, August.

Boulding, W., Staelin, R. and Ehret, M. (2005), 'A customer relationship management roadmap: what is known, potential pitfalls, and where to go', *Journal of Marketing*, vol. 69, no. 4, pp. 155–166.

Bowen, D.E. and Lawler, E.E. (1992), 'The empowerment of service workers: what, why, how and when?', *MIT Sloan Management Review*, vol. 33, no. 3, pp. 31–39.

Bowen, D.E., Ledford, G.E. and Nathan, B.R. (1996), 'Hiring for the organization, not the job', in J. Billsberry (ed.), *The Effective Manager: Perspectives and illustrations*, Sage, London.

Bowman, C. and Asch, D. (1996), *Managing Strategy*, Macmillan Business, Basingstoke.

Bozarth, C. (2006), 'ERP implementation efforts at three firms', *International Journal of Operations & Production Management*, vol. 26, no. 11, pp. 1223–1239.

Branson, R. (1999), *Losing My Virginity*, Virgin Books, London.

Brass, D. J. (1984), 'Being in the right place: a structural analysis of individual Influence in an organization', *Administrative Science Quarterly*, vol. 29, no. 4, pp. 518–540.

Bratton, J. and Gold, J. (2007), *Human Resource Management* (4th edn), Palgrave, London.

Brews, P.J. and Hunt, M.R. (1999), 'Learning to plan and planning to learn: resolving the planning school/learning school debate', *Strategic Management Journal*, vol. 20, no. 10, pp. 889–913.

Brewster, C. (1994), 'European HRM: reflection of, or challenge to, the American concept?', in P. Kirkbride (ed.), *Human Resource Management in Europe*, Routledge, London.

Brookfield, S.D. (1987), *Developing Critical Thinkers*, Open University Press, Milton Keynes.

Brown, S. (1996), *Strategic Manufacturing for Competitive Advantage*, Prentice Hall International, Hemel Hempstead.

Bryson, J. M. (2004), 'What to do when stakeholders matter', *Public Management Review*, vol. 6, no. 1, pp. 21–53.

Buchanan, D. (2001), *The Lived Experience of Strategic Change: A hospital case study*, Leicester Business School Occasional Paper 64.

Buchanan, D. and Badham, R. (1999), *Power, Politics and Organizational Change: Winning the turf game*, Sage, London.

Buchanan, L. and O'Connell, A. (2006), 'A brief history of decision making', *Harvard Business Review*, vol. 84, no. 1, pp. 32–41.

Burnes, B. (2004), 'Kurt Lewin and the planned approach to change: a re-appraisal', *Journal of Management Studies*, vol. 41, no. 6, pp. 977–1002.

Burns, J.M. (1978), *Leadership*, Harper & Row, New York.

Burns, T. (1961), 'Micropolitics: mechanisms of organizational change', *Administrative Science Quarterly*, vol. 6, no. 3, pp. 257–281.

Burns, T. and Stalker, G.M. (1961), *The Management of Innovation*, Tavistock, London.

Butt, J. (ed.) (1971), *Robert Owen: Prince of cotton spinners*, David & Charles, Newton Abbott.

Cairncross, F. (2001), *The Death of Distance 2.0: How the communications revolution will change our lives*, Orion, London.

Camuffo, A., Romano, P. and Vinelli, A. (2001), 'Back to the future: Benetton transforms its global network', *MIT Sloan Management Review*, vol. 43, no. 1, pp. 46–52.

Cannon, T. (1996), *Basic Marketing: Principles and practice* (4th edn), Cassell, London.

Carroll, A.B. (1989), *Business and Society: Ethics and stakeholder management*, South Western College Publishing, Cincinnati, OH.

Carroll, A.B. (1999), 'Corporate social responsibility', *Business and Society*, vol. 38, no. 3, pp. 268–295.

Chaffey, D. (2002), *E-business and E-commerce Management*, Financial Times/Prentice Hall, Harlow.

Chaffey, D. (ed.) (2003), *Business Information Systems* (2nd edn), Financial Times/Prentice Hall, Harlow.

Chandler, A.D. (1962), *Strategy and Structure*, MIT Press, Cambridge, MA.

Chapman, D. and Cowdell, T. (1998), *New Public Sector Marketing*, Financial Times Management, London.

Chatterjee, S. (2005), 'Core objectives: clarity in designing strategy', *California Management Review*, vol. 47, no. 2, pp. 33–49.

Chen, M. (2004), *Asian Management Systems*, Thomson, London.

Cherns, A. (1987), 'The principles of sociotechnical design revisited', *Human Relations*, vol. 40, no. 3, pp. 153–162.

Child, J. (1972), 'Organizational structure, environment and performance: the role of strategic choice', *Sociology*, vol. 6, pp. 1–22.

Child, J. (1984), *Organisation: A guide to problems and practice* (2nd edn), Harper & Row, London.

Child, J., Chung, L. and Davies, H. (2003), 'The performance of cross-border units in China: a test of natural selection, strategic choice and contingency theories', *Journal of International Business Studies*, vol. 34, no. 3, pp. 242–254.

Child, J. (2005), *Organization: Contemporary Principles and Practice*, Blackwell Publishing, Oxford.

Child, J. and Tsai, T. (2005), 'The dynamic between firms' environmental strategies and institutional constraints in emerging economies: evidence from China and Taiwan', *Journal of Management Studies*, vol. 42, no. 1, pp. 95–125.

CIPD (2006), *Recruitment, Retention and Turnover, Annual Survey Report*, Chartered Institute of Personnel and Development, London.

Clarke, F.L. (2003), *Corporate Collapse: Accounting, regulatory and ethical failure*, Cambridge University Press, Cambridge.

Coggan, P. (2002), *The Money Machine*, Penguin, Harmondsworth.

Conger, J.A. and Kanungo, R.N. (1994), 'Charismatic leadership in organizations: perceived behavioral attributes and their measurement', *Journal of Organizational Behavior*, vol. 15, no. 5, pp. 439–452.

Cooke, B. (2003), 'The denial of slavery in management studies', *Journal of Management Studies*, vol. 40, no. 8, pp. 1895–1918.

Cooke, S. and Slack, N. (1991), *Making Management Decisions* (2nd edn) Prentice Hall, Hemel Hempstead.

Cooper, C. and Taylor, P. (2000), 'From Taylorism to Ms Taylor: the transformation of the accounting craft', *Accounting Organizations and Society*, vol. 25, no. 6, pp. 555–578.

Corfield, R. (1999), *Successful Interview Skills*, Kogan Page, London.

Cornelius, P., Van de Putte, A. and Mattia, R. (2005), 'Three decades of scenario planning at Shell', *California Management Review*, vol. 48, no. 2, pp. 92–109.

Crosby, P. (1979), *Quality is Free*, McGraw-Hill, New York.

Cummings, S. and Angwin, D. (2004), 'The future shape of strategy: lemmings or chimeras', *Academy of Management Executive*, vol. 18, no. 2, pp. 21–36.

Currie, G. and Proctor, S.J. (2005), 'The antecedents of middle managers' strategic contribution: the case of a professional bureaucracy', *Journal of Management Studies*, vol. 42, no. 7, pp. 1325–1356.

Cusumano, M. (1997), 'How Microsoft makes large teams work like small teams', *MIT Sloan Management Review*, vol. 39, no. 1, pp. 9–20.

Cusumano, M.A. and Nobeoka, K. (1998), *Thinking Beyond Lean*, Free Press, New York.

Cyert, R. and March, J.G. (1963), *A Behavioral Theory of the Firm*, Prentice-Hall, Englewood Cliffs, NJ.

Czarniawska, B. (2004), *Narratives in Social Science Research*, Sage, London.

Daniels, A., Daniels, J. and Abernathy, B. (2006), 'The leader's role in pay systems and organizational performance', *Compensation and Benefits Review*, vol. 38, no. 3, pp. 56–60.

Daniels, J.D., Radebaugh, L.H. and Sullivan, D.P. (2004), *International Business: Environments and operations* (10th edn), Pearson/Prentice-Hall, Upper Saddle River, NJ.

Davenport, T.H. (1998), 'Putting the enterprise into enterprise systems', *Harvard Business Review*, vol. 76, no. 4, pp. 121–132.

Davenport, T.H. and Harris, J.G. (2005), 'Automated decision making comes of age', *MIT Sloan Management Review*, vol. 46, no. 4, pp. 83–89.

Deal, T.E. and Kennedy, A.A. (1982), *Corporate Culture: The rites and rituals of corporate life*, Addison-Wesley, Reading, MA.

Dearstyne, B.W. (2005), 'BLOGS: the new information revolution?', *Information Management Journal*, vol. 39, no. 5, pp. 38–44.

Deery, S., Iverson, R.D. and Walsh, J.T. (2006), 'Towards a better understanding of psychological contract breach: a study of customer service employees', *Journal of Applied Psychology*, vol. 91, no. 1, pp. 166–175.

De Hoogh, A.H.B., Den Hartog, D.N. and Koopman, P.L. (2005), 'Linking the big five factors of personality to charismatic and transactional leadership: perceived dynamic work environment as a moderator', *Journal of Organizational Behavior*, vol. 26, no. 7, pp. 839–865.

Delmar, F. and Shane, S. (2003), 'Does business planning facilitate the development of new ventures?', *Strategic Management Journal*, vol. 24, no. 12, pp. 1165–1185.

Deming, W.E. (1988), *Out of the Crisis*, Cambridge University Press, Cambridge.

Dent, C.M. (1997), *The European Economy: The global context*, Routledge, London.

de Wit, B. and Meyer, R. (2004), *Strategy: Process, content and context, an international perspective*, International Thomson Business, London.

Dibb, S., Simkin, L., Pride, W.M. and Ferrell, O.C. (2006), *Marketing: Concepts and strategies* (5th edn), Houghton-Mifflin, New York.

Dimbleby, R. and Burton, G. (1992), *More Than Words: An introduction to communication* (2nd edn), Routledge, London.

Dirsmith, M.W., Heian, J.B. and Covaleski, M.A. (1997), 'Structure and agency in an institutional setting: the application and social transformation of control in the big 6', *Accounting, Organizations and Society*, vol. 22, no. 1, pp. 1–27.

Dobson, P., Starkey, K. and Richards, J. (2004), *Strategic Management: Issues and cases*, Blackwell, Oxford.

Donachie, I. (2000), *Robert Owen: Owen of New Lanark and New Harmony*, Tuckwell Press, East Linton.

Donaldson, L. (1995), *Contingency Theory*, Dartmouth, Aldershot.

Donaldson, L. (1996), *For Positive Organization Theory*, Sage, London.

Donaldson, L. (2001), *The Contingency Theory of Organizations*, Sage, London.

Drucker, P.F. (1954), *The Practice of Management*, Harper, New York.

Drucker, P.F. (1999a), *Innovation and Entrepreneurship* (2nd edn), Butterworth-Heinemann, Oxford.

Drucker, P. (1999b), *Management Challenges for the 21st Century*, Butterworth/Heinemann, London.

Drummond, H. (1996), *Escalation in decision-making*, Oxford University Press, Oxford.

Drury, C. (2004), *Management and Cost Accounting*, Thomson Learning, London.

Druskat, V.U. and Wheeler, J.V. (2004), 'How to lead a self-managing team', *MIT Sloan Management Review*, vol. 45, no. 4, pp. 65–71.

Duncan, R.B. (1972), 'Characteristics of organizational environments and perceived environmental uncertainty', *Administrative Science Quarterly*, vol. 17, no. 3, pp. 313–328.

Echikson, W. (2001), 'When big oil gets connected', *Business Week e-biz*, pp. 19–22.

Eden, C. and Ackerman, F. (1998), *Making Strategy: The journey of strategic management*, Sage, London.

Edvardsson, B. and Enquist, B. (2002), 'The IKEA saga: how service culture drives service strategy', *Services Industries Journal*, vol. 22, no. 4, pp. 153–186.

Egan, J. and Wilson, D. (2002), *Private Business – Public Battleground*, Palgrave, Basingstoke.

Elliott, B. and Elliott, J. (2006), *Financial Accounting and Reporting* (11th edn), Financial Times/Prentice Hall, Harlow.

Engel, J., Kollatt, D. and Blackwell, R. (1978), *Consumer Behavior*, Dryden Press, Boston, MA.

Equal Opportunities Commission (2006), *Facts about Women and Men in Great Britain*, EOC, London.

Ezzamel, M., Lilley, S. and Wilmott, H. (1994), 'The "new organization" and the "new managerial work"', *European Management Journal*, vol. 12, no. 4, pp. 454–461.

Fayol, H. (1949), *General and Industrial Management*, Pitman, London.

Feigenbaum, A.V. (1993), *Total Quality Control*, McGraw-Hill, New York.

Feng, K.C., Chen, E.T. and Liou, W.C. (2004), 'Implementation of knowledge management systems and firm performance: an empirical investigation', *Journal of Computer Information Systems*, vol. 45, no. 2, pp. 92–104.

Fiedler, F.E. and House, R.J. (1994), 'Leadership theory and research: a report of progress', in C.L. Cooper and I.T. Robertson (eds), *Key Reviews of Managerial Psychology*, Wiley, Chichester.

Finkelstein, S. (2003), *Why Smart Executives Fail: And what you can learn from their mistakes*, Penguin, New York.

Fleishman, E.A. (1953), 'The description of supervisory behavior', *Journal of Applied Psychology*, vol. 37, no.1, pp. 1–6.

Fletcher, M. and Harris, S. (2002), 'Seven aspects of strategy formulation', *International Small Business Journal*, vol. 20, no. 3, pp. 297–314.

Florance, I. (2006), 'Ability testing: avoiding the pitfalls and reaping the rewards', *Management Services*, vol. 50, no. 2, pp. 23–25.

Floyd, S.W. and Wooldridge, B. (2000), *Building Strategy from the Middle: Reconceptualizing the strategy process*, Sage, Thousand Oaks, CA.

Fogel, R.W. (1989), *Without Consent or Contract: The rise and fall of American slavery*, Norton, New York.

Follett, M.P. (1920), *The New State: Group organization, the solution of popular government*, Longmans Green, London.

Fombrun, C., Tichy, N.M. and Devanna, M.A. (1984), *Strategic Human Resource Management*, Wiley, New York.

Ford, H. (1922), *My Life and Work*, Heinemann, London.

Foss, N. J. (2003), 'Selective intervention and internal hybrids: interpreting and learning from the rise and decline of the Oticon spaghetti organization', *Organization Science*, vol. 14, no. 3, pp. 331–349.

Foster, R. and Kaplan, S. (2001), *Creative Destruction*, Doubleday/Currency, New York.

Fox, A. (1974), *Man Mismanagement*, Hutchinson, London.

Francis, H. and Keegan, A. (2006), 'The changing face of HRM: in search of balance', *Human Resource Management Journal*, vol. 16, no. 3, pp. 231–249.

Freeman, R.E. (1984), *Strategic Management: a stakeholder approach*, Pitman, Boston, MA.

French, J. and Raven, B. (1959), 'The bases of social power', in D. Cartwright (ed.), *Studies in Social Power*, Institute for Social Research, Ann Arbor, MI.

Fried, Y. and Slowik, L.H. (2004), 'Enriching goal-setting theory with time: an integrated approach', *Academy of Management Review*, vol. 29, no. 3, pp. 404–422.

Friedman, M. (1962), *Capitalism and Freedom*, University of Chicago Press, Chicago, IL.

Frooman, J (1999), 'Stakeholder influence strategies', *Academy of Management Review*, vol. 24, no.2, pp. 191–205.

Fu, P.P. and Yukl, G. (2000), 'Perceived effectiveness of influence tactics in the United States and China', *Leadership Quarterly*, vol. 11, no. 2, pp. 252–266.

Furst, S.A., Reeves, M., Rosen, B. and Blackburn, R.S. (2004), 'Managing the life cycle of virtual teams', *Academy of Management Executive*, vol. 18, no. 2, pp. 6–20.

Gabriel, Y. (2005), 'Glass cages and glass palaces: images of organization in image-conscious times', *Organization*, vol. 12, no. 1, pp. 9–27.

Gamble, J., Morris, J. and Wilkinson, B. (2004), 'Mass production is alive and well: the future of work and organization in east Asia', *International Journal of Human Resource Management*, vol. 15, no. 2, pp. 397–409.

Geare, A., Edgar, F. and McAndrew, I. (2006), 'Employment relationships: ideology and HRM practice', *International Journal of Human Resource Management*, vol. 17, no. 7, pp. 1190–1208.

Geerlings, W. and van Veen, K. (2006), 'The future qualities of workforces: a simulation study of the long-term consequences of minor selection decisions', *International Journal of Human Resource Management*, vol. 17, no. 7, pp. 1254–1266.

Gerwin, D. (1979), 'Relationships between structure and technology at the organizational and job levels', *Journal of Management Studies*, vol. 16, no. 1, pp. 70–79.

Ghoshal, S. and Bartlett, C.A. (1998), *The Individualized Corporation*, Heinemann, London.

Gilbreth, F.B. (1911), *Motion study: A method for increasing the efficiency of the workman*, Van Norstrand, New York.

Gilbreth, L.M. (1914), *The Psychology of Management*, Sturgis & Walton, New York.

Gillespie, R. (1991), *Manufacturing Knowledge: A history of the Hawthorne experiments*, Cambridge University Press, Cambridge.

Glaister, K.W. and Falshaw, J.R. (1999), 'Strategic planning: still going strong?', *Long Range Planning*, vol. 32, no. 1, pp. 107–116.

Glass, N. (1996), 'Chaos, non-linear systems and day-to-day management', *European Management Journal*, vol. 14, no. 1, pp. 98–106.

Goffman, E. (1959), *The Presentation of Self in Everyday Life*, Doubleday, New York.

Gooderham, P.N., Nordhaug, O. and Ringdal, K. (1999), 'Institutional and rational determinants of organizational practices: human resource management in European firms', *Administrative Science Quarterly*, vol. 44, no. 3, pp. 507–532.

Goold, M. (1997) 'Institutional advantage: a way into strategic management in not-for-profit organizations', *Long Range Planning*, vol. 30, no. 2, pp. 291–293.

Govindarajan, V. and Gupta, A.K. (2001), 'Building an effective global business team', *MIT Sloan Management Review*, vol. 42, no. 4, pp. 63–71.

Graham, P. (1995), *Mary Parker Follett: Prophet of management*, Harvard Business School Press, Boston, MA.

Grant, R.M. (1991), 'The resource-based theory of competitive advantage: implications for strategy formulation', *California Management Review*, vol. 33, no. 3, pp. 114–135.

Grant, R.M. (2002), *Contemporary Strategy Analysis* (4th edn), Blackwell, Oxford.

Greenley, G.E. (1986), 'Does strategic planning improve company performance?', *Long Range Planning*, vol. 19, no. 2, pp. 101–109.

Greenwood, R.G., Bolton, A.A. and Greenwood, R.A. (1983), 'Hawthorne a half century later: relay assembly participants remember', *Journal of Management*, vol. 9, Fall/Winter, pp. 217–231.

Greenwood, R. and Lawrence, T.B. (2005), 'The iron cage in the information age: the legacy and relevance of Max Weber for organization studies', *Organization Studies*, vol. 26, no. 4, pp. 493–499.

Greer, C.R. (2001), *Strategic Human Resource Management*, Prentice-Hall, Upper Saddle River, NJ.

Gronroos, C. (2000), *Service Management and Marketing: A customer relationship management approach* (2nd edn), Wiley, Chichester.

Groves, K. S. (2005), 'Linking leader skills, follower attitudes, and contextual variables via an integrated model of charismatic leadership', *Journal of Management*, vol. 31, no. 2, pp. 255–277.

Guest, D.E. (1987), 'Human resource management and industrial relations', *Journal of Management Studies*, vol. 24, no. 5, pp. 502–521.

Gupta, A.K. and Govindarajan, V. (2000), 'Knowledge management's social dimension: lessons from Nucor Steel', *Sloan Management Review*, vol. 42, no. 1, pp. 71–80.

Guthrie, D. (2006), *China and Globalization: The social, economic and political transformation of Chinese society*, Routledge, London.

Hackman, J.R. (1990), *Groups that Work (and Those that Don't)*, Jossey-Bass, San Francisco, CA.

Hackman, J.R. and Oldham, G.R. (1975), 'Development of the Job Diagnostic Survey', *Journal of Applied Psychology*, vol. 60, no. 2, pp. 159–170.

Hackman, J.R. and Oldham, G.R. (1980), *Work Redesign*, Addison-Wesley, Reading, MA.

Hackman, J. R. and Wageman, R. (2005), 'A theory of team coaching', *Academy of Management Review*, vol. 30, no. 2, pp. 269–287.

Hage, J. and Aiken, M. (1967), 'Program change and organizational properties: a comparative analysis', *American Journal of Sociology*, vol. 72, pp. 503–519.

Hagel, J., and Brown, J.S. (2001), 'Your next IT strategy', *Harvard Business Review*, vol. 79, no. 10, pp. 105–113.

Hales, C. (2001), *Managing through Organization*, Routledge, London.

Hales, C. (2005), 'Rooted in supervision, branching into management: continuity and change in the role of first-line manager', *Journal of Management Studies*, vol. 42, no. 3, pp. 471–506.

Hall, W. (1995), *Managing Cultures*, Wiley, Chichester.

Hamm, S. (2007), *Bangalore Tiger*, McGraw-Hill, New York.

Handy, C. (1988), *Understanding Voluntary Organizations*, Penguin, Harmondsworth.

Handy, C. (1993), *Understanding Organizations* (4th edn), Penguin, Harmondsworth.

Hardaker, M. and Ward, B. (1987), 'Getting things done', *Harvard Business Review*, vol. 65, no. 6, pp. 112–120.

Hargie, O.D.W. (1997), *Handbook of Communication Skills*, Routledge, London.

Harris, M. and Rochester, C. (1996), 'Managing relationships with governing bodies', Chapter 3 in Osborne, S.P. (ed.) (1996), *Managing in the Voluntary Sector*, International Thomson, London.

Harris, N. (1999), *European Business* (2nd edn), Macmillan Business, Basingstoke.

Harrison, E.F. (1999), *The Managerial Decision-Making Process* (5th edn), Houghton Mifflin, Boston, MA.

Harrison, M. (2005), *Diagnosing Organizations: Methods, models and processes* (3rd edn), Sage, London.

Hartley, J., Bennington, J. and Binns, P. (1997), 'Researching the roles of internal change agents in the management of organizational change', *British Journal of Management*, vol. 8, no. 1, pp. 61–74.

Hayes, N. (1997), *Successful Team Development*, International Thomson Business Press, London.

Heffcutt, A.I. and Arthur, W. (1994), 'Hunter and Hunter (1984) revisited: interview validity for entry-level jobs', *Journal of Applied Psychology*, vol. 79, no. 2, pp. 184–190.

Heil, G., Bennis, W. and Stephens, D.C. (2000), *Douglas McGregor Revisited*, Wiley, New York.

Helgesen, S. (1995), *The Female Advantage: Women's ways of leadership*, Currency/Doubleday, New York.

Heller, R. (2001), 'Inside Zara', *Forbes Global*, 28 May, pp. 24–25, 28–29.

Hellriegel, D. and Slocum, J.W. (1988) *Management* (5th edn), Addison-Wesley, Reading, MA.

Henry, D. (2004), 'Fuzzy numbers', *Business Week*, 4 October, pp. 79–87.

Herzberg, F. (1959), *The Motivation to Work*, Wiley, New York.

Herzberg, F. (1987), 'One more time: how do you motivate employees?', *Harvard Business Review*, vol. 65, no. 5, pp. 109–120.

Hill, C.W.L. and Pickering, J.F. (1986), 'Divisionalization, decentralization and performance of large United Kingdom companies', *Journal of Management Studies*, vol. 23, no. 1, pp. 26–50.

Hill, T. (2004), *Operations Management* (2nd edn), Palgrave Macmillan, London.

Hillman, A. J. (2005), 'Politicians on the board of directors: do connections affect the bottom line?', *Journal of Management*, vol. 31, no. 3, pp. 464–481.

Hinds, P.J. and Pfeffer, J. (2003), 'Why organizations don't "know what they know": cognitive and motivational factors affecting the transfer of expertise', in Ackerman, M.S., Pipek, V. and Wulf, V. (eds), *Sharing Expertise: Beyond knowledge management*, MIT Press, Cambridge, MA.

Hofstede, G. (1989), 'Organizing for cultural diversity', *European Management Journal*, vol. 7, no. 4, pp. 390–397.

Hofstede, G. (1991), *Cultures and Organizations: Software of the mind*, McGraw-Hill, London.

Hofstede, G. (2001), *Culture's Consequences: Comparing values, behaviors, institutions and organizations across nations*, Sage, London.

Hofstede, G. and Hofstede, G. J. (2005), *Cultures and Organizations: Software of the Mind* (2nd edn), McGraw-Hill, New York.

Horngren, C.T., Datar, S.M. and Foster G. (2005), *Cost Accounting* (12th edn), Financial Times/Prentice Hall, Harlow.

House, R.J. (1996), 'Path–goal theory of leadership: lessons, legacy and a reformulation', *Leadership Quarterly*, vol. 7, no. 3, pp. 323–352.

House, R.J., Hanges, P.J., Javidan, M., Dorfman, P.W. and Gupta, V. (2004), *Culture, Leadership and Organizations: The GLOBE study of 62 societies*, Sage, Thousand Oaks, CA.

House, R.J. and Mitchell, T.R. (1974), 'Path–goal theory of leadership', *Contemporary Business*, vol. 3, no. 2, pp. 81–98.

Howard, J.A. and Sheth, J.N. (1969), *The Theory of Buyer Behavior*, Wiley, New York.

HR Focus (2006), 'Workforce planning is new key to productivity and efficiency', vol. 83, no. 10, pp. 8–9.

Huczynski, A.A. (2004), *Influencing Within Organizations* (2nd edn), Routledge, London.

Huczynski, A.A. and Buchanan, D.A. (2007), *Organizational Behaviour* (6th edn), Financial Times/Prentice Hall, Harlow.

Huselid, M.A. (1995), 'The impact of human resource management practices on turnover, productivity and corporate financial performance', *Academy of Management Journal*, vol. 38, no. 3, pp. 635–672.

Ibbott, C. and O'Keefe, R. (2004), 'Transforming the Vodafone/Ericsson relationship', *Long Range Planning*, vol. 37, no. 3, pp. 219–237.

IPD (1999) *Organisational Development: Whose responsibility?* Institute of Personnel and Development, London.

Iyengar, S.W. and Lepper, M.R. (2000), 'When choice is demotivating: can one desire too much of a good thing?', *Journal of Personality and Social Psychology*, vol. 79, no. 6, pp. 995–1006.

Jackall, R. (1998), *Moral Mazes: The world of corporate managers*, Oxford University Press, Oxford.

Jackson, T. (1993) *Organizational Behaviour in International Management*, Butterworth/Heinemann, Oxford.

Jacobs, D. (2004), 'The human side of enterprise in peril', *Academy of Management Review*, vol. 29, no. 2, pp. 293–296.

Janis, I.L. (1972), *Victim of Groupthink*, Houghton-Mifflin, Boston, MA.

Janis, I.L. (1977), *Decision Making: A psychological analysis of conflict, choice and commitment*, Free Press, New York.

Jennings, D. (2000), 'PowerGen: the development of corporate planning in a privatized utility', *Long Range Planning*, vol. 33, no. 2, pp. 201–219.

Jobber, D. (2007), *Principles and Practices of Marketing* (5th edn), McGraw-Hill, London.

Johns, G. (2006), 'The essential impact of context on organizational behavior', *Academy of Management Review*, vol. 31, no. 2, pp. 386–408.

Johnson, G., Scholes, K. and Whittington, R. (2006), *Exploring Corporate Strategy* (7th edn), Financial Times/Prentice Hall, Harlow.

Jones, O. (2000), ' Scientific management, culture and control: a first-hand account of Taylorism in practice', *Human Relations*, vol. 53, no. 5, pp. 631–653.

Jones, R.A., Jimmieson, N.L. and Griffiths, A. (2005), 'The impact of organizational culture and reshaping capabilities on change implementation success: the mediating role of readiness for change', *Journal of Management Studies*, vol. 42, no. 2, pp. 361–386.

Judd, V.C. (2003), 'Achieving customer orientation using people power – the 5th P', *European Journal of Marketing*, vol. 37, no. 10, pp. 1301–1313.

Judge, T.A., Piccolo, R.F. and Ilies, R. (2004), 'The forgotten ones? The validity of consideration and initiating structure in leadership research', *Journal of Applied Psychology*, vol. 89, no. 1, pp. 36–51.

Juran, J. (1974), *Quality Control Handbook*, McGraw-Hill, New York.

Kalb, K., Cherry, N., Kauzloric, R., Brender, A., Green, K., Miyagawa, L. and Shinoda-Mettler, A. (2006), 'A competency-based approach to public health nursing performance appraisal', *Public Health Nursing*, vol. 23, no. 2, pp. 115–124.

Kanter, R.M. (1979), 'Power failure in management circuits', *Harvard Business Review*, vol. 57, no. 4, pp. 65–75.

Kanter, R.M. (2001), 'The ten deadly mistakes of wanna dots', *Harvard Business Review*, vol. 79, no. 1, pp. 91–100.

Kaplan, R.S. and Norton, D.P. (1992), 'The balanced scorecard: measures that drive performance', *Harvard Business Review*, vol. 70, no.1, pp. 71–79.

Kaplan, R.S. and Norton, D.P. (1993), 'Putting the balanced scorecard to work', *Harvard Business Review*, vol. 71, no. 5, pp 134–142.

Kaplan, R.S. and Norton, D.P. (1996), *The Balanced Scorecard: Translating strategy into action*, Harvard Business School Press, Cambridge, MA.

Katzenbach, J.R. and Smith, D.K. (1993), *The Wisdom of Teams*, Harvard Business School Press, Boston, MA.

Kay, J. (1993), *Foundations of Corporate Success*, Oxford University Press, Oxford.

Kay, J. (1996), *The Business of Economics*, Oxford University Press, Oxford.

Keaveney, P. and Kaufmann, M. (2001), *Marketing for the Voluntary Sector*, Kogan Page, London.

Keen, P. (1981), 'Information systems and organization change', in E. Rhodes and D. Weild (eds), *Implementing New Technologies*, Blackwell/Open University Press, Oxford.

Kennedy, G., Boddy, D. and Paton, R. (2006), 'Managing the aftermath: lessons from The Royal Bank of Scotland's acquisition of NatWest', *European Management Journal*, vol. 24, no. 5, pp. 368–379.

Ketokivi, M. and Castañer, X. (2004), 'Strategic planning as an integrative device', *Administrative Science Quarterly*, vol. 49, no. 3, pp. 337–365.

Khaneman, D. and Tversky, A. (1974), 'Judgement under uncertainty: heuristics and biases', *Science*, vol. 185, pp. 1124–1131.

Kim, E. Nam, D.-I. and Stimpert, J.L. (2004), 'The applicability of Porter's generic strategies in the digital age: assumptions, conjectures, and suggestions', *Journal of Management*, vol. 30, no. 5, pp. 569–589.

Kipnis, D., Schmidt, S.M. and Wilkinson, I. (1980), 'Intra-organizational influence tactics: explorations in getting one's way', *Journal of Applied Psychology*, vol. 65, no. 4, pp. 440–452.

Kirby, M.W. (2003), *Operational Research in War and Peace: The British experience from the 1930s to the 1970s*, Imperial College Press, London.

Kirkman, B.L., Lowe, K.B. and Gibson, C.B. (2006), 'A quarter century of *Culture's Consequences*: a review of empirical research incorporating Hofstede's cultural values framework', *Journal of International Business Studies*, vol. 37, no. 3, pp. 285–320.

Klein, G. (1997), *Sources of Power: How people make decisions*, MIT Press, Cambridge, MA.

Klein, N. (2000), *No Logo: Taking aim at the brand bullies*, Flamingo, London.

Kleiner, A. (2003), *Who Really Matters: The core group theory of power, privilege and success*, Doubleday, New York.

Knapp, M.L. and Hall, J.A. (2002), *Non-verbal Communication in Human Interaction*, Thomson Learning, London.

Knights, D. and Murray, F. (1994), *Managers Divided: Organizational politics and information technology management*, Wiley, Chichester.

Kochan, T.A. (1992), *Principles for a Post-New Deal Employment Policy*, Sloan School of Management, MIT, Working Paper 5.

Kochan, T.A. *et al.* (2003), 'The effects of diversity on business performance: report of the diversity research network', *Human Resource Management*, vol. 42, no. 1, pp. 3–21.

Kolb, D., Rubin, E. and Osland, J. (1991), *Organizational Psychology*, Prentice-Hall, Englewood Cliffs, NJ.

Kolk, A. and Pinkse, J. (2005), 'Business responses to climate change: identifying emergent strategies', *California Management Review*, vol. 47, no. 3, pp. 6–20.

Komaki, J. (2003), 'Reinforcement theory at work: enhancing and explaining what workers do', in L.W. Porter, G.A. Bigley and R.M. Steers (eds), *Motivation and Work Behavior* (7th edn), Irwin/McGraw-Hill, Burr Ridge, IL.

Komaki, J.L., Coombs, T., Redding, T.P. and Schepman, S. (2000), 'A rich and rigorous examination of applied behavior analysis research in the world of work', in C.L. Cooper and I.T. Robertson (eds), *International Review of Industrial and Organizational Psychology*, Wiley, Chichester, pp. 265–367.

Kotler, P. (2003), *Marketing Management* (11th edn), Prentice-hall, Upper Saddle River, NJ.

Kotler, P. and Keller, K. (2006), *Marketing Management* (12th edn), Financial Times/Prentice Hall, Harlow.

Kottasz, R. (2004), 'How should charitable organizations motivate young professionals to give philanthropically?', *International Journal of Non-Profit and Voluntary Sector Marketing*, vol. 9, no. 1, pp. 9–27.

Kotter, J.P. (1982), *The General Managers*, Free Press, New York.

Kotter, J.P. (1990), *A Force for Change: How leadership differs from management*, Free Press, New York.

Kotter, J. and Cohen, D. (2002), *The Heart of Change: Real-life stories of how people change their organizations*, Harvard Business School Press, Boston, MA.

Kotter, J.P. and Heskett, J. (1992), *Corporate Culture and Performance*, Free Press, New York.

Kotter, J.P. and Schlesinger, L.A. (1979), 'Choosing strategies for change', *Harvard Business Review*, vol. 57, no. 3, pp. 106–114.

Krackhardt, D. and Hanson, J.R. (1993), 'Informal networks: the company behind the chart', *Harvard Business Review*, vol. 71, no. 4, pp. 104–111.

Krajewski, L.J. and Ritzman, L.P. (2004), *Operations Management: Strategy and analysis* (7th edn), Pearson Education, London.

Kramer, R. M. (2006), 'The great intimidators', *Harvard Business Review*, vol. 84, no. 2, pp. 88–96.

Kumar, N. (2006), 'Strategies to fight low-cost rivals', *Harvard Business Review*, vol. 84, no. 12, pp. 104–112.

Kumar, V., Venkatesan, R. and Reinartz, W. (2006), 'Knowing what to sell, when, and to whom', *Harvard Business Review*, vol. 84, no. 3, pp. 131–137.

Lancaster, G., Massingham, L. and Ashford, R. (2002), *Essentials of Marketing*, McGraw-Hill, London.

Laudon, K.C. and Laudon, J.P. (2004a), *Management Information Systems: Managing the digital firm* (8th edn), Prentice Hall, Upper Saddle River, NJ.

Laudon, K.C. and Laudon, J.P. (2004b), *Management Information Systems: Organization and technology in the networked enterprise*, Prentice Hall, Harlow.

Lawler, E.E. (1976), 'Control Systems in Organizations', in Dunnette, M.D. (ed.), *Handbook of Industrial and Organizational Psychology*, Rand-McNally, Chicago, IL.

Lawrence, P. and Lorsch, J.W. (1967), *Organization and Environment*, Harvard Business School Press, Boston, MA.

Lawson, P. (2000), 'Performance-related pay', in R. Thorpe and G. Homan (eds), *Strategic Reward Systems*, Prentice Hall, Harlow.

Leach, S. (1996), *Mission Statements and Strategic Visions: Symbol or substance?*, Local Government Management Board, London.

Legge, K. (1978), *Power, Innovation and Problem Solving in Personnel Management*, McGraw-Hill, London.

Legge, K. (1995), *Human Resource Management: Rhetorics and realities*, Macmillan, London.

Lei, D. and Slocum Jr., J.W. (2005), 'Strategic and organizational requirements for competitive advantage', *Academy of Management Executive*, vol. 19, no. 1, pp. 31–45.

Lengel, R.H. and Daft, R.L. (1988), 'The selection of communication media as an executive skill', *Academy of Management Executive*, vol. 11, no. 3, pp. 225–232.

Levitt, T. (1960), 'Marketing myopia', *Harvard Business Review*, vol. 38, no. 4, pp. 45–56.

Levitt, T. (1983), 'The globalization of markets', *Harvard Business Review*, vol. 61, no. 3, pp. 92–102.

Lewin, K. (1947), 'Frontiers in group dynamics', *Human Relations*, vol. 1, pp. 5–41.

Lewis, D. (2001), *The Management of Non-Governmental Development Organizations*, Routledge, London.

Lezaun, M., Pérez, G. and de la Maza, E.S. (2006), 'Crew rostering problem in a public transport company', *Journal of the Operational Research Society*, vol. 57, no. 10, pp. 1173–1179.

Likert, R. (1961), *New Patterns of Management*, McGraw-Hill, New York.

Likert, R. (1967), *The Human Organization: Its management and value*, McGraw-Hill, New York.

Lindblom, C.E. (1959), 'The science of muddling through', *Public Administration Review*, vol. 19, no. 2, pp. 79–88.

Lock, D. (2003), *Project Management* (8th edn), Gower, Aldershot.

Locke, E.A. (1968), 'Towards a theory of task motivation and incentives', *Organizational Behavior and Human Performance*, vol. 3, pp. 157–189.

Locke, E.A. and Latham, G.P. (1990), *A Theory of Goal Setting and Task Performance*, Prentice-Hall, Englewood Cliffs, NJ.

Locke, E.A. and Latham, G.P. (2002), 'Building a practically useful theory of goal setting and task motivation: a 35-year odyssey', *American Psychologist*, vol. 57, no. 9, pp. 705–717.

Lorsch, J.W. (1986), 'Managing culture: the invisible barrier to strategic change', *California Management Review*, vol. 28, no. 2, pp. 95–109.

Luthans, F. (1988), 'Successful vs effective real managers', *Academy of Management Executive*, vol. 11, no. 2, pp. 127–32.

Lynch, R. (2003), *Corporate Strategy* (3rd edn), Financial Times/Prentice Hall, Harlow.

Macbeth, D.K. and Ferguson, N. (1994), *Partnership Sourcing: An integrated supply chain approach*, Financial Times Pitman, London.

Magretta, J. (2002), *What Management Is (and why it is everyone's business)*, Profile Books, London.

March, J.G. (1988), *Decisions and Organizations*, Blackwell, London.

Margolis, J. D. and Walsh, J.P. (2003), 'Misery loves companies: rethinking social initiatives by business', *Administrative Science Quarterly*, vol. 48, no. 2, pp. 268–305.

Martin, J. (2002), *Organizational Culture: Mapping the terrain*, Sage, London.

Martinko, M.J. and Gardner, W.L. (1990), 'Structured observation of managerial work: a replication and synthesis', *Journal of Management Studies*, vol. 27, no. 3, pp. 329–357.

Maruca, R.F. (1998) 'How do you manage an off-site team?', *Harvard Business Review*, vol. 76, no. 4, pp. 22–35.

Maslow, A. (1970), *Motivation and Personality* (2nd edn), Harper & Row, New York.

Massey, A.P., Montoya-Weiss, M.M. and Holcom, K. (2001), 'Re-engineering the customer relationship: leveraging knowledge assets at IBM', *Decision Support Systems*, vol. 32, no. 2, pp. 155–170.

Mayer, M. and Whittington, R. (2004), 'Economics, politics and nations: resistance to the multidivisional form in France, Germany and the United Kingdom, 1983–1993', *Journal of Management Studies*, vol. 41, no. 7, pp. 1057–1082.

Mayo, E. (1949), *The Social Problems of an Industrial Civilization*, Routledge & Kegan Paul, London.

McAdam, R. and Walker, T. (2003), 'An inquiry into balanced scorecards within best value implementation in UK local government', *Public Administration*, vol. 81, no. 4, pp. 873–892.

McAfee, A. (2006), 'Mastering the three worlds of information technology', *Harvard Business Review*, vol. 84, no. 11, pp. 141–149.

McClelland, D. (1961), *The Achieving Society*, Van Nostrand Reinhold, Princeton, NJ.

McCrae, R.R. and John, O.P. (1992), 'An introduction to the five-factor model and its applications', *Journal of Personality*, vol. 60, no. 2, pp. 175–215.

McEntire, L.E., Dailey, L.R., Holly, K. and Mumford, M. (2006), 'Innovations in job analysis: development and application of metrics to analyze job data', *Human Resource Management Review*, vol. 16, no. 3, pp. 310–323.

McGregor, D. (1960), *The Human Side of Enterprise*, McGraw-Hill, New York.

McKeen, J.D. and Smith, H.A. (2003), *Making IT Happen: Critical issues in IT management*, Wiley, Chichester.

McLaren, D.J. (1990), *David Dale of New Lanark*, Heatherbank Press, Milngavie.

McSweeney, B. (2002), 'Hofstede's model of national cultural differences and consequences: a triumph of faith – failure of analysis', *Human Relations*, vol. 55, no. 1, pp. 89–118.

Megone, C. and Robinson, S.J. (2002), *Case Histories in Business Ethics*, Routledge, London.

Melancon, S. and Williams, M. (2006), 'Competency-based assessment center design: a case study', *Advances in Human Resource Management*, vol. 8, no. 2, pp. 283–314.

Mellahi, K., Jackson, P. and Sparks, L. (2002), 'An exploratory study into failure in successful organizations: the case of Marks and Spencer', *British Journal of Management*, vol. 13, no . 1, pp. 15–29.

Mercado, S., Welford, R. and Prescott, K. (2001), *European Business*, Financial Times/Prentice Hall, Harlow.

Mezias, J.M. and Starbuck, W.H. (2003), 'Studying the accuracy of managers' perceptions: a research odyssey, *British Journal of Management*, vol. 14, no. 1, pp. 3–17.

Michaels, E.G. (1982), 'Marketing muscle', *Business Horizons*, May/June, pp. 63–74.

Micklethwait, J. and Wooldridge, A. (2003), *The Company: A short history of a revolutionary idea*, Weidenfeld & Nicolson, London.

Miller, S., Wilson, D. and Hickson, D. (2004), 'Beyond planning: strategies for successfully implementing strategic decisions', *Long Range Planning*, vol. 37, no. 3, pp. 201–218.

Mintzberg, H. (1973), *The Nature of Managerial Work*, Harper & Row, New York.

Mintzberg, H. (1979), *The Structuring of Organizations*, Prentice-Hall, Englewood Cliffs, NJ.

Mintzberg, H. (1994a), *The Rise and Fall of Strategic Planning*, Prentice Hall International, Hemel Hempstead.

Mintzberg, H. (1994b), 'Rethinking strategic planning. Part I: Pitfalls and fallacies', *Long Range Planning*, vol. 27, no. 3, pp. 12–21.

Mintzberg, H., Ahlstrand B. and Lampsel, J. (1998), *Strategy Safari*, Prentice Hall Europe, Hemel Hempstead.

Mintzberg, H., Raisinghani, D. and Theoret, A. (1976), 'The structure of unstructured decision processes', *Administrative Science Quarterly*, vol. 21, no. 2, pp. 246–275.

Mitroff, I.I. (1983), *Stakeholders of the Organizational Mind*, Jossey-Bass, San Francisco, CA.

Monbiot, G. (2000), *The Captive State*, Macmillan, Basingstoke.

Moore, F. (2005), *Transnational Business Cultures: Life and work in a multinational corporation*, Ashgate Publishing, Aldershot.

Moore, J.I. (2001), *Writers on Strategies and Strategic Management* (2nd edn), Penguin, London.

Morgan, G. (1997), *Images of Organization*, Sage, London.

Morse, J. and Lorsch, J. (1970), 'Beyond theory Y', *Harvard Business Review*, vol. 48, no. 3, pp. 61–68.

Moutinho, L. (1995), *Cases in Marketing Management*, Addison-Wesley, Wokingham.

Mowday, R.T. and Colwell, K.A. (2003), 'Employee reactions to unfair outcomes in the workplace: the contribution of Adams' equity theory to understanding work motivation', in L.W. Porter, G.A. Bigley and R.M. Steers (eds), *Motivation and Work Behavior* (7th edn), Irwin/McGraw-Hill, Burr Ridge, IL.

Mumford, E. (1997), 'The reality of participative systems design: contributing to stability in a rocking boat', *Information Systems Journal*, vol. 7, no. 4, pp. 390–322.

Mumford, E. (2006), 'The story of socio-technical design: reflections on its successes, failures and potential', *Information Systems Journal*, vol. 16, no. 4, pp. 317–342.

Mumford, E. and Weir, M. (1979), *Computer Systems in Work Design: The Ethics method*, Associated Business Press, London.

Munro, E. (2004), 'The impact of audit on social work practice', *British Journal of Social Work*, vol. 34, no. 8, pp. 1075–1095.

Nauta, A. and Sanders, K. (2001), 'Causes and consequences of perceived goal differences between departments within manufacturing organizations', *Journal of Occupational & Organizational Psychology*, vol. 74, no. 3, pp. 321–342.

Neely, A. and Al Najjar, M. (2006), 'Management learning not management control: the true role of performance measurement', *California Management Review*, vol. 48, no. 3, pp. 99–114.

Newell, S. (1999), 'Ebank: a failed knowledge management initiative', in H. Scarbrough and J. Swan (eds), *Case Studies in Knowledge Management*, Institute for Personnel and Development, London.

Newell, S. (2006) 'Selection and assessment', in Redman, T. and Wilkinson, A. (eds), *Contemporary Human Resource Management*, Financial Times/Prentice Hall, Harlow, pp. 65–98.

Newell, S. and Tansley, C. (2001), 'International uses of selection methods', in C.L. Cooper and I.T. Robertson (eds), *International Review of Industrial and Organizational Psychology*, Wiley, Chichester.

Newman, A.J. and Patel, D. (2004), 'The marketing directions of two fashion retailers', *European Journal of Marketing*, vol. 38, no. 7, pp. 770–789.

Nonaka, I. and Takeuchi, H. (1995), *The Knowledge Creating Company*, Oxford University Press, New York.

Noordegraaf, M. and Stewart, R. (2000), 'Managerial behaviour research in private and public sectors: distinctiveness, disputes and directions', *Journal of Management Studies*, vol. 37, no. 3, pp. 427–444.

Nugent, N. (ed.) (2004), *European Union Enlargement*, Palgrave Macmillan, Basingstoke.

Nutt, P. C. (2002), *Why Decisions Fail: Avoiding the blunders and traps that lead to debacles*, Berrett-Koehler, San Francisco, CA.

Oakland, J. (1994), *Total Quality Management*, Butterworth/Heinemann, Oxford.

O'Connell, J.F. and Williams, G. (2005), 'Passengers' perceptions of low cost airlines and full service carriers', *Journal of Air Transport Management*, vol. 11, no. 4, pp. 259–272.

Ogbonna, E. and Harris, L.C. (1998), 'Organizational culture: it's not what you think', *Journal of General Management*, vol. 23, no. 3, pp. 35–48.

Ogbonna, E. and Harris, L.C. (2002), 'Organizational culture: a ten-year, two-phase study of change in the UK food retailing sector', *Journal of Management Studies*, vol. 39, no. 5, pp. 673–706.

O'Gorman, C., Bourke, S. and Murray, J.A. (2005), 'The nature of managerial work in small growth-oriented businesses', *Small Business Economics*, vol. 25, no. 1, pp. 1–16.

Orlicky, J. (1975), *Material Requirements Planning*, McGraw-Hill, New York.

Orlitzky, M., Schmidt, F. and Rynes, S. (2003), 'Corporate social and financial performance: a meta-analysis', *Organization Studies*, vol. 24, no. 3, pp. 403–441.

Osborne, S.P. (ed.) (1996), *Managing in the Voluntary Sector*, International Thomson, London.

Ouchi, W.J. (1981), *Theory Z*, Addison-Wesley, Reading, MA.

Paik, Y. and Choi, D. (2005), 'The shortcomings of a standardized global knowledge management system: the case study of Accenture', *Academy of Management Executive*, vol. 19, no. 2, pp. 81–84.

Pajunen, K. (2006), 'Stakeholder influences on organizational survival', *Journal of Management Studies*, vol. 43, no. 6, pp. 1261–1288.

Pan, S.L. (1999) 'Knowledge management at Buckman Laboratories', in Scarbrough and Swan (1999).

Papke-Shields, K.E., Malhotra, M.K. and Grover, V. (2006), 'Evolution in the strategic manufacturing planning process of organizations', *Journal of Operations Management*, vol. 24, no. 5, pp. 421–439.

Parker, D. and Stacey, R. (1994), *Chaos, Management and Economics: The implications of non-linear thinking*, Hobart Paper 125, Institute of Economic Affairs, London.

Parker, L.D. and Ritson, P.A. (2005), 'Revisiting Fayol: anticipating contemporary management', *British Journal of Management*, vol. 16, no. 3, pp. 175–194.

Parker, M. (2000), *Organizational Culture and Identity: Unity and division at work*, Sage, London.

Pascale, R. (1990), *Managing on the Edge*, Penguin, London.

Pedler, M., Burgoyne, J. and Boydell, T. (1997), *The Learning Company: A strategy for sustainable development* (2nd edn), McGraw-Hill, London.

Pedler, M., Burgoyne, J. and Boydell, T. (2004), *A Manager's Guide to Leadership*, McGraw-Hill, Maidenhead.

Peloza, J. (2006), 'Using corporate social responsibility as insurance for financial performance', *California Management Review*, vol. 48, no. 2, pp. 52–72.

Peters, T.J. and Waterman, D.H. (1982), *In Search of Excellence*, Harper & Row, London.

Pettigrew, A. (1985), *The Awakening Giant: Continuity and change in Imperial Chemical Industries*, Blackwell, Oxford.

Pettigrew, A. (1987), 'Context and action in the transformation of the firm', *Journal of Management Studies*, vol. 24, no. 6, pp. 649–670.

Pettigrew, A., Ferlie, E. and McKee, L. (1992), *Shaping Strategic Change*, Sage, London.

Pettigrew, A.M. and Whipp, R. (1991), *Managing Change for Competitive Success*, Blackwell, Oxford.

Pfeffer, J. (1992a), *Managing with Power*, Harvard Business School Press, Boston, MA.

Pfeffer, J. (1992b) 'Understanding power in organizations', *California Management Review*, vol. 34, no. 2, pp. 29–50.

Pfeffer, J. (1994), *Competitive Advantage Through People*, Harvard Business School Press, Cambridge, MA.

Pfeffer, J. (2005), 'Producing sustainable competitive advantage through the effective management of people', *Academy of Management Executive*, vol. 19, no. 4, pp. 95–106.

Pfeffer, J. and Sutton, R.I. (2006a), 'Evidence-based management', *Harvard Business Review*, vol. 84, no. 1, pp. 62–74.

Pfeffer, J. and Sutton, R.I. (2006b), *Hard Facts, Dangerous Truths and Total Nonsense*, Harvard Business School Press, Boston, MA.

Phillips, P. (2003), *E-Business Strategy: Texts and cases*, McGraw-Hill, Maidenhead.

Pierce, J.L. and Gardner, D.G. (2004), 'Self-esteem within the work and organizational context: a review of the organization-based self-esteem literature', *Journal of Management*, vol. 30, no. 5, pp. 591–622.

Pinder, J. (2001), *The European Union: A very short introduction*, Oxford University Press, Oxford.

Pinto, J. (1998), 'Understanding the role of politics in successful project management', *International Journal of Project Management*, vol. 18, no. 2, pp. 85–91.

Porter, M.E. (1980a), *Competitive Strategy*, Free Press, New York.

Porter, M. (1980b), *Competitive Advantage*, Free Press, New York.

Porter, M.E. (1985), *Competitive Advantage: Creating and sustaining superior performance*, Free Press, New York.

Porter, M.E. (1990), *The Competitive Advantage of Nations*, Free Press, New York.

Porter, M.E. (1994), 'Competitive strategy revisited: a view from the 1990s', in P. B. Duffy (ed.), *The Relevance of a Decade*, Harvard Business School Press, Boston, MA.

Porter, M.E. (2001), 'Strategy and the Internet', *Harvard Business Review*, vol. 79, no. 3, pp. 63–78.

Prastacos, G., Soderquist, K., Spanos, Y. and Van Wassenhove, L. (2002), 'An integrated framework for managing change in the new competitive landscape', *European Management Journal*, vol. 20, no. 1, pp. 55–70.

Pugh, D.S. and Hickson, D.J. (1976), *Organization Structure in its Context: The Aston Programme I*, Gower, Aldershot.

Quinn, J.B. (1980), *Strategies for Change: Logical incrementalism*, Irwin, Homewood, IL.

Quinn, R.E., Faerman, S.R., Thompson, M.P. and McGrath, M.R. (2003), *Becoming a Master Manager* (3rd edn), Wiley, New York.

Recardo, R. (1991), 'The what, why and how of change management', *Manufacturing Systems*, May, pp. 52–58.

Redman, T. and Wilkinson A. (2006), *Contemporary Human Resource Management: Text and Cases* (2nd edn), Prentice Hall, London.

Reiter-Palmon, R., Brown, M., Sandall, D., Bublotz, C. and Nimps, T. (2006), 'Development of an O*Net web-based job analysis and its implementation in the US Navy: lessons learned', *Human Resource Management Review*, vol. 16, no. 3, pp. 294–309.

Ring, P.S., Bigley, G.A., D'Aunno, T. and Khanna, T. (2005), 'Perspectives on how governments matter', *Academy of Management Review*, vol. 30, no. 2, pp. 308–320.

Rivard, S., Bennoit, A.A., Patry, M., Pare, G. and Smith, H.A. (2004), *Information Technology and Organizational Transformation*, Elsevier/Butterworth-Heinemann, Oxford.

Robbins, S.P. (2001), *Managing Today!*, Prentice-Hall, Englewood Cliffs, NJ.

Robbins, S.P. and Coulter, M. (2005), *Management* (8th edn), Prentice-Hall, Upper Saddle River, NJ.

Roberto, M.A. and Levesque, L.C. (2005), 'The art of making change initiatives stick', *MIT Sloan Management Review*, vol. 46, no. 4, pp. 53–60.

Roberts, J., McNulty, T. and Stiles, P. (2005), 'Beyond agency conceptions of the work of the non-executive director: creating accountability in the boardroom', *British Journal of Management*, vol. 16, Supplement 1, pp. S5–S26.

Roberts, P. and Dowling, G. (2002), 'Corporate reputation and sustained superior financial performance', *Strategic Management Journal*, vol. 23, no. 12, pp. 1077–1093.

Robertson, I. (1996), 'Personnel selection and assessment', in P. Warr (ed.), *Psychology at Work* (4th edn), Penguin, Harmondsworth.

Robey, D., Schwaig, K.S. and Jin, L. (2003), 'Intertwining material and virtual work', *Information and Organization*, vol. 13, no. 3, pp. 111–129.

Roddick, A. (1991), *Body and Soul*, Ebury Press, London.

Roddick, A. (2000), *Business as Unusual*, Thorsons, London.

Rodriguez, P., Uhlenbruck, K. and Eden, L. (2005), 'Government corruption and the entry strategies of multinationals', *Academy of Management Review*, vol. 30, no. 2, pp. 383–396.

Roethlisberger, F.J. and Dickson, W.J. (1939), *Management and the Worker*, Harvard University Press, Cambridge, MA.

Rosen, S. (1998), 'A lump of clay', *Communication World*, vol. 15, no. 7, p. 58.

Rosener, J.B. (1997), *America's Competitive Secret: Women managers*, Oxford University Press, Oxford.

Ross, S., Westerfield, R. and Jordan, B. (2005), *Fundamentals of Corporate Finance* (7th edn), McGraw-Hill/Irwin, New York.

Rousseau, D.M. (1995), *Psychological Contracts in Organizations: Understanding the written and unwritten agreements*, Sage, London.

Rousseau, D.M. and Schalk, R. (2000), *Psychological Contracts in Employment: Cross-national perspectives*, Sage, London.

Royle, E. (1998), *Robert Owen and the commencement of the millennium: a study of the Harmony community*, Manchester University Press, Manchester.

Rugman, A. (2000), *The End of Globalization*, Random Books, New York.

Ryals, L. (2005), 'Making customer relationship management work: the measurement and profitable management of customer relationships', *Journal of Marketing*, vol. 69, no. 4, pp. 252–261.

Sadler-Smith, E. and Shefy, E. (2004), 'The intuitive executive: understanding and applying "gut-feel" in decision-making', *Academy of Management Executive*, vol. 18, no. 4, pp. 76–91.

Sandberg, A. (ed) (1995), *Enriching Production*, Avebury, Aldershot.

Saunders, C., Van Slyke, C. and Vogel, D. R. (2004), 'My time or yours? Managing time visions in global virtual teams', *Academy of Management Executive*, vol. 18, no. 1, pp. 19–31.

Scarbrough, H. and Swan, J. (1999), *Case Studies in Knowledge Management*, IPD, London.

Schein, E. (2004), *Organization Culture and Leadership* (3rd edn) Jossey-Bass, San Francisco, CA.

Schonberger, R.J. (1983), *Japanese Manufacturing Techniques*, Free Press, New York.

Schor, J.B. (2004), *Born to Buy: The commercialized child and the new consumer culture*, Scribner, New York.

Scullion, H. and Leineham, M. (2005), *International Human Resource Management: A criticial text*, Palgrave Macmillan, London.

Schwartz, B. (2005), *The Paradox of Choice*, Ecco, New York.

Schwenk, C.R. (1984), 'Cognitive simplification processes in strategic decision making', *Strategic Management Journal*, vol. 5, pp. 111–128.

Semler, R. (2003), *The Seven Day Weekend: Finding the work/life balance*, Century, London.

Shao, L. and Webber, S. (2006), 'A cross-cultural test of the "five-factor model of personality and transformational leadership"', *Journal of Business Research*, vol. 59, no. 8, pp. 936–944.

Sharp, B. and Dawes, J. (2001), 'What is differentiation and how does it work?', *Journal of Marketing Management*, vol. 17, no. 7/8, pp. 739–759.

Shaw, C.T., Shaw, V. and Enkit, M. (2004), 'Relations between engineers and marketers in the UK and Germany', *European Journal of Marketing*, vol. 38, no. 5/6, pp. 694–719.

Shaw, M.E. (1978), 'Communication networks fourteen years later', in Berkowitz, L. (ed.), *Group Processes*, Elsevier.

Shaw, W.H. (1991), *Business Ethics*, Wadsworth, Belmont, CA.

Simon, H. (1960), *Administrative Behavior*, Macmillan, New York.

Simons, R. (1995a), 'Control in an age of empowerment', *Harvard Business Review*, vol. 73, no. 2, pp. 80–88.

Simons, R. (1995), *Levers of Control: How managers use innovative control systems to drive strategic renewal*, Harvard Business School Press, Boston, MA.

Sine, W.D., Mitsuhashi, H. and Kirsch, D.A. (2006), 'Revisiting Burns and Stalker: formal structure and new venture performance in emerging economic sectors', *Academy of Management Journal*, vol. 49, no. 1, pp. 121–132.

Sinha, D.K. (1990), 'The contribution of formal planning to decisions', *Strategic Management Journal*, vol. 6, pp. 479–492.

Skinner, B.F. (1971), *Contingencies of Reinforcement*, Appleton-Century-Crofts, East Norwalk, CT.

Slack, N. and Lewis, M. (2002), *Operations Strategy*, Financial Times/Prentice Hall, Harlow.

Smith, A. (1776), *The Wealth of Nations*, ed. with an introduction by Andrew Skinner (1974), Penguin, Harmondsworth.

Smith, J.H. (1998), 'The enduring legacy of Elton Mayo', *Human Relations*, vol. 51, no. 3, pp. 221–249.

Smith, N.C. (1990), *Morality and the Market*, Routledge, London.

Smith, R.J. (1995), *Strategic Management and Planning in the Public Sector* (2nd edn), Longman/Civil Service College, Harlow.

Sparrow, P., Brewster, C. and Harris, H. (2004), *Globalizing Human Resource Management*, Routledge, London.

Sparrowe, R.T. and Liden, R.C. (2005), 'Two routes to influence: integrating leader–member exchange and social network perspectives', *Administrative Science Quarterly*, vol. 50, no. 4, pp. 505–535.

Sparrowe, R.T., Liden, R.C., Wayne, S.J. and Kraimer, M.L. (2001), 'Social networks and the performance of individuals and groups', *Academy of Management Journal*, vol. 44, no. 2, pp. 316–325.

Sprague, L. (1990), 'Operations management: productivity and quality performance', in E.G.C. Collins and M.A. Devanna, *The Portable MBA*, Wiley, New York.

Spriegel, W.R. and Myers, C.E. (eds) (1953), *The Writings of the Gilbreths*, Irwin, Homewood, IL.

Stavins, R.N. (1994), 'The challenge of going green', *Harvard Business Review*, vol. 72, no. 4, pp. 38–39.

Steers, R.M., Mowday, R.T. and Shapiro, D.L. (2004), 'The future of work motivation theory', *Academy of Management Review*, vol. 29, no. 3, pp. 379–387.

Steinbock, D. (2001), *The Nokia Revolution*, American Management Association, New York.

Stern, N. (2007), *The Economics of Climate Change*, Cambridge University Press, Cambridge.

Sternberg, E. (2004), *Corporate Governance: Accountability in the market place* (2nd edn), Institute of Economic Affairs, London.

Stewart, R. (1967), *Managers and their Jobs*, Macmillan, London.

Storey, J. (1992), *Developments in the Management of Human Resources*, Blackwell, Oxford.

Sull, D. (2005), 'Strategy as active waiting', *Harvard Business Review*, vol. 83, no. 9, pp. 120–129.

Sull, D.N. and Spinosa, C. (2005), 'Using commitments to manage across units', *MIT Sloan Management Review*, vol. 47, no. 1, pp. 73–81.

Swartz, M. and Watkins, S. (2002), *Power Failure: The rise and fall of Enron*, Aurum, London.

Symon, G. and Clegg, C.W. (1991) 'A study of the implementation of CADCAM', *Journal of Occupational Psychology*, vol. 64, no. 4, pp. 273–290.

Tannenbaum, R. and Schmidt, W.H. (1973), 'How to choose a leadership pattern: should a manager be democratic or autocratic – or something in between?', *Harvard Business Review*, vol. 37, no. 2, pp. 95–102.

Tayeb, M.H. (1996), *The Management of a Multicultural Workforce*, Wiley, Chichester.

Tayeb, M.H. (2000), *The Management of International Enterprises: A socio-political view*, Macmillan, Basingstoke.

Tayeb, M. H. (2005), *International Human Resource Management*, Oxford University Press, Oxford.

Taylor, B. (1997), 'The return of strategic planning: once more with feeling', *Long Range Planning*, vol. 30, no. 3, pp. 334–344.

Taylor, F.W. (1917), *The Principles of Scientific Management*, Harper, New York.

Thomas, A.B. (2003), *Controversies in Management: Issues, debates and answers* (2nd edn), Routledge, London.

Thompson, J.D. (1967), *Organizations in Action*, McGraw-Hill, New York.

Thompson, M.P.A. and Walsham, G. (2004), 'Placing knowledge management in context', *Journal of Management Studies*, vol. 41, no. 5, pp. 725–747.

Thompson, P. and McHugh, D. (2002), *Work Organizations: A critical introduction*, Palgrave, Basingstoke.

Toffler, B.L. and Reingold, J. (2003), *Final Accounting: Ambition, greed and the fall of Arthur Andersen*, Broadway Books, New York.

Torkzadeh, G., Chang, J.C.-J. and Hansen, G.W. (2006), 'Identifying issues in customer relationship management at Merck-Medco', *Decision Support Systems*, vol. 42, no. 2, pp. 1116–1130.

Tran, T. and Blackman, M. (2006), 'The dynamics and validity of the group selection interview', *Journal of Social Psychology*, vol. 146, no. 2, pp. 183–201.

Trevino, L.K. (1986), 'Ethical decision-making in organisations: a person–situation interactionist model', *Academy of Management Review*, vol. 11, no. 3, pp. 601–617.

Trist, E.L. and Bamforth, K.W. (1951), 'Some social and psychological consequences of the Longwall Method of coal getting', *Human Relations*, vol. 4, no. 1, pp. 3–38.

Trompenaars, F. (1993), *Riding the Waves of Culture: Understanding cultural diversity in business*, The Economist Books, London.

Tuckman, B. and Jensen, N. (1977), 'Stages of small group development revisited', *Group and Organizational Studies*, vol. 2, pp. 419–427.

Turner, M.E. and Pratkanis, A.R. (1998), 'Twenty-five years of groupthink theory and research: lessons from an evaluation of the theory', *Organizational Behavior and Human Decision Processes*, vol. 73, no. 2, pp. 105–115.

Tyson, S. and Fell, A. (1985), *Evaluating the Personnel Function*, Hutchinson, London.

Uhl-Bien, M. and Graen, G.B. (1998), 'Individual self-management: analysis of professionals' self-managing activities in functional and cross-functional teams', *Academy of Management Journal*, vol. 41, no. 3, pp. 340–350.

Van der Heijden, K. (1996), *Scenarios: The art of strategic conversation*, Wiley, Chichester.

Van Der Vegt, G.S. and Bunderson, J.S. (2005), 'Learning and performance in multidisciplinary teams: the importance of collective team identification', *Academy of Management Journal*, vol. 48, no. 3, pp. 532–547.

van Veen-Dirks, P. and Wijn, M. (2002), 'Strategic control: meshing critical success factors with the balanced scorecard', *Long Range Planning*, vol. 35, no. 4, pp. 407–427.

Voelpel, S.C., Dous, M. and Davenport, T.H. (2005), 'Five steps to creating a global knowledge-sharing system: Siemens' Sharenet', *Academy of Management Executive*, vol. 19, no. 2, pp. 9–23.

Vogel, D. (2005), *The Market for Virtue: The potential and limits of corporate social responsibility*, Brookings Institution Press, Washington, DC.

Volberda, H.W. (1997), 'Building flexible organizations for fast-moving markets', *Long Range Planning*, vol. 30, no. 2, pp. 169–183.

Vroom, V.H. (1964), *Work and Motivation*, Wiley, New York.

Vroom, V.H. and Yetton, P.W. (1973), *Leadership and Decision-making*, University of Pittsburgh Press, Pittsburgh, PA.

Walsham, G. (1993), *Interpreting Information Systems in Organisations*, Wiley, Chichester.

Walton, E.J. (2005), 'The persistence of bureaucracy: a meta-analysis of Weber's model of bureaucratic control', *Organization Studies*, vol. 26, no. 4, pp. 569–600.

Walton, R.E. (1985) 'From control to commitment in the workplace', *Harvard Business Review*, vol. 63, no. 2, pp. 76–84.

Watson, T.J. (1994), *In Search of Management*, Routledge, London.

Weber, M. (1947), *The Theory of Social and Economic Organization*, Free Press, Glencoe, IL.

Weber, M. (1978), *Economy and Society*, transl. and ed. G. Roth and G. Wittich, University of California Press, Berkeley, CA.

West, M. and Allen, N. (1997), 'Selecting for teamwork', in Anderson, N. and P. Herviot (eds), *International Handbook of Selection and Assessment*, Wiley, Chichester.

West, M.A., Guthrie, J.P., Dawson, J.F., Borrill, C.S. and Carter, M. (2006), 'Reducing patient mortality in hospitals: the role of human resource management', *Journal of Organizational Behavior*, vol. 27, no. 7, pp. 983–1002.

Whetten, D.A. and Cameron, K.S. (2007), *Developing Management Skills* (7th edn), Prentice-Hall International, Upper Saddle River, NJ.

Whipp, R., Rosenfeld, R. and Pettigrew, A. (1988), 'Understanding strategic change processes: some preliminary British findings', in Pettigrew, A. (ed.), *The Management of Strategic Change*, Blackwell, Oxford.

Whitley, R. (1999), *Divergent Capitalisms: The social structuring and change of business systems*, Oxford University Press, Oxford.

Wieder, H., Booth, P., Matolcsy, Z.P. and Ossimitz, M.-L. (2006), 'The impact of ERP systems on firm and business process performance', *Journal of Enterprise Information Management*, vol. 19, no. 1, pp. 13–29.

Williams, K., Haslam, C. and Williams, J. (1992), 'Ford vs Fordism: the beginnings of mass production?', *Work, Employment and Society*, vol. 6, no. 4, pp. 517–555.

Willoughby, K.A. and Zappe, C.J. (2006), 'A methodology to optimize foundation seminar assignments', *Journal of the Operational Research Society*, vol. 57, no. 8, pp. 950–956.

Winstanley, D. and Woodall, J. (2000), 'The ethical dimension of human resource management', *Human Resource Management Journal*, vol. 10, no. 2, pp. 5–20.

Womack, J.P. and Jones, D. (1996), *Lean Thinking*, Simon & Schuster, New York.

Womack, J.P., Jones, D.P. and Roos, J. (1990) *The Machine that Changed the World*, Macmillan, Basingstoke.

Woodward, J. (1958), *Management and Technology*, HMSO, London.

Woodward, J. (1965), *Industrial Organization: Theory and practice*, Oxford University Press, Oxford (2nd edn 1980).

Woodward, J. (1997), *Construction Project Management*, Thomas Telford Publications, London.

Wright, P.M., Gardner, T.M. and Moynihan, L.M. (2003), 'The impact of HR practices on the performance of business units', *Human Resource Management Journal*, vol. 13, no. 3, pp. 21–36.

Yip, G.S., Loewe, P.M. and Yoshino, M.Y. (1988), 'How to take your company to the global market', *Columbia Journal of World Business*, vol. 23, no. 4, pp. 37–48.

Yukl, G.A. (2004), *Leadership in Organizations* (6th edn), Prentice-Hall, Upper Saddle River, NJ.

Yukl, G. and Falbe, C.M. (1990), 'Influence tactics in upward, downward and lateral influence attempts', *Journal of Applied Psychology*, vol. 75, no. 2, pp. 132–140.

Yukl, G. and Tracey, J.B. (1992), 'Consequences of influence tactics used with subordinates, peers and the boss', *Journal of Applied Psychology*, vol. 77, no. 4, pp. 525–535.

Zeithaml, V.A., Parasuraman, A. and Berry, L.L. (1990), *Delivering Quality Service: Balancing customer perceptions and expectations*, Free Press, New York.

Zheng, C., Morrison, M. and O'Neill, G. (2006), 'An empirical study of high performance HRM practices in Chinese SMEs', *International Journal of Human Resource Management*, vol. 17, no. 10, pp. 1771–1803.

Zolkiewski, J. (2004), 'Relationships are not ubiquitous in marketing', *European Journal of Marketing*, vol. 38, no. 1/2, pp. 24–29.